T0399490

CONTEMPORARY THOUGHT ON NINETEENTH CENTURY CONSERVATISM

CONTEMPORARY THOUGHT ON NINETEENTH CENTURY CONSERVATISM

Edited by Richard A. Gaunt and Angus Hawkins

Volume IV

1850–1874

Editor: Angus Hawkins

Routledge
Taylor & Francis Group

LONDON AND NEW YORK

First published 2021
by Routledge
2 Park Square, Milton Park, Abingdon, Oxon OX14 4RN

and by Routledge
52 Vanderbilt Avenue, New York, NY 10017

Routledge is an imprint of the Taylor & Francis Group, an informa business

British Library Cataloguing-in-Publication Data
A catalogue record for this book is available from the British Library

Library of Congress Cataloging-in-Publication Data
A catalog record for this book has been requested

ISBN: 978-1-138-05209-3 (set)
eISBN: 978-1-351-27068-7 (set)
ISBN: 978-0-367-63651-7 (volume IV)
eISBN: 978-1-003-12016-2 (volume IV)

Typeset in Time New Roman
by Apex CoVantage, LLC

CONTENTS

CONTENTS

CONTENTS

Part 3

CONSERVATISM AND THE CHURCH, 1852–1874

Benjamin Disraeli, *'Church and the Queen': Five Speeches Delivered by the Rt Hon B. Disraeli MP, 1860–1864* (London: G. J. Palmer, 1865), 1–79

Worcester College Library, XXB.6.6(6)

Religion and the Church of England, as the Established Church, were central to mid-Victorian Conservatism. They were also fundamental to the thinking of the two most prominent Conservatives of the 1850s and 1860s, Lord Derby and Benjamin Disraeli. Both saw the Anglican Church as an integral part of the constitution and essential to the life of the nation.

For Derby, the Church and its liturgy safeguarded the moral character of the nation as the bedrock of its institutions. Instructed in evangelical Anglicanism by his mother as a boy, he published *Conversations on the Parables* in 1828 and *The Miracles of Our Lord Explained* in 1839. However, his defence of the Church establishment never hardened into harsh Protestant bigotry. He never regretted his vote, as a young Whig, for Catholic Emancipation in 1829, although his hope that the measure would attach Catholic subjects in Ireland more firmly to the Union was disappointed. As party leader, he opposed exciting Protestant prejudice as a Conservative rallying cry. He defended the Maynooth Grant against the hostile motions of the ultra-Protestant Conservative backbencher Richard Spooner during the 1850s. The vehemently anti-Catholic National Club, largely Conservative in membership, he regarded as 'a mischievous body whose extreme pretensions and views must not be encouraged' (Derby to Disraeli, 15 November 1853, Derby Mss., 920 DER (14) 182/1). The passions of ultra-Protestant Conservative MPs such as Charles Newdegate, William Beresford, and Richard Spooner were to be discouraged, he insisted in 1853, 'by the negative means of avoiding in debate, or in meetings of the party, language which may unnecessarily *frossier* their . . . views' (*Ibid.*).

Yet, for Derby, the British national identity was rooted in the Reformation, when Papal authority was cast off. The Protestant constitution was enshrined in the monarch as both 'supreme governor' of the Church of England and head of state. The Providential blessings of Britain's stability and ordered freedoms were embodied in the Anglican Church. Derby believed that all Protestant and Catholic British subjects should have full and free exercise of their religion. Nevertheless, the status of the Church of England as the Established Church was fundamental to institutional stability and social order. His ideal of ecclesiastical preferment embodied scholarly clergy of moderate views, inclining to Low Church sympathies. While prime minister, he assured the Queen that he held 'as strong an objection to the Ritualist clergy as Her Majesty' (Derby to General Grey, 19 October 1867, Derby Mss., 920 DER (14) 194/1).

Although discounted by some recent scholars, religious faith was also central to Disraeli's thinking. However, his mind engaged with the philosophical discussion

3

of religion, rather than dogma. He rejected rigid doctrinal dispute fostering sectarianism and religious factionalism. Rather, he believed that the individual and the nation were incomplete without God and recognition of the moral duties and stewardship each member of society owed to others. Disraeli and his father, Isaac D'Israeli, wrote about the vital role of religious faith to the health of a nation. Doctrine, as peoples evolved, was amended, but transcendent religious truths were intrinsic to the well-being of society. The nation, defined by its distinct historical experience, was a moral entity. In 1835, Disraeli declared religion and the future welfare of the people to be of greater importance to the English nation than their political condition.

Amid the pervasive theological controversy and intellectual contention of the nineteenth century, preserving England's religious faith through the Church of England was a major theme in Disraeli's novels, writings in which Byronic Romanticism, his study of Jewish history, the quest for genius, and his belief in England as a great ordained nation, came together. The moral void of Utilitarianism and scientific materialism, as he saw it, and sectarian disputes splitting society were the threats to be determinedly resisted. His 'Young England' trilogy of the 1840s elaborated the necessity of faith to political stewardship and wisdom. His 1870 novel *Lothair* portrayed the requirement of belief to face down the forces of irreligion and unbelief. Disraeli's novels also explored the potency of religious belief in shaping leaders, societies, and nations, within narratives influenced by Old Testament accounts of exile, redemption, and kingship, the great leader, possessing spiritual insight, rising up and delivering the nation back to truth.

For Disraeli, the Jews offered the prototypical example of a people whose religion gave them an enduring identity and a sacred place in human history. Divine revelation was granted to the ancient Jews. Through them God had entered the human narrative. The Jewish theocracy had been the core of their traditional institutions, rituals, and religious practice. Disraeli saw a theological continuity between Judaism and Christianity. The fundamental Jewishness of Christianity was a theme in Chapter 24 of Disraeli's 1852 biography of Lord George Bentinck. Medieval Catholicism, before the Reformation, also represented, for Disraeli, a venerable creed promoting unity and concord. Embodying reverence, mysticism, and faithfulness to ritual and tradition, it supported a moral stewardship towards society upheld by an elite aware of the duties inherent in privileged status. For his contemporaries Disraeli saw the Church of England as the sacred constitutional embodiment of the same religious truth, safeguarding the moral basis of English society.

A baptised and practising Anglican, Disraeli regarded the England of his day as a nation, like the Jews, blessed by Providence. England was the Israel of his imagination, its Anglican constitution shaped by its historic identity. Like the Jews, the English were a 'chosen' people with a sacred constitution. Land, the soil of England, and aristocracy buttressed the Providential status of the nation. The link between the Anglican faith and the soil of England was indissoluble. Land ownership, the basis of the territorial constitution, he asserted, was a form of religious inheritance. Just as the Holy Land held the key to the religious revelation imparted to the Jews, the geographic genius of place, so the soil of England rooted the moral identity of the English race. For Disraeli the term 'race' was synonymous with 'people' and 'nation'. It was a cultural historical concept, not a biological or genetic construction. Like 'people' and 'nation', it brought together an historic cluster of cultural characteristics. Racial differences comprised, he believed, variations in spiritual and religious capacity. Influenced by scripture, it formed part of the larger Providential narrative framing England's special status as a 'chosen people'.

The nineteenth century saw the urgent attempt to revitalise the Church of England, marking a remarkable institutional and spiritual revival. This was accompanied by increasing tensions between the Protestant, Catholic, and liberal traditions within Anglicanism, the Evangelical revival and the Oxford Movement. From the 1840s to the 1870s theological controversy, especially the rise of scientific materialism and the impact of German Biblical criticism, increasingly occupied Disraeli's thinking on religion. A concern that was prompted by Darwin's *On the Origin of the Species*, English translations of David Strauss's *Life of Christ* and Ludwig Feuerbach's *The Essence of Christianity*, Francis Newman's *The Soul*, W. R. Greg's *The Creed of Christendom*, the liberal Anglicanism of *Essays and Reviews* (1860), and Bishop Colenso's disputing of the authenticity of the Pentateuch in 1860. The authors of *Essays and Reviews* refuted the existence of miracles, denied the doctrine of eternal punishment, and proposed that the Bible be studied as a book like any other. The subsequent controversy, Disraeli lamented, rendered the state of the Anglican Church critical, from dissension and heresy among its own children, handing the Church over to narrow-minded and ignorant fanaticism.

An important part of Disraeli's practical religious faith, inextricably bound up with his sense of social order, moral duty, and political stewardship, was rooted in the parish of his country house at Hughenden. When at Hughenden he regularly attended services and received communion. He exercised with care his patronage of the living at Hughenden. The rituals and responsibilities of parish life constituted an integral part of his vision of himself as a benevolent conscientious landowner and gentleman. Disraeli requested that, after his death, he be buried at Hughenden Church. Since the 1830s, however, the Anglican parochial system had been the object of a sustained parliamentary campaign by Nonconformists to abolish Church rates: a parish tax levied on all occupiers of land or a house for the benefit of the Anglican parish church. In July 1859 leading Liberals such as Palmerston, Russell, and the Home Secretary, Sir George Cornewall Lewis, declared their support for the abolition of Church rates. The conversion of such prominent national politicians to the cause of Church rates abolition added to Disraeli's sense of crisis concerning the standing of the Established Church, striking at its parochial foundations that were woven into the fabric of local communities.

In the 1860s, Disraeli embarked on a full-scale rebuttal of scientific materialism and Anglican sectarianism, calls for the disestablishment of the Church, and unbelief. He campaigned for a faithful nation and a robust Church–State alliance. Supported by Bishop Samuel Wilberforce, he delivered a series of speeches calling for a unified Church, and diocesan and parochial reform. In a speech at Aylesbury in November 1861, he declared the Church in danger from German Biblical criticism, the heretical arguments in *Essays and Reviews*, and the call for disestablishment. At High Wycombe in October 1862, he proposed a strengthening of the Church as a national institution by continuing its influence over education, by an extension of the Episcopate, by increasing the lay presence in the Church's administration, by maintaining the existing parochial system, and by giving its clergy sufficient remuneration. His call to fortify the Anglican Church as the sacred depository of Divine truth culminated in his 'Apes and Angels' speech, delivered at the Oxford Sheldonian Theatre in November 1864. In the debate on whether man was 'an ape or an angel', he pronounced, 'My Lord, I am on the side of the angels'.

1

BENJAMIN DISRAELI, 'CHURCH AND THE QUEEN': FIVE SPEECHES DELIVERED BY THE RT HON B. DISRAELI MP, 1860–1864

(London: G. J. Palmer, 1865), 1–79

Church rates

At a meeting of clergy and laity of the rural deanery, held at Amersham, December 4th, 1860, Rev. T. EVETTS, R. D., in the Chair,

The Rt. Hon. B. DISRAELI said,—In this practical country great issues are generally tried on collateral points. It is now generally announced and accepted that the discussion of the question of Church-rates involves that of a National Church. It is, therefore, of the last importance that Churchmen should not make a mistake in this matter. I will view the question now only secularly, and even in that limited sense I shrink from realizing what would be the consequences to this country of the termination of the connection between Church and State. The political and social relations of the National Church to England must be considered. As for the political, the termination of the alliance must break up our parochial constitution. Our political constitution is built upon our parochial constitution. The parish is one of the strongest securities for local government, and on local government mainly depends our political liberty. As to the social relations of the Church with the community, they are so comprehensive and so complicated, so vast and various, that the most far-seeing cannot calculate the consequences of the projected change. It is not merely the education of the people that is concerned, it is even their physical condition. I would almost say, that if, by some convulsion of nature, some important district of the country, one on which the food and the industry of the community mainly depend, were suddenly swept from the surface, the change would not be greater than would arise by the withdrawal of the influence of the Church from our society. The fact is, the Church of England is part of England—a point of view not sufficiently contemplated by those who speculate on changes in her character and position.

It may be asked how it happens that, when so much is at stake, the movement for the abolition of Church-rates has been so active and progressive of late years.

I attribute it to the want of union and organization among Churchmen. When Churchmen are united, the Church is never endangered. This is shown in the years that elapsed between 1831 and 1841. During that period England was in a state of semi-revolution, Ireland of semi-rebellion; the Church of England was the chosen arena for the fierce struggle of parties, and governments were formed on the principle of appropriating its property to secular purposes. But the Church baffled all these attempts, because Churchmen were united and organized. Why are they not united and organized now? There has been no union and organization among Churchmen since 1841. I will state what I deem to be the causes of this condition of things. I have been asked to speak frankly: I will do so, without reserve.

I attribute this want of union and organization to two causes: first, to the disruption of political parties; secondly, to disputes among the clergy themselves. Are these permanent causes? This is not the first time, by many instances, that political connections have been broken up in this country; but there is an irresistible tendency in our public life, that parties both in and out of Parliament should reflect opinion, and not personal interests and feelings. Time, therefore, inevitably adjusted, as it is now adjusting, the proper balance of political connections. With respect to the controversies among the clergy themselves, as distinguished from the Church generally, I think that upon this head there is exaggeration and greater misconception. It is impossible—and were it possible, it is not perhaps to be desired—that in a National Church of a free country like England, there should not be discrepancy of opinion among the clergy on matters of ritual, and even, in some degree, of doctrine. It has always been so. Where there is opinion, and especially religious opinion, there will be periods of excess. We live in one of these periods. They are periods of trial, but not necessarily of danger; and those who too readily augur from them the worst consequences show an ignorance alike of human nature and the history of their own country. You should remember that before this a cardinal's hat has been offered to an Anglican archbishop, while there was also a time when a Socinian prelate sat on the Episcopal Bench; but the Church of England has survived these temptations and experiments. The great body of the community has always rallied round that *via media* which has been eulogized and vindicated by the most eminent of our divines, by Hooker, by Taylor, by Barrow. The period of excess has passed away, and the influence of the Church has remained only greater and more beneficial.

But then arises the question, Suppose Churchmen were again united and organized, as I hope they may be, on what course shall they agree with regard to Church-rates? We cannot conceal from ourselves that on this subject there are two opinions among our friends. Some are for compromise. What does compromise mean? Does it mean improvement? If so, I am for compromise. It may be expedient that the Church-rate levied in a district should be applied to the Church of that district; that when the rate is levied, the purposes to which it is to be applied should be more precisely defined; that the means of obtaining the rate when voted should be more prompt and effective; that there should be no particular charge called Church-rate, but a general parochial rate from which the necessary expenses for the fabric and the service of the church should be deducted by the wardens under certain limitations. All these may be improvements, but all these are matter of detail; and what is the use of attempting to legislate on matters of detail when the principle is not only contested but rejected in one branch of the Legislature? Some of our friends would go further than this. They would exempt the Dissenter from the charge. That is not compromise; that is surrender. It is acknowledging that the Church of England is no longer a National Church. But it is conceding more even than that. This is a public charge of which all the circumstances are of a popular character. It is ancient; it is for a general not to say a common purpose; it is levied by public votes. If in a country where the majority decide everything, the minority are, on the ground of conscientious scruple, to be exempted from a public payment, on what principle can society be held together? Landowners might have a conscientious scruple against paying the public creditor; peace societies might have a conscientious scruple against paying war taxes. What the Dissenter demands is, in fact, an oligarchical privilege; and the principle, if conceded and pursued, may lead to general confusion.

But there is one more objection urged by our friends against levying the Church-rate: that it is impracticable. Is it impracticable? In the vast majority of parishes it is raised with facility. But then it is urged that the parishes which refuse are the parishes of large towns, and that their aggregate population is scarcely inferior to that vast majority of parishes in which it is raised. Yet their immense population are not Dissenters. They are not the votaries of rival creeds and establishments. They are ignorant, or indifferent, or more, unfortunate. Are we, then, to maintain that the Church is to retire from the duty of contending with their unsympathizing and unbelieving mass? The greatest triumphs of the Church have been accomplished in great towns. If the influence of the Church in great towns is limited, it is not because her means are ineffective, but because they are insufficient. When we consider the nature of the religious principle, he is a bold man who will maintain that in our teeming seats of industry there may not be destined for the Church a triumphant future. Who can foresee the history of the next quarter of a century? It will not probably be as tranquil as the last. What if it be a period of great religious confusion and excitement? The country will cling to a church which combines toleration with orthodoxy, and unites divine teaching with human sympathies. Is it wise, then, publicly to announce by legislation that the Church of England relinquishes the character of a National Church?

On these grounds I cannot recommend the present meeting to sanction the principle of exemption. I feel deeply the responsibility of giving such advice. I know I am opposing the recommendation of the Committee of the House of Lords, in 1859, and of what was then at least the unanimous opinion of the Bench of Bishops. I need not say that for the House of Lords I entertain profound respect. In maturity of judgment and calmness of inquiry I think the labours of the great committees of the Lords superior to those of the House of Commons; in acuteness of investigation they are not inferior; but in the interpretation of public opinion, I think, and it is perhaps in the necessity of things, that the Commons have the advantage. I think that the Lords' Committee were precipitate in their course in the matter of Church-rates; I think they have mistaken public humour for public opinion. I am sustained in the difficult and painful course I am taking by the recollection of what occurred in the spring and at the last meeting of the clergy and laity in this deanery. At that time the second reading of Sir John Trelawny's bill had been carried by a much reduced majority, and the advocates of what is fallaciously called compromise were strongly in favour of what they called seizing the opportunity for a settlement. I was of a different opinion. I did not think that the advantage the Church had then obtained was only a happy casualty. I thought it was the break of dawn. I did my utmost to dissuade my friends from relinquishing the contest, and ultimately, on my sole responsibility, opposed the third reading of Sir John Trelawny's bill. The whole country was agitated on the occasion by the opponents of the Church to regain the lost ground. Instead of that, the majority against Church-rates, which had sat like an incubus on the Church for twenty years, virtually disappeared. We owe to that division our commanding position. It is in our power, if we choose it, to close this controversy for ever, not by a feeble concession, but by a bold assertion of public right. We sent 5,000 petitions to the House of Commons last session in favour of that public right; let us send 15,000 this. Every parish should have its petition; they should not be merely signed by the incumbent and churchwardens, as they are in some cases; or by rate-payers merely, as in many cases; but by as many persons as they can obtain. It is the cause of all. There is no greater mistake than to suppose that petitions produce little effect on the House of Commons. They produce great effect. The number of petitions, the number and nature of their signatures, the classes from which they proceed, are all weighed and canvassed. There is a report every week sent by a select committee to every member of Parliament on these heads. The clergy never extensively move in this manner without exercising great authority. You cannot petition too much. You should not wait for the attack. You should send in your petitions as soon as Parliament meets, on a broad issue, in favour of maintaining the union between Church and State, and incidentally in favour of Church-rates. You should also encourage and establish Church defence associations in every part of England. You should habituate the laity to act with the clergy in all matters of public moment to the Church. There is also a third course to take, and here I will address myself particularly to my clerical friends. The laity, through that excellent body the Committee of Laymen, have done their duty in that respect. I have always discouraged the clergy from entering into mere party politics, but now I tell you frankly that, if you want to succeed, you must bring your influence to bear on members of the House of Commons. The question of Church-rates has fortunately not yet fallen into the catalogue of party politics. More than one member of the present Cabinet records at least his vote in their favour. The clergy must make members of Parliament understand that, though this is not a party, it is a political question, and a political question on which in their minds there ought not to be, and there could not be, any mistake. I can assure you of my own knowledge there are many members of Parliament who on this question give careless votes, and think that by so doing they are giving some vague liberal satisfaction without preparing any future inconvenience for themselves. Let our clerical friends, Whig or Tory, Conservative or Liberal, make these gentlemen understand that in their opinion in the union of Church and State depend in a large measure the happiness, the greatness, and the liberty of England.

The present position of the Church

At the annual meeting of the Oxford Diocesan Church Societies, held at Ayles-bury, Nov. 14, 1861, the BISHOP OF OXFORD presiding, the Right Hon. B. DISRAELI spoke as follows:—

MY LORD BISHOP, I have great pleasure in seconding the resolution which has been proposed by the Venerable Archdeacon Bickersteth. Your lordship has with such comprehensive clearness placed before this meeting the object of the dioc-esan societies, and the venerable archdeacon has with such lucid precision stated to us the results of their operations, that it will not be necessary for me to weary this meeting with much detail. Although each of these societies has an indepen-dent constitution, and proposes to itself a specific object, they, in fact, form one great whole. They propose to provide the people of this diocese with education upon those principles which we believe to be sound and true; to provide for the spiritual supervision of the population of this diocese, and to supply the deficien-cies of our parochial system wherever it is incomplete or inadequate. Lastly, they propose to provide for the people of this county sufficient and decorous means of worshipping Almighty God. These, then, are the three great purposes at the attain-ment of which a Church should always aim—education, spiritual supervision, and public worship. It will be clear, therefore, to all present that if these societies were perfectly developed and powerfully supported, they would greatly increase the influence of the Church of England in these three counties; and I conclude that none of those who now hear me will deny that increasing the influence of the Church of England is a means of promoting the welfare of our population, both here and hereafter. Are these societies, then, perfectly developed and pow-erfully supported? That, I apprehend, is the question which we are called upon to consider to-day. We do not assemble merely to hear a report or to audit an account, but rather to reflect and confer upon the condition of these societies; to see whether they completely effect their object; and, above all, whether it is in our power to augment their efficiency.

I will take in the first instance the Diocesan Board of Education. I look upon the constitution of that board as most wise, especially in introducing a due pro-portion of the lay element into its management. I regard the administration of that board, thus constituted, as admirably effective. Yet what do I find? Why, that its efforts are sustained by an annual subscription clearly inadequate to its purpose; and even of that inadequate subscription two-thirds are actually contributed by the clergy themselves. The venerable archdeacon has referred to some possible expression of mine to-day on the important subject of national education, and on the changes which have recently been introduced with respect to it. Neither upon that subject nor upon any other will I now make a controversial remark, but will rather content myself with merely repeating to-day the opinion I have long entertained—viz., that it is impossible that the education of the people of this country can be extended too far if it be founded on sound principles, and that in proportion as it is so extended the influence of the Church of England will be increased. Well, let me now look at the position of the other two societies—the one for building and restoring churches, the other for supplying additional spiritual aid to parishes. What do I find there? Why, that there are demands upon both of these institutions which their resources cannot meet, and that even these scanty resources, I am sorry to hear, are anticipated. That is not, in my mind, an entirely satisfactory state of affairs. When we consider what is the practical object which these societies are instituted to accomplish, I think there are none present who will not concur in that remark. We live in a diocese remarkable for its large parishes, its scattered population, and its numerous hamlets. It is of all dioceses in England the one, perhaps, that most requires this collateral assistance and ancillary aid. Where there is a Church there is a school; where there is a Church there is one being at least whose duty it is to console and to civilize. I am certainly not going to question the conclusion which has been drawn by the venerable archdeacon in the resolution which he has proposed; indeed, I have risen to second it. I will not for a moment controvert the proposition that these diocesan societies have aided, and greatly aided, the action of the Church in this diocese; the details we have listened to to-day satisfactorily prove that; but we have to consider whether the support which those societies have given to the action of the Church in this diocese is sufficient, whether it can be increased, and whether the advantages which have been attained are not rather an incentive to animate us to obtain greater results and to accomplish greater conclusions.

Upon an occasion like the present, when we are met not merely to indulge in idle phrases and conventional congratulations, but rather to examine the condition of these important societies—although I am perfectly justified in supporting this resolution,—I should conceal my own convictions if I did not confess that it does appear to me that the results of these societies do not offer that due relation which they ought to bear to the wealth, intelligence, and sound Churchmanship of the diocese. What is the cause of this,—for I apprehend there must be a cause for a consequence of such importance? There is no want of Churchmen in the diocese of Oxford, and, even in the presence of my Lord Bishop, I cannot refrain from remembering with pride that of all dioceses in England it is one remarkable for the zeal and ability with which it is administered. There is no want of Churchmen in the diocese of Oxford, but that is wanting in the diocese of Oxford which is wanting in the country generally—namely, union among Churchmen. Until union among Churchmen is accomplished, I feel persuaded that the action of these important societies and the good which they can do—being in themselves, in my opinion, incalculable and illimitable—will be an influence which, unfortunately, can be calculated, and will be limited.

I propose to-day, with great brevity, to try whether we cannot come to some understanding upon this important point,—to inquire why there is a want of union among Churchmen; what are the feelings which cause it; and whether there is not some common ground upon which Churchmen of all sections may meet together. If we can come to some satisfactory resolution upon this point, then I do not believe but that that increased and powerful support will be given to these diocesan societies which the right rev. prelate in the chair so ardently wishes for, and that those results will be accomplished which every sincere Churchman and every lover of his century must desire. This want of union among Churchmen in this county—and I apprehend this county is a fair picture of the country generally—appears to me to arise from three feelings, which in different degrees influence different sections of Churchmen. I would describe them as a feeling of perplexity, a feeling of distrust, and a feeling of discontent.

The feeling of perplexity, I am told, arises from what is usually styled the state of parties in the Church, which, from their apparently opposite courses, distract and enfeeble the efforts of Churchmen. This feeling appears to me to be entirely without foundation. Parties have always existed in the Church of England. Nay, more, there never has been a Christian Church, even those which have most affected the character of unity, in which parties have not equally prevailed. But there is this peculiarity in the Church of England, that parties within its pale have been always permitted, nay, recognized and sanctioned. Our Church, always catholic and expansive in its character, has ever felt that the human mind was a manifold quality, and that some men must be governed by enthusiasm, and some controlled by ceremony. Happy the land where there is an institution which prevents enthusiasm from degenerating into extravagance, and ceremony from being degraded into superstition! No doubt, during the last thirty years there have been periods of excess on both sides. But in such great matters we cannot draw a general conclusion from so limited an observation, and the aggregate of experience, in my opinion, fully justifies the conviction that parties in the Church are not a sign of its weakness, but rather a symbol of its strength.

I come now to the feeling of distrust among Churchmen. That I hesitate not to say is mainly attributable to the speculations on sacred things which have been recently published by certain clergymen of our Church. I deeply regret that publication. For the sake of the writers—for no other reason. I am myself in favour of free inquiry on all subjects, civil and religious, with no condition but that it be pursued with learning, argument, and conscience. But then I think we have a right to expect that free inquiry should be pursued by free inquirers. And in my opinion, the authors of "Essays and Reviews" have entered into engagements with the people of this country quite inconsistent with the views advanced in those prolusions. The evil is not so much that they have created a distrust in things; that might be removed by superior argument and superior learning. The evil is, that they have created a distrust in persons, and that is a sentiment which once engendered is not easily removed, even by reason and erudition. Setting, however, aside the characters of the writers, I am not disposed to evade the question whether the work itself is one which should justify distrust among Churchmen. Perhaps it may not be altogether unsuitable that a layman should make a remark upon this subject, and that the brunt of comment should not always be borne by clergymen. Now, the volume of "Essays and Reviews," generally speaking, is founded on the philosophical theology of Germany. What is German theology? It is of the greatest importance that clearer ideas should exist upon this subject than I find generally prevail in most assemblies of my countrymen. About a century ago, German theology, which was mystical, became by the law of reaction, critical. There gradually arose a school of philosophical theologians, which introduced a new system for the interpretation of Scripture. Accepting the sacred narrative without cavil, they explained all the supernatural incidents by natural causes. This system in time was called Rationalism, and, supported by great learning, and even greater ingenuity, in the course of half a century absorbed the opinion of all the intellect of Germany, and indeed, greatly influenced that of every Protestant community. But where now is German Rationalism, and where are its results? They are erased from the intellectual tablets of living opinion. A new school of German theology then arose, which, with profound learning and inexorable logic, proved that Rationalism was irrational, and successfully substituted for it a new scheme of Scriptural interpretation called the mythical. But, if the mythical theologians triumphantly demonstrated, as they undoubtedly did, that Rationalism was irrational, so the mythical system itself has already become a myth; and its most distinguished votaries, in that spirit of progress which, as we are told, is the characteristic of the nineteenth century, and which generally brings us back to old ideas, have now found an invincible solution of the mysteries of existence in a revival of Pagan Pantheism. That, I believe, is a literally accurate sketch of the various phases through which the intellect of Germany has passed during the last century. Well, I ask, what has the Church to fear from speculations so overreaching, so capricious, and so self-destructive? And why is society to be agitated by a volume which is at the best a secondhand medley of these contradictory and discordant theories? No religious creed was ever destroyed by a philosophical theory; philosophers destroy themselves. Epicurus was as great a man, I apprehend, as Hegel; but it was not Epicurus who subverted the religion of Olympus. But, it may be said, are not such lucubrations to be noticed and answered? Both—I reply. Yet, I may observe in passing, that those who answer them should remember that hasty replies always assist well-matured attacks. Let them be answered, then, by men equal to the occasion, and I doubt not that many such will come forward. That a book of that character, written by clergymen of the Church of England, should pass unnoticed by authority, would have been most inconsistent. The conduct of Convocation in this matter appeared to me to be marked by all that discretion and sound judgment which have distinguished its proceedings ever since its revival, and which are gradually, but surely, obtaining for it public confidence. It denounced what it deemed pestilent heresies, but it did not counsel the prosecution of the heretics. And here I am bound to say that I wish this frank and reasonable course had been followed in high places. The wisest of men has said, "For everything there is a season;" and the nineteenth century appears to me a season when the Church should confute error, and not punish it.

Having touched upon the causes of perplexity and distrust, I will now say a word upon the third cause of the want of union among Churchmen,—the feeling of discontent. That is a feeling which prevails among a certain body of our brethren, who entertain what are deemed by some exalted notions respecting ecclesiastical affairs. I know that recent appointments to high places in the Church, and other public circumstances, in their opinion equally opposed to the spread and spirit of sound Church principles, have made some look without any enthusiasm on the connection between Church and State, and even contemplate without alarm the possible disruption of that union. It is impossible to speak of those who hold these opinions without respect, and I would say even affection, for we all of us to a great degree must share in the sentiments of those who entertain these opinions, though we may not be able to sanction their practical conclusions. But I think myself that these opinions rest on a fallacy, and that fallacy consists in assuming that if the dissolution of the tie between Church and State took place, the Church would occupy that somewhat mediæval position which, no doubt, in its time was highly advantageous to Europe, and to no country more than to England. My own opinion differs from theirs. I do not believe that in this age or in this country the civil power would ever submit to a superior authority, or even brook a rival. I foresee, if that were to take place, controversy and contest between Church and State as to their reciprocal rights and duties; possible struggle, probable spoliation. I for one am not prepared to run such hazards. I should grieve to see this great Church of England, this centre of light, learning, and liberty, sink into a position, relative to the nation, similar to that now filled by the Episcopal Church of Scotland, or possibly even subside into a fastidious, not to say finical, congregation.

I hold that the connection between Church and State is one which is to be upheld and vindicated on principles entirely in unison with the spirit of the age, with the circumstances with which we have to deal, and with the soundest principles of political philosophy. The most powerful principle which governs man is the religious principle. It is eternal and indestructible, for it takes its rise in the nature of human intelligence, which will never be content till it penetrates the origin of things and ascertains its relations to the Creator—a knowledge to which all who are here present well know that unaided, and alone, human intelligence can never attain. A wise Government, then, would seek to include such an element in its means of influencing man; otherwise it would leave in society a principle stronger than itself, which in due season may assert its supremacy, and even, perhaps, in a destructive manner. A wise Government, allying itself with religion, would, as it were, consecrate society and sanctify the State. But how is this to be done? It is the problem of modern politics which has always most embarrassed statesmen. No solution of the difficulty can be found in salaried priesthoods and in complicated concordats. But by the side of the State of England there has gradually arisen a majestic corporation—wealthy, powerful, independent—with the sanctity of a long tradition, yet sympathizing with authority, and full of conciliation, even deference, to the civil power. Broadly and deeply planted in the land, mixed up with all our manners and customs, one of the main guarantees of our local government, and therefore one of the prime securities of our common liberties, the Church of England is part of our history, part of our life, part of England itself.

It is said sometimes that the Church of England is hostile to religious liberty. As well might it be said that the monarchy of England is adverse to political freedom. Both are institutions which insure liberty by securing order. It is said sometimes that the Church in this country has proved unequal to its mission, and has failed to secure the spiritual culture of the population. It is perfectly true that within the last fifty years there has been a vast and irregular increase of our population, with which the machinery of the Church has been inadequate to cope. But the machinery of the Church, in that respect, was incomplete only; it was not obsolete. It is said that the Church has lost the great towns; unhappily, the Church has never found the great towns. They are her future, and it will be in the great towns that the greatest triumphs of the Church will be achieved; for the greater the population and the higher the education of the people, the more they will require a refined worship, a learned theology, an independent priesthood, and a sanctuary hallowed by the associations of historic ages.

Here, then, is a common ground on which, dismissing unsubstantial and illusory feelings of perplexity, distrust, and discontent, all sections and parties of Churchmen may unite and act together in maintaining the religious settlement of this realm. Is it unnecessary? Can any one now pretend that the union between Church and State in this country is not assailed and endangered? It is assailed in the chief place of the realm, its Parliament, and it is endangered in an assembly where, if Churchmen were united, the Church would be irresistible. Nothing can exceed the preparation, the perseverance, the ability, and, I will willingly admit, the conscience with which the assault upon the Church is now conducted in the House of Commons. Churchmen would do wrong to treat lightly these efforts, because they believe that they are only the action of a minority in the country. The history of success is the history of minorities. During the last session of Parliament alone a series of bills was introduced, all with various specific objects, but all converging to the same point—an attack upon the authority of the Church and the most precious privileges of Churchmen. Our Charities are assailed; even our Churchyards are invaded; our law of Marriage is to be altered; our public Worship, to use the language of our opponents, is to be "facilitated." Finally, the sacred fabrics of the Church are no longer to be considered national. It is true that all these efforts were defeated. But how defeated? By a strain upon the vigilance and energy of those who repelled the attack, which cannot be counted on hereafter, unless Churchmen, and the country generally, come forward to assist us.

I said that there should not be a subject to-day on which I would make a controversial remark, and I am not going to depart from that rule, though I am going to make a remark on the subject of church-rates. My opinions on church-rates are

16

well known. I hold that the carrying of a measure for the total and unconditional abolition of church-rates would be a signal blow to the alliance between Church and State, and that under no conceivable circumstances—at least, under no circumstances that I can conceive—should it be conceded. But there is a general opinion that legislation on the subject of church-rates is necessary and desirable, and that, without any relinquishment of principle, the law may be improved and adapted to existing circumstances. Be it so; only this I would venture to impress most earnestly on all Churchmen who may be present—and perhaps I may presume to say, on some who are not here—that if there is to be legislation on church-rates, none can be satisfactory which is not introduced with the authority of her Majesty's Government. Sure I am that no member of Parliament, whether he sits in the Lords or the Commons, can, with his own resources and on his own responsibility, succeed in such an enterprise. It would lead only to renewed defeat and increased disaster. The subject is at present in that position that the Government of this country is most happily placed in regard to it if it wishes to legislate. One-half of the House of Commons sitting opposite to them will support any just measure, waiving any points of difference on matters of detail among themselves; and therefore it is in the power of the Government to secure a large majority on the subject. I think myself, on the whole, that it is now their duty to deal with it. The question of church-rates is the great domestic question of the day, and it ought not to be left in the position which it now occupies, after what has occurred in the two Houses of Parliament of late years. The very fact that opinion in the House of Commons as against the Government is equally divided, and that in the other House of Parliament there is an overwhelming majority against any rash and unconditional change, indicates that it is the duty of those who are responsible for the good government of the country to come forward, and with all the authority of an Administration to offer their opinion on the question and to act upon it.

I would venture, my Lord Bishop, to ask your permission to offer one observation on this subject, which I hope those Churchmen who minister to us in things sacred will not think presumptuous. I am myself, I need hardly say, in public life a party man. I am not unaware of the errors and excesses which occasionally occur in party conflicts, but I have a profound conviction that in this country the best security for purity of government and for public liberty is to be found in the organized emulation of public men. Nevertheless, I have ever impressed on my clerical friends the wisdom of the utmost reserve on their part with regard to mere political questions. Not that I question their right to entertain opinions on all public questions, and to act upon them. An English clergyman is an English gentleman and an English citizen. But I have always felt that in proportion to their political activity will the integrity of their spiritual and social influence be diminished; and I think that influence of far greater importance than their political activity. But there is a limit to this reserve. What I would presume to recommend is this:—When institutions are in question, and not individuals, the clergy ought to interfere, and when, of all institutions, that to which they are specially devoted, and on which their daily thoughts and nightly meditations should be fixed, is at stake, their utmost vigilance and determination should be summoned. When the interests of the Church, of which they are the sacred ministers, are concerned, the clergy would be guilty of indefensible apathy if they remained silent and idle. The clergy of the Church of England have at this moment one of the greatest and most glorious opportunities for accomplishing a great public service that was probably ever offered to any body of public men. It is in their power to determine and to insure that Church questions in this country shall no longer be party questions. They, and they alone, can effect this immense result, and that by a simple process—I mean by being united. Let them upon general public affairs entertain that which I trust they always will entertain as free Englishmen, their own general opinions. Let them be banded in the two great historical parties in the State, Whig or Tory. It would be a very unfortunate thing for this country if in any great body of respectable men there should ever cease to be such differences of political opinion. But let them say that Church questions are not questions which they will permit to enter the province of political party. If the clergy are united in that determination, rest assured that the laity will soon become united too, and we shall be spared hereafter the frightful anomaly of seeing conscientious Churchmen recording their votes and exerting their influence against the Church. Depend upon it that nothing in this country can resist Churchmen when united, and if they are only united on Church questions, they will add immensely to the strength of good government and to the general welfare of the people. Then I believe that these admirable institutions, the object of which is to ameliorate the whole body of society, will assume that character in their action which is so devoutly to be desired—then the great aims of the Church, the Education of the People, their perfect spiritual Supervision, the completion of our Parochial System, and, above all, the free and decorous Worship of the Almighty, will be securely effected.

My Lord Bishop, I am sometimes apt to think that there is nothing unsuitable in this diocese taking the lead in bringing about such a result, not merely because it is presided over by one who possesses that energy of character and that fertility of resource which indicate his capacity for dealing with great affairs, but also for other reasons. The two things which Englishmen love most are religion and liberty. Now, in this diocese over which you rule are included those districts which in the history of this country are most memorable for sacred learning and for public spirit. May their united influence guide your lordship and your clergy at this grave and critical moment in the history of the Church, and you will prove a shining light and a powerful example to other dioceses; and then we need not despair, under the favour of Divine Providence, of seeing the Church of England for ever established on the catholic sympathies of an enlightened and religious people.

The future position of the Church

At a public meeting in aid of the Oxford Diocesan Society for the Augmentation of Small Benefices, held at High Wycombe, Thursday, October 30, 1862, the Right Hon. B. DISRAELI spoke as follows:—

My Lord Bishop, I rise to second the resolution moved by the Archdeacon of Buckingham. He has placed the scope of the question so fully before this meeting, that it is unnecessary for me to dilate upon it in detail. The condition of the mass of the benefices in this diocese is not satisfactory; but I hope that the result of this meeting, and the result of many meetings like the present throughout the country, will prove that we have no cause for despondency. No doubt for a long time a very erroneous impression has subsisted as to the remuneration received by the clergy of our Church, and the amount of property which it possesses. I think that time has to a certain degree removed this false impression; but when errors have long prevailed and have been made use of for hostile purposes, it is difficult entirely to remove their first consequences. The fact is, that the clergy of the Church of England are a poor clergy, and not a rich clergy; and it is for the sake of the country, not principally for the sake of the clergy, that I venture to lay down that we should take care that the clergy should be fairly remunerated. If you wish to engage the highest education and the highest sense of duty in the performance of the sacred offices of the Church, it is most inexpedient that you should offer to those from whom you expect such a high fulfilment, rewards and remunerations which no class of society in service would accept.

With regard to the present excellent Association, which is in its infancy, I may remark, it has already effected some good. Of the small livings in this county, although we have only laboured one year, twenty-two have received some aid; and I observe of these twenty-two there are eleven of which the highest do not exceed 80*l.* per annum, while the lowest is under 50*l.* a year. Indeed it is a fact, which will no longer be disputed, that the clergy of our Church, who have been so long described as a wealthy and an over-paid clergy, contribute to the service of the Church from their private resources more than they receive from it. I believe that it is now on record, that of their income at least two-thirds is provided from their own private resources. Well, that is not a position of affairs which is honourable to the country. But I do not wish to recommend the cause which I am advocating to-day upon a mere sentimental plea. It is not merely that it is not honourable to the country, but it is highly disadvantageous to the country. If it be of the first importance that the highest education and men who are impressed with the highest sense of duty should be engaged in the ministration of our sacred offices, we cannot expect such a result—it would be foreign to the principles of human nature—if we hold out to them none of those inducements which animate the other classes of mankind.

It is not surprising that the Church of England should be a poor Church, because the Church in this country has been despoiled. That is not a fate peculiar to the Church of England. Other Churches too have been despoiled; but there is a peculiarity with regard to our Church in this matter. In other countries, when the Church has been deprived by the State of its property, at least that property has been applied to public and national purposes. That has not been the case of the Church in England. The property of the Church in England has been granted by despots and tyrants to their minions, and has been made the foundation and establishment of powerful families, who, by virtue of that property, and not from any public services of their own, have had for generations a great portion of the government of this country and of its power and patronage. Well, I find in these circumstances of aggravation in the case of the spoliation of the Church in this country, compared with the spoliation of Churches in other countries, circumstances of consolation and hope, because we live in an age when communities are governed by the influence of opinion, and when individuals are regulated in their conduct to a great degree by the influence of conscience, I cannot but believe that the estimable descendants of those original appropriators of Church property, when they learn—and in a country of free discussion like the present they must now all of them be well informed upon that subject—that men of the highest education, who, from a sense of duty and devotion, dedicate their lives to comforting the people, receive for their labours stipends which even menials would refuse—I cannot but believe the estimable descendants of those original appropriators, in the satiety of their splendour, must feel an impulse that will make them apply a portion of that property, ages ago thus unjustly obtained, to purposes of a character which society would recognize, and by its approbation reward. And I think, my Lord, that what we have heard to-day, and what we know of the action of this Society, justifies that expectation. What the Archdeacon has just mentioned in the instance of our highly-esteemed neighbour Lord Howe, is a most gratifying case; and I learn that shortly after the formation of this Society—it is but due to the Duke of Bedford to mention it—a communication was received from his Grace, couched in a spirit worthy of his high position, which showed that he completely recognized the justice of the principle I have indicated. His Grace feels it to be his duty, as it has been his performance, with respect to miserably paid livings on his own estate, possessing, as it is well known his family does, large ecclesiastical property, to raise all the low livings to an amount which is at least adequate to sustain a clergyman who is performing parochial duty. Well, then, I say, we have a right to expect—and I am more sanguine than the Archdeacon on that head—that a portion of the property which was alienated from the Church, under circumstances which could not prevail and be justified in the present age, will yet find its way to the increase of these livings.

But I should not be acting with candour to your Lordship if I concealed my opinion that there is little hope of any large action on the part of the class to which I have referred in this respect; or, indeed, I will say that there is much hope of any great exertion being made by the laity and the Church generally, unless the Church itself takes a more definite and determined position than it has occupied during the last five-and-twenty years. During that period there has been a degree of perplexity and of hesitation—I will say even of inconsistency—in the relations between the Church and the nation, that has damped the ardour and depressed the energies of churchmen. I think it is not difficult to indicate the probable cause of that conduct; and it is only by ascertaining it that we can perhaps supply the remedy which may remove those injurious consequences.

Society in this country is now established upon the principle of civil and religious liberty; and, in my opinion, it is impossible—and, if possible, not desirable—to resist the complete development of that principle. At the same time, you have a Church established by law; that is to say, a National Church; and there is an apparent inconsistency in the principle which you have adopted as the foundation of your social system and the existence of that Established Church; because the principle of civil and religious liberty has placed legislative power in the hands of great bodies of the people who are not in communion with that Church, and they have used that power during the last five-and-twenty years, with caution at first, with much deliberation at first, but, as time advanced, with more boldness and with more energy, till, within the last few years, they have made an avowed attack upon that Church, an attack which they have conducted with great ability and with great courage. That being the case, you have what has occurred during the last quarter of a century; you have an apparent want of sympathy between that which, by the Constitution, is the National Church and a great portion of the nation; a state of affairs which is to be highly deprecated.

Twenty years ago, when this inconvenience was first generally felt, ardent churchmen, as sincere churchmen as ever lived, thought they had found a solution for this difficulty by terminating the union between Church and State. They said, "Terminate the union between Church and State, as the whole of the nation is no longer in communion with the Church, and you will put an end to the dissatisfaction that partially, but to a considerable degree, prevails." That, no doubt, is a very plausible suggestion, and one that has been accepted by ingenuous and able minds; but if it is examined into, it will be found one that may lead to results very different from those which are anticipated by the persons who are favourable to it, and results perhaps unsatisfactory and injurious to the country; because it cannot be supposed for a moment that in this age the civil power will tolerate an *imperium in imperio,* and allow a great corporation, in possession of vast property—for the property is considerable, though, if distributed, it may not offer adequate compensation to those who are labouring in its service—to act in independence of the State. Therefore, there is no concealing it from ourselves that it would soon end in another spoliation, and the Church would be left without the endowment of the estates which it at present possesses. The principles of Divine truth, I admit, do not depend upon property; but the circulation of the principles of divine truth, by human machinery, depends upon property for its organization. And there is no doubt that, deprived of the means by which the divine instruction which it affords to the people is secured, the Church would of course lose immensely in its efficiency.

But in the case of the Church of England, it is not merely the question of the loss of its property, but it is also a question of the peculiar character of that property. The property of the Church of England is territorial. It is so distributed throughout the country that it makes that Church, from the very nature of its tenure, a National Church; and the power of the Church of England does not depend merely on the amount of property it possesses, but, in a very great degree, on the character and kind of that property. Then, I say, the result would be, that the Church, deprived of its status, would become merely an episcopal sect in this country; and, in time, it is not impossible it might become an insignificant one. But that is not the whole, or, perhaps, even the greatest evil that might arise from the dissolution of the connection between Church and State, because in the present age the art of government becomes every day more difficult, and no Government will allow a principle so powerful as the religious principle to be divorced from the influences by which it regulates the affairs of a country. What would happen? Why, it is very obvious what would happen. The State of England would take care, after the Church was spoiled, to enlist in its service what are called the ministers of all religions. The ministers of all religions would be salaried by the State, and the consequences of the dissolution of the alliance between Church and State would be one equally disastrous to the Churchman and to the Non-conformist. It would place the ministers of all spiritual influences under the control of the civil power, and it would in reality effect a revolution in the national character. In my opinion, it would have even a most injurious effect upon the liberties of the country; and I cannot believe that after the thought and discussion that have been devoted to the subject for now the twenty years since it was first mooted by ardent and sincere men, I cannot believe there can be among those who have well considered it, any great difference of opinion, but that all men—I would say the Churchman, the Dissenter, the Philosopher—would shrink from a solution of the difficulty by such means.

Well, then, what would you do? I maintain that you have only one alternative; that if you do not favour a dissolution of the union of Church and State, you must assert the Nationality of the Church of England.

I know it will be said, "Assert the Nationality of the Church in a nation where there are millions not in communion with the Church? These are words easy to use, but practically, what would be the consequence of a mere phrase?" Well, I think that is a point worthy of some grave consideration; and in the first place it is expedient to ascertain, What is the character of those—I will acknowledge it—millions who are not in communion with the Church? They consist of two classes. They consist of those who dissent from the Church, and of those who are indifferent to the Church; but these classes are very unequally divided.

Now the history of English dissent will always be a memorable chapter in the history of the country. It displays many of those virtues—I would say most of those virtues—for which the English character is distinguished—earnestness, courage, devotion, conscience; but one thing is quite clear: that in the present day the causes which originally created dissent no longer exist; while, which is of still more importance, there are now causes in existence opposed to the spread of dissent. I will not refer to the fact that many, I believe the great majority, of the families of the descendants of the original Puritans and Presbyterians have merged in the Church of England itself; but no man can any longer conceal from himself that the tendency of this age is, not that all creeds and Churches and consistories should combine,—I do not say *that,* mind,—but I do say, that the tendency of the present age is, that all Churches, creeds, and consistories should cease hereafter from any internecine hostility. That is a tendency which it is impossible for them

22

to resist; and therefore, so far as the spread of dissent, of mere sincere religious dissent, is concerned, I hold that it is of a very limited character, and there is nothing in the existence of it which should prevent the Church of England from asserting her nationality. For observe, the same difficulties that are experienced by the Church are also experienced by the dissenters, without the advantage which the Church possesses, in her discipline, learning, and tradition.

But I come now to the more important consideration; I come to the second division of the English population that is not in communion with the Church of England. And here I acknowledge that, at first, the difficulty seems great, because here you do count them by millions; but, in the first place, observe that these are not dissenters from the Church; these are not millions who have quitted the Church. There are great masses of the population who have never yet entered into communion with the Church of England. The late Archbishop of Canterbury, a most amiable and pious man, and by no means deficient in observation of the times, passed many of his last years in anxious perplexity about the anomalous position of that National Church of which he was the Primate. I was a member of a committee formed of members of the two Houses of Parliament, who had to confer together upon the conduct to be pursued in the Houses of Lords and Commons by the friends of the Church, upon some momentous questions in which the interests and the character of the Church were concerned. The Archbishop of Canterbury was our Chairman, and in every instance when we had to confer together, the late Archbishop always counselled surrender, and surrender without conditions. Fortunately, there were other opinions upon that committee, and I am glad to say, that in every instance the late Archbishop of Canterbury was outvoted. It so happened, that in all these cases, when they were brought before the Houses of Parliament for decision, it was proved that the opinion of the Archbishop had been erroneous, and that he had miscalculated the feeling in favour of the Church which existed in the country, because the decision of the Houses of Parliament, and especially the House of Commons, is only a reflection upon such subjects of the feeling of the country. The year before the Archbishop died, he did me the honour of seeking a conversation with me, and the object of that conversation was to explain the course he had taken with regard to these questions, in which he admitted that, so far as recent occurrences were concerned, he had been mistaken; but he said: "Although I may have formed an erroneous judgment, and although I admit you and your friends were right in your view of the case, still I went upon a great fact. My conduct was based upon a great fact, which no one can deny, and it is this,—No one can deny that the population has outgrown the Church." No one can deny that. I do not deny it; but I draw from that fact a conclusion exactly opposite to that of the late Archbishop of Canterbury. My inference is the very reverse of the one which he drew, and the conduct which he consequently recommended.

If, indeed, the Church of England were in the same state as the pagan religion was in the time of Constantine; if her altars were paling before the Divine splendour of inspired shrines, it might be well, indeed, for the Church and for the ministers of the Church, to consider the course that they should pursue; but nothing of the kind is the case. You have to deal, so far as regards the millions who are not in communion with the Church, and whom I will describe, distinguishing them from the dissenters, as those who are indifferent to the Church—you are dealing with millions of the English people. And who are the English people? The English people are, without exception, the most enthusiastic people in the world. There are more excitable races. The French, the Italians, are much more excitable; but for deep and fervid feeling, there is no race in the world at all equal to the English. And what is the subject, of all others, upon which the English people have always been most enthusiastic? Religion. The notes on the gamut of their feeling are few, but they are deep. Industry, Liberty, Religion, form the solemn scale. Industry, Liberty, Religion—that *is* the history of England. Now, upon these three subjects they have periods of exaltation. They have had periods of deep feeling within our own experience, alike with regard to *toil* and with regard to *freedom;* and it is not impossible, nay, I would not hesitate to say, there may be many in this room who may witness a period of exaltation in the public mind of the country, and especially among these millions, with regard to *religion,* that has certainly not been equalled in our times, or in the times of our fathers. But what an opportunity is that for a Church! When great bodies of the nation, who have never been in communion with the Church, have their minds, their feelings, and their passions, all exalted in the direction of religion, and influenced by the religious principle, what an opportunity for a Church, with her learning, her organization, and the ineffable influences of her tradition, with her sacred services, with her divine offices, with all the beauty of holiness in which she worships, to advance and address them! What an immense field for any Church! But what a field for a corporation which is not merely a Church, but which is the Church of England; blending with divine instruction the sentiment of patriotism, and announcing herself, not only as the Church of God, but as the Church of the Country! I say that, with these views, instead of supposing that the relations which exist between a large body of our fellow-subjects and the Church—relations at this moment of indifference and even of alienation—are causes why the Church should not assert her Nationality, they are causes and circumstances which peculiarly call upon the Church to exert herself; and to prepare for a coming future which will demand her utmost energies, as I believe it will yield her greatest rewards.

I know it may be said that this is a practical country; and though this view of the character of the English people may be abstractedly just, and though the advice which you give may be generally well founded, still what are the practical measures by which the Nationality of the Church may be asserted? I do not think we ought to blink the question, and in considering those means, I am brought intimately and nearly to the resolution that is in my hand. It would not be convenient for me now to enter at any great length into a subject of this kind; but inasmuch as it is utterly impossible that we ever can put societies of this character upon the foundation that we desire, and infuse into them the spirit which is necessary, without a clear conception of what the conduct and the career of the Church should be, I will briefly advert to some of them, especially as they all, to a certain degree, refer to the cause of our meeting to-day.

Well, then, if I am to consider what are the means by which the Nationality of the Church may be asserted, I say certainly, in the first place,—it is hardly necessary for me to say that,—the Church should Educate the people. But though we have lived during the last quarter of a century in times not very favourable to the Church; though the Church has gone through great trials during that period, and has trials even at the present moment, not merely from its avowed enemies, still I think the Church may congratulate herself upon the whole on what she has accomplished in the education of the people. It is possible that the means which have been at the command of the Church may be reduced. It is possible that there may be fresh assaults and attacks upon the machinery by which the State has assisted the Church in that great effort; but I think that no impartial man can shut his eyes to the conviction that the Church of England during the last five-and-twenty years has obtained a command over the education of the people, which fifty years ago could not have been contemplated, and so much having been done, we have no right to believe that the command will be diminished. On the contrary, whatever may be the conduct of the State, I express my belief, that the influence of the Church over the education of the people will increase. Well, so far, on that head, the result is favourable.

There is another important means by which the Nationality of the Church may be, in my opinion, asserted. It is one on which there is controversy; but it is only by controversy that truth is elicited and established. I am in favour, not of any wild, indiscriminate, or rashly-adopted, but, on the contrary, of a moderate and well-considered extension of the Episcopate. And I form my opinion upon the advantages that would arise from an extension of that character, from the consequences of the extension of the Episcopate to our colonies, which have been signal, and, to a considerable degree, upon the consequences that have resulted from the establishment of the two new Dioceses in England. In the diocese of Ripon, I think, the effects have been very considerable. More might have been done in the diocese of Manchester, where the occasion was golden; but something has been gained, and at least we have the consolation of hoping that a glorious future there awaits us.

Then there is a third means and measure by which, I think, the Nationality of the Church of England may be asserted; and that is by a further development of the lay element in the administration of affairs which are not of a spiritual character. We must erase from the mind of the country the idea that the Church of England is a clerical corporation. The Church of England is a national corporation, of which the clerical element, however important, is only a small element; and except—a great exception no doubt—the ministering to us of sacred things, there is nothing that concerns the Church in which it is not alike the privilege and the duty of laymen to take an active part. Now, I believe, if such a prudent development of the lay element in the management of the affairs of the Church takes place, you will have a third great means of asserting the Nationality of the Church.

There is a fourth measure, which is, in my mind, of great importance, and that is the maintenance of the Parochial system. Unfortunately in this country, so far as the Church is concerned, very erroneous ideas exist upon the subject of our parochial constitution. In consequence of the great changes that have taken place of late years with regard to parochial administration,—as, for example, mainly in the Poor Law and in some other measures,—there is a too general idea that the parochial constitution has been subverted; but so far as the Church is concerned, the parochial constitution is complete and inviolate. It is not in any degree affected by any of those changes, and the right of visitation, both by the parishioner and the parish priest, remains intact; and if properly acted upon, is a source of immense and increasing influence, especially in those large towns of which we hear so much, and where the right is now considered as not even in existence.

The fifth means by which the Nationality of the Church may be asserted brings me closely to this resolution; and I mention it last, not because I think it inferior in importance to any of those which have preceded it. You must render your clergy more efficient, whether in the great towns you increase the staff of curates, which perhaps is more advantageous than building churches without making preparations for their maintenance, and still less for their endowment; or whether you avail yourselves of those means which other societies in this Diocese for the increase of spiritual assistance afford; or whether, lastly and chiefly, you take the great subject in hand which has brought us together to-day, and make an effort throughout the country for putting an end to those low stipends which are now almost in mockery appended to the discharge of laborious parochial duties. I can say from my own experience, what I have no doubt many gentlemen in this room can confirm, that in innumerable cases at this moment the clergyman of the Church of England, devoting his life, his health, the fruits of a refined education, to the service of God and the comforting of the people, is not only not remunerated, but is absolutely, by his contributions to local and parochial objects and institutions, out of pocket at the end of the year in the parish which he serves.

Well, these are five great practical means by which the Nationality of the Church may be asserted. Still they are but means and machinery, and they must be inspired by that spirit of zeal and devotion which alone can ensure success, and which alone deserve success; but in the present state of this country, after the analysis of its population which I have presumed to sketch to-day, I say that a great corporation like the Church of England, where the clergy and laity act in union, may look forward by means of measures such as I have now mentioned under these five heads, to great, triumphant, and final success.

There is only one other topic upon which I will make a remark before I conclude. It will be observed, that the five measures which I have ventured to recommend, with one exception, can be adopted by the Church without any appeal to the Legislature—a great advantage; and in the exceptional instance, namely, that which refers to the extension of the Episcopate, if an application were made to the Legislature, couched with the discretion becoming the subject, I have little doubt it would be successful. We must not shut our eyes to this fact, that the time has

26

gone by when we could ask for new powers and privileges from Parliament to establish the position of the Church of England. That time is gone. I myself do not undervalue a public recognition of the Church by the Legislature of the country. I think its importance is great, perhaps cannot be overestimated. I believe that in its action it gives the Church an authority with many minds which, without that position, she would not possess or exercise. It is because we believe that a public recognition of the Nationality of the Church by the Constitution is of that great value, that I, and others who have acted with me in that behalf, have resisted all those attacks which during the last few years in Parliament have been directed at the privileges and the public status of the Church. We have so acted, because we believed that public status would give the Church an immense advantage when the opportunity offered of asserting her Nationality. If we had not believed such would be the consequence, we should have declined contending for privileges which would otherwise be obsolete, and for a public status that was barren. But because we thought that, when the hour arrived for a great effort in the Church,— and I think that hour has arrived,—a public recognition by the ancient constitution of the country of her national status would be of immense advantage, and give it great vantage-ground, we made those efforts and entered into that struggle. I would venture to hope that this meeting to-day may be of some use; I will venture to hope that the effort of this diocese will be great, and that it will not be confined to this diocese. I hope we shall be no longer appalled and paralyzed by indefinite estimates of the hostility and the obstacles we have to encounter. I hope, above all, that those faint-hearted among our brethren, who seem to me of late years only to be considering how they could decorously relinquish a position of great respon- sibility, will learn that the wisest course with regard to the Church of England, as with regard to all other cases in which a great duty is involved, is to be coura- geous, and endeavour to perform that duty. Then I am confident that this Church of England will show to the world that it has powers of renovation which have not been suspected by some. For my own part, I uphold it, not merely because it is the sanctuary of Divine Truth, but because I verily believe it is our best security for that civil and religious liberty of which we hear so much, and which we are told is opposed to its institution.

Uniformity Act Resolution

In the House of Commons, June 9, 1863, Motion made and Question proposed,— "That in the opinion of this House the subscription required from the clergy to the Thirty-nine Articles, and to the Prayer-book ought to be relaxed."—Mr. BUXTON.

The Previous Question having been moved, Mr. DISRAELI said: It is with reluc- tance that I rise, Sir, after the very able speech of my noble friend (Lord R. Cecil), who has touched, with so much force, on many of the important topics that we have discussed this evening. But really I cannot reconcile it to myself to pass over in silence the course which the House has resolved, partly, I believe, from accident, to take this evening—a harmless one, no doubt, if followed with a clear understanding, on both sides, of the feelings and opinions under which it was adopted. I cannot myself at all agree that moving the previous question was a proper mode in which to encounter the motion of the hon. member for Maidstone, and I believe that is not an opinion peculiar to myself. From circumstances of a technical and passing nature, the House has adopted that course; and my right hon. friend the member for the University of Cambridge having acquiesced in it—I fancied with some reluctance—I do not think it becoming towards one whom I always wish to treat with that deep respect which he deserves, to disturb the arrangement at which the House has arrived. But feeling the importance of this question, and knowing that the vote given and the procedure adopted to-night may be hereafter represented to the disadvantage of those who object to the motion, I beg to say, that though after the speech of the Chancellor of the Exchequer the course we are about to adopt is, I am happy to believe, perfectly harmless, and one not altogether devoid of propriety, it is not the one which I myself should have suggested. The hon. gentleman the member for the University of Dublin said he should give a cordial vote for the motion of the previous question. I have, in the course of my time, voted occasionally for the previous question, but I never gave a cordial vote for it; and, of all the motions made in this House, it is one which I should least expect, and which I have never previously known, to receive the cordial adhesion of any hon. gentleman. I should never adopt voting for the previous question as a testimony of the ardour of my feeling, or of the strength of my conviction.

This important discussion, the result of which will not pass away with the transient debate of to-night, commenced with the motion of the hon. gentleman the member for Maidstone, in which he appeared, as I understood him, to counsel the relaxation of the subscription to the Articles and the Liturgy, in deference to the overwhelming power of public opinion. The hon. gentleman feels that his case is irresistible, because he is supported and animated by the invincible power of public opinion. The hon. member for Pontefract, who followed, giving a partial adhesion to the views of the hon. member for Maidstone, counselled us to take, not an identical, but a limited course in the same direction, on a ground totally adverse—namely, that public opinion cannot be trusted, that its deleterious tendencies must be fenced out and guarded against. The House, after hearing the statement of the Minister, agreed not to support either the original motion or the amendment; but it consented to a course which, without explanation, gives an implied assent to the position of the hon. member for Maidstone, and also to the gentleman who proposed the amendment, by admitting that there are grounds entitling the question to the consideration of this House. Now, what are those grounds? Subscription to the Articles and to the Prayer-Book is objected to—I am now trying to give a general description of the main arguments we have heard—because they are opposed to that comprehensive character which I suppose all of us are agreed that the Church should assume and maintain. No one is more in favour of the comprehensive character of the Church of England than myself; but I would make this condition—that the comprehensiveness of the Church of England should be based on Church principles. The hon. gentleman the member for Maidstone, as others before him have done, pointed out the origin of the Act of Charles II., to which he supposes such injurious effects upon the comprehensive character of the Church may be ascribed. He has shown us how many, who might be included in the pale of the Church, are no longer found in its fold; and he has denounced the ancient legislation, the consequences of which may be found in our present situation. I doubt very much the general justice of this criticism, and I doubt whether it was possible at that time, or at any time, in this country, or perhaps in any country, to prevent in matters of religion what is called Dissent. I look upon Dissent—I am sure the hon. member for Sheffield will pardon me for saying it—as a weakness incident to humanity. Look at the case of the Roman Catholic religion. I will be bound I could show, if it were necessary, that there has been as much dissent, as much heresy, as much schism, in the Church of Rome as in the Church of England. But the dissent has occasionally been forcibly suppressed, the schism has in some instances been adroitly managed, and the heresy has found a safety-valve in the institution sometimes even of monastic orders. You have found this in a religion established on the principle of infallibility, and in countries where that religion has been supported by the civil power, assuming, generally, an arbitrary character. What, then, can we expect in a country where, instead of infallibility, religion is founded upon the principle of free inquiry—and where, though that religion has, generally speaking, been supported by the civil power, that civil power has yet been established on the principle of civil liberty?

It is only as politicians and as statesmen that we may presume to speak in this House upon this subject, and I maintain that in modern times, since that year 1662 which has been just quoted to the House, no English statesman has ever contemplated that the Church of England, though founded on a catholic creed, should at the same time command a catholic communion. For the last two hundred years no statesman has contemplated that the whole population of England should be within the pale of the national Church. What has been contemplated in these centuries of what I may call the practical working of our Constitution, has been this—that there should be a standard of religious truth established by the State in the country; that the religious principle should be recognised as one of the most important and influential in the conduct of Government; that the Government of this country should not be reduced to a mere question of police; but that we should seek to influence the conduct of men by the highest sanction which can be conceived. Sir, I say that object has been successfully accomplished by the Church in its connection with the State in England during the last two centuries. We have to-night a new system commended to our notice, which is to bring about a state of affairs more comprehensive. The first principle of this new system is, that not only the creed of the Church should be catholic, but that the communion should be catholic, and that we should all belong to the same Church—a doctrine not very favourable at the outset to that principle of religious liberty which, I believe, is still much esteemed in this country. When you analyze this doctrine it comes to this:—The comprehensive Church is, in fact, to be a Church founded very much on the same principles as that federal constitution of America, of which in this House we have heard so much and so often, and with regard to which recently we have witnessed such strange and startling experiences. All creeds are to belong to one Church, but all creeds are to retain their own particular opinions. But that experiment has been tried to a great degree on the Continent of Europe. You have had it in Germany; you may see its defects to a certain degree in France; and you may trace them not only in Europe, but in America. You have what without offence may be called an infidel Church, composed of various sections of the population, some of them often influenced by fanatical impulses. If on the Continent such an experiment has not been over success-ful, what are our chances of success in England, where feelings on religious subjects are so deep and enthusiastic? No one can doubt that the consequences would be of a perilous character, perhaps disastrous to the State, and entailing results which none would dare to contemplate, and all must wish to avoid. Therefore, I very much doubt whether this system of comprehension on which the relaxation of these tests is recommended is a sound one. A Church may be so comprehensive that no one may comprehend it.

It is really a question for us to consider, if this Act of Charles II., which has been so much vituperated to-night, had not been passed, what might have been the historical fortunes of this country? It is perfectly absurd to consider the Act of Uniformity in an abstract sense without reference to the spirit of the time in which it was passed, and without any relation to the events which preceded it. The hon. member for Poole (Mr. D. Seymour) told us that it was passed in a time of pas-sion. It is very well for us to describe a period as a time of passion; but what we describe as a time of passion was, in fact, a time of feeling. Men thought and felt, and they did something. All the great things done in the history of England were done in a time of passion. If you scrutinize the means and motives by which the great statutes and the great charters of English liberties were obtained, on which were established the deep foundations of the glorious edifice of our social life, you may make as good a case out against them as against Archbishop Sheldon. Take the Grand Remonstrance. It was carried by a casting vote, or something of the sort. You might say who cares for a political document which depends on such a pedigree; and yet I do not suppose any one would be swayed by a criticism of that sort on the great doctrines which were vindicated and upheld by the Grand Remonstrance. The language of these tests has been much criticised to-night. Some hon. gentlemen have expressed their approbation of them as a whole, but they say there is a word here which does not please them, an expression which might be altered. But is this the tone in which we ought to view the ancient docu-ments of the nation, upon which its most important conditions depend? Take the Bill of Rights. I will be bound to say, that if I were to give notice that on going into Committee of Supply on Friday night, I would call the attention of the House to the Bill of Rights, and make a motion upon it, I would make such a case out against the Bill of Rights by criticising its articles, that I should stand in almost as eminent a position as the hon. member for Maidstone. I dare say I should have some followers, if not many in this House, at least out of it; and no doubt it would take a position among Parliamentary questions. But I do not think that any sane man, without any reference to the justice of my criticisms, would say that it was a wise thing, or for the welfare of the country, to call the Bill of Rights into question; on the contrary, I am quite sure that any person who took such a course would assume that position in political life to which he was fairly entitled. I would say, therefore, with all respect for the hon. member for Maidstone, that that part of his case which rests upon the expediency of making the Church comprehensive, and upon the injurious effect which the Act of Uniformity has had on its comprehensive character, is neither sound nor true; and that, in fact, if you are to indulge in what I would presume to call *dilettante* criticism, there is scarcely any record of our rights—scarcely anything which was ever done by the great men who preceded us in this and the other House of Parliament which may not be cavilled at, questioned, and improved. But the result would be that the edifice of our rights and liberties—of our political and social life, which has been raised at so much pains and so much risk, would be reduced to nothing—it would be resolved into its original elements—the fabric would crumble into dust.

I admit that there are grave reasons for the hon. gentleman bringing forward this question, other than the argument that by relaxing the terms of subscription you may render the Church more comprehensive in her character. I have no doubt that there are reasons peculiar to the present time which act with great force, and have great influence on masses of society, more especially on that youthful portion of society to which we must look forward, whether as clergymen to continue the ministration of the offices of our Church, or as laymen to be among its ardent supporters. The existence of these reasons has been frankly admitted to-night, and especially by recent speakers. I think there is in the times in which we live a circumstance which disturbs the public mind, which has influenced the spirit of youth, and has acted very injuriously on those who would otherwise enter into holy orders. It is quite unwise to conceal it, and it is idle to explain it, as is the fashion even in high places, by statistical arguments. I do not believe that the want of candidates for Ordination is to be accounted for by the enormous nuggets which are to be discovered in Australia, or by the large fortunes said to be realized by civil engineers. I believe the youth of England are actuated by more noble and generous feelings. I was myself once young, and committed many follies; but at that time of life I can most frankly declare I was not influenced by such considerations, and I believe the generation to which we look forward with hope and confidence is equally free from such degrading ideas and sordid motives. Still, it cannot be concealed that there is much in the theological studies of this country, much in the theological productions of the day, which naturally would influence and disturb the ardent and susceptible mind of youth.

The hon. gentleman who seconded the motion informed us, and I agree with him, that it is likely that for many years questions respecting the Church and religion may be brought under the consideration of the British Parliament. I trust, however, that we shall be able to discuss those questions in a manner becoming our position—that we shall remember that we are not a lay synod, but that we are the Reformed Parliament of England. I hope that when those questions come before us we shall not discuss them like those members of the Long Parliament, who on occasion pulled their thumb Bibles from their waistcoat pockets, and enforced their arguments *pro* and *con.* by quoting chapter and verse. On the contrary, I hope that we shall remember the constitutional and social position which we occupy, and meet the difficulty without exciting any feelings but those which are suited to the unimpassioned sphere of the British Parliament. But without entering into any religious controversy, I would venture to say that there is nothing very new, nothing very original, and nothing very alarming in this periodical appearance of a particular branch of literature which is supposed to have affected the opinion of the country, and to have rendered it necessary that we should suddenly and precipitately alter the Act of Uniformity. It is important that we should remember this. I would venture to say to those who are young—because, though they have devoted themselves with so much care to the cultivation of their minds, they may be pardoned for not being perfectly aware of what has happened with reference to this subject before—that there is nothing new in these doubts which have been thrown out, and which appear to have recently agitated some portions of the public mind. A century and a half ago, at a time when England was in a state of great civilization, these views were very prevalent in this country—much more prevalent than at present. It was a natural reaction from that immense triumph of Puritanism which had destroyed the institutions of the country, and which apparently had effected an enduring change in the national character. That Puritanic spirit passed away, however, and left behind, as a consequence, great latitudinarianism, ending in a general spirit of scepticism. The state of things was far more alarming then than now. The most alarming thing now, it is said, is that an infidel may be made a bishop; but infidels then were actually made bishops. There was at that time a large body of the ablest writers and most eminent men that England ever produced devoted with greater courage, and in a far more unblushing manner than is now the fashion, to the propagation of those ideas which are now circulated with more modesty, and perhaps with a more timid spirit. You had men of high position, Ministers of State, and other distinguished persons among the educated and influential classes of society adopting these opinions in the reign of George I. What happened? A century passed away, and what permanent effect was produced by these opinions, although they produced a literature of their own, which was second to none in acuteness and learning, and although they were sanctioned by persons in high places? What have been the consequences, I will not say to the Church of England, but to the faith accepted by that Church? Why, there never was a period in which the religion of this country, and especially the religion embalmed in the offices of the Church of England, was more influential, or more expansive, or flourished more than in the century that has elapsed since that time. And I defy any one to bring me passages impugning the faith of the Scriptures in any works recently published in which these doctrines are urged with more power or more learning than by the writers of that period.

But then it may be said that England is an insular country, and that English-men are a peculiar people; that they have an aristocracy, and a Church possessing territorial power; that the middle classes are bigoted, and the aristocratic classes interested in preserving the Church, and that by a combination of circumstances it has happened that a natural result has not been attained. But we have seen the same causes at work on a much larger scale, and at a period more recent, in a neighbouring country—a country that is not insular, that has destroyed its aris-tocracy, subverted its priesthood, plundered its Church, and left no prizes to be competed for in it. We have heard that the reason why there are less candidates for orders in the Church of England is that so many prizes have been taken away. But what happened in the Church of France when all its property had been taken? The whole institutions of the land, ecclesiastical and otherwise, were erased; yet, as if by magic, parish churches have re-appeared in the 30,000 districts of France; and although they have had monarchies, empires, and republics, and may have in the future a combination of government which no one can anticipate, yet the Chris-tian Church in that country counts at present more powerful and more numerous adherents than ever. Therefore, I say, that it is a great mistake, and an opinion not sanctioned by experience, to suppose that we are encountering a novel and revolutionary phase of opinion, and that in consequence of views which have before this been advanced, have flourished, and then disappeared, the House of Commons is to meet in a panic to revise the great title-deeds of the Church of England, and to say in this hasty moment of the introduction of a new philosophy that the measures taken by the great statesmen and Churchmen of the days of the Stuarts at an important crisis were a profound mistake, seeing that they have only secured for England two centuries of tranquillity and repose! Totally repudiating as materials for legislation on such a subject the passing accidents of the hour, which, however, naturally influence the youthful mind of the country, I will make one remark on the character of the subscription, and on the Creeds and Articles which are now brought forward as unsuited to the age in which we live, and which are regarded as so objectionable that a Ministry to whom is intrusted the defence of the institutions of the country are not resolute enough to come forward and oppose the very crude resolution before the House, but are obliged to meet it with the previous question.

I have understood from every gentleman who has spoken to-night, except the candid member for Sheffield, that he is in favour of maintaining the Established Church of this country. The advantages which accrue from the existence of the Church of England have been adverted to by different speakers; and from the hon. gentleman who introduced the motion, and the hon. member for Pontefract, who moved the amendment—I have not heard from any of the speakers any objec-tion or insinuation against the wisdom of maintaining the Church of this country. Well, but what do you mean by a Church? I say, No Creed! no Church! How can you have a Church without a creed, articles, formularies, and a subscription? If you object to a creed, to formularies, and to articles, tell us so, and then we shall understand the question before us. We will discuss that question, and the nation must decide which side they will adopt. But if you are to have a Church, I maintain you must have symbols of union among those who are in communion with that Church. That I hope is not bigotry, for we must speak on this subject as politicians, and not intrude our private religious convictions on any member of this House, but consider this weighty matter with reference to the happiness of society, and the means of lofty and virtuous government, by the aid of which we may prevent government from degenerating into a mere machinery of police. We are agreed, then, that we shall have a Church, and that it shall be maintained. Well, I want to know how are we to have a Church without a symbol of union among those who are in communion with it? No one has told us. If we are to have a Church without articles, creeds, or formularies, we shall have the most pernicious and the most dangerous institution which ever yet existed in any country, the means of which for evil, under the disposition of able men, are entirely incalculable. We are often favoured by the hon. member for Warwickshire (Mr. Newdegate) with bulletins on the progress of Jesuitism. The Jesuits have done vast things, and we may hope that they may not rival their past achievements; but whatever conception the hon. gentleman may form of the evils which the Jesuits have inflicted or may inflict upon society, they never contemplated or acquired a more fatal influence than that which a Church may possess and must exercise in a country like England, when it is a Church without a creed, without articles, or formularies.

I would say one word on the course which the Government have taken and may take on the religious controversies before us. How ought we to act? I think that no case has been made out at present to justify the course taken by the Government. I think that the Chancellor of the Exchequer misunderstood an expression of my hon. friend the member for Stamford, when he laid it down that my hon. friend's words justified the course of the Government. I agree with the Chancellor of the Exchequer—every man of temperate mind must agree with him—that neither the Articles of the Church nor the Prayer-book are perfect. There may be blots in their composition. The Prayer-book may be Divine, but it is also human. But I do not see anything in the present state of affairs that justifies the course taken by Government. Suppose there were circumstances that justified the course taken by the hon. member for Maidstone. Is the course taken by the Government that which they ought to take? I do not think it is. If this House be ever of opinion that the title-deeds of the Church require to be revised, in however modified a manner, it does appear to me that the inquiry should not originate in either House of Parliament. It has been said in the course of this debate that the Act of Uniformity at present in question is an Act of Parliament, and that as it originated in Parliament, its revision and formal reconstruction ought to take place there. With regard to that, I say the character of Parliament in the reign of Charles II. and of Victoria is decidedly and essentially different. Parliament is no longer a lay synod, and therefore it cannot of right and with propriety assume such a function. No doubt, if a revision were to take place, the opinion of Parliament must ultimately be given on the general merits of the question. But it would not enter into every ecclesiastical detail and religious difference of opinion, if for no other reason, from that innate sense of propriety which always guides it. But, I say, if revision be necessary, it is from the temporal head of our Church that measure should flow, and by the Queen, and by the Queen alone, it should be indicated. A Royal Commission is the proper medium by which any change which may be necessary either in the Articles or Liturgy of the Church could alone be brought under the consideration of authority. What authority? The hon. member for Poole (Mr. Henry Seymour) says, "Who would trust the discussion of this question to Convocation? I regret that Convocation has ever been called into existence, and I trust its attributes and functions will soon be terminated." [*Cheers from below the gangway on the Government side.*] I cannot agree with that opinion; I cannot sympathize with that cheer. It seems to me—and I say it with the greatest courtesy—extremely bigoted and narrow-minded. Why should Convocation be silenced? Convocation is a representative body, and should therefore recommend itself to the Liberal party; it is a body which carries on its affairs by public discussion, and therefore should be regarded, I think, with some respect by those who are devoted to reformed Parliaments. And I must say this of Convocation: I admit that as at present constituted there are elements which render Convocation not altogether a satisfactory tribunal. But it does not follow that Convocation should be therefore altogether abrogated. Let us be just to Convocation. It was recalled into existence after a long lapse of time. It was unused to the functions which it was summoned to exercise. It consisted entirely of clergymen, and loud were the predictions that it would fail, and fail ignominiously. But I ask sensible and temperate men on both sides of the House, is it fair to give that character to the labours of Convocation since it has been revived? I say myself, revived as it has been after a long desuetude, trammelled as it has been, checked and controlled as it has been in a manner that would have broken the spirit and crushed the energies of any assembly; it has done many things deserving approval, and, what is more, has done that which all predicted it would not do in the brief term it has been permitted to exercise its powers—it has shown an extremely practical character. I would wish its basis were more comprehensive, and I cannot see how any appeal could be made to Convocation on such a question as that which has formed the subject of controversy to-night unless that basis were more comprehensive. You must associate with it the other province and the Church of Ireland, and I myself think you ought to introduce something of that lay element to which the Church of England has been so much indebted. Nor do I doubt that there are lay members of the Church at the present moment who, from their learning, their knowledge of men, and their high character, might bring to Convocation such ability and reputation as Selden and Chillingworth might have brought in former days. But if it be the opinion of Government that it is necessary to revise the Liturgy and Articles, they ought to proceed, not by moving the previous question, but by the initiatory act of the Crown whom they counsel; and after a Royal Commission had been instituted and had terminated its labours, the result might, with propriety, be submitted to a Convocation constituted on the broad basis I have indicated. It may be said these are difficult questions; but it is the province of Government to cope with difficulties; and whatever the decision arrived at might be, it would be ultimately laid before Parliament, for no one contemplates that any decision upon such subjects would be satisfactory unless Parliament were consulted.

We have heard to-night from the hon. member for Pontefract (Mr. Monckton Milnes) a warning not to submit to a sacerdotal despotism. I entirely agree with the hon. gentleman that no evil can perhaps be conceived for any country, but at all events none for a country like England, greater than to fall under a sacerdotal despotism, or that we should be at all interfered with in our free life by any priestly power. But it appears to me that the hon. member for Pontefract has entirely misapprehended the question upon which he proposed an amendment, and which one would think he did not resolve on until he had given sufficient consideration to the subject. Sir, my idea of a sacerdotal despotism, in the times in which we live, is not that the inquisition will appear in this country, or that Archbishop Laud, in the form of the mild and benignant Metropolitan of Lambeth, may summon us again to a High Commission Court. But my idea of sacerdotal despotism is this, that a minister of the Church of England, who is appointed to expound doctrine should deem that he has a right to invent doctrine. That, sir, is the sacerdotal despotism I fear. And it appears to me, that if the course which has been recommended to our consideration to-night is adopted, in that false guise in which such propositions are sometimes exhibited in this House and out of it, we shall not be secure from arriving at such a goal. I warn the House, however improbable it may appear, from the seemingly innocent form in which these simple and enlightened propositions have been brought before us, that they are propositions in favour of the priesthood and not of the laity; and the more their consequences are traced, the more plainly that will be found to be the inevitable result. No doubt there are men of genius among the clergy, fine writers, men of learning and imagination, who can easily picture to themselves what would be the consequence of the success of these endeavours. No doubt the mere clergyman would soon become a prophet. No doubt you would have many churches, and the abounding eloquence, the exquisite learning, the fine sentiment, and the admirable ingenuity, which pervade many of the publications which are put upon our tables, would produce consequences to the Church of England very different from what have proceeded from this reviled Act of Uniformity. But what I feel is this—if that course be pursued, I see no security for two hundred years of tranquillity and toleration. I see no security for two hundred years which have resolved as great a problem in spiritual life as we have in political. It is the boast of this country that in politics it has reconciled order with liberty. What in its religious affairs is a greater triumph than this—it has combined orthodoxy with toleration. What security have you for such results if you pursue the course which is insidiously recommended to you now in so many ways and by so many changes? I prefer to stand upon the ancient ground. I see no reason whatever why, if the occasion demands it, our attention should not be duly called to necessary changes in our Articles and Liturgy. But though I see no reason, if the occasion requires it, why that should not be done, I can most sincerely say that hitherto no satisfactory case has been made out in favour of that course. I prefer to stand as we are—on a Church which lives in the historic conscience of the country, which comes down with the title-deeds of its great Liturgy which we all can understand, because our fathers and our forefathers have contributed to its creation. Sir, I regret the course which we have taken to-night, although I trust, after this discussion, it will not be misunderstood, and that the country will feel that it is the determination of Parliament to stand in its spirit by the Church of England.

Church policy

At a meeting in aid of the Oxford Diocesan Society for the Augmentation of Small Benefices, held at Oxford, November 25, 1864, the Bishop of Oxford presiding,

The Right Hon. B. DISRAELI said: My Lord Bishop, I can heartily second the motion that has been made by my right hon. friend, because it only expresses a resolution which, in that part of the diocese with which I am more immediately connected, and which, in a certain sense, I may say, I represent to-day, I have heretofore exerted myself to the utmost to uphold. I must say, however, that though some degree of sympathy has been found—and among some individuals that sympathy has been expressed in a manner most energetic,—the general result there has not been, in my opinion, adequate to the greatness of the cause and to the character of those institutions which have been established in this diocese.

My Lord, it is perhaps a delicate subject to touch upon; but it is expedient that upon this matter we should have clear ideas. These institutions, as established in this diocese, and not so fully and completely, but in some degree, I believe, established in all the dioceses of England, sustain, or rather would sustain and complete, the parochial system of this country, and their object is to adapt the machinery of the Church to the ever fluctuating circumstances in the condition of the nation. There are two reasons why I think that these institutions have not yet received in the country that support which I sometimes flatter myself by foreseeing they will acquire. In the first place it must be remembered that these institutions are of a novel character. They have, comparatively speaking, only recently been established in the country.

In the next place—and that is a much more important circumstance, which we should clearly apprehend—these diocesan institutions have been established in England during a period in which the Church has been with reference to the State in a condition of transition. Some forty years ago or less, a great change took place in the constitution of this country. It was, in fact, a revolution; but, like all revolutions in England, comparatively silent, and perfectly tranquil. But when religious liberty was adopted as a principle in the political constitution of this country, an effect was produced immediately upon the position of the Church. That party who are opposed to the Church in this country—and we cannot flatter ourselves that there ever will be a period, in a country like England, when there will not be an anti-Church party—that party with much plausibility, for the purpose of advancing their views, called public attention to the anomaly which the Church in this country presented, the moment that the political Constitution had adopted the principle of religious liberty. The Parliament of England had been a lay synod until that change, and they naturally said if you have a Legislature in the hands of those not in communion with the Church, your boasted union between Church and State must expire, and the fall of the Church is at hand. Under these circumstances, if we had had only to meet the natural opponents of the Church, I think the prospects of the Church would not have been so difficult. But unfortunately some of the best friends of the Church—men who, from their elevated character, sincere principle, learning and devotion, could not for a moment be looked upon with an eye other than friendly by the Church and Churchmen—became so alarmed by what they considered the logical consequences of that revolution, that they, although for perfectly distinct and contrary purposes, counselled the same policy as the anti-Church party: dissolution of the union between Church and State. The consequence of this state of affairs was a condition of great perplexity among Churchmen—much timidity, painfully apparent inconsistency of conduct, sometimes apathy, because they did not know to what objects they should devote their energies, sometimes, perhaps, a fantastic and unnatural action; but the practical result was that there was no longer cordial co-operation among all classes of Churchmen for those objects in which the interests of the Church were concerned; and all those diocesan societies so admirably adapted to the wants of the age, and which would in practice as well as in theory have completed the parochial system, were launched at a time when cordial co-operation was, for the reasons I have alleged, impossible. That is one of the many causes why these institutions have not received that support which they might have counted upon. For during this period, especially during the last few years, while the principle of religious liberty—which I am sure no Churchman now wishes to disturb or distrust—has been developed to its completeness, there was a paralysis on the united action of Churchmen.

This remarkable result, however, happened—which, indeed, in matters of this character and import, has happened before in this country—the question of Church and State has been so discussed by the nation, generally; it has been so deliberated upon, so considered and pondered, that the country has arrived at a conclusion which may not be so logical as that of the anti-Church party or of our alarmed friends, but is a solution, like all solutions of great questions in England, essentially practical—for the country has come to a conviction that the union between Church and State is perfectly consistent with the existence and complete development of the principle of religious liberty. All the points which were argued during the period of transition have been considered and solved by the country. The country has felt that if you terminate the connection between Church and State, it is not probable, for example, that in this age and nation, an *imperium in imperio* would be tolerated by the State. They saw that it was most improbable that if the alliance were terminated the Church would be allowed to remain in possession of her property and privileges. They knew very well that the Government of the country, seeing the importance of the religious principle as one of the chief elements for the government of mankind, would not allow it to run waste and wild in society. They knew what had happened in other countries where the alliance between Church and State had been terminated, or where churches had been confiscated and plundered,—namely, the process by which what are called "the ministers of all religions" are salaried by the State, and there was a general feeling that if that did occur, there would be something besides religious truth that would be endangered, and that political liberty might be imperilled. Thus after years of discussion the public voice arrived at a practical conclusion on this main question.

Then there was another point. It had been held that it was impossible that the Church could long maintain itself in this country in consequence of the spread of Dissent. But, during this period of transition, we fell upon a statistical age. Statistics were studied by the nation, and they discovered that there had not been a spread of Dissent, that, on the contrary, Dissent had diminished—I speak of true religious Dissent—that the descendants of the Puritan families, whom I shall always mention with that respect which their high qualities and historical character deserve, had almost all merged in the Church itself; that the tendency of the age was no longer favourable to hostile rivalry among religious bodies, but rather led to virtual, though not formal, co-operation between churches and consistories; and that, in short, there was no reason for supposing that the Church, on the ground of Dissent, could not be maintained in its original and constitutional position.

Well, then, there was another very important point which occupied public attention, and that was the contrast placed so prominently by the anti-Church party before the country, between the state of the Church and the millions of the population who had escaped its influence, though not in communion with any other religious body. Well, but the result of deliberating over that startling state of affairs was that the country came to a conclusion exactly the reverse of that which the opponents of the Church wished to instil into the public mind. They knew the religious character of the people of England, they argued that if there are millions not in communion with the National Church because they have never had the opportunity, it is a duty to provide competent machinery to deal with this population, and instruct them in those great truths which they have hitherto neglected. The progress of the Church of late years in great towns justifies this conclusion. Therefore, it has happened that the country—in a manner which may not be logical, but which is essentially practical—has solved the whole question. And while the anti-Church party and a considerable and most respectable section of Churchmen were prepared to dissolve the alliance between Church and State, the period of the transition passed, because the nation had arrived at the resolution that the union between Church and State should be upheld.

I take this to be the result that they arrived at after many years' discussion, as is customary in England when great principles of policy are at stake, and that, I believe, is the secret reason and the real cause of the change which took place in Parliament three years ago upon the subject of church-rates. The matter of church-rates is one in itself, no doubt, of main importance; but when we consider that in the Parliament which had abolished them by a large majority there was in the course of a few years a majority in their favour, the change can only be accounted for by the fact that the country had fixed upon the question of church-rates to prove their determination to support the union between Church and State, and their conviction that, practically, the alliance was consistent with the full development of religious liberty. But the consequence of such a state of affairs is most significant. Thirty or forty years ago there was an alternative. It might have been open to the Church to abdicate its nationality, or to assert it, but there was never a middle course. The country has resolved that its nationality should not be abdicated, and the consequence is that the Church must assert its nationality.

I remember some three years ago, at a meeting of one of these diocesan societies which I attended—I am not sure whether it was not this identical society—I ventured to point out the measures[1] by which I thought the nationality of the Church might be practically asserted; and though I will not now enter into any details, I will notice them briefly, because they will complete the position from which I wish to draw some inferences that may affect our meeting this day. I said then I thought there were five modes by which the nationality of the Church might be asserted, it being now, as I say, not only the duty, but the necessity, of the Church that it should be asserted in a practical character. And, in the first place, I said the nationality of the Church might be asserted with regard to the question of education. I hold that it is of the utmost importance that the Church should not in any way compromise the legitimate position she occupies now with reference to the education of the people, which the Church has obtained by natural circumstances, and which is sanctioned by law. Secondly, I said another practical mode of asserting its nationality was to support, not a wild and extravagant, but a temperate and matured plan for the extension of the episcopate. The third measure was that in all ecclesiastical matters which were not of a strictly spiritual nature, the assistance of the laity should be called into co-operation with the clergy (cheers), in order that we should erase from the public mind that vulgar but pernicious error that the Church is a merely clerical corporation. The fourth measure I then ventured to say should be pursued was to assert the rights and duties of Churchmen existing in our parochial constitution, and which are secured to them by law. And the fifth course I then impressed on the assembled diocese was to uphold these diocesan institutions, to support one of which we are this day assembled.

Now, in my opinion, these are measures temperate in conception, and practical in execution, which, if carried—and I believe they might be carried, for they are entirely adapted to the temper of the times—would add amazingly to the efficiency of the Church. As I am upon the subject, I will venture to say there are three other subjects or measures which I think ought now also to engage the attention of Churchmen. And the first is, that we should favour in every possible manner the formation of Convocation on a broader basis, and with a fuller representation of the parochial clergy. It is not necessary now, nor would it be convenient, to enter into details on the subject. But I would just intimate that if the two provinces were united, the basis would be much broader; and at this moment in the province of York the parochial clergy are more fully represented than in the province of Canterbury. There is something, I think, ridiculous in the diocese of London, for example, with 1,000 clergy, being only represented in Convocation by two paro-chial clergymen.

The next measure I hope we shall induce my right hon. friend (Mr. Cardwell) to undertake, and that is to place the relations of our Colonial Church—which, remember, is not an Established Church—with the metropolis in a more satisfac-tory condition than they are at present.

And the last measure, which in my own mind is paramount, is the reconstitu-tion of the tribunal of last appeal in matters spiritual, which it appears to me the circumstances of these times imperatively demand. I know the difficulty, I know the delicacy of that question, but still I am apt to believe, after giving it that con-sideration which its importance deserves, that these difficulties may be overcome, and that the most delicate circumstances connected with it may be treated in a happy manner. I do believe that with entire deference to the principle of the Royal Supremacy, which I trust may never be lost sight of for an instant, it may be pos-sible to reconcile the requirements of the State with the conscience of the Church. Now, allow me to repeat what on a previous occasion, some years ago, I had the honour of stating—that the object of these measures is to restore the Church to its natural—and I may say its original—efficiency by means which I think are essen-tially practical, and which are in tone and harmony with the spirit of the age in which we live; and I could not but believe that, with cordial co-operation among Churchmen, those eight measures might be carried. My Lord, they form a Church policy, temperate, practical, yet perfectly efficient. There is no argument that I can well collect that can be urged against them of a valid character; and yet it appears to me that if these eight objects were obtained, the Church in this country would occupy a position of just influence and salutary power which it has not for a long time filled.

Well, my Lord, I had hoped that when I should have the honour of address-ing you again on matters connected with these societies, I should have had to congratulate ourselves that that inconsistency, and timidity, and perplexity which have paralyzed the efforts of Churchmen for so many years, had entirely dis-appeared. I did think that cordial co-operation might have been obtained from all classes of Churchmen after the significant manner in which the country has decided that no disunion between Church and State should take place, but that the old constitution was, in its opinion, consistent with the fulfilment of the prin-ciple of religious liberty. I thought we might then have forgotten all our dif-ferences, and that we in this hearty and united spirit might have laboured with perseverance, with temper, with no anxiety for precipitate success, but with the determination of men who clearly see a practical object before them, for the attainment of the measures which I have noticed to-day, and which, as I have stated, form in my mind a complete Church policy. But I am sorry to say I still find, at least in that part of the diocese with which I am particularly connected, difficulties existing, and, though they are different from those we have encountered before, paralyzing to a great degree the efforts which would be made for the support of the diocesan societies, and especially that which has called us together today. My right hon. friend has touched on them with delicacy, but with clearness. We are now told that the Church is in a very difficult position—that its condition is not satisfactory, and these are made the arguments, and, no doubt, the conscientious grounds, for keeping aloof from associations like the present. But then I observe, in contrast with the difficulties which we had to encounter three or four years ago, that the nature of the difficulty is now very different. In old days, during the period of transition which I have sketched, the Church was accused of apathy, of having no hold on the feelings of the great mass of the population, of exercising little influence, and its fall was predicted in consequence. But the case is now changed. No one now accuses the Church of apathy, no one now accuses the Church of not possessing influence, of wanting intelligence; but it is still doomed; the Church must still fall; it is still in as great danger as ever; and that danger comes not from an anti-Church party, but from its own intestine condition, and the parties that exist in its own bosom.

My Lord, I am not here to deny, or to regret, the existence of parties in the Church. Parties in the Church have always existed. They existed in the Church at Jerusalem. They existed in the Church at Ephesus. They existed always in the Church at Rome. And it would be most wonderful indeed if in a country like England, where party has always been recognized as the most efficient and satisfactory means of conducting public affairs, party should not be found in the Church alone. My Lord, what is Party? Party is organized opinion. And so long as the nature of man is of that various and varying character which we all know it is, so long will there be various and varying modes by which it will express itself, or by which it may be counselled, upon religious matters. There are some who find solace in symbolic ceremonies, and who feel that the religious sentiment can only be adequately satisfied by ecclesiastical services in that vein. There are others with whom the soul requires to be sustained by the ecstasy of spiritual enthusiasm. But so long as they who counsel or pursue these modes meet on the common platform of true Church principles—and I hold that the acknowledgment of the Church as the sacred depository of Divine truth is the truest Church principle—I do not think that such courses are to be regretted, but on the whole I have no doubt both schools of religious feeling have been beneficially and equally advantageous to the country and the Church. And doubtless the two great parties in the Church have effected as eminent service for true religion as the two great parties in the State have achieved for public liberty and the good government of the country.

But there is yet another party to which I must for a moment refer, because, no doubt, the influence of that party upon that cordial co-operation of Churchmen

42

by which alone these societies can be effectually supported is considerable, and I cannot pretend that it is advantageous. Now, that is a party described by an epithet which I observe a distinguished prelate of the Church has adopted in a recent address to his clergy, but which appears to me to be an epithet that I should not use within these walls, for it has hardly as yet entered into the category of classical expression. It is an epithet, my lord, that would imply a particular degree of comprehension. But whilst fully acknowledging the abilities, the eloquence, and the knowledge of this new Church party, I must say that there is a peculiarity about the comprehension which they attempt to accomplish. Hitherto there has been nothing new in a Church party aiming at the comprehensive; but then they have always wished to include all those who believed anything; whereas the remarkable peculiarity of the comprehension of the party to which I now refer is, that they seem to wish to include everybody who believes nothing. Now, there is no doubt that the influence of the new party is very injurious to the Society whose interests have called us together today; and if we attempt to get rid of the difficulty by avoiding to speak about it, we in fact do not remedy our position, but the deleterious process from which we are suffering goes on without any effort on our part to oppose its evil consequences. The Church having, as I think, successfully encountered the unsatisfactory condition of mind among Churchmen, which was the consequence, and the long consequence, of the change in the Constitution; having overcome that difficulty, and Churchmen having it in their power, by the measures to which I have referred, to place, by their cordial co-operation, the Church in its proper position in this country, I will make a few remarks upon the new difficulty with which we have to deal—for it would be unwise to treat the existence and influence of this new party with contempt—and consider whether the difficulties which no doubt exist are insuperable, whether we must yield to them, or whether we have a prospect of overcoming them.

Now, this new party is not founded upon the principle of Authority—on which all Church parties hitherto in this country, and in all countries to some degree, have been founded. But it is founded upon a very singular principle. It is founded upon the principle of Criticism. Now, doubt is an element of criticism, and the tendency of criticism is necessarily sceptical. I use the epithet in a philosophical and not in a popular or odious sense. It is quite possible, for example, that a party founded upon the principle of criticism may arrive at conclusions which we may deem monstrous. They may, for example, reject inspiration as a principle and miracles as a practice. That is possible. And I think it quite logical that, having arrived at such conclusions, they should repudiate creeds and reject articles of faith, because creeds and articles of faith cannot exist or be sustained without acknowledging the principle of inspiration and the practice of miracles. All that I admit; but what I do not understand, and what I wish to draw the attention of this assembly and of the country generally to is this—that, having arrived at these conclusions, having arrived conscientiously at the result that, with their opinions, they must repudiate creeds and reject articles, they should not carry their principles to their legitimate end, but that, repudiating creeds, and rejecting articles, they are still sworn supporters of ecclesiastical establishments,—fervent upholders of dignitaries of the Church—even of rectors, vicars, and curates. Now this is a matter of most serious importance, not merely for us to consider, as Churchmen, but for the country generally to consider, whatever may be its opinions or forms of faith—for the consequences may be very critical. If it be true, as I am often told it is, that the age of faith has passed, then the fact of having an opulent hierarchy, supported by men of high cultivation, brilliant talents and eloquence, and perhaps some ambition, with no distinctive opinions, might be a very harmless state of affairs, and it would certainly not be a very permanent one. But then, my Lord, instead of believing that the age of faith has passed, when I observe what is passing around us—what is taking place in this country, and not only in this country, but in other countries, and even hemispheres—instead of believing that the age of faith has passed, I hold that the characteristic of the present age is a craving credulity. Why, my Lord, man is a being born to believe. And if no Church comes forward with its title-deeds of truth, sustained by the tradition of sacred ages and by the conviction of countless generations to guide him, he will find altars and idols in his own heart and his own imagination. But observe this. What must be the relations of a powerful Church, without distinctive creeds, with a being of such a nature? Why of course the chief principle of political economy will be observed. Where there is a great demand there will be a proportionate supply; and commencing, as the new school may, by rejecting the principle of inspiration, it will end by every priest becoming a prophet; and beginning as they do by repudiating the practice of miracles, before long, rest assured, we shall be living in a flitting scene of spiritual phantasmagoria. There are no tenets however extravagant, and no practices however objectionable, which will not in time develop under such a state of affairs; opinions the most absurd, and ceremonies the most revolting—

——— Qualia demens
Ægyptus portenta colat"—

perhaps to be followed by the incantations of Canidia and the Corybantian howl.

But consider the country in which all this may take place. Dangerous in all countries, it would be yet more dangerous in England. Our empire is now unrivalled for its extent; but the base—the material base—of that empire is by no means equal to the colossal superstructure. It is not our iron ships; it is not our celebrated regiments; it is not these things which have created, or indeed really maintain our empire. It is the character of the people. Now I want to know where that famous character of the English people will be if they are to be influenced and guided by a Church of immense talent, opulence, and power without any distinctive creed. You have in this country accumulated wealth that never has been equalled, and probably it will still increase. You have a luxury that will some day peradventure rival even your wealth. And the union of such circumstances with a Church without a distinctive creed will lead, I believe, to a dissoluteness of manners and of morals rarely equalled in the history of man, but which prepares the tomb of empires.

There is another point in connection with this subject which I cannot help noticing on the present occasion. It is the common cry—the common blunder—that articles of faith and religious creeds are the arms of a clergy, and are framed to tyrannize over a land. They are exactly the reverse. The precise creed and the strict article are the title-deeds of the laity to the religion which has descended to them. And whenever these questions have been brought before Parliament I have always opposed alterations of articles and subscriptions on this broad principle— that the security and certainty which they furnish are the special privileges of the laity, and that you cannot tell in what position the laity may find themselves, if that security be withdrawn.

Perhaps I ought to apologise for having touched upon this subject; but it appears to me—I know it from my own experience—to be one vitally connected with the affairs that have called us here to-day, because the opinions of the new school are paralyzing the efforts of many who ought to be our friends. Let us venture to ask ourselves this question:—Will these opinions succeed? Is there a possibility of their success? My conviction is that they will fail. I wish to do justice to the acknowledged talents, the influence, and information which the new party command; but I am of opinion they will fail—for two reasons. In the first place, having examined all their writings, I believe without any exception—whether they consist of fascinating eloquence, diversified learning, and picturesque sensibility—I speak seriously what I feel—and that too exercised by one honoured in this University, and whom to know is to admire and regard; or whether you find them in the cruder conclusions of prelates who appear to have commenced their theological studies after they had grasped the crozier, and who introduce to society their obsolete discoveries with the startling wonder and the frank ingenuousness of their own savages; or whether I read the lucubrations of nebulous professors, who seem in their style to have revived chaos; or, lastly, whether it be the provincial arrogance and the precipitate self-complacency which flash and flare in an essay or review, I find that the common characteristic of their writings is this, that their learning is always second-hand.

I do not say that because learning is second-hand it may not be sound, or that knowledge, because it is second-hand, may not be true; but this I do say, without any fear of denial from any man competent to give an opinion upon the subject, that there is something in original research so invigorating to the intellect, and which so braces and disciplines the human mind, that those who have undergone that process arrive at their conclusions with great caution and with great circumspection; but when a man of brilliant imagination has to deal with a vast quantity of facts furnished by the labours of others, he is tempted to generalize with a fatal facility, and often arrives at conclusions which in time he has not only to repudiate, but which sometimes he is destined to refute.

In the second place, when I examine the writings of those who have been the masters of the new school in this learning; men who undoubtedly have gone through the process of original research, and have not found their equals for learning and perseverance and erudite assiduity for many generations—the great scholars of Germany—I find this in their labours: doing full justice to their eminent qualities, I find this in their labours, that there is really nothing new. I admit their distinguished qualities. As Hebraists they are equal to the great scholars of the eighteenth, and who flourished at the end of the seventeenth century. In their knowledge of the cognate Semitic dialects they are infinitely superior. In the new theory, or science of language, as it is justly called, they have of course an advantage over the old scholars, because it is a science that has only been developed in our own time. But this I do say, that in all important conclusions, from the alleged materials of the Book of Genesis down to the formation of the Canon, and in every important event, historical, literary, and spiritual, that occurred in that long interval, they have been anticipated by the great Hebrew scholars who flourished in the eighteenth and at the end of the seventeenth century.

I know it may be said that the suggestions of an Astruc and the investigations of a Father Simon were known only to those who like them lived in their cells and colleges; but this is a vulgar and delusive error. The learned labours of those men formed the mind and inspired the efforts of the two most intellectual bodies of men that have existed certainly since the Greek philosophers,—for I think they were superior to the schoolmen,—the freethinkers of England and the philosophers of France. Therefore the conclusions of these eminent scholars were thoroughly placed before the public mind. All that inexorable logic, irresistible rhetoric, bewildering wit, could avail to popularize those views, were set in motion to impress the new learning on the minds of the two leading nations of Europe—the people of England and the people of France. And they produced their effect. The greatest of revolutions was, I will not say, occasioned by those opinions, but no one can deny that their promulgation largely contributed to that mighty movement popularly called the French Revolution, which has not yet ended, and which is certainly the greatest event that has happened in the history of man. Only the fall of the Roman empire can be compared to it; but that was going on for centuries, and so gradually, that it cannot for one moment be held to have so instantaneously influenced the opinion of the world. Now, what happened? Look at the age in which we live, and the time when these opinions were successfully promulgated by men who, I am sure, with no intention to disparage the new party, I may venture to say were not unequal to them. Look at the Europe of the present day and the Europe of a century ago. It is not the same Europe. Its very form is changed. Whole nations and great nations, which then flourished, have disappeared. There is not a political constitution in Europe existing at the present time which then existed. The leading community of the continent of Europe has changed all its landmarks, altered its boundaries, erased its local names. The whole jurisprudence of Europe has been subverted. Even the tenure of land, which of all human institutions most affects the character of man, has been altered. The feudal system has been abolished. Not merely laws have been changed—not merely manners have been changed—but customs have been changed. And what happened? When the turbulence was over—when the shout of triumph and the wail of agony were alike stilled—when, as it were, the waters had subsided, the sacred heights of Sinai and of Calvary were again revealed, and amid the wreck of thrones and tribunals, of extinct nations and abolished laws, mankind, tried by so many sorrows, purified by so much suffering, and wise with such unprecedented experience, bowed again before the Divine truths that Omnipotence in His ineffable wisdom had entrusted to the custody and the promulgation of a chosen people!

Well, then, because all their learning is secondhand; because their conclusions are not new; because they have already been placed before the mind of man with a power and a spirit that it is vain to expect will be again equalled; because mankind have tried and rejected this new learning now bolstered up for our edification; I believe that the efforts of this new school, powerful as they are and influential at this moment, and most injurious to these diocesan societies, will fail.

Before sitting down, there is only one other point on which I will venture briefly to touch. We are told every day that all I have feebly expressed to you may be true; but at the same time there is a characteristic of the present age which never existed in preceding ages, and which must be destructive to the Church and to all religious establishments, and that is the progress of science. The discoveries of science are not, we are told, consistent with the teachings of the Church. Now, I am sure there is not one in this theatre who is not prepared to do full justice to the merits of scientific men, and who does not fully appreciate those discoveries of science which have added so much to the convenience of life, and to the comfort of man. But it is of great importance, when this tattle about science is mentioned, that we should annex to the phrase precise ideas. I hold that the function of science is the interpretation of nature—and the interpretation of the highest nature is the highest science. What is the highest nature? Man is the highest nature. But I must say that when I compare the interpretation of the highest nature by the most advanced, the most fashionable and modish, school of modern science with some other teachings with which we are familiar, I am not prepared to say that the lecture-room is more scientific than the Church. What is the question now placed before society with a glib assurance the most astounding? The question is this—Is man an ape or an angel? My lord, I am on the side of the angels. I repudiate with indignation and abhorrence the contrary view, which is, I believe, foreign to the conscience of humanity: more than that, even in the strictest intellectual point of view, I believe the severest metaphysical analysis is opposed to such a conclusion. But on the other hand, what does the Church teach us? What is its interpretation of this highest nature? It teaches us that man is made in the image of his Creator—a source of inspiration and of solace—a source from which only can flow every right principle of morals and every Divine truth. I say, therefore, that when we are told that the teachings of the Church are not consistent with the discoveries of science, and that in that sense the inferiority of the Church is shown, I totally deny the proposition. I say that the scientific teaching of the Church upon the most important of all subjects is, in fact, infinitely superior to anything that has been brought forward by any of those new discoveries. In fact, it is between those two contending interpretations of the nature of man, and their consequences, that society will have to decide. Their rivalry is at the bottom of all human affairs. Upon our acceptance of that Divine interpretation for which we are indebted to the Church, and of which the Church is the Guardian, all sound and salutary legislation depends. That truth is the only security for civilization, and the only guarantee of real progress.

Now, it is to promote, to foster, and to extend in this country—but mainly, of course, to-day in this diocese—the teaching of that Church that we are assembled here. Let us support in spirit the resolution which has been moved by my right hon. friend; let us act with united energy, with that cordial co-operation which, if Churchmen share, they will carry everything before them; and having successfully discarded all the attempts which for some time appeared to paralyze our efforts, and circulate distrust among us by those who are the avowed opponents of the Church, let us equally discard the fanciful ideas of this new party in the Church, which have extended only because persons are always captivated by assumed novelty, but which I think I have shown have no genuine claim to that title. And let us, by our united efforts, support that Church policy to which I adverted at the commencement of my observations, and especially the action of these Diocesan Institutions.

Note

1 *Vide* p. 39.

Gathorne Hardy, *The Speech of Mr Gathorne Hardy on the Irish Church Question, in the House of Commons, 31 March, 1868* (London, NUCCA, 1868).

British Library, 016981716

The son of a wealthy ironworks owner and MP for Bradford, Gathorne Hardy (1814–1906) attended Shrewsbury School and then went up to Oriel College, Oxford, in 1833. After a successful career in the law, he was elected Conservative MP for Leominster in 1856. Retiring from the law, he thereafter devoted himself to Conservative politics. A staunch defender of the Established Church, he was a devout life-long High Churchman. An enthusiast for field sports, he was also a determined defender of property rights and law and order. In Derby's 1858–1859 government he served as Under-Secretary of the Home Office. In opposition after 1859, he established a formidable reputation as a combative and effective speaker, contributing to the withdrawal of Russell's Reform bill in 1860 and opposing the exemption of Nonconformists from Church rates in 1862. He expressed the views of Conservative backbenchers with a trenchant directness that endeared him to many in the party. In 1865, he defeated Gladstone on becoming MP for Oxford University.

In July 1866, Hardy became President of the Poor Law Board in Derby's third government. On Spencer Walpole's resignation as Home Secretary in May 1867, Hardy succeeded him. Unenthusiastic about all aspects of the Conservatives' Reform proposals, nonetheless, Hardy accepted that party loyalty required him to support Disraeli in the Commons. During Commons debate of the government's Reform bill, Hardy further enhanced his reputation as one of the best and most passionate speakers the party possessed. On the passing of the Reform Act for England and Wales, he privately noted that, if the gentry played their part, they would be accepted as leaders by the newly enfranchised. If they did not, then disastrously all would be left to the demagogues.

When Derby stepped down as prime minister, for reasons of ill health, in February 1868, to be succeeded by Disraeli, Hardy doubted the ability of the Conservative government to survive for long. In March, Gladstone introduced three resolutions in the Commons calling for the disestablishment of the Church of Ireland, its gradual disendowment, and the placing of the Crown's interest in the Church temporalities at the disposal of parliament. Conservative MPs received Hardy's statement opposing the resolutions on 31 March, though hastily prepared, with great enthusiasm. Their prolonged cheers were lasting and the spirits of the party rallied. Derby immediately wrote privately to Hardy praising the great force and ability with which he placed the whole question of the Irish Church on its proper footing. The National Union of Conservative and Constitutional Associations quickly published a copy of the speech.

2

GATHORNE HARDY, *THE SPEECH OF MR GATHORNE HARDY ON THE IRISH CHURCH QUESTION, IN THE HOUSE OF COMMONS, 31 MARCH, 1868*

(London, NUCCA, 1868).

UPON the order of the day for resuming the adjourned debate upon the Established Church in Ireland,

Mr. G. HARDY rose, and was received with loud cheers from the Ministerial side of the house. He said—There is no member of this house who is more inclined to rate highly the gravity of the question involved in this motion than I am. I quite admit that it is one of those questions which long ago it was thought must engage the attention of the house at no distant period; and, though we take exception to the particular period at which it is brought before the house, it is a question which we are prepared to meet on any occasion, and under any circumstances (cheers.) It has been brought before the house in a speech of great power and eloquence, and by one who, from his position as a leader in it, and as a man of the greatest ability, is entitled to claim the attention, not only of the house, but of the country itself. But I cannot help observing that this question, which is of such momentous gravity, has been treated upon the opposite side of the house, not merely as a question affecting the Church of Ireland, but with a degree of bitterness and acrimony against the ministry who sit on these benches which makes it at once an attack upon the Church of Ireland and upon the ministry (cheers); and not only have we met with this reception in front, but even on our flank we have been assailed (renewed cheers). I will for a moment speak upon the subject of the ministry that is attacked, and, if I am permitted, of myself, who have been personally attacked. I feel that it is one of the highest honours that I ever achieved that of sitting in the same cabinet with my noble friend (Lord Cranborne). No one felt more the resources of his genius, eloquence, and power which he brought to the ministry of which he formed a part; and I acted with him with cordiality and sincerity in all the transactions between us. The noble lord, in the position he has assumed in this house, that of speaking as the censor of the ministry, and of attacking them one by one for the course they thought proper to pursue last year, has forgotten, I think, how far he himself proceeded in the path they followed (cheers). He has forgotten that his objection was, not on account of lowering the franchise to the point to which it was lowered, but on account of the want, as he thought, of sufficient checks to moderate that enfranchisement; he has forgotten that we, having the same view as himself, were defeated on it, not merely by those who sit opposite, but by the overwhelming feeling of gentlemen who sat behind the government. I do not mean to say that the Reform Bill of last year is in everything such as I could have wished for if I could have controlled it (laughter and cheers); but I should like to know where is the man who has sat in any cabinet, or in any assembly of men, that has not been obliged in some respects to compromise his opinions, and to give way to those sitting with him, so that they might act with unity together. That I consider is all I have done. I have sacrificed no principle (oh, oh, and cheers). I say I sacrificed no principle. I consider that the question of Reform brought before the house was a question, not of principle, but of degree (cheers). We had been parties to lowering the franchise, we had assented to the second reading of the bill introduced by the other side of the house, which effected that lowering to a great extent, and we had assented to the lowering of the franchise in the bill of 1866; and I say that it became evident—not on account of disturbance out of doors, but on account of the parliamentary attitude that the question had assumed, that it became absolutely necessary to settle it. I say it was a question of degree and not of principle. I should not have said a word about myself if my noble friend had not brought my name forward somewhat unnecessarily. He complimented my sincerity at the expense of my pliability (hear, hear), but I trust that as concerns principle, I shall be found as ready to maintain those principles in which we both agree as he himself has been (hear, hear). Let me advert in passing to the course my noble friend has thought proper to take this year. My noble friend has been the firm consistent advocate of church rates, but this year he has taken a different view, and this suddenly—unexpected no doubt by those sitting near him, and certainly by those who have hitherto acted with him. Far be it from me to say that this was from any want of principle. I believe that he acted from a patriotic feeling, and from that principle for which I hope he will give credit to others (cheers). I now come to the question before the house. We are called on at a special and peculiar moment to go into committee upon a question of the greatest possible importance, and one that cannot be settled or terminated—I will not say in this parliament—but possibly in the next; nor for many years to come, in my opinion. This is met by an amendment on the part of my noble friend, to which great exception has been taken. I will for a moment take notice of a remark that has been made on that amendment. My noble friend claimed for himself freedom of acting in future sessions on this great question, without expressing an opinion now; but at the same time he said that he wished to make it manifest by the earlier part of his resolution that it was no mere abstraction on the part of those who sit on these benches; that there were things to redress and reform in the Irish Church; and though some might wish to go far beyond what I am prepared to do, yet I am free to confess, as I said in

1865, and as has been said by bishops and clergy and attached friends of the Irish Church, that with a view to strengthen and give more effect to that Church, there are needed great reforms, alterations, and, if I may use the word, "modifications" are necessary (hear). It would have been idle and absurd, after having assented to a commission upon the Irish Church, if the Government had not been prepared to act upon the facts adduced before that commission—to ameliorate where it was found necessary (hear, hear). I do not mean to say that the present parliament is not competent to deal with the subject, because it is obvious that so long as the house is in existence, it must have all the powers and functions of a legislative assembly. It is not a question of competence, but of time, occasion, and opportunity. The facts are these:—At a comparatively late period of the session, with very little progress made in supply; with boundary bills, involving the interests of 81 boroughs, and of one or two counties; and with two reform bills—one for Scotland and one for Ireland—in which amendments of great importance will be moved, and which must take a long time—it is with these things before us, and with the necessity of calling for an early dissolution of the house, and an appeal to the country—I say, with these things before us, are we not right in saying that the house is encumbered with business, measures of great importance are pressing upon us, and therefore this is not the time to come forward with an abstract resolution? (loud cheers). The first resolution of the right hon. gentleman is distinctly and solely an abstract resolution, which cannot pledge the new parliament that will have to assemble in a few months, and which he himself admits cannot be carried into effect by legislation in the course of the present session. I say then, that this question is one which has been suddenly started upon the country, and it has taken the people by surprise (hear, hear). If it had not been started so suddenly, if it had not come but recently on the minds of those who produced it, why, when the opportunity was afforded by the notice given by the hon. member for Cork to go into committee on the state of Ireland, of submitting this question of the Irish Church to the consideration of the house, why did not the right honourable gentleman produce his resolutions then, and ask the house to consider them in connection with the state of Ireland? (hear, hear). Is it unreasonable that we should ask for time to consider so important a matter? Is it unreasonable to ask for time in order that the country should consider the question upon which it must eventually decide? Even within the short week we have had the rustle of petitions increasingly heard from both sides of the house day by day, and as the question becomes better understood, I have reason to believe that there will be as many more petitions on this side of the house, not from churchmen only, but, as I know already, from the nonconforming body (cheers.) And after all, the right hon. gentleman himself stated last night he did not anticipate that this great measure which he had in hand could be carried into effect under much less time than thirty years (hear, hear). Nevertheless he has made it a matter of hours. Moreover, the proposition is one which evades the chief difficulties of the question, and only deals with those portions of it upon which unity of action can be obtained. Whereas, if the right hon. gentleman had developed his whole plan, it would be certain to split the house into many sections. The resolutions aimed a blow at that which had admittedly existed for 300 years, though I believe that that Church had existed for a long period previously. I will not, however, enter now into that quest on, because if I did so I might possibly call up opposition on the other side. But I contend that when we are dealing with a mass of property of so much importance and of so long prescription, it is not a matter for haste, and you have no right to force it upon the country until it has the whole case before it, and until we have an opportunity of consulting it upon it. Supposing we had met these resolutions by a direct negative—which, as far as I am concerned, I should be perfectly prepared to do (cheers)—and I think you will find that not only I personally, but all who sit on this side of the house would be ready to take the same course (hear, hear)—but supposing, I say, that we had met these resolutions with a direct negative, what would be said by hon. gentlemen opposite? I know what would be said. It would be said that we object to enter into an inquiry upon this question—that we object to go into committee, and that we are not prepared to admit that there is any reformation needed in the Irish Church. Whereas, by the amendment we propose, we say that if it were shown before the commission that reformation was needed, we are prepared to act upon such report, and to show that when we assented to the commission being issued, we were prepared to abide by its decision (hear, hear). The hon. member for Edinburgh, in his speech last night, did me the honour of calling attention to something I said in 1865. I have only to say now that I have nothing to alter as to the opinions which I then expressed I expressed those opinions in all sincerity and candour in favor of the Establishment of the Irish Church and the retention of its endowments. I do not mean to express a difference of opinion, and I speak now precisely as I spoke then (cheers). But I am told I am to renounce all the old arguments in favour of that Church. The right hon. gentleman said yesterday that those arguments were of such a character that no one would think of using them now. Sir, I trust I shall be able to show that there are authorities which might even have influence with the right hon. gentleman—authorities who have used these arguments, and who, like myself, are not ashamed to use them still, because they are just and apposite to the purpose we have in hand (hear, hear). I have on a former occasion called attention to a speech of the right hon. gentleman. I should not enter into this matter now, but the right hon. gentleman himself has challenged discussion as to the propriety of his bringing this question forward and as to the consistency he has shown in doing so. The right hon. gentleman said that for a period of 25 years his opinions have been forming on this subject, and that they have gradually arrived at the position which led him to assume the position he now occupies (hear, hear). The right hon. gentleman said that in the year 1846 it was impossible for him to pledge himself on principle to maintain the Irish Church. Now, I wish to ask him to whom he made that statement known (cheers).

Mr. GLADSTONE.—To my committee (laughter).

Mr. G. HARDY.—The right hon. gentleman must have had a singularly judicious committee, for until he rose last night the secret had never been revealed to the public (oh, oh, and laughter). Before I conclude I think it but right to call the attention of the right hon. gentleman to statements which have appeared in the public press, so that if they be incorrect the right hon. gentleman will be enabled to state under what circumstances they had been made public, and if not, how he can reconcile his statements last night with his former conduct and professions (hear, hear). I say nothing of the right hon. gentleman's opinions now: but I say I have a right to assume those to be his professions at the time these statements appeared in the public newspapers—newspapers which then strenuously advocated his own interests. The writers themselves of the articles I refer to must have been taken by surprise at the opinions which the right hon. gentleman has now expressed, although he made a statement last night to the house that in 1865 he gave a warning to his constituents of the course he was to take on the question of the Irish Church. The speech alluded to was no doubt a warning that the right hon. gentleman saw something unsatisfactory in the Irish Church, but it was certainly not a warning of the course which he has now taken (hear, hear). The right hon. gentleman now states that this is not a question of surplus or of amendment, but a question whether the Irish Church Establishment should be disendowed. In 1865 the right hon. gentleman said "It will be our duty to consider, surplus or no surplus, what obligations of the Act of Union remained to be fulfilled, and how they ought to be performed." And now I find in a letter published in the newspapers it is stated by a gentleman—who does not certainly sign his name (cries of "oh, oh")—although he has not signed his name to this letter he undertakes to produce the document to which he refers if any doubt be thrown upon his statement (cheers). It is, I presume, very well known that many letters are published in newspapers anonymously—nay, it is the commonest thing, I believe, for gentlemen to have their letters published without their names being attached to them, at the same time to furnish their names privately to the editors, with the intention of coming personally forward to substantiate their statements in case they should be questioned. The right hon gentleman had said that in 1865 he looked for action in the coming parliament; and therefore it was that he had made that speech. But did he look for action in the coming parliament? Was not the speech of 1865 a statement that the difficulty was so great, the problem was so difficult of solution, that he could not make up his mind when the subject could be brought before parliament with any chance of its settlement? (cheers). The writer of the letter I have referred to stated that a "mutual friend was the medium of communication"—this was just before the Oxford election—"and the reply contained the following assurance which was then deemed to be as satisfactory as it was intended to be." The document itself is at your disposal. This is the passage referred to—"The question of the Irish Establishment is remote and apparently out of all bearing upon the practical politics of the day" (hear, hear). Did the right hon. gentleman write that to one of his committee or supporters? If he did it seems wholly inconsistent with his statement last night, that he looked for action in the coming parliament (hear, hear). The right hon gentleman was also stated to have said "I think I have marked strongly my sense of the responsibility attaching to the opening of such a question. One thing I may add, because I think it a clear landmark, that in any measure dealing with the Irish Church—I think though I scarcely can expect to be called on to share in such a measure (hear, hear)—the Act of Union must be recognised, and must have important consequences, especially with reference to the position of the hierarchy" (cheers). (Here the right hon. gentleman handed the letter across the table to Mr. Gladstone).

An Hon. MEMBER.—Where does it come from?

Mr. G. HARDY.—The letter came from the *Morning Herald,* in which paper it appeared (hear, hear). The right hon. gentleman has the letter now in his own hands. I brought it before him because I thought it was my duty to do so. If the right hon. gentleman did not write the words attributed to him I should, of course, apologise for having brought it forward, and for having used it as I have done (hear, hear). But having seen the letter in the columns of the *Morning Herald,* I think it would not have been my duty to abstain from submitting it to the consideration of the house (hear). Whether the letter was really written by the right hon. gentleman or not, it is clear that his opinions had not been openly professed, and that he was using what is called by divines, economy and reserve, and abstained from professing those opinions which in this great emergency he has so suddenly professed (hear, hear). Another right hon gentleman sitting opposite in 1863 made this statement, "I believe this house will not surrender the principle of the Established Church. I believe it will not alienate the property of the Church. from the ecclesiastical purposes to which it has been devoted" (cheers). When I see these things I think we have a right to say that these resolutions have come suddenly upon the house and upon the country. And that those who have not known that the right hon. gentleman has changed his opinions within the last twenty-five years, have a right to say whether they had the same confidence in him now that they had entertained before (hear, hear). I will now pass from this which I consider the personal question (hear, hear, and some derisive cheers from the Opposition). Yes, if it be a personal question to ask the right hon. gentleman whether he has expressed such and such opinions without seeing anything inconsistent in his conduct? (hear, hear). If the right hon. gentleman says he has not written the letter in question, I should at once apologise to him and withdraw all I have said upon that point. Those gentlemen who appear now to be so averse to what is called personal questions were the loudest in their cheers that greeted the most envenomed shafts which were shot last night at the members of the government by a person sitting on this side of the house (cheers). I would ask whether this question of the Irish Church is to be disposed of hastily and without discussion. Is this Church which has stood for so long a time and has battled for centuries in defence of the truth, to be at once given up without consideration, and are all the arguments of the many great men who had defended her in former days to be ignored or declared to be of no avail? Am I to be afraid to say that the Union of Great Britain and Ireland was a compact—a treaty of a solemn and a binding character? (cheers.) Am I to be forbidden to say that the 5th article of that Union was so important that it was made the fundamental basis and the very essence of that Union? (cheers.) That same article was put forward by the first minister of the Crown of that day as the main inducement to the Irish Protestants to assent to this Union, and unite their Church with the Church of England indissolubly (cheers.) This being the case, is it right now, because the Irish Church might be considered by some persons as a burden, for us to say that we will renounce our union with it and leave it to take care of itself? Lord Chief Justice Ellenborough, in respect of the Act of Union, on the 13th May, 1805, used the following language, "By the 5th article of the Union, it is declared that the continuance and preservation of the said United Church, as the Established Church of England and Ireland, shall be deemed and taken as the essential and fundamental part of the Union—to be such an integral part of the compact of union between the two kingdoms as is absolutely necessary to sustain and support the whole fabric of the Union; and such as, being removed, would produce ruin and overthrow of the political union founded on that article as its immediate basis" (cheers). The right hon. gentleman sought to escape from this point by denying that Mr. Pitt meant to do this or that in conformity with the opinions which he had expressed—not upon the Union, but in a speech and in papers now accessible. But the fact is, there was no engagement on the part of Mr. Pitt to do more than was done by the statute. The right hon. gentleman said there were other inducements to the Act of Union, and that the Irish parliament was a corrupt one. Admitting this, I ask whether the English parliament at the time was also corrupt? (here Mr. Bright made some gesture.) The hon. member for Birmingham says it was, and, therefore, I suppose he would argue that the acts of that parliament are not to be attended to in the same way as the acts passed by a more perfect legislature.

Mr. BRIGHT.—I did not say so.

Mr. G. HARDY.—I thought I might assume that to be the meaning of the gesture of the hon. member for Birmingham. If it be meant that the Irish parliament was corrupt, and that being a corrupt parliament that that fact invalidated the act it had passed, all I can say to that argument is that if we should be induced to admit it we shall then get into a position of much embarrassment. I am afraid that many creditors would find themselves placed in a most unfavourable situation as regarded the recovery of their debts. The right hon. gentleman the member for South Lancashire has stated that whatever else might be the ultimate effect of his resolutions, they could not be injurious to the Protestant faith, and he went into statistics as to population and the proportions of different creeds. But I will only say I think that those who heard his statement as to the sources from whence those statistics were drawn will not be inclined to attach much credit to them as demonstrative statements in respect to the population of Ireland. The only figures thoroughly gone into were those of 1834 and 1861. The right hon. gentleman said that when the penal laws were most strictly enforced the Protestants had increased, but that when the penal laws ceased the Protestants began to diminish in proportion to the Roman Catholics; the right honourable gentleman taking those things as cause and effect (hear, hear). Now, if there were a period during which there was a more general relaxation of the penal laws it was that between 1834 and 1861, and yet it will be found that the proportions of the populations had then increased in favour of the Protestants (cheers). I know that the right hon. gentleman says that such increase is to be accounted for by the emigration of the labouring classes, whom he assumes to be all of the Roman Catholic faith. But the right hon. gentleman has made no allowance whatever for the large emigration of Protestants from Ireland (hear, hear). I appeal to those who are acquainted with the facts of the case whether there has not been a large proportion of Protestants amongst the emigrants from Ireland? (hear, hear.) But the right hon. gentleman says that the disestablishment of the Protestant Church in Ireland will not be injurious to the Protestant faith. I should certainly be ashamed of the religion I profess if I said I had the slightest fear of its stability either with or without endowments. But if we are to contend for the faith encumbered with large endowments why, I ask, should you object to my Protestant friends retaining the belief that they are of service to their Church, and that it has a right to them? (hear, hear.) In respect to the voluntary principle there is a great part of Ireland in which the voluntary principle is hardly applicable—parts where the Protestants are but thinly scattered, and where they would be obliged to seek other means in addition to their own for the support of their Church. At all events in such parts it would, of course, be necessary to supply them with those means to which they are entitled by law (hear, hear). The right hon. gentleman forgets how many of the clergy and others interested in the maintenance of the Church are suffering from want and distress. We are here, as it were, lookers on at a picture which is passing before us in the distance. It touches the hearts and the homes of many. It is to such both a fundamental grievance and a practical wrong. They feel deeply upon the matter. Is it, then reserved to us, in our apathetic indifference, to give up the dearest interest of all those with whom we are united by the ties of religion, of honour, of treaty, and of compact—to allow such considerations to be thrown over without regard to their feelings, with the view of reconciling others who may, after all, remain hostile to us, whilst we alienate our old friends who have ever been faithful to us? (cheers.) The right hon. gentleman said he did not think that any one would venture to use the argument that the subversion of the Irish Church would tend also to the subversion of property. It is, however, an argument that has been used by some of our greatest authorities, and not the least, by that great man, Sir Robert Peel, whose memory probably the right hon. gentleman opposite respects (hear, hear.) It was an argument that Sir Robert Peel did not disdain to use, and urge with great force, on more than one occasion. In speaking of the Appropriation Clause, Sir Robert Peel said—"If long possession and the prescription of three centuries were not powerful enough to protect the property of the Church from spoliation there is little safety for any description of private property, and much less for that property which is in the hands of lay corporations" (cheers). And it was no idle fear, for there are symptoms that property in the hands of lay corporations is in danger, for language has been used in this house on the Irish land question which seemed to verge very near it (hear, hear); and, with regard to the City corporation, language has been used with reference to their possession of land in Ireland which must certainly give them the hint that the time may come when they might have to set their house in order (cheers.) And with reference to the Law Life Association language has been used which shows there is a design in some persons to carry the attack beyond the property of the Irish Church, and not stop short of the landlords (cheers); for I do not hesitate to state that the schemes proposed for dealing with the land in Ireland are in themselves on a revolutionary scale (loud cheers). These schemes do not attack the rights of property, and those who argue that you might take corporate property from the Church depend upon it they will not be very squeamish hereafter in dealing with other property (loud cheers). Well, sir, in speaking of this question I will not hesitate to adopt what might be considered a legal statement upon the question of the corporate property made by the Lord Chancellor. He says that the right to land by corporate bodies remains so long as the property is not greater in amount than can be usefully applied by the corporate body, and that there is no right or principle on which parliament can interfere to alienate property of that kind. It was a principle acted on with respect to all charity property by the Court of Chancery. I believe it is a just rule, and one which we cannot violate without assailing the interests of property (cheers). The right hon. gentleman says he is going to deal tenderly with our victim, for we are going to preserve vested rights, and we even propose going beyond that; but at that moment the cheer which had greeted the maintaining of vested rights died away—and at the more than vested rights, the interests of curates and those who had entered on some miserable benefice. I found that cheering checked: and it will not be so easy for the right hon. gentleman to carry out his tender regard for those who have no vested interests, but only for those who have vested interests in property (cheers). It is not a question of the clergy, for I freely admit you may deal with them, so far as they are personally concerned, by paying them off, pensioning them, or by dealing with them in any other manner you please; but when you come to the vested interests of the laity, which are held in trust for them by the bishops and clergy, and not for themselves, how are you going to compensate them for the vested interests you are going to rob them of? (loud cheers). The right hon. gentleman has told us it is absurd for us to refer to that which has been said in order to obtain concessions in former days—the hopes held out that something would happen that would bring peace and harmony to Ireland—but certainly those who fondly anticipated and fairly prophecied such results had been disappointed (hear hear). It is undoubtedly a most serious misfortune that the hopes held out of extension of rights to the Roman Catholics were not fulfilled to the promises—the promises of Plunkett, Blake, and Peel to the Roman Catholic prelates as a body, and the canonists of Maynooth, have not been fulfilled, the latter of whom had declared that the title of the Irish Church to her property was recognised by the Church of Rome (cheers), that they only required a prescription of 100 years, whereas the Protestant Church had at least a prescription of 300 years (hear, hear). On this occasion I am bound to say there is no danger of our being led away by any promise that what we are asked to do will in any degree tend to the pacification of Ireland (loud cheers), because there are questions of far greater magnitude behind, and it will be remembered that the calm men of Limerick which the right hon. gentleman, the member for Calne, referred to a night or two ago, are of opinion that nothing will satisfy the people of Ireland, or do justice to Irish interests, except the repeal of the union, and the committing of Irish interests to an Irish parliament in Dublin (hear, hear). The hon. member for Honiton, in his speech last night, quoted a very remarkable passage, which I will venture to repeat, showing that those who are interested in tenant-right have put aside the question of the Established Church as a grievance nothing in comparison to it, if it be a grievance at all. At a meeting of a tenant-right association, of which the Roman Catholic Bishop of Meath is the president, and over which the vicar general presided, this resolution was proposed, viz., "The one, the great, the sole question for Ireland is the land question; and other agitations, such as that against the Established Church, are got up for party purposes" (loud cheers). Why introduce an element of bigotry into the laity and disturb the relations between landlord and tenant, which would effect the ruin of thousands of tenants, and precipitate that social catastrophe which we are anxious to avert? (renewed cheering.) And yet we are told that by holding out this olive-branch to the Irish people we are doing all that is required; whilst Lord Russell has thrown the land question over as unworthy of his consideration, and the Roman Catholics themselves say the Church question is a matter of infinite insignificance ("no, no," and "hear, hear.") We now come to an important part of the resolutions, with reference to which the right hon. gentleman has offered us no solution, and without which, I say, we cannot fairly vote for or against these resolutions (hear, hear). It is essentially necessary that we should know the whole of the scheme that is to be proposed (hear, hear); and before we are asked to secularise the revenues of of the Irish Church we ought to be told how it proposed to apply them (cheers). We are told, however, by the right hon. gentleman, that it is a weak feeling on the part of those who object to the secularisation of the funds of the Church, and that it is one that ought at once to be put aside. The late Sir James Graham, who was a colleague of the right hon. gentleman, entertained very different feelings, and expressed them in the most solemn and almost affecting terms; and he ended a great speech on the subject in very strong and decided language, and in which be avowed he possessed that feeling of weakness which the right hon. gentleman pities, but which Sir James Graham was not ashamed to avow. He says "Church property is property that was set apart by our fore-father to properly maintain the Christian religion. I tell you it is sacred, and must be applied to that purpose. Those who minister at the altar must live by the altar. Their claim is as high as Heaven, and as strong as the Almighty, and you cannot overthrow it. It is as lasting as the Eternal, and can never cease to be binding, (oh, oh; and cheers). It is binding on you as Christian legislators, and as Christian men, and for one there is no consideration on earth which shall induce me to compromise or violate it (cheers (cheers)." I can quite understand that some hon. gentlemen will condemn the weakness of feeling of Sir James Graham, but I am content to feel with him, and to express the opinion which he expressed, and to avow that there is in this secularisation of Church property something inconsistent in such an application of the funds (hear, hear). Lord Brougham had also expressed a strong opinion upon the subject—viz.: that not one farthing of the money of the Church should be diverted to other purposes until sufficient had been taken for the purposes of the Church, and then it should only be taken for Church education; and, above all, on no consideration on earth would he give one farthing of it to assist the Roman Catholics (loud cheers). The right hon. gentleman has revealed to a certain extent a part of his plan. He has told us that he would deal tenderly with it, and not disturb the parsonages and residences of the clergy in Ireland; but I want to know whether parsonage, houses or residences are to be provided for the priests and ministers of every other creed, Presbyterian, Roman Catholic, or any other sect or denomination in Ireland, because I find it is put forward in a pamphlet by an Irish Roman Catholic and M.P. (who might be then in the house) that, so far from the right hon. gentleman's plan giving satisfaction, it would give the greatest dissatisfaction (loud cheers); and, so far from its being a prudent thing to leave their residences in the hands of the clergy without providing similar residences for the Roman Catholic clergy, nothing could be more irrating and vexatious (cheers). It is a hopeful prospect that this gentleman has put before us, and I have no doubt that he and other Roman Catholic members will express their opinion to the house as to the effect such a scheme will have in producing discontent and irritation (hear, hear). The right hon. gentleman in his speech in 1865, said it was essential in any well-considered measure—and nothing but a well-considered measure should be brought before parliament—that they should arrive at the conclusion whether the Church property should be applied one way or the other; but in the resolution before us there is nothing to guide us as to what is to become of this money. I can quite understand that hon. members will say it is badly applied, but there are worse purposes to which it may be applied, and probably many others will consider that, until they know to what uses it is to be applied, there is no scheme before them upon which they can be honestly called to vote (cheers). The right hon. gentleman says also that to show that he is in earnest, he proposes immediate legislation upon the subject; but let us consider what it means. It is not to settle the question, but to stay our hands and let there be a suspension of everything in Ireland relating to the Church until the next parliament meets (hear, hear). And what, I ask, is that but prejudging the question? (cheers). The period at which we have arrived precludes the possibility of our considering, discussing, and passing a bill through both houses of parliament (hear, hear). That is the way in which all great questions are treated, and as they ought to be. The right hon. gentleman says that nothing can be so bad as an abstract resolution, and I defy any one to show that the first resolution is anything but that (cheers). I want, therefore, to know if the other house of parliament is also to be tested on the resolutions, in order to ascertain what prospects there are of obtaining their assent to such a bill; or is this house to usurp the whole power of the two houses, and its opinion to guide the whole? In that case it would be an unconstitutional proceeding, and if you are to pass resolutions of this kind and addresses to the Crown, they ought to be joint resolutions and joint addresses (cheers). The main question after all is, what are you going to do with the funds of the Irish Church? It is not enough to get a number of persons to vote on one side of the question without any idea of the principles that are to guide them hereafter. The hon. member for Westminster has a scheme for applying the funds to unsectarian education as a means of conciliating the Roman Catholics of Ireland, but if there is one thing more than another against which they set their faces, it is that (cheers). And then with regard to the tithe: it belongs to no particular part or locality, but is for the general purposes of the Church and the improvement of the religious instruction of the people, and it might be fairly applied to any part where it was so wanted. I pass by Earl Russell's scheme of distribution, which no one is ready to adopt, and which the noble lord himself condemned with such great effect before he adopted it (hear, hear). We might, therefore, rely on his condemnation as sufficient for our purpose. The hon. member for Birmingham would leave something, but he would take away a good deal and secularise it, but he has not told us the particular mode in which the money is to be dealt with; and we have arrived at this point, that instead of everything being clear there is nothing clear (hear, hear). You complain that this being a sentimental grievance, it is not enough for persons to resent it. I do not say it is not, but when you have it on one side and you make more of it than the other side, it is only fair that those upon whom you are going to make the experiment should know the destination of the funds of which you are about to despoil them (loud cheers). But I am told that it is not legitimate to say in this debate that the question of the Irish Church affects the stability of the English and Scotch Churches. I can quite understand that there are those who, like the mother in her extremity, who would throw away her children to save herself from the devouring wolf; but it is not a very happy instance of maternal feeling. The course taken by that unhappy mother does not commend itself to those who feel themselves bound to Ireland by sympathy and the ties of blood and religion (hear, hear). I am not so disposed to throw her overboard, and I am still less disposed to do so when a course is taken which materially affects the principles upon which the Church Establishment rests in the sister country (cheers); for whatever might be said, the minor arguments which might be used by the right hon. gentleman and hon. members who sit below the gangway, and with perfect consistency by the latter, in support of these resolutions, are in favour of religious equality (hear, hear). Now, religious equality I do not understand either in principle or practice to apply to only one part of the empire (loud cheers). I say, therefore, it is not unreasonable in us to object, if you are going to touch part of our Church, because on that principle you are in fact touching the whole, and upsetting the principle upon which alone the establishments of the country— Church and State—can be defended (cheers). If it is necessary for religious equality that there shall be no endowments or privileges accorded to the ministers of the Established Church, then I understand the argument. It is the voluntary system pure and simple, and one fairly to be debated and argued, but you cannot justly put forward religious equality when you are only going to apply it to a small part of the empire (cheers). What will be gained by this great sacrifice of principles on our parts if we are to accede to it? You have promised us nothing, and you have brought nothing before us to justify such a sacrifice, but if you can show that by it you can bring perfect harmony and concord in every part of our dominions, Heaven knows how many prejudices, how many sacrifices of a deeper nature everybody would be ready to make to obtain so desirable an object (cheers). If justice requires that a man should give up those things which his heart is set on— that the interests of the whole country require it, and there is before us a certainty of obtaining that which we all desire, I for one would at least go out of my way and let others carry this measure, if I felt it was for the benefit of all. But when I do not see it is so, when I am advocating on this side of the house principles which I advocated from the opposite side of the house—if I change them it should not be by my hand that the stab was given (cheers), nor should it be from these benches that the change was made (a burst of cheering, which was renewed again and again). But should I be in a position of trust when any change of that kind is made, I will take care to be in a position to be able to give a proof of my honesty, and that I was acting on a principle which I could not resist (hear, hear). Well, sir, what is the great emergency that has arisen calling on us to make these enormous sacri- fices? (loud cheers)—which, likewise, if we had made, we should have been taunted for making on an occasion which did not require it to be done. Is it the miserable Fenianism that has prevailed in this country, or the base Fenianism in Ireland, spoken of the other night calling on us to make this sacrifice of our time, of our duty, of all that was dear to us, in order to get rid of what would not be affected by it for a moment? Was it the suspension of the Habeas Corpus Act? We have had the suspension of the Habeas Corpus Act for many years. Has it inter- fered practically with the liberties of Ireland? Has it interfered in the way it has been used? Has it interfered with the ordinary progress of business? Has it inter- fered with religious freedom? Has it interfered with ordinary freedom of inter- course? Has it not rather been used as an earnest to check that which it was feared, but for it, would have proved inconveniently lawless? (hear, hear.) If you are to take this ground you will only be adding another to the right hon. gentleman's list of dates which were last night cited to prove the imbecility and weakness of the English parliament—its injustice, its unfairness, its readiness to do wrong so long as the wrong could be done with impunity, and he told us that up to the present time we had abstained from doing justice to Ireland, but that now he said these things must be swept away, and he threw it in the teeth of parliament that it had never done an act of justice to Ireland without having been compelled to do so (hear, hear). If that be so, it was to the disgrace of parliament, and not an example to be imitated upon the present occasion (hear, hear). I think, sir, I owe an apology to the house for trespassing so long (go on). Well, I think I have shown that the present is not a fitting time at which such a change, if it were necessary, should be made, and I state boldly that nothing which has been put forward by the right hon. gentleman is sufficient to convince the house that the people of this country reposes any confidence in the views of the right hon. gentleman the member for South Lancashire on this question. Surely, then, the people ought to be consulted before such a change is made. I further say that first resolution is not binding on the parliament to which it will pass. I say that if you throw aside a compact, a statute made as a treaty, and say, "that is not to bind parliament," how can you say, that this resolution, passed by a dying parliament, is to bind its successor? I say this is a position which you have no right to take, and I say that when you are calling on us to proceed on what has been termed this "revolutionary task" by the right hon. gentleman the member for Morpeth, you ought to call to counsel that branch of the legislature without which, at all events, you cannot legislate. Again, I say, suppose you carry the resolution, you do not show us the object in view or that you obtain the peace of Ireland. On the contrary, you would increase many of her evils You complain of absenteeism. I believe that carrying such a resolution would increase it among the laymen, and at all events among the clergy. Have the clergy been found remiss, and will not go among their own flocks, but among their Roman Catholic neighbours? Has not the right hon. gentleman, on the contrary, admitted that they have rendered the most important services in relieving the poor, and probably conferred more benefit upon the Roman Catholic population than any other class of men? If, in spite of the objections I have urged, the amendment is rejected, the Conservative party would oppose the resolutions themselves (hear, hear). If you ask what we would do—not in this parliament, because it would have no opportunity of doing anything in the matter—but in the next parliament, in the event of the resolutions being carried, my reply is that I will give the right hon. gentleman no other pledge than this—that we will act in accordance with the former part of the resolution, and if on the report of the commission we are satisfied that it would be for the benefit of the Irish Church that certain modifications in it should be made, we will make them with a fearless hand (hear, hear). But if you ask us to go further, I will say, at least for myself, as I have upon former occasions, that I will not be a party to a measure for disestablishing the Irish Church (much cheering). I am not prepared to sever Ireland from England in religious matters, and present the spectacle of a government in Ireland of a purely secular character, and a government in England partially religious (a growing laugh)—I beg pardon for a slip of the tongue; but what I meant to say was, that I will not consent that Church and State should be dis-severed in Ireland, and remain connected in England (hear, hear). The right hon. gentleman said that the disestablishment of the Irish Church would, as respected the Irish people, "Pluck from the memory a rooted sorrow, and raze out the written troubles of the brain," but he quite omitted to quote the preceding line, "Can'st thou not minister to a mind diseased" (hear, hear). It is the diseased state of the mind of Ireland to which they ought to direct their attention (cheering). It was diseased by a long traditionary hatred of the Saxon, kept alive by constant agitation and misrepresentation (cheers). That it is believed, which has diseased the great and generous mind of Ireland. But for that pernicious agitation I believe that it would have been in harmony with us at the present moment. The drug, however, which the right hon. gentleman proposed to administer would not be "a sweet oblivious antidote," but rather a nauseous, and, as I believe, not a corrective drug, and if they took it it would require many other remedies to cleanse their system before they got rid of its bad effects (hear). The measure proposed by the right hon. gentleman would not tend in any degree to the desired end—to concilliate those who first of all told them that the land question was to be settled on a basis and in a way to which the present parliament would never assent, and that in the end there was to be a repeal of that union the inviolable and fundamental basis of which was the United Church of England and Ireland (a burst of cheering). I look in vain to the speeches which have been made on the Opposition side of the house for any indication of to whom the funds are to be given which they propose to take from those now in possessson. I say your resolutions are founded on principles of repugnance, away from the principles and the practice of the constitution of the country, and will be provocative of strife, of enmity, and of dissension, instead of paving the way for peace and harmony between England and Ireland. If they conciliated one party, they would irritate another; and, although I will never believe that the Protestants of Ireland would become disloyal, yet there can be no doubt that the dis-establishment of the Irish Church would incite among them discontent and disaffection, and that the injustice which is done them must in the end react upon England. I feel bound, where a wrong is about to be done and property to be taken away from those to whom it belonged, to protest against the spoliation. I feel doubly bound, both as a member of parliament and as an Englishman, to be true to the treaty which is in force between the two countries; and as a Churchman I cannot be indifferent to the condition of my brethren of the faith in Ireland, or to the fate of the clergy who have so nobly performed their duty, and in whose behalf I call as witnesses those who are most opposed to the old endowments; and, finally, I cannot be a party to severing that Church and State under which it is the glory and the privilege of the state to uphold the light of the Reformation in the midst of Ireland. (The right hon. gentleman was greeted with repeated rounds of applause on resuming his seat).

Part 4

CONSERVATISM AND REFORM, 1852–1868

John Wilson Croker, 'The Reform Bill'
The Quarterly Review, March 1854, 558–605

In 1848, Lord John Russell publicly stated that the 1832 Reform Act required modification. In February 1852, as prime minister, he introduced a Reform bill. The measure proposed the extension of the borough franchise to occupiers of property worth £5 per annum and the vote in counties to £20 occupiers. Russell also proposed a direct taxation franchise of 40s per annum, operative in both towns and counties. The abolition of property qualifications for MPs, the abolition of the requirement that ministers face re-election on taking up office, and amendment of the parliamentary oath rendering it less objectionable to Catholics and possible for it to taken by practising Jews were also included. Any redistribution was conspicuous by its absence. Russell characterised the measure as a supplement to the 1832 Reform Act, not a substitute for it.

On Russell's announcement of his bill, Disraeli responded that, prior to careful consideration of its specific proposals, it was not prudent to pass judgement. The merit of any measure would depend on its details. Russell, he commented, had suggested two tests for enfranchisement, numbers of population and property. While not objecting to these tests, Disraeli suggested that Reform legislation at this moment was of questionable propriety. Any change to parliamentary representation should be permanent. While supporting the admission of the working classes to the suffrage, he doubted whether the £5 borough franchise would achieve this object. At the same time, proceeding with Reform would divert parliamentary attention away from other necessary legislation.

In the event, Russell's resignation as prime minister on 21 February foreclosed further consideration of his Reform proposals.

In February 1854, Russell introduced another Reform bill to the Commons. Its main provisions were the lowering of the borough franchise to those occupying property with a £6 annual rateable value. In the counties, the vote was extended to £10 occupiers. 'Merit franchises' would give the vote to men receiving an annual salary of £100 or more, those receiving £10 or more annually from funds or stock, university graduates, and those with savings of £50 or more deposited in a Savings Bank in the borough in which they resided. Redistribution would enable a third MP to be given to 46 two-Member counties and nine boroughs with populations of more than 100,000. In these new three-Member constituencies, electors would possess only two votes. This was a protection of minority representation.

John Wilson Croker's article 'The Reform Bill' condemned Russell's measure as experimental and destructive. Legislation distinguished by dangerous innovation. In 1832, Croker had resigned from the Commons in protest over the Reform

Act. He did so because it exposed venerable institutions, which custom suggested were unchangeable, to refashioning. It conceded the principle that numbers, not just property, were a consideration in conferring the privilege of the vote. As a result, for the past 20 years, he pronounced, the country had slid down the inclined plane of democracy. In 1848, Russell had abandoned 1832 as a final settlement of Reform. This, Croker believed, inoculated a cancerous disease into the vitals of the constitution. Russell's motive for doing so, Croker suggested, was Russell's realisation that 1832 had neither pacified the demand for democracy, nor secured the official domination of the Whigs.

Croker saw the object of Russell's 1854 Reform measure as the attempt to extend the numerical principle through the whole representative system, all political power being passed to numerical majorities. This was a path, Croker warned, that led ultimately and ineluctably to universal suffrage. In France since 1848, universal suffrage had led to despotism, marked by Louis Napoleon's apotheosis as Emperor Napoleon III. In the United States there existed, often unrecognised, constitutional checks on government by numbers. Russell's redistribution proposals confirmed, Croker argued, that his great object was to give all power to selected numerical majorities – a subversion of the principle that the Commons should represent property and 'interests'.

3

JOHN WILSON CROKER, 'THE REFORM BILL'

The Quarterly Review, March 1854, 558–605

A<small>RT</small>. VIII.—1. *The Constitution of the United States compared with our own.* By H. S. Tremenheere. London. 1854.

2. *The English in America.* By (Mr. Justice Halyburton) the Author of 'Sam Slick,' &c. 2 vols. London. 1851.

3. *Parliamentary Reform: a Letter to Richard Freedom, Esq., on the Re-distribution, Extension, and Purification of the Elective Franchise.* By a Revising Barrister (Sir J. Eardley Wilmot, Bart.) 2nd Edition. London. 1853.

4. *Minorities and Majorities, their relative Rights: a Letter to Lord John Russell, M.P., on Parliamentary Reform.* London. 1853.

5. *Electoral Facts from* 1832 *to* 1853, *impartially stated; constituting a complete Political Gazetteer.* By C. R. Dod, Esq. London. 1853.

W<small>E</small> are told that most of the members of the House of Commons who heard Lord John Russell's speech on the introduction of his present Reform Bill—as well as the majority of persons out of doors—appear to consider and treat the proposition as a *sham*. This may account for the cold dissatisfaction with which it was received by those with whom the very name of a *New Reform Bill* promised to be so popular, and the surprising indifference with which it has been regarded by the Conservative party both in the House and in the country. It seemed to be viewed in no more serious light than as an experiment addressed *ad captandum* to the Radicals on one side, and *in terrorem* to the Conservatives on the other, which the Ministers thought it prudent to have in hand, though with very vague intentions as to employing it. These surmises were very much confirmed by the remarkable shilli-shalliness of the Ministerial press as to its *opportunity*. One day it was questioned whether it was wise to begin a foreign war and a domestic revolution simultaneously, but the conclusion arrived at was that the attack on the Russians at Cronstadt or Sebastopol need be no impediment to an assault on the freemen of our towns or the freeholders of our counties. A few days after the opposite opinion prevailed, and we were advised that the Government had on their hands so much to *do,* that they could not pursue with sufficient vigour their schemes to *undo.* Then came some meetings of the friends of Reform, who thought the new scheme not worth a trial; and others—the most favourable—would only accept it as a small instalment, little better than nothing: and at the late moment that we write these lines we still are in doubt what course the Ministers mean to take.

We on our part believe that the motive and the object were more simple as well as more serious. Our conjecture is that Lord John Russell has long seen that his original Reform Bill had failed—that it had neither pacified the Democracy, nor, what he had still more relied on, secured the official domination of the Whigs, and that stronger measures, though in the same direction, would be necessary to secure these points. He has also a little personal monomania—that *he alone* has a right to be the *reformer* of the age, and that if any further reform is called for, *his* hands must prepare and *his* single voice propound it. In the last years of his own ministry, he found his followers unmanageable, and in the agony of its final months of feeble and feverish existence, he saw that both power and popularity were slipping away from him, and that he had no resource but in a new Reform Bill, of which he would be of course the leader, and eventually the chief beneficiary. The embarrassment of his government—in spite of his attempted Reform Bill in 1852—drove him to resign—not unwillingly—for he probably calculated that it was only *reculer pour mieux sauter*. He foresaw that he would be in a condition either to storm the Cabinet in a new tempest of reform, or make it the subject of a compromise with some new combination of men, in which he, whatever else might happen, should still be the grand Missionary of the measure. This has happened, and we have little doubt that he was so far consistent in his negotiation with his new colleagues, that a new Reform Bill was his *sine quâ non,* and became the fundamental basis of the Coalition.

We confess ourselves astonished at his success on this point. We had fancied that there were parties to these negotiations whom nothing could have induced to pass under the *Caudine Forks* of reform; but it may have been thus brought about. Lord John Russell, no doubt, felt that in accepting, first, secondary office, and, subsequently, the leadership of the House without office, with and *under* his oldest political antagonists, he was making a great sacrifice and entitled to an adequate consideration. That consideration probably was that he should mark his own importance and the total acquiescence of his new colleagues, by having his great object recognised and sanctioned by the solemnity of being announced in the *Speech from the* THRONE—an honour with which he had not ventured to invest his own measure of 1852.

This we suspect to be something very near the secret history of the new Reform Bill, and convinces us that it is no *sham*—at least on the part of Lord John Russell, but that, on the contrary, it is a measure on which he has staked his political existence, and that any hesitation or reluctance as to its progress can only have arisen from those of his colleagues, who, though they may have acquiesced in his general views, may have discovered that it is pregnant with more difficulties and dangers of various kinds than they had at first imagined—as little acceptable to the people as it is discordant with their own former principles; and that the safest and perhaps the only possible course now left to them would be to abandon it.

This can only be a mere conjecture on our part—but neither the secret reluctance of Lord John's colleagues, if it exists, nor the postponement nor even modification of the measure itself, would make any essential and ultimate difference in the state of the case, or alleviate the alarm with which we view this revival of the whole Reform question—not as the inflammation or fever of a season—it has lost all those transient symptoms—not as a question of this session or the next—but as a cancerous disease now inoculated into the vitals of our Constitution. Whether the Ministers had originally more or less intention of forcing on the Bill, or more or less hope of carrying it, can have little importance compared with the more permanent influence which such a proposition solemnly made by a *Cabinet* that professes to be *conservative* as well as liberal, with the sanction of the *Crown,* must ultimately have, sooner or later, on what still remains of the old English Constitution.

We wish on so serious a subject to exaggerate nothing; and we will therefore not say that this is the last nor even the penultimate blow which that Constitution, mutilated as it is, may be able to bear. We do not mean to represent the operation of the Ministerial measure as inevitably sudden, though we believe it to be inevitably certain. We are well aware of the vitality that must exist in a government so old—so tried—so rooted—so successful—so honoured as ours has been. We know that in such a case forms will long survive spirit—that life will still linger under a mortal wound—that the hectic blush of decay may look like a transient bloom of health—that, after a spendthrift has been ruined, he may continue for a time deceiving himself and those who have dealings with him on a hollow and factitious credit—and that, in short, a Constitution, by the illusion of departed strength, by the *prestige* of its ancient vigour, and by the force of a *post mortem* and galvanised action, may be like the hero of romance—

'Andava combattando—ed *era morto!*'

This has been exemplified by the state of the country, which for the last twenty years has been sliding down the inclined plane of democracy with little other visible check or jolt than—a most unprecedented and remarkable circumstance to be sure—our having had within that period no less than *fifteen changes of Ministers;* and we think that, even as things stand, no one can reasonably expect more stability for the future; while, on the other hand, we shall show in the course of this paper that if this new Bill is to pass, some of the main causes of that very precarious stability will be utterly destroyed. In short, we have taken a slow poison; and though in the interval we may seem to talk as wisely and as calmly as Plato tells us that Socrates did on the mortuary couch, the event is equally certain, and the awful power stands at the bedside to administer fresh doses, if what we have already taken should be found insufficient.

Let us recapitulate some of the main facts of the case. The Reform Bill of 1832 was made, as its promoters admitted, extravagantly large, in order that party fanaticism should have no excuse for attempting to extend it. Lord John Russell called it a *revolution,* and so great a one that he was determined, he said, not to risk another; and he had so deeply pledged himself to this principle as to entitle him from his own partisans to the discourteous title of '*Finality John*'—a designation which, however, we should cite as even more honourable than the title he derives from his birth, if he had really merited it by political wisdom and personal consistency. Lord John Russell, we say, in spite of these antecedents—but under the new impressions created by the failure of his own administration, which we have before noticed—produced in 1852, in the character of First Minister of the Crown, a new Reform Bill, or, to use his own term, attempted a *new Revolution.* Three changes or modifications of the Government have since taken place, all notoriously produced by the weakness of the governing power and the growth of the democratic one in the House of Commons; and yet *He,* who had been himself driven by the caprices of that unmanageable body from the station of Prime Minister into Opposition, and from Opposition to the Foreign Office, and, finally, to leave the Foreign Office for no office at all, but that of leading old enemies against old friends—and all this within two years—*He,* we say, *Finality John,* now proposes another and worse revolution, of which the obvious and indeed the almost avowed result must be to render *any* administration still more precarious, and the democracy still more unmanageable.

We are, therefore, not surprised that an impression should have prevailed that a course so inconsistent, and so absurd, was never expected nor intended to succeed; but we are satisfied, as we have just stated, that this impression was erroneous, and that the measure was proposed in the most sincere of all tempers—party zeal and individual *amour-propre!* How else could it have received the solemn sanction of a *recommendation from the Throne*—which, on such an occasion, is not a *proposition,* but a *pledge*—a *confession* on the part of the Sovereign that her power, which is hardly sufficient to keep a ministry together for twelve months, is *too great,* and that the already irresistible force of her electoral subjects requires a large addition.

But we have other evidence of the seriousness of this proposition earlier, and *in these times* more authoritative, than the speech from the Throne. We have lately heard much of the divulgation of Cabinet secrets, but nothing we think more curious than as to this new Reform Bill, which contains, besides the old obvious and hackneyed encroachments on the Constitution, with which the former one had rendered us but too familiar, some provisions of so novel and, as they seem to us, so absurd a nature as would have astonished the world if it had not been prepared for them by certain publications, which, if not originally suggested by the resolutions of the Cabinet, must inevitably have been borrowed and adopted by it. We must leave the common sense and intelligence of mankind the choice of the alternative whether the Cabinet prompted those publications, or whether it drew its inspiration of public policy and public duties from such sources. However that may be, the fact is certain that an article in the 'Edinburgh Review' of two years ago and another in that for last October, and the pamphlet by a 'Revising Barrister,' since avowed in a second edition by Sir Eardley Wilmot, first opened to the wondering eyes of the public the very minute and accurate details of some of the most extravagant innovations which we have since found in the Ministerial Reform Bill—*election by minorities—saving banks' franchise—members for the Inns of Court and London University—placemen not vacating*—nay, the *names* of places to be disfranchised, and the very scale and lines that were to govern disfranchisement were all distinctly suggested. We do not mention this as a complaint that Ministers should pay attention to the suggestions of their supporters in private or in the press—nothing more natural; we are only surprised to find that our colleagues, gentlemen of the pen, have become the advisers of Cabinet measures and the harbingers of the embryo intentions of the Crown. Sir Eardley Wilmot is, as far as we know, a respectable gentleman, though we should regret to find verified a rumour that has reached us that his Ministerial pamphlet has been rewarded with a County Judgeship. We have heard that the author of the article in the 'Edinburgh Review' is also personally as respectable as he is as an essayist; but somehow we do not think it was quite seemly to put these gentlemen forward as the first heralds and organs of the determination of her Majesty the Queen some months before it was communicated to Parliament. But even upon that anomaly we lay little stress, and we notice it only as an additional proof that this Reform Bill is a serious and premeditated design. Its absurd details should not induce us to divert our alarm from its formidable object. It is like what we sometimes read of in the Italian carnivals, where the foulest murder is perpetrated under the masquerade of a jack-pudding.

That ultimate object is to carry out through our whole representative system the *numerical principle*—the power of mere NUMBERS, and especially of AGGREGATE NUMBERS—in short, *physical force*. This was for the first time in the legislative history of Governments attempted in the original Reform Bill, but rather covertly and with some appearance of bashfulness, as if the naked proposition was too indecent to be exhibited. In the present Bill it is more shamelessly avowed, and the slight adjuncts which are hung round it to divert the eye remind us of the female figure in the Great Exhibition, of which the nudity was rather marked than tempered by the adventitious addition of a bracelet round the wrist and a fetter round the ankle. Of no more value for either decency or substantial importance are the pretences of the *educational franchises,* the *protection of minorities,* the *votes for taxes,* and other similar delusions, which are to be attached to the *wrists* and *ankles* of the colossus of *Universal Suffrage,* of which, and of nothing else, this Bill is really the model and the mould.

This scarcely veiled principle of Representation by *numbers* is, in our view, the whole Bill, and it is to it that we think it our duty to endeavour to direct the attention of the country by a closer analysis of that principle than we have before had either the opportunity or the necessity of attempting; and we cannot but hope, that late as it may seem, we may still make some impression on the public mind by a more practical elucidation of the case than we have yet seen.

The *verbal* import of the word 'Representation' has been, in our opinion, very mischievously confounded with its real, and, in this country, constitutional *essence.* Undoubtedly the abstract principle of *representation* assumes *numbers* as the fundamental basis of political as they are of physical power, and if a Constitution were a mere arithmetical question, any *thousand* men would have a claim to ten times the political weight of any *hundred;* and the logical result of that unlimited principle would be *Universal Suffrage.* But the danger of such an extension, and its incompatibility with the safety of individual persons, the security of private property, or the steady administration of civil government, are so axiomatically obvious, that no country, not even the most democratic republics, have ever ventured on a practical adoption of the unrestricted principle.

If any one should at first sight, and it could only be at first sight, object that the recent, experiment in France, and the longer one in the United States of America, are exceptions to this statement, we reply that these are, in fact, no exceptions, but on the contrary pregnant instances of the justice of our opinion. The French republic of 1848 attempted a Government on the basis of *universal suffrage;* but it and all its provisions were summarily swept away within two years by a military usurpation, which Universal Suffrage was also *pro hac vice* called in to cover with its delusive authority, and to constitute an absolute despotism, in which neither universal nor indeed any suffrage but the *sic jubeo* of one man is of the slightest weight or importance. France has now for a second time accomplished that sagacious prophecy of Burke's, that her attempts at a republic would end '*in the most complete arbitrary power that has ever appeared on earth.*' Whether it will ever happen that universal suffrage shall be really and *bonâ fide* admitted to any effective share in the government of that country is more than we can guess; but we may safely say that there is no rational man in France who wishes that it should. Certain it is that all numerical influence is now extinguished, and that the two great trials thus made of it in 1848 and 1851 have ended not merely in failure but disgrace—the first producing an insupportable *anarchy,* and the second a *despotism,* which will, we venture to prophesy, at no distant period be found equally intolerable.

The example of the United States is more specious; but it is very far from being anything like a case in point, and indeed on the contrary exhibits, when well considered, the most striking illustration, both in principle and in practice, against a merely *numerical* representation. As this is the only precedent which we have ever seen or heard produced in favour of the numerical principle, and as the supposed success of the American experiment is frequently and confidently urged against us, we think it our duty to enter into it with a detail which would otherwise seem supererogatory.

Several of the checks which the *natural* condition of the States and the deliberate provisions of their constitutions have interposed against the direct power of *numbers* are obvious; but they, as well as some others less notorious, have been brought together and stated with great clearness and force in the very able and *timely* work of Mr. Tremenheere, which we earnestly recommend to the special attention of our readers as well for its interesting exposition of the political and social condition of America as for its more general views of the theory and practice of constitutional government, which are applicable to all countries, and particularly to ourselves in our present very precarious circumstances. Mr. Tremenheere's work is the result not merely of his own personal observations in the States, but of an able examination and digest of the opinions of the greatest American writers, Adams, Jay, Hamilton, and above all, Mr. Justice Story and Chancellor Kent, whose legal authority is not only supreme in America, but of as much and merited weight in our English courts as any text-books of our own. From them we shall see three most important points:—*First,* The natural causes that tended to limit the numerical principle within innocuous bounds. *Secondly,* The political pains taken by the framers of the Constitutions both federal and separate to check it still further. *Thirdly,* The incompatibility of that principle with the very existence of even the Republican Constitution, on which, as is its nature, it is gradually—and as these great jurists think fatally—encroaching. Each of these heads will be found to contain matter well deserving our attention in the present crisis of our constitution.

I. The American Union was, we may say, born a Republic, and inured from its cradle to the direct action of popular government. Even before their independence the royal authority over the internal affairs of the colonies was but a name, and the population was such, both in composition and numbers, as to preclude any undue influence from the masses—in fact there were no *masses* to dread—there was no populace—no idle hands itching for other people's property, and the western expanse was—we will not rate it so low as a safety valve, but—a broad and boundless channel for the overflowings of every species of enterprise and ambition; and we see in Mr. Justice Haliburton's work—which we can also recommend to any one desirous of understanding the elements of American Society—how exceedingly slight were the social, and, above all, the *legal* and *constitutional* changes that ensued on their passing from their colonial to their independent state.

II. The able and judicious framers of the American constitution, while proclaiming as its basis the *sovereignty of the people,* were not blind to the practical danger of the unlimited principle, and they therefore preserved not only all of the antagonistic elements which they found in the original *provinces,* but they endeavoured to consolidate them with new guarantees and preservatives against what they well knew was the greatest, if not the only, constitutional danger—the excess of *merely popular* influences. There was a struggle of many years, while the federal Constitution was in progress, between three conflicting principles—the absolute right of the sovereign people—the restrictions with which the most judicious and influential statesmen wished to bridle that impetuous power—and an immense diversity of local and personal interests and opinions. It was at last, as Judge Story says—

'a system of compromise and conciliation, in which the strictness of abstract theory was made to yield to a just consideration for particular interests and even prejudices; and some irregularity of benefit was submitted to for the common good.'

—*Apud Tremenheere,* p. 39.

The first check on the omnipotence of Numbers is the independent authority of the President. Once elected, he, and with him the ministers and all the subordinate public servants, whom he chooses and displaces at his own absolute will and pleasure, are wholly independent of Congress, and of course of any elective power. He has an original veto upon all legislation, with a provision in certain cases, that if after such a negative the law should be again proposed by a majority of two-thirds of the legislature the veto is annulled. There have been frequent instances of the exercise of the Presidential veto, but no instance is stated in the works before us of the veto having been overruled—but if it were to be so, it would not displace either the President or his ministers, and they would continue to administer the government, as has already twice happened, though notoriously in a minority of both Houses of Congress. Here is a check on numerical legislation with which we presume none of our reformers would think of investing an English ministry. But there occurred in the formation of the American system an earlier, an easier, and yet still more important check, namely, the maintaining the territorial divisions of the old colonies in their new character of *States*. This decision slightly, if at all questioned at the time, and little noticed since, was, both directly and in its consequences, a most powerful exception and antidote to the numerical principle. Delaware, with an extent of about 2000 square miles, and a population of perhaps 100,000, is as much a sovereign State, and as such of equal authority in the Union, as its gigantic neighbour, New York, of near 50,000 square miles, and perhaps 3,000,000 of population. From this datum followed others of more practical importance. Each State is governed in all its internal interest by its own separate and independent constitution and jurisdiction. These constitutions exhibited a great *variety* of modes for the election of its legislators, its officers and magistrates; and it is hardly necessary to add that when their representatives arrive at the federal Congress at Washington, they bring with them a great variety of antagonist interests, and will be considerably influenced by the peculiarity that exists in the constitutional principles and practice of each individual State; and finally, when arrayed in Congress, though each State sends members to the *House of Representatives* proportionable to its *population,* they have all an *equal* representation in the *Senate*—Delaware with its population of 100,000, and New York with its 3,000,000, have each two senators. This direct repudiation of the numerical principle, first in the President's independence, and again in the legislative power of the Senate, is of the greatest importance, and in the case of the Senate at least of the greatest advantage.

'It has been demonstrated,' says Judge Story, 'that the Senate *in its actual organization* is a most important and valuable part of the system, and the *real balance-wheel* which adjusts and regulates its movements.'

—p. 74.

We wish we could say as much for the practical and permanent power of our House of Lords; and we almost equally wish that we could believe that the

78

'balance-wheel' of the American constitution may be maintained in its undis-
turbed operation. We shall see presently that, whatever may be our wishes, there
is more ground for fear than hope. But even as the case thus stands, we think that
those of our reformers who press the American extension of suffrage upon us,
should, in common fairness, tell us how they would supply the two counteracting powers which we have just shown to exist in the American case, and without
which we do not believe that the American constitution would have survived General Washington.

But even in the election for Representatives the numerical power is by no
means so extensive as it is represented. To the assertion that every individual has
a right to vote, the American commentators, in common with both the principles
and practices of all other representative governments, show that it is not an inherent *natural* right, but a civil privilege conferred by society, modified in a variety
of instances by age, by different capacities, and by that grand distinction which
everywhere has denied the right to *at least one-half* of the human race, who must
be contented to be constructively represented—even though Lord John Russell
were to erect the ward of Billingsgate into a separate borough.

'The truth seems to be,' says Judge Story, 'that the right of voting, like
many other rights, is one which, whether it has a fixed foundation in
natural law or not, has always been treated in the practice of nations as a
strictly civil right, derived from and regulated by each society, according
to its own circumstances and interests. * * * * If, therefore, any society
shall deem the common good and interests of the whole society best
promoted, under the particular circumstances in which it is placed, by a
restriction of the right of suffrage, it is not easy to state any solid ground
of objection to its exercise of such an authority.'

—p. 89.

As a corollary to those principles, he adds an important matter of fact:—

'That no two of the States have fixed the qualification of voters upon
the same uniform basis. From this,' he adds, 'it will be seen how little
even in the most free of Republican Governments any abstract right of
suffrage or any original indefeasible privilege has been recognized in
practice.'

—p. 90.

The fact itself is thus stated and illustrated by Mr. Tremenheere:—

'At the time of the framing of the Constitution of the United States the
differences in the manner in which the franchise was settled in the different States was remarkable. In Virginia the exclusive right to vote was
in the freeholders; in Rhode Island and Connecticut in the freemen; in

Massachusetts in persons possessing a given amount of personal property; in other states in persons paying taxes or having a fixed residence. The question was much debated by the Convention which drew up the Constitution, whether it would not be more fair and equal, and more likely to ensure a direct and immediate representation of the popular opinion, if a uniform qualification for voting were adopted for the House of Representatives. It was, however, unanimously decided otherwise; and upon grounds precisely similar to those which are held to justify and recommend *the very great diversity of qualifications for the elective franchise that has so long existed in this country.*'

—p. 92.

Perhaps we may be interrupted here by an objection, that we are not menaced by anything like a *uniform franchise;* that, on the contrary, the proposed Reform Bill would extend even extravagantly the diversity of the right. We shall show, when we arrive at the consideration of the bill itself, that this is a mere delusion, that the intended diversities, extravagant and even absurd as they may be, all tend to the one general principle of the extension of the numerical power, and that these diversities are mere cloaks, and very thin ones, to cover that greater design. And here again the American precedent detects and exposes the fallacy and danger of the attempt, and this brings us to the third head of this portion of our discussion.

III. We have seen the pains taken by the framers of the American Constitutions, to adopt where they existed, and to create where they did not, all the checks within their reach to the numerical principle—of the encroaching activity of which they were sagaciously jealous, and which has exhibited itself more strongly and rapidly than, we believe, even they expected. We copy Mr. Tremenheere's extract from the Commentaries of Chancellor Kent—a name not second in American, and we may say European authority to those of Blackstone and of Story:—

'*The progress and impulse of popular opinion is rapidly destroying every Constitutional check, every conservative element,* intended by the sages who framed the earliest American Constitutions as *safeguards against the abuses of popular suffrage.*

'Thus in *Massachusetts,* by the Constitution of 1780, a defined portion of real or personal property was requisite in an elector; that qualification was dispensed with by the amended Constitution of 1821.

'By the practice under the Charters of *Rhode Island* and *Connecticut,* a property qualification was requisite to constitute freemen and voters. This test is continued in Rhode Island, but done away in Connecticut by their Constitution of 1818.

'The *New York* Constitution of 1777 required the electors of the Senate to be freeholders, and of the Assembly to be either freeholders or to have a rented tenement of the yearly value of forty shillings. The amended Constitution of 1821 reduced this qualification down to payment of a tax, or performance of militia duty, or assessment and work on the highways. But the Constitution as again amended in 1826, swept away all these impediments to universal suffrage.

'In *Maryland,* by their Constitution of 1776, electors were to be free-holders, or possessing property to the amount of 30*l*.; but by legislative amendments in 1801 and 1809 (and amendments are allowed to be made in that State by an ordinary statute, if confirmed by the next succeeding legislature) all property qualification was disregarded.

'The Constitution of *Virginia* in 1776 required the electors to be free-holders, but the Constitution of 1830 reduced down the property qualification to that of being the owner of a leasehold estate or a householder.'

—p. 113.

And in 1851, this 'once aristocratic State of Virginia' abolished all qualification, and adopted the ultra-democratic form of Constitution by a vote (under the former right of suffrage) of 75,748 to 11,060 against it.—(p. 114.)

'In *Mississippi,* by the Constitution of 1817, electors were to have been enrolled in the militia, or paid taxes; but those impediments to universal suffrage were removed by the new Constitution of 1833.

'So the freehold qualification, requisite in certain cases by the Constitution of *Tennessee* of 1796, is entirely discontinued by the Constitution of 1835.

'*All* the State Constitutions formed since 1800 have omitted to require any property qualifications in an elector, except what may be implied in the requisition of having paid a State or county tax, and even that is not in the Constitutions more recently formed or amended, except in the *Rhode Island* Constitution of 1843. * * * *

'*Such a rapid course of destruction of the former Constitutional checks is matter for grave reflection;* and to counteract the dangerous tendency of such combined forces as universal suffrage, frequent elections, all officers for short periods, all offices elective, and an unchecked press, and to *prevent them from racking and destroying our political machines,* the *People* must have a larger share than usual of that wisdom which is "first pure, then peaceable, gentle, and easy to be entreated" ' [James, iii. 17].

—p. 114.

Such a pure, calm, and manageable wisdom no people ever will or ever can possess; and accordingly, even in the nine years that have elapsed since Judge Kent published his Commentaries, the evil has rapidly advanced. Of the thirty-one States, and the six *Territories* (candidate States), eight only, and these the older states, 'retain the semblance of a qualification of the suffrage;' but it is only a semblance; and the whole case is thus summed up:—

> '*This almost entire destruction, in so short a period, of all those* "constitutional checks and conservative elements," *in the franchise of the individual States, which had been regarded by the framers of the Constitution as essential to genuine liberty, has entirely altered the basis on which those able men placed the Constitution, and on which they relied for its continuing to be what their prudence and wisdom left it.*'
>
> —p. 117.

Such are the direct results of democratic encroachment, but the collateral consequences, though not so visible, are not less important. The Senate—a few years since the *balance-wheel* of the State—is already deranged.

> 'In determining that the Senate of the United States should be elected by the State legislatures, they expected that those legislatures would be composed, first, of a Senate returned by a class of electors representing the more stable elements of the community; and, secondly, of a House of Representatives resting on similar elements, namely, on the electoral qualifications of property, residence, and the payment of taxes.
>
> 'The process of change in this short space of time has swept away these expectations; and the Senate of the United States is now elected by State legislatures, based on a franchise unrestricted by any of the above qualifications, except in the very few instances above noticed; and the members of the House of Representatives of the United States are returned by direct election, by voters having, in twenty of the States, no property qualification at all, and in nine next to none, the remaining two only having retained any valid qualification.'
>
> —p. 117.

But this, bad as it is in a constitutional view, is still worse as to the internal administration of justice. We suppose that we need not insist to any man in England, except Lord John Russell, on the expediency—until these late days, we should have said necessity—of keeping the law and the Judges as clear as the nature of our social institutions would permit, apart from political influences; but see how the democratical encroachments have affected the judicial authority in America:—

> 'The above great change is far from being the only proof of the progress of ultra-democratic opinions which the legislation of that country has afforded of late years. Among the most remarkable has been the adoption, in more than two-thirds of the States, of the practice of electing the Judges by popular vote and for short periods only; thus striking at the root of their independence, and violating a principle which has ever been held to be among the first elements of freedom, and of protection to life and property.'
>
> —*Tremenheere*, p. 119.

From all this we deduce, and think we have proved, two important points—first, that the American Constitution never meant to give that preponderance to the numerical principle that has been vulgarly attributed to it; and, secondly, that any opening, however small, however guarded, to numerical preponderance is certain to enlarge itself—like *a rat-hole in a Dutch dyke*—to so irresistible and irremediable an extent, as to spread devastation over all the interests that the dyke had formerly protected.

Most earnestly requesting our readers to ponder on and calmly estimate the opening, the progress, the present state, and the probable results of the great American experiment, and to decide in their unbiassed judgment whether it is not rather an awful warning than a seductive precedent, we conclude by a single observation, perhaps the most important of all—namely, that supposing the American precedent were ever so perfect and successful in all its points, what guide would it be to a country that *professes* to maintain an hereditary monarchy and an hereditary House of Lords? To those who are not prepared for *that,* of what use to their argument would be the most perfect success of the American system? Let us, therefore, now return to our own constitutional questions.

Representation was from the earliest times an important ingredient in all European governments, and traces of it existed in the most despotic countries of the continent, even before the American and French revolutions had given a new impetus to the popular principle; but in England alone it had maintained its vitality and constitutional importance. This is attributable no doubt, in a main degree, to our insular position, that relieved us from the necessity of standing armies and fortresses, and of such a concentration of powers and such unity and celerity of action in the hands of the monarch as are hardly reconcileable with the delays and other still more serious difficulties that must arise from the counterbalance and probably the counteraction of an independent and deliberative assembly. But the circumstances which rendered it impossible to our monarchs either to destroy our parliamentary system, or to reduce it, as in France, to merely judicial and remonstrative functions, would not have prevented its destroying itself if the antagonism of its *component* parts had not been, by a fortunate combination of design, accident, and the amalgamating power of time and experience, brought into a working state of harmony and co-operation.

The mode in which this result was accomplished was anomalous, it must be admitted, but rational and effective. Ever since the Revolution of 1688, it is not to be questioned that the real power of Government was—not legally nor avowedly, but practically—exercised, we will not say *by* but *in* the House of Commons. The theory was that the counteraction of three equal forces might in politics, as in the physical problem, keep the central body in equilibrio. That was a fallacy. Power, like a house, divided against itself cannot stand. There must be unity somewhere. That unity was in the House of Commons. The King and the Lords were independent only in theory—neither, nor even both, could resist a strong and fixed determination of the House of Commons. A House of Commons might indeed be, and not unfrequently has been, dissolved on some special points of difference with the Crown, and the succeeding House has sometimes adopted and ratified the views of the Crown; but still the *ultima ratio* was in the House of Commons. How then was it that this all-powerful body was kept in such general harmony with what were theoretically called the antagonist branches of the Constitution? Such a sober and steady result was contrary to what might be *à priori* expected from the very nature of a popular assembly.

The first moderating cause was the fact that the House of Commons itself was, as we shall see presently, in a very mitigated degree the representative of the numerical principle. The constituencies in themselves comprised a great variety of counteracting classes—freeholders in both counties and towns—in some boroughs, copyholders—leaseholders—corporators of various denominations, aldermen, common councilmen, jurats, burgesses, portmen, freemen by inheritance, by servitude, and by purchase—householders—burgage tenants—scot-and-lot men—and in some very few instances *potwallers* and inhabitants, with little other qualification than mere residence within the district. This variety of constituent classes—which grew to be more numerous and more distinctive as the House of Commons advanced in weight and importance—seems to have been designed— some of them, such as the burgage tenures and the corporations, avowedly were— to divide, and thereby check the impetus of the masses of population—and this diversity Mr. Justice Story cites with approbation as the example by which the constitutions of the several American States maintained similar varieties as conducive to 'a mixed system, embracing and representing and combining distinct interests, classes, and opinions.'

> 'In England,' adds the enlightened commentator, 'the House of Commons as a representative body is founded *on no uniform principle either of numbers, classes, or places, such diversities being important checks upon undue legislation,* as facilitating the representation of different interests and opinions, and securing a well-balanced and intelligent representation of all the various classes of society.'
>
> —*Com.,* § 585.

But even these local and personal diversities would have not been enough, if the House of Commons, however otherwise well constituted, had been exclusively the organ of popular interests and feelings: for its inevitable antagonism with the Lords and the Crown would not have been sufficiently provided against.

That conciliatory result was only to be obtained by, as it were, calling into council the Crown and the Lords, whose opinions should be conveyed to the House of Commons and infused into its discussions by the means of constituencies, more or less sympathising with the royal and aristocratical influences. *There* was the true balance of power—the real amalgam that brought and kept the three otherwise conflicting authorities together. The final decision of the Lower House no doubt settled all questions, but not without a previous conciliatory discussion, and generally mutual concessions, in which the Crown and the Lords had their reasonable weight, and which discussions and concessions in ninety-nine cases out of the hundred either rendered an open negative unnecessary, or showed that it would be unavailing, and thus prevented a direct collision between the powers of the State.

This compromise—anomaly, if you will—is the true secret not merely of the success but of the very existence of our mixed constitution, of which it is really the *mixing* process, for without it the constitutional elements would be not *mixed* but *repulsive*. It is that harmony and *concent* of powers which Shakspeare, the great master of all arts, describes in the character of that wise statesman—the Duke of Exeter, uncle of Henry V.:—

> 'For government, though *high, and low, and lower,*
> Put into parts, doth keep in *one concent;*
> *Congruing* to a full and natural close,
> Like music.'[1]

This passage, which condenses the spirit of any practical representative government, so much resembles one in Plato, and another in Cicero's Republic, preserved by St. Augustine (since found in Cardinal Mai's MS. of the '*Republic*'), that Shakspeare's commentators are at a loss to know how his 'small Latin and no Greek' should have got at Plato and St. Augustine. He probably found the doctrine in his own sagacity, and decorated it by his own fancy. The sagacity and wisdom of Mr. Burke summed up the whole case in the following remarkable paragraph:—

> 'Mr. Fox and the "friends of the people" well know that the House of Lords is, by itself, the feeblest part of the Constitution; they know that the House of Lords is supported only by its connexions with the Crown and with the House of Commons; and that without this double connexion the Lords *could not exist a single year*. They know that all these parts of our Constitution, whilst they are *balanced* as opposing interests, are also *connected* as friends; otherwise nothing but confusion could be the result of such a complex constitution. It is natural therefore that they who wish the common destruction of the whole, and of all its parts, should contend for their total separation. But as the House of Commons is that LINK which connects both the other parts of the constitution (the Crown and the Lords) *with the mass of the people,* it is to that link (as it is natural enough) that their incessant attacks are directed;—that *artificial* representation of the people, being once discredited and overturned, all goes to pieces, and nothing but a plain French democracy or arbitrary monarchy can possibly exist.'
>
> —*Observations on the Conduct of the Minority,* vol. vii. p. 257.

What wisdom! what truth! the eye of a master engineer looking into all the hidden springs and motives of the great political machine! This harmony—*concent* of powers—was, as Mr. Burke saw, attained in our constitution by what were called the close boroughs, and it was to the loss of this beneficial influence that the Duke of Wellington alluded in his celebrated question—'How is the King's Government to be carried on?' We shall see as we proceed, that this question has become so pressing, and is rapidly growing so much more urgent, that the very authors of the Reform Bill are devising means to remedy the mischief which they were thus warned against doing.

And let it not be thought that this collateral interference of the Crown and the Lords was any real encroachment on the power of the Commons. In fact it had existed from the earliest parliamentary times, and was, as we have before said, a *sine qua non* to the existence of the constitutional balance: the '*burgage tenure*' boroughs, for instance, a large class—not fewer, we believe, than five and twenty, and the closest—were exercising—on the day that the Reform Bill abolished them—the *same* purpose for which they were originally created six centuries ago—that of representing the local and personal interests of the great landed proprietor (of old, the feudal Baron), at whose will they held ancient tenements situated within the precincts and protection of the ancient *burgh* or castle. In a still more extensive and important class of boroughs, the small Corporations, the franchise was limited for the protection of the middle and upper ranks of a concentrated population against the power of numbers; and they too, from the earliest times, were sensitive of and responsive to the influences of adjacent property.

But independently of such considerations (important as they are both in fact and in principle), it cannot be said that the influence of the Crown and the Lords *within* the Lower House was any encroachment on the power of the Commons—quite the reverse. According to the strict legal and constitutional theory, the Commons were but *one-third* of the legislative power, and were liable to be overborne by the union of the other two, and even nullified by the opposition of one: but when the Crown and Peers were admitted to mingle their influence, through the medium of Commoners adopting their opinions, they were no longer constitutional *antagonists,* but voluntary auxiliaries and *contributors* to the power of the Commons— giving up a harsh theoretic claim, the frequent exercise of which would have been dangerous if not impossible, for a lighter but constant influence—never strong enough to overbear or even to impede the action of the greater body, but only to infuse a spirit of accommodation and compromise—the only spirit in which human affairs, public or private, can be permanently and successfully managed. It was the *oil of the wheel,* invisible from without, but counteracting continually the destructive heat that would have been otherwise inevitable; and thus securing the smooth, equable, constant, and successful action of the whole machine.

Such had been the working state of our Constitution, which, with all its anomalies and irregularities, had not only blessed us with as large a share of internal prosperity and of external glory as any country ever enjoyed, but had commanded the respect and even emulative envy of every foreign people on whom any idea of rational and regulated liberty had dawned. And we think we may conclude, without fear of contradiction, that the secret of that unparalleled success was not in the theoretic balance of three independent powers (which really never existed), but in the occult union and amalgamation of these elements in that *officina imperii,* in the House of Commons. The Reform Bill of 1831, under the delusion, or we rather believe, the pretence of *restoring* what never had existed, *first* introduced the direct *numerical principle,* and adopting the arbitrary population line of 4000, condemned those boroughs whose inhabitants should be under that number, to lose one member, and those under 2000 to total disfranchisement. We have no desire to revive heats and animosities that accompanied that most unfortunate, and by the not tardy avowal of its own framers, unsuccessful measure; but as the same principle and the same practices are reproduced in the New Bill with which we are menaced—prepared too and presented by the *same hand*—it is absolutely necessary to recall them to, we trust, the sober and more deliberate consideration and as we expect condemnation of the Country.

When the number 4000 was first announced in 1831, no one could conjecture why that number had been selected more than what numerically seemed more obvious—5000, or 10,000—or what magic there was in that number of 4000, or its *half,* that arbitrarily made them the

'*certi* denique fines
Quos ultra citraque nequit consistere rectum.'

It was evident enough, from the *prima facies* of the Bill, that the secret object of its framers was to make the disfranchisement fall as heavily as possible on the Tory boroughs, and as lightly as possible on those possessed by the Whigs; but the motive of this particular line of demarcation was not detected till it was found that in the Population Returns of 1821, on which the scale professed to be founded, Lord Fitzwilliam's borough of *Malton* was returned at '*four thousand and—five!*' We need not remind our readers of the weight and importance of Lord Fitzwilliam to the Whig party; and as soon as it was discovered that Malton—'*fortunate Malton,*' as it was termed by acclamation—had a population of 'four thousand and—*five,*' the enigma was solved, and no doubt existed as to the motive that determined the 4000 line. But, though Malton was probably the first and ruling object, a more detailed examination soon proved that the lines of 4000 and 2000 accommodated themselves very aptly to several other cases of favouritism; and even where they did not at first sight seem to do so, they were ingeniously twisted and stretched to accomplish the double purpose of Tory disfranchisement and Whig immunity. A large volume would not suffice to explain and expose all these manœuvres; but a few leading cases (most of which also figure in the New Reform Bill) will serve as guides and warnings as to the delusive and hypocritical pretences on which these reforms are proposed and perpetrated.

The population returns of 1821, which the Government professed to take as their basis in 1831, happened to be made on no uniform principle of *local denomination.* In fact, the parliamentary franchise was so little connected with extent or population, that, except in counties, it formed no territorial division of the country. The consequence was that the Returns were made with considerable local diversities. Sometimes the population of the *actual town,* when it happened to be defined, was given. Sometimes adjoining *districts,* greater or less, were added. Sometimes, when an ill-defined town stood in a large parish, the whole *parish* was given without distinguishing the town. Sometimes, when the town stood in *two parishes,* the population of both were given; sometimes that of the *predominant parish* only. All this diversity was of no importance to the object of ascertaining the population of the county; but it was a very different case when it came to be employed as a scale for the partition of rights and franchises amongst contiguous localities. By a dextrous handling of these diversities, which, in truth, were mere clerical discrepancies (which the slightest inquiries would have explained and reconciled), the Ministry were enabled by a secret legerdemain to perform some most extraordinary, but to themselves most important jobs, and to exercise proscription against their opponents, and favouritism towards their friends and supporters.

The first town on the list of proscription, Schedule A, happened to be APPLEBY—the *County-town* of, and *only borough* in, the county of Westmoreland—circumstances which, if there had been any doubt about its bonâ-fide place in the scale of population, should have entitled it to special consideration. But no special consideration was necessary, for its right was clear—but it was supposed to be, or likely to be, under Tory influence, and therefore *coûte qui coûte* it *must* be disfranchised. Appleby stood in two contiguous parishes, called *St. Michael's* and *St. Lawrence's,* both under one corporate government, and having been perambulated time out of mind as one borough—these parishes contained respectively 1341 and 1275 inhabitants; together 2616—it therefore passed the 2000 line, and was entitled to stand in Schedule B, retaining one member. How was this to be prevented? The remedy was not very rational, but it was easy and bold—the Ministers cut the Gordian knot, by asserting, without any shadow of proof or reason, that one only of the two parishes, St. Michael's, constituted the whole borough, and as that had only a population of 1341, Appleby was totally disfranchised, and placed at the head of Schedule A. This decision, contrary to common sense, to all evidence, and to general notoriety, was monstrous; but it was nevertheless confirmed by a large majority; who however were soon stultified by a ministerial confession that they were wrong in point of *fact,* and that the borough did actually extend into both the parishes; but, having predetermined that Appleby should be disfranchised, they contrived, by inventing an *imaginary* boundary excluding the larger portion of both parishes, to still keep it in Schedule A.

There was hardly one of the disfranchised Tory boroughs which was not thus moulded and *manipulated,* so as to attain the ministerial purpose; and very few indeed, if they had been dealt with in the same way that the Whig boroughs in the same circumstances were treated, would not have equally preserved their franchise. We solicit our readers' attention to this *Appleby* case—not merely because it was a County-town and the only borough in the county, but because it was the *first case* discussed, and is therefore not, by us, invidiously selected—for it was no worse than many others; but because also it affords a curious illustration of the mode in which Ministers played at fast and loose with their own precedents—for it presented two important precedents. It was disfranchised in the *first* Bill as belonging to one parish only, and when that *fact,* though voted by a large ministerial majority, was eventually admitted by the Ministers to be *false and untenable,* it was disfranchised in the *second* Bill, because, though it stood in two parishes, neither were to be taken into account.

Now let us see how these precedents were subsequently applied to Whig boroughs.

And first as to 'fortunate Malton.' We have seen under what suspicious circumstances MALTON found itself within the *asylum* line; but, going a step farther, we find that it was *screwed* into that asylum by the very process that had been denied to Appleby. Malton, like Appleby, stood in two parishes—*St. Michael's* and *St. Leonard's*—there was really no other difference between the cases than that the second parish was called at Appleby, *St. Lawrence,* and at Malton, *St. Leonard's.* But by lopping off St. Lawrence's parish from Appleby, it was totally disfranchised, and by including St. Leonard's in Malton—*'fortunate Malton'*—it preserved its entire franchise. With what results Mr. Dod's 'Electoral Facts,' a work now it seems of ministerial authority[2]—shall tell us:—

> MALTON.—'Influence—*almost wholly in the hands of Earl Fitzwilliam— there has been no contest for nearly half a century.'*
>
> —*Dod, loco.*

Do we blame this junction of parishes at Malton? not at all—but, it being right *there,* what can be said for the adoption of the direct contrary proceeding at Appleby? A similar case soon followed with similar motives and results.

HORSHAM is a small rural town, little better than a village, but it returned two members, one always, and two generally, at the nomination of the *Duke of Norfolk.* We need not dwell on the weight and influence of that Duke with the Ministers, nor on the motives that existed for maintaining and if possible increasing his Grace's influence. Here is the description of the place given officially by the Government Commissioners, and laid before Parliament by the Ministers themselves:—

> '*The town is small and inconsiderable—irregularly and poorly built, many of the houses being of timber, and rarely exceeding a single story in height; it is neither lighted nor watched, and very indifferently paved.'*
>
> —*Boundary Report,* vol. v. p. 71.

The population of this poor place was only 1887; but it happens to stand in the midst of a very large parish, eight miles long and four wide; and so, by reckoning-in the whole parish, and confounding it with the borough, the population was run up to 6000; and thus this poorly-built village retained its ancient privilege of returning two members, while the County-town of Appleby was reduced, by the exclusion of its parishes, to total disfranchisement.

A similar but more complicated *tour de force* was performed on MORPETH, a corporate borough surrounded by an admittedly-distinct rural district, called the *township*. The population of the *borough* being under 2000, it should have been disfranchised altogether. This would no doubt have been extremely disagreeable to *Lord Carlisle,* then a member of the *Reform Cabinet,* who had always nominated to *one* of the seats. This inconvenience, however, was obviated by doing what was rejected at Appleby, and, by reckoning the *township* into the borough, it was raised to the combined total of 3415, so as to retain *one* member. This would have left the *Cabinet Minister*—Lord John Russell's colleague—no worse off than he was before; but a still better result was discovered. Morpeth, like Horsham, was in the centre of a large *parish;* it was obviously just as easy to throw in the *parish* as the *township*—'in for a penny in for a pound'—and accordingly the *Reform* Ministry amended their *first* proposition by adding not only the *township* of Morpeth, but *seven other townships, parish and all,* to the borough, and *both* the members were preserved—and with what effect Mr. Dod shall again testify:—

> MORPETH.—'INFLUENCE was *formerly* divided between Mr. Ord, of Whitfield Hall, and the Earl of Carlisle; *but since the Reform Act* WHOLLY *in the hands* of the Earl.'
>
> —*Dod, loco.*

To be sure this was *making things pleasant,* and it must have been an agreeable surprise to the noble Minister to find that his friend and colleague's bill, which professed to destroy nominations, had, on the contrary, secured him *two* instead of *one.*

Another case requires special notice in contrast to the second Appleby precedent. We have said that in order to insure its disfranchisement the Ministers, by a new *legerdemain,* gave it an *imaginary* boundary. This was done by drawing through the very body of the town *four straight lines* which they said comprised the sites of all the ancient burgage tenures, and they thus excluded not only the adjacent *parishes* but considerable portions of the actual *town*—a boundary not merely imaginary but absolutely unheard of and absurd, and never in any other case so much as attempted, though equally applicable to all the other burgage-tenure boroughs in the kingdom.

Now mark what happened in an analogous case! MIDHURST is a small town, hardly more than a village, and, like Appleby, was a burgage franchise; but at Appleby the burgages were scattered through the town. At Midhurst they were fewer, and collected within a very small but strictly defined space; and if any imaginary line had been drawn round them, as was round those at Appleby, Midhurst had not a pretence to escape utter disfranchisement. Nothing of the kind was done. But even with the addition (denied to Appleby) of the circumjacent *parish,* Midhurst could be carried no higher than 1335, and so in the first *five* editions of the Reform Bill Midhurst stood in Schedule A, like Appleby, totally disfranchised. But as the discussions proceeded, the Ministers found that the inconsistency and errors of their original data were indefensible, and they produced a new one, compounded (by the ingenuity of one Lieutenant Drummond) of several statistical elements into a scheme much celebrated at the time, but for nothing more than its elaborate unintelligibility. By this scheme, however, Midhurst was carried up a little higher than the Drummond line, whatever that was, and in the *sixth* edition of the Reform Bill Midhurst was safely housed in Schedule B, with the retention of one member.

Now comes perhaps the most curious of all those curious circumstances. *Cui bono,* for whose benefit?

The small portion of the parish—a very few acres, 30 or 40 we believe—that included the burgage tenures, and of course the borough, had been no doubt originally a dependence on the old castle of Cowdray, belonging to the ancient family of Browne Lords Montecute; but it had in process of time been detached from Cowdray and had become the property of Lord Carrington. His influence was destroyed by the disfranchisement of the burgage tenures, and the votes being thrown into the 10*l.* householders of the extensive *parish,* the *nomination* borough was, of course, and in accordance with the spirit of the Reform Bill, annihilated! Not so fast! It turned out fortunately, almost miraculously, that the ancient Cowdray property (*all except the burgages*) had passed into the possession of *Mr. Poyntz,* a gentleman of large fortune and great respectability, who happened to be a staunch Whig, and more lucky still, *uncle to Lord Althorpe,* then Chancellor of the Exchequer, who, luckiest of all, was, in conjunction with Lord John Russell, charged with the conduct through the House of the Bill for the destruction of nomination-boroughs—and the ultimate result was, that in right of this Cowdray property Mr. Poyntz found him by the sixth and *final* edition of his *nephew's* Reform Bill created the patron of a new nomination borough as close as Old Sarum; the first member for which in the Reformed Parliament was Captain (now Lord) Spencer, the brother of the Chancellor of the Exchequer, both Mr. Poyntz's nephews; and for the three next *Reformed* Parliaments the member was Mr. Poyntz himself—who we well remember at the time appeared as much surprised as any one at this sudden accession of patronage, and very candidly exclaimed, 'Only see! *they have made me*—staunch reformer as I was—a *boroughmonger* in my old age.'

There was, we believe, hardly one—perhaps *not* one—of the 120 boroughs practised upon by the original bill, concerning which we could not produce circumstances as little creditable to the framers of that Bill as the few that we have thus exhibited as *specimens;* and in the selection of these specimens we have been guided, as we shall now proceed to show, not by the flagrancy of the particular cases—not merely to make a *show-up* of the old Reform Bill (though that would be a not unimportant historical object), but for the more practical and, as we hope, the more useful purpose, of exposing the new one. We know that the latter is in the same hands that manufactured the former, and the examination that we have made of it satisfies us that its provisions are liable if not to similar suspicions of favouritism—the times are too sharp and keen for such petty frauds—but, in a constitutional point of view, to still more serious objections.

We confess that we cannot look back at the impudent partiality and gross injustice of those old Schedules without indignation—but as Conservatives we never opposed nor regretted that portion of the result which preserved those Whig influences, which were as precious in a constitutional view as those of the *Tories;* and it is to the fortunate but dishonest preservation of the Whig boroughs we have alluded to, and of several Tory boroughs *whose cases could not be separated from them,* that we attribute a great share of whatever degree of stability our government has since exhibited. These nomination boroughs, though so rashly diminished in number, and so unjustifiably garbled as to their limits, do still afford some auxiliary help to the Crown and the Peers, without which Lord John Russell's first Revolution would have already, we are satisfied, made a more rapid movement and taken a much deeper colour.

They are now, however, to undergo a new proscription—the great majority of them are not merely to be destroyed, but, what is worse, their weight is to be thrown bodily into the opposite scale—that is, distributed on the mere principle of *numbers.* Instead of *Calne,* we are to have *Chelsea,* and for *Knaresborough, Kensington.* We will not venture to prophesy what new parliamentary phenomena are likely to be produced by *Cheyne Walk* and *Blackland's Lane,* or by the *Gore* and the *Gravel Pits*—the chief features of this new borough; but we are pretty certain that they will not exceed, in personal character, public services, and historical illustration, the members for *Calne* and *Knaresborough,* which they are thus destined to replace.

On this topic—no inconsiderable one in a comparison of representative systems—we should do injustice to our argument and our opinions if we did not at once declare that we believe that, in the composition of the old House of Commons, the members for nomination seats were *as a class*—next to the County representatives—the most respectable for station, character, and real independence of any in the House. We remember Sir Francis Burdett once confessing, even while voting for the Reform Bill, that, 'after all, he never had been his own master, except while he sat for a close borough.' We could exemplify this view by a long list of illustrious instances, but we shall confine ourselves to the cases of the boroughs we have already mentioned, which will suffice to show the principles on which such men as Lords Lonsdale, Carlisle, and Fitzwilliam, the Duke of Devonshire, and the Marquis of Lansdowne, executed the great trust that had devolved upon them. The weakness with which they may be reproached, was lending themselves to the first Reform Bill, but we honour them for the use they had always made of the great and useful power which these nomination boroughs placed in their hands.

We begin by observing the singular coincidence that the first two boroughs that we have been comparing (both *annihilated* in the first Bill)—APPLEBY and MID-HURST—should have had the honour of opening parliament and public life to *William Pitt* and *Charles Fox*. If we have, or hope to have, new Pitts and Foxes, we know not where their young and untried abilities are likely to find an opportunity of making them known—not certainly in *Blackland's Lane* or *Kensington Gravel Pits*. MIDHURST also first introduced *Lord Plunket* to the Imperial Parliament. When *Mr. Burke* was driven from the representation of Bristol for the early expression of those great principles which have immortalised his name, MALTON was indeed 'fortunate' in affording him for the rest of his public life a station equally independent of the influences of the Court and the caprices of the people. So also MALTON had the honour of first introducing *Mr. Grattan* to the Imperial Parliament, at a season when he undoubtedly could not have been chosen by any popular constituency. MORPETH first brought forward *Mr. Huskisson*—as well as the late and the present *Lords Carlisle,* men of taste, talents, and character which have illustrated their titles, and the present *Earl Granville*. KNARESBOROUGH returned, for no less than *six parliaments,* two as accomplished men as ever adorned the House of Commons, *Mr. Hare* and *Lord John Townshend*: and, later, one of the ablest men that ever adorned either House—*Henry Brougham*. And CALNE could boast for near *fifty years* of such names as *Dunning, Barré, Baring, Jekyll, Henry Petty, Speaker Abercrombie,* and—at the moment of its semi-disfranchisement—for up to the time of the old Reform Bill it returned two members—*Mr. Macaulay*. In the debate of the 16th December, 1831, Mr. Macaulay took the course—strange in a man of his information, stranger still in a man in his peculiar position—of vituperating the nomination system, which he represented as useless even for the purpose of bringing forward eminent abilities; and he enumerated four or five celebrated statesmen who had been chosen by popular constituencies. To this Mr. Croker replied at the time *ad hominem* and *in locum:*—

'It was true that the eminent men in question were chosen for popular places. But how did they become known to the electors in those popular places? Did they not all *first* sit for *nomination boroughs;* and was it not by the talents which they displayed while they sat for those nomination boroughs that they recommended themselves to the electors of popular places? Let him ask the learned gentleman which of the names he had arrayed would have been heard of had there been no nomination boroughs? In his (Mr. Croker's) opinion, one of the greatest merits of the nomination boroughs was, that they afforded a preliminary trial, a sort of political apprenticeship, which enabled the electors of large and popular places to ascertain the qualifications of individuals with whom they would otherwise have been wholly unacquainted.

'He (Mr. Croker) had said that this answer was in the mouths of all who were familiar with the political history of the country; but he would add that it ought especially to have been present to the mind of the learned gentleman himself. Did not the learned gentleman owe the honour of an invitation to become the representative of the town of Leeds, *should the Bill pass,* to his representing a nomination borough? (*Would to God that so much of the Bill might pass*—separated from the dangers and difficulties attendant upon the rest of its provisions—*as would enable the learned gentleman to represent the town of Leeds!³*) How did the learned gentleman become known in Leeds? How had he an opportunity of showing his great talents? By sitting for one of those nomination boroughs which he now so loudly condemned. Let him not blush at following the traces of those eminent men whose names he had mentioned. If he must blush, let it be at the momentary ingratitude which had induced him to stigmatise with such offensive epithets the very system to which he was indebted for the high station which he himself held in public opinion.'

—Hansard, loco.

Our readers will have observed that in this latter recapitulation we have taken no notice of HORSHAM, so conspicuous in the contrast between its treatment and that of twenty or thirty Tory boroughs, which would have been preserved on an honest application of the same principles—but we have only postponed it because it has a very particular bearing on the new Bill. Horsham ought to have been in the first Schedule A. It was subsequently jobbed into Schedule B, where it still remains—one, we believe, of the most insignificant places in the list; but by the new Bill we are astonished to find that, while Calne and Knaresborough are to be totally disfranchised, Horsham is to be released from the purgatory of Schedule B, and restored to its full representation. We do not suspect that this strange result is produced by any *additional* foul play in the new schedules—we rather suppose it to be an accidental but absurd consequence of the *fictitious boundary* assigned to Horsham in the first Bill, by throwing in the large *parish,* eight miles long and four wide, of which the borough was really so insignificant a portion; and, *now,* proceeding on that fictitious basis, Horsham is passed off as a large substantial town with 6000 inhabitants, 1000 houses, and 350 electors. So that Calne and Knaresborough are to be wholly disfranchised, and such *Cities* and *County-towns* as *Lichfield, Chichester, Dorchester, Guildford, Hertford, Peterborough,* and twenty-six other considerable *towns—bonâ-fide* towns—are to be reduced to Schedule B, while this poor village of Horsham, which has not even a nucleus sufficient to admit of municipal government, is to return two members.

Thus this *Horsham* case becomes of most serious importance; and it is evident that the basis that produces such an absurd, and, to fifty considerable towns so unjust, a distribution of the franchise, cannot be blindly acquiesced in—the boundaries, if the Bill be persisted in, must be revised and rectified by some approximation to sense and truth; and the cathedral and corporate cities of Lichfield and Chichester cannot be mutilated of *one* member in order that the rural hamlets for eight miles round the poor village of Horsham should be favoured with two.

This case of Horsham and many others of the old Act, some of which are adopted in the new Act, suggest another important constitutional question—are we to have, as of old, representation connected with bodies of men collected and associated by local ties and interests, as in Counties, Cities, and Boroughs? or are we, under the delusive name of towns and *boroughs*, to have *electoral districts* of a scattered population, with no other bond of union or community of interest, or measure of electoral capacity, than the mere *numbers* which may be found within what the Government may please to constitute an electoral district, and call by the old but now fraudulent title of a *borough?*

A second question, of equal importance, and which is the basis of Sir Eardley Wilmot's plan, and of course of the Government Bill, is whether—throwing over all considerations of ancient rights, prescriptive interests, real importance, and concentration of intelligence—representation is to be ambulatory, and to move every ten years with the varying tide of mere population? In short, are Chelsea and Kensington, Bradford and Birkenhead, and Burnley and Staleybridge, and in process of time *every other* district in which the Minister of the day may find, or *by arbitrary limits* create, a population of 10,000 souls, to extinguish the franchises of no less than *seventy* existing boroughs that happen to have a less population? Will even the present House of Commons venture on such a sweeping and disorganising approach to the omnipotence of numerical force?

The first Reform Bill was originally based on mere proportions of population; but when it was discovered that that test would not thoroughly accomplish the secret wishes of its authors, other ingredients were introduced by the Drummond and some similar juggles, and so mixed and combined, often unintelligibly, as to produce the desired result. So, in the present schedules, Lord John proposes a junction of two elements, *either* of which would have been intelligible, and at all events liable to no legerdemain—the number of existing electors OR the amount of the population. He totally disfranchises all who have not 300 electors AND 5000 inhabitants, and takes one member from those that have not 500 electors AND 10,000 inhabitants. Now, if change were necessary, we think assuredly that the best test of the respectability of a place was the number of electors of the class to which the former Reform Bill delegated the representation of the empire; but by the combination with the two arbitrary lines of electors AND population the Ministers are enabled to arrive at the following strange results. Of the 19 towns totally disfranchised, 6 have populations over 5000, and 5 have more than 300 electors—so that, if either test had been adopted, those respective numbers of boroughs would have escaped; and, what is additionally curious, if Lord John had adhered to his former asylum line, only 2 of the 19 would have lost even one member, and none have been totally disfranchised. The new Schedule B presents still stranger anomalies. Of the 33 boroughs mutilated, no fewer than 15 have above 500 electors—most competent and respectable constituencies we should have thought; but because they have not a population of 10,000 (of which in such a case a majority must rather be populace), these respectable towns are to be thus degraded.

In fact, the whole of that schedule offers the predominance of the numerical principle on which the other—we might almost call it pretended—gradation of *electoral* respectability has little perceptible effect—or indeed none, and might, in fact as in fairness, have been wholly omitted. This will be explained by the following summary of the *ten* cases next *below* and the ten cases next *above* the line of demarcation. The ten cases above the line, and therefore preserved in their *full franchise,* contain 3404 electors; the ten below, and therefore disfranchised, contain more than double the number—7228: thus by this popular reform 7228 electors are sacrificed to 3404; and, what is still more monstrous, this mutilated Schedule B happens to contain *four* Cathedral Cities and no less than *ten* County-towns—besides such places as Stamford, Tamworth, Tiverton, Weymouth, and Windsor, each of which contains more than 9000 inhabitants. Even the nerves of Sir Eardley Wilmot himself, though tried by seven years' employment under the old Reform Bill, and strengthened by Ministerial confidence and favour, failed him at the aspect of surrendering *four* County-towns to Chelsea and Staleybridge; and he accordingly would have spared Dorchester, Guildford, Hertford, and Huntingdon; but Lord John, who deserves—preferably to the old Demetrius—the appellative of *Poliorcetes,* has with a bolder hand swept them all away. We know very well that Lord John is valorous after a certain Bobadil fashion; but we cannot but think that, in consequence of the exigencies of his Radical allies, very much helped by two defeats by the Chartists of the family interests in *Tavistock,* so elaborately guarded against in the first Bill, he has become personally very indifferent to what he should propose.

We should not trouble ourselves, and still less our readers, with these details, if they did not so strongly show that the great object of the Bill is to transfer all political power not merely to numerical majorities, but to *selected* numerical majorities; and that the checks and limits, here and there apparently applied, are in truth but cloaks to the ultimate design. We will frankly confess that we think it would be less dangerous to see the whole country—counties, cities, and all—carved out into electoral squares, and represented by an avowed and recognised principle of representation proportionate to numbers, than to be at the mercy of such arbitrary if not fraudulent divisions and distribution of the franchise as every clause of this Bill seems to us to make with as little decency as necessity—for certainly in all our reading or experience we do not recollect any measure so entirely uncalled for by the public, and so wholly at variance with the professed principles of its propounders, or so irreconcileable with either the theory or practice of our constitutional policy.

But if these disfranchising enactments are thus both unjust and insidious, the enfranchisement clauses are still worse—they are really insulting to good faith and common sense.

In the first place, there was no call, no pretence for this disfranchisement of *fifty* boroughs, but just to create a fund of 66 seats, by which the Ministry should be able to purchase favour, not only in certain large populations, but with the whole Radical party, who, affecting to be much displeased at some provisions of the Bill, very justly consider the movement as a great increase of their absolute strength at the moment, and a pledge to the future concession of *all* their expectations.

Our first attention is naturally directed to the proposed new boroughs, some of which seem derisory in their details, though all are formidable in the principles they involve.

We entreat our readers not to lose sight of the main fact in this portion of the case—that the *disposable seats* are only obtained by the *arbitrary disfranchise-ment* of—*inter alias*—no less than *ten County towns* and *Cathedral Cities* which have returned members from the most remote parliamentary times, and which have not been so much as charged with any misconduct whatsoever in the exercise of their ancient trust. If the Ministers had had ten *forfeited* seats to dispose of, we should still quarrel with the distribution that they have made; but the question is much more serious—whether the franchises of Chichester and Poole, which have been enjoyed for upwards of *five centuries,* are to be wantonly confiscated and thrown into a raffle between Chelsea and Staleybridge? What pretence can there be for reckoning Chelsea and Kensington as a *town?* What community of interests and feelings can there be between these districts? Have they any more unity of feeling than Brompton and Barnet? Nay, have they not already shown symptoms of mutual jealousy and complaint? But if such an agglomeration of suburban resi-dences is a principle, why is not Hammersmith included, as Sir Eardley Wilmot proposed? and why not Clapham—Battersea—Fulham—Walham Green—Shep-herd's Bush—Bayswater—Pancras—Highgate—Hampstead—and all the other continuous environs of the metropolis? But all in good time—*l'appétit vient en mangeant*—and *Durham, Lincoln, Hereford,* and *Salisbury* may in Lord John's *next* Bill be all swallowed up in some new metropolitan combination. Why not? Chelsea alone has a greater numerical population than those four cathedral cities all together. Where is all this to stop, if these constitutional landmarks, *as old as England itself,* are to be levelled by the usurping deluge of *numbers?*

The two new boroughs proposed for Cheshire, or rather indeed for Lancashire, to which they more properly belong, are specimens of the same handling. Of *Birkenhead,* 'a chapelry near Liverpool,' which in 1841 contained 8222 inhabit-ants, the Population Returns of that year say:—

'The great increase of population in Birkenhead is attributed to its prox-imity to the town of Liverpool.'

The last Returns (1851) carry it up to 24,284, and add this note:—

'The population of the chapelry of Birkenhead has increased in a three-fold degree since 1841, arising from extensive improvements and

building speculations, which, combined with the facilities of steam communication on the Mersey, have caused it to become *the residence of a
portion of the mercantile community of Liverpool.'*

A description not very promising for the construction of a borough, and which
would rather point to its political annexation to its natural parent Liverpool; and
the rather as we find by another clause of the Bill that Liverpool is to be endowed
with a *third* member.

Staleybridge is a town adjoining the borough of Ashton, created by the first
Reform Bill; and it will be seen in the Boundary Reports of that day that the Commissioners thought that it should have been included in Ashton, but the Staleybridge people declined the honour; they have now, it seems, thought better of it,
and *Windsor* must lose a member because *Staleybridge* has changed its mind. The
last of these new boroughs is Burnley, of which all we know is, first, that in Lord
John's bill of 1852 *Burnley* was wholly disregarded, while a smaller place in the
same immediate neighbourhood, called *Colne,* was to be admitted to a share of the
representation of the borough of Clitheroe. Observe these shiftings and changes
within a few months in the same localities—Colne was to be enfranchised yesterday—Burnley is substituted to-day. What to-morrow? But, secondly, all these
places are in the same favoured district of Lancashire which, after having obtained
13 new seats by the first Reform Bill, is also to receive 11 *more* by the new one;
and with how little success as to satisfying the appetite of the people, we may
judge by the assembling the celebrated '*Wages Parliament*'—still, we believe,
sitting—and all the other symptoms of disorder and disorganisation which that
county at this moment unhappily exhibits.

We next come to a distribution of new seats, which proves beyond doubt that
the great disfranchisement was made to furnish means for increasing the *numerical* power, even in cases where no one expected and no one desired it. Who ever
complained that *Counties* had only *two* members? though since the extension of
the numerical principle they might justly have done so; but the County members
and their constituencies were equally satisfied—*stare super vias antiquas*—and
even received with no great favour the provisions of the last Reform Bill for dou-
bling the representation of certain counties by dividing them into two portions.
But this has been followed up in the new Bill by a more insidious and much more
dangerous scheme. The County constituencies are known to be the *stronghold of
the Conservative* party; and yet Lord John proposes to add about forty members
to the County representation: how generous, how elevated above all party feeling,
must the Ministry appear who volunteer—nobody asking for or dreaming of—a
large and unimportant accession to the Conservative influence! If any Tory was
deluded by such a fraud, we can only exclaim—

'Oh miseri, quæ tanta insania, cives?
Creditis avectos hostes? aut ulla putatis
Dona carere dolis Danaum? *Sic notus Ulysses?*'

Did they not know *Lord John Russell?* This liberal and impartial proposition was only the precursor of another more liberal and impartial. The proposition is made to a Parliament in which the Conservatives—though decidedly the strongest individual party—are notoriously in the minority, and therefore Lord John announced, with peculiar grace and characteristic sincerity, that the rights of a *minority* should, for the first time in the representative systems or even theories of mankind, be represented. Alas! *sic notus Ulysses.* A very slight consideration detected that the boon was like Sinon's horse, and meant to ensure the speedier destruction of the very interests it pretended to protect. We do not recollect in the annals of political deception so bold a stroke as this. The plausible scheme was, that *Minorities* were to be represented, and this was to be thus effected. Certain constituencies were to have *three* members, but each man only *two* votes; so that, supposing a majority of even two to one, it would carry but two seats, and the third party would secure the third candidate. Mighty fine! but mark what the practical result would be. In the Counties, *ex hypothesi,* as well as, generally speaking, in fact, the Tories had been in the habit of carrying *all the members;* the *minorities,* therefore, in the counties were Whigs or Radicals, but, by this new sleight of hand, which is to secure one member to the Minority, it turns out—we say again *ex hypothesi* (for there will be insulated exceptions)—the Whigs would obtain *thirty-six* members. On the other hand, with that kind of fairness which marks all Lord John Russell's proceedings, he could not refuse to extend the same privilege to the *towns* in which, *ex eadem hypothesi,* his own party was supposed to be predominant, and which he also proposes to increase to three members, one of which should accrue to the Tory minority. Admirable impartiality! But when this equitable scheme comes to be sifted, it turns out that this tripartite representation is extended but to *eight* towns. So that the Ministers, by this device, would gain at one stroke *thirty-six* county members, and lose but *eight* borough members; balance in their favour twenty-eight! So impudent a pretence of impartiality, so flagrant an abuse of a pretended principle, never was, we believe, before heard of. It is worse than the schoolboy cheat of 'heads, I win; tails, you lose.'

If the principle—objectionable as at best, we think, it would be—were to be extended to *all* the constituencies of the kingdom, it might have some plausibility; but when it is to act on only selected cases, and that the result of the selected cases is—under the pretence of protecting one interest—really to transfer *at once* twenty-eight seats from *that very interest* to its antagonists, we are really astonished at the boldness of such a proposition.

This application of a principle so startling in itself to the purposes of such flagrant partiality and usurpation, is, as it seems, too strong for any nerves but those of the Government; and, accordingly, of the many writers who have shown some favour to the principle of protecting minorities, there is *not one,* as far as we remember, who ventures to recommend the special proposition.

The motives of most of the advocates of the cause of the Minorities are just enough—that by the abolition of the small boroughs, and the extension of the general franchise, so great a preponderance has been given to the masses, that the very existence of society seems to require that the force of these masses should be broken and mitigated. Quite true, no doubt; but their remedies would only inflame the disease. What can be said for the political logic and consistency of men who—having created the evil by the disfranchisement of 80 boroughs in 1832, and being now ready to sacrifice 50 more—can find no more rational corrective than that, contrary to the universal practice and common sense of mankind, *both* majorities and minorities should be represented? *In terms it is an Irish bull,* and in practice would be speedily swept away by the power, as well as the right, of the insulted and exasperated Majorities. In what imaginable state of society can you preserve the influence of both majorities and minorities?

The various details suggested by these theorists also are as contradictory and as visionary as their main project.

The plan, so partially adopted in the Government bill, of giving each elector of certain selected localities a number of votes smaller than the number of candidates, was first suggested by Lord Grey in the debates on the Irish Municipal Bill in 1836, namely, that in electing town councillors, &c., each man should vote for only *one-half,* or at most *five-eighths,* of the numbers to be elected. This proposition was plausible, and perhaps might be advantageous in such cases, viz., of bodies of two or three dozen municipals elected for *administrative* functions within respective districts—but is obviously ill suited to parliamentary representation, and wholly inapplicable where there shall not be *at least* three choices. There was no such case (except only London) in our old parliamentary system: there are but seven under the existing Reform Bill: and when the new bill proposes to bring this scheme into play, it is forced to create—as we have seen—57 more of these triple representations on which it is to operate. It is evident that if it is ever to be *honestly* tried, *all* the constituencies in the empire must be remodelled into groups, none having fewer than three members.

With the solution of that theorem we need not, we suppose, at present trouble ourselves; but we must notice two other modes proposed for solving this *minority* problem. The first is that of Mr. Garth Marshall of Leeds, who proposes what he calls the *cumulative* vote, that is, that every elector should have as many votes as there are vacancies, but should bestow all if he pleases on any one candidate. Mr. Marshall professes to be an ardent reformer, and it is evident he is one of those who cordially concurred in the disfranchisement of the old boroughs, on account of the anomalies which they exhibited to the *strict principles* of representation. Yet observe the main feature of his own proposal—which is, that an elector intrusted by the Constitution with the power of electing three members should be not only at liberty but encouraged to abuse that power by accumulating all those votes upon one. We presume Mr. Marshall, from his connexion with Leeds, may be a man of business, and we therefore venture to ask him what he would think of a trustee or assignee who, having received 6s. 8d. in the pound to be distributed to each of three creditors, should execute this duty by giving the whole sum, twenty shillings in the pound, to one, and leaving the others to shift as they might.

But passing over this abuse of the electoral principle, as gross as anything that can be reproached to Calne or Knaresborough, we confess our inability to see how this scheme would break the power of majorities; for, supposing that each elector was a Cerberus with three *voices,* he would still be but *one* Cerberus; and presuming that he would employ his three voices cumulatively (as is Mr. Marshall's hypothesis), how would the case differ from his having but one?—the numbers would be tripled, but the voters and the results must be the same. To be sure there might be three times the latitude for jobbing, for combination, for conspiracy, for bribery, for all sorts of tricks and frauds; but the final result, as regards the honest protection of minorities, would not—that we can see—be essentially different.

Another scheme admits the absurdity of the *cumulative* vote, and proposes what is distinguished as the *single* vote—that, instead of as many votes as candidates, each elector should have but *one*. This looks more consistent with natural justice, and would certainly be simpler in all its operations. Every elector would vote for the man who came nearest to his own ideas; and, except in those cases created by the last Reform Bill where there is but one member, the minority would be pretty sure of being represented: and if (as we presume the advocates of the single vote would require) these single representations should be done away, it seems the most plausible of any, but yet, quite as impracticable as the others. For at the very root of *all* these plans for the protection of minorities there is this *inherent* inconvenience, anomaly, or, perhaps we might say, danger, that in many cases the majority and minority, even though very unequal in numbers, might be *equally* represented, and that the political weight of the individual place might be thus neutralized, and the general administration of the country brought into such a balance of small majorities and large minorities, as could only be adjusted by *blows.*

This would be peculiarly felt in the *single-vote* scheme, and above all in the places returning three members—for in any such place the majority of the electors, to secure the return of one favourite candidate, must give him a majority of votes—say, for instance, 451 out of 900 electors, while two others of opposite politics might divide the minority between them—249 and 200; and so the constituency might be represented *two to one* against the wishes, and indeed the votes, of the majority. In short, we cannot but conclude that all these schemes are fitter for Laputa than for England, and we should not have thought them worth even the notice we have taken of them if they were not the reluctant confessions of the Government and its advocates of the danger of the numerical preponderance which their own innovations have so greatly inflamed—of the necessity that they feel of inventing some counteracting agency—and of the futility and conflicting absurdities of the expedients hitherto proposed for attaining it. One thing, however, we think that we may safely conclude—that the gross injustice of the application of the minority principle to fifty county seats, and half a dozen boroughs only, cannot be persisted in; and that we shall not have—under the pretence of checking numerical preponderance—so heavy an addition *smuggled* into the already overloaded scale.

For the next class of enfranchisements, called the *Educational,* we are really unable to arrive at any satisfactory motive; they appear so supererogatory—so uncalled for—so little likely to produce any popular effect, and so sure to produce a ludicrous and eventually an inconvenient one, that we know not to what to attribute them. We at first thought—and we are still not sure that we were wrong—that the appetite for the destruction of the small-town constituencies was so great that, rather than not disfranchise them, the Ministers were willing to make, as the phrase is, *ducks and drakes* of the acquired seats: but, on further consideration, we suspect that this may have been a compromise and concession to that coxcombical portion of their supporters who, while unscrupulously helping to extend on every side the brute power of numbers, are glad to interject a few specious and hypocritical commonplaces on the claims of 'intelligence,' 'education,' and 'literature,' just as solemnly as if it were not notorious that every successive advance of the numerical power must, more than proportionably, diminish the weight of literature, education, and intelligence in the representative assembly.

Whatever the motive may be—and we confess that we do not much rely on conjectural reasons for proceedings so apparently unreasonable—the facts themselves are extremely curious, and not a little amusing. Lord John announces that his system of disfranchisement has furnished him with 66 seats to dispose of. Sixty-six seats! *Io triumphe!* What an opening for the *educated* and *intellectual* classes of the *three kingdoms*—what a mine of erudition for the reformed council of the nation! What an ample counterbalance will be provided to the honourable, though perhaps not highly intellectual, members for Kensington and Staleybridge! But, as we proceed in the items, we are somewhat disappointed at finding that this intellectual addition consists—out of 66 seats which have been, as it seemed, *going a begging*—of an allotment of *two* to the Inns of Court and *one* to the London University! 'O monstrous! but one halfpennyworth of bread to this intolerable deal of sack!' We cannot in fairness reckon the two *odd* men added to the Universities of Oxford and Cambridge, who themselves desired no such addition, and on whom they are *forced* only to deteriorate the rank and value of those really intellectual eminences by the proposed rule that is to saddle them with a third-rate representative, the choice of the *minority.* Sir Eardley Wilmot is, as far as we know, the proposer of this educational addition—his distribution, however, was more liberal, and as a special curiosity is worth exhibiting to the admiration of our readers:—

TABLE No. X.
The additional Educational Members.

Oxford University, additional member 1
Cambridge University, additional member 1
London University, 2 members 2
Edinburgh University, 2 members 2
Glasgow University, 2 members 2

The Physicians of the United Kingdom, 2 members . . 2

The Surgeons and Apothecaries of the United Kingdom 2

The Bar of the United Kingdom, 1 member 1

The Attorneys, Solicitors. Proctors, and Writers to the ⎫ 1
Signet of the United Kingdom . . . . ⎭

Educational members 14

—p. 68.

Sir Eardley Wilmot's legal practice must, we think, have apprised him that, before a commissioner of lunacy, two or three instances of decided insanity will convict the patient, even if he appeared rational in ordinary matters. If the same rule were to be applied to Sir Eardley's pandect of reform, we cannot but think that the four last items of this *table* would raise some doubts as to the political sanity of the proposer. The whole *Bar—all* the attorneys, solicitors, proctors, and writers to the signet—*all* the physicians—*all* the surgeons and apothecaries *of England, Scotland, and Ireland*—to form each ONE Constituency! We hardly know whether the ridicule or the mischief of this scheme predominates,—but we need only deal with the latter, for the Government, afraid of such a schedule's being laughed out of the House—*solvuntur risu tabulæ*—have here abandoned their guide, slipped out of the ridicule, and only adopted the mischief. We are *not,* at present, to have national and provincial synods of doctors and apothecaries, nor electoral convocations of writers and attorneys, nor the interminable comicalities that would arise when the revising barrister should have to decide on the distinctive qualifications of the various practitioners; but the *Bar* question is more serious. What is the *Bar* that is to constitute the new borough? The terms of the 25th section of the Act would include, and are apparently meant to do so, all *the Judges*—those of the superior courts of Law and Chancery as well as all the inferior Judges—in bankruptcy, insolvency, county and other local courts, recorders, revising barristers, stipendiary and police magistrates, &c.,—a body daily increasing in numbers, in administrative power, and local authority, and whom it has always been hitherto, on general grounds, thought wise to disconnect as much as practicable from political influences, but who are now to be, *nolentes volentes,* forced into the vortex of politics. 'Tis true that at present all those Judges may vote, and frequently—particularly the inferior ones—do so; but that occasional, unobtrusive right, exercised in a *private capacity,* and arising out of some *private qualification,* is a very different thing from a vote imposed by law, in right of the *legal,* and consequently of the judicial character, and bringing the voter into direct conflict with all his colleagues of all the Benches, and all his brethren of all the Inns of Court. It is one thing to see a Sir William or Sir Thomas going down to York or Winchester to vote as one of many thousand freeholders in the county of his patrimonial property, and another to see *my Lord Chief Justice* or *my Lord Chief Baron* coming, *as such,* to a hustings in *Lincoln's Inn Hall,* and mixing in the parties and the passions to which the relative positions and close professional

103

connexions of both candidates and electors could not fail to give additional heat, if not acrimony.

So far as to Judges: as to the Bar at large, this franchise would be of wider and, even individually, of hardly less injurious effect. At present, or at least till late times, the politics of individual barristers were seldom conspicuous. The limited number of eminent lawyers who aspired to public office found, or were provided with, seats in nomination boroughs, without passing through the embarrassing ordeal of popular canvass, or being subjected to the trammels of popular pledges; and they were in fact, as a class, as independent as any in the House. A great number—the majority, we believe, of the puisne Judges—never were in Parliament at all; and we think it may be safely said that, up to the Reformed Parliament, the *Bar* (whatever might be the personal partialities or the *private* rights and qualifications of individuals) was more free from strong party bias than could *à priori* have been expected. The curtailment of the nomination boroughs, and the system which has grown out of it of not *finding* seats for law officers, but being forced to make law officers of those who could find seats for themselves, have given a great stimulus to the political propensities of the *Bar,* and have, of course, carried a rapidly increasing number of political partisans to judicial stations of all degrees—an evil which, if not wholly to be avoided, is always to be deplored, but to which this new legal franchise would give universal and inevitable effect—for the *whole* Bar will be now forced to adopt a party and take a part. A barrister will be no longer free to wait for years—perhaps for his whole life—without committing himself as a Whig or a Tory; he will be driven, possibly before he has had a brief, to give a vote; and the candidate for legal office will no longer pursue it in the higher arena of Westminster Hall, but in the subaltern canvass of the *Blackacre* district extending from Gray's Inn Lane to Paper Buildings. We need not expatiate on the great and injurious change that this would immediately operate on the profession itself, and eventually on the whole judicial economy of the empire. And for what?—to throw away two surplus and superfluous seats on that peculiar class which is already universally thought to possess a more than proportionate share of parliamentary influence.

We say nothing of the neglect in the Government scheme of the Irish and Scotch Bars. It would be—if the Ministers had any faith in their own project—offensive and unjust to them—but we have no disposition to urge the Government to a consistency in its faults or follies. We are for the same reason silent as to the University of Dublin, which we have no doubt congratulates itself on being despised or forgotten. That *we* may not be suspected of treating the London University in the same way, we will just say that we shall be curious to hear, if ever the Bill should come to a real examination in Committee, how far the numbers, literary distinctions, and general educational importance of that institution entitle it to an equality with the University of Dublin, and a preference to that of Edinburgh.

Besides these clauses creating educational *seats,* there follows another important one for educational *votes,* which we shall presently notice under that head.

We have thus tediously, we fear, though we confess very imperfectly, examined the distribution of *seats*. We now proceed to the creation of new *votes,* which are as absurd, as contradictory, and for any useful purpose as illusory as all the rest.

The first is the most surprising—that every person *enjoying a yearly salary of* 100*l., public or private, should be entitled to a vote.* 'This franchise will bring in,' said Lord John, 'a very intelligent body of men;' and the reports add that this announcement was received with *cheers.* The *proposition* and the *cheers* may be very justifiable; but at least they are somewhat surprising from the Whigs—the same party that carried Mr. Dunning's celebrated resolution that '*the power of the Crown has increased, is increasing, and ought to be diminished*'—a vote equally factious and absurd, for its very success proved its falsity; but it was long a Whig shiboleth—the leading theme of Whig oratory, and the favourite test of Whig principles. As a consequence of this vote Mr. Fox introduced, by the hands of Mr. Crewe, a bill—long trumpeted as a great effort of Whig patriotism—for depriving all officers in the Customs, Excise, and Post-office of their elective franchise. These Whig triumphs—the first false in fact, the last unjust in principle—we are not sorry to see condemned, however tardily, by themselves—but we cannot suffer it to be done under false pretences. The repeal of these Whig dogmas cannot have been designed for the single object of adding 'an intelligent class of men' to the constituencies, because it is accompanied by a large addition of those who must be the least intelligent classes, by lowering the county franchise from 50*l.* to 20*l.* and even to 10*l.,* and the town qualification from 10*l.* to 6*l.,* and the repeal of the *rate-paying* clauses. We have no doubt that it is a double-faced measure. To the democratic portion of Lord John Russell's followers it has been represented as a large extension of the suffrage; and to those of any Conservative feelings as an accession to the power of the Crown: both views we think are illusory; first, a great proportion of those enjoying salaries of 100*l.* a-year will probably possess some household franchise; and as to the second, if the rest of the bill, or anything like it, is carried, such checks as these would be mere cobwebs which might perhaps facilitate the jobbing of borough interests, but would give no real strength to the Crown in its antagonism with the democracy. It may be worth notice as an additional objection that the making a *private* salary, paid yearly, half-yearly, or *quarterly,* a ground of political franchise, is a novelty which seems contrary to public policy, open to all the worst species of corruption, and likely, where it does not end in corruption, to create oppression and ill blood amongst the parties to whom it may apply.

The next franchise is proposed to be derived by the receipt of 10*l.* a-year from the public funds, or Bank or East India stock;—this we believe to be still more illusory than the former, for how many *men* are there likely to be worth 10*l.* a-year dividends who will not have some household franchise? And what sort of claim to a voice in the government of the country can 10*l.* a-year confer—equivalent to about 7*d.* a-day and 300*l.* capital? Without discussing the principle of making money-value a political test, we may venture to say that, if money-value is taken as a principle, it should at least amount to something that shall denote respectability and independence.

Next comes the grand discovery of two or three years ago, that the Savings-banks might be made a source of political regeneration. We have always been warm advocates for the Savings-banks, and we would make every reasonable effort to extend their popularity and real utility, but not by claptraps of electoral franchises and political power. It is very wise and right to induce poor men to economise their savings; but we believe that a vote once in seven years would be a visionary inducement, unless accompanied by not only a hope, but some practical experience, that the voter would receive the old *quid pro quo*. Mr. Bright's complaint at the Manchester meeting that, if a man who had banked up the prescribed 50*l*. should draw out 3*l*. to apprentice his child, he should lose his vote, was a shallow objection in the case, for wherever you draw a line you must abide by it, and whether it be 10*l*. or 30*l*. or 50*l*., if you fall short of the privileged limit, you must needs forfeit the privilege. The real objection is to any such narrow and fugacious grounds for rights that are public, and ought to be permanent. Lord John was eloquent we think two years ago on the elevating effect on the working-man of the prospect of obtaining a vote by economising his earnings; we much doubt, as we just said, the effect of such a long-sighted ambition for so dubious and distant an object; but if such a feeling does exist, and that Lord John really then thought or now expects that the elective franchise should be so strong an inducement to industry and economy, why did he propose to reduce the 10*l*. franchise to 5*l*., and so destroy the stimulus in the great masses that inhabit houses between 10*l*. and 5*l*.? and why does he *now* draw his line at 6*l*. and diminish *pro tanto* the poor man's ambition to improve his every-day comfort and permanent respectability by a *better house*, equally accompanied by the incentive, which Lord John Russell considers so powerful, the lottery of a septennial suffrage? But above all, and this we think will conclusively expose the futility, not to say fraud, of this theory—why does this same Bill that values so highly the incentive influence of the elective franchise, why, we ask, does it in the next page remove all the existing *rate-paying* clauses? If the incentive be so powerful, is there any more legitimate, more respectable, more effective way in which it could show itself, than in making a man stand in his own neighbourhood as one who is solvent, and able to pay his taxes and his rates? That feeling ought to be, and would be, the first pride, as it is the first duty, of an independent man; but *that* natural and honest stimulus Lord John removes, while he relies on its efficacy for a remote and speculative object. In truth this whole scheme of Savings-bank voting seems to us a mere *ad captandum* declamation which cannot stand investigation. The plan if carried would not fulfil its purpose, and the purpose itself is not worth fulfilling: while on the other hand the repeal of the *rate-paying* clauses cannot fail to have a large and injurious effect on the respectability of the lower classes of electors. It is a mere sop to Cerberus, which will only make him more greedy.

Sir Eardley Wilmot closes what he chooses to call his educational views by proposing a wide enfranchisement of what the French more intelligibly call *capacities:*—

> 'In addition to the above, I would so far confer educational franchise
> that I would admit *every officiating clergyman* of *every denomination,*
> every practising barrister, physician, and surgeon, all officers on full-pay,
> half-pay, or on the retired list in the army, navy, or East India Company's
> service, all fellows and graduates of royal and learned societies, and also
> every certified schoolmaster.'

—p. 44.

To all this we reply that the Constitution of England never recognised any doctrine so vague and disputable as that of *capacities.* Its first principle was *property*—not merely as property, but as the safest and most comprehensive test,
under which all the various classes of *capacities* would find themselves eventually included and represented; and accordingly it gave no political power unconnected with some determined locality, some definite duties, some fixed, tangible,
and measurable rights. Some at least of the classes above enumerated would make
excellent electors, and most of them, we dare say, are already so, under distinct
qualifications: if we *professed* to be framing a new theory of constitution, these
capacities might be very properly recognised as likely to form a kind of aristocratic nucleus in a popular body. But we are not dealing with such theorems, and
the only immediate importance of Sir Eardley's 'educational' scheme is that the
Government, not venturing upon this new aristocracy and hierarchy, have contented themselves with introducing the *point of the wedge,* and have adopted only
the '*Graduates of all the universities*'—omitting, *for the present,* 'clergymen of
all denominations, schoolmasters,' and the like, who might have embarrassed
their first steps in this 'capacity' line, but who are sure to follow in good time if the
'*Graduates* of all universities' are to be admitted to equal rights with Freeholders
and Householders.

There is another franchise proposed, also, we presume, as a conservative one,
which is, in every view, worse than delusive—we mean the payment of 40*s.* a year
in the Income or Assessed taxes. The sum is petty, but the principle is a very large
one. In the earlier days of reform the fashionable theory was that taxation and representation should be commensurate, but it soon went out of favour, even with the
reforming theorists who broached it, because they saw that, though it tended at first
sight to universal suffrage, since every man who eats or drinks is indirectly, even
if not directly taxed, its practical application would involve details as to the nature
and proportion of the requisite contribution, unfavourable to the mere democratic
influence, which was from the beginning, and will be to the end, their ultimate
and indeed only object. The Ministerial proposition is the first direct attempt at
inoculating our system with this mere money-voting, and is, though so petty in
itself, such a wanton innovation as to require a word of protest. Whatever theorists
might allege in favour of the abstract principle, or practical men might expect from

107

such a wide and proportionate application of it as should be of some substantial influence on either taxation or elections, nothing rational can be said for rating a vote at 40s.—not even a voluntary 40s., but a compulsory one, which must be paid whether it confer the vote or not. The *sum* we suppose was chosen from some confusion in the projector's head between a 40s. freehold and a 40s. tax, but he forgot first that the 40s. freehold is but the sign of a territorial interest as old as parliaments, and that secondly, small as the sums are, there is an essential difference between *plus* and *minus*—between 40s. which you have the advantage of receiving, and 40s. which you are forced to pay. These are trifles, which we only mention because, unintelligible as they seem to us, there may lurk under them some *arrière pensée* that we do not detect; but there is a more practical and important observation to be made, which is the permanency which it supposes in the Income-tax, as well as the Assessed taxes. We cannot forget how odious the 'inquisitorial Income-tax' had been to the Whigs—nor the pledges of the Peelites that it was to last but for three years, just to get us out of a special crisis—nor the joint proposition of the Whigs and Peelites just now made, of taking a proposed addition to it for only six months. These grave, and to the payers of the income-tax very disagreeable inconsistencies, Lord John Russell, having no better excuse, endeavoured to meet with what his followers seem to have taken as a capital joke:—

'Those who pay income-tax will receive votes for the present; and when they lose their votes, they will have the compensation of getting rid of the tax.' (*Cheers and laughter.*)

Are these fit grounds, and is this a proper spirit, for the framing and discussing a great constitutional compact?

To all this must be added an arithmetical difficulty, which would be serious if anything in the proposition were serious. What do 40s. mean? When the bill was introduced, a 40s. tax represented about 70l. income—before the bill is read a second time, the tax is doubled, and 40s. represents only an income of 35l. Perhaps Lord John's answer may be as facetious as his former, and be received with equal 'cheers and laughter'—viz. that *there are no incomes subject to so low a tax as* 40s. So it seems—but then what becomes of the franchise? and why not have at once said that any one paying any income tax should be placed on the register? The same observations apply in principle to the increase or diminution (shall we ever see any such diminution?) of the Assessed taxes. But, after all, what is the value, the meaning of such a rate of franchise? and may we not once more protest against such uncertain and fugitive, as well as insufficient tests of constitutional rights?

The last of the anomalies of Lord John Russell's proposition that we have to notice is of a piece with the repeal of Mr. Crewe's bill—the proposition that Ministers are no longer to vacate their seats on the acceptance of office from the Crown—a measure the most Whiggish that had passed since the Revolution, and the most prominent and decidedly popular exposition of the old Whig jealousy of the power of the Crown. This inconsistency Lord John endeavours to excuse, by, as his speech is reported, essentially misstating the case for the purpose of borrowing a kind of countenance from what he calls the Tory doctrines of 150 years ago; but he cannot conceal the fact that the existing practice was the proposition of the Whigs, which he now finds it convenient to throw overboard, as he has done the Whig enactments against Popery—Mr. Dunning's Whig denunciation of the overgrown power of the Crown—and Mr. Crewe's Whig disenfranchisement Bill. It is not for us to complain of Lord John Russell's apostacy from the principles of Whigs; on the contrary, we congratulate ourselves at finding him forced to make this tardy and awkward, but complete confirmation of the objection of the Duke of Wellington and of all the Tory statesmen (and of ourselves, if we may be permitted to allude to our humble labours), that the old monarchical government could not be carried on under the first Reform Bill. It is a precious admission from the godfather of that Reform Bill that it cannot work the Constitution that it affected to restore; he finds it too strong for him, and—

'Half a patriot, half a coward grown,
He flies from petty tyrants to the throne'—

that is, he flies from the constituencies he has created to the uncontrolled power of the Crown. *Habemus confitentem reum.* The consequence was foretold to Lord John and his colleagues—they denied it; and now we find him, in a Bill that professes to enlarge the constituencies and to increase their power and independence, depriving them of one of their most important constitutional privileges.

We admit to Lord John that this question, like almost every other detail of our Constitution, has been essentially changed and dangerously deteriorated by his Reform Bill, but we are not at all disposed to adopt his remedy—which indeed, so far from being a remedy, is, either through insidious design or a marvellous blindness, an aggravation of the evil. Lord John Russell's proposal shelters itself under the ancient dogma—never quite true, but now a notorious fallacy—that ministers are the spontaneous and *mero motu* choice of the Crown. It has never been so since the Revolution, nor indeed since the Restoration—though, up to the Reform Bill, the monarchical power tacitly exerted in the House of Commons, and often backed by the constituencies, had, if not an absolute choice, yet a great weight, and generally a predominant authority in the choice of the ministry: *that,* Lord John admits, is gone, but he does not tell us (though it was no doubt the thing uppermost in his thoughts) whither that power has been transferred: to be sure he need not have told us—everybody sees it; it has passed—not partially—not influentially—but directly and exclusively—to the majority of the reformed House of Commons. Can that fact be questioned? The Sovereign, no doubt, still possesses, from the traditional respect of her subjects and the dutiful courtesy of the heads of parties whom the House of Commons have *hitherto* presented to her as Ministers, some voice in the preference of individual persons and in the distribution of particular employments; but as to the *Ministry as a body,* or as to the general

109

tenour of their policy, she has less choice than any of the leaders of parties or factions—even very small ones—in the House of Commons.

What, then, is this proposition of Lord John Russell for the alleged protection of the old constitutional right of the *Crown* in the choice of its ministers, but the real annihilation of the last shred of its independent power—the appeal to the people? An incapable, an obnoxious, an offensive Minister may be forced on the Closet—the Closet cannot resist—but a Constituency may; and, by its actual opposition to the re-election, or (which is more common) by the apprehension of that opposition, the Closet escapes the intrusion of the obnoxious personage. *Nous aurons changé tout cela,* and the check which Lord John Russell proposes to remove is, therefore, not on the patronage of the Crown, but on the power of the House of Commons, which has become the real dispenser of that patronage. We see, or fancy we see, not only in the retrospective history of all popular assemblies, but by what is passing under our own eyes, the power of the House of Commons approaching to an absorption of all the other elements of the Constitution—we find its committees busied, day after day, with details which ought to belong to ministerial responsibility—we see them invested with some of the executive and many of the administrative functions of the Government. No one questions that the majorities of the House of Commons have, ever since the Revolution at least, made and unmade ministers and ministries; but neither can it be denied that the influences of the Crown and the Lords were, prior to the Reform Bill, powerful ingredients in those majorities, and moderated and counteracted those impulses, caprices, passions, or factions, inseparable from popular assemblies, whom all experience shows to be at once insatiable of power, and incapable of giving it the unity and stability necessary to the good government of a state. The application of these facts and arguments we leave to the judgment of every man who observes the practical working of our present system; and we think that most people will be of opinion that—in the true spirit of the Constitution—the celebrated *Dunning Declaration* ought to have been directed, even at that early day, and would be infinitely more opportune and more necessary in ours, against the power of the *House of Commons* rather than that of the *Crown.* It is therefore that (in addition to our alarm at the general spirit of innovation now afloat) we should be reluctant to give up the appeal to the constituencies, now imposed on candidate placemen, which, slight as it may seem, has already, we believe, been found, and is likely every day to become more so, a *protection* to the Crown and to its Ministers against personal pretensions and the dictation of parties, which, without this check, it might be difficult to resist.

We have now gone through the chief features and objects of this extraordinary bill, both in its principle and its details. Our objections to the principle appear to us so strong and so decisive that no modification of its details could either have attenuated, nor—we, at first sight, thought—increased them. Our readers will have seen that this last impression was erroneous. *Every one* of the details is elaborately calculated to help the main mischief—every pretence at conservatism turns out to contain an additional germ of destruction—every seeming deference to property, to intelligence, to education, to moral sentiment, resolves itself into a fresh accession to the power of *aggregated numbers*. Where a decent consideration of existing interests or ancient rights was professed, the result is found to be innovation and spoliation. In short, the whole appears to us the most extraordinary and laborious combination of mischief and absurdity—of audacious inconsistency, and gigantic injustice, that we have ever seen or read of; and if it, or anything like it, is to pass, the Revolution, already we fear but too certain, will become not merely inevitable, but *rapid* in its consummation, beyond either the hopes of its advocates or the alarm of its opponents.

But though we see too much reason to fear that the democratical spirit of this bill—*recommended as it is from* THE THRONE, *and produced by* MINISTERS, *some of whom at least were never, till now, suspected of democratic tendencies,* will eventually prevail, we cannot persuade ourselves that it can be carried in its present form—nay we cannot believe that the Government will even attempt it—they will manage to find some cause or expedient for postponing it to a more inflammable season. But should they persist in the attempt, we hope to see a great rally made against the second reading of the bill, of *all* who (under whatever other shades of political opinions) are attached to the old Constitution, and adverse to a democratic Republic. If that should fail, which—if the bill be adequately examined and discussed—we hardly think possible under present circumstances, it is open in committee to such an exposure of its nonsense and its deceptions, as may—not improve it, that is hopeless—but encourage the HOUSE OF LORDS and awaken even in the CROWN, or in some of the MINISTRY (who cannot, we would fain persuade ourselves, have seen the full scope of the measure)—a sense of the great and *wanton* danger of such a tremendous experiment, so uncalled for by the public voice, and so little congenial to public feeling, that it has been approved in no quarter—has been treated by those whom it was intended to cajole either with contempt or dissatisfaction, and has filled everybody else, that it has been our chance to meet, with disgust and alarm—tempered—we are sorry to add—by the very feeble and dangerous consolation of persuading themselves, '*that it is too monstrous to pass.*'

Notes

1 Henry V., i. 2.
2 Sir E. Wilmot's pamphlet takes it as the base of all his calculations and suggestions.
3 It is worth notice, perhaps, in reference to this passage, that Mr. Croker, who was so strenuous an opponent of the *wholesale* Reform Bill, was the first and the last of his party to advocate such *a timely and moderate concession* as might safely avert the greater dangers. In 1820 he drew up, at Lord Liverpool's request, a paper of reasons why the franchise of the two then delinquent boroughs of Grampound and Penrhyn should be transferred to *Manchester* and *Birmingham,* and of the two next that might be convicted to *Leeds* and *Sheffield;* and he supported this proposition on two grounds—first, that 'being borough franchises they would be more naturally and constitutionally transferred to towns than merged in the counties;' secondly, 'that if we neglected to draw off the accumulating discontent by the natural sluices that so luckily presented themselves, we

were *in danger of a deluge that would sweep all away.'* And again in February, 1830, he declined to vote with his party for the transfer of East Retford to the county, and wrote to Sir Robert Peel earnestly pressing the transfer of both Retford and Grampound to *Manchester, Birmingham,* &c., concluding with this warning, that the anti-Reformers *'will not be able to prevent a torrent if they refuse to pacify us by the concession of two drops.'*

Scheme for a Reform of Parliament by an Ex-MP and a Tory (London: Thomas Hatchard, 1858), pp. 3–22

Published anonymously by an ex-MP and a Tory, the *Scheme for a Reform of Parliament* revealed the range of opinion within, as well between, the parties regarding the very complex and highly technical issue of Reform. The variety of different problems commentators saw with the existing electoral system also led to diverse proposals for curing disparate current ills.

In constituencies with more than one MP, voters possessed as many votes as Members for the constituency. Therefore, in constituencies with two MPs, voters had two votes. In those with three MPs, voters possessed three votes. The pamphlet argued that every adult male paying rates and taxes as a resident should be given a single vote, provided they were not receiving alms or charity, that they could sign their name, that they had not been fined or imprisoned in the last five years, and that they were not convicted of drunkenness. The recent history of universal suffrage in France, it argued, shows that a broad 'popular' suffrage was not inimical to Conservatism. Further proposals were that all parliamentary candidates must be rate-paying residents in the constituency. 'Strangers', candidates coming from outside the constituency, it argued, offered an opportunity for those able to 'speechify', but with no knowledge of the community, nor could the community have sufficient knowledge of the candidate. Lastly, it proposed the abolition of the requirement that those accepting ministerial office must face re-election. This was originally a Whig measure of 150 years earlier, passed in order to require the electoral endorsement of ministers appointed by the Crown as a constraint on the prerogative.

While undoubtedly eccentric in some regards as a Conservative contribution to the Reform debate, the pamphlet served to illustrate the complexity, technicality, and diversity of view, even within parties, the issue generated. Moreover, the different problems commentators diagnosed with the electoral system could generate very different remedies.

4

SCHEME FOR A REFORM OF PARLIAMENT BY AN EX-MP AND A TORY

(London: Thomas Hatchard, 1858), pp. 3–22

Reform of Parliament has been so long regarded as the peculiar property of Blue and Buff politicians, and latterly of Red Republicans, that Lord Derby's announcement that the Government, of which he is the head, would in due time introduce a measure for the amendment of the representation of the people, has been received with wonder by his own party, and by the jeers of his opponents. It is, in truth, to take the bread out of the mouths of these latter—to leave them without the shred of a flag to wave on the hustings—to make them "poor indeed." But, on the other hand, the Conservative party cannot understand how a measure, which they have always considered as the *ne plus ultra* of destructiveness, can ever be made to blend with their sincere and honest principles of opposing Reform, because it has been hitherto nothing less than Revolution; and they cannot understand how to enunciate a considerable change can be reconciled to their watchword of "leaving well alone." They already begin to fear that their leader has determined to finish his course by relapsing to his old Whiggery, and that they possibly may (when again sacrificed by their chiefs and leaders) have to play the game of 1846 over again, even before the splinter of Peelism has been yet returned to the old stock of Conservatism.

They may, however, remember, for the consolation of their principles, that their great Apostle (Pitt) was, three quarters of a century ago, the first to enunciate a measure of Reform in Parliament. There would, therefore, be some political justice if Reform should be completed by the party who acknowledge the first Reformer as their "great example, as he is their theme."

Abstracted, however, from great names and obsolete reminiscences, the mind of every Tory or Conservative must at once perceive how great the difference is between that principle which could have induced him of old "to die in the last ditch of Old Sarum," from now laying a less reverend hand upon the modern structure raised by the Whigs, with the almost avowed object of merely damaging their opponents, and of ousting them from their long prescriptive tenure of government. The old Constitution had worked well, notwithstanding its defects in theory; had raised up generations of mighty men for the service of the State;

and had safely carried the country through dangers, domestic and foreign, of the most fearful imminence to the old timbers of the vessel. Now, on the contrary, when to deal with an institution only of the other day, the working of which has confessedly disappointed its own authors, and has certainly not reared a larger supply than the old system did of men qualified to serve God "in the State," it has not had to withstand any very severe shock,[1] but has brought matters to such a stand by its divisions and sub-divisions of opinion, that "the Queen's Government cannot be carried on without difficulty;" there is now a general concurrence of opinion among all political parties, that some change has become necessary—not in the interest of any class in the country—Whig or Tory, Conservative or Destructive, but for its own practical everyday working. To make such real and effective changes that may enable the Government to be carried on, a Conservative Government is surely as well suited to the task as any other.

Reform of Parliament has, indeed, only become, in comparatively modern times, the by-word for the increase of the democratic influence in the State. Pitt never took up the question with that view; nor was it until after the French Revolution had inaugurated Republicanism in its worst form, that its violent admirers in this country adopted the cry for Reform as a means of overthrowing all the hallowed institutions of England. Liberty, as then exhibited with its blood-stained cap, became repulsive to the sober and temperate Reformers in Parliament; and for a time it fell into great disrepute, until a very insignificant section, called Chartists, again lighted their farthing rushlight, and threatened physical force.

The Whig party did not take up extreme or inflamed views of the question until long exclusion from office had made them desperate. Then, indeed, the hustings—the dinner-table—Covent-Garden and Palace-Yard—rang with sentiments that a former generation of the most extreme party had never dared to avow; the physical force of the Birmingham Association was encouraged and established; and Lord John Russell screamed out in the House of Commons his bravado against "the whisper of faction."

The same Lord John would have readily stopped when the passing of the Reform Bill had attained one of its greatest objects, the possession of power; but the dogs of war had been let loose and blooded, and after an attempted stand on "finality," he has been pushed on again to try his "'prentice hand" in mending his own handiwork of the Reform Bill, which does not appear quite genial to his Lordship.

But why must Reform and Revolution be identical? Why should Reform lead us to transfer the most sacred duties of legislative reconstruction to the lowest, least respected, and most violent men, who go headlong into every violent and outrageous theory, founded on no reason, nor justified by present dangers, while the great body of the country, Conservative in their nature and best interests, sit by apparently indifferent, or deeming themselves powerless to stay the course of the overpowering torrent?

The opinion of the most eminent writers on this country, native and foreign, is disposed to consider that the Conservative element is the most remarkable characteristic of the English people; and that its practical ingredient is a desire to assist, with all its energies, "to carry on the Queen's Government."[2] How is it, then, that in the working of the Reform Bill this result is not apparent? Is it possible that Lambeth, and Finsbury, and Manchester, and Burnley, and all the new boroughs created by that Act, have no Conservatives among the constituency? or is it that their representatives do not fairly reflect all opinions in those constituencies, but only one? If it be replied, that in all these boroughs Conservatism is at a discount, it may reasonably be answered, How can this be so? Is there not something rotten in the law which can, in all these places, quench altogether the characteristic spirit of the country, known to be totally different in its tendency? and is it not grossly unjust, that in all the new boroughs there should arise no one member to represent this really prominent ingredient in the Legislature? It might be urged, that this result negatives the supposition of those who hold to the opinion that Conservatism is the natural element of our people, were the contrary not too palpable to be gainsayed. Again, it might be said that it is entirely owing to the fault of the Conservatives themselves—in their want of organisation, in their want of management, in the defect of their chiefs and leaders; but this can be hardly said with truth of the new constituencies only, while it is palpably false in all the old. It only remains to rest upon the almost admitted fact, that it is the natural consequence of the new constituencies, obeying as they do the main object of their formation, in the annihilation or suppression of the Conservative element for the sole benefit of its opponents, the Whigs and Radicals. But how, then, does it act in this way, and how does it produce the effect I have stated? Mainly by the facility which is offered to combinations among the dominant and most active leaders to prevent altogether any representation of the minority. The same result has been made apparent in a contrary direction in the county constituencies—the county of Hertford, for example, where three Conservative members were returned in 1852; and but for the chance balance of a few votes, three Whigs might have as readily come in to the exclusion of any one Conservative. The evil, to my mind, is owing palpably to the old principle still existing in our system, that each voter should have as many votes as is given to the population and presumed importance of the entire constituency. Thus, for the four members returnable by the city of London, or the three members by the county of Hertford, or two members by the borough of Sheffield, or one member by the borough of Clitheroe, each voter has four, three, two, or one vote respectively, merely because on some theory of population and wealth these proportions have been established. But why should a liveryman of London have four times as many votes to give away for his parliamentary representatives, while the manufacturer of Clitheroe has only one? No one man either needs, or is entitled to, four representatives of his interests or opinions; and constituents thus employed in counteracting each other are finally left without any effective voice at all: for if one side of the question is represented absolutely to-day, the other side may become as exclusively in the ascendant to-morrow. That the metropolitan city, with its rich companies and its world-wide commerce, should have a larger number of members in the aggregate, may not appear unreasonable; but that is no reason whatever for giving this manifold power to each individual voter. It is notorious that this is the great evil and abuse to be protected from. The jobbings, combinations, coaxings and contrivances, by which men are cajoled into giving their two votes, upon the fictitious excuse that the popular candidate may be secured, and that his success may not be neutralised by a Conservative colleague, have brought things to that pass, that the great city of Westminster, containing more of the aristocratic element than any constituency in the kingdom, has never returned a Conservative member in the memory of man. Is this justice? Is this a fair reflex of our representative system? Surely it is this which calls loudly for reform; and to this point it is of first importance to direct our attention.

I would therefore propose in the new Reform Bill, *that every man of full age, duly registered as having paid his rates and taxes as an inhabitant, and not receiving alms or charity, shall have one vote, and one vote only, for the borough or county in which he is so registered.*

It may at first be supposed, that this is "universal suffrage,"—and so much depends on a name that I may hardly be listened to for even suggesting it; but it is believed that, in its effect, it will not increase materially, if at all, the number of votes now given, while it increases the number of persons voting. There is no question that the principle that makes this proposal approach to universal suffrage is, that every man contributing to the necessities of the State should be entitled to his suffrage, and this is coeval with the most ancient right of voting, or "scot and lot," as it was called; and on this account, whatever fear may be excited on the score of universal suffrage, its antiquity is not unworthy of the attention of Conservatives. Indeed, the strong Conservative Government which has resulted lately in France from "universal suffrage," may well encourage us not to be frightened by the name, more especially when, as there, it is limited to one vote.

Universal Suffrage, as the child of Radicalism, was a very differently constituted animal. It was intended to introduce the power of the mob against property, to raise the power of the masses against what was called "the privileged orders." "Scot and lot," on the contrary, was the representation of property. The poorest man that pays his rates and taxes has "a stake in the hedge," and whilst he may be now still represented in Marylebone, Manchester, and the large constituencies, he is unfairly shut out from the representation in those quarters where Conservatism is strongest—namely, the rural populations.

The normal principle for the elective franchise was unquestionably *personal*.[3] The true reason for requiring any qualification of property in voters, is to exclude such as are esteemed to have no independent will. The ordinary franchise was scot and lot until Henry VI. introduced the forty-shilling freehold.[4] Allowing, however, the qualification as to property to be tested by the due payment of every rate and tax due from the voter at the time of registry, these further tests should be imposed:

1. That no alms or charity shall have been received since the registry.
2. A test as to education. This may be difficult, but cannot be impossible; and it is peculiarly in the spirit of the times, and fitting that it should be prominently

118

asserted, that a man requires to be educated, as well as to be able to pay his way, to entitle him to the franchise. One way by which a man's education may be tested may be by his being required by the registering officer to write in a book openly before the public, and in his presence, "I claim to vote," &c. and to sign his name in full.

3. A test of character. No man who has been fined or imprisoned under a verdict of a jury for five years preceding the registry, should be entitled to the franchise, let his other qualifications be what they may.

4. A test as to the matter of drunkenness. This is an evil so universally admitted, but which so completely evades all the expedients that have been hitherto adopted to check it, that it is well deserving of consideration whether, in any measure of Reform of Parliament, it shall not be admitted to disparage and to disallow a man of confirmed habits of intemperance to have a vote for Members of Parliament. To check the evil by fines, is known to be only to aggravate the misfortune to the wretched man's family. To preach drunkenness out of a man rarely, if ever, succeeds. The Maine Liquor Law is a foolish, visionary attempt, in defiance of all common sense, and can be no more practicable than the proposal to root up all the vineyards. Perhaps, therefore, all attempts to stay the evil are futile; but, nevertheless, make it a test of disqualification, on the score of want of respectability, to a voter, that if he shall have been punished for a second or third offence before a petty session, at which at least three of the quorum shall be present, a conviction under their hands and seals shall supersede every other qualification to be admitted upon the registry for the same year.

It may be named, in passing, that neither the property qualification nor the other tests can be applied to the University constituencies, which should be left to the right of voting which at present constitutes their peculiar franchise.

But I desire also to see a Reform introduced in the constituencies, rural and commercial, in the quality of the candidate as well as in the voter. What can be more contrary to common sense, than that some Counsellor Silver-tongue, with no better recommendation than the gift of speaking fluently, should have the power of running down to a borough with which he is utterly unconnected, and, by dint of the most lavish professions and confident promises, steal away the hearts, or at least the votes, of the lieges, with the very honest and earnest intention of advancing himself in his profession? Worse than this is another class of trading politicians, men without any character or respectability at home, but who can recommend themselves to the ignorant constituency of some metropolitan borough, and obtain the reputation of a patriot, though they would scarcely find a man who knows them to trust them with a five-pound note. These men should not be assisted, if they cannot be altogether excluded, in their political trade and vocation. They are a bad blister on the State, weakening rather than strengthening the influence of Parliament; misleading the meritorious and well-intentioned out of doors by a species of will-worship; and within the walls of St. Stephen's putting obstacles in the way of all government, whether of one party or another, by keeping up a school of demagogism very injurious to the character of that assembly, and almost destructive of doing any business in the way of legislation.

I therefore would propose,—

> *That no Candidate shall be eligible to stand for a constituency of which he is not a member, paying rates and taxes, and being registered as the inhabitant of a tenement within its limits.*

It has been already determined by the law and custom of Parliament, that no minor nor alien, no person in holy orders, no one attainted of treason or felony, no persons concerned in the collection of taxes, nor any persons holding certain offices, or executing certain duties, are eligible to sit and vote in the House of Commons. Until 14 Geo. III. c. 58, all ought to have been inhabitants of the places for which they were chosen. (See 1 Hen. V. c. 1. 23 Hen. VI. c. 15.) Knights of the shire were to have estates in their counties sufficient for the dignity of a knight, and the property qualifications now substituted, both in county and town elections, must be situated in England, Scotland, or Ireland, as the case may be; from which it is clear, that it is strictly in a Conservative sense that this condition should be introduced: and if government is to be carried on through the medium of the House of Commons, it is most important, if not indispensable, that we should resort to ancient practice, and require a plan by which the elected shall be better known to the electors of either counties or towns before he can be admitted to be their representative in Parliament.

I purpose, nevertheless, to leave an opening for the admission of strangers to come into a constituency, because it is probable that a fit representative could not always be supplied from a population, excepting through the doctors, apothecaries, or solicitors of the district. As every man may have a town and country residence, a shooting-box or a villa, so any one may have a tenement for his residence among the constituency he may desire to represent, for which he shall pay rates and taxes, and be considered a resident competent to represent the place. What is to be prevented is the seeking for candidates at the moment of an election; the raising a chance-medley and interested cry, in order to obtain the expenditure of money, either for the sake of lawyers, innkeepers, or the vast train of idlers and adventurers that belong to every large population; and, above all, at last to send up to the Legislature a man to represent a place in its body who cannot be properly their representative, because he is utterly unknown to them, excepting on the spur of the moment.

There can be no doubt that it would be a good measure of Reform to require strangers who may represent constituencies in Parliament to domicile themselves some little time (say six months) before they are rendered eligible to become candidates; and this is to the interest of the constituencies themselves. They may thus learn a little of the administrative qualities of men who can readily enough spout and speechify, but who may be clumsy impostors in everything else, before they entrust them with power which they are to exercise in acts rather than mere words.

The third and last measure of Reform I would introduce is a change in the law that requires a seat of Parliament to be vacated on acceptance of office. This provision (6 Anne, c. 7), which was introduced in the interest of the constituency against the influence of the Crown, has operated injuriously to both. Against the Crown, and consequently to the national prejudice, in preventing office being given to the most deserving men, by making it dependent on a power of re-election only; and to the injury of the elective body, by enabling the elected men to escape from their service by obtaining from the Crown such a nominal office as Steward of the Chiltern Hundreds, or by some more substantive reward of party devotion, altogether irrespective of the interests or wishes of those who first opened to him the offer and possession of this piece of fortune or advancement.

I would therefore propose, that the Act of Queen Anne should be repealed, and that, instead of a seat in Parliament becoming vacant by the acceptance of office,—

No member should be permitted to vacate his seat in the middle of the Parliament without the consent of his constituents.

The power that confers the seat in Parliament is the only one that should justly be regarded as sufficient to annul it; and it is an abuse of power given to the Crown, to enable the Ministers of the day to remove their servant from reach of their praise or censure, which ought to be suspended over a man who has accepted and who holds a trust committed to his keeping, until he has rendered "an account of his stewardship," and which he ought not to be permitted to relinquish until he has received his *quietus* from those who trusted him.

Until the Act of Queen Anne, no Member could resign; and although there may be some inconvenience in returning to so absolute a condition as this, there is no doubt but that the mere nomination to office is no check whatever in the interest of the constituency, since the Member by this means may slip altogether through their fingers; and the expedient, as it affects the changes of Government, is felt by every one to be a positive evil.

Although very great abuses unquestionably exist in the matter of the Property Qualification for a seat in the Legislature, yet, on the other hand, very great hardships are often found to exist, especially to commercial men, in the matter as it stands, all of which might render it desirable that this question should be settled in any great question of Reform. But, whatever relief or security may be introduced into the matter of a qualification, care should be always had that a Member of Parliament should be of the class which has a substantial stake in the hedge: he must be a ratepayer, according to a previous suggestion, but he should also be a man of considerable property, of one sort or another. If it be totally impossible to prevent or impede the captivating influences of places or titles, even in the possessors of large property; yet these evils are venial in comparison with what must occur from similar influences on men who are without such pecuniary means as would

121

classify them with the gentry of the land: and the nearer that a sound system of qualification can secure the admission of gentlemen into the Legislature, the better for the country, and the more acceptable will it prove to the national taste, which regards the character of a "gentleman" as worthy of all confidence; as we may remember it was also esteemed by so great an authority as the late Emperor of Russia, in the celebrated correspondence of Sir H. Seymour.

This, then, is the measure of Reform propounded to the public by one who was a Tory in times gone by, but who is indifferent under what appellation of party he may now be classed in offering to the Legislature a plan to remedy existing evils without driving them into "others that they know not of." I do not name the Ballot, since I trust that no Parliament of British gentlemen will ever sanction a proposition so un-English and so mean-spirited. It can only suit a most craven, abject mind in a man, to desire to have it supposed that he is voting one way, when he is really voting diametrically the other way; and such a fellow is sure to be found out. In America, the ballot does not conceal the votes; and, in truth, it would not answer the purpose of a mere self-interested man, that his friend or enemy should long remain ignorant of what he has done to serve or to spite him. I propose to leave the whole machinery for the election of Members of the House of Commons intact. The Crown Office to issue the writs as now—the High Sheriff to send them to the same returning-officers as now—the same number of members to be returned by the counties and boroughs as now—the same proclamation to call them up to the consideration of divers important matters as now—the same forms of Parliament to continue as now—the same durations of Parliament to exist as now. Nothing to be changed or affected but these three things:—

1. The true opinion of the country, either Conservative or Liberal, to be represented by the Members elected, by affording privileges to the minority.
2. The Members returned to be known before they are trusted.
3. No Member to be allowed to escape from his trust without yielding up a just account of it.

It is to be hoped that, as a corollary to these manifest improvements in the representation, the services of men of eloquence will continue to be secured to the State, as well as those of administrative ability; and that the Conservative plan of Reform, whatever it shall be, will be more successful in this respect than that of the Whigs has proved.

It would be desirable, in any new measure of Reform, in order to approach "a finality" upon the most inconvenient and undesirable condition to a country, that its representative system should be always suspended over our heads, to provide the means of admitting to the right of sending members, such towns as are from time to time rising into eminence, and to discontinue the right to those that are falling into decay. The former right should be retained permanently by the Sovereign and Council, who should have the right to order writs to issue from the Crown Office to send up one or more representatives, as the case may be. The right of the elective franchise being everywhere the same, no new machinery will be required to be introduced for such a purpose; and all that would be called for would be to nominate a returning-officer, and to denote the polling-places that are to be united in forming the new constituency. The other right, of declaring a constituency unfit to exist, should arise upon an address from Parliament to the Crown, under which the writ should be withheld; and the Home Office, or some other department of Government, should direct the distribution of the voters to other constituencies.

In conclusion, I repeat, the principle of my Reform is to secure a representative for each shade of opinion, and to prevent that a Conservative residing in Manchester and Birmingham should be absolutely excluded from having any voice in the House of Commons.

Notes

1 Perhaps in fairness I ought to except that great day of popular Conservatism, April 10, 1848, when the Parliamentary system successfully resisted the menaces of brute force.
2 No one can have forgotten the eloquent remarks of Montalembert on this subject, in a recent publication.
3 Oldfield.
4 Blackstone.

Lord Robert Cecil, 'The Theories of
Parliamentary Reform'
Oxford Essays (London: John W. Parker
and Son, 1858), 52–79

The sceptical and incisive Tory intelligence of Lord Robert Cecil (who became Lord Cranborne in 1865 and Lord Salisbury in 1868) grouped the various arguments proposed for further parliamentary Reform into three schools. First, those who were seeking to give a preponderance to intellect. Second, those 'democratic' Reformers who wished to give a preponderance to numbers. Third, those 'symmetrical' Reformers who sought to avoid the preponderance of any single class, but whose sense of order was shocked by existing 'anomalies'. All these arguments he found wanting. Having dismissed the practicality of such plans, Cecil concluded with the argument that property and the 'influence' that pertained to it had always been and should continue to be the basis for engagement in political society.

5

LORD ROBERT CECIL, 'THE THEORIES OF PARLIAMENTARY REFORM'

Oxford Essays (London: John W. Parker and Son, 1858), 52–79

It seems probable that one of the principal subjects of public discussion possibly for many years to come, will be the reform of the representation. The present state of public opinion is certainly more favourable to such inquiries than that of any previous period. Delusions on all sides have been cleared away; the battle-field of the contending parties is narrower; strongholds of argument have been abandoned, on either hand, which were once deemed impregnable. On the one hand, the claim to a property in close boroughs has become impossible; and anything like an assertion of class privileges would be hooted down by the spirit of the age. On the other side—thanks to the increase of historical knowledge—reforming orators have ceased to appeal to the 'ancient constitution of the House of Commons' as a popular model; and for many years we have heard no more of the inalienable rights of free-born Britons. The rights of caste and the rights of man have been alike consigned to a blessed oblivion. Indeed, the tacit unanimity with which this generation has laid aside the ingenious network of political first principles which the industry of three centuries of theorists had woven, is one of the most remarkable phenomena in the progress of thought. In politics, at least, the old antithesis of principle and expediency is absolutely forgotten: expediency is the only principle to which sincere allegiance is paid. It is true that men often appeal to what they call principles, because it is a traditional habit to do so, and it saves the necessity of thinking; and, moreover, the word, from its frequent use in reference to religion, has a kind of religious flavour about it, and seems to give a dim, shadowy hint of a claim to some superhuman sanction. But no one acts on them, or reasons from them. It is convenient still to employ, for instance, the great party names, and still to appeal to Conservative and Liberal principles; but their perfect vagueness has become a proverb. The Conservative professes that 'he is opposed to all unnecessary changes, but will not resist those that are really beneficial.' The Liberal, on the other hand, 'while he is far from promoting violent or ill-considered changes, will always be the consistent advocate of progressive measures'—which comes very much to the same thing. It is not that there is not a real difference between a Conservative and a Liberal; but it is not a difference of principles, but a difference of bias. The Conservative has a prepossession against change; the Liberal has a prepossession in its favour. But if you ask them to formulate their 'principles,' each will lay down a proposition which is the mere converse of the other. The same fate has overtaken 'constitutional principles,' and all other first principles whatever, except those which belong purely to religion. 'First principles' once were living springs of action—solid starting-points of thought; now they take rank among the many fictions from which all vitality has disappeared, and which only serve, like fossils, to chronicle systems that have passed away. The only principle upon which, in the present day, any thinking politician really acts, is 'the greatest happiness of the greatest number.' And therefore, in any discussion upon Reform, this is the only question which it is really worth while to entertain. 'Antiquity'—precedent—the spirit of the Constitution—the rights of the people—will be plentifully appealed to on both sides in the progress of the debate. But they are mere figures of speech—they will not influence the nation's course. I do not enter upon the question whether this temper of thought is a gratifying or a lamentable one; but I do not think its existence can be denied. There is, however, one consideration to which even more than its due logical weight will probably be attached; and that is, the English dislike of disturbing the *status in quo;* and the recollection of this probability should determine the form of any discussion on the subject. Under any circumstances, change is abstractedly an evil, and the onus of showing the advantages of any particular change must lie on those who advocate it; but in advocating any change in English institutions the onus is practically much heavier. The most practical way, therefore, of considering the question of Reform will be to consider in detail the theories and arguments of those who call for it, in order to ascertain whether they have a *primâ facie* case for legislation.

There are many persons calling for Reform; but they are far from having the same object in view, or attaching the same signification to the word. Each man has his own idea of the abuse which ought to be rectified, and of the only remedy which will be adequate to meet it. For the purposes of argument, however, it will be sufficient to class the Reformers under three heads:—1. The Educational Reformers; or those who seek to give a preponderance to intellect: 2. The Democratic Reformers; or those who seek to give a preponderance to numbers: and 3. The Symmetrical Reformers; or those who do not wish to give any particular preponderance to any single class, but whose sense of order is shocked by the 'anomalies' which exist in the Representation.

The Educational Reformers may be dismissed very briefly. They are students of politics more than politicians, and their schemes, though founded on truth, are too hard of execution to find favour with a popular Government. They have the advantage of a truism for the basis of their reasoning, when they urge that Government should be in the hands of the wisest. But the old difficulty pursues them—'how are the wisest to be selected?' It is easy to say that intellect should be represented in the House of Commons; but how is intellect to be ascertained? Public examination is warranted to do many things. It is supposed to be capable of discovering, not only retentive memories, but such qualities as honesty, business habits, powers of administration, knowledge of the world; but few people, out of China, have ever thought of employing it for the choice, immediately or secondarily, of a legislative body. We must have recourse, therefore, to some more circuitous test. The professions have been suggested as a criterion; and the proposal seems plausible at first sight, for no man would think of betaking himself to some at least of the professions unless he had intellect and education enough to give him a chance of success. But the scheme breaks down when you come to examine its details. An electoral qualificacation is a mockery, unless it be impossible, or at least difficult, for contending parties artificially to create them in any large quantities. And this would apply with especial stringency to a professional constituency, because it would be a very limited constituency, and a very small proportion of fagot votes would materially bias its decision. Now, in the cases of the clerical and medical professions, the danger of fagot votes would be almost an insuperable difficulty. If the constituency could be confined to the Episcopal communions, or to the Presbyterian Church in Scotland, the difficulty in the case of the clergy would disappear; for the mode of ordination in all those bodies is recognised by the State, and ascertainable in a court of law. But any attempt so to confine it would safely land the Intellectual Reform Bill in the religious difficulty—the Goodwin Sands of legislative projects. But suppose that the Bill boldly included Dissenting ministers in the new constituencies. It would be only shifting the burden from the back of the House of Commons to the back of the revising barrister. What test would he have to determine who was or who was not a minister of the Primitive Methodists, the Bible Christians, or the Latter-day Saints? In the larger sects some sort of security might be afforded for the *bona fides* of an elector's ministrations, by the existence of a formula of ordination prescribed by a governing body; though even in this case a schism, such as those that have more than once occurred in the Wesleyan body, would open a perennial fountain of perplexity. But in the case of the many fragmentary sects, whose existence is attested by Mr. Horace Mann's Report, there would be absolutely no security at all; and it is obvious that, under cover of our religious differences, unscrupulous partisans might easily swamp the register with manufactured votes, and set the acumen of the revising barrister at defiance. All that has been said of the clergy will apply with equal force to the medical profession. The *odium theologium* has an ample counterpart in the cognate science; 'sectarianism' is nearly as great a difficulty to the legislator in medicine as in religion. The Homœopathists, Hydropathists, and Morisonians stand in much the same relation to the College of Physicians as that in which the Dissenters stand to the Established Church; and their relative positions offer precisely the same difficulties. It is only to the Bar that these objections do not apply; since in this profession the body recognised by the State has an absolute monopoly of practice. But a professional franchise, which excluded the clergy and the medical profession, would hardly answer the expectations raised by its name; and would in effect reduce itself to the proposition of giving representatives to the Inns of Court, which was made by Lord John Russell in 1854. It is to be presumed that in any proposal that is likely to be made, a professional franchise would be limited to these three professions. By the nature of the case, it would be a perfectly useless gift to the diplomatists. There have been advocates for the inclusion of army and navy officers in the new intellectual or educational constituencies; but the minuteness of the connexion between intellectual merit and advancement, in the early stages at least, of those services, is so well known, that such a proposal is never likely to meet with any general support. It is hardly necessary to dwell upon the still deeper objection which the number of persons *excluded* raises to any scheme limiting the intellectual or educational constituencies to the professions. The professions may be highly intellectual, but they do not contain a tithe of the intellect of the country. To entrust to them the office of representing it would neither do justice to it, nor be fair to the far greater number whose claim to such a privilege is equally good.

Impracticable as this proposal is, it is impossible to dismiss it without regret. It is a step in the direction of a system which departs widely indeed from our own, but which, if it were practicable, would be the very Utopia of representation. It seeks to represent men, not places: the classes and interests into which mankind are divided, not merely the bits of soil on which they dwell. Regarded from the point of view of those who insist on a logical justification in favour of every institution which they suffer to remain, nothing can be more rude or more irrational than a geographical representation; for, in respect to far the greater number of localities, there is no distinction between the interests of separate places to support the distinct representation. This, however, is only an objection on the score of symmetry, and therefore of no real importance. But there is a demerit most practical in its nature, which belongs to geographical constituencies, and which deserves to be more seriously considered; and that is the enormous power which it gives to interested classes to oppose legislation which they imagine will prove injurious to themselves. The popular idea is, that class representation would produce class legislation. The truth is exactly the reverse. The idea seems to be that by distributing a class in fragmentary portions among a number of constituencies you neutralize its power, and make it harmless by dilution; just as has been sometimes done with a mutinous regiment. But, in point of fact, it is this very distribution which gives it such an enormous power of obstruction. Few members in these days hold their seats with such certainty as to be able to disregard the wishes of any tolerably influential section of their constituents. The section may be a small one, but it may be strong enough to turn a close election; and therefore its behests must be obeyed. A small section thus wields the power of the whole constituency; much in the way in which, some six or seven years ago, the Irish members tried to wield the power of the English Government. No one can have watched the utter impotence of Parliament to raise its hand against the attorneys or the licensed victuallers, or the extreme difficulty with which even so small a body as the ecclesiastical lawyers have been dealt with, without perceiving how effectively these tactics operate. Now, if any such class had a number of members proportioned to its importance wholly given over to it, and were debarred from any other suffrage, their power in the House of Commons would be limited to that number of members. Whereas, now they command, or at least greatly influence, the vote of every member, of whose constituency some of them form a part; and from this position it is impossible to dislodge them, until some popular ferment arouses the inert mass of the electors to overbear the active and interested few. The result is, that legislation in matters where these classes are concerned, can only advance by a series of jerks: it lies in a chronic state of prostration with an intermittent fever of Reform. Now, this is a state of things which can be satisfactory to no shade of politicians, to whatever party they may belong. If this power of obstruction, which depends, not on any real difficulty in the questions at issue, but merely on the apathy of the nation and the alertness of the interested class, really checked in the long run the progress of change, there would be many statesmen who would be loth to interfere with it. There is a great deal to be said in the abstract for the opinion that, though inaction is bad, recklessness is worse; and the golden mean between the two is so rare that it is more prudent to take the safest alternative, and to be content with the *status in quo*. But experience shows that this wise timidity has long become impossible in England. Changes that are really wholesome are only made noxious by being put off. The stream is not arrested—it is only dammed into a flood. The only excuse for repeating commonplaces now so trite is, that the same old story is being again and again re-enacted before our eyes. Changes neither organic, nor seriously contested by any disinterested person, are advocated, assented to, year after year; and year after year are got rid of by the secret machinery of obstruction. A number of such intended changes, all in a chronic state of temporary postponement, at last accumulate; and the farce becomes so ridiculous that energetic men turn away in disgust from a hopeless struggle with an inert resistance, and seek for aid from without to bring it to a close. They attempt to raise a popular excitement, and perhaps they succeed in doing so; and then the remedy is worse than the disease. Once handed over to the tender mercies of a popular hurricane, it is fortunate if the institution or privilege operated upon escapes entire annihilation. And this necessity for having recourse to the dangerous expedient of popular pressure, in order to forward the necessary business of legislation, is in a great measure due to the vantage ground which is conceded to the principle of obstruction by a system of geographical constituencies.

The Democratic Reformers, who are the next class, are, at all events, not open to the objection that they are mere students and not practical politicians, or that their doctrines rest on an admitted truism. But they are much more likely to influence the policy of Parliament; for, in asking for a lower and more democratic suffrage, they appeal to the personal interest of the masses, and therefore command a numerous following. They are too confident of their power to affect argument very much; in fact, their ordinary style of persuasion is somewhat in this strain:— 'The people are bent upon having reform; you may stave it off for this year, or the next, by one device or another, but the will of the people will be carried out sooner or later; and you had better submit to it at once with as good a grace as you can.' This argument, in one form or another, is the substance of most of what is said and written on the democratic side of the controversy, and is evidently the argument which is most relied upon to make an impression on the enemy. Not a notion ever seems to cross the minds of those who use it, that it involves a principle which, if it were carried out, would be absolutely fatal to all government, or that the use of it implies the deepest contempt for the honesty and courage of their opponents. The principle involved is this, that it is the duty of an English minister, or legislator, to legislate in exact obedience to every popular demand. Now, it is perfectly true that there are a great number of measures whose salutary operation depends entirely on the perfect concurrence of those on whom they are to operate. Instances of this class of measures occur every session, especially in matters affecting the moral and intellectual condition of the people. The course that was taken on the Sunday Beer Bill is one of the most notable recent instances. On the other hand, it is equally true that there are rare conjunctures in the history of a nation, when discontent and excitement have risen to such a height that the soundest institutions will not bear the strain, and the evils of conceding even the most ill-judged measures become less than the evils of resistance. The late Duke of Wellington was of opinion that such a case had arisen in 1829, in respect to Roman Catholic Emancipation; and he passed it contrary to his avowed convictions. But between these two extremes there lie a very large class of measures, which are fraught either with great benefit or with great peril, and yet on whose fate no civil war is likely to depend. They are the measures which try men's honesty and courage; for the course of wisdom in regard to them lies not unfrequently in an opposite direction to that dictated by the popular clamour. To this class it will hardly be denied that a Reform Bill, at the present time, belongs. The object of all the constitutions that have been, since the world began, has been that, in respect of such measures, the popular will should not be blindly followed; but that the calmer wisdom of a few educated men, selected in a great variety of ways, should intervene between the violent and ignorant impulses which often sway the masses and actual legislation. But if this calmer wisdom is never to operate—if 'the people will it' is to be a conclusive argument—all the costly and toilsome machinery of legislation becomes a superfluous luxury. And it is not a fiction like those which concern the Royal power, and which are innocent because they are notorious, but it is one which the actors in it struggle stoutly to conceal. It really does leave the public in doubt as to the real depositaries of power. It shifts the responsibility from the shoulders of those who do rule to the shoulders of those who do not. The journalist and the platform-orator, who, if such a theory be really true, are the actual rulers of the country, feel none of the responsibilities of power, because their power is unavowed and indirect. They trust to the authorities above them to temper proposals which may be hasty, and to supply any counterpoises that may be needed; while the authorities above them are only waiting to choose their course, in accordance with the exact direction of the kick which they may receive

132

from below. But in England this contradiction between theory and practice—a Parliament that professes to rule, but, in truth, only indexes the pressure from without—is peculiarly pernicious. By the practice of the Constitution it necessitates dishonesty. If a Minister were to come down to Parliament on the occasion of every important measure in respect to which his convictions were at issue with the popular voice, and to say, 'I believe this measure which I am going to recommend to you to be madness, but I bow to the opinion out of doors, and entreat you to do the same, and to pass it,' he would at least be honest; and so would a member at the hustings if he were to say, 'I abominate the Ballot, and I do not object to Maynooth; but, in deference to your wishes, I will, if you select me, vote contrary to my convictions;' but, with a few rare exceptions, they never do so. The Minister knows that he would be called on to stand aside, and to allow those who really believed in the popular policy to carry it out. The candidate knows that no electors would care to send a mere hireling voter to represent their honest convictions in the House of Commons. So Minister and candidate, if, in an important matter, they do yield to pressure, have no choice but to be dishonest. The Minister is not ashamed to use all his powers of argument in support of the bill which he has been forced, against his will, to introduce; and the candidate argues in a tone of honest independence in behalf of the nauseous pledges he was made, and will be made again to swallow at the hustings. And this degrading dishonesty—which, everybody knows, is very far from being an ideal state of things—is the direct and necessary result of the maxims propounded by so many honourable men, touching 'the wisdom of bowing to the people's will, and conforming to the spirit of the age.' And so distorted is the prevalent morality on this point, that those statesmen, living or dead, are upheld as the most patriotic who have 'yielded their own predilections to the nation's will;' that is, who have come forward to argue in favour of measures in which they do not believe, and which they only adopted in order to conciliate popular goodwill. It is strange that such homage should be paid to what, in every other matter, would be denounced as fraud. Perhaps it is that the agitators and writers who, by their influence on opinion, possess the substance of power, do not care to reprobate the system which secures it to them, or to expose the pliant puppets who act with so much gravity the pageant of independent statesmanship.

When the Democratic Reformers are forced from the haughty position in which they rely on the *sic volo* of the people, the arguments to which they have recourse are various enough. As generally happens, those which are employed the most frequently, and which exercise the widest influence, scarcely deserve the name of arguments, while those which really appeal to facts and pay some regard to logic, are almost put aside. No reasoning, no statistics have exercised half as much influence in making converts to the present necessity of Reform as the supposed connexion between Reform and Liberal principles. Liberals have always advocated Reform, and therefore Liberals must advocate it still. They and their predecessors have always travelled in one direction, and in that direction they will continue to travel. Whether the road is, as heretofore, tolerably safe, or whether it is leading them into a morass, these reasoners stop not to inquire. The extent to which this delusion has penetrated is evidenced by the fact that even so liberal an organ as the *Edinburgh Review* openly laments it. A refutation of such a cry would be a waste of words. Even those who admit to the fullest extent all the benefits that are claimed for bygone Liberal victories, must see that a stereotyped policy is as alien to this varying world as stereotyped institutions.

Another very favourite argument for an extension of the suffrage has been found, during the last two or three years, in the expectation that it would put a stop to the system of favouritism in the exercise of patronage which paralyses the efficiency of the public service. That such favouritism should exist is very much to be lamented, and no effort should be spared to root it out. But the remedy ought to have some sort of relation to the disease. How will favouritism be arrested by the transfer of power from one class to another? The causes of it are, the human frailty which makes men prefer the well-doing of their relatives to the public weal, joined to the necessity—it may almost be said—under which the Minister of a Representative Government lies, of bartering patronage for votes. Are men more pure from these frailties in proportion as they descend in the grade of society? Would the selection of our rulers from the poorer instead of the wealthier section of the population, secure us a distribution of patronage on the score of merit alone? I imagine that a very slight acquaintance with parochial affairs would convince a fair inquirer that a preference for the interests of their friends whom they do know, over those of the public whom they do not know, is not confined to aristocrats. It is, however, undoubtedly true, that if corrupt appointments are to continue to exist, it is not fair that they should exist for the benefit of any single class, and that the poorer classes would certainly share in their fruits, if a large transfer of political power was made to them. Perhaps this is the view taken by the Administrative Reformers; and the real definition of Administrative Reform is a fairer distribution of the spoils of corruption: and in that case they certainly are right in pressing for an extension of the suffrage. But, otherwise, the connexion in their minds between the two is utterly mysterious. It can only be classed among the baneful delusions with respect to Reform which used to prevail thirty years ago, when so many of the working classes were led to look upon it as a panacea for commercial, manufacturing, and agricultural distress, and every other conceivable evil to which the body politic is liable.

But by far the strongest argument employed on this side lies in the maxim that representation involves taxation. The poor man pays taxes as well as the rich. He does not pay them in the direct form of income-tax or succession duty, but in the enhanced price of tea, sugar, beer, and spirits. Every shareholder takes part in the management of his railway, every rate-payer has a voice in the vestry; why is not every tax-payer to be represented in the body to whom the taxes are entrusted? If it be a rule that taxes ought not to be levied nor disbursed except by the representatives of the taxed—a rule which the Americans thought so sacred, that a breach of it seemed to them just cause for rebellion,—why is the poor man to be unrepresented, on whose scanty means a wasteful finance presses with such terrible effect?

134

Such is the argument: and assuming that representation and taxation ought to be co-extensive, and in practice are so in every other respect, the argument is unanswerable. Whether they *ought* to be co-extensive, is one of those disputes on first-principles which are rather a pastime for subtle intellects than fruitful of any practical result; but, as regards the practice of the British Constitution, it is easy to show that, apart from the case of the unenfranchised, they *are* not. Generalities are vague and hazy. Let us confine our attention to one particular section of the electorate of England, and see how, in that selected constituency, the existing system succeeds in making representation co-extensive with taxation—setting aside, as I have said, the case of those who are excluded from the franchise. Let the constituency be somewhere in the metropolis—say Finsbury or the Tower Hamlets. There is a great capitalist who possesses an enormous revenue—say of 200,000*l.* a year; and pays taxes in proportion. It would not be difficult, I apprehend, to append several names to this description. This capitalist possesses a single vote for each representative of his borough; he can possess no more: he is surrounded by twenty or five-and-twenty thousand ten-pound householders; any one of these possesses as much influence in the councils of the nation as he does; any two of them, though they be publicans not making 50*l.* a year between them, are more powerful than he is. Setting aside the measures which originate in our religious disputes, Parliament exists almost exclusively for the purpose of regulating taxation and guarding property, as any one may see by turning to the statute book of any single session. And yet 50*l.* may possess more influence in Parliament than 200,000*l.* It may be proposed to abolish Customs and Excise, and to exempt a large section of the smaller incomes from direct taxation: of course the capitalist would resist such an attempt to lay the burden of the national expenditure on himself and his wealthy fellows, but he would be outvoted and overborne by the grocer and the publican next door. Or it might happen that the country was cursed with a wasteful or a warlike Minister, and all the capitalists in the City might groan in concert over a commerce stifled by some punctilious quarrel, and their own enormous payments to the Exchequer squandered in costly armaments; but they would be outvoted and overborne by thousands of ten-pounders, who, with little to lose, whatever might chance, and few taxes to damp their vicarious courage, would merrily throw up their caps for 'a vigorous and energetic prosecution of the war.' And this superiority of two men with 50*l.* to one man with 200,000*l.* is not confined to any single category of wealth.

The landowner and the manufacturer, though disturbing causes to which I shall presently advert have secured to their wealth its due consideration in the Legislature, are, according to the theory of the Constitution, as much in the hands of the poor ten-pounders as the capitalist or the merchant. The poor voters are numerous, the rich voters are few; and the few voters are absolutely and entirely at the mercy of the many. On the other hand, a very large proportion of the taxes—it is impossible to tell how large—is levied from the rich. Therefore, as the theory stands, it is the poor man who levies the taxes and spends the taxes, while to the rich man is reserved only the privilege of paying. It is poverty that settles how property shall be bled. The State is a joint-stock company to all intents and purposes. It is the combination of a vast number of men for well-defined objects—the preservation of life and property. But it has this monstrous and unheard-of peculiarity, that it is a joint-stock company in which the shareholders vote, not by shares, but by heads. True, that every one has invested, so to speak, his life in the concern, and that the lives of all are equal; but, over and above this, every one has invested his property, and properties are not equal; and the legislation, to carry on which the votes are given, is almost entirely concerned with the security and rights of property. That the shareholders should vote by numbers, and not by their share in the concern, is a principle which any man of business would at once dismiss as iniquitous and absurd. No joint-stock company could adopt it without an absolute certainty of failure. And yet it is the principle on which the existing theory of the Constitution proposes to raise equitably a revenue of sixty-four millions, and to guard the property of the richest nation in the world.

It would not be difficult to devise a graduated suffrage, in which a man's importance as a voter should bear some sort of proportion to his importance as a citizen, instead of lifting him at one leap from political nonentity to the level of the millionaire, at the magic point of the 10*l.* house. If such a scheme were feasible, it would remedy the injustice of the present arrangement. But no one of any eminent position has ever advocated such a measure, and it may therefore be assumed that the practical difficulties which lie in its way have been thought insuperable.[1] But the gross unfairness of the uniform suffrage is what makes the extension of it to the lower strata of society a matter of such grave importance, and in the eyes of those who oppose a Reform bill, a matter of such serious peril. Let the representation be really coextensive with the taxation, if that be possible. But while they remain so grossly disproportioned on the one side, there would be no sort of fairness in adjusting them on the other. The votes accorded to the rich, by the theory of the Constitution—what the practice is we shall consider presently—are, as it is, frightfully inadequate to the maintenance of the rights of property; but, in such a position of affairs, to double the votes on the side of the poor, would be only to aggravate the disproportion past repair. And the uniform suffrage has the further disadvantage, that it places the unenfranchised in this position, that they cannot ask for their just share in the representation: they must either ask for too much, or for nothing at all. It is common to talk of the extension as a slight thing, and to make a kind of appeal *ad misericordiam* to the existing electors, as though it was churlish to refuse your neighbour a share in the privileges you enjoyed yourself. And it is sometimes argued that a little more admixture of the industrial element would wholesomely leaven the governing body. But this tone of argument entirely misstates the case. It is not a question of admitting—as a recent manifesto proposed—'all the males of full age in the towns, and all 10*l.* householders in counties,' to a *share* in the government of the country. The word 'share' is entirely out of place; if they have anything, they must have it all: there is no middle point—such is the operation of the uniform suffrage—between exclusion and monopoly. If admitted, they are so numerous, that they would swamp at a single blow all the existing electors. We are apt to forget how the classes of society increase in numbers as you go down; how disproportionately the social pyramid widens at its base. Even the more moderate extension to 6*l.* householders, which was proposed in 1854, and which the genuine Reformers scarcely deigned to look at, would have doubled the constituency of Manchester, and quadrupled the occupancy constituency of Liverpool. Any extensive enlargement of the franchise is, therefore, no light constitutional change, no question of admission to a 'share;' it is an entire and absolute transfer of power. It will be an overwhelming and irresistible reinforcement to the poorer class of voters, whose preponderance in the Constitution is already so enormous and so unjust. And if the uniform suffrage is adhered to, the wealthier classes will be more and more over-matched, the deeper the enfranchisement penetrates the strata of society. It is not pretended that any proposition which is now made is to be accepted as a final adjustment of the question. Reformers open before us a long vista of successive Reform bills, terminating at last in the promised land of Universal Manhood Suffrage. When that goal has been reached, the operation of the uniform suffrage—the one vote and no more to every man—will place the wealth of the capitalist and the landowner, the manufacturer and the merchant, within the grasp of the poor—the poor, whose industry is in England weighted with such a terrible debt, and whose wretchedness is too often keen enough to misguide the stoutest principles and the clearest reason.

There is still an argument for a wider suffrage, to which I have not hitherto adverted, because, though its force is deeply felt by many, it is scarcely ever openly employed; and that is, the argument derived from the moral effect of an extended suffrage on the loyalty and the contentment of the population. So far as it goes, and so far as it is not qualified by weightier considerations, I think that its truth must be unreservedly admitted. There can be no doubt of the greater contentment of a population—even of that part of it who are hostile to the policy of their rulers—if they feel that it is in their hands that the powers of Government ultimately reside. It seems absurd that each man should repose any confidence upon the microscopic influence which his own vote, in choosing a representative, may exert upon the nation's policy. Perhaps it is partly that his vanity is gratified by the thought that he is something in the national councils—partly that his jealousy is pacified by the fact that his neighbour is, at all events, not a bit more important than himself; but probably it is mainly because the suspicions are lulled which all men so readily entertain of the management of affairs from which they themselves are wholly shut out. But, whatever the cause may be, the effect is certain. That Government will always meet with the readiest submission which the masses think they have had the greatest share in selecting. Unfortunately they are not famous for making the wisest selections. The results of the appearance, and the results of the reality of popular power, unluckily, do not coincide. While the appearance secures contentment, the reality, if carried too far, does not secure sagacity. So that it may be said that the best form of Government (setting aside the question of morality) is one where the masses have little power, and seem to have a great deal. That it is so, is no necessary disparagement to them. Mr. Carlyle's epigrammatic expression, that no machinery will grind a wise representative out of a constituency of fools, is of course an exaggeration, if generally applied to the existing state of things. But it *is* true that ignorant and impulsive men, preoccupied generally by some single exciting question, are not likely to choose sage and cautious rulers; and ignorance of State affairs is the necessity of their busy and leisureless condition, impulsiveness is the inseparable attribute of numbers. And there is a point where ignorance and recklessness in a legislature become graver evils than even popular discontent. This furnishes the limiting principle to the undoubted axiom that a popular suffrage makes a contented people. Supposing, of course, that property is sufficiently represented to insure due consideration to its rights, then, as long as the standard of representatives does not degenerate, the legislator cannot extend the suffrage too liberally or too far. But when this mark begins to fail, he is bound to hold his hand. The test is not hard to apply to the English representation. It is true that, partly owing to the difference in the county qualification, partly to more irregular causes, the present House of Commons does not at all represent the class of ten-pound voters; and it therefore furnishes no criterion of what are the real results of that franchise thoroughly carried out, still less of the probable results of any change. But there is a portion of the House of Commons which exhibits its action scarcely tempered by any disturbing influence whatever. The representatives of the metropolis—excluding the City, where there is a more varied franchise—may be accepted as perfect representatives of the mind of the ten-pound householders, or at least of such of them as choose to vote. They may fairly serve as an index to warn a prudent legislator, if his policy is becoming dangerous—a regulator to check the velocity of his progress when it becomes rash. Their intellectual position will indicate exactly the limit at which the advantages of liberality are crossed and neutralized by the dangers of deterioration. So long as the metropolitan representatives are favourable specimens of the national intellect and sagacity, the experiment may be safely continued; there is no fear that a lower suffrage will lower the character of the House of Commons. But such a measure is full of danger as soon as the indexes begin to point the other way.

The third class of Reformers hold a central position between the students who advocate the claims of intellect, and the agitators who are not afraid to intrust the Government to the uninstructed masses of the people. The symmetrical Reformers have no professed or necessary leanings towards democracy, though the result of their policy would tend in that direction. They only seek 'to rectify certain anomalies in the representation.' They are the representatives of a school of thought which has never been even listened to in England at any previous period in our history, but in the present age has become a considerable party. They are the children of Abbé Sieyes and the *doctrinaires:* their mania is to introduce the accuracy of a machine and the proportions of a geometrical figure into the institutions which are to secure the happiness and carry out the wishes of capricious, inconsistent, illogical mankind. Like all earnest believers in a one-sided theory, they are perfectly fearless as to results;—they would probably be willing to sail their ships and build their houses by *à priori* reasoning. Everything that is theoretically absurd, or ill-adjusted, or 'contrary to all sound principle' must be rooted up, no matter how long it has endured, or how well it has practically worked; and they have no fear in venturing on the hazardous, unknown future of institutions that have nothing but logic to guarantee them. That the rule of thumb is safer than the rule of science—that institutions which ought by every rule to fail, may be practically made to succeed by the common sense of those who work them—that the magic force of habit and traditional attachment will give to the rough contrivances of ruder times an ease, and an elasticity, and a practical efficiency which are denied to the newest masterpiece of the wisest schemer in Laputa—are ideas which they would consign to the limbo of mediæval superstitions with a complacent nineteenth-century sneer. Assuredly they have shown no common courage in undertaking to reconstruct on symmetrical principles the political organism of England. They have need of Herculean strength, for an Augæan stable of anomalies lies before them.

It is an old observation, that every one of our institutions, from the highest to the humblest, has not been created, but has grown. Each in its own sphere, and independently of every other, has hardened, first from casual contrivance into custom, and then from custom into law; and, in the absence of any single controlling mind, has developed and gathered strength without any fixed limit to its application, or any adjustment of its relations to its neighbours. Thus, first the Church and the aristocracy, and afterwards the popular power grew up, independent and self-existent, side by side with the Crown; and thus the canon law, and the common law, and the powers of equity, each sprung up into independent jurisdiction without recognising the existence of the others: thus, tenants *in capite* became mighty feudatories; and, later on, military retainers became lessees, and squatting villeins strengthened into copyholders: and every corner of the kingdom teemed with peculiar rights and customs, often incompatible, but for the time, until they had found their mutual level, all bearing the force of law. Then came, in the history of each, sooner or later, the era of collision. That two supreme jurisdictions could not long exist with respect to the same subject-matter, was an eternal law, which soon found its expression in fact, and forced itself into notice. It was inevitable that one of the rivals should be subordinated to the other; but in almost every case the course taken was to seize the substance but to spare the shadow of power—to leave the name of independence while securing the reality of subordination. It is often a subject of perplexity to our contemporary critics abroad, how this spirit can have grown up, and imbedded itself in the character of the people, to the extent that it has done. In part, no doubt, the motive was policy and a dislike of conflict; it seemed wiser, on the one side, to throw a sop to the vanity which mostly makes men cling to power, than to fight for a mere name; on the other, to yield to the inevitable, rather than plunge into a war that should only end in the destruction of both. But in part it was also due to the lavish use of legal fiction, which had been forced upon the Church of Rome by her multiform practice and unchanging theory. The ecclesiastics, who in early times formed the majority of statesmen, were thoroughly trained, by the system of which they formed a part, to the idea of what we now call 'shams.'

But, however it arose, it soon became a national characteristic. The regular process was, that the co-ordinate powers should clash, should pass through a period of conflict, and then, that one should either take its place as an avowed subordinate, or, more commonly, should retain only the name of its former power. The contest between the courts of law ended in an avowed submission on the weaker side. The canon law has given way to the common law, the common law to the Court of Equity; and this latter has itself yielded to the stereotyping action of tradition, has lost its living use as a fountain of discretionary relief, and become a mere court of law. But more often the weaker power withered silently away, retaining still the outward pomp and circumstance of its old estate. How this operation has been illustrated in the case of the English Crown, is a matter of notoriety. The House of Lords is another instance, though somewhat less glaring. The mighty Chancellor, the first lay subject of the Crown, and in former times the wielder of all its power, has yielded to the superior claims of finance, and has sunk into the Prime Minister's principal law-adviser. And so it has been with the feudal institutions: long before they were abolished, the military tenures had become, in effect, independent leaseholds, with a vexatious species of quit-rent; and copyholds are so still. The Church, which resisted the longest, has been bent the lowest. Her emancipation from Rome plunged her from a deep to a still deeper depth of legal fictions, for she bears all that have been imposed on her for State reasons in later times, in addition to those which she inherited from her unreformed condition.

The oaths still stand on the statute-book which were enacted to make Church conformity binding on all servants of the State. But numbers never did conform; and it was always hopeless to make them. Parliament is not inclined to commit itself to an abandonment of the old theory of an establishment, and is still less disposed to accept its practical results. Accordingly, it has not wholly repealed the law; but year by year, for more than a hundred years, it has given to those who have neglected so to qualify for their offices, a year of grace to do so. And year by year it gravely inserts the proviso, that nothing in that act contained shall make void any judgment pronounced, or penalty inflicted, on any person for neglecting to qualify, it being, of course, simply impossible that any man who has been the subject of such a penalty can be now alive. But it is within the precincts of the Church itself that the English taste for anomalies and shams luxuriates in its most startling forms. They have a peculiar effect from the perfect freedom with which the name of the Deity is used to give a completeness and a finish to the performance. The young gentleman who has been brought up from his earliest infancy to look to the family living as his livelihood, is solemnly asked by the Bishop whether he believes himself 'to be moved by the Holy Ghost to undertake the office and ministration' which is to introduce him to its revenues, and as solemnly answers that he does. With a like engaging simplicity, the Archbishop announces that he 'trusts the Holy Ghost hath called to the work' of a bishopric the gentleman whom it suits the political purposes of the Prime Minister of the day to appoint to a seat in the House of Lords. But the most shameless instance of this ecclesiastical profanity is, when the Dean summons his Chapter to elect a Bishop, and prays with solemn unction that the Deity will deign to assist their choice with His inspiration, when the result of that choice has already been in the newspapers several days before. Nothing can show more strongly how deep-seated this taste for legal fictions is in the English mind, than that the nation should care to maintain, even at the expense of blasphemy, the semblance of an independence which is notoriously utterly crushed.

The utter want of symmetry which is the natural characteristic of a wild, irregular, neglected growth, shows itself in every part of the Constitution. The inferior judges are selected with the utmost care, and scrupulously removed from the influence of the Crown. The chief justices are selected for their prowess, not in law, but in political debate, and for their services to the Minister of the Crown. Of the higher courts of appeal, the judges in one—the judicial committee—are, or may be, selected in each case by the sovereign; while the other consists generally of political lawyers who have served their time—sometimes of the very judge from whom the appeal is made. The relation of the courts of law to the Houses of Parliament is so perfectly undefined, that neither owns the supremacy of the other, and both occasionally go to war by imprisoning each other's subordinates. Indeed, an eminent statesman has lately promised us that, in case the House of Lords continues to reject the Jew Bill, the edifying fray shall be renewed during the present year. But it would be endless to run through the whole string of anomalies which the slightest glance at the working of our polity discloses. The desperate chaos of the statute-book—the hopeless tangle of the relations between the Court of Chancery and its own offspring, the Court of Bankruptcy—the unjust limitation of local taxes to real property—the intricate jurisprudence which clogs the sale and therefore lowers the value of land,—all point with equal distinctness to the law, if law it can be called, which has governed the growth of our institutions. It is a law of lawlessness, a spirit antipathetic to forced regularity, a genius of untamed independence, which can work out its own well-being in its own free fashion, and will not endure to be caged in the scientific formulæ of abstract politicians. Taken one by one, many of these things seem foolish and indefensible—some of them even detestable. What is their defence? It is a defence which in this country is happily still worth any amount of argumentative triumph or successful invective. It is that, *as a whole,* they have worked well; that they have secured a greater amount of individual happiness than any set of institutions upon earth. In other words, the same spirit that has worked the evil has worked the cure. The self-reliance, the habit of mutual concession, the exclusive regard to practical ends, have, it is true, been patient of blundering laws, but they have known how to elicit from them a result of happiness and order. And their success is a practical protest against the criticism—now so common—which would estimate our laws according to their symmetry, and view the British Constitution through the eyes of a Dutch gardener. Those who wish to lay it out in well-clipt paths and accurately drawn figures must be content to plough it up and lay it out anew; for it has not a vestige of a principle of regularity in its construction. And what is true of the whole is true of its parts. The criticism I have referred to is equally delusive in measuring the merits of the representative system. To say that that system is 'anomalous,' 'irregular,' 'absurdly disproportioned,' may not, indeed, be far wide of the truth; but it is, in effect, simply to say that it is of a piece with the British Constitution.

The considerations advanced above have not, of course, had for their object to deprecate any change whose practical advantage can be proved. It has rather been to protest against persons coming to the consideration of this or any other great organic question in English politics, with so bigoted an attachment to symmetry, as to amount practically to the proposition, though they would shrink from stating it in words, that 'irregularity is of itself a sufficient ground for legislative change.' But there is a more positive and obvious reason against permitting a taste for symmetry to influence us in dealing with the representation. The anomalies in it are not superficial blemishes which can be removed without injuring the strength and soundness of the whole. They are an integral part of it, and to remove them would be to change its nature. The representative system, after many vicissitudes, has settled itself down into an equipoise. To change or remove one part, anomalous or not, without readjusting the whole, would upset that equipoise.

The 'anomalies in the representation' against which the objections of the Symmetrical Reformers are almost exclusively aimed, are the smaller boroughs and the Chandos clause. Now, that these are anomalies, and very flagrant ones, it would be ludicrous to deny. Not only are the smaller boroughs invested with an importance utterly at variance with their real weight, but the entire absence of any principle to regulate the distribution of power extends right through the representation. It pays no consistent regard to population, or to intelligence, or to wealth. The smaller boroughs are only extreme instances of the general confusion. That an inhabitant of the obscure town of Thetford should in reality be the most powerful voter in England—that he should alone be more powerful than eighty-two Manchester voters, or eighty-four Liverpool voters, or one hundred and twenty-nine Tower Hamlets voters—is, no doubt, very startling: but it is only an instance of what can be said, in a greater or less degree, with respect to almost every borough in the kingdom. The disproportion is universal and all-pervading. It is impossible to conceive anything more disheartening to the eye of a geometrical politician. It seems, and indeed is, a chaos without principle, and apparently without object, piled together during the lapse of ages by blind chance. It is a monument of the days when wealth was in the South of England, and desolation in the North—when a seaport near to the Continental coast gave the same kind of pre-eminence which is now given by the neighbourhood of a coal-field—when Shoreham was summoned to furnish more ships to the king's fleet than Newcastle or even London. As centuries have gone by, wealth, and with it population, have slowly migrated to the North; but the apportionment of the representation has not kept pace with the change. Of course this is an anomaly. It is theoretically quite indefensible that political power should be devised in mortmain—that the living generation should be ruled by the power that has mouldered and the pre-eminence which belonged to ages that have passed away. And it is, of course, clear enough that these decaying constituencies, as well as the Chandos clause, practically throw a great amount of political power into the hands of the wealthier classes. But it will not be hard to point to anomalies and changes in the other direction which are quite as glaring, and which, to say the least, fully rectify the balance. The most notable of these are of two kinds—those which affect the relative positions of counties and towns, and those which affect the relative position of the wealthy and the poor.

The representatives of the counties are 159; the representatives of the cities and boroughs are 339. It is notorious, and need hardly be repeated, that the importance which this disproportion gives to the towns is in startling contrast with the numerical inferiority of their population. But, whenever this argument has been used, the retort has always been ready, that the disproportion was a fair consequence of the difference of franchise, and that the constituencies were fairly represented, although the populations were not. It will be worth while to examine whether this allegation is borne out by the figures.[2] The county electors are 520,729 in number; the county members are 159. Consequently the proportion of members to voters is one to every 3275. The town electors are 430,311; the town members are 339. Consequently there is one town member to every 1263 voters. So that, even admitting the principle that representatives ought to be apportioned according to the numbers of the constituencies, and not according to the population, the proportion of a county voter's influence in political affairs to that of a town voter is as one to more than two and a half. In other words, two town voters have on the average a larger share in the government of the country than five county voters. It may give a better idea of the extent of the injustice which is thus committed towards the counties to add that, in order to rectify the disproportion, it would be necessary to take 113 members from the towns and give them to the counties. But a vague idea is sometimes entertained that towns are the centres of wealth, and therefore deserve to have a preponderance in the legislature, even though the rural districts may out-number them in actual voters. Any such notion will be best tested by reference to a return which was obtained by Mr. Disraeli during the session of last year, on the subject of the comparative value of the rateable property—the only property with which the franchise is concerned—in counties and represented towns. From that paper it appears that the rateable value of counties is 59,086,989*l.*, which gives one member as the representative of every 371,623*l.* The rateable value of represented towns is 34,588,866*l.*, giving one member to every 102,032*l.* Two pounds, therefore, in a town is better represented, on the average, than seven pounds in a county; and the number of members which, in order to rectify the disproportion in this point of view, it would be necessary to take from the towns and give to the counties, is 155.

But the political defencelessness to which property is reduced by the uniform suffrage is a far greater anomaly, and one that more than outweighs any advantage that property may derive from the irregularities of the franchise. Property is very unequally divided in this country: those who are in easy circumstances are comparatively few; those whose struggle for a livelihood is close and constant, are the large majority. Many legislative questions, but, above all, that of taxation, give frequent opportunities for one class to ease itself by the spoliation of the other. As the needy are ever the readiest for plunder, and the rich are the most tempting victims, it should have been the special care of the law to protect the rich from the inroads of the needy. Nor would such a protection be a reflection upon the poorer classes any more than the institution of a police. The law has no right to leave open the path to crime, in the generous confidence that it will not be used. It is its business to presuppose that all human beings may be wicked, and to guard beforehand against the wrong that their wickedness may do. Therefore the Constitution, if it rightly performed its functions, should have guarded against the possibility of the poor making use of the powers of legislation to satisfy their own needs at the expense of the superfluities of the rich. Instead of taking this precaution, it has given to each of the many poor voters the same power as to each of the rich few, in a contest where victory is to the majority. The result is that, according to the theory of the Constitution, the rich are left absolutely and helplessly at the mercy of the poor. But it may be said that the uniform suffrage is coeval with Parliament itself; and if it is pregnant with such perils, it has been a long time in bringing them to the birth. The answer is, that it has not existed alone. The barons who set up the House of Commons never dreamt of its becoming the supreme power in the State. For many centuries it would have been curbed by the other two estates, even if its constitution had inclined it to democratic excess. Even after the power of the Crown had been broken at the Revolution, the House of Lords, a body mainly composed of large proprietors, retained an effective check up to the time of the Reform Bill. It was, however, impossible that the powers of the House of Lords should survive that memorable struggle. When once the fact was ascertained by experiment that any bill could be forced through the Lords at the will of the Commons by the simple threat of marching in new peers, the independence of the Upper House was destroyed for ever. It now enjoys a position very similar to that of the old Parliaments of Paris. In matters of detail its decisions are received with very great respect, from the fact that those decisions are independent, and not given, like the decisions of the House of Commons, under the ever-present terror of constituents. But in great organic questions it only possesses an indefinite power of protest, which may at any moment be set at nought by an enterprising Minister of the Crown. In truth, so thoroughly is this recognised, that the debates in the House of Lords seem generally to proceed on the assumption that there is a point beyond which the votes of the House of Commons cannot be safely disregarded. This state of things is painful enough to those who value the historical and theoretical position of the House of Lords; but it is a stubborn fact, which must be fairly faced when we are thinking to readjust the construction of the House of Commons.

It is, however, in the anomalies of that construction, still more than in the power of the House of Lords, that property has, up to this moment, found its defence

144

against the natural tendency of the uniform suffrage. The 'influence' which, in one way or another, possessors of property have been able to exercise over voters—in some few cases based on neighbourly attachment, but more generally resulting from actual dependence—has, from the time that the House of Commons emerged into importance until now, largely tinctured its constitution, and neutralized the mere representation of numbers. Before the Reform Bill this influence, in too many instances, took the form of mere buying and selling, the practical result of which was an enormous demoralization of the bought; and much of the political power which it secured to property was concentrated in the hands of one or two individuals, who were thus put in a position to dictate to the Government. Whatever else be said of the Reform Act, it certainly had the merit of checking the prevalence of these evils. But the influence in other forms, and more equably diffused among men of property, remains. A glance at Dod's *Electoral Facts,* which only indicates it in the most salient cases, will show how few constituencies there are which are perfectly free from its operation. Town populations of a large extent are undoubtedly the most independent, because in them the contact between the wealthy and the poor is less immediate; but probably the metropolitan constituencies are the only places where the real mind of the average ten-pound householder is expressed in the choice of representatives. But the backbone of this influence undoubtedly lies in the counties and the smaller boroughs. And the destruction of it in the counties by a ten-pound suffrage, in the smaller boroughs by simple disfranchisement, is the point on which the Symmetrical Reformers unite with the Democratic.

Now this 'influence' may not be by itself a very desirable thing. It sometimes bears hard on men of strong opinions, and turns them into sullen martyrs. Moreover, as the subjects of it are all the while treated as independent in the eye of the law, and in the decorously-guarded language of public men, it must take its rank among the foremost of English shams. But it must not be considered by itself; it must be considered along with the other anomalies whose operation it counteracts. It is the counterweight to that great and monstrous anomaly that the theory of the representation gives to wealth no security whatever. It is better than its alternative—spoliation in the first political tempest that may arise. True, it is illegitimate, and so far hurtful; but it is one poison counteracting another: the irregular but necessary antidote to an iniquitous law. Those who hold property are compelled to resort to it in self-defence; for in an old country, where the pressure of poverty is constant and severe, the rich who are not strong will soon cease to be rich. If, therefore, the law is to be altered, let it be reconstructed altogether; if that is impossible, let the equipoise remain as it stands. To remove one anomaly and leave the other—to destroy the influence of the rich without cutting down the overwhelming numerical superiority of the poor—is to strip property of the single bulwark which secures it from the power of impoverished and uninstructed masses. Language has been held, as though another such bulwark might be found by the wealthy classes in the 'cultivation of social influences'—in other words, by assiduity in dinner-giving and visiting, in smirking and small-talk. The experience of America has shown that you cannot rely upon that unattractive species of industry in any large class of refined and educated men; and that they had rather face any political risks, in the hope that the existing state of things may possibly last their time, than endure to pass their existence in a lifelong canvass.

The present movement in favour of Reform is so gentle, that it is hard to decide whether it is a real current of popular feeling, or only one of those eddies on the surface which active politicians can always create at will. But if it be indeed the beginning of a popular movement, there seems to be a strange misconception on the part of its leaders as to the exact nature of the battle they are fighting. To judge by the language often used, one would imagine that they were striking down some dominant and oppressive caste analogous to the old French *noblesse*. If such be their object, they are fighting the air. The very semblance of aristocratic privilege—with the exception of the House of Lords, which is not now the object of attack—has passed away. Some peers are powerful, not because they are peers, but because they are rich, and rich in the most influential kind of property. But a poor peer is not more powerful than his neighbours. Indeed, the progress of events has left him stranded in a very pitiable condition. The practice of Parliament forbids him to interfere as a peer with the financial policy of the House of Commons in the slightest degree; and the orders of that House forbid him to take an elector's part in their decisions by voting at the elections. So that in reality the poorest 'potwalloper' has more weight than a poor peer in the control of the public purse. This phantom of aristocratic privilege is only another proof of the tenacious vitality of party watchwords. Those who *are* preponderant in England—who are struggling to retain their preponderance, because it is a condition of their existence, and against whom therefore this movement is really directed—are the possessors of property. No doubt it is easy to see that there are many who are keen for democratic progress, but who would not raise a hand against the rights of property. Such men, gaining a temporary popularity by the abnegation of their class's rights, have ever been the heralds and main agents of great organic change. Their tone has always been one of indignant wonder that anybody can suspect their clients of making an interested use of supreme power; and so it is in the present day. They have what they flatter themselves is a generous confidence in the people of England; they will not believe that any attempts at spoliation will ever meet with general support. Public morality, they say, is too high, and the holders of property, great and small, form too influential a portion of the community for such a policy ever to be possible. This is true enough of avowed spoliation. A bald proposition to seize the property of Lord Overstone would probably be rejected by the most democratic assembly that could be got together, unless the country was in a state bordering on revolution. But there are measures which would effect the objects of spoliation without any such open defiance of morality. It is sufficient to mention one, the most powerful and the most simple—a graduated income-tax. Conceive a Parliament elected by manhood suffrage in the great towns, and a ten-pound suffrage in

146

the counties; conceive that by the suppression of small constituencies its members represented this mob-suffrage as accurately as the metropolitan members represent the tradesman-suffrage of their boroughs; and conceive a ministry selected from men of that stamp of character and opinion. Would they scruple to impose an income-tax—it is even now called for—which should take a larger per-centage from the richest, and a lower per-centage as the scale went down? And as the needs of the public purse and the impatience of taxation increased, would not the weight be increased on the necks of the wealthy few who were not represented, rather than on those of the poorer many who were? Is there any conceivable limit to the extent to which, in times of excitement and pressure, a mob-Parliament might carry the process? Mr. Cobden professes an unlimited confidence in the judgment and wisdom of 'aggregate humanity.' Unhappily, 'aggregates of humanity' are chargeable with half the crimes that redden the page of history, from the massacre of Melos to the Reign of Terror. Of course, a 'generous confidence' may believe anything. It may believe that if you lend a starving man a loaf, he will not eat it; or it may believe that a poverty-stricken class with the government in their hands will not use it to relieve themselves. Of course we cannot certainly *know* what the lowest classes of England would do if they were placed in power, for we have not tried. The experiment, unfortunately, is a nervous one to make, for if it fails it cannot be retraced. Political power that has descended from a higher class in society to a lower, is never yielded back except to a despot. But a specimen of what their leaders' views on the subject of property are, was given to the world a short time ago. A number of working men in London were suffering from having been thrown out of employ. A demagogue of some note assembled them to propose to them a project of relief; and his proposition was, simply and without any circumlocution, to seize the estates of some of the largest landowners, and to divide them among the sufferers. This is not reassuring as to what his conduct would be if he was Chancellor of the Exchequer under the new *régime*. As this gentleman is said to enjoy considerable popularity among the classes who would rule us if manhood suffrage were adopted, there is nothing chimerical in saying that a new Reform Bill would place the rights of property in issue. In truth, every indication which comes to the surface shows that the present unequal division of property is regarded with great jealousy by the multitudes who are almost or altogether excluded from a share; and it is not credible that there should be so much enthusiasm among certain sections for the Charter, especially in times of distress, unless they expected from it something more substantial than a mere political privilege. To give them political supremacy—or even to give them such a preponderance of power as shall enable them, by future Reform bills, to gain the rest—is to give them the means, which they will not fail to use, of satisfying these desires. It is needless to dwell on the stupendous magnitude of the interests which are thus imperilled, or of the danger of such agrarian efforts not only to the wealthy, but to all. Industry is the radiating centre of all social well-being; and industry thrives in precise proportion as property is secure. That the fruits of industry should be enjoyed in peace is the main object for which civilization exists.

The result, then, to which a review of the Reformer's arguments inevitably leads us, is that we must either change enormously or not at all. It is undoubtedly to be desired that every anomaly should be removed at which hostile critics can laugh or cavil; still more that every person in the kingdom should have exactly his just share, and no more than his just share, in the government of the country. On the other hand, it is of vital importance that the Legislature should not be deteriorated, or the safety of property endangered. A system of representation might doubtless be devised in which all these objects should be regularly and exactly attained; but most statesmen will hesitate before they prefer a paper constitution to the time-hardened trusty machine whose working they have thoroughly tried. But to remove one evil without removing that which is its counterpoise, to withdraw one poison from the prescription without withdrawing the other which is its antidote, is the maddest course of all. Political justice to one side and not to the other, is worse than a set-off of injustice on both sides; political symmetry on a faulty plan is worse than chaos. Better far to reconstruct the whole; better still to let that which has worked well, work on. But, whichever course is taken, the condition in the representative system which it is our duty to maintain, even at the cost of any restriction or any anomaly, is that the intellectual *status* of the Legislature shall not be lowered, and that sufficient weight, direct or indirect, shall be given to property to secure it from the possibility of harm.

Feb. 1, 1858. R. G. C.

Notes

1 The Legislature of Victoria have lately adopted the system of plurality of votes in combination with universal suffrage. The result of the experiment of course depends entirely on the proportion in which wealth is allowed to confer votes. But it is the only combination which is at once logically unassailable, and yet likely to work fairly in practice.
2 The figures used are those which were prepared for Lord John Russell's Reform Bill in 1854.—*Parl. Pap.* 69.

Benjamin Disraeli, *Parliamentary Reform, Speech in the House of Commons, February 28, 1859* (London, 1859)

Bodleian Library, (Weston Stack) G.Pamphlet 2512(1)

In August 1858 Derby began consideration of the Conservative Reform bill promised for the 1859 session. Since 1851 he had indicated his willingness to modify the 1832 settlement, while being opposed to very extensive changes. His major concern was the intrusion of urban freeholders into the county electorates. In June 1858, two Commons votes had shown that Whigs and Liberals supported the equalisation of the borough and county franchises and were staunchly opposed to the ballot. Derby appointed a cabinet committee to draw up a measure, made up of himself, Disraeli, Sir John Pakington, Lord John Manners, Lord Salisbury, and the Commons chief whip Jolliffe. More recalcitrant ministers, such as Spencer Horatio Walpole, Joseph Henley, and Lord Hardwicke, were excluded. Derby indicated his flexibility on any new suffrage, being prepared to adopt an £8 rating franchise in the boroughs. The keystone of the whole, however, was urban freeholders being restricted to borough, not county, elections.

During the autumn, Russell kept publicly silent on Reform, preferring to await the emergence of Conservative differences. In October, however, the radical John Bright broke ground. In a series of public addresses in Birmingham, Manchester, and Glasgow, he demanded the borough franchise for all who paid rates and the county franchise for all lodgers who paid a rent of £10 or more. The public response to Bright staking out his position on Reform helped the government in defining a more moderate proposal acceptable to those alarmed by radical demands.

In November, Derby drafted a cabinet committee report. Its main recommendations were that the Reform bill should be confined to England and Wales, with the franchise and redistribution dealt with in one measure, and that the borough franchise be retained at its existing level and the county franchise lowered to a £10 rated suffrage. Whigs and Liberals had supported the equalisation of the franchise the previous June. Also, it recommended that a £20 rental lodger franchise be introduced in the boroughs, while freeholders enfranchised by urban property should be confined to voting in borough constituencies. On redistribution, it was proposed that boroughs with a population less than 500 be disfranchised and some two-Member borough constituencies with a population of between 5,000 and 15,000 lose a Member. County constituencies with a population above 100,000 were to be given three MPs, an additional 48 MPs in total, and an additional 18 MPs to be given to borough constituencies. The use of polling papers was to be made an option and the ballot to be resisted in any form.

Walpole and Henley fiercely objected to the committee recommendations, while some other ministers complained the recommendations did not go far enough. In the face of this dissension, in January Derby floated an alternative scheme

149

proposing an £8 rating borough franchise and a rating franchise of £16 in the counties. However, Walpole and Henley persisted in their objections. At the same time, the Conservative election agent Philip Rose reported that Conservative constituency organisations and landowners supported the cabinet committee recommendations. In late January, Derby reverted to the proposals made in the committee report. Walpole and Henley subsequently resigned.

On 12 February 1859 the Conservative cabinet agreed to a £10 borough and £10 county franchise. The equalisation of the franchises being linked to the removal of urban freehold votes from the county electorates. A number of 'merit franchises', similar to those proposed by Russell in 1854, were also agreed. Those receiving pensions of £20 per annum, with deposits of £60 in Savings Banks, possessing £50 of shares or stock, university graduates, ministers of religion, barristers, attorneys, registered medical men, and certified schoolmasters were to be enfranchised. No skilled workman, on this basis, it was argued, need be long excluded from possessing a vote. The original redistribution of seats was dramatically reduced, with just 15 seats being reallocated. On the eve of the Reform measure being presented to the Commons, John Delane, editor of *The Times*, declared he would give the bill every support. The moderate Liberal Robert Lowe declared it showed the government's wish to deal with the question on honest and intelligible principles.

Disraeli introduced the Conservative Reform bill to the Commons on 28 February 1859. At a meeting of Conservative MPs in Downing Street on 1 March, Derby urged them to vote unflinchingly for the entirety of the measure, individual clauses that might seem Liberal or extreme in isolation to be seen in the context of the bill as a whole. At a gathering of Conservative peers on 5 March, held by Derby, the measure was endorsed unanimously. On 10 March, Russell gave notice of a motion on the Second Reading of the bill objecting to the expulsion of urban freeholders from county electorates. Early in the morning of 1 April Russell's motion passed by 330 to 291 votes. Derby received permission from the Queen to hold a general election, and parliament dissolved on 19 April.

In a full Lords on 4 April, with an election in prospect, Derby stated that the distracted state of parties in the Commons threatened the very basis of parliamentary government. Not bound by any common tie, parties combined to eject governments from office, but were unable to provide a strong stable ministry themselves. Over Reform in April, the 'motley and heterogeneous materials' making up the opposition had succumbed to faction and ignored the interest of the nation. The Conservative Reform bill had been defeated by ingenious manoeuvre, rather than by fair parliamentary process. Derby then plotted Russell's political career as a lifetime of self-interested intrigue. In 1835, Russell had turned out Peel from office on an impracticable pretext. In 1852, he overthrew Derby's ministry with an objectless coalition. In 1855, he ejected Lord Aberdeen from office in a personal *coup d'état*. In 1858, he overthrew Palmerston, only to combine with Palmerston during the past session over a cunning resolution sabotaging a moderate Reform settlement.

6

BENJAMIN DISRAELI,
PARLIAMENTARY REFORM, SPEECH IN THE HOUSE OF COMMONS, FEBRUARY 28, 1859

(London, 1859)

Sir, it is my duty to-night to draw the attention of the House to a theme than which nothing more important can be submitted to their consideration. Those which are often esteemed the greatest political questions—those questions, for example, of peace or war which now occupy and agitate the public mind, are in fact inferior. In either of those cases an erroneous policy may be retraced; and there are no disasters which cannot be successfully encountered by the energies of a free people; but the principles upon which the distribution of power depends in a community when once adopted can rarely be changed, and an error in that direction may permanently affect the fortunes of a State or the character of a people.

But, grave as is the duty, and difficult as is the task which have devolved upon Her Majesty's Government in undertaking to prepare a measure to amend the representation of the people in this House, these I admit—and cheerfully admit— are considerably mitigated by two circumstances—the absence of all passion on the subject, and the advantage of experience. Whatever may be the causes, on which I care not to dwell, I believe that on this subject and on this occasion I appeal to as impartial a tribunal as is compatible with our popular form of Government. I believe, there is a general wish among all men of light and leading in this country that the solution of this long-controverted question should be arrived at; and that if public men occupying the position which we now occupy, feel it their duty to come forward to offer that solution—one which I trust in our case will not be based upon any mean concession or any temporary compromise, but on principles consistent with the spirit of our constitution, which will bear the scrutiny of debate, and which I trust may obtain the sympathy of public opinion— I feel persuaded that in the present conjuncture of our political world such an attempt will meet from this House a candid though a discriminating support. And equally, it may be observed, that the public mind of this country has for the last quarter of a century, and especially during its latter portion, been so habituated to the consideration of all questions connected with popular representation, the period itself has been so prolific of political phenomena for the contemplation and study, and I may add, the instruction of the people of this country, that we are in a much more favourable position, than the statesmen who in 1832 undertook the great office which then devolved upon them, because we address not only a Parliament, but a country which has upon this subject the advantage of previous knowledge; and all will agree that this greatly facilitates both discussion and decision. Although some of those who took a leading part in the transactions of 1832, happily for us, still sit in both Houses of Parliament, yet so long is the space of time that has elapsed since those occurrences I think it is not impossible to speak of them with something of the candour of history. I do not doubt that our future records will acknowledge that, during some of the most important political events of modern history, those events were treated with the energy and the resource becoming British statesmen. If we judge of the Act of 1832 by its consequences, in the measures of this house and in the character of its Members, it must be admitted that that policy was equal to the emergency it controlled and directed. I cannot, indeed, agree with those who attribute to the legislation of 1832 every measure of public benefit that has been passed by this House during the last twenty-five years. I know well that before the reform of this House took place the administration of this country was distinguished by its ability and precision. I believe, indeed, that, especially in the latter part of the administration of Lord Liverpool, this House was rather in advance of the opinion of the country at large. But I think that the reform of the House of Commons in 1832 greatly added to the energy and public spirit in which we had then become somewhat deficient. But, Sir, it must be remembered that the labours of the statesmen who took part in the transactions of 1832 were eminently experimental. In many respects they had to treat their subject empirically, and it is not to be wondered at if in the course of time it was found that some errors were committed in that settlement; and if, as time rolled on, some, if not many deficiencies, were discovered. I beg the house to consider well those effects of time, and what has been the character of the twenty-five years that have elapsed since the Reform of 1832. They form no ordinary period. In a progressive country, and a progressive age, progress has been not only rapid, but, perhaps, precipitate. There is no instance in the history of Europe of such an increase of population as has taken place in this country during this period. There is no example in the history of Europe or of America, of a creation and accumulation of capital so vast as has occurred in this country in those twenty-five years. And I believe the general diffusion of intelligence has kept pace with that increase of population and wealth. In that period you have brought science to bear on social life in a manner no philosopher in his dreams could ever have anticipated. In that space of time you have, in a manner, annihilated both time and space. The influence of the discovery of printing is really only beginning to work on the multitude. It is, therefore, not surprising that in a measure passed twenty-five years ago, in a spirit necessarily experimental, however distinguished were its authors, and however remarkable their ability, some omissions have been found that ought to be supplied, and some defects that ought to be remedied. In such a state of things a question in England becomes what is called a public question. Thus Parliamentary Reform became a public question; a public question in due course of time becomes a Parliamentary question; and then, as it were, shedding its last skin, it becomes a Ministerial question. Reform has been for fifteen years a Parliamentary question; for ten years, it has been a Ministerial question. It is ten years since the Prime Minister of that day, who sat in this House, after resisting for some time a series of Motions, the object of which was to change the settlement of 1832, declared it to be the opinion of himself and his colleagues that some alteration ought be made in it. Public events prevented that Minister from immediately acting on that public declaration. But in 1852, I believe in this very month of February, that Prime Minister counselled Her Majesty to address Parliament from the Throne in these terms:—It appears to me that this is a fitting time for calmly considering whether it may not be advisable to make such amendments in the Act of the late reign, relating to the representation of the Commons in Parliament as may be deemed calculated to carry into more complete effect the principles upon which that law is founded. I have the fullest confidence that in any such consideration you will firmly adhere to the acknowledged principles of the Constitution by which the prerogative of the Crown, the authority of both Houses of Parliament, and the rights and liberties of the people are equally secured. In consequence of that announcement from the Throne, a measure of Parliamentary Reform was brought forward by the Ministry of the day. It was not pressed in consequence of a change of Government which then took place. But two years afterwards another Minister being at the head of affairs,—a Minister who, in the general tenor of his politics afforded a contrast to the one who introduced the measure of 1852—a Minister born and bred in what is termed the Tory camp, as his predecessor was born and bred in the Whig camp—this Minister being called on to form a Government, having to consider the requirements of the country, as every individual with that responsibility is bound to consider them, felt it his duty to counsel Her Majesty, in February, 1854, to address to Parliament this language from the Throne:—Recent experience has shown that it is necessary to take more effectual precautions against the evils of bribery and corrupt practices at elections. It will also be your duty to consider whether more complete effect may not be given to the principles of the Act of the last reign, whereby reforms were made in the representation of the people in Parliament. In recommending this subject to your consideration, my desire is to remove every cause of just complaint, to increase general confidence in the Legislature, and to give additional stability to the settled institutions of the State. In consequence of that announcement, another measure was brought forward by the Ministry of Lord Aberdeen, which was considered stronger than the measure of 1852, proposed by Lord John Russell—for it is not against order thus historically to mention that distinguished name. But circumstances again changed, and prevented the Legislature from proceeding with that measure of Reform. The country became involved in a war with a first-rate power—a war that might be described as European. Before it terminated a change of Government again occurred. Another statesman, who may well be compared with the two distinguished men who preceded him—a statesman renowned, not only for his ability, but his great experience, and whose political prejudices—if he has any (laughter and cheers)—well, then, I will say, whose superiority to prejudice—at any rate a statesman who has no morbid sympathy with advanced opinions. Then what did that noble Lord deem it to be his first civil duty to accomplish when he accepted the responsibility of office, and peace had been concluded? In the same solemn and impressive manner adopted by the noble Lord the Member for the City, and by the Earl of Aberdeen—the noble Lord, in 1857, on the termination of peace, counselled his Sovereign to address Parliament in these words:— Your attention will be called to the laws which regulate the representation of the people in Parliament, with a view to consider what Amendments may be safely and beneficially made therein. The House will therefore see that during three Ministries the subject of Parliamentary, Reform has been formally brought before the attention of the Legislature. And let me remind hon. Gentlemen, that although circumstances have prevented the Ministers who preceded us from either proceeding with the measures which they introduced, or with the measures which they proposed, this House has shown during that interval no disposition to wait, and no reluctance to deal with it. The consequence is, that you have had, up to the end of the last Session of Parliament, independent Members of this Assembly continuing that course which was pursued before any of those messages from the Throne were delivered to the Legislature—namely, that of carrying a Reform of Parliament by measures of detail, instead of taking a general view and bringing forward a comprehensive plan which should effect a fair adjustment of all the points in controversy. This, Sir, was the state of the question when, a change of Government again occurring, the Earl of Derby became responsible for the administration of this country. Let me now ask the House what, in their opinion, was our duty under these circumstances? That, from the peculiar position at which this question had arrived, it might have been practicable by evasion for a time to stave off a solution, I do not say is impossible; but that is a course which, speaking for my colleagues and myself, I may respectfully observe is not at all congenial with our tastes. Were you to allow this question, which the Sovereign had three times announced was one that ought to be dealt with—which three Prime Ministers, among the most skilful and authoritative of our Statesmen, had declared it was their intention to deal with—to remain in abeyance? Was it to be left as a means of re-organizing an opposition? Is that the opinion of either side of this House? Is it the judgment of this House that that is a wholesome position for political questions of the highest quality to occupy? Was Parliamentary Reform—a subject which touches the interests of all classes and all individuals, and in the wise and proper settlement of which the very destiny of this country is concerned—to be suffered to remain as a desperate resource of faction; or was it a matter to be grappled with only at a moment of great popular excitement, and settled, not by the reason, but by the passion of the people? Were we to establish, as it were, a chronic irritation in the public mind upon this subject, which, of all others, should not form the staple of our party contests? Were the energies of this country—an ancient country of complicated civilization—were they at this time of day, boasting as we do of a throne that has endured for a thousand years, to be distracted and diverted from their proper objects—the increase of the wealth and welfare of the community, and wasted in a discussion of the principles of our constitution and of what should be the fundamental base of our political institutions? I cannot for a moment believe that this House would think that a posture of affairs which would be free from danger to the Empire, or which it would be honourable for any public man to sanction. Having, then, to consider the state of the country with reference to this question, and recalling all those details Which on this occasion I feel it incumbent on me to place before the House, the Government of the Earl of Derby, on their accession to power, had to inquire what it was their duty to fulfil. And, Sir, it was the opinion—the unanimous opinion of the Cabinet of the Earl of Derby—that this subject must be dealt with, and dealt with in an earnest and sincere spirit.

But I am told that, although it might be necessary that a solution should be effected, although three Prime Ministers who had made the attempt had withdrawn from the effort, yet it was not for the Earl of Derby—even if he deemed it for the interests of his country, and held it to be his paramount duty in the position that he occupied—to undertake such a task. Sir, I dispute that statement. I say it is not a just statement, and cannot in discussion be at all maintained. What is there in the previous career of the noble Earl at the head of Her Majesty's Government which should preclude him from taking this course? The noble Lord the Member for the City of London has connected his name with the question of Parliamentary Reform to his enduring honour. I do not grudge the well-earned celebrity which he enjoys. But the noble Lord can remember the day when Earl Grey summoned himself and Mr. Stanley to his cabinet in 1832; and the noble Lord knows well that, had it not been for their ability and energy, probably the Reform Bill, and certainly in its present shape, would never have been passed into law. I think, therefore, it cannot for a moment be contended that there is anything in the position or antecedents of the head of the Government that should preclude him from dealing with this question. What is there in the position of hon. Gentlemen who sit on this side of the House to render it an inconsistent act, on their part, to adopt the course which I shall recommend to-night? Why, when the noble Lord introduced his measure, and also when the measure of the Earl of Aberdeen was introduced into this House, I, acting with the complete sanction and at the personal request of many now sitting behind and around me on these benches, expressed our views upon the course pursued by the Government of that day, I stated then, on their behalf, that we should offer no opposition to any measure which might be brought in, the object of which was to effect a reconstruction of this House. I said that we were prepared to adhere to the Conservative compact which was wrung from the Conservative party in 1835 by taunts and reproaches as to their insincerity in professing to be bound by the Act of 1832. I said, that by that Conservative compact, which was made by those who then represented the Conservative party in this House, we were ready to stand; but that if those who themselves made the settlement questioned its propriety and proposed to amend it, we should offer no opposition, but would give to those proposed Amendments our candid consideration, making every effort on our part to improve the representation of the people. Therefore I cannot understand the justness of the taunts which have been so freely used against our undertaking a task which, in my mind, no one who occupies these benches can avoid, or ought to shrink from. Sir, it is in pursuance of the pledge which we gave when we acceded to office that, on the part of the Government of the Earl of Derby, I am, with your permission, to-night to call your attention to the measures which we think it politic that this House should adopt.

Now, Sir, it appears to me that those who are called Parliamentary Reformers may be divided into two classes. The first are those whose object I will attempt to describe in a sentence. They are those who would adapt the settlement of 1832 to the England of 1859; and would act in the spirit and according to the genius of the existing constitution. Among these Reformers I may be permitted to class Her Majesty's Ministers. But, Sir, it would not be candid, and it would be impolitic not to acknowledge that there is another school of Reformers, having objects very different from those which I have named. The new school, if I may so describe them, would avowedly effect a Parliamentary Reform on principles different from those which have hitherto been acknowledged as forming the proper foundations for this House. The new school of Reformers are of opinion that the chief, if not the sole, object of representation is to realize the opinion of the numerical majority of the country. Their standard is population; and I admit that their views have been clearly and efficiently placed before the country. Now, Sir, there is no doubt population is, and must always be, one of the elements of our representative system. There is also such a thing as property; and that, too, must be considered. I am ready to admit that the new school have not on any occasion limited the elements of their representative system solely to population. They have, with a murmur, admitted that property has an equal claim to consideration; but, then, they have said that property and population go together. Well, Sir, population and property do go together—in statistics, but in nothing else. Population and property do not go together in politics and practice. I cannot agree with the principles of the new school, either if population or property is their sole, or if both together, constitute their double standard. I think the function of this House is something more than merely to represent the population and property of the country. This House, in my opinion, ought to represent all the interests of the country. Now, those interests are sometimes antagonistic, often competing, always independent and jealous; yet they all demand a distinctive representation in this House; and how can that be effected, under such circumstances, by the simple representation of the voice of the majority, or even by the mere preponderance of property? If the function of this House is to represent all the interests of the country, you must of course have a representation scattered over the country; because interests are necessarily local. An illustration is always worth two arguments; permit me, therefore, so to explain my meaning—if it requires explanation. Let me take the two cases of the metropolis and that of the kingdom of Scotland to the representation of which the hon. Gentleman opposite (Mr. Baxter) is so much afraid that I should not do justice. The population of the metropolis and that of the kingdom of Scotland are, at this time about equal. The wealth of the metropolis and the wealth of the kingdom of Scotland are very unequal. The wealth of the metropolis yields a yearly income of £44,000,000—upon which the assessment under the great schedules of the income tax is levied; while the amount upon which such assessment is levied under those schedules in Scotland is only £30,000,000. There is, therefore, the annual difference between £44,000,000 and £30,000,000; yet who would for a moment pretend that the various classes and interests of Scotland could be adequately represented by the same number of Members as represent the metropolis? So much for the population test. Let us now take the property test. Let us take one portion of that very metropolis to which I have this moment referred. This is an age of statistics. I do not place more value upon them than they deserve; but this is, I believe, at least an accurate memorandum. Let us look to the wealth of the City of London. The wealth of the City of London is more than equivalent to that of 25 English and Welsh Counties returning 40 Members, and of 140 Boroughs returning 232 Members. The City of London, the City proper, is richer than Liverpool, Manchester, and Birmingham put together. Or take another and even more pregnant formula. The City of London is richer than Bristol, Leeds, Newcastle, Sheffield, Hull, Wolverhampton, Bradford, Brighton, Stoke-upon-Trent, Nottingham, Greenwich, Preston, East Retfurd, Sunderland, York, and Salford combined—towns which return among them no less than 31 Members. The City of London has not asked me to insert it in the Bill which I am asking leave to introduce for 31 Members. I have heard that there is another measure of Reform, in hands, probably, more able to deal with the subject than myself, and in hands which, perhaps, are much interested in ascertaining the claims of the City of London. Whether the noble Lord has made his arrangements according to the statistical return we shall probably know some day or other; but, as far as I am concerned, the citizens of London have acted with modesty and propriety. They seem to be satisfied with their representation, and to consider that, probably, no place requires a greater number of Members than the City of London at present possesses. Perhaps they have some suspicion that, if they had more Members, they would find some difficulty in obtaining men who were competent to discharge that office. So much for the population test, and so much for the property test, if you are to reconstruct this House on either of those principles; but the truth is, that men are sent to this House to represent the opinions of a place and not its power. We know very well what takes place at a Parliamentary election in this country. The man of princely fortune has, when he goes to the poll, no more votes than the humble dweller in a £10 house; because we know very well that his wealth, his station, and his character will give him the influence which will adequately represent his property; and the Constitution shrinks from a plurality of votes in such a case. The constitution also shrinks from the enjoyment of a plurality of votes by large towns by means of seats in this House. It wants the large towns and cities of England to be completely represented. It wishes to see the Members for Liverpool, Manchester, and Birmingham in their places, ready to express the views of those powerful and influential communities; and it recognizes them as the representatives of the opinions of those places, but not as the representatives of their power and influence. Because what happens to the rich man at a contested election will happen to these places. Why, Sir, the power of the city of London or that of the city of Manchester in this House is not to be measured by the honourable and respectable individuals whom they send here to represent their opinions. I will be bound to say that there is a score—nay, that there are three score—Members in this House who are as much and more interested, perhaps, in the city of Manchester than those who are in this House its authoritative and authentic representatives; and when a question arises in which the interests of Manchester, Liverpool, or Birmingham are concerned, the influence of those places is shown by the votes of persons so interested in their welfare as well as by those of the respectable and respected individuals who are sent here to represent them. Look at the metropolis itself, not speaking merely of the City of London. Is the influence of the metropolis in this House to be measured by the sixteen hon. Members who represent it, and who represent it, I have no doubt, in a manner perfectly satisfactory to their constituents, or they would not be here? No! We all of us live in the metropolis; many of the Members of this House have property, a few of them very large property, in it; and, therefore, the indirect influence of the metropolis in this House is not to be measured merely by the number of Members which it returns to Parliament. So much for that principle of population, or that principle of property, which has been adopted by some, or that principle of population and property combined, which seems to be the more favourite form. It appears to me that the principle, as one upon which the representation of the people in this House ought to be founded, is fallacious and erroneous. There is one remarkable circumstance connected with the new school, who would build up our representation on the basis of a numerical majority, and who take population as their standard. It is this—that none of their principles apply except in cases where population is concentrated. The principle of population is, although I cannot say a favourite doctrine, because I do not think it is so, a very notorious doctrine at the present moment; but it is not novel, although introduced at a comparatively recent period into our politics. It was broached in the discussions which took place when the former Reform Bills were brought in by preceding Governments. It was the favourite argument of the late Mr. Hume. His argument for Parliamentary Reform—a subject which he frequently brought before the house—was generally this:—He took some unfortunate borough in the west of England; he described it as a borough with a very small population and with very little business, and he said:—This borough returns two Members to Parliament, while the great city of Manchester, with its population of hundreds of thousands and with half the business of the world concentrated in its circle, only returns the same number. Can anything be more monstrous? Disfranchise the small borough, and give its Members to the city of Manchester.

158

Such was the argument which for several years passed in this House unchallenged. Mr. Hume brought forward his Motion for Parliamentary Reform in 1852, when, by a somewhat curious coincidence, I was occupying the same seat which I now fill, and it fell to my lot to make a reply to him. I stated then what I had long felt, that although I entirely rejected the principle of population, still, admitting it for the sake of argument to be a right principle, we must arrive at conclusions exactly the reverse of those which Mr. Hume and the school which he founded were perpetually impressing upon the public mind. The principle, in my opinion, is false, and would produce results dangerous to the country, and fatal to the House of Commons. But if it be true—if it be our duty to reform the representation upon it—then I say you must I arrive at conclusions entirely different from those which the new school has adopted. If population is to be the standard, and you choose to disfranchise small boroughs and small constituencies, it is not to the great towns you can, according to your own principle, transfer their Members. Perhaps the House will allow me to refer to a note of some returns which I quoted in 1852, because they are perfectly germane to the argument which I am now offering to the House. When Mr. Hume used the illustrations, a sample of which I have just cited, I asked him to look to the case of North Cheshire, a county with a population of 249,000; with two great towns, Macclesfield and Stockport, together possessing a population of 93,000 and returning four Members to Parliament, while the residue of the county population, (156,000) returned only two Members. I asked him to look to the case of South Cheshire, a county with 206,000 inhabitants, with one town of 28,000 returning two Members to Parliament, but with the rest of the county population, (178,0000,) returning only the same number. I brought before him the remarkable case of South Derbyshire. The population of that county was 166,000. It had only got one town, Derby itself, with 40,000 inhabitants, who returned two Members to Parliament, while the residue of the county population (126,000) had also only two Members. I called his attention to the case of North Durham with a population of 272,000. There are four great towns, Durham, Gateshead, South Shields, and Sunderland, with a conjoint population of 136,000, returning six Members to Parliament, while the county population of identically the same number, (136,000.) return only two Members. I referred him to the case of West Kent. That county has a population of 400,000. There are four great towns—Maidstone, Chatham, Rochester, and Greenwich,—with a joint population of 172,000, returning seven Members; while the remaining inhabitants 228,000 in number, return only two. I likewise cited the case of East Norfolk, with a population of 250,000. Two towns—Norwich and Yarmouth, with a population of 100,000, return four Members; but the county residue of 150,000, return only two. I asked hire to take the case of the East Riding, with a population of 220,000. Hull and another town return four Members; the residue of the county population, (126,000,) return only two. I told him to look at the West Riding, with its population of 1,300,000, reduced by nine considerable towns to 800,000. Those 800,000 return only two Members; whereas the nine considerable towns, representing a population of 500,000, return sixteen Members. Finally, I referred him to the case of South Lancashire, with a population of 1,500,000. Ten great towns in South Lancashire, with a joint population of 1,000,000, return fifteen Members to Parliament, but the county residue of 500,000 return only two. Why, Sir, it is notorious that, if you come to population in round numbers, 10,500,000 of the people of England return only 150 or 160 county Members, while the boroughs, representing 7,500,000, return more than 330 Members. Admitting, then, the principle of population, which is the principle of the new school, I say you must disfranchise your boroughs, and give their Members answer to this argument. It cannot have to die counties. Sir, I never heard an been misunderstood, because it was not offered in a corner, but in this House; and I repeat that, although seven years have elapsed since it was advanced, in 1852, I never heard an answer given to it. I have watched the recent agitation, when I was told that a new English constitution was to be created on the principle of population, to see if that argument was answered. It has, indeed, been said that there are some, nay, that there are many boroughs through which the landed interest is represented in this House. That may or may not be a sufficient answer to the demand of the landed interest to be more represented in this House; but it is no answer to the inhabitants of the counties. What proves that my argument is sound, and enters into the public mind, and is accepted as authentic, is, that the noble Lord the Member for the City in 1854, acknowledged, with generous can dour, that it had influenced him in the arrangements which he had made, and a large proportion of the seats—certainly two-thirds—which formerly belonged to the small constituencies that he proposed to disfranchise he transferred to the county representation.

Let us now, see, Sir, what will be the consequence if the population principle is adopted. You would have a House, generally speaking, formed partly of great landowners and partly of manufacturers. I have no doubt that, whether we look to their property or to their character, there would be no country in the world which could rival in respectability such an assembly. But would it be a House of Commons—would it represent the country—would it represent the various interests of England? Why, Sir, after all, the suffrage and the seat respecting which there is so much controversy and contest are only means to an end. They are means by which you may create a representative assembly that is a mirror of the mind as well as the material interests of England. You want in this House every element that obtains the respect and engages the interest of the country. You must have lineage and great territorial property; you must have manufacturing enterprise of the highest character; you must have commercial weight; you must have professional ability in all its forms: but you want something more,—you want a body of men not too intimately connected either with agriculture, or with manufactures, or with commerce; not too much wedded to professional thought and professional habits; you want a body of men representing the vast variety of the English character; men who would arbitrate between the claims of those great predominant interests; who would temper the acerbity of their controversies. You want a body of men to represent that immense portion of the community who cannot be ranked under any of those striking and powerful classes to which I have referred, but who are in their aggregate equally important and valuable, and perhaps as numerous. Hitherto you have been able to effect this object, you have effected it by the existing borough system, which has given you a number of constituencies of various dimensions distributed over the country. No one for a moment pretends that the borough system in England was originally framed to represent all the classes and interests of the country; but it has been kept and cherished because the people found that, although not directly intended for such a purpose, yet indirectly it has accomplished that object; and hence I lay it down as a principle which ought to be adopted, that if you subvert that system, you are bound to substitute for it machinery equally effective. That is all I contend for. I am not wedded to arrangements merely because they are arrangements; but what I hope this House will not sanction is, that we should remove a machinery which performs the office we desire, unless we are certain that we can substitute for it a machinery equally effective. Now, there is one remarkable feature in the agitation of the new school. It is, not that they offer for the system they would subvert a substitute; it is nut that they offer us a new machinery for the old machinery they would abrogate; but it is a remarkable circumstance that they offer no substitute whatever. They lay down their inexorable principle; they carry it to its logical consequences, and the logical consequences would be that to this House, in the present state of the population, no doubt you would have men returned by large constituencies who would, in most instances represent great wealth. I will make that concession;—but when this House is assembled, how will it perform the duties of a House of Commons. I will tell you what must be the natural consequence of such a state of things. The House will lose, as a matter of course, its hold on the Executive. The House will assemble; it will have men sent to it, no doubt, of character and wealth; the great majority of them matured and advanced in life; and, having met here, they will be unable to carry on the Executive of the country. [An hon. MEMBER: Why?] Why? asks an hon. Member. Because the experiment has been tried in every country, and the same result has occurred; because it is not in the power of one or two classes to give that variety of character and acquirement by which the administration of a country can be carried on. Well, then, if this House loses its hold over the Executive of the country, what happens? We fall back on a bureaucratic system, and we should find ourselves, after all our struggles, in the very same position which in 1640 we had to extricate ourselves from. Your Administration would be carried on by a Court Minister, perhaps a Court minion. It might not be in these times, but in some future time. The result of such a system would be to create an assembly where the Members of Parliament, though chosen by great constituencies, would be chosen from limited classes, and, perhaps, only from one class of the community. There is a new school of philosophers, who are of opinion that there is no such thing as progress—that nations move in a circle, and that after a certain cycle they arrive at exactly the same place, and stand in precisely the same circumstances which they quitted two or three centuries before. I have no time now to solve a problem of that depth. Questions so profound require the study and abstraction of the Opposition benches. But if the population principle be adopted I should give in my adhesion to the new school of philosophy; and I feel persuaded that the House of Commons, after all its reform and reconstruction, would find itself in the same comparatively ignominious position from which the spirit and energy of the old English gentry emancipated it more than two centuries ago. Therefore I need not inform the House that it is no part of my duty to recommend it to adopt that principle. We cannot acknowledge that population, or property, or even property and population joined together, should be the principle on which the legislative system shall be constructed. But before I refer to that part of the subject there appears to me to be one branch of the utmost interest, and which it is my duty rather to touch on before I advert to any other, and that is the state of the franchise. If there be One point more than another on which public feeling has been most shown, it has been in the desire to exercise the suffrage. That was the first claim that was made when the settlement of 1832 began to engage the critical spirit of the nation; and as tile prosperity of this country increased, and as its wealth, population, and intelligence increased; as new interests arose, and as new classes were, as it were called into social existence, that desire became stronger, and it is, I think, hardly necessary to admit that it was founded on a natural feeling, and one which we should by no means infer is entertained by those only who are disaffected with the institutions of the country. On the contrary, in most instances that desire arises, no doubt, from a desire to participate in privileges which are appreciated.

In considering this question, I would make, first of all, one general observation, as to the object which the Ministry have had in view in preparing their measure of Reform. We have never, in any of the arrangements which we shall propose to Parliament to adopt, considered for a moment whether they would increase or whether they would diminish the constituent body. Our sole object has been to confer the franchise on all of those to whom we thought that privilege might be safely entrusted, and who would exercise it for the general welfare of the country. I will, with the permission of the House, address myself first to the borough franchise. The Reform Act of 1832, acknowledging to a certain degree some of the old franchises of the boroughs, which exist but to a limited extent at present, established the franchise in boroughs on the occupation of a house of £10 annual value. There is a wish—I would once have said a very general wish—that instead of the household suffrage being founded on value, it should be founded by preference on rating. I am not at all surprised that more than one hon. Gentleman has received this observation with marks of assent and sympathy. I confess myself that I was always much biased in favour of that idea. It appears to me that if you could make—to use a common phrase—the rate-book the register, you would very much simplify the business of election; but, when you come to examine this matter in detail, in order to see how it will act, you will find that it is involved in difficulties—great, all acknowledge, and I am sorry to be obliged to confess, to my mind insurmountable. For the purpose of securing the advantage of having the rate-book the register, you must, of course, leave per-feet discretion to the overseer. The overseer has an interest in raising rates, people may say; or he may be a very hot political partisan. Are you prepared to leave to the overseer the absolute discretion of appointing those who are to exercise the suffrage? Some will say, We must have some check. But what is a check but an appeal? And if you appeal, you cannot do better than appeal to the revising barrister. If you have an appeal to some other parochial officer, you appeal to an inferior tribunal to that which you now enjoy; and, indeed, unless you permitted the overseer to be unchallenged you could not make the rate-book the register. But even beyond this, there are other difficulties which you will find most perplexing. Notwithstanding the Parochial Assessment Act, the rating of this country is most unequal; and it is only those whose business it has been to examine into this subject in its minute details, who can be aware of the preposterous consequences which would arise from adopting a rating instead of a value qualification. Take the present qualification of £10 value, which it is very generally and popularly supposed might be supplied by an £8 rating. Now, let us see what would be the consequence upon the present constituency of adopting an £8 rating instead of a £10 value? I will take the instance of Boston, represented by my hon. and learned Friend behind me (Mr. Adams). The borough of Boston consists of two parishes; the rating of one of them is upon one-half the value, and of the other upon two-thirds of the value. The practical consequence of having an £8 rating in Boston would be to disfranchise 400 of the electors of that borough, who may or may not be supporters of my hon. and learned Friend. Then taking the case of another borough—Dovor,—if you had in that borough a franchise based upon £8 rating, instead of £10 value, you would exactly double the constituency. I have taken these two instances from a great number of others, and the House will see that the idea of establishing a franchise based upon rating instead of upon value, is by no means the simple process it is by some persons supposed to be. The great objection to such a measure, which led us entirely to relinquish all idea of adopting it, is its tendency to disfranchise many of the constituencies.

I will now proceed to consider the franchise of boroughs based upon a value qualification. The £10 qualification has been severely assailed, and I think the objections to it may be ranged under two heads. First, it is said that there is no principle in a franchise founded on a £10 qualification; and secondly, it is said that a constituency based upon such a qualification must be extremely monotonous. It is said that there is such an identity of interest in a constituency so founded, when we ought to seek for variety of character, that that alone is an objection; and it has really become almost a phrase of contumely to speak of a constituency as "only ten-pounders." I will in the first place touch upon the objection that a £10 borough qualification is one founded upon no principle. Now, I demur to that objection. It appears to me that that qualification is founded on a principle. It is said, "Why should a man who lives in a £10 house be more fitted for the suffrage than a man who lives in a £9 house?" That appears to me to be no argument. It is a mere sophism and cavil. If it be an argument, it is an argument against all tests, and not in favour of a £9 qualification. But the £10 qualification was intended as a test; and the question is, Is it a test that is effective? It is a test easily accessible; it is a test which, if adopted, is universal in its application; and it is a test which affords a fair presumption that the holder possesses those qualities which entitle him to perform the acts of citizenship. It is, therefore, founded upon a principle; and the objection urged against it appears to me to be a sophism. The other objection to the £10 qualification is that it gives a monotonous character to a constituency; that from extending the suffrage only to men who live in £10 houses you have merely one sentiment and one class of ideas represented. That appears to me to be altogether a fallacy, resting upon the false assumption that every man who votes under a £10 qualification necessarily lives in a £10 house. But that is not the case. On the contrary, under that £10 qualification all orders of men exercise the suffrage—the most affluent and the most humble. A man who lives in a house worth £400 a year yet votes under the £10 qualification, and, instead of rendering a constituency monotonous, it secures within its range a great variety of interests, of feelings, and of opinions. But, Sir, I am ready to admit that there are many persons quite capable of exercising the suffrage who do not live in £10 houses, and whom I should wish to see possessing the suffrage. But should we obtain that result by—I won't call it the vulgar expedient, because the epithet might be misinterpreted, though I should not use it in an offensive sense—but by the coarse and common expedient which is recommended of what is called "lowering the franchise in towns?" Now, I beg the House to consider for a moment what must be the effect of lowering the franchise in towns. Suppose that, instead of a £10 borough qualification, you had a £5 borough qualification? Well, the moment that you had a £5 borough qualification you would realize all those inconvenient results which are erroneously ascribed to the £10 qualification. You would then have a monotonous constituency. You would then have a constituency whose predominant opinions would be identical. You would then have a constituency who would return to Parliament Members holding the same ideas, the same opinions, the same sentiments and all that variety which represents the English character would be entirely lost. You would then have in your borough constituency a predominant class; and certainly the spirit and genius of our constitution are adverse to the predominance of any class in this House. It certainly would be most injudicious, not to say intolerable, when we are guarding ourselves against the predominance of a territorial aristocracy and the predominance of a manufacturing and commercial oligarchy, that we should reform Parliament by securing the predominance of a household democracy. I am convinced that that is not the mode in which you must improve and vary the elements of the present borough constituency. We think, Sir, that there are modes by which that object can be adequately and efficiently attained; and if the House will permit me, I will now proceed to describe them.

We propose to introduce into these borough constituencies new franchises. In the first place we shall introduce, as qualifying for the suffrage a class of property which hitherto has not formed an element out of which voters have been created—I mean personal property. We shall propose to allow persons who have funded property, property in Bank Stock, or in East India Stock and Bonds, to the amount of £10 per annum, to exercise the suffrage. I know the objection which may be urged by some persons against the introduction of this qualification. They will point out the obstacles to a genuine exercise of the suffrage, if that element is introduced. The House will pardon me on this occasion, when I have to travel over a vast field, and when I must confine myself to the chief features of the measure I am recommending to their notice, if I abstain from now entering into that question. Enough for me now to say, that the Bill which I have here, and which, with the permission of the House, I shall introduce, provides, in our opinion, a satisfactory and secure machinery by which this and all other similar franchises to which I am about to advert may be exercised. Now, Sir, there is another franchise which we shall also recommend the House to adopt; and that is one which depends upon the possession of a certain sum in the savings banks. A man who has had £60 for one year in a savings bank will, under this Bill, if it become law, be an elector for the borough in which he resides. Again, a man who has a pension for public service, but who has ceased to be employed in that service, whether it be Her Majesty's naval, military, or civil service to the amount of £20 a year, will under this Bill, if it become law, be entitled to a vote wherever he may reside. Then, again, Sir, the occupant of a portion of a house, the aggregate rent of which amounts to £20 a year—which would be 8s. a week,—will also be entitled to a vote. The House has heard much of late years of what is called an educational franchise. I am bound to say that no plan for the creation of all educational franchise—in a precise sense of that word—which in their opinion would work satisfactorily, has been brought under the consideration of the Government. It has, indeed, been proposed that the basis of such a franchise should be sought for among the members of the various learned societies. But, as it has been aptly observed, it does not follow that the members of learned societies should be learned. In these days we frequently see name followed by an amount of alphabetical combination which is almost appalling; yet, though we associate the highest learning, great antiquarian and scientific acquirements, with those persons it sometimes turns out that they only possess a respectable character and pay ten guineas a year. An educational franchise according to that high empyrean of imagination which some have attempted to reach, has baffled all our practical efforts. But it will be our duty to recommend to the House that the privilege of a vote irrespective of the more formal qualification arising from property, should be conferred upon those classes whose education has involved some considerable investment of capital, many of them, no doubt, exercising the franchise under the previous qualifications which I have described. We have thought it advisable that the suffrage should be conferred upon graduates of all Universities; upon the ministers of religion—whether clergymen and deacons of the Church, or ministers of other denominations,—under regulations which the House will find in the Bill; upon the members of the legal profession in all its branches, whether barristers, members of the Inns of Court, solicitors, or proctors; and upon all members of the medical body who are registered under the late Medical Act. To these we have added such schoolmasters as possess a certificate from the Council. Sir, there are some other franchises which it is our intention to give to the borough constituencies; but before I touch upon them it will be convenient that I should call the attention of the House to the subject of the county franchise. Previous to the Reform Act of 1832, the general franchise of England may be described popularly—though technically, perhaps, such a description is not quite correct—as a franchise which in the counties arose from property, and in the boroughs from occupation. When the measure passed in 1832 was first introduced, that distinction was recognized by the statesmen who had the preparation and conduct of the Bill. I have no doubt they deeply considered that question at the time; nor can it be denied that, if the constituencies had remained as they proposed them, the principle thus established would have been a distinct and a clear one. Whether, however, the distinction could have been long maintained, I may, with great humility, be permitted to doubt. Looking at the expansion of the country, at its vast increase in wealth and population, and not only in wealth and population, but in those distinctive interests which seek representation in this House—remembering the 10,500,000, inhabitants of counties to whom I have already alluded,—I venture humbly to doubt whether that distinction could have been long kept up. That its maintenance was convenient to the statesmen of 1832, who had immense difficulties to contend with, I can easily conceive; but whatever was their intention, they were disappointed in the plan which they had prepared, and circumstances occurred in this House which changed the character of the franchise and destroyed that distinction between property and occupation which the Ministry of Lord Grey had sought to establish. Now, the individual responsible for that change was the noble Duke who was my predecessor in the seat which I now unworthily fill; and as his conduct in this respect has often been challenged, and as there are many who now deplore the course which he then took, perhaps the House will for a moment permit me, who am well aware of the motives which influenced him, to state the reasons which induced Lord Chandos to move successfully in this House the celebrated clause that bears his name. When the Reform Bill was introduced in 1831, it was generally avowed that the object of that measure was to give a legitimate position in the Legislature to the middle classes of England. That was the object avowed by the Ministry, and its propriety was generally acknowledged by the country. Now, when the principle that the middle classes should be represented in this House was laid down, Lord Chandos, who was then the Member for the county of Buckingham, being a man who lived much among his neighbours, and who was familiar with the character and the interests of rural society, naturally felt what he considered great absurdity that the most important portion of the middle classes—the most important even at this day, because they are the greatest employers of labour,—I mean the farmers of England—should not possess the suffrage; and it was with that view that Lord Chandos moved the clause. The sympathy of the House was so great in its favour (a sympathy not confined to party—Mr. Hume was a supporter of the Chandos clause) that the noble Lord who then led this House—Lord Althorp—felt it his duty to yield to it. But that happened then which sometimes does happen when great measures are brought forward by a Ministry and an important Amendment is introduced successfully by an eager Opposition.

166

Those who have had the preparation of great and important measures,—and I see present many upon whom that task has devolved,—know the great difficulty, the long anxiety, the constant hesitation which are involved in such a task, and know how hard it is to adapt one part to another, and to obtain that general harmony which will meet public wants, and which will give you a chance of carrying your measure successfully through. But when a leader of Opposition carries an Amendment, which he believes to be necessary, he thinks only of the proposal which he is making to the House, and if the Ministry are obliged to adopt it, it very often does not fit in with their previous design; it does not display the harmony and unison which would perhaps have been the case had they themselves devised it with a due regard for the other details of the measure. I have no doubt that had the Government thought fit in 1831–2 to introduce the principle of occupation in the county franchise, they might have rendered it so homogeneous with their general scheme that it would have worked with perfect facility,—that we should long ere this have been quite accustomed to its operation; and then those distinctions and difficulties which have since arisen might never have been heard of. But there is no doubt that from the moment, or shortly after, this £50 occupation clause was put into operation, feelings of dissatisfaction and suspicion were excited in the minds of the community. Occupiers in the county of less than £50—say of £40 or £20,—who, if the principle had not been admitted, would probably never have thought themselves injured, naturally looked with great soreness on the man who had voted in a borough because he had an occupation of £10. That feeling of dissatisfaction was unfortunately followed by those industrial controversies, respecting the origin or end of which it is unnecessary to say anything, but which were prolonged, and which undoubtedly occasioned great bitterness among all classes. The feeling of dissatisfaction became a feeling of distrust. It was said that commercial changes were prevented in this country chiefly by this £50 tenancy clause. The men who acted under that clause—and, take them altogether, I do not believe that a more valuable class to whom to intrust the franchise could be found—were described in this House as men void of all patriotism and public spirit, exercising the suffrage without the slightest effort of intelligence, merely at the beck of their landlords. Nothing can be more exaggerated or even groundless than the opinions which have been expressed in this House on the effect of the Chandos clause, and on the influence which it has had on popular election. In the first place, voters under the Chandos clause at no time ever exceeded one-fifth of the constituent body of counties. Therefore, had they all voted the same way, they never could have exercised that influence upon public events which has been ascribed to them. But the proprietary of the soil does not rest alone with Tories and Conservatives. There are Whig landlords, and very considerable Whig landlords. The proprietary of the soil is distributed among proprietors of all opinions; and the consequence is, that if you look at the elections, you will find that those who voted under this Chandos clause were much divided—often equally divided. It is not true, therefore, that those who vote under this qualification have exercised any very great influence upon the legislation of this country, or that they are a class who have acted always without intent or meaning. But there is no doubt that dissatisfaction, followed by distrust and misrepresentation, did raise in the country an idea that the county representation was an exclusive representation; that it was animated only by one object; that it had a selfish interest always before it, and that it had not that sympathy with the community which we desire in that body to whom the privilege of election is intrusted. An effort was made by means of the 40s. freehold, which was retained in counties, to counteract the exaggerated influence of the £50 tenancy voters. A manufacture of votes—from the facts before me I am entitled so to call it—was carried on in the boroughs, by which it was supposed that the injurious influence of the tenants living upon the land, dwelling in the counties, might be counteracted. For the last fifteen years—for the last ten years at a very great rate—this has been going on, until it has really arrived at this point, that the number of county voters who do not dwell in the counties now exceeds the number of those who vote under the £50 clause. It was proclaimed with great triumph that when a gentleman stood for a county, his neighbours who dwelt in the county might vote for him, but some large town in the district would pour out its legions by railway, and on the nomination of some club in the metropolis would elect the representative for the county. The dwellers in the county found themselves not represented in many instances by those who lived among them. A sort of civil war was raised in this manner; and if hon. Gentlemen look into the statistics on this point, they will see that what I may call an unnatural state of things was brought about; because there is no doubt that a man should vote for the place where he resides, or for the locality in which he is really and substantially interested. A man who votes for a place where he resides, or in which he has an interest, votes with a greater sense of responsibility than a more stranger. Where, then, when we are considering the condition of the constituency of the country; when we are endeavouring to reconstruct it on a broad basis, which will admit within its pale all those who are trustworthy,—shall we look for means by which we may terminate these heart-burnings, and restore the constituencies of England to what I will venture to call their natural elements? No doubt it is a labour of great difficulty. Are we to attempt to do it by restrictions?—by artificial arrangements? It might be possible to pass a law which would remove these strangers from the sphere of their political power. But, whether possible or not, who would be rash enough to propose it? How could we terminate these misunderstandings, how restore that good feeling,—that which Lord Clarendon called the "good-nature of the English people,"—if we took a course which would give occasion to a perpetual agitation for the removal of the restrictions which we had succeeded in establishing? Her Majesty's Government have given to this subject the most anxious consideration. I may say, that if labour, if thought, could assist us to arrive at a proper solution; neither labour nor thought has been spared. Is there any principle on which we can restore the county constituency to its natural state, and bring about that general and constant sympathy between the two portions of the constituent body which ought to exist? Her Majesty's Government are of opinion that some such solution does exist. We think there is a principle, the justness of which will be at once acknowledged, the logical consequences of which will be at once remedial, and which, if applied with due discretion, will effect all those objects which we anxiously desire with respect to the county constituency. We find that principle in recognizing the identity of suffrage between county and town. I will proceed to show the House what, in our opinion, would be the practical consequences of recognizing that identity. If the suffrages of the town are transferred to the county, and the suffrages of the county transferred to the town, all those voters who, dwelling in a town, exercise their suffrage in the county in virtue of a county suffrage, will record their votes in the town, and the freeholder, resident in a town—subject to provisions in the Bill which would prevent this constitutional instrument being turned to an improper use,—will have a right to vote for the borough in which he resides. This, as well as the franchise founded on savings-banks, will open another avenue to the mechanic, whose virtue, prudence, intelligence, and frugality entitle him to enter into the privileged pale of the constituent body of the country. If this principle be adopted, a man will vote for the place where he resides, and with which he is substantially connected. Therefore the first measure would embody this logical consequence—that it would transfer the freeholders of the town from the county to the town. But if this principle be adopted, there are other measures which, in our opinion, it would be the duty of Parliament in this respect to adopt. Since the year 1832 there has been a peculiar increase in the population of this country irrespective of the ratio of increase, with which we are acquainted. The creation of railways in particular districts has stimulated that increase; and this has come to pass in England, that in a great many of the boroughs there is a population resoling, who, for all social and municipal purposes, are part and parcel of the community, but who for Parliamentary purposes are pariahs. A man votes for a municipality; he pays his parochial rates and taxes; he is called upon to contribute to all purposes of charity and philanthropy in the borough; but, because he lives in a part of the borough which exceeds the boundary that was formed in 1832, he is not, though he lives in a £10 house, permitted to vote for Members of Parliament. Now, all this extramural population in fact and in spirit consists of persons who ought to be electors in the boroughs in which they reside; and we therefore propose that Boundary Commissioners should visit all the boroughs of England, and re-arrange them according to the altered circumstances of the time. I know that the title of Boundary Commissioners may cause some alarm in this country. I know there are traditions of party arrangements effected by that machinery which, whether true or not, left an unpopular recollection in the House of Commons. I believe that in the present state of public feeling on this subject, so moderate as it is, and in the present balanced state of parties, no partial or improper conduct of that character, if it ever did take place, could be repeated. But it is quite unnecessary for me to dwell upon this point, because Her Majesty's Ministers are so circumstanced that they can, in that respect, make a proposition to the House which will at once divest it of all suspicion. Since the Reform of 1832, machinery has arisen in this country perfectly competent to effect that which we believe to be so necessary—I mean the

Enclosure Commissioners. There is a body of men totally independent of all party; and we purpose to delegate to them the fulfilment of this office. They will appoint Deputy Commissioners, who will visit the boroughs. The Deputy Commissioners will make their reports to the Secretary of State, the Secretary of State will embody them in a Bill, and that Bill will be subjected to the criticism of this House. After that, no one can for a moment suspect that there will be any opportunity of making arrangements favourable to any party.

The House has a right to ask me whether Her Majesty's Government have formed any estimate of what may be the consequence of the change which we propose in the number of the county constituencies. That is, no doubt, a point upon which one must speak with some degree of hesitation; but there are some materials in existence which are furnished by the papers before the House, and there are others which are at our command. This morning there was put into my hand a pamphlet—probably a proof—published to day. It is by a gentleman who ranks, I believe, as the most eminent statistical authority in the country, who is well known to Gentlemen in this House, and who has often been examined before our Committees—Mr. Newmarch. Mr. Newmarch estimates that the gross increase that would be occasioned in the county voters by a £10 county franchise would be 103,000. I have no time to ascertain what are the data on which Mr. Newmarch makes his calculation, but I should be disingenuous if I did not acknowledge to the House that the estimate formed by Her Majesty's Ministers is much more considerable. I should suppose the addition to the county constituency would be not less than 200,000, one-half of which would be furnished by what statisticians call the north-western and the south-eastern groups of counties—that is to say, Cheshire, Lancashire, and the West Riding on the one hand; and Kent, Sussex, and part of Surrey, on the other. With reference to those gentlemen who have on various occasions expressed their opinion that a £20 occupation franchise is one which they should prefer to see adopted, I would observe that the number between a £20 and a £10 franchise would, I think, be described by the figures 100,000. But, with reference to the change of the county constituency from £50 to £20, I would venture to observe that, having given to this subject very considerable pains, so far as I can form an opinion, there is nothing which would make me trust the loyalty and respectability of one who lived in a £20 house in a county, in preference to one who lived in a £10 house. I am also bound to say that the estimate of 200,000 voters has been made irrespective of what the effects of the labours of the Boundary Commissioners may be. I have heard many arguments against this proposition, but only to one of them would I attach much weight, and to that not for its strength, but for the phrase which is used to clothe it. I allude to the objection that the identity which this proposition would introduce between the county and the town constituencies, may lead to what are called "electoral districts." Now, if the only protection of the English people from electoral districts is a difference of £10 in an occupation franchise between the county and the town, then I am afraid that electoral districts cannot be resisted. But, believing, as I do, that there is nothing more unpopular in this country than electoral districts, and that they are alien to all the customs, manners, and associations of the people, I have no fear whatever that that scheme will be adopted until Englishmen have lost all pride in their country and all fondness for the localities in which they have lived. Why, Sir, electoral districts can never be established until you recognize the voice of a numerical majority as the right principle of representation in this House. They can be formed upon no other principle; and the measures which it is my duty to introduce on the part of the Government to the House to-night have no other object but to assert these contrary but, as we believe, right principles upon which the representation in this House has always been based.

I have now, very imperfectly, and omitting many points, placed before the House a general view of what we propose to do with the constituent body of the country. Our object is to reconstruct that body, with no mere view of increasing its numerical amount, but solely with the object of improving it, by the addition of various classes and individuals to whom the privilege of the franchise may be trusted with safety to the State and benefit to the community. If the measure we recommend be adopted, you will have a great homogeneous constituency, with much variety of character—for variety in the franchise is perfectly consistent with identity of the suffrage;—you will have a great homogeneous body, between the different sections of which there will no longer exist feelings of dissatisfaction and distrust. The elector will elect a man of the community in which he lives, and he will exercise the right under the high sense of duty that influences Englishmen in performing it. I have always thought the ideal of the constituent body in England should be this—It should be numerous enough to be independent, and select enough to be responsible; and that is the constituency Her Majesty's Ministers believe will be formed by the measure I propose to the House to-night.

Having laid before the House the character of the elective body it becomes me to state how we propose it shall be registered, and how it may vote. The House is aware that under the present system there is a difference in the method of registration in counties and boroughs. In counties, an elector makes his own claim to be placed on the list; in boroughs, the list is made out by a public officer. It is well known that great difficulty attends the county registration; nothing proves it more than the fact that, notwithstanding the increase in the population and wealth of the country, the county registration is a decaying one. This must always be the case if you surround it with every obstacle. We propose to amend that system entirely; we propose, in fact, that there shall be a self-acting registry. The overseer in every parish will make out a list of owners as well as occupiers. I believe there will be no difficulty whatever in doing it, and clauses will be found in the Bill to ensure its accomplishment. If any one is omitted from the list, whether owner or occupier, he may make his claim, and in a supplementary list his name will be inserted and sent to the clerk of the peace, and the revising barrister. That is the great change we propose with regard to registration. There are other regulations of considerable importance, but I have still other points to allude to; and though the House has treated me with much indulgence, I feel I must not dwell on this head.

Now, being registered, how is the elector to vote? We wish to put an end to those scandals that have of late years been discussed in the House, and the bitter feelings and controversies raised by the question, Are the travelling expenses of electors to be paid by the candidates? Is there no mode of terminating for ever what may be a scandal, and is always a controversy? When we are re-constructing the constituent body of the country, and completing its representation in this House, is it not the fitting occasion to make an effort, not merely to improve the registration, but to insure the registered vote being given in the simplest and safest manner we can devise? We propose, in the first place, that the number of polling places throughout the country shall be greatly increased. We propose that in every parish containing 200 electors there shall be a polling place. If a parish does not contain 200 electors, then it will form one of a group reaching that number, which will have a polling place. Every man who votes will vote at the place where he resides, wherever his qualification may be. To effect that object, there will not only be a qualification register, but a residence register. It may be said these additional polling places will be a great expense to candidates; but the Bill provides that candidates shall not bear the expense of them. If left to the candidate, the expense would be very heavy; if left to the county, it will be very little. Where there is a petty Sessions, there is generally a Police Station, or a room that may be hired; and there are provisions in the Bill which will satisfy hon. Gentlemen that this can be effected in a reasonably cheap manner. If a man chooses to vote as he always has voted, he may go to the polling place of his district and do so; but we propose also to allow the elector to vote, though he may not choose to go to the poll, that he may vote by what are called voting papers. This is not an experiment, or a thing adopted for the first time,—there is nothing empirical about it. For many years the people of this country have been familiar with it: in the election of Poor Law Guardians, the votes are taken by voting papers; the Metropolis Act, recently passed by the House, provides that the elections under it may be taken by voting papers. What is the result of giving this supplementary power to a constituency? Why, it renders the expression of public opinion more complete than under the existing system. Of the constituent body under the Poor Law Act, 90 per cent. records its votes; but, in the great electoral body of England called on to elect the representatives of the British people, and form this famous House of Parliament, that affects the opinions of the world, how is that high privilege treated? Not more than 50 or 60 per cent. of that constituency records its votes in the performance of that solemn duty. But it may be said, voting by papers may lead to personation; as if there was no personation now! In the history of man there never was any improvement proposed which the interests and passions of some would not distort; we believe the electors can vote by polling papers without personation, and in an honest and satisfactory manner. Sir, I shall always go myself to the hustings; but if a man wishes to vote for his Member by a voting paper, instead of going to the hustings, I see no objection to his being allowed to do so. All he will have to do is to write to the public officer and ask for a voting paper, the form of which will be found in the schedule of this Bill. A voting paper will be sent to him by the public officer in a registered letter; and, therefore, you will have evidence of its transmission. He will sign this paper in the presence of two witnesses, one of whom must be a householder, and then return it to the public officer, also in a registered letter. Thus we shall have evidence of its transmission both ways; and the paper will be opened before the proper authorities, and the man's vote will be duly rerecorded. I believe a vote given by this instrumentality may be honestly and properly given, and that there will be no more deception or personation practised under this machinery than under the open system which at present prevails. But lest there should be any personation, we provide against it by making it a misdemeanour under this Bill.

I have now placed before the House—much more briefly than I ought, perhaps, to have done, but they will pardon me if, in consequence of the largeness of the theme, I may omit some of the details which will be found in the Bill,—I have now placed before you the leading features of what we propose to do with the registration of the constituent body, and the method in which their votes shall be taken. I have next to touch upon a certainly not less important portion of my subject. In attempting to deal with the question popularly designated Parliamentary Reform, Her Majesty's Government have endeavoured, as far as their intelligence could guide them, to offer a proposition to the House which, consistently with their conception of the principles upon which the English constitution is founded, should secure for this country a complete representation. One of our first considerations was, of course, the electoral body, upon which I have treated at such length. But a complete representation does not depend merely upon the electoral body, however varied you may make its elements, however homogeneous its character. It also depends upon whether, in your system, the different interests of the country are adequately represented. Now, discarding for ever that principle of population upon which it has been my duty to make some remarks; accepting it as a truth that the function of this House is to represent not the views of a numerical majority—not merely the gross influence of a predominant property, but the varied interests of the country, we have felt that on this occasion it was incumbent on us diligently and even curiously to investigate the whole of England, and see whether there were interests not represented in this House whose views we should wish to be heard here; and whether the general representation of the country could be matured and completed. In undertaking this office, it must not be supposed that we have been animated by a feeling that we would only do that which the hard necessity of the case required. Had we been so influenced, it is possible we might have brought forward a measure that would have served the purpose of the moment, and yet left seeds behind us which might have germinated in future troubles, controversies, and anxieties. We have been sincerely desirous to adapt the scheme of 1832 to the England of 1859, and to induce the House to come to a general settlement, whether as regards the exercise of the franchise or the direct representation in this House of the various interests of the community which should take this question for a long period out of the agitating thoughts of men. We have sought to offer to the country, in the hope that it will meet with

173

its calm and serious approval, what we believe to be a just and—I will not say a final, but—conclusive settlement. Finality, Sir, is not the language of politics. But it is our duty to propose an arrangement which, as far as the circumstances of the age in which we live can influence our opinion, will be a conclusive settlement. And we have laid it down as our task to consider, without any respect to persons, what we honestly think are the interests of the country that are not represented, but which we should at this moment counsel the House to add to their numbers.

I venture to divide this branch of the subject into the cases where there is a want of representation, and those where a representation exists, but not an adequate one. We find both of these circumstances characteristic of the West Riding of Yorkshire and South Lancashire. There, there are distinct interests which are not represented in this House, and some also which are very inadequately represented. I mean by the term "inadequately represented," to say that there are several distinct interests, while the present Members are returned to this House by the predominant interest; the other interests, which are considerable enough to challenge and claim our consideration, being virtually unrepresented. We propose, therefore, to add to the representation of the West Riding of Yorkshire four Members. Here I will not speak of population or property, because we are not about to offer a proposition to the House formed merely upon population or property. In the West Riding we find a great territory seventy miles in length, which is purely agricultural. We find another great division studded with towns, none of them important enough, or having distinctive interests powerful enough to be represented, yet in their aggregate constituting a wonderful hive of industry and energy; and there is still another portion of the West Riding where there are blended and varied interests. We propose, therefore, to add four Members to the West Riding of Yorkshire, and to divide it, not according to a mathematical arrangement as to population, but according to its separate interests. This principle of division will be in accordance with the local demarcations of wapentakes. If property be the test, the property here is identical; for, however varied is the number of their population, the property of the wapentakes is as follows:—We propose that there should be a West Yorkshire, with a population of 472,000. That is the division in which you will find Keighley, Dewsbury, and a score of towns which you cannot summon here, but which, if you adopt these principles for your constituent body, would be voting for county Members; and therefore they ought to vote with the distinct interest with which they are connected. We propose that there shall be a North-West Yorkshire, with a population of 129,000, and a South Yorkshire, with one of 225,000. We propose these divisions, instead of an endless division and sub-division without names, which is little in harmony with our habits, and because these are the names which are used in the locality. With regard to the property of these divisions, varying as they do in interest and population, its amount is almost identical in each. In one of them the annual assessment to the county rate is £963,000, in another £809,000, and in the third £808,000. We propose to add two Members to South Lancashire—that is to say, we propose to distribute the county of Lancashire into three divisions. One will be the hundred of West Derby, and one the hundred of Salford. These divisions are the same as those proposed by the noble Lord the Member for London, except that one of the hundreds of North Lancashire was inserted in West Derby in his Bill, and it now remains with North Lancashire. This will be an addition of six to the number of county Members. There is another county to which we propose to add two Members—that is, the county of Middlesex—which we propose to divide. By dividing Middlesex, the claims of Kensington, and Chelsea, and Hammersmith, and other suburban districts, the claims of which have been urged in this House, will be provided for. They will form part of South Middlesex, while the distinctive interests of the other portion of the county, the northern division, will also be represented in this House. These are all the additions that we propose to make to the representation of the counties—eight Members.

It is now, Sir, my duty to call the attention of the House to those places which, because they possess distinct interests, which are not duly represented in this House, ought, in our opinion, to be represented here. The first place which, in our opinion, ought to be represented in the House of Commons is the town of Hartlepool and its immediate district. There is no place in England more distinguished by the energy of its inhabitants, its rapid progress, and the character of its industry. In North Durham there are four great towns which are represented, and there are two county Members; in South Durham there are two county Members and no town which is represented. I will not dwell on the population of Hartlepool; I will not rest the granting of a Member on that basis, though the population is very considerable—upwards of 30,000; but I rest it upon the rapid development of its considerable industry, and the very fact that at this moment its importation of foreign goods is larger than that even of Newcastle. We, therefore, propose that there should be a Member for Hartlepool. For the same reason that it is a place where the shipping and mercantile interest of the country are conspicuous, we are of opinion that Birkenhead ought to be represented. There is a part of Staffordshire which we think deserves and requires the consideration of this House. It is that district which is called "The Black Country," where an immense distinctive industry has arisen since the passing of the Reform Act; and we therefore propose that West Bromwich and Wednesbury shall return a Member to this House. I said that we had allotted only two additional Members to South Lancashire, because we thought that there were two towns in that county whose interests require to be represented in this House, and therefore we recommend that Members should be allotted to Burnley and Stalybridge. That will be five additional borough Members. Turning now to the South of England, we find a place in Surrey, which ought to be represented—namely, Croydon; and in the county of Kent we propose that a Member should be allotted to Gravesend—a very ancient town, with a distinctive character, and in every sense of the word, I think, entitled to a representative. Now, Sir, I will not say we have studied the map of England—we have done more than that; at this moment I declare that, if you are to complete the representative of England according to the principle which influences Her Majesty's Ministers—the principle that this House is to represent not the numerical majority, but the interests of the country—I do not see any other Member required to complete that representation; and I believe that if we have erred, we have erred rather by anticipating the destiny of what I believe, will in time be great and thriving communities.

Well, Sir, how are these fifteen Members to be supplied? That is the question. They are to be supplied in the spirit of the English constitution. Adopting a policy which has been recognized on previous occasions, and which for two centuries has been adopted by the Sovereigns and Parliaments of England—assuming in which I hope I am correct, that it is the opinion of this House that its Members ought not to be increased, we must find the means of representing these new interests as means have been found before under similar circumstances and in the same constitutional spirit. It is sometimes said that there are constituencies in this country so small that it is an indefensible anamely to permit them to exist. [Hear, hear!" and a laugh!] I entirely disagree with the Gentleman who cheered me. I do not think that better arguments can be urged in favour of a constituency of 1,000 than one of 500; and I should be very much surprised if the hon. Gentleman, ingenious as he may be, could urge them. There are, it is true, some constituencies which certainly cannot be defended if the numerical majority is to govern England; but there are some very small constituencies which may perform a very important part in the representation of the principles upon which the English constitution is founded, which are still upheld in this House and still revered in this country. I will take an instance. In all those rattling schemes of disfranchisement with which we were favoured during the autumn, when every Gentleman thought that he could sit down at his table and reconstruct the venerable fabric of the English constitution—if there was one point more than another on which those Utopian meddlers agreed—if there was one enemy which they were all resolved to hunt to death—it was the borough of Arundel. There every vice of the system seemed to be congregated—a small population, a small constituency, absolute nomination. Well, now, Sir, that is very well for autumnal agitation; but let us see how it practically works in this ancient and famous community in which it is our pride and privilege to live. There are 900,000 Roman Catholics in England, scattered and dispersed in every town and county,—of course a minority. What means have they of being represented in this House, especially in the present, as I deem it, unfortunate state of feeling in England with regard to our Roman Catholic fellow-subjects? There is one English Roman Catholic Member of Parliament, a man who bears a name that will ever be honoured by England and Englishmen: and practically, and in the spirit of the English constitution, the 900,000 Roman Catholics of England, men, many of them, of ancient lineage and vast possessions, whose feelings all must respect, even if they do not agree with them in every particular, find a representative in the borough of Arundel. That is the practical working of our constitution. You talk of the small numbers of the constituency of Arundel,—900,000 Roman Catholics! Why, it is more than the West Riding of Yorkshire; it is double the Tower Hamlets. Therefore, Sir, we are not to say, because a constituency small, that is the source from which we must inevitably

176

draw the constitutional means of completing the representation of England. The House will do me the justice of observing that by the measure which, on the part of the Government, I have placed before them to-night, whatever arrangements may be made with existing boroughs to find means of effecting the representation of interests not represented without increasing the numbers of this House, no man will be disfranchised. By adopting this principle of identity of suffrage, even if a man loses the Member who has represented his borough, he still may go to the poll or send his voting paper; and, under all circumstances, that is a compensation which was never offered in previous schemes of Parliamentary Reform. We do not feel it our duty to recommend to Parliament that any borough represented by a single Member, like Arundel, should lose that Member. We want, in order to complete the representation of the country fifteen seats in this House. To procure those seats we must fix upon some rule that must necessarily be arbitrary. The only condition that the House has a right to make, and which all should be glad to concede, is that that rule should be impartially applied. In the last Census, if you throw your eye over its Parliamentary results, you will find that there are fifteen boroughs represented by two Members each, and the population of which is under 6000. Only fifteen boroughs? It will be an admirable opportunity for a display of patriotism—an opportunity seldom offered by the circumstances and occasions of society—to the Members of those places. I have no personal feeling on this subject. I do most sincerely and ardently hope that when there is a new Parliament we may all meet again; but if these fifteen boroughs now represented by two Members each, though with a population under 6000, would consent, without our using force to compel them to make this concession, we should complete the representation of the country according to the principles that I believe to be those upon which our representation ought to rest. Therefore, Sir, in the Bill, which soon will be in the hands of Members, there are provisions that the fifteen boroughs in question shall in the next Parliament be represented by only one Member each. [Cries of "Name, name!"] The House, I am sure, will consider my feelings. I shall take care that every Gentleman, I hope to-morrow morning, will receive the schedule containing the name of these boroughs; but I see no necessity, while I think it would be invidious, to mention them now. [Cries of "No, no!" and "Name!"] I regret to be compelled to introduce personal details into this statement; but as the House insists upon it, I suppose I must read the names of the boroughs which, at present represented by two Members, are in future to return only one each. They are—Honiton, Thetford, Totness, Harwich, Evesham, Wells, Richmond, Marlborough, Leominster, Lymington, Ludlow, Andover, Knaresborough, Tewkesbury, and Maldon.

I have now, Sir, touched upon those topics which it was my duty to lay before the House this evening. I have omitted many things that I ought to have said, and I have no doubt I may have said some things that I ought to have omitted. Such errors are inevitable in treating so large and so various a theme, but I am sure the House will remember that there will be many opportunities for me to enter into necessary explanations, and will treat an occasion like the present with generous forbearance. Sir, having described as clearly as I could the principal provisions of our Bill to the House, I shall say no more. I believe that this is a measure wise, prudent, and adequate to the occasion. I earnestly hope the House may adopt it. I believe, Sir, it is a Conservative measure, using that epithet in no limited or partial sense, but in the highest and holiest interpretation of which it is capable. I can say sincerely that those who framed this measure are men who reverence the past, are proud of the present, but are confident of the future. Such as it is, I now submit it for the consideration of the House of Commons, convinced that they will deal with it as becomes the representatives of a wise and understanding people.

The right hon. Gentleman concluded by moving, That leave be given to bring in a Bill to amend the Laws relating to the Representation of the People in England and Wales, and to facilitate the Registration and Voting of Electors.

Spencer Horatio Walpole, 'Parliamentary Reform,
or the Three Bills and Mr Bright's Schedules'
The Quarterly Review, October 1859, pp. 541–562

Spencer Horatio Walpole, 'Reform Schemes'
The Quarterly Review, January 1860, pp. 220–266

After Eton and Trinity, Cambridge, Spencer Horatio Walpole (1806–1898) entered a career in the law, becoming a QC in 1846. The same year he became MP for Midhurst as a Protectionist. From 1856 he sat for Cambridge University. A strong Church-man, Walpole was a staunch defender of the claims and privileges of the Church of England. He spoke out forthrightly against removing Jewish disabilities in 1848, denounced 'Papal aggression' in 1851, opposed any traits he detected of Jesuitism and Catholic ritual, and opposed the admission of Dissenters to Oxford and Cam-bridge in 1854. Abandoning Protectionism in 1851, Walpole became Home Secre-tary in Derby's first ministry in 1852. He subsequently entertained hopes, encouraged by his wife, of being elected Speaker of the Commons. He blamed Disraeli for his failure to achieve this, encouraged by his wife's anti-Semitic smears. This rendered him a querulous and vehemently anti-Disraeli presence in Conservative counsels.

In 1858, after some persuasion, Walpole resumed the office of Home Secretary in Derby's cabinet. He gave active support to the abolition of property qualifica-tions for MPs, describing the requirement as a sham. But, as Derby's cabinet began discussion of their Reform bill, Walpole became deeply alarmed that a radical measure was being foisted on Derby by an unprincipled Disraeli. Wal-pole opposed the equalisation of the county and borough franchises, eradicating, he argued, a county vote based on property and a borough vote based on occu-pancy. In late December, Derby received 'a Chancery brief, 87 folios' written by Walpole objecting to the recommendations of the cabinet committee on Reform, particularly the equalisation of the borough and county franchises. Upon Derby reaffirming, in late January, the committee recommendations as the basis for their measure, Walpole informed the prime minister of his determination to resign.

During the Commons debate of the Second Reading of the Reform bill and Rus-sell's motion in March, Walpole, from the backbenches, gave a long speech. In the course of his statement, he reiterated his objection to equalisation of the franchise in counties and boroughs, eradicating the distinction between the two electorates. He could not support the Second Reading of the Reform bill in its present form, but hoped for suitable amendments in Committee, a settlement of Reform being necessary. He urged the ministry not to regard equalisation of the franchise as vital to their measure. In the event of Russell's motion being passed, he pressed the government to persevere with their bill, not to withdraw it, not to resign, and not to dissolve parliament. Walpole voted against Russell's motion, though he regarded it as unusual, but not irregular.

Walpole's two essays in the *Quarterly Review,* 'Parliamentary Reform, or the Three Bills and Mr Bright's Schedules' and 'Reform Schemes', surveyed the long historical experience and continued usage that produced the existing electoral system. The result was not the product of experimental innovation, *a priori* arguments, or abstract reason, but practical experience. Walpole then examined the Reform bills of 1852, 1854, and 1859; extension of the suffrage; the distribution of seats; electoral corruption; and the duration of parliaments. He deprecated the drawing of arbitrary lines in extending the vote, the disfranchisement of boroughs because they were small, and the redistribution of seats in proportion to numbers. 'Public opinion', he observed, was not in favour of extensive Reform. He regretted the tendency, since 1832, for MPs to regard themselves as representatives of their respective constituency, ambassadors from distinct communities, rather than as elected custodians of the national interest. The great question confronting parliament, Walpole concluded, was not what sort of Reform was likely to be passed by parliament, satisfy supporters, or conciliate critics, but what was right, wisest, and best.

7

SPENCER HORATIO WALPOLE, 'PARLIAMENTARY REFORM, OR THE THREE BILLS AND MR BRIGHT'S SCHEDULES'

The Quarterly Review, October 1859,
pp. 541–562

Art. IX.—1. *A Bill to extend the Right of Voting for Members of Parliament, and to amend the Laws relating to the Representation of the People in Parliament.* Prepared and brought in by Lord John Russell, Sir George Grey, and the Chancellor of the Exchequer (Sir Charles Wood), and ordered by the House of Commons to be printed, 12th February, 1852.

2. *A Bill further to amend the Law relating to the Representation of the People in England and Wales.* Prepared and brought in by Lord John Russell and Sir James Graham, and ordered by the House of Commons to be printed, 16th February, 1854.

3. *A Bill to amend the Laws relating to the Representation of the People in England and Wales, and to facilitate the Registration and Voting of Electors.* Prepared and brought in by the Chancellor of the Exchequer (Mr. Disraeli), Lord Stanley, and General Peel, and ordered by the House of Commons to be printed, 28th February, 1859.

4. *Information for Reformers respecting the Cities and Boroughs of the United Kingdom, Classified according to the Schedules of the Reform Bill proposed by John Bright, Esq., M.P.* Prepared, at the request of the London Parliamentary Committee, and also showing the Results of the Government Reform Bill, by Duncan Mc Cluer.

In his speech at Aberdeen, Lord John Russell assigned it as a reason for discussing the principles upon which a Reform Bill should be framed, that we were now in the autumnal time, free from the heat of the House of Commons' debates. It is, indeed, most desirable that the public should arrive at some definite conclusions upon this momentous question, and not leave it to be settled according to the accidental combinations and interests which may sway the House of Commons at the moment. If the good sense of the country is brought to bear upon the subject, we have no fear of the result. The danger is in the apathy which abandons legislation upon this vital topic to a few hundred persons, who will act according to their particular predilections and interests without any effectual control from the community. We cannot but think that the mere fact, that three such bills as those mentioned at the head of this article have been brought into Parliament, by three different Administrations, within the short period of nine years, should furnish food for grave and serious reflection. Nor will the gravity and seriousness of that reflection be at all diminished, rather, we should say, it will be immensely increased, by a careful consideration of the fourth document—the Information for Reformers—published under the authority of Mr. Bright.

A quarter of a century has scarcely passed away since the Reform Bill of 1832 became the law of the land. According to the opinions of those who framed it, the measure was both decisive and extensive in its character; more decisive and more extensive than it otherwise would have been, in order that it might rest, so far at least as its principles were concerned, on something like a permanent foundation. Lord Althorp, as the leader of the Government in the House of Commons, observed that, 'He had every reason to hope, from the satisfaction it had already given, that the change that they had proposed would be permanent;'[1] and he added on another occasion:—

'It appears to me that the good sense of the people of England will be satisfied when they see that the crying evil of the present system will be then got rid of, and that they will have their proper influence in the representation of the country. *I am sure that the people of this country are not so fickle as to give reason to apprehend that when they have no practical evil to complain of, they will still wish for change, for the sake of change itself.* It has been truly said that what this country requires is quiet, and a cessation from anxiety and agitation; and I consider this Bill as the most effectual means for attaining that object.'[2]

During the discussions which followed in the House of Lords, Lord Grey remarked:—

'It has been said that a measure of a more contracted nature than this would have satisfied the people. I doubt whether, in such a state of things, this could have been reasonably expected. It seemed to me that permanent contentment could only be produced by a decisive and extensive measure; and the object which the King's Government had in view was to produce such a settlement of this long-agitated question as might prevent its being brought into renewed discussion in those seasons of distress and difficulty when experience has shown that it has constantly revived, calling into action all the elements of political division and discontent. *It surely was desirable, if this question was to be entered into at all, it should be done in such a manner as to afford a hope that it might be effectually and permanently adjusted.*'

These opinions, thus strongly expressed, were the declarations of statesmen who had the good of their country at heart. They knew full well that this was the *first* and *only* time in the history of this country when an attempt was made to remodel and define our representative system by statutory enactment. They believed that the real justification for such an attempt was the existence of defects or the growth of abuses, clearly acknowledged and practically felt, which could only be remedied by actual legislation. They proceeded—as our forefathers have always proceeded—not by theorizing on the best form of government, but by making that which they thankfully enjoyed suitable to the wants and wishes of the community. Therefore they concluded, most wisely and most justly, that when they were dealing with a prescriptive Constitution, the grafting into it of any new and untried project must always be uncertain and often dangerous; that the policy of England has ever been to observe whether a practical evil exists, and, having applied a practical, not a fanciful remedy, to discourage that morbid and rest-less desire for change which indicates a state of feverish excitement rather than a sound and healthy condition. The declarations made by Lord Althorp and Earl Grey were plainly the result of some such reasoning as this; and, if they were alive, they would probably consider that the reopening of the question of Parlia-mentary Reform, except so far as it may at any time be necessary to redress some practical grievance, would be little less than a severe reflection on their want of foresight or their want of honesty: their want of foresight in not being able to frame a measure which would last beyond a quarter of a century—their want of honesty in not avowing the whole of their intentions, or not abiding by them when they were avowed. In saying this, we do no more than repeat what Lord John Russell has himself urged: for in his memorable Letter to the electors of Stroud, he announced to the country his mature conviction that if, after the declaration made by the heads of Lord Grey's Cabinet, any member of it were to propose to begin the whole question anew, the obvious remark would be, 'You have either so egregiously deceived us that we cannot trust to your public engagements, or you have so blindly deceived yourselves that we cannot believe in the solidity of your new scheme.'[3]

We refer to these facts not with the view of throwing out taunts or casting reproaches, but to recall to the recollection of our present statesmen the leading principles upon which alone they can venture to touch our representative system with prudence. There is need of this caution. With three Bills proposed by three different Administrations within the last decade—that is to say, from 1850 to 1860; with the prospect of a fourth from a fourth Administration before that decade is brought to a close; with various schemes propounded by others, especially those of Mr. Roebuck and Mr. Bright; with different principles embodied in each of them, some of which are positively at variance with, and some of which are altogether unknown to, the Constitution, not merely in its practice, but also in its theory; and with no demand for what is called Reform, which has yet assumed a tangible shape from any large section of the intelligent part of the community, we own we feel not a little apprehensive lest we should soon arrive at that state which Sir James Graham once described as the very worst in which Parliament could find itself—the state where everybody says that something must be done, but nobody knows what that something is to be. The fact is, that the moment Parliament shall really find itself in that condition, it can only be likened to those 'unhappy persons who live, if they can be said to live, in the statical chair—who are ever feeling their pulse, and who do not judge of health by the aptitude of the body to perform its functions, but by their ideas of what ought to be the true balance between the several secretions.'[4]

The healthy action, however, of the body politic, like the healthy action of the natural body, is not kept in order by such quackery as this. Our history is a remarkable one; and there is nothing for which it is more remarkable, than for the sound judgment and the resolute good sense with which the nation, as a whole, has always set to work to remove or to cure any positive malady that might disturb its functions. At the same time, it has never troubled itself with imaginary evils, nor sought to make itself speculatively better, when the result would probably only be to make itself practically worse. From the earliest times down to the present— from our Saxon institutions to the Great Charter, from the Great Charter to the Reformation, from the Reformation to the Revolution, from the Revolution to the Act of Settlement, from the Act of Settlement to the Reform Act—the two most significant features in our political annals unquestionably are—first, that whenever a movement has been made for the purpose of demanding a change in the laws, or, at least, in the administration of them, that movement has always been directed against some palpable wrong, some tangible grievance, some proved abuse; and secondly, that the demand for which this movement was commenced has always been urged in a Conservative spirit. So much has this been the case, that it has generally been confined to a declaration of rights which have been called in question, or to a restoration of rights which have been abused, or to an extension of right which, owing to new and accidental circumstances, a part of the community have ceased to enjoy. The plain reason for all this is that the constitution of England is a prescriptive constitution which has grown up with us, and adapted itself to our wants and wishes. It is not a constitution which has been made by Parliamentary enactment. It is not the creature of positive law, and never ought to be. It is based on long, constant, immemorial usage, which implies the choice, not of one day or of one set of people, but the choice of a nation; the deliberate choice of successive ages founded on reason, justified by experience, and confirmed by enjoyment. Any attempt to alter what may be called its primary and most essential characteristic would be fatal to its freedom as well as to its power. Experience, not experiment, has hitherto been our guide. May it never be said, by those at least who profess to be our rulers, that experiment, not experience, is hereafter to be our motto.

And yet there is some danger lest this should happen. In these days the House of Commons is too much regarded as a mere machine for making laws; whereas its original and principal functions were rather to see that the laws were observed than that the laws are changed; that is to say, to provide by means of the existing Institutions that the rights of the people should be steadily maintained, their interests protected, and their grievances redressed. As incident to these functions the House of Commons is a Legislative as well as a Representative body. But even the statutes which it makes in that character may be chiefly considered as the declaration of laws already existing when their requirements have been invaded, the expansion of those laws where the judicial power without the interposition of a higher authority would hesitate to extend them, and the adaptation of those laws to all the new wants and exigencies of society. It will generally be found that the correction of our laws has been confined to the instances in which the principles upon which they are established have either been perverted or misapplied. If any one will take the trouble to examine the huge volumes of Statutes which are issued yearly under the authority of Parliament he will soon discover that, with the exception of those Acts which empower the Crown to carry on the government of the country (and which cannot be passed until the House of Commons has had the opportunity of seeing that the wants of the people are attended to, and their grievances are redressed), the remainder are almost if not altogether employed in dealing with former Acts. The policy of this country ought clearly to be what it always has been in the best periods of our history, which is to look upon our institutions 'as the subjects of prudent and honest use, and thankful enjoyment, and not of captious criticism and rash experiment.' We should be slow to legislate until the necessity for it is clearly made out; and as soon as that necessity is established, we should be wise and circumspect in adapting the remedy to the malady to be cured.

There are very few occasions in which Parliament has thought it necessary to touch the constitution of the House of Commons; none whatever, until the Reform Act, in which it has been attempted on a large scale to remodel and define our representative system. On all such occasions there was almost invariably a substantial ground of complaint with reference to which some legislative action was required. On all such occasions also the Parliament acted, or at least professed to act, on the acknowledged principles of the Constitution. On none did it hunt after new experiments, such as dividing the country into electoral districts—apportioning the representatives among the constituencies according to mathematical or arithmetical calculations—basing the franchise on a personal right, or assuming that every one should be personally represented. What Parliament insisted on, was that its proceedings should not be unduly interrupted by the authority of the Crown; that the existence of the House of Commons should not be prolonged so as to make it independent of public opinion; that all classes and all interests should there have a voice; that as new classes and new interests sprang up, the same privileges should be conferred on them which had been enjoyed by others; that the preferable way of accomplishing this object was to have recourse to known communities which possess something like a common tie, rather than to the mere aggregation of numbers which have nothing to connect and bind them together; and that thus, by removing proved abuses or by supplying ascertained defects, 'the representative body should be the image of the represented,' not in the sense of making it the mere mirror of popular clamour, passion, or caprice, but in the sense that it should be an 'assembly united with the people by the closest sympathies.'[5] The design was that it should reflect not indeed every misty cloud that may pass over its disk, but the clear judgment and the matured opinions, the property and the industry, the virtues and the intelligence, of a free community.

Let us recall to our recollection for a few moments the only occasions in which Parliament has substantially interfered as regards its own functions or composition, and let us see how carefully it has adapted its remedies to the actual disorder or to the country's wants.

In the first place, when encroachments had been made by Edward I. for obtaining the 'aids, tasks, and prises given to him aforetime for his wars and other business,' Parliament felt that it was necessary to prevent such encroachments from growing into a custom or 'bondage' to the people. Wherefore, in his celebrated confirmation of the Charter, which he made in the 21st year of his reign, he granted for himself and for his heirs 'that for no business from thenceforth would they take such aids, tasks, and prises, but *by the common consent of all the realm* and *for the common profit thereof,*' saving the ancient aids and prises due and accustomed. This was simply a declaration of rights coeval with the Constitution.

In the next place, when the proceedings of Parliament were inconveniently interrupted by the neglect of the Crown to convene the two Houses, it was enacted first in the reign of Edward II.,[6] that 'forasmuch as many people be aggrieved by the King's ministers against right, in respect of which grievance no one can recover without a common Parliament,' and secondly, in the reign of Edward III.,[7] that 'for the redress of divers mischiefs and inconveniences which *daily* happened,' Parliament should be holden every year once, and 'oftener, if need be.' This was simply the taking security against an actual abuse. It required that Parliaments should be frequently held, not that the House of Commons should be frequently chosen.

The next instance is a very remarkable one, for it is the only case in which Parliament has put a limit on the County franchise. Down to the year A.D. 1429, the elections for counties were made *in pleno comitatu,* that is to say, in the presence and with the concurrence of all men of free condition who owed suit and service in the County Court.[8] But vast confusion is said to have occurred: for it was found, according to the recital in the 8 Hen. VI., c. 27, that the elections were made by very great, outrageous, and excessive number of people, of which the most part was of small substance or of no value, whereby manslaughter, riots, batteries, and divisions among the gentlemen and other people of the same county were very likely to arise. Therefore it was enacted[9] that the knights of the shire should be chosen by people dwelling and resident in the same counties, whereof every one of them shall have free land or tenement, to the value of forty shillings by the year at the least, above all charges.

There is no other example of any importance in which Parliament interfered by legislative acts with reference to itself until we arrive at the end of the reign of Charles I. The old statute of Edward III. had fallen into desuetude during the wars of the Roses, and it had not been acted upon in the reign of the Tudors. There were long intermissions in the meetings of Parliament; 'the mischiefs and inconveniences' which had been apprehended 'daily happened.' Wherefore, in the reign of Charles I., provision was made for convening Parliament at least once in every three years; and though that statute was repealed after the Restoration at the special request of the King, yet, in the great declaration of our rights, it was specified as one that, 'for the redress of all grievances, and for the amending, strengthening, and preserving of the laws, Parliament ought to be held frequently.'

The next occasion on which Parliament legislated with respect to itself was to limit the duration of its own existence. When once chosen under any king's writs, it was in reality chosen for the life of that king, unless he should think fit to put an end to it by dissolution. One Parliament had been convened for eleven years in the reign of Elizabeth, another for seventeen years in the reign of Charles II. This evil was strongly felt, for the representatives were placed by the security of a long but still uncertain tenure beyond the reach of that public opinion which alone could control it, and within the influence of the only power upon which it depended for its vital breath. Hence it was that the Triennial Bill became the law of the land in 1694; but it was soon found that the shortness of the period increased the animosity and expenses of elections, and weakened the authority of Parliament itself. There was imminent danger, too, at a particular crisis of our history, that the ordinary Triennial dissolution would be taken advantage of by the adherents of the Pretender to throw the country into confusion, and endanger at once our English constitution and our Protestant faith. Therefore the Septennial Act was passed. According to the opinion of Mr. Speaker Onslow (no mean judge in such matters as these), 'The passing of the Septennial Bill formed the era of the emancipation of the House of Commons from dependence on the Crown and the House of Lords.'

The next instance in which Parliament interfered with reference to the condition of its members, was to introduce what may be called a novelty in the Constitution—the requirement that the English representatives should possess an estate of specified value. It is true, indeed, that, in the encroaching times of Henry V. and Henry VI., residence, property, and gentle birth were attempted to be made the conditions for membership, at least in the counties. But the feeling of the country was so much opposed to this kind of restriction, that it does not appear to have ever been acted on; and with regard to one of those statutes, it was judicially determined,[10] in 1681, that 'little regard was to be had to it, because the common practice of the kingdom had been ever since to the contrary.' In the 9th of Queen Anne, however, under the pretence of 'securing the freedom of Parliament,' and the independence of its members, but really for the purpose of checking the efforts of the commercial classes to raise themselves into an equality with the territorial aristocracy,[11] a landed qualification of 600*l.* a-year in counties, and 300*l.* a-year in boroughs, was for the first time required. A qualification arising out of personal property,[12] as well as a qualification out of landed estates, was afterwards allowed, but both were repealed, and the old law was restored in 1858.

These are the only important instances in which Parliament has interfered by legislative action, either as regards its own functions or composition, up to the time of the Reform Act. And what is the inference to be drawn from this? Is it not that our Government, as a Representative Government, was complete in its theory from its very inception, and that all our efforts have been always directed to make the practice and the theory accord? This completeness it owed to the fact that the

Constitution was a prescriptive Constitution, and had grown out of 'the peculiar circumstances, occasions, tempers, dispositions, and moral, civil, and social habitudes of the people, which declare themselves only in a long space of time. It was a vestment which had accommodated itself to the body.' Such is the language of Edmund Burke. We doubt much whether a vestment taken from any other country, even from our Anglo-Saxon brethren on the other side of the Atlantic, would be so well suited to the English frame, or the peculiar requirements of our political atmosphere. Let them enjoy their institutions, while we enjoy ours. The best parts of their laws they derive from ourselves, and where they deviate we question the improvement.

But when we say that the English Constitution was complete in its inception, and that this was owing to the fortunate circumstance that it was a prescriptive, and not a written Constitution, and that it is, therefore, a vestment which has accommodated itself to the principal requirements of the body politic, we are aware that we are entering more or less into the field of controversy. The controversy, however, is not so much with those great Statesmen who, in all the improvements made in our laws, have endeavoured to keep up a connexion with the past, by basing alterations on former experience and traditional associations, as with that new party which is fond of going to the other side of the Atlantic for their notions of Government and Representative Institutions. By exaggerating the faults and depreciating the advantages of everything they possess, and by magnifying the merits and glossing over the defects of that which they only see at a distance, they draw a comparison to the detriment of the one, and in favour of the other. And yet this new party is too often confounded with those from whom we are entitled to look for better things, merely because they happen to sit on the same side of the House, and assume for themselves the common name of Liberals. The difference, however, between those who call themselves by that name is really enormous. Mr. Disraeli, with great justice, described the House of Commons as now made up of two classes of Reformers. The one, he said, consisted of those who would adapt the Constitution of 1832 to the England of 1859, and would act in the spirit and according to the genius of the existing Institutions. The 'other considered that the chief, if not the sole object of representation was to realize the opinion of the majority.' Their standard, he added, is population. It is necessary to keep this distinction in mind; for it would be absurd to include and confound two classes of politicians in the same category, merely because they choose to adopt a common name, and appear to unfurl a common banner.

Whatever may have been our opinion of the Reform Act at the time it was proposed, one thing is certain, that the authors of that measure supposed they were acting according to the acknowledged principles of the Constitution. This was the view of the old class of reformers. Whether they were justified in that supposition by the measure itself, or whether they succeeded in settling the question of parliamentary reform, either permanently or satisfactorily, we still take leave to doubt. But we cannot deny to them the high merit of avowing, boldly and distinctly, the only sound principles upon which they could act; nor shall we be slow to give them credit for the manner in which, by adhering to those principles, they endeavoured to make the practice of our Constitution accord better with its original theory.

Undoubtedly owing to time and accidents the constitution of the House of Commons had declined from its original foundation, and therefore it demanded both propping and repair. In the first place, according to the true theory upon which the Constitution was framed, every part of the country with a definite community of interest was entitled to be heard in the great council of the nation; and in the second place, every person of free condition who contributed directly either to the burdens of the State, or to those of the place in which he dwelt, was entitled to have a voice in choosing the Member whom he wished to represent him. There can hardly be a question that this was the fact; for as soon as Parliament assumed its present shape the writs of the Crown required two knights to be returned for each county or shire, and two burgesses for every city or borough within the same. There was therefore, at that time, no part of the country which had a known community of interests without its representative. At the same time also there was no man of free condition without his vote, if he contributed any thing to the direct burdens either of the State or of the place in which he dwelt. In the counties the knights were elected down to the reign of Henry VI. by all the freeholders who did suit and service in the county courts, without regard to their holding by military or soccage tenure, and without reference to their being or not being immediate tenants of the Crown.[13] In the towns and boroughs not only did the freeholder, the burgage tenant, and the member of the corporation possess the electoral franchise, but every person who became a resident householder in a borough, and was capable of paying scot (*i. e.* his share of local taxation), and of bearing lot (*i. e.* of discharging in turn the local offices),[14] was sworn and enrolled at the borough leet and became a burgess. In both these respects the original building had swerved from its perpendicular.

With respect to the places entitled to representation, the sheriffs, either from negligence or partiality, had omitted towns that had previously received writs; and the Crown, out of gratitude for services rendered, or to obtain dependants in the House of Commons, created new boroughs without regard to their wealth or importance. The first of these evils ceased with the Tudors; for none of the cities and towns which returned members at the accession of Henry VIII. intermitted their privilege down to 1832; and in the reigns of James and Charles I. thirty-six places which had lost their privilege had the right restored to them. But the second evil had greatly increased by an undue addition to the smaller boroughs, while no counteracting remedy was offered by any attempt to include the larger towns. From the reign of Henry VIII. to the accession of Charles I. the House of Commons received an addition of 156 members. In Cornwall alone twelve members were added by Edward VI., four by Mary, and ten by Elizabeth. The last occasion on which the Crown thus exerted its prerogative was in the reign of Charles II. Had it only been possible to renew its exercise by depriving those places which had fallen into decay of the right to return members, while it transferred that right to the flourishing communities which had since sprung up, the reason alleged for a great portion of the Reform Act would never have arisen.

Next as to the franchise. If other kinds of property (besides the freehold) which was the subject of local as well as imperial taxation, had not been subsequently brought into existence, the county franchise might reasonably have rested on its original basis. But that was not so. Copyholders and leaseholders had acquired substantial rights of property which were not recognised or even known in the earlier periods of our history. In the cities, towns, and boroughs, the corporations themselves, as well as the Crown, had made encroachments on the electoral franchise by limiting it in such a manner as to answer better their own ends than the public good. The corporations, acting by their corporate seal, and as an aggregate body, monopolized authority wherever they could, retained that authority among a small number of persons, and exercised the power of selecting burgesses from those who were non-residents, often to the exclusion of the great body of the inhabitants who had property in the place. The Crown at the same time began to grant Charters of Incorporation, with clauses[15] which gave exclusive powers to certain officers or to certain select bodies. Thus the electoral as well as the municipal system had widely declined in most of our boroughs from its original state; and it cannot be doubted that the restoration of its primitive characteristics, at the time of the Reform Act, was one of the main objects contemplated by its authors. This is clear, both from the preamble of the Statute, and from the language which the King himself was recommended to use in his speech from the throne.

Now, however much politicians or parties may be inclined to differ with reference to the Act, either as regards its necessity or expediency, or as regards the particular mode in which the intentions of its authors were reduced into practice, no one can entertain a moment's doubt as to what their objects were, nor can he disapprove of the avowed principles upon which it was sought to carry them into effect. There was a practical grievance and an actual injustice. The practical grievance was the non-representation of those large manufacturing and commercial towns, which had grown into a mighty existence since the Crown had exercised the power of creating any new boroughs. The actual injustice was the exclusion of many persons from the exercise of the franchise who by their position, intelligence, and independence were justly entitled to it; and this wrong was occasioned either by the encroachments made through the close corporations and Royal Charters, or by the omission to extend the privilege to those new kinds of property which had become as important in the course of time as the original freehold. To remedy the practical grievance forty-two new boroughs were created, twenty-two of which return two members and ten return one member each, including in the country at large such places as Manchester, Leeds, Birmingham, Sheffield, Sunderland, Wolverhampton, Devonport, Bolton, Bradford, Blackburn, Halifax, Stroud, Macclesfield, Oldham, Stockport, Stoke-upon-Trent, Ashton-under-Lyne, Bury, Dudley, Frome, Gateshead, Huddersfield, Whitehaven, Whitby; and in the metropolis and its adjacent districts Marylebone, Lambeth, Finsbury, Greenwich, and the Tower Hamlets. In addition to this, and partly as a counterpoise to the large influence which was thus acquired by the town constituencies, the county members were increased from 95 to 159. To remedy the actual injustice, copyholders and leaseholders, with specified interests, were admitted for the first time to the county franchise, while the occupation of a house and premises of 10*l.* annual value, with other conditions as to registry, residence, and the payment of rates and assessed taxes, was made to constitute the main foundation upon which the borough franchise has since rested.

It can hardly be denied, in point of principle, that this was a restoration rather than an alteration of our representative system. But, without renewing those fierce controversies which naturally took place in the discussion of such a measure, it may be questioned whether this principle was carried into operation in the manner which was best calculated to bring the theory and practice of the Constitution into harmony with each other. It may be questioned, for example, whether it would not have been wiser, both in the creation of new, and in the extension of the area of the old boroughs, to make them identical with some distinct community of interest; so that their members should have been the representatives of known societies, where the inhabitants were bound and connected together by something like a common tie, instead of being what they are now in too many instances—the representatives of a population rather than the representatives of a people. Had this been done, we should not have heard that nonsense talked at public meetings which ignorantly assumes that the mere aggregation of numbers is the people, or that the people is the particular assemblage which the orator addresses, or that the people can mean anything else than the whole collective body of the nation in its fullest sense, or, in its more limited sense, those communities within the nation which are allied to each other by an agreement of laws or a communion of interests. 'Res publica—res populi. Populus autem non omnis hominum cœtus quoquo modo congregatus, sed cœtus multitudinis juris consensu atque utilitatis communione sociatus.'[16] In this sense, but in no other, can we justly talk of the people of England—the people of Huddersfield, the people of Manchester, the people of Yorkshire, or the people of Kent. It may also be questioned whether it would not have been wiser, in settling the franchise, to place it on a foundation more certain, more varied, and, we will add, more durable than a 10*l.* occupation value. For what is a 10*l.* occupation value? It represents a totally different class of persons in different parts of the country. It is one thing in one place, and another thing in another. It furnishes no reason why one man should have a vote when he is just able to reach the mark, while his next door neighbour is not to enjoy it because the supposed value of his tenement falls below that mark by a few shillings. Neither does such a franchise, in spite of its inequalities, provide that variety of qualifications which is necessary to satisfy the variety of interests that have since grown up and become a part of our social system. Lord John Russell himself admitted in 1852 the force of the last objection. 'By taking,' he said, 'an uniform 10*l.* value franchise in 1832, and by abolishing all those intricate franchises which then existed, Lord Grey's Government' (he ought to have said Lord Grey's Administration, for it was the King's Government, and not Lord Grey's) 'confined themselves too much to one species of franchise and did not make it sufficiently various, and therefore it was not sufficiently comprehensive.'

It is clear, then, that, in the minds of our ablest statesmen, the word Reform, down to the time when the Reform Act was passed, has never meant the demolition of one system and the reconstruction of another. With them it meant the continuance of a system which experience and reason had equally approved of, and which

191

only required reparation, expansion, and adaptation, that it might comprehend the old as well as the new requirements of a growing community. They may have been wrong in their mode of action, but we have already pointed out that in the principle of action they were undoubtedly right, and had nothing in common with those who are now confounded with them under the same name of Reformers or Liberals. The distinction was palpable. Sir Robert Peel and the Conservatives had wisely acquiesced in the Settlement of 1832. Lord John Russell and the Whigs with equal wisdom had determined to abide by it. Both indeed would be willing to rectify any actual grievance; but as the settlement had been recently made, both would be slow to disturb it hastily, and both would refuse to change the basis upon which our Constitutional and Representative System has always rested. But with the new party which has now risen up everything is to be treated in a different manner. The spirit of change seems to have taken such possession of their minds that the more sweeping it is, the better the Reform; the wilder the promises, the greater the Liberal. According to them the experience of the past is to be set aside—our connection with the past is to be severed, and we are to begin our history as it were *de novo*. Or if we are to refer to any previous period, it is for the purpose of holding up that Constitutional system, which has certainly blended authority and liberty more effectually than any State either ancient or modern, as little less than a gigantic fraud raised and fostered for the benefit of the few at the expense of the many. Hence, as an improvement forsooth, we are to have, instead of the present system, a redistribution of seats; a creation of constituencies which may or may not have any community of interest; an apportionment of Members among those constituencies by an arithmetical calculation; an extension of the franchise upon no intelligible principle, except the principle of mere numbers; such an alteration in the mode of voting as will neither enable us to detect fraud, nor ensure responsibility; and such a limitation of the duration of Parliament, as would probably destroy its authority and efficiency. The germ of these propositions was authentically recorded in the Journals of the House of Commons, when Mr. Hume submitted to it the following motion on the 5th of June, 1849: 'That leave be given to bring in a Bill to amend the national representation, by extending the elective franchise so as to include all householders; by enacting that votes shall be taken by ballot; that the duration of Parliament shall not exceed three years; and that the appointment of Representatives be rendered more equal to the population.'[17] The growth of these propositions is more fully developed in a series of resolutions passed by the Committees of Parliamentary Reformers at the King's Arms Tavern, Palace Yard, with Mr. Roebuck in the chair;[18] and the application of these propositions, or at least of one of them, is manifested in those extraordinary 'schedules of the Reform Bill proposed by John Bright, Esq., M.P., and prepared at the request of the London Parliamentary Reform Committee.' According to this plan, twenty-three places are to return three members each, for no earthly reason except that they possess a few hundred inhabitants more than some others; thirteen places, namely, London, Sheffield, Bristol, Edinburgh, Leeds, Southwark, Birmingham, Westminster, Lambeth, Dublin, Tower Hamlets Division A! and Tower Hamlets Division B!! are to return four Members each, as if they were all equal in wealth and importance; while five places, namely, Manchester, Finsbury, Glasgow, Marylebone, and Liverpool, are to be so much regarded as the cream of all the constituencies in the kingdom, that no less than six Members are to be allotted to each of them! Can Mr. Bright be really serious when he submits to the country propositions like these?

In such a state of things, it might be thought that the course to be taken by our parliamentary leaders was plain and simple. Mr. Hume's motion had divided the House upon this subject into two classes—those who sought to build up for themselves a representative system on an entirely new model, and those who were resolved to adhere to the existing system, but were willing at the same time to correct any errors in it, supply deficiencies, and remedy abuses. The former proceeded upon mere theory, partly founded on inventions of their own, and partly drawn from the other side of the Atlantic. The latter insisted on past experience, historical proofs, and constitutional practice. The former were a small, compact, and active body, but they did not include more than four men of any parliamentary note—Mr. Hume, Mr. Roebuck, Mr. Bright, and Mr. Cobden. The latter were much more numerous, and were certainly not inferior to them in political knowledge and public virtue. They comprehended, in fact, the first men of the day; but as they came out of two rival camps, arrayed and marshalled each against each on other questions, and struggling for power, they had upon this subject no bond of union which could keep them together beyond a division or two. The small but active party persevered in its attack, while it was ready to accept as much as it could get from either of the others. The others, for fear of losing popularity in their race for power, began to consider how far they could go without compromising their credit. To this cause we must trace the three bills at the head of this article. To the same cause, also, we may trace their failure. The framers of these measures knew full well that they did not intend to concede to this new and, we must call it, this revolutionary party, the only demands which it really cares for. At the same time, we grieve to say events had brought things to that pass that they could not afford to lose its support. That party, therefore, is apparently in the ascendant: it has gained for a time this advantageous position, that it can accept anything by way of instalment, but it will accept nothing by way of settlement. And thus we have reached the wretched state of things so graphically described by Sir James Graham as the very worst in which Parliament can find itself, namely, the state where every body says that something must be done, but nobody knows what that something is to be.

Under such circumstances there is only one way by which Parliament can extricate itself from its present difficulties, and that is, carefully to consider what ought to be admitted according to established principles, and steadily to resist any other demand. If there be a grievance, let it be redressed; if there be an injustice, let it be remedied; if there be a want, let it be supplied. But make no assumptions. The moment it is assumed, for instance, that seats should be distributed according to number, or that a man should have a vote because he is of full age, irrespective altogether of other considerations, these positions must necessarily carry with them electoral districts and universal suffrage. Nobody who reflects can doubt this for a moment. And yet it is almost demonstrable that ideas of this kind have largely influenced the framers of the three Bills at the head of our article, and they must have been uppermost in the thoughts of Mr. Bright when he prepared his Schedules. Let us only take a few examples. In the first of these bills several places were added to boroughs, with which they have no connexion whatever, merely for the purpose, as far as we can judge, of increasing the constituencies.[19] In the second of these Bills nineteen boroughs were altogether disfranchised, and thirty-three boroughs were deprived of one member, principally with the view of adding a *third* representative to certain counties and divisions of counties, and to such towns as Birmingham, Bristol, Bradford, Leeds, Liverpool, Manchester, Sheffield, and Wolverhampton. But the framers of that Bill seemed so conscious of the objections that must have been instantly taken to such a proposition, that, according to another clause, no one was to vote for more than two candidates in any of these places. In the third of these Bills, among much that was sound, there was an unfortunate attempt to add to the number of county electors, by assimilating the county and the borough franchises, there was the strange creation of a variety of franchises, some of them nicknamed not inaptly as fancy franchises, and all of them unconnected with the places in which they would have to be exercised, except by a miserable twelvemonths' residence. There was also an entire alteration of all the old franchises, by not deducting from the value of the property composing the franchise the annual charges which rested upon it; so that the elector might have had any or no interest at the time when he registered or exercised his vote. Now no one can look at the foregoing propositions in any of these Bills, without concluding that even our best and ablest Statesmen are too much carried away by mere statistics and arithmetical calculations, when they begin to touch and try to reduce within the plausible symmetry of positive law, the varied requirements and the numberless complexities of a moral, social, and political system. If we turn to the schedules of Mr. Bright, we cannot discover that he is guided by any higher consideration than the mere standard of population; for though he gives us the comparative income supposed to be enjoyed by the inhabitants of each borough, as well as the direct taxes payable by them, we are at a loss to perceive upon what principle he proceeds, except upon the principle of proportionate numbers. It is impossible to comprehend why eighty-six places are disfranchised altogether, and why twenty-three places are to have three representatives, twelve places four, and five places six, unless he takes the standard of population as his rule or measure. The disfranchising line seems to be a population of 8000; the privileged lines apparently include for three members a population of more than 54,000 (why 54?), and less than 120,000; for four members, a population of more than 120,000, and less than 300,000, and for six members a population of 300,000 and upwards. What is all this but making constitutions for a moral, social, and intellectual being like man, not by reference to all those agencies, habitudes, and associations, by which such a being must necessarily be governed, but rather by reference to the first four rules in arithmetic, with a partial smattering in the rules of proportion?

194

But it will be said, If you thus find fault with others, what do you recommend your-selves? It is easy to criticise, difficult to prescribe. Will you have any or no changes? If you have any, what are they to be? If none, how will you redeem the pledges given, not by individuals, but by Parliament itself, that this is a subject which must be taken into immediate consideration? The appeal is a fair one, and we will fairly reply to it.

We think it is now too late to refuse to entertain the question. It might have been wiser not to have re-opened it. But four Administrations have advised the Queen to recommend from the throne the further consideration of it. Lord John Russell began this course in 1852; Lord Aberdeen continued it in 1854; Lord Palmerston acquiesced in 1857; and Lord Derby, feeling the immense inconvenience of leav-ing such a subject dangling in the air, endeavoured to bring it to a direct decision in 1859. On these occasions the recommendation from the Throne has always been agreed to without amendment. The Queen is pledged; Parliament is pledged; every party in the State is pledged. But to what are they pledged? The answer is on record. In 1852 they were pledged calmly to consider 'whether it may not be advisable to make such amendments in the Act of the late reign relating to the Representation of the Commons in Parliament, *as may be deemed calculated to carry into more complete effect the principles upon which that law is founded.*'[20] In 1854 they were pledged to nearly the same effect, 'and they thanked Her Maj-esty,' at the same time, for assuring Parliament 'that, in recommending the subject of Reform to their consideration, her desire was to *remove every cause of just complaint, to increase general confidence in the Legislature, and to give addi-tional stability to the settled institutions of the State.*'[21] In 1857 they were pledged 'to direct their earnest attention to the laws which regulate the representation of the people in Parliament,[22] *with a view to consider what amendments may be safely and beneficially made therein.*' And in 1859 they were pledged to give to this great subject 'that degree of calm and impartial consideration which is pro-portionate to the magnitude of the interests involved in the result of their discus-sions.'[23] The pledges thus given are therefore general and specific: general, as to the necessity of considering the subject with a view to such safe and beneficial amendments as may be made in the Reform Act; specific, as to the duty of main-taining and promoting the *principles* of the Act. 1st, by removing every just cause of complaint; 2nd, by increasing general confidence in the Legislature; and 3rd, by giving additional stability to the settled institutions of the State. These are the tests by which any measure must properly be tried.

If these tests are applied to the demands made for Parliamentary Reform by those who have renewed the agitation on this subject, it will at once be seen that they are totally at variance with their schemes. Their demands are the nearest approximation to manhood suffrage which circumstances will admit; a redistribution of seats, so as to bring the places to be represented and the members who shall represent them in closer proportion relatively to each other; the substitution of secret for an open system of voting, and of triennial for septennial Parliaments. Can any one pretend that the refusal of these demands constitutes with the working and intelligent part of the community a just cause of complaint? Will any one assert that the concession of these demands would really increase general confidence in the Legislature? Does any one believe that such a concession would give additional stability to the settled institutions of the State? The idea is preposterous. But if we put these demands into a different shape, it may be reasonable to consider—1st, whether there are not some classes of persons and some kinds of property to which the franchise may properly be extended; 2nd, whether there are still any unrepresented places to which representation might advantageously be given; 3rd, whether the present system of voting may not be improved, so as to ensure as much as possible its freedom, without intimidation and without corruption; 4th, whether the existing duration of Parliament is upon the whole the best which can be devised; and 5th, as a corollary from these propositions, whether the supposed advantages to accrue from a change would or would not in all or any of them be more than counterbalanced by the inconveniences attending it? These questions we propose to discuss fully and frankly in our next Number. When the time for the assembling of Parliament approaches, the details of the question are likely to receive more attention than at present; and if our Statesmen will only agree that this vital subject shall not be made the mere battlefield for Place and Power, we believe that a fair adjustment may be contrived which will satisfy nearly all persons—high and low, rich and poor—who really desire on the one hand to remove practical grievances, and on the other to resist wild and purposeless changes, which hold out no prospect of good, and may inflict an enormous amount of evil.

Notes

1 Parliamentary Debate, Sept. 21, 1831.
2 Ibid., March 19, 1832.
3 See the Letter, p. 27.
4 Burke.
5 Mr. Pitt's phrase.
6 5 Edward II. c. 29.
7 4 Edward III. c. 14.
8 This has been sometimes doubted, but see Hallam's 'Middle Ages,' vol. iii., pp. 22, 29. The better opinion is that stated in the text.
9 8 Henry VI. c. 7.
10 Onslow *v.* Ripley, King's Bench.
11 See Hallam, vol. iii. p. 402.
12 1 and 2 Vict. c. 48.
13 See Creasy's little work on the 'Rise and Progress of the Constitution,' p. 193.
14 Creasy, p. 261.
15 See Creasy, p. 263.
16 Cicero de Republicâ, lib. i., c. xxv.
17 Hansard, vol. cv., 3rd Series, p. 1171.
18 The following statement was issued by the Committee of Parliamentary Reformers:—

> 'Fellow-countrymen,—We, whose names are hereunto subscribed, disclaiming all right or desire to dictate, but anxious to elicit a definite expression of your will, and waiving abstract rights, recommend you to insist upon the following leading features of Parliamentary Reform, as calculated to unite in

support of them the largest number of voices, as capable of being attained by resolute and united efforts, and as promising, if adopted, to secure a real and effective representation of your political interests:

1. The extension of the borough franchise in England and Wales to every male person of full age, and not subject to any legal incapacity, who shall occupy as owner or tenant in part or whole any premises within the borough which are rated to the relief of the poor.
2. The extension of the county franchise in England and Wales to all 10*l.* occupiers at least; and the assimilation, as far as possible, of the franchise in Scotland and Ireland to those of England and Wales.
3. Protection to the voter by the ballot on a plan similar to that adopted in the Australian colonies.
4. A reappointment of seats, that shall make such an approach to an equalisation of constituencies as shall give in the United Kingdom a majority of members to a majority of electors.
5. Abolition of property qualification for members.
6. The calling of a new parliament every three years.

Fellow-countrymen,—If this broad outline of parliamentary reform meets your view—if, in your judgment, it is adapted to the occasion—*if it comprehends as much as you can hope to get, and as little as you could be satisfied to accept*—it is for you to say so, and to say so in time. This business is yours, and if you wish it done you must do it yourselves. On our part we are ready to aid you, as best we may, in placing this sketch of reform, properly filled in, upon the statute book of the realm.'

19 See Section 18 and Schedule B, and the maps which accompanied that Bill.
20 Hansard, 3rd Series, vol. cxix., p. 75.
21 Ibid., vol. cxxx., pp. 114–118.
22 Ibid., vol. cxlviii., p. 98.
23 Hansard, 3rd Series, vol. clii., p. 67.

8

SPENCER HORATIO WALPOLE, 'REFORM SCHEDULES'

The Quarterly Review, January 1860, pp. 220–266

ART. VII.—1. *A Bill to extend the Right of Voting for Members of Parliament, and to amend the Laws relating to the Representation of the People in Parliament*. Prepared and brought in by Lord John Russell, Sir G. Grey, and the Chancellor of the Exchequer (Sir C. Wood), and ordered by the House of Commons to be printed, 12th February, 1852.

2. *A Bill further to amend the Law relating to the Representation of the People in England and Wales*. Prepared and brought in by Lord J. Russell and Sir J. Graham, and ordered by the House of Commons to be printed, 16th February, 1854.

3. *A Bill to amend the Laws relating to the Representation of the People in England and Wales, and to facilitate the Registration and Voting of Electors.* Prepared and brought in by the Chancellor of the Exchequer (Mr. Disraeli), Lord Stanley, and General Peel, and ordered by the House of Commons to be printed, 28th February, 1859.

4. *Information for Reformers respecting the Cities and Boroughs of the United Kingdom, Classified according to the Schedules of the Reform Bill proposed by John Bright, Esq., M.P.* Prepared, at the request of the London Parliamentary Committee, and also showing the Results of the Government Reform Bill, by Duncan McCluer.

It was once observed by that remarkable man whose sad and almost sudden loss the whole country has had so recently to deplore,[1] that history, when we look at it in small fragments, may prove anything or nothing; but that it is full of useful and precious instructions when we contemplate it in large portions, or rather when we take in at one view the whole lifetime of great societies. This observation is so just, and yet at the same time it is so little regarded, that in our last number we thought it advisable to bring into one continuous review all the instances in which Parliament has interfered by legislative action either with reference to its own functions, or as regards its own composition. At the same time the reasons which led to that interference, and the principles which guided it when any change was introduced, were stated and explained. Moreover, we endeavoured to fix in our own minds, as well as to make present to the minds of others, 'the whole lifetime of the great society' in which we are living, before we would break up or even propose any material alteration in that very remarkable but prescriptive form of government, which, according to the remark of a distinguished American, made to Lord John Russell on the eve of his proposing the Reform Bill, has lasted so long and has been so strong.[2] It is indisputably clear from that review that our ablest statesmen, whenever they suggested any material changes in the constitution of the State, have declined to proceed upon mere theories of their own. They have always required, in justification of such changes, the plain proof of some actual grievance, some tangible abuse, some practical injustice, to which they might apply an actual, tangible, or practical remedy. As soon as they ascertained that a remedy was needed, they never failed, at least in intention, carefully to adapt it to the malady to be cured. We scarcely know of a single instance in which they have had recourse to innovating experiments or crude empiricism.

To ignore the past; to speculate on the future; to act on mere theory, however ingenious; or to import any novelties which may work well in other Institutions, but which are not in harmony or consistent with our own—these are notions totally at variance with that wise, safe, and practical policy which has always characterised the legislation of this country through all its history. We may therefore learn from that history—whenever it is contemplated, as it ought to be, according to the remark of Lord Macaulay, in large portions, and not fragmentally—that if we are to make any further alterations in our representative system, such alterations should always be effected by the same methods, and based as it were upon the same principles, as those by which we have hitherto been guided. Since the question has been completely reopened by four administrations in no less than four successive Parliaments, it would be most inconvenient, as Lord Derby stated when he accepted office in 1858, to leave such a subject still dangling in the air, to be tossed about in this or that direction as chance or folly might happen to carry it. However desirable it may have been that the subject should not have been re-opened, Parliament is now bound to consider it fully; and that with the view, as both Houses have themselves declared, 'of removing every just cause of complaint, of increasing general confidence in the Legislature, and of giving additional stability to the settled institutions of the State.'[3] Acting in that spirit, and desirous of lending a helping hand towards the attainment of so important an object, we now propose to redeem our pledge by discussing the whole matter in all its bearings. We shall disguise nothing, and we shall flinch from nothing; for the constitution of this country and the well-being of the people are matters too serious to be hastily taken up or lightly passed by.

The questions which arise are these:—First, whether there are not some classes of persons and some kinds of property to whom or to which the franchise may be extended; secondly, whether there are still any unrepresented places to which representatives might advantageously be given; thirdly, whether the present law relating to elections might be further improved, so as to ensure their more perfect freedom, without intimidation and without corruption; fourthly, whether the existing duration of Parliament is upon the whole the best which can be devised; and fifthly, as a corollary from these propositions—or rather as an incident to be borne in mind in considering each of them—whether the supposed advantages to accrue from such changes would or would not be more than counterbalanced by the inconveniences attending them. These points will necessarily embrace the whole subject; and they may be stated broadly, as challenging our decision on certain matters which are the very essence of our representative system,—that is to say, the extension of the suffrage, distribution of seats, freedom of elections, and the duration of Parliaments.

I. The first point is the extension of the Suffrage. All parties are more or less agreed that certain classes whose intelligence, industry, station, and independence would entitle them to the franchise, are now shut out, or at least they are debarred by the limited character of our electoral arrangements, from the power of exercising it. We believe that this is mainly owing to two causes:—first, to the circumstance that many descriptions of property have not, among their incidents, the incident of the suffrage; though, on every ground of reason and policy, they deserve it as much as those other kinds of property to which that incident was originally attached, or has subsequently been extended; secondly, it is owing to that sharp and unmeaning line of demarcation which was drawn by the Reform Act between the elector and the non-elector, when a house and land of 10*l*. occupation value was made almost the single substitute in the borough constituencies for the many franchises which then existed, or which might have been introduced. The amount and extent of this exclusion it is difficult to determine, but we are firmly persuaded that it is not near so great as it is convenient for those who pander to popularity roundly to assert. Four or five,[4] or even six millions, are glibly talked of as the aggregate minimum which ought to be found in the English constituencies. This assumes (and even then it is an exaggeration) that every adult male is entitled to a vote. But if any test whatever is to be applied by which we are to insure independence of action, honesty of purpose, freedom of choice, and power of deliberation—it is perfectly clear that every adult male cannot be included. Some abatements must necessarily be made. What those abatements are or ought to be is another matter. In truth it is there that the whole gist of the question will be found to lie; and yet, under the cover of vague generalities, this is the point which is usually evaded. The difficulty of the problem is no doubt great; but if we are in earnest, it must be grappled with; and we shall therefore make no apology for troubling our readers with such details as will enable us to form a judgment upon it.

The total number of electors in England and Wales is about 506,000 in the counties, and 439,000 in the boroughs. That at least was the estimated number in 1856–7.[5] The aggregate, therefore, at that period, was somewhere about

945,000. At the same time, the population may be taken, in round numbers, at 19,000,000—of which one-half were females, reducing the males to 9,500,000. One-half of these again were under 21, reducing the adult males of all descriptions to 4,750,000. The problem to be solved, therefore, is how many of these adult males which constitute the difference between 945,000 who have the franchise, and 3,805,000 who have it not, should be entitled to claim it.

The Radicals would solve this problem at once by saying, 'All, or, at least, very nearly all;' and they would rest their case upon that kind of hypothetical right, whereby they assume that every one is entitled, either directly or indirectly, to a voice in the Government under which he lives. As a corollary to this they jump to the conclusion that the supposed right can only be secured by personal representation, or universal suffrage; or if that be unattainable, as they know it is, then that it should be aimed at in an imperfect degree by manhood suffrage, or in a degree still more imperfect by that which has been called, though very loosely, household suffrage. Now, whatever decision Parliament may come to, we are satisfied it may be shown that these, at any rate, are not the modes by which the problem can be satisfactorily solved.

Personal representation is simply an impossibility, unless there be any one so ingenious as to find out a way by which each voter may actually return his own member. It is obvious that the minority, of whatever number that minority consists, must still remain in an unrepresented state. Some dissatisfaction has always been felt at a circumstance which is the plain and necessary result of all elections; but this dissatisfaction would be enormously increased if personal representation were interpreted to mean a personal right to exercise the franchise, irrespective of all other qualifications; for then the choice would be transferred to mere numbers, and the minority who were beaten by mere numbers would be more discontented than a minority which was beaten by those whose opinions they had some respect for. As long as the arrangements by which a majority binds the minority are so constituted that upon the whole they fairly declare the corporate mind, and signify honestly the general will of a free, independent, and intelligent community, they answer in the main the great ends for which men are brought by specific conventions into different states of civil society. In such a case the minority submits to the decision of the majority, because it knows that the corporate opinion is reasonably ascertained and legitimately acted upon; but if that majority, instead of being composed of the intelligence, virtue, and industry of a people, should be a majority, told by the head, whether good or bad, diligent or idle, educated or ignorant, the better part of the community, finding that their opinions were drowned or lost in the tumult of the mass, would feel, and justly, not only that they were unrepresented, but also that they were misrepresented. Any attempt to mitigate the evil by giving to the minority a potential voice, so that they might have a member of their own, would be totally at variance with the whole theory of personal representation, and consequently we dismiss that kind of proposition as a simple impossibility.

Universal suffrage is open to all, or almost all, of the same objections as those which apply to personal representation; but with those who talk most loudly about it, it has this absurdity in addition—that it never means what the words convey, or what its advocates intend. The meaning which the words convey would include all persons of every kind, whatever might be their sex, age, or condition. The advocates for this system say that it is unfair to push their argument to this extreme, that every rule has its exceptions, and that the exceptions in this case must qualify the rule to a certain extent—that is to say, that every male person who is not a minor, a criminal, a bankrupt, or a pauper, is entitled to have a voice in the making of those laws which he is bound to obey. Well, but if that be so, do not the advocates for this system perceive that, by their own showing, they have admitted themselves, as lawyers phrase it, entirely out of court? Why exclude women? Because it is better that they should confine themselves to their own more appropriate and domestic sphere. Why exclude minors? Because a line must somewhere be drawn between those whose judgments are uninformed and immature, and those who are supposed, by reason of their age, to exercise the franchise with prudence and discretion. Why exclude criminals? Because their dishonesty is a just disqualification. Why exclude bankrupts, insolvents, and paupers? Because their circumstances do not imply a sufficient amount of independence to enable them to vote freely. Some exceptions therefore, even with the advocates of universal suffrage, must plainly be admitted; and these exceptions are as plainly founded on considerations of a social and a moral character.[6] Station, position, mental capacity, and pecuniary circumstances, are all of them elements which must needs be regarded, unless we are to give an undue preponderance to ignorance, idleness, and even vice, over industry, education, independence, and virtue.

Upon similar grounds, if this reasoning be correct, Manhood suffrage will also require very numerous exceptions. The contrary opinion is based on the assumption that every adult male is entitled to have an equal voice in the enactment and administration of those laws which he is bound to obey. The fallacy of this assumption is so transparent, that it hardly demands an answer. But the answer given by the most philosophical and the ablest advocate of that kind of suffrage is so conclusive, and withal it is so much to the point, that we cannot refrain from recapitulating it here in his own words. Speaking of these advocates he observes:—

'They say that every one has an equal interest in being well governed, and that every one, therefore, has an equal claim to control over his own government. I might agree to this, if control over his own government were really the thing in question: but what I am asked to assent to is, that every individual has an equal claim to control over the government of other people. The power which the suffrage gives is not over himself alone—it is power over others also. Whatever control the voter is enabled to exercise over his own concerns, he exercises the same degree of it over those of every one else. Now, it can in no case be admitted that all persons have an equal claim to power over others. The claim of different people to such power differs as much as their qualifications for exercising it beneficially. *If it is asserted that all persons ought to be equal in every description of right exercised by society, I answer, not until all are equal in worth as human beings. It is the fact that one person is not as good as another, and it is reversing all the rules of rational conduct to attempt to raise a political fabric on a supposition which is at variance with fact.*'[7]

The remainder of the passage is an apt illustration of the foregoing reasoning, and it is well worth referring to, though too long to quote.

We should have thought that these observations of Mr. Mill were absolutely conclusive against Manhood as well as against Universal suffrage. But not so: that philosophical writer, whose reasoning and conclusions we thus far concur in, would still desire to give every one a vote. He goes on to say that, 'when all have votes, it will be both *just in principle* and *necessary in fact* that some mode be adopted of giving greater weight to the suffrages of the more educated voter! Some means must be devised by which the more intrinsically valuable member of society, the one who is more competent for the general business of life, and possesses more of the knowledge applicable to the management of the affairs of the community, *should,* as far as practicable, be *singled out and allowed a superiority of influence in proportion to his higher qualifications.*' Accordingly he would establish, if the time were ripe for it, a gradation of voting among different classes. Assuming, for example, that the ordinary unskilled labourer had one vote, he thinks that the skilled labourer should have two; the foreman or superintendent of labour ought perhaps to have three; the farmer or manufacturer three or four; a member of any profession requiring a long, accurate, and systematic mental cultivation—such as a lawyer, physician, surgeon, clergyman, or artist—should have five or six; and a graduate of any University, or a person freely elected a member of any learned Society, should be entitled to at least as many. But since, in his opinion (and here again we entirely concur with him), the time is not come for obtaining, or even asking for, a representative system founded on such principles, he would only recognise them so far at present as to pave the way for their future introduction by making a considerable extension of the suffrage subordinate to an educational qualification. This kind of qualification he afterwards describes, and if we interpret his conclusions rightly, he seems to mean that every person[8] who can copy a sentence of English in the presence of the Registering Officer, and perform a common sum in the Rule of Three, should be placed on the Parliamentary electoral roll.

Now, without commenting, except by way of passing remark, on the great dissatisfaction which such a scheme, when fully completed, would certainly occasion, by giving to the easy combination of a few an enormous superiority over the general mass, which they would not be much disposed to concede, it is sufficient to observe that the plan in every shape absolutely negatives, on unanswerable grounds, the very notion of Manhood suffrage. For if Manhood suffrage means, as we conceive it does, an equal voice or share in the representation, there cannot be a doubt that no system would be more unequal than that proposed; none would excite greater dissatisfaction; none would provoke more bitter jealousies. The observation, however, is not unimportant, for it will help us most materially to the solution of the problem which invites an answer, namely, 'How many of the adult males which constitute the difference between 945,000 who have the franchise, and 3,805,000 who have it not, should be entitled to claim it?' Mr. Mill says, those who can copy a sentence in English and perform a sum in the Rule of Three. Well, how many are those? It appears by the last Report of the Registrar-General,[9] that more than one-third of the males who were married in 1858 made their marks when signing the register—so that the number of adult males who could fulfil even the easiest part of Mr. Mill's qualification could not be more than two-thirds; and though there are no means of ascertaining the number of adult males who can perform a sum in the Rule of Three, we fear we are much within the mark when we assume that a fourth or fifth of the whole number would hardly be equal to that task. If taken at a fourth, this would reduce the adult males, who, according to Mr. Mill, ought to have the franchise, from 4,750,000 to $\frac{4,750,000}{4}$, that is to say, to about 1,875,500; or if taken at a fifth, it would reduce them from 4,750,000 to $\frac{4,750,000}{5}$, that is to say, to 950,000, or about the number of the present constituencies.

Setting then aside Personal representation, Universal suffrage, and Manhood suffrage, as things impracticable, or morally and socially prejudicial to the community, what shall we say to Household suffrage? Here again we are met *in limine* by an ambiguity of phrase. What is meant by a householder? The matter was discussed, at least cursorily, when Mr. Hume's motion in the House of Commons on National Representation was brought forward in 1849. And as near as any definition could be arrived at, even in the minds of those who originated and supported that motion, it seemed to signify, if it signified anything, not a person who held a house, but a person whom a house held. Whether he was the owner or occupier of the whole, or whether he were a lodger or temporary occupier of any part, of it, he was, according to the author of that motion, to be entitled to a vote; provided only he had claimed to be rated to the relief of the poor. Now, whatever may have been the value of such a proposition in the estimation of those who supported it originally, it has clearly given way, and has in fact been given up, in the face of free and open discussion. Even with those who formerly stood up for it, that kind of suffrage is hardly insisted upon. A clearer proof could not be adduced that loud cries and bold assertions are not to be taken, or rather mistaken, for the true voice of public opinion. At that time Mr. Hume's proposition was supported and defended as just and reasonable and highly expedient. But is that the language now used by those who voted for it? We consider Mr. Bright as perhaps on the whole the ablest exponent of that class of politicians who may be called, for want of a better name, Ultra-Liberals. Now Mr. Bright voted, though he did not speak, in favour of Mr. Hume's motion. In the last two years we have been made acquainted with most of his views on Parliamentary Reform. Vote by ballot, redistribution of seats, and extension of the suffrage are the principal objects at which he aims. But what does he intend by extension of suffrage? Does he intend that particular Household suffrage which Mr. Hume recommended and for which he voted? Nothing like it. He felt that this would introduce into the constituencies (we are going to quote his own words) 'scores,' and 'hundreds,' and 'thousands' of persons, many of them 'intemperate,' some of them 'profligate,' some of them 'naturally incapable,' and '*all of them in a condition of dependence* such as to offer no reasonable expectation that they would give their votes in a manner not only consistent with their own opinions and consciences (*if they have any in the matter*), *but consistent with the representation of the town or city in which they live.*'[10] In confirmation of this view, he refers to the opinions of 'the working men' who had corresponded with him; and he illustrates it most fairly by that which takes place in Scotland. There he finds that it is the custom in Edinburgh not to rate those who live in a house of lower value than 4*l.* a-year, because they are among the most helpless of the population. Consequently he admits that a rating suffrage in Edinburgh at 4*l.* a-year would at once exclude all that class; and he is prepared to maintain that it would 'be advantageous rather than otherwise that such persons should not be admitted on the electoral roll.' But then he points out a difficulty which might arise from taking that test, since the custom in England with reference to rating is different from that which prevails in Scotland. In England, he says (and he says truly), that the custom has obtained, sometimes by law and sometimes by agreement, that the landlords pay the rates even of the lowest and poorest class of dwellings—consequently, he argues, a rating franchise would admit a class in England which would exclude the same class in Scotland; that this would be a distinction which Parliament could not be expected to support; and that then comes the question whether you are to make some rule by which that unfortunate class in Scotland would be admitted, or a rule by which the corresponding unfortunate class in England would be excluded. Very candidly, as well as rationally, Mr. Bright has furnished us with a plain answer to his own question; and this will help us still further to the solution of the problem which has to be solved:—

'I should propose,' he says, 'a plan something like this. It is almost impossible, I fear, to make this matter quite clear to everybody here, but I have received so many letters about it, and I have found it so much a matter of discussion, that, with that perfect candour with which I have treated the public on every matter connected with reform, I feel it necessary now, on perhaps the only opportunity I may have before Parliament assembles,[11] to meet the question and briefly to discuss it. I think

206

it is extremely likely that if Parliament were to entertain a proposition so extensive as I have proposed, *they would say it is far better that the corresponding class in England, whom you admit to be so utterly dependent in Scotland that your own plan excludes them, should be excluded.* They might, however, propose that the clause should enact that, *down to a certain point of assessment,* as low as they like it to go, whether the tenant paid the rate or the landlord, *the tenant should be enfranchised,* but *below that line* which is supposed to set apart this very dependent and unfortunate class, if there be any man ambitious of having a vote, *let him tell the officer who is connected with the rating that he wishes not only to be rated, but that he wishes himself, as tenant and occupier, to pay his own rate,* which sum of course he might by arrangement deduct from the amount of his rent; and then let him be as free as any of those above him in circumstances to be placed upon the list of the electors.'

Thus then it is perfectly clear that 'Household suffrage,' without at least a very large qualification which destroys its plain and obvious meaning, is no more admissible than Manhood suffrage, Universal suffrage, and Personal representation. We are evidently gaining something by these discussions. The truth is gradually peeping out. Mr. Bright's admission is a most important one—and we agree with him that such a franchise as Household suffrage would place on the parliamentary roll, many persons unfit to exercise the electoral franchise, though we forbear from calling them, as he does, 'profligate,' 'intemperate,' and 'devoid of all conscience in the matter.' It is sufficient for our purpose simply to state that such a franchise would place on the parliamentary electoral roll many persons who, unhappily but most certainly, are in such a situation and condition of life that they would not be free and independent voters within the meaning of Mr. Fox's definition of the best plan for a representative system. According to him, *'the best plan of representation is that which shall bring into activity the greatest number of independent voters; and that plan is defective which would bring forth those whose situation and condition take from them the power of deliberation.'* Now Mr. Bright has shown most distinctly that household suffrage would bring forth a large class whose condition of life did take from them the power of deliberation; and the opinion thus expressed by him is irresistibly confirmed by the evidence taken before the House of Lords' Committee on the Bill of 1850–51 which proposed to amend the Municipal Reform Act. From that it will appear that the Municipal franchise, as settled by that Act, was strangely altered by a subsequent Statute, passed for the purpose of further assessing and collecting the poor and highway rates in respect of small tenements; and this alteration has so impaired the respectability and independence of the different constituencies, that in truth they are at the mercy of those classes who are at the same time the least educated, the least wealthy, and the most corrupt. The subject is a serious one, and it deserves investigation. By the former of these

Acts, a three years' residency, coupled with rating and the payment of rates, except those which had become due in the six months immediately preceding the time of registration, constituted together the necessary qualification for the municipal franchise. By the latter, a clause entirely foreign to the purpose of the Act was introduced in Committee—that clause declared that the *occupier* should be entitled to all municipal privileges and franchises when the *owner* had been rated and had paid the rates. In consequence of this change, the poorest occupier is enabled to claim the same Municipal rights and privileges as the other inhabitants of the Town and Borough, although in all cases he is contributing less by one-third, and in some cases less by one-half to the municipal expenses of such Town and Borough, than he would have to do if he himself were rated and paid his own rates.[12] The effect of this has been and is most detrimental to the Municipal constituencies, and it shows pretty clearly what a similar change in the Parliamentary Constituencies would be likely to produce. It appears from the evidence, that in general, and more especially in the large towns like Newcastle-on-Tyne,[13] the bulk of this class are far less qualified by education, independence, and sobriety, to exercise electoral privileges than the direct ratepayers. They are described as belonging to the lowest grade of operatives; as consisting in some districts principally, or in great part, of Irish immigrants, unsettled in character and occupation; as taking no interest in municipal elections, unless it is one merely temporary and selfish; as so uneducated that few of them can read and write; as usually under some external influence, by the necessity of ignorance and poverty; as open to the highest bidder; and as taking this bidding in the form of drink and breakfasts given at public-houses, or of a payment in the name of compensation for loss of work, amounting very often to more than a day's wages. In short, they are shown, not only to be dependent, but also corrupt, for without such compensation it seems they would seldom take part in the election, since they care but little, if at all, about it—except as affording them the opportunity of having a 'good tuck out:' that is to say, of drinking and feasting at the expense of the candidate. To this we should add what appears in another part of the same report, that the rateable value of the tenements rated under the Act is generally but a small, often an insignificant portion of the whole rateable property of a ward. The small tenement voters frequently form an absolute majority. In one case the Act has increased the number of voters from 381 to 948, the minority representing property of the value of 26,000*l.*, while the majority represents property of the value of 4000*l.* only. In another case, 302 small tenement voters are able to control the elections of a ward, though their rating is no more than 66*l.*, out of a total of nearly 16,000*l.* In Bridgewater, where the small tenement occupiers are of so low a class that numbers of them receive parish relief during the winter, they form two-thirds of the constituency; and in Sunderland,[14] which affords a striking example of this state of things, it appears that, out of 5300 voters, 1000 pay on 29,000*l.*; while 4300 pay on 7000*l.* only. From this state of facts the Committee have drawn two important conclusions. In one place they say—

'The result then of the clause enfranchising the small tenement hold-ers has been in these and similar cases to transfer the power of elect-ing those who have the management of the municipal funds, from the persons who pay the rates, to those who at most only bear indirectly an insignificant proportion of the burthen, and sometimes pay noth-ing, either directly or indirectly, to the municipal revenues.' And they add,—'In numerous cases, wherein the clause in question has come into full operation, the owners and occupiers of a very small part of the rated property have paramount influence in the taxation and expendi-ture of the borough.'

In another place they observe:—

'While there is no doubt that the Act is of great service in facilitating the collection of rates, it is quite clear that it has produced, wherever large numbers of small tenement occupiers have been admitted to vote, a serious deterioration in the character of the Constituent body. Taking different wards of the same town, the evidence before them justifies the Committee in believing that those in which the small tenement voters are most numerous are the most noted for the prevalence of malprac-tices. *No trifling deterioration of the constituency is implied in the mere fact, that in many cases the direct ratepayers are completely outnum-bered by those who either pay no rates, or pay them so indirectly that they are hardly aware of the payment, and whose ignorance of munici-pal affairs is not enlightened by the self-interest of contributors to the local taxation.*'

After this we think we may say that the present state of the Municipal franchise, which, through a mistake, has thus been placed on the worst possible footing, is abso-lutely conclusive, like Mr. Bright's reasoning on the smaller occupiers in Scotland and in England, against the introduction of Household suffrage. Nay, more; it shows, as plainly as facts can do, that, unless the suffrage is carefully limited and restrained to those who are capable of exercising it honestly, as well as freely, the greatest mis-chiefs are likely to arise. Where, then, should the limit be put? The evidence taken before the House of Lords' Committee would seem to indicate, as a matter of justice as well as of policy, that it should be made to commence with those tenements where the rates cannot be compounded for by the landlord. In other words, the line should be drawn, as in all principle and fairness it ought to be drawn, where the occupier must contribute, in proportion to the value of his own holding, an equal share with the rest of the inhabitants towards the usual municipal expenses. That limit cannot be put higher than a 6*l.* rating, or its equivalent an 8*l.* value. Below that amount it is perfectly clear that the smaller occupiers are, as a body, really dependent on the influence of others. They are not, in fact, when taken as a class, in such a situation and condition of life as to enable them to exercise that power of deliberation which Mr.

Fox's rule very reasonably requires. There may be some, doubtless there are, who have that power, but these might be provided for in a different way, without including them in the general mass, which would make their votes of no avail. For the sake, therefore, of the better class of voters, as well as for the sake of the Constituencies generally, it is absolutely necessary that those whose position will not allow them to act freely should be excluded. Rather, we should say, that, according to the temperate reasoning of Mr. Mill, they cannot be admitted to the same privileges as the rest of their fellow-citizens until they are raised to the same level of intelligence and independence. Horne Tooke once declared that justice and policy alike required that a share in power and contribution to power should be proportionate to each other. But this is a result which will never be attained if those who, from their poverty, neither do nor can be expected to contribute to the municipal burdens are placed upon an equality with those whose rates must be paid in full, and by themselves, instead of being compounded for at a lower figure and paid by another. Any other limit would unquestionably fulfil the prophetic language of Sir E. Lytton, and place capital and knowledge 'at the command of impatient poverty and uninstructed numbers.'

The limit, therefore, which ought to be put on that vague generality, Household suffrage, is tolerably plain. No doubt it brings down the number of persons who may be admitted to the franchise, consistently with its free and independent exercise, to a much smaller amount than the actual number of adult males for whom it is sometimes very loosely claimed. We have estimated the number of adult males in England and Wales at 4,750,000. The number of inhabited houses in 1857 was 3,275,000. So that the number of adult males who are actually householders could not be more than 3,275,000. Now, out of these 3,275,000, not less than 1,700,000 houses—that is to say more than one-half—were under the value of 6*l.*, according to Mr. Newmarch's electoral statistics.[15] The exact proportions we shall have no means of determining accurately until we are furnished with those returns which the Government has recently directed to be made. But, with such figures alone before us as those to which we have just adverted, we can approximate, at all events, towards the truth. For, taking Mr. Fox's rule as our guide, and deducting the occupiers of those tenements whose rates may be compounded for and paid by the landlord, the number of adult males will be reduced at once from 4,750,000 to $\dfrac{3,275,000}{2}$ —that is to say, to 1,637,500. Further deductions, however, according to the same rule, must also be made. For some of these tenements are occupied by women, some are unoccupied, and in some of them, moreover, and even others of a higher value, there are many lodgers who are not so well off as those who are occupiers of a tenement rated at 6*l.* only; and, therefore, in no respect are they so independent as those under whose roof they obtain a temporary and precarious abode. To ascertain the number of these lodgers is not very easy. But the great majority—in fact, almost all of them—would come within the class whose circumstances, according to any rule (whether we take Mr. Fox's, Mr. Mill's, or Mr. Bright's), would disqualify them from exercising it as they ought. A considerable number, therefore, must be further deducted from the former residue of 1,637,500, and when that is done, there could not be more than 1,400,000 or 1,500,000 adult males to whom the franchise, according to Mr. Fox's rule, could properly be given. But, as we have already about 950,000 electors, it follows that an addition of 400,000 or 500,000, either by the reduction of the old franchise, or by the introduction of a new franchise, will probably place on the electoral roll every person who may properly and prudently be admitted to it. And it is not altogether unworthy of remark, that this result, with respect to extension of the suffrage alone, would produce a Reform Bill as extensive as that which was passed in 1832. At that time the total constituency of England and Wales was raised from 430,000 or 450,000 to 800,000, or thereabouts. An addition to it now of 400,000 or 500,000 electors would raise it more than as much again.

But, in order to make any new measure of reform not merely an extensive but a beneficial measure (the great aim which should always be kept in view, however strangely it has always been neglected), it would be most unwise simply to have recourse to the clumsy expedient of reducing the occupation value of the voter's tenement in counties and boroughs—that is a line which must necessarily be arbitrary, usually uncertain, and often unintelligible. All the bills at the head of our article, the Bill of 1852, the Bill of 1854, and the Bill of 1859, have recommended the introduction of new franchises. The reason for that recommendation was not ill put by Lord J. Russell, when he said, in the year 1852, that, 'by taking a uniform 10*l.* value, and by abolishing all those intricate franchises which previously existed, the authors of the Reform Bill had confined themselves too much to one species of franchise. They did not make it sufficiently various, and, therefore, it was not sufficiently comprehensive.' Nobody can doubt that this confession of the original error is well-founded. A varied franchise will furnish, in fact, the only means of representing equitably a variety of interests. The difficulty consists in ascertaining and defining of what kind those franchises should be, and what are the conditions which ought to attach to them. Each of the bills professes to deal with this part of the subject, but they do not deal with it in the same way, or to the same extent. By the first of these bills every male person of full age, and not subject to any legal incapacity, was to be entitled to register his vote in the county or borough in which he lived, if he had been charged either under any assessment of the duties of assessed taxes (except certain licences), or under any assessment of the duties payable from properties, trades, and professions. The conditions attached to this franchise were a twelve months' charge previous to the day when the register was made up; payment of so much of the charge as was due on the 5th of January then next preceding; and a six months' residence within the place, or seven miles of its boundary, in respect of which the vote was claimed. Such an addition is clearly right in point of principle, because it makes taxation and representation go along with each other. The only question would be, whether the conditions attached to the franchise are sufficient to secure a community of interests in the place where this franchise would have to be exercised.

By the second of these Bills the franchise was intended to be conferred,—

1st. On persons in receipt of salaries, from public or private employment, of not less than 100*l.* per annum, payable quarterly or half-yearly.[16]

2nd. On persons in respect of 10*l*. per annum derived from the Government funds, or from Bank or East India Stock.

3rd. On persons paying 40*s*. per annum, either as assessed taxes or under the Property and Income Tax Act.

4th. On Graduates of any University in the United Kingdom.

5th. On persons who have for three years possessed a deposit of 50*l*. in any savings-bank.

The conditions to be attached to these franchises were—first, a twelvemonth's residence in the county or borough where the vote was to be registered; secondly, a twelvemonth's receipt of the annual income; thirdly, a twelvemonth's payment of the 40*s*. charge; and fourthly, in the case of a savings-bank deposit, a three years' possession of it. In point of principle there could be little opposition to these additions, except as regards the first; but as regards the first, we must express our doubts whether a suffrage from salaries given as such would not open the door to many influences which it is desirable and almost necessary to control.

By the third of these Bills the *new* franchises intended to be introduced were as follows:—

1st. Persons in the beneficial enjoyment of 10*l*. per annum from the Government funds, or Bank or East India Stock.

2nd. Persons in the beneficial enjoyment of 20*l*. per annum, as a pension, pay, or superannuation allowance, in respect of any past employment in Her Majesty's Naval, Military, East Indian, or Civil service.

3rd. Depositors in a savings-bank to the amount of 60*l*.

4th. Graduate of any University.

5th. Minister of any religious denomination.

6th. Barristers-at-law, sergeants-at-law, certificated pleaders or conveyancers.

7th. Certificated attorneys, solicitors, or proctors.

8th. Members of the medical profession.

9th. Certificated schoolmasters.

10th. Lodgers who shall pay a rent of not less than 8*s*. a-week, or 20*l*. per annum.

The conditions to be attached to these franchises were—first, the receipt of the annuity or income, or the possession of the savings-bank deposit, for twelve calendar months previous to the 21st day of June in each year of registration; secondly, residence in all cases (except the case of a lodger) for the same twelve calendar months within the county or borough for which the claim to be registered is made; thirdly, as regards lodgers, actual occupation for a similar period of twelve calendar months; and fourthly, registration in one place only, when the party claiming has two or more places of residence. In point of principle we doubt No. 2—namely, the pensions and superannuation allowances; and we believe No. 5, No. 6, No. 7, No. 8, and No. 9—or those which are called the fancy franchises—would be probably unnecessary, and often objectionable. The other propositions, to which we have taken no specific exceptions, have much to rec-ommend them. It is right, for example, that those who contribute to the revenues of the country by the direct taxation which is imposed upon them, should have, if possible, a voice in the matter. It is right moreover, since personal property has acquired an interest which it did not possess when the framework of the constitu-tion was originally compacted, that this kind of property, as well as that which principally consists of real estate, should be represented. It is further right that those who are trying to acquire such property by deposits in a savings-bank, and have thereby given the strongest proof of economy and foresight, of intelligent prudence, and a desire for independence, should be entitled to place themselves upon the register, although they may neither invest their money in a forty-shilling freehold, nor happen to be occupiers of a 10*l*. tenement. It is also right that many industrious and painstaking persons—born perhaps to poverty, but rising in the world—well educated, but struggling hard with little more than professional incomes—should have the means of placing themselves on the register, if they should not come within any of the qualifications above allowed. The persons to whom we here refer are the unbeneficed clergy; unmarried members of the learned professions; half-pay officers in the navy and army; young architects, sculptors, and painters; hundreds who are employed in study or tuition; and thou-sands of clerks, foremen, shopmen, and skilled artisans, who are in the receipt of good salaries or wages. These might be reached to a certain extent by giving votes to those who had previously graduated in an University; and they might also be reached to a much greater extent by allowing lodgers, at a certain rental, to acquire the franchise. Both these additions are therefore admissible; but then in this, as in most of the cases herein enumerated, it would be absolutely neces-sary, by the most careful provisions, to connect them by feeling as well as by interest with the county and borough where their vote is to be exercised, so that they might have that *juris consensum et utilitatis communionem* with the rest of the constituency which alone can make an incorporated people. We believe that in such cases there is no way whatever of accomplishing this object, except by the obligation of continuous residence. Nor should it be forgotten that, without more guards than those which were introduced into the last Bill, frauds in regis-tration and personation in voting might easily be practised, if an abstract quali-fication, unconnected with visible property, were made the basis of the electoral right. Certainty of possession and continuity of residence are therefore prelimi-nary and essential conditions which ought to attach to such franchises as these. Without these conditions, abuses would be endless.

For the reasons adverted to above we have purposely excluded from the new franchises all those which might either be derived from quarterly salaries, as pro-posed by the second Bill, or from pensions and superannuation allowances, or from a professional and educational status, as proposed by the third. Not only will such franchises be open to abuse which it would be difficult to control, but they would not be necessary if the others were allowed. Taking the qualifications which are assumed as starting-points in the other new franchises, it is hardly possible to conceive a person, claiming to be registered for a franchise from salaries, or from pensions, or from a professional or educational test, who would not be entitled to exercise his right from money in the funds, from the payment of direct taxation, from a deposit in a savings-bank, from an University degree, or from apartments or lodgings; but suppose there were one or two such persons, they would probably at all events attain their rights by having recourse to one of the old franchises, if they were only varied to such an extent as a due regard to the proper working of our representative system would require or suggest. And this observation leads us at once to that part of the subject which has been so much talked of, and, we ought to add, so little considered. Nothing can be easier than to reduce an occupation value from one figure to another; but if it be desirable still to maintain a due regard to the numerous rights and the varied interests which we know to exist—if it be wise to adhere to those principles which time and experience have equally sanctioned, instead of having recourse to those novelties which a thirst for change and a love of experiment alone recommend—if reason and good policy alike declare, as they seem to do in the thoughtful reflection of Mr. Mill, as well as in the glowing indignation of Mr. Bright, that a predominance should be given to property over poverty, knowledge over ignorance, industry over idleness, and honest independence over thoughtless incapacity—we cannot conceive anything more foolish than to place the County and Borough franchises on one uniform level, or to bring them down to such a standard that it would be vain to expect from them either power of deliberation or freedom of action.

In the three Bills at the head of our article the old franchises are dealt with in the following manner. By the first of these Bills the occupation-value in Counties was intended to be reduced from 50*l.* to 20*l.*, and the value of the copyhold and leasehold franchise was intended to be reduced from 10*l.* to 5*l.* above all rents and charges; while in boroughs the occupation-value of 10*l.* was reduced to a *rateable* value of not less than 5*l.*, and for the purposes of registration it could not be compounded at a less amount. By the second of these Bills the occupation-value in counties was reduced from 50*l.* to 10*l.*, of which not less than 5*l.* was to arise from some dwelling-house or holding, and not from land only; while in boroughs the occupation-value of 10*l.* was reduced to a rateable value of 6*l.*, with a power to the tenant, whose rates had been compounded for, to claim to be rated at the compounded amount. By the third of these Bills the occupation-value in Counties was reduced from 50*l.* to 10*l.*, and the value of the copyhold and leasehold franchise was reduced from the clear yearly value of 20*l.* over and above all rents and charges to the clear yearly value of 5*l.* over and above all charges and incumbrances, but without any deduction on account of rent. By the same Bill the occupation-value in Boroughs was left where it was, with the view of endeavouring to identify the suffrage both Town and County: requiring on the one hand the 40*s.* freeholders resident in towns to vote for the Town, and enabling on the other the 10*l.* occupier resident in the county to vote for the County.

The mere recapitulation of these propositions shows how unsettled men's opinions are when once they begin to draw arbitrary lines and theorise upon government, instead of acting on the less ostentatious, but still the wiser and more practical, plan of requiring some proof of the defects to be supplied and the abuses to be remedied before they disturb the regular action of a most valuable but very complicated machine. Any one who considers the full effect of introducing such new franchises as suggested above, will see that the variation or reduction of the old franchise may be deemed almost a secondary object. Most of the persons who by station and respectability are entitled to have votes, would, through the new franchises, be enabled to obtain them. But there may, and probably would, be some who now are excluded by the arbitrary line which the law has drawn, and who could not take advantage of the new franchises; and such men, with some degree of justice, may complain that they are entitled on *other considerations* to the benefit of the suffrage quite as much as their next-door neighbours who are only preferred to them by the unequal operation of an arbitrary rule. According to the original framework of our Constitution this is a complaint which never could have arisen. For, as we have shown in our former article, every person of free condition who contributed directly either to the burdens of the state, or to those of the place in which he dwelt, was entitled to have a voice in the choice of his representative. The nearer we go back to that framework, the better will be our chance of enlarging as well as adapting the building to the reasonable exigencies of the age in which we live. This is a result, however, which can never be accomplished simply by drawing an arbitrary line unconnected with the duties and burdens which the inhabitants may be called upon to discharge or to bear. Some test must necessarily be taken; and it would be well to take that which the legislature has imposed as the proper criterion for measuring the capacity of the different inhabitants to discharge the one or bear the other. Such a test we have both in Counties and Boroughs—in Counties, where the juror's qualification commences, implying thereby a due assessment to imperial taxation,—in Boroughs, where the tenant's obligation is fixed for contributing, like his neighbours, without composition and without abatement, a full share to the local burdens. Acting on these principles, every householder[17] in a county who is rated or assessed to the poor-rate or to the inhabited house duty on a value of not less than 20*l*.; and every occupier in a borough[18] assessed at a sum exceeding 6*l*. a-year (being therefore a person whose local burdens could not be compounded for at one-third of their value), would, as a general rule, be entitled to vote. Until the returns which the Government have asked for are placed in our hands, it would be premature to lay down, with any degree of accuracy, how many would be added by such a reduction in the counties and boroughs to the two sets of constituencies. But judging from returns which are now before us,[19] we believe it would include (if every one claimed for such qualifications) at least 200,000 in the one, and nearly that number in the other. This, with the new franchises above recommended, would clearly raise the Constituencies of the kingdom to that amount, which in point of number as well as capacity would include all those who, by their position and social station, may fairly be considered as well entitled to claim and exercise the electoral privilege.

And thus, while everything is justly conceded, so far as regards the extension of the suffrage, the grounds upon which that extension is made would not introduce that fatal principle which two of these Bills unhappily suggest, that large numbers may be added to a constituency who do not bear the same burdens as those which attach on the rest of the community with whom they reside. We are convinced that the course which has recently been pursued of extending municipal or political power to those who are exonerated at the same time from a proportionate share of direct taxation, whether local or imperial, is one which cannot be justified in reason, and must in the end be absolutely fatal to all good government. A vast inroad was made in this principle, when the window-duty, affecting most of the tenements which conferred the franchises, was transferred by substitution to those houses only which were above the value of 20*l.* a-year. Another great inroad was made upon it when the composition of rates, on the ground of poverty, was allowed to give Municipal privileges to those who were exempt from Municipal burdens. That these inroads may not be carried farther—that powers and responsibility may always go together—let the juror's qualification and Imperial taxation form the basis of the occupation franchise in Counties, and let equal rating and the payment of rates form the basis of the same kind of franchise in cities and boroughs. On any other hypothesis, power and privilege will be permanently vested in one set of men, while the duties of citizenship and the burden of taxation are cast upon another. Responsibility and power will be finally severed. 'They who govern will not pay, and they who pay will not be allowed to govern.'[20]

II. Such are the modes in which the suffrage may with least danger be extended. The next point which we have to consider is the distribution of seats.

This has been dealt with in very different ways by those who profess to set themselves up as authorities on this subject. Mr. Hume[21] moved vaguely, 'That the apportionment of representatives be rendered more equal to the population.' Mr. Roebuck advances with great boldness, and urges at once, as the organ of the Committee of Parliamentary Reformers, 'A reappointment of seats that shall make such an approach to an equalisation of constituencies as shall give in the United Kingdom a majority of members to a majority of electors.'[22] The first of the three Parliamentary Bills made Birkenhead and Burnley new boroughs, and added to 65 of the existing boroughs 106 unrepresented towns, which had no connexion whatever with them, except the connexion of a supposed proximity. The second of the Bills proposed to disfranchise 19 boroughs altogether, to take away the second member from 33 more, to add a third member to 37 counties or divisions of counties, to divide Lancashire into three divisions, and the West Riding of York into two, to confer on 8 of the existing boroughs the privilege of sending a third member to Parliament, and to enable Salford to return two, the Inns of Court two, and the University of London, Birkenhead, Burnley, and Staleybridge, one each. The third of these Bills would have taken away the second members from 15 boroughs which now return two; would have separated Middlesex and South Lancashire into two divisions, and the West Riding of

Yorkshire into three; and would have created seven new boroughs, namely, West Bromwich, Birkenhead, Burnley, Staleybridge, Croydon, Gravesend, and Hartlepool. Mr. Bright's Schedules[23] would have absolutely disfranchised 86 places, leaving the counties exactly as they are. They would have entirely recast the borough constituencies by allotting one member to 110 places, where the population was more than 8000, and less than 25,000; two members to 43 places, where the population was more than 25,000, and less than 54,000; three members to 23 places, where the population was more than 54,000, and less than 120,000; four members to 12 places, where the population was more than 120,000, and less than 300,000; six members to 5 places, where the population was more than 300,000, and less than 400,000; and since the Tower Hamlets exceeded the last number by 100,000 at least, that favoured suburb was to be divided into two divisions, each of which was to have the privilege of returning four members, that is to say, eight in the whole!

Can anything be more unsatisfactory than these different propositions? Can anything be wanted more than the recapitulation of such suggestions to show conclusively that those who profess to be our ablest public men are little better than children groping in the dark, when their principal guides in framing Constitutions are a few figures of arithmetic? Can anything lead more directly to the belief that they prepare such measures with a view to success or personal popularity, and not because they believe them to be right? or must we conclude that they are simply attempting to do something, because they are told that something must be done, without having an idea in their own minds as to what that something ought really to be? Very different was the way in which our statesmen formerly acted. Even in the midst of the Reform excitement in 1832, the authors of that measure disclaimed the idea of proceeding on mere theories of their own. The acknowledged principles upon which the Constitution had always been based were the only guides which they professed to recognise. They acted on the conviction that there was a grievance to be redressed, and an injustice to be remedied. They found that the fabric of our representative system had swerved from its foundations in two particulars. They saw, in the first place, that there were many of the great seats of manufacture and corn trade which had not been brought within its pale; and, in the second place, that there were several boroughs which had fallen so completely into decay, that, according to Lord John Russell, 'They did not and could not represent the opinions of the inhabitants.' To cure these defects they never sought or pretended to 'give a majority of members to a majority of electors,' as Mr. Roebuck proposes, or to adjust the representation in proportion to numbers, as Mr. Bright suggests; but they took from those places which 'did not and could not represent the opinion of the inhabitants' a certain number of seats, and transferred them to those places which had an undeniable claim (in any change that might be introduced) to be heard for themselves and by their own members. Had they done what they are now asked to do, they must have destroyed that variety of representation which alone can provide for a variety of interests. But they knew that this variety is essential to our system;

and they also knew that it can only be maintained by still preserving, as part of that system, different constituencies, and of a different character. This was one of the principal grounds upon which Lord John Russell successfully resisted the vague proposition made by Mr. Hume in 1848. After adverting to the fact that, before the Reform Bill, there were many large towns with no representatives, and several decayed boroughs in possession of two, he tells us that the authors of the Bill did not jump to the hasty conclusion that all should be levelled, or nearly assimilated, that he approves, as they approved, of still keeping alive constituent bodies of various kinds—some large and others small—and he gives his reasons very distinctly, and without reserve:[24]—

> 'Considering,' he said, 'the varied character of the people of this country—considering their varied occupations—considering how many men there are of great intelligence who take little part ordinarily in political conflicts—considering how many men there are who give their labours to the world in the shape of works on political science, it may be, or who are conversant with commerce, but who do not enter into the agitations relating to the immediate political questions of the day—I certainly am of opinion that the country, taken as a whole, is far better represented by the varied kind of representation I have just mentioned, than it would be if we had nothing but two large divisions, the counties sending agricultural members, and the large cities commercial members, or representatives of the manufacturing interest.'

The same reasoning is equally applicable to Mr. Roebuck's plan of ensuring everywhere a majority of members to a majority of electors. If this were honestly and fairly attempted in England and Wales, it ought to give a member to every 50,000 of the present population. But, to accomplish that end in the different counties and boroughs as they now exist, there should be two members for every 100,000 of inhabitants, three for 150,000, four for 200,000, and so on until the maximum is reached. What would be the result? The rural element of the nation, the scattered and quieter, but not the least valuable part of the community, would be entirely overwhelmed by the pushing, restless, fluctuating element, which characterises, more or less, the population of our towns and cities. According to this principle there would be fifteen counties, partly agricultural and partly commercial, which ought to have four members, four which ought to have five, Lancashire North seven, Lancashire South ten, the West Riding fifteen; while in the boroughs, Leeds and Southwark should have four, Westminster and Birmingham five, Lambeth six, Manchester and Finsbury seven, Marylebone and Liverpool eight, and the Tower Hamlets eleven. Such are the results which the principle contained in Mr. Roebuck's proposition would naturally bring with it, and there is only one way of maintaining the principle, and avoiding the absurdity to which it would lead; and that is, by dividing or subdividing the different constituencies into equal portions. But should that be done, we are landed at once in electoral districts, not, indeed, with geometrical areas, but within the limits of an arithmetical calculation. Where, then, would be that variety of representation which now opens the door to all classes, all interests, and all kinds of talent? Obviously and plainly it must be destroyed, and an uniform standard established in its stead. This will appear all the more glaring if we take along with it the other part of Mr. Roebuck's proposition,[25] namely, 'the extension of the county franchise to all 10*l*. occupiers at least;' that is to say, an assimilation of the County and Borough franchise, for then we should have a complete subversion of the existing system. The total number of persons rated at 10*l*. and upwards is 613,680; of these the lower part of the constituency, or those rated at sums under 50*l*., is more than twice as many as the higher class, or those rated above 50*l*. The former amount to 415,517, while the latter amount to 198,163 only. The two classes would be divided into three; of which the higher would have one part, and the lower two. In a trice, therefore, the whole character of the county constituency is changed, and identified with that of boroughs. What would be the consequence? Mr. Mill's opinion upon that point is decisive and just:—

'Except in the few places where there is still a yeomanry—as in Cumberland, Westmoreland, and, in some degree, North Yorkshire and Kent—there exists in the agricultural population no class but the farmers intermediate between the landlords and the labourers. A 10*l*. franchise will admit no agricultural labourer, and the farmers and landlords would collectively be far outnumbered by the 10*l*. householders of all the small towns in England. To enable the agricultural population to hold its fair share of the representation, under any uniform and extensive suffrage short of universal, it seems absolutely necessary that the town electors should, as a rule, be kept out of the county constituencies. And the sole alternative is to form them, or the great bulk of them, into constituencies by themselves.'

Mr. Mill is right. The smaller towns in England and Wales, with a population of more than 4000 in each, which an occupation franchise of 10*l*. would bring into the county constituency, are 378. This would overwhelm that property franchise which now forms the principal basis of the country constituencies. For, taking the year 1856 as our guide, the total number of county electors rated to the relief of the poor was then about 415,000, of whom not one-half, or about 198,000, were rated at 50*l*. and upwards; but with an assimilated franchise for counties and boroughs, the total number of county electors rated at 10*l*. and upwards would have been at the same period 613,680, of whom more than two-thirds, or 415,517, would have been rated at 10*l*. and under 50*l*. Thus the tables would be turned. In the one case, property would outweigh occupation; in the other, occupation would outweigh property. Take another test—the test of contribution to the taxes of the country, as derived from property under Schedules A and B, and compare them with that which arises from trades and professions under Schedule D. The following will give the average result in counties:—

	£	s.	d.
The Property under Schedule A is per head................	5	15	6
The Property under Schedule B is per head................	3	13	10
The Property under Schedule D is per head................	1	14	0
Total................	11	3	4
In the Boroughs, including the City of London—the Property under Schedule A is per head................	5	15	3
In the Boroughs, including the City of London—the Property under Schedule B is per head................	0	6	7
In the Boroughs, including the City of London—the Property under Schedule D is per head................	7	9	7
Total................	13	11	5
In the Boroughs, excluding the City of London—the Property under Schedule A is per head................	5	11	8
In the Boroughs, excluding the City of London—the Property under Schedule B is per head................	0	6	7
In the Boroughs, excluding the City of London—the Property under Schedule D is per head................	5	15	0
Total................	11	13	3

From these tables it will be seen, that in the Counties the majority is composed of those who now contribute to the revenue of the country from that which is called real property; while in the Boroughs, the majority is composed of those who contribute to the revenue from professional incomes. Can we want a stronger proof of the wisdom of continuing that old 'well-founded and important distinction' between the county and the borough franchise, whereof property is principally the basis of the one, while occupation and residence is the basis of the other? Very little need be said of the first of the three Parliamentary Bills, with reference to a change in the distribution of seats, as it did not receive much favour at the time; and we believe its authors are not over partial to it. No objection would possibly be made to the formation of Birkenhead and Burnley into boroughs: both are populous and growing communities, and the former is likely hereafter to command a prominent position as a commercial town. But when we consider the strange proposition of adding to 65 of the existing boroughs 106 unrepresented towns; and when we examine the plans by which that proposition was intended to be worked and carried into effect, we see at once the danger and the difficulty of extemporising theoretical and paper constitutions. The farther we recede from the original framework of our representative system, which recognises for its basis social communities existing as it were within the same limits, subject to the same regulations and law, and bound together by the same ties and interests, the more rapidly we shall descend to electoral districts and the representation of numbers. The towns to be added to the smaller boroughs by the Bill of 1852, had little or no connection between them, except the connection of a supposed proximity. Even that connection, however, was almost always severed by distance, and sometimes interrupted by other boroughs. In Essex—Harwich was to take in Manningtree, which was tolerably near; Halstead, which was some way off; and Coggeshall, which was interrupted by the town of Colchester. In Hampshire—Lymington was to ally itself to Lyndhurst, and to pass by Southampton that it might reach Romsey. In Shropshire—Ludlow was to wander away to a considerable distance in three directions, that it might marry itself to three wives: Cleobury Mortimer, Church Stretton, and Bishop's-Castle. In Surrey—Dorking was to be united to Reigate; while Croydon, which is one of the most considerable of the unrepresented towns, was left unnoticed. In Wiltshire—the four boroughs of Chippenham, Calne, Devizes, and Westbury were to intersect each other in the strangest confusion. Calne was to take in Melksham to the south; Chippenham, which is a little to the south-west of Calne, was to go still further south to get at Bradford; Westbury was to be joined to Trowbridge, which is nearer to Bradford, that was to be added to Chippenham; and Devizes boldly passed by Westbury, that it might be quietly absorbed into Heytesbury and Warminster. We need not pursue this matter further, except as a warning against all attempts, however ingenious, to break up into fragments that community of interests which must form the basis of every kind of representation, if representation is to mean, in future, anything more than the representation of numbers.

With regard to the second of the Parliamentary Bills, one of its main objects appears to have been to give to minorities a right to choose their own member. For that purpose it disfranchised entirely 19 boroughs, partially 33, and it apportioned the representation thus set free to the extent at least of 45 members, by adding a third member to 8 boroughs and 37 counties. And whenever any place returned three members or more, no person was to be entitled to vote for more than two candidates. Now the objections to this measure are twofold. In the first place it would be impracticable, and probably impolitic, to introduce into our system the representation of minorities; and if that part of the Bill were rejected, as it would be, then the addition of a third member in the larger boroughs would only give to the preponderating interest in these boroughs a larger power of overpowering the minority, and weakening its influence. In the second place, it would destroy *pro tanto* that varied representation of various classes and various interests which is partly obtained through the smaller boroughs. The first of these objections is in itself fatal; the second opens up the whole question of the existence of smaller and larger constituencies. In their favour is prescription, against them is theory; and we believe that prescription, founded on experience and long usage, is ten times more valuable than all theory, however ingenious, unless it can be shown that the practical working of an existing system is really bad, and that the projected change would probably be better. But is this working of our present system practically bad? We will not reply in our own words, but we will take our answer from the authors of the Reform Act. Their reasons for preserving in the different constituencies that variety which still exists, were stated at the time by Lord J. Russell:—

'In the representation as we propose to leave it,'[26] he observed, 'there will still be a class, which some may think a blot on our system, *but the existence of which I think will add to the permanence of Parliament, and to the welfare of the people.*[27] I mean that there will be a hundred or more members from places of *three, four, five,* or *six* thousand inhabitants, who will not perhaps immediately represent any particular interest, and who may therefore be better qualified to speak and inform the House on great questions of general interest to the community. If we had proceeded, as some recommended, viz., to destroy the existing system, and to allow none but members from counties and large cities and towns—although it would have been a representation of the landed, commercial, and manufacturing interests—something would still have been wanting to its completeness. That something I find in a number of persons not connected either with the land, commerce, or manufactures, but who are certainly well worthy to enter these walls, and able to give advice and advance opinions important to the welfare of the community.'

This opinion, thus expressed at the time, he always adhered to; for he again remarked,[28] after an interval of twenty years' experience,—

'In the Bill of 1832 we proposed, as I have said, a large and wide disfranchisement, and we did that on the ground that there were certain boroughs that did not and could not represent the opinions of the inhabitants, and therefore were unfitted for admission to the representation. We did it likewise on the ground that there were many great towns and places of manufacturing industry which could not otherwise obtain members, as it was desirable not to increase the numbers of the House: but in looking to the present state [that was in the year 1852] *I cannot see that there is any such ground of necessity as should induce us now to have recourse to any absolute disfranchisement.* It appears to me, as I have stated more than once, and stated at the time of the discussion on the Reform Bill, that *nothing but an absolute necessity should induce you to resort to an arbitrary and absolute disfranchisement.* What we propose by the name of disfranchisement is simply this—to disfranchise in every case of proved corruption.'

If this reasoning be just, as we conceive it is, it would be unwise to have recourse to absolute disfranchisement in any case, unless there is a proved necessity for it. We should always remember that an addition to the franchise, as before suggested, would raise the constituencies even in the smaller boroughs a third; and it would be very difficult, without destroying the principle of prescription and landing ourselves at once in electoral districts, to lay down as a general rule that in this or that borough the population or the electors are so few that it ought not to return any members in future. Should seats be wanted for other places of growing wealth or increased importance, it would be far preferable to adopt in this respect the course recommended in the last Bill, that is to say, instead of disfranchising any borough altogether, to take away the second member from those which have less than 5000 electors, in order that they may be transferred to the selected places where a fuller or more immediate representation may be deemed desirable. But can it be said that any such necessity really exists, according to the principles upon which the Reform Act was originally framed? If it does, one of two things should clearly be shown. Either it should be shown that there are some places, still unrepresented, of such importance that they ought to have members; or it should be shown that some constituencies are so large that it would be right to subdivide them still further. But can this be shown? In the first place, it is to be observed that there are no unrepresented towns with 40,000 inhabitants, and only five with more than 20,000, viz., Birkenhead, Burnley, Staleybridge, West Bromwich, and Croydon. In the second place, the only large county not subdivided, which has been left with only two members, is strangely enough the metropolitan county of Middlesex; and the only subdivided parts of a county which may fairly require a further subdivision, on account of their wealth as well as their population, are the West Riding of Yorkshire and South Lancashire. The only cases where it might be advisable to give representation and addition to the places above enumerated would be the University of London; and, if that were done, it would be worthy of consideration whether the four Universities in Scotland, and the three Queen's Colleges in Ireland, ought not to be formed into separate constituencies. However that may be, or to what extent it might be prudent to go in each or any of the foregoing instances, the existing vacancies occasioned by the disfranchisement of Sudbury and St. Albans, and the withdrawal of a second member from those boroughs where the population was less than 5000, would provide the means by which such places could obtain members, without increasing the aggregate number of the whole House of Commons. This then is the safest rule by which any disfranchisement can reasonably be regulated; for if we adopt any other, it is a mere wrangle about figures, without any principle whatever to guide us.

Mr. Bright's schedules, in point of principle, are so nearly similar to Mr. Roebuck's theories, that the same objections which apply to the one are quite as applicable to the other also. Both remind us of Mr. Canning's joke at the crazy schemes of Tom Paine and his disciples:—

'Where each fair burgh, numerically free,
Shall choose its members by the Rule of Three.'

Seriously speaking, however, we are glad to find that Mr. Bright is disposed to drop these schedules, if he can only get that more moderate Reform Bill which he hopes Lord John Russell will be prepared to give him. But, as it is not clear that Lord John Russell will be likely to accommodate him to the full extent of his wishes—while it is perfectly notorious that other members of the Government cannot, if they are true to their former opinions, disfranchise and redistribute the different constituencies to anything like that extent—it may be as well to analyse this plan in some detail, in case it should ever be seriously propounded.

In these famous schedules, Mr. Bright proceeds on the principle of population. It is true that he adds columns in which he refers to the direct taxes payable in each borough; but any one who takes the trouble to examine these schedules will see that population is his only test. The first thing to be remarked on such a scheme is its partial character, even assuming that population is or ought to be the standard of any wise representative system. In redistributing the seats disfranchised, he allots to English counties[29] 18 members and no more, while he allots to English boroughs, either in addition or by enfranchisement, no less than 78. But the English counties, with a present population of 10,495,000, would (after deducting the boroughs enfranchised, and so taken out of them, and the boroughs disfranchised, and so thrown into them) still have a population of 10,629,791; while the population of boroughs, which now stands at 7,443,822, would, under Mr. Bright's Bill, be no more than 7,309,961. With an augmented population thus apportioned to counties, and a diminished population thus limited to boroughs, one would have expected that, according to Mr. Bright's own principles, more of the disfranchised seats should be allotted to the former instead of to the latter. Yet how stand the facts? The counties of England and Wales now return 159 members, and under Mr. Bright's Bill they would return 177. The boroughs, exclusive of the two Universities, now return 333 members; they would return, under Mr. Bright's Bill, 290. So that, while an augmented county constituency—consisting of 10,629,791 persons—is to have a representation of 177 members, a diminished borough constituency—consisting of 7,309,961 persons—is to have a representation of 290 members; and thus these schedules which, proceeding upon population, would find on an average every county member representing a population of 66,000 persons, would leave them still representing a population of 60,000 persons; while, as regards boroughs, they would find every borough member now on an average representing a population of less than 26,000 persons, and would leave them representing a population of less than 25,000 persons. If equality be justice, where is it here? All is unequal; and this inequality would be quite as striking if the whole were worked out in complete detail. Upon his own principles, therefore, Mr. Bright's plan would be clearly partial; and, what in our judgment is not less important, this partiality would appear as strong if property and not population were taken as the standard. Taking the aggregate wealth of the counties and also of the boroughs in England and Wales, under Schedules A, B, and D, of the property

224

and income taxation, we believe, according to the best calculations which we have been able to obtain, the county members, one with another, would each of them, under the existing system,[30] represent very nearly 740,000*l.* of that aggregate wealth, and under Mr. Bright's Bill 660,000*l.*, or a little more; whilst the borough members, one with another, would each of them represent a little less than 300,000*l.*, and under Mr. Bright's Bill a short 350,000*l.* In other words, the property which county members represent will be nearly twice as great as that which borough members represent, while the number of the former is to be 177 only, and the number of the latter 290. Can Mr. Bright have seriously weighed the effect and the consequences of his own proposal? Or can anything more be needed to show that the attempt to make constitutions and governments by arithmetical rules must always fail?

But this is by no means our only objection to these famous schedules. The inequality and injustice which we have just pointed out are enough to condemn them. There is another principle, however, embodied in them which would be as inequitable and also as impolitic, as the unequalness and injustice above adverted to. We allude to the principle of multiplying members in the same constituencies in proportion to population. According to Mr. Bright's plan, this would be done by destroying the representation of smaller places and adding to the representation of the larger. If that were accomplished, the variety in the system, which all statesmen desire to preserve, would be immensely curtailed. At the same time, the dissatisfaction which is now felt by the beaten minority, in not obtaining a single representative, would be proportionately aggravated. Under the present system, different classes may obtain a voice in different localities; different interests are not swallowed up by that which predominates. But, if these classes and interests are either disfranchised or consolidated in any one place, that which predominates must, by reason of that very consolidation, unduly prevail. It is, therefore, a false step to give, as Mr. Bright proposes to do, four, five, and six members to any one place. The predominating interest, as a general rule, will return them all of one colour, and the remaining interest will be unrepresented. In quiet times there may be a compromise, and here and there it would occasionally take place for the sake of peace; but, if there be an agitation or popular excitement on any subject, the minority will be overpowered by the same voices which swell the cry. They would have no chance whatever of success, and it is more than possible, in such an event, that passion, not reason, would everywhere be triumphant.

On a careful review of the first two points which we had to consider, and the only propositions which have yet been made by those who may be considered the leading men of the day, we think that the first of these bills at the head of our article is best adapted for the first of those points, or extension of the suffrage, and the third is the best for the second of those points, or the redistribution of seats.

By maintaining the distinction which has always existed between the county and the borough franchise, we provide more effectually than we otherwise could

for the fair representation of those two great interests, in which all others collect and unite—the agricultural and the commercial. By resting the occupation
franchise in the one on a juror's qualification and imperial taxation, and in the
other on rating and the payment of rates, we make the duties and privileges of
citizenship, as near as may be, co-relative terms. By introducing into both those
who contribute to the direct taxation of the State—those whose stake in personal property is as great as that of others in real property or land—those whose
means and social position are quite as good as the tenant who occupies the whole
of a house, though they themselves only occupy a part of it—and those whose
industry and commercial prudence raise a presumption of electoral fitness which
ought to be encouraged, we confer on many an electoral capacity, whom an arbitrary line, like a 10*l.* occupation value, must often exclude. Moreover, by conferring these qualifications, with such a residence as will give them an interest in
that community where the right is claimed, it is almost demonstrable that every
person who is entitled to the franchise by reason of his intelligence, station, and
independence, will either have or be capable of attaining it; and this he could do
without more difficulty than that which pre-supposes the necessary guarantees
for discharging the trust thereby reposed in him. As regards disfranchisement
we may also add that, by still preserving those varied constituencies which tend
to secure a varied representation; by not breaking up those prescriptive usages
which form for the present a connecting-link with the past and the future, and so
give life and continuity to a nation; and by limiting our changes to those cases
where a practical grievance is shown to exist, and a practical remedy requires to
be applied, we shall make, or retain, an infinitely better distribution of seats than
fanciful theories, ingenious calculations, or mere experiment can ever supply us
with.

III. The two other points which remain to be considered are, the freedom of
elections and the duration of Parliaments. To ensure the first, Mr. Roebuck and
Mr. Bright would have recourse to the Ballot; and to limit the last in such a manner as to bring our legislature more completely under the control of public opinion, they would shorten the duration of Parliaments by at least four years. All the
Bills at the head of our article are silent on both subjects. But the third, by the
introduction of voting papers,—not in substitution of, but in addition to the present mode of taking the poll,—sought to facilitate the elector's freedom in giving
his vote, and at once to do away with any necessity, either real or supposed, for
providing him with refreshment, or paying his expenses in going to the poll.

With regard to the Ballot, so much has been said that but little new light can be
thrown upon the subject. We need only observe here that the advantages of such a
system are all founded on a false assumption—a moral error—and a political mistake. The false assumption is, that a man's opinions, especially in a free country,
can ever be kept secret. In the United States we know that the voting is not secret,
and we are sure that in England no man's opinions would be hidden from his neighbour, nor indeed is it desirable that they should be. Acting on this conviction, Burke
once said, in his usual clenching and powerful style, 'All contrivance by ballot we

know experimentally to be vain and childish to prevent a discovery of inclinations. Where they may best answer the purposes of concealment, they are sure to produce suspicion, and this is a still more mischievous cause of partiality.'[31] Let us suppose, however, that it is possible to preserve secrecy. Then will be seen the moral error into which we shall have run, namely, the error that a man's conscience will work as well in the dark as in the light—thence will follow the political mistake that any one, and every one, can exercise a trust or discharge a duty which may have either a bad or good effect on all his neighbours as well as himself, uncontrolled by public opinion, and entirely exempt from all responsibility, excepting that which he chooses to impose on his own conduct. Can anything be more irrational on abstract reasoning? or can anything be more perilous if we consult experience? Once, we know, that a plan of secret, instead of open voting, was recommended and adopted in the decline of the Roman Empire; and a contemporary witness has given us his opinion of it. He tells us, in one passage, why this remedy was sought.—'Quæ nunc, immodico favore corrupta, ad tacita suffragia, quasi ad remedium decurrerunt.' Soon afterwards he points out his apprehensions on the subject; and he does not withhold his reasons for them.—'Sed vereor, ne, procedente tempore, *ex ipso remedio vitia nascantur.* Est enim periculum, ne tacitis suffragiis impudentia irrepat. *Nam quoto—cuique eadem honestatis cura secreto, quæ palam?* MULTI FAMAM, PAUCI CONSCIENTIAM, VERENTUR.'[32] Subsequently he shows that his fears were realised: 'Scripseram tibi, verendum esse, ne ex tacitis suffragiis vitium aliquod exsisteret. *Factum est.*' And then in another passage, which was quoted by the late Sir Robert Peel with great effect in the House of Commons, the result of this change on the public mind is strikingly given:—'Tantum licentiæ pravis ingeniis adjicit illa fiducia—*Quis enim sciet? Poposcit tabellas, stylum accepit, demisit caput, neminem veretur, se contemnit.*'[33] With the knowledge of such results we would rather retain the open manliness of the English character, with the means of detecting, and therefore of punishing all attempts to corrupt and deprave it, than knowingly enable some future historian to say of us what Gibbon said of Rome:—

'As long as the tribes gave their voices aloud, the conduct of each citizen was open to the eyes and ears of his friends and countrymen; the aspect of a pure magistrate was a living lesson to the multitude. *A new method of secret voting abolished the influences of fear and shame, of honour and interest, and the abuse of freedom accelerated the progress of anarchy and despotism.*'

The history of Parliamentary corruption in England has yet to be written—so said Lord Macaulay,[34] and we believe he is right. But when it is written we also believe the only modes by which it has ever hitherto been checked, or by which alone it can be prevented, are—first, by raising the standard of public morals; and, secondly, by passing such laws as enable us to define and detect the offence, and so to stop by punishing the commission of it. Secret voting never can accomplish either one or the other.

227

In former times, corruption was most prevalent within the walls of Parliament itself: now, it is manifested most strongly outside those walls. We know how mercenary members had become in the reign of Charles II.: nay more, they were shameless pensioners in a French king's pay. To Clifford is attributed the infamous demerit of introducing this plague-spot into our system. He is said to have discovered that a noisy patriot, whom it was no longer possible to send to prison, might be turned into a courtier by a goldsmith's note. 'Often the wits said that when a pump appears to be dry, if a very small quantity is pumped in, a great quantity of water rushes out; and so when a Parliament appears to be niggardly, 10,000*l*. judiciously given in bribes will often produce a million in supplies.'[35] The evil was not diminished—it was aggravated, if anything—by that revolution[36] which freed our country from so many other evils. Happily for us, this state of things has long since passed away: partly through the shame which has gradually attached to the reception of a bribe, though not to the giving of it; partly from the publicity with which that shame was made known; and partly by the condemnation of many offenders to heavy fines or imprisonment in the Tower. The corruption of members is now seldom, if ever, heard of. The other kind of corruption, by which the elector's vote was reached, at first took the form of expensive entertainments. This was in the reign of Charles II. A short time afterwards, that is to say in 1701, the buying of votes was scandalously set on foot as a novel practice by the merchants concerned in the new East India Company. According to Burnet,[37] there was so little decency about it, that the electors engaged themselves by subscription to choose a blank person before they were trusted with the names of the candidates. The flood-gates of bribery, however, were not fully opened till the general elections of 1747 and 1754. Hallam[38] then traces it to the increase of wealth by which the rich capitalists sought to counteract the influence of the territorial aristocracy. About this time the sale of seats commenced; and this 'extraordinary traffic' was accompanied in other places by the sale of votes. As soon as this noxious seed sprung up, of course it spread, as all weeds do, until the soil on which they grow is better cleaned. Laws were passed with a view of eradicating it: to a certain extent they succeeded. The riot and debauchery which we can still see in Hogarth's pictures, and read of in Smollett's novels, and the frightful expenses which half-ruined the unhappy candidates, are certainly not what they once were. Still, if the truth must be spoken, we fear it will appear that the corruption and extravagance, which all parties desire to put down, exist as much in the larger Towns as in those Boroughs which are peculiarly the theme of Liberal abuse and the convenient scapegoat of Liberal disfranchisement.

On this subject we do not speak without book. We have now before us some curious returns of those places which have been convicted of bribery between 1851 and 1859. It will be interesting to analyse them.[39] From 1831 to 1851 there were 76 boroughs convicted of bribery; and according to the testimony of a Liberal[40] contemporary 'of these only 21 can properly be called small as having fewer than 500 electors, while some of the more constantly and frequently impure places number their votes by thousands.' A Table of them may not be uninstructive—we therefore subjoin a list of those places where the election has been avoided on the ground of bribery, treating, or corrupt practices, distinguishing those cases where the electors were less than 500 from those where they exceeded 1000, and putting in Italics the boroughs created under the Reform Act.

Year.	Places where Electors were less than 500.	Places where Electors were more than 1000.
1833	None.	Oxford city.
		Southampton.
1835	None.	Canterbury.
		Ipswich.
1837–8	Evesham.	Kingston-upon-Hull.
		Newcastle-under-Lyne.
1839	Ludlow.	Cambridge town.
1840	Totness.	
1841	Lyme Regis.	Ipswich.
	Sudbury.	Newcastle-under-Lyne.
		Northampton.
		Southampton.
1842	None.	Newcastle-under-Lyne.
		Durham.
1847–8	Bewdley.	Aylesbury.
	Harwich.	Carlisle.
	Horsham.	*Cheltenham.*
		Derby.
		Lancaster.
		Leicester.
		Lincoln.
		Yarmouth.
1851	Harwich.	Aylesbury.
	Total 9.	Total 22.

So much for the prevalence of corruption down to the end of 1851. Three general elections have since taken place: one in 1852, one in 1857, and one in 1859. All these elections were attended with nearly similar results as regards the corruption of the smaller and larger boroughs. The proportions were still on the side of the latter. Subjoined is a list of these results:—[41]

Places where Electors were less than 500.	Places where Electors were more than 1000.	
1. Harwich.	1. *Blackburn.*	7. Kingston-on-Hull.
2. Peterborough.	2. Cambridge town.	8. Lancaster.
	3. Canterbury.	9. Maidstone.
	4. *Chatham.*	10. Plymouth.
	5. Derby.	11. Durham.
	6. *Huddersfield.*	12. Liverpool.

After the general election of 1857 there were only two places in England and Wales in which the returns were actually avoided on the ground of bribery or treating—namely, Great Yarmouth and Oxford city. Both of these were among the larger boroughs. The petitions presented after the general election in 1859 have not as yet been all of them heard; but out of those which have been heard—namely, fifteen in all—seven returns[42] have been avoided for bribery by agents. In one of these there were less than 500 electors, while in the remaining six there were upwards of 1000:—

Place where Electors were less than 500.	Places where Electors were more than 1000.	
Dartmouth.	Aylesbury.	Kingston-upon-Hull.
	Beverley.	Norwich.
	Gloucester city.	*Wakefield.*

When we add to this statement, that the cases for which Commissions of Inquiry have been issued, under the 15th and 16th Victoria, chap. 57, upon the ground that corrupt practices have extensively prevailed, are—

Canterbury, with a constituency of	1564	Barnstaple, with a constituency of	733
Maldon, with a constituency of	1071	Tynemouth, with a constituency of	1062
Cambridge town, with a constituency of	1797	Gloucester city, with a constituency of	1721
Kingston-upon-Hull, with a constituency of	5526	*Wakefield,* with a constituency of	952

we are driven to the conclusion that bribery and treating, and undue influences, are as actively at work, to say the least of it, in the larger towns as they are in the smaller boroughs. Nor can we say that the new boroughs created by the Reform Act are so free from corruption, or so moderate in their expenses, as one could wish to find them. Blackburn, Chatham, Cheltenham, Huddersfield, and Wakefield, have all had adverse reports upon them; and the revelations at Wakefield, under the recent Commission, are not very cheering to those who would calculate on purity of election as the probable consequence of a 10*l.* constituency. Moreover, when we look at the expenses of others, as the same have been returned through election auditors, we own we are astonished at some of the sums which the unfortunate candidates have had to pay at some of these elections. The returns for the general election of 1859 are not yet published; but the returns for the general election of 1857 will show that contests may be as costly, or even more costly, in boroughs than in counties. We will give a few instances of these expenses:—

Name of New Borough.	No. of Candidates.	Expenses of Candidates.	Total.		
			£.	s.	d.
Manchester...............	4	For 2	2253	3	6
		2	4546	9	9
			6799	13	3
	3	1	412	0	10
		1	736	11	7
		1	2308	12	11
			3457	5	4
Tower Hamlets..............	3	1	806	2	10
		1	1337	13	11
		1	1133	16	6
			3277	13	3
Southwark..................	3	1	684	2	11
		1	1219	14	1
		1	3880	7	7
			5784	4	7
Lambeth	3	1	1708	0	0
		1	2688	15	7
		1	5339	0	1
			9735	15	8

It is singular enough that the winning candidate in these places is usually the man who paid the most; and there are only two of the old boroughs which can at all vie with them in expense: these are Liverpool and London. But the expenses of Liverpool with three candidates are not near equal to those of Manchester with four; while the expenses of London with five candidates are under those of Southwark, and far less than those of Lambeth, which had only three candidates each. We recommend the consideration of the foregoing facts to those who seek for purity of election either in an extended suffrage or in secret voting. An extended suffrage beyond the point where intelligence and independence may be reasonably assumed, will augment instead of diminish the evil; and the Ballot will wholly prevent its detection, and so increase the temptation to indulge in it. Unless certain impunity is the best preventive of crime, the Ballot would neither put down corruption nor stop intimidation, nor diminish expense. Exposure, detection, conviction, and punishment, not disproportioned, but suitable to the nature and character of the offence, are the things most needed. Secret voting will give us none of them; but it will give us dark intrigue, private spite, cunning treachery, mean suspicion, reckless indifference to public opinion, and a licensed immunity not only from punishment but also from censure. Having obtained under Lord John Russell's Act the power of inquiring into the fact of bribery before the proof of agency is established, and having further obtained in the last Act (which consolidated the whole of the laws on this subject) a clear definition of the three offences of bribery, treating, and undue influence, we believe that the desiderata now most requisite to be added are—a readier mode of detecting the offences than that which is furnished by the costly machinery of the Election Committees; a revision of the statutes by which Commissions of Inquiry are regulated, so that the two Houses may be enabled to act in a more judicial manner than they have hitherto done in the disfranchisement of voters or of whole constituencies; and such a punishment, when the delinquency is proved, as will prevent its repetition by destroying the advantage expected to be gained from it. In making this remark, we allude more particularly to a disqualification of the party bribing and the party bribed from sitting in Parliament or exercising his franchise, for such a number of sessions, or such a number of years, as may be deemed suitable, without being excessive. These are matters however which ought to be originated by the responsible advisers of the Crown; and we trust that they will state their views on the subject very early in the session, and appoint a committee to inquire into and report upon it.

IV. Upon the last of the four great points into which this subject appropriately divides itself—the duration of Parliament—nothing is said in any of the three Bills at the head of our article; but Mr. Roebuck's Committee of Parliamentary Reform would limit their existence to three years. Now it may be difficult to determine the exact duration which would probably be the best; but we have no hesitation whatever in saying that three years would certainly be the worst. Once it was tried, and it signally failed. Every one who has watched the proceedings of Parliament, knows full well that the sessions which follow and precede dissolution are the least advantageous for real business and useful legislation. The experience of the Triennial Bill taught the statesmen of that day how much those sessions were wasted and thrown away.

> 'The first year of a triennial Parliament,' said Sir Richard Steele, 'has been spent in vindictive discussions and animosities concerning the late elections; the second session has entered into business, but rather with a spirit of contradiction to what the prevailing set of men in former Parliaments had brought to pass, than of a disinterested zeal for the public good; the third session languished in the pursuit of what little was intended to be done in the second; and the approach of an ensuing election terrified the members into a servile management, according as their respective principles were disposed towards the question before them in the House.'[43]

If such was the experience of those times, we must confess it is amply confirmed by our personal observations in these. Nothing is less conducive to deliberate counsel on the part of Ministers, or definite views on the part of the House,

232

than the doubtful state in which they meet after a general election. The right to seats has first to be determined; inquiries broken off have again to be resumed; the opinions of members just fresh from their constituents are imperfectly ascertained; the feeling of the House is rather a feeling of uncertainty and suspense, than that which settles down to practical business and immediate action; and under such circumstances prudent administrations (as it was once observed somewhat quaintly, though not less truly) are slow to resolve upon any measures of consequence, until they have 'felt not only the pulse of Parliament, but the pulse of the people.' Hence it happens that the first session after a dissolution is generally unproductive, and in some measure lost. The session which precedes an expected dissolution has still less to recommend it. Nothing is more deplorable than the way in which members then speak to their constituents, and even abandon their fixed convictions, for fear of giving offence to those whom they believe to be wrong, but dare not say 'No' to. The year 1859 will furnish us with more than one example of this—shall we call it vacillation or degradation?—in some among the foremost of our public men.

The last observation points directly to the great evil of frequent elections. It will make men delegates instead of representatives, and the character of the Legislature would be materially affected and lowered by it. If elections were so frequent as to make the House the accurate mirror of the popular feeling, according as it happened to cry up or cry down either men, or things, or opinions; there is just as much chance of its reflecting these prejudices or hasty resolutions, as that it would represent their reason and deliberate judgment. Nothing is more difficult than to define exactly what 'public opinion' really is. A wit, once asked to define orthodoxy, said 'Orthodoxy is my doxy.' In the same way many popular orators seem always to be saying 'Public opinion is my opinion.' But the true sense of public opinion—by which we mean the settled determination of a nation's choice, founded on reason, thought, and reflection—can only be acquired after much deliberation and constant discussion. Many proposals, which sound plausible at first, would be found to be most mischievous if they were at once adopted. Many others are entirely altered and almost remodelled before it would be wise to pass them into a law. Some, which appear theoretically right, may often turn out to be practically wrong—and some few are so far in advance of the general mind that it requires time, patient investigation, and repeated trials to give them a chance of settled acceptance. Now in all those cases where the mere dictates of the popular will would be strongly insisted on, through a frequent appeal to popular prejudice or popular passion, a blind attention to that will would be a positive curse instead of a blessing. Even in the last instance—where the theory of the thing is assumed to be true, but the time for the recognition of it is found to be premature—it is infinitely better that this recognition should for a time be delayed in order that it may be canvassed, discussed, and improved, instead of being forced by pressure from without on an unsatisfied and unwilling minority. Unless they feel that they have had fair play, they will constantly renew agitation upon it. But if fair play has been accorded to them, it is the character of Englishmen then to acquiesce, because they know that they are fairly beaten. 'Le gouvernement d'Angleterre est plus sage, parcequ'il y a un corps qui l'examine continuellement, et qui s'examinaient continuellement lui-même; et telles sont ses erreurs qu'elles ne sont jamais longues, et que par l'esprit d'attention qu'elles donnent à la nation elles sont souvent utiles.'[44]

These reflections are sufficient to convince every friend to order and good government, that the existence of Parliament may be too short as well as too long. On the one hand it may be conceded that it is necessary that new Parliaments should be summoned so often as to ensure in the members full justification of the confidence reposed in them, by compelling them to go before their constituents at stated intervals, for a renewal of their trust. But, on the other hand, we are equally confident that the interval between two general elections should be sufficiently long to enable its members to legislate thoughtfully for the whole community, instead of giving an undue preponderance to those interests which are purely local, or to those feelings which are temporary and occasional. If it be the duty of Members to attend carefully, as it certainly is, to the clear voice of an honest and intelligent public opinion, it is equally their duty to take a large and comprehensive view of the functions of Government, and the interests of the people, without being exposed to every change in the popular sentiment and will, and without acting as mere canvassers for popular favours, or as miserable caterers for popular applause. Whether seven years is the very best limit which could be fixed upon, we will neither pretend to assert nor deny. But when a measure has answered its purpose, and answered it well, the desire to change it, merely from a fancy that something else might be possibly as good, can hardly be characterised by any other name than political pedantry.

We have now gone through the whole of this interesting and important subject; and we have considered in detail every proposition which has been submitted to Parliament, or suggested by any of those public men who are usually deemed Parliamentary leaders. Of other plans worked out in the closets of political philosophers, but not adopted by practical statesmen, we forbear to speak on the present occasion. The science of constructing or reforming a government is an experimental science; and it cannot be taught by *à priori* arguments, however ingenious, or by abstract reasoning, however plausible. Moreover it is a science which has to deal with the most complicated of all things in the most complicated of all relations—man in a social and highly civilised state; united and formed into separate societies of various kinds, and placed here in England with no other restrictions on his natural freedom than those which the necessity of the case requires, but nevertheless with such restrictions as will not enable him to employ that freedom either to the injury of himself or others. Being therefore a science so practical in itself, and intended also for such practical objects, our statesmen must confine themselves, at the present moment, to the practical duty of seeing whether those objects are reasonably obtained, or how far and in what way they can better be realised. Without indulging in vain speculations, we have therefore endeavoured simply to lay down such practical rules, and define at the same time such general principles, as ought to guide and determine our judgment. For some reasons probably it might have been better—under ordinary circumstances we believe it would be—to leave to the Government the sole duty and the exclusive responsibility of originating such measures as they conceive to be most conducive to the well-being of the country, without volunteering any opinions of our own. But there is so much confusion in the present state of parties, the sentiments and opinions of our public men seem so uncertain and so unsettled, the race for power has been and is so close, and the struggle for victory depends so much on conciliating the opposition of those whom the leaders on both sides of the House entirely disagree with, that we own we are anxious to strengthen the hands of Government itself against the attacks of its own followers; and to keep the Conservatives true to their convictions, in spite of the temptation to win power by means of allies who cannot support them in their general policy.

The constitution of a state is not a matter to be lightly dealt with. It is made for enjoyment and thankful use, not for altercation or speculative experiment. Nothing can be weaker or more unwise than to propose alterations merely to satisfy an artificial demand. Unless it is certain—reasonably certain—that those alterations are really required—that they will harmonise and fit in with other parts of our social system—and that they will not lead, by their novelty or incongruity, to other alterations which would then become necessary—they cannot be recommended, and ought not to be entertained. All changes are sure to be attended with some inconvenience. Change for the sake of change, indicates a morbid and restless feeling which seems to be one of the fatal characteristics of the present day. But change which leads to ulterior change is the very worst of all the courses which any prudent or thoughtful statesman will ever have recourse to. On that ground alone it is above all things important that we should now proceed in such a manner as will give us some chance of permanence and stability in our legislation on this subject. Arbitrary lines—and occupation-values, irrespective altogether of social obligations—the extension of the suffrage for the purpose of increasing the electoral roll, without regard to those local considerations which ought to accompany the right to exercise it—the disfranchisement of boroughs merely because they happen to be small—and the distribution of seats, consequent on that disfranchisement, in proportion to numbers or according to any rules of arithmetical computation—these are changes which cannot be deprecated in terms too strong, since they are sure to be uncertain, unstable, and insecure. In addition to the evils already pointed out, they must bring with them this one above all, that they cannot offer a firm foundation upon which the Government can permanently rest.

Few will pretend that among the intelligent portion of the community there is any demand for such changes as these, and fewer still will venture to assert that, in their judgment, the constitution of Parliament would be actually improved by them. Three general elections have now taken place since the question of Reform was again taken up by a minister of the Crown. But that question was not the question upon which any one of these elections turned. In 1852, in 1857, and in 1859, the main and almost the only point upon which the constituencies went to the poll was the degree of confidence which ought to be placed in Lord Derby or Lord Palmerston, both of them being opposed—except so far as they have been pushed on by others—to extensive measures of Parliamentary change. The inference is obvious. Public opinion is not in favour of it; and, except so far as there is or may be some practical grievance which requires redress, we doubt much whether public opinion, by which we mean the reason and intelligence of the public mind, will ever be in favour of it. The people of the country know full well that though the Reform Act allayed some discontent, cured some defects, corrected some abuses, and removed some anomalies which had silently crept in with the inroads of time, it has not improved the character of the House of Commons. Its members as a body possess many qualities which the original Reform Act has probably increased—great local knowledge, professional skill in many departments, a considerable capacity for the details of business, untiring activity, and restless ambition; but it cannot altogether be forgotten or concealed that they have not exhibited a proportionate improvement in those qualities which enabled our statesmen in former days to take a large and comprehensive view of the higher functions of government and legislation. The tendency of members since the Reform Act has been, unfortunately, to become representatives of their respective constituencies rather than representatives of the entire kingdom. If this tendency were still further increased by similar legislation, the House of Commons would resemble still more a delegation of ambassadors from distinct communities, and there would be danger at all events, to say the least of it, that 'being provided with several and often conflicting instructions, they would every day become less capable of united action'[45] either with themselves or with the House of Lords. This was one of the principal evils which the opponents of Reform instinctively dreaded and uniformly denounced. Mr. Canning's warnings were, like the man, brilliant and emphatic; and we have them not only in his recorded speeches, but in the heads for speeches, carefully prepared, which Mr. Stapleton has preserved in his recent biography of that eminent statesman.[46] The Duke of Wellington's sagacity conveyed his views in one short question, 'How is the Queen's Government to be carried on?' and that is a question which administration after administration has been striving to answer ever since, but with doubtful success. Even Sir Robert Peel, the most powerful minister since the Reform Act, was forced to confess that the greatest difficulty which he had to encounter was to reconcile, if possible, an ancient monarchy, a proud aristocracy, and a reformed House of Commons. If that difficulty were so formidable then, let our statesmen beware lest they unduly increase it now. For that purpose let them always remember that the only questions which they have to ask themselves are not, as they seem inclined to do, what kind of Bill is most likely to pass? or what will satisfy unwilling supporters? or what will conciliate unscrupulous criticism?—but what is right? what is wisest? what is best? In short, what will give us the surest guarantees for still preserving that mixed form of government under which it is our happiness and privilege to live?

Notes

1 Lord Macaulay.
2 See Hansard, xcix. 920. 'I remember,' said Lord John Russell in 1847, 'on the night before I was to bring in the Reform Bill, speaking to an American of distinguished talents, who then represented his country at this Court. I said to him, "I cannot but feel great anxiety in proposing to make an alteration in the Constitution which has lasted so long." "Yes," he replied, "so long and so strong." ' That is past the truth with regard to our constitution.
3 See the Address in answer to the Speech from the Throne in 1854.
4 See Mr. Hume's Statement in 1847. Hansard, 3rd Series, vol. xcix. p. 884.
5 Mr. Bright's returns show a little difference. According to them the population was 19,857,000, and the voters 943,248. See No. 121, Sept. 1859. But these returns were taken for the year 1858.
6 See Mr. Gregg's 'Essays on Social and Political Science,' vol. ii. p. 478.
7 See Mr. Mill's 'Thoughts on Parliamentary Reform,' pp. 22 and 23.
8 See pamphlet, p. 29.
9 Registrar-General's Report, 1859. See pp. vii.-ix.
10 See his speech at Rochdale.
11 This speech was delivered before Parliament met in February 1858.
12 See 13 and 14 Vic., c. 99.
13 See Report, iv.
14 See Report, p. v.
15 See pp. 190, 199.
16 Sect. xxiii.
17 6 Geo. IV., c. 50.
18 13 and 14 Vict., c. 99.
19 See and compare Mr. Knight's return, sess. 1859, No. 112; Mr. J. S. Smith's return, same session, No. 7.
20 This epigrammatic sentence is borrowed from the *Times*. We hope that influential journal will still maintain it.
21 See our last number, pp. 556, 557.
22 See former note.
23 It ought to be remembered that these Schedules refer to the whole kingdom, while the Government Bills were confined to England and Wales.
24 Hansard, 3rd Ser., cv., p. 1214.
25 See note to last Number, p. 557.
26 3 Hansard, iv. 338.
27 See on this subject Lord Grey, 64 and 86.
28 Hansard, cxix. 258.
29 In the schedules, as published separately, English counties are not named; but they will be found in the plan as set forth in the *Times* of January 18, 1859.
30 See Sir Stafford Northcote's returns, which differ very little from Mr. Bright's and Mr. J. B. Smith's.
31 See his Works, vol. v., p. 368.
32 Plin., lib. iii., ep. xx.
33 Lib. iv., ep. xxv.
34 Vol. iii., p. 541.
35 Ibid., p. 145.
36 Ibid.
37 See 'His Own Times,' vol. ii., p. 268.
38 'Constitutional History,' vol. iii., p. 402.

39 See 'House of Commons Returns,' 1853, No. 431; and see 'Edinburgh Review.'
40 See 'Edinburgh Review,' No. 200, p. 589. The Review makes the number 72 instead of 76, but we believe we are right according to the returns.
41 See 'House of Commons Returns,' 1854, No. 63, No. 460.
42 See 'House of Commons Returns,' 1859, No. 220, Sess. 2.
43 Lord J. Russell's 'Modern Europe from the Peace of Utrecht,' vol. i. p. 364.
44 Montesquieu.
45 See 'A Plan for the Constituency,' 1859, by Mr. Austin, in which the remarks on this subject are characterised by the author's usual power and juridical ability.
46 See pages 337 et seq.

Sir John Eardley-Wilmot, *A Safe and Constitutional Plan of Parliamentary Reform: In Two Letters to a Member of the Conservative Party* (London: William Ridgway, 1865), 1–32

Corpus Christi Library, XIII.63

Sir John Eardley-Wilmot (1810–1892) was educated at Rugby, Winchester and Balliol College, Oxford. Entering the law, he became a Judge serving in the county court at Bristol from 1854 to 1863 and the Marylebone district in London from 1863 to 1871. He wrote several works on legal and political subjects, including editing his father's *Abridgement of Blackstone's Commentaries* in 1853. Eardley-Wilmot was Conservative MP for South Warwickshire from 1874 to 1885.

Eardley-Wilmot's *A Safe and Constitutional Plan of Parliamentary Reform* sought to enlarge the electorate, while maintaining the equilibrium of the constitution and preventing any one class acquiring a preponderant power. Payment of direct taxation, Eardley-Wilmot argued, provided the basis for doing so. He proposed that, in the counties, adult males paying income tax, as well as copyholders of the annual value of 40s, leaseholders paying an annual rent of £10 or more, tenants paying rent of £20 or more per annum, and those paying taxes to the annual amount of 40s, be given the vote. In the boroughs, those occupying premises of an £8 rated value, those paying income tax, and those paying local taxes to the amount of 40s, should be enfranchised. With regard to redistribution, he proposed enlarging the Commons to 700 MPs. A total of 30 additional seats should be allocated to existing English boroughs, ten new borough constituencies, the University of London, and existing county constituencies. In Scotland, a total of seven additional seats should be allocated to one city, one borough, one county, and the Universities of Edinburgh and Glasgow. In Ireland, a total of five additional MPs should be allocated to the city of Dublin and the counties of Cork, Tipperary, and Down.

9

SIR JOHN EARDLEY-WILMOT, *A SAFE AND CONSTITUTIONAL PLAN OF PARLIAMENTARY REFORM: IN TWO LETTERS TO A MEMBER OF THE CONSERVATIVE PARTY*

(London: William Ridgway, 1865), 1–32

> "It being the interest as well as intention of the people to have a fair and equal representation, whoever brings it nearest to that, is an undoubted friend to and establisher of the Government."
> —*Locke on Government,* Book II. ch. 10.

Letter I. On the extension of the franchise

DEAR SIR,

Before and during the late elections a nearly unanimous wish was expressed by the candidates for Parliamentary honours that some temperate and well-digested plan of Electoral Reform should be brought forward, entitled, irrespectively of party, to public support. This wish found utterance from a conviction, very generally entertained, at least by those who had thought much upon the subject, that a vast portion of the intelligence of the community is at the present time excluded from the privilege of voting, chiefly in consequence of the qualification for it being too limited and one-sided. What is felt to be required is such an extension or rather expansion of the franchise as shall admit to the representation a numerous section of the industry of the working classes, and also many in professions and trades, who from the accidental circumstance of their not being either freeholders or householders, or from their being unpossessed of any other of the present legal qualifications, are unable to find their way into the registration lists.

Since the following pages were prepared for the press the death of the late lamented Statesman who had so long presided over Her Majesty's councils with the greatest advantage to the nation, and the appointment of his successor, have reopened discussion upon this important question, and a general opinion is entertained that the settlement of it can no longer satisfactorily be postponed.

With an experience of seven years as a revising barrister, and having on three former occasions submitted to the public, by whom it was favourably received, a plan very similar to the one I am now about to propose, I shall not, I trust, be deemed presumptuous in endeavouring to point out the defects of measures introduced into Parliament by the leaders of both parties, which defects necessarily resulted in their failure.

I may add that the substance of this letter, with its details, was actually in type some weeks ago, with the intention of its being published prior to the elections, and with the view of giving to the Conservative party safe ground and vantage ground upon which they might stand, touching the question of Parliamentary reform. The unavoidable length of the letter, however, and unforeseen circumstances, prevented its appearance in print at the period when I considered the publication of it would be most valuable. It may at the present time be not without its importance, especially as no statesman, with the exception of Lord Stanley, propounded at the time of the elections any specific plan for the correction of certain anomalies in the representative system as they at present exist.

That the progress in the wealth and prosperity of the country since the period of the Reform Act of 1832, a progress mainly due to the skill and industry of the productive classes, has been most rapid and marvellous, may be demonstrated by very few figures.

In 1831 there were 390,504 depositors in Savings Banks, and deposits to the amount of £12,677,163. In 1864 there were 1,275,981 depositors, and deposits representing £34,650,298. In addition to these, last year there were 431,937 depositors in Post Office Savings Banks (for which most useful measure we are indebted to the present Chancellor of the Exchequer), and deposits of the value of £4,687,891. The above figures show an increase in 33 years of the number of depositors of 1,317,414, and in deposits, in the same period, of £26,661,026, inclusive in both cases of Post Office Savings Banks deposits. The population of represented boroughs in England and Wales was, in 1831, 5,207,520. In 1861 it was 8,638,569, showing an increase of 65·9 per cent. In 1832 there were 285,077 registered electors for the Cities and Boroughs in England and Wales;[1] in 1864 there were 491,229, or an increase of 72·3 per cent. There has been an increase in the number of inhabited houses in England and Wales, since 1801, to the amount of 2,163,582. Of this increase we find 461,666 in the 10 years occurring from 1851 to 1861, as compared with 221,581 in the 10 years from 1801 to 1811. In the 60 years from 1801 to 1861 the population of England and Wales has increased 11,173,688, the increase of the last 10 years, from 1851 to 1861, being 2,138,615, as compared with 1,271,720 occurring in the 10 years from 1801 to 1811. Since 1831 the population of Liverpool has increased 242,187, of Manchester 170,957, of Birmingham 152,090, of Birkenhead 47,454, of Brighton 45,323, of Marylebone 195,958, of Portsmouth 44,410, of Plymouth and Devonport 51,848, of Sheffield 93,480, and of other large towns in an equal proportion. In the city of London alone we find the decrease, easily to be accounted for, in the same period of 10,468. Let us now come to the item of exports and imports. In 1854 the value of exports and imports into and from the United Kingdom was £268,210,145. In 1860 it was £375,052,224. In 1864 it was £487,520,466, showing an increase in 10 years amounting to £219,310,321. The total amount of Income and Property Tax for the years 1863, 1864, amounted in England and Wales to £8,443,906.

I am aware that figures are distasteful to the general reader, but the above are important as demonstrating the immense and rapid advance in our country's prosperity during the present century, and especially during the last ten years; and we may calculate, under the blessing of Divine Providence, upon its still more gigantic development, as facilities of communication between countries increase, and their moral relations are improved and strengthened, as the springs of commerce become still more elastic, and as the wonderful improvements in machinery and mechanical science are wrought out and perfected.

Assuming, from the above figures, that the Representative System cannot be expected to remain as it stood in 1832, the question necessarily arises, how, in enlarging its area, we shall best maintain the equilibrium of the Constitution, and extend its privileges, without handing over a preponderating portion of the power inherent in them to any particular class, the object being that every section of the community should be fairly and adequately, but not exclusively, represented. Could this object have been attained by either the Bill of Lord Derby in 1859, or that of Earl (then Lord John) Russell in 1860? The former proposed to make the Borough and County Franchise identical, by reducing the tenant occupation from £50 to £10; the latter created the same reduction of the County Franchise, but at the same time reduced the Borough Franchise from a £10 to a £6 qualification. Let us consider carefully what would be the result of both these proposals if they should become law. As regards the first, it is quite clear, although we have no figures at hand to demonstrate our argument, that if we reduce the tenant occupation in Counties from £50 to £10 we should totally subvert the character of the County Franchise, as representing the element of property, and transfer it to the *unrepresented* towns. Take for example North and South Warwickshire, the one a district partly agricultural and partly manufacturing, and the other purely agricultural. In North Warwickshire the thickly populated but straggling towns of Nuneaton, Bedworth, Foleshill and Atherton, putting aside Birmingham itself, would completely absorb the representation of the Division, while in South Warwickshire the town of Leamington would turn the scale; and although for some time a majority in the House of Commons affirmed the principle of Mr. Locke King's measure, nevertheless that majority gradually dwindled down, as men considered seriously the extent to which political power would be affected by its adoption, until ultimately it was negatived by its own original supporters by a majority of 28. It will be recollected that Mr. Walpole and Mr. Henley both quitted Lord Derby's Government rather than assent to such a reduction, and public opinion now fully recognises the wisdom and prudence of their course. At the same time they were willing to lower the tenant qualification to £20, whereby a large number of small farmers and occupiers would have been added to the lists of voters, without swamping the

County constituency. The limit of £20 appears the best that can be fixed upon; at that point the house tax commences, and the annual rent of £20 renders the occupier liable to be summoned as a juror. The present plan of Electoral Reform cannot do better than commence by a reduction of the £50 qualification to £20.

It would have been more methodical perhaps to deal separately with the County and with the Borough Franchise; but I turned aside from my first intention, in consequence of having to notice the objectionable part of Lord Derby's Bill of 1859. Let us now pass on to the principal feature contained in that introduced by Earl Russell in 1860, namely, that embodying the £6 Franchise in Boroughs. I may observe that both those Bills had reference only to England and Wales, as will also be the case with the scheme proposed in my present Letter, though it is very desirable in any alteration of the electoral system to render the qualifications of voters throughout the United Kingdom as uniform as possible. For the purpose of explaining what would be the electoral results of a £6 Franchise I am obliged to use the returns moved for in Parliament by Mr. Villiers in 1860, and by Mr. White in 1861, no later returns upon this question having been published. But although the present number of £10, £8 and £6 occupiers in Boroughs may greatly exceed their number in 1860 or 1861, yet it may be reasonably assumed, that as regards *proportion,* for which purpose I am about to cite them, they exhibit no material difference. Looking then over Mr. White's and Mr. Villier's returns, which seem to have startled the House of Commons when published, and to have greatly thinned the ranks of reformers there, we shall, I think, come upon figures which will assist us very materially in settling the question of a reduction of the Borough Franchise. If we begin with Manchester, with its 18,334 registered electors in 1860, we shall find that under a £6 Franchise there would have been an addition of 22,492 male occupiers, which, after deducting 20 per cent. for disqualified and unregistered persons, would have left 17,994 electors to be added to the list of voters as it stood in 1860. Under an £8 Franchise the accession, with the reduction of 20 per cent., would have been 6472. At Wolverhampton, with its 4025 registered electors in 1860, there would have been added, under a £6 Franchise, 9346 male occupiers, which, after a reduction of 20 per cent., would have given us 7477 more electors to be placed upon the list. With an £8 Franchise, in a similar way, we shall find an addition of 1600. At Preston, with its 2657 registered voters in 1860, there would have been, under a £6 Franchise, 5287 more voters inclusive of the above reduction. With an £8 Franchise the addition would only have amounted to 1758. At Bolton, with 2057 registered electors in 1860, we should have added to the list 2432 voters with a £6 Franchise. Under an £8 Franchise there would have been an accession of 574. At Macclesfield, with 4207 registered electors in 1860, there would have been 3803 more voters under a £6 Franchise, while under one at £8 the addition would have amounted to 768. We will now take two or three of the smaller boroughs. Frome, with its 385 registered electors in 1860, would have given us 323 more voters under a £6 Franchise; under one at £8 we should have found an addition of 87, after making the usual reduction of 20 per cent. At Poole, with 547 registered electors in 1860, we should have placed, under a £6 Franchise,

447 more voters on the list, whereas under one at £8 we should have an accession of 128 only. Lewes, with 697 registered electors in 1860, would have gained 379 more voters under a £6 Franchise, while with one at £8 the addition would have been 113. At Rye, with 470 voters in 1860 there would have been 268 more persons upon the list; under one at £8 we should have added 64 more. Kidderminster, with 487 electors in 1860, would have shown an addition of 779 voters under a £6 Franchise—under one at £8 there would have been 148 more added to the lists. At Lincoln, with 1435 electors in 1860, of whom 513 were freemen, we should have had 1061 more voters under a Franchise at £6. Under one at £8 there would have been an addition of 251.

Then taking the figures generally from the returns obtained by Mr. White and Mr. Villiers, it appears that taking the gross estimated rental, and without the reduction of 20 per cent., there would have been admissible to the Register under a £6 Franchise the immense number of 288,889, of which the male occupiers at the rent of £6 and under £8 amounted to 189,323. The addition under an £8 Franchise would have been 99,566, a very considerable accession of numbers, but within a few thousand less than half of the addition under a Franchise at £6. In 1861, at the time Mr. White's return was made (20th February), there were 442,210 occupiers at £10 and freemen on the Borough lists. It will be apparent from the above figures, that the great mass of small occupiers of houses in Boroughs (and it may be inferred in unrepresented towns) ranges at the limit between £6 and £8 annual rental, and that while we might safely lower the Borough Franchise to £8, we could not descend lower without surrendering the whole electoral power into the hands of men, by their habits, their dependence upon others and their education, least justified to exercise it. On the other hand, by lowering the Borough Franchise to £8, we should admit a large number of the working classes, without depriving property of its just and legitimate influence. I therefore propose to reduce the Borough Franchise to that amount. But even with such a reduction, there would remain a considerable number of respectable inhabitants of Boroughs, by their position in society and their education, professional men, tradesmen, skilled workmen, and artizans, well qualified to possess the electoral suffrage, and yet who do not happen to be freemen or householders. How are these to be admitted to representative rights? For this purpose a lodger Franchise, a wages Franchise, a Franchise by deposits in Savings Banks, an educational Franchise, a fundholder Franchise, have at various times been either suggested, or actually been made the basis of proposed legislation. All these modes of meeting the difficulty are open to objection, though they do not merit the ridicule cast upon them by Mr. Bright, by whom they were styled fancy Franchises.

The Educational Franchise, already recognised and admitted in our principal Universities in England and Ireland, would on the whole perhaps be best amplified and extended by conferring representatives on additional seats of learning. Lodgers, on the other hand, are often shifting and migratory, and the lower class of them not unfrequently found by experience to be very unsteady and uncertain in their payments. The payment of wages differs very materially in different places and at different periods of the year. The industrious man with the largest family, who best brings up his children, cannot afford to put much into a Savings Bank. The proof of such deposits, by its inquisitorial character, is alien to our feelings and habits; and the latter objection is equally applicable to a Franchise to be obtained by holding money to a certain amount in the public funds. It would be almost as well to give every man the suffrage who could afford to pay 40s. per annum for it to the public purse.

A simpler and readier method of conferring the Electoral Privilege exists in the payment of taxation to a certain amount, and we possess the machinery for testing this qualification in our rate books. Lord John Russell in 1854 proposed the qualification by payment of Government and parochial taxes to the amount of 40s., and in addition to the adoption of that portion of his plan of Parliamentary Reform, I propose (as I did in 1861) that the payment of income tax to any amount should give the person (not otherwise disqualified) a right to be placed on the register. Such a qualification is in unity and consistent with constitutional rights, which presume that every person paying taxes ought to have a voice in their administration. We all however know that in a form of government so nicely balanced as ours, and harmonizing at times by its very inconsistencies, we cannot carry abstract political rights to their full extent. This therefore completes my plan for the extension of the Borough Franchise in England and Wales, viz., 1st., a reduction of the £10 qualification to £8; 2ndly, the introduction of qualification by payment of income tax; 3dly, a qualification by the payment of Government and parochial taxes in all to the annual amount of 40s.

Before leaving this branch of my subject, I must not disguise the fact that to a certain extent the test of a rental or rating value for a house is unsatisfactory, inasmuch as the amount of rent varies so much in different localities. This was pointed out forcibly by Lord Brougham, then Mr. Brougham, in 1831. In Westminster, according to the figures already cited, a £6 franchise would only have added in 1860 about 750 voters to a list of 13,791 existing at that time. Marylebone would only have furnished, with the same reduction, 500 additional voters, with a list of 21,031. Lambeth, with 21,737, would have given an addition of 2,111. It must, however, be recollected that in the Metropolis this smallness of additional numbers would be far more than made up for by the introduction into Boroughs of a qualification by the annual payment of income tax and assessed and parochial taxes.

My letter has already reached such a considerable length that I shall have less space to devote to Counties, where, however, the paths are much smoother and the difficulties obviously less. I have already, for reasons I have given, placed the reduction of the tenant qualification at the limit of £20. The freeholders naturally remain as they are. Next come the copyholders, entitled at present to vote if they hold copyhold lands of the annual value of £10. This franchise was first successfully introduced into Parliament in 1832, but we find that Mr. Pitt as far back as 1784 proposed it to Mr. Wyvill and made it the subject of a Bill in Parliament in the following year. He placed the annual value at 40s., making it identical with the freehold franchise. A valuable Parliamentary return, moved for by Mr. Blake in the last Session, has been lately published, exhibiting the several qualifications of electors in the Counties of England and Wales for the year 1864. By this return we find how small a proportion the copyholders bear to the other electors. In my own county, Warwickshire, where I know many small copyholders are to be found, and where the freeholders in both Divisions amount in all to 6918, the copyholders number only 132. In Gloucestershire, where we find freeholders in both Divisions to the number of 13,373, there are only 218 copyholders. In Leicestershire, with 8210 freeholders in both Divisions, we find only copyholders 127 in number. In Wilts, where much copyhold property exists, we find 6132 freeholders, and only 265 copyholders in both Divisions. There is reason to believe, that if we should carry out Mr. Pitt's proposition we should place on the list of voters a very large additional number of small holders of copyhold property. We come next to the leaseholders, whose qualification was also created by the Reform Act, but with such restrictions as to term that it is altogether nugatory, insomuch so that during the many years I acted as a Revising Barrister, I do not recollect ever having admitted a single leaseholder to the registration lists. By the provisions of the Reform Act leaseholders for the term of 60 years, or any part then unexpired, and paying a rent of £10 per annum, or for the term of 20 years, or any part then unexpired, and paying £50 per annum, were privileged to vote. Looking at Mr. Blake's returns, we shall at once perceive that those provisions have not worked satisfactorily. Referring once more to Gloucestershire, a large agricultural county, with 7515 electors now on the list for its Eastern, and 9368 for its Western Division, we shall find that there are only 108 leaseholders in the former and 119 in the latter Division. Middlesex, with 14,847 electors on its books, has only 938 leaseholders. Nottinghamshire, with 4065 electors for its Northern and 3427 for its Southern Division, has only 11 leaseholders in the one and 8 in the other. Warwickshire again, with 10,127 electors in both Divisions, has in the aggregate only 595 leaseholders. Wilts, with 5146 electors in its Northern and 3343 in its Southern Division, has in all only 481 leaseholders. A considerable addition in the number of county voters would be realized, and that without altering the fundamental character of the County Franchise, which represents the element of property, if we should substitute for the present leasehold qualification one for a term of seven years and upwards, and subject to a rental of (say) £10 and over. By these means we should obtain a class of voters both in the rural districts and in unrepresented towns very different from the £10 occupier from year to year, while facilities afforded to the granting of such leases must necessarily occasion the improvement of property. Lastly, in Counties as in Boroughs, I would admit a numerous body of men, not qualified either as freeholders, copyholders, leaseholders, or occupying tenants, by the annual payment of income tax and of Government and parochial taxes to the amount of 40s. per annum.

I have thus submitted to public consideration and criticism, and very possibly to public censure, a plan for extending without unduly lowering the Electoral Franchise, not supposing for a moment that it has not its defects or that it cannot be improved; but with the hope that it may not be without its use in directing men's minds to what they require, and by what channel, and in what quarter they may obtain that requirement. In a subsequent Letter, I propose to deal with what is usually called the question of redistribution of seats, but which I should prefer to style the reconstruction of the representatives of the people in the Commons House of Parliament, which I was desirous of keeping distinct from that of the Extension of the Franchise. I shall endeavour, hereafter, as in the present Letter, to substantiate my arguments by reference to figures. In the meantime, I will conclude with a recapitulation of the scheme as it relates to the extension of the Electoral Franchise in Counties and Boroughs in England and Wales.

COUNTIES.

Qualification.

1. Freeholders, holders of offices, &c., as at present.
2. Copyholders of the annual value of Forty Shillings (now £10).
3. Leaseholders for terms of seven years, and upwards, paying annual rent not less than £10.
4. Occupying tenants paying rent not less than £20 per annum.
5. All persons (not legally incapacitated) paying annual income tax to any amount.
6. All persons (not legally incapacitated) paying Government and Parochial Taxes, in all to the annual amount of Forty Shillings.

BOROUGHS.

1. Freemen, Potwallers, Scot and Lot Voters, as at present.
2. Resident Occupiers of Premises (not legally incapacitated) of annual (rated) value of £8.
3. All persons (not legally incapacitated) paying annual Income Tax to any amount.
4. All persons (not legally incapacitated) paying Government and Parochial Taxes in all to the annual amount of Forty Shillings.

I remain,

Yours &c.[2]

Letter II. On the enlargement of parliamentary presentation

DEAR SIR,

In my former Letter I submitted to your consideration what appeared to me, after much reflexion upon the subject, a moderate and yet comprehensive plan for the extension of the Electoral Franchise. I pointed out to you how, notwithstanding the immense advance of our country in civilization, industry, and wealth, and notwithstanding the extraordinary increase in its population within the last few years, a great portion of its intelligence and independence are still excluded from the privilege of voting, and I argued that though there exists no popular excitement on the subject of Parliamentary Reform, there is still a general feeling entertained that the question ought to be dealt with and settled in a statesmanlike manner, without further equivocation or evasion. The present time appears especially favorable to its discussion. We have peace, we have contentment, and we have soberness of feeling and moderation on political topics. We have also a Government identified with, and to a certain extent committed to Reform.

The subject for consideration in this Letter is one generally joined with the Extension of the Franchise, but really quite distinct from it, namely, what is usually termed the Redistribution of Seats in the House of Commons. In almost every scheme put forward since 1832, it has been proposed either partially or entirely to deprive certain Boroughs of their members, and to hand over the seats thus rendered vacant to other places considered to be more worthy of representation in consequence of their greater wealth and population. There is no doubt that the Reform Bill of 1832 finally settled the question of the Legislature having the power of disfranchisement. Some years previously, Mr. Pitt had experienced such opposition when proposing a similar plan, that, as a compromise, he offered the small Boroughs a pecuniary grant as a compensation for the surrender of their privilege of sending members to Parliament. It will be interesting to take a brief survey of the representation as it stood in 1832. Before the Reform Act (2 Wm. 4, c. 45), there were as now 658 representatives in the Lower House, but they were thus divided:—England and Wales had 513, Ireland (by the Act of Union, A.D. 1800) 100, and Scotland 45. These proportions were altered by the Reform Act. England and Wales had afterwards 500, Scotland 53, and Ireland 105. By the same Act, 56 English Boroughs were disfranchised, beginning with Old Sarum, having a population of 12 persons only, Newtown, I. W., with 68, then St. Michael's and Bramber, with a population of 97 each, and ending with St. Germains and East Grinstead, having populations respectively of 2586 and 3364. Proceeding thence to the Boroughs which lost one member by the Reform Act, we find Clitheroe and Shaftesbury the largest, 8915 and 8518, and Droitwich and Wareham the lowest, 2487 and 2325. It is remarkable that both Wareham and Droitwich have more than doubled their population since the Census of 1831, and many other towns which then lost one member have greatly increased. By the Act of 1832 twenty-two unrepresented towns had two members given to them, the highest in population being sections of the Metropolis, viz., the Tower Hamlets, 361,783; Marylebone, 240,294, and Finsbury, 234,629; the lowest, Blackburn, 27,091, and Macclesfield, 23,129; at that period, the population of other towns having two members given them was for Manchester 187,022, for Birmingham 143,986, for Leeds. 123,393.

We come next to twenty towns having a single member conferred upon them, the highest in the list Salford, with a population, in 1831, of 40,786, the next Tynemouth, 23,206, the lowest Frome, Kendal, and Whitby, with populations respectively of 12,240, 11,577, and 10,339. Many of these twenty-two towns, made Boroughs by the Reform Act, show an enormous increase of population since 1831, especially Ashton-under-Lyne, Bury, Dudley, Salford, and Cheltenham.

The number of Registered Electors in most of these Boroughs has more than doubled since 1831. Cheltenham shows an increase of 1657, Huddersfield of 1268, Salford of 3640, Bury of 791, Walsall of 653, Gateshead of 538, Rochdale of 761. In all these there are more than twice as many electors as there were in 1831. Even many of the Boroughs which were wholly disfranchised by the Act of 1832 show a considerable increase of population; for example, Minehead, Brackley, Heytesbury, and Stockbridge. I have cited these figures for the purpose of proving that the present times are altogether different from those preceding the Reform Act, and that the question of redistribution of Parliamentary seats cannot be approached in the same manner as it was then. Some very interesting returns on the subject of population and electors were moved for by Mr. James White, and ordered by the House of Commons to be printed on 10th May, 1864. By these tables we find a list of English Parliamentary Boroughs with less than 8000 inhabitants in 1831, which still return members to Parliament, with their increase or decrease in population from that period to 1861. The Boroughs are 75 in number, and return collectively 118 members, beginning with Bewdley, with a population of 7939 in 1831, and ending with Arundel, with 2803 at the same period. Among these 75 Boroughs there are only eleven which show a decrease of population, viz., the two above mentioned, also Westbury, Knaresborough, Launceston, Lymington, Northallerton, Dartmouth, Honiton, Ashburton, and Lyme Regis. These eleven Boroughs send collectively 14 members to Parliament. The remaining 104 members are returned by towns which, though they had only 8000 inhabitants in 1831, show a considerable increase. Great Grimsby shows an increase of 8471, Bedford of 6454, Peterborough of 5224, Morpeth of 7028, Bridgewater of 4041, Stafford of 4949, Reigate of 6578. The nett increase of population in these 75 Boroughs since 1831 is 104,810. Their aggregate population at the present time is 537,388. In the same returns we find 53 English Boroughs with a population in 1861 of 314,005 returning 83 members to Parliament, beginning with Newport, I.W., with a population of 7934, and ending as before with Arundel, with 2498. Within the last ten years, however, the population of many of these Boroughs has been steadily on the advance. Maldon shows an increase of 373, Dorchester of 429, Chippenham of 792, Buckingham of 443, Petersfield of 105. In most of them we also find since 1851 a considerable increase in the number of Registered Electors. The increase in the population and wealth of the Counties we shall advert to hereafter. But the question meanwhile arises, is it desirable at the present time, with so many evidences of advancing prosperity around us, to deprive even partially of their existing privilege of sending members to Parliament Boroughs, which, with very few exceptions, evince no sign whatever of decay or impending dissolution, but on the contrary are running their race with the general prosperity of the country. And can no other mode of meeting the difficulty short of disfranchisement be resorted to? For in the first place it will not be a liberal or enabling statute which takes from one class of citizens, not shown to be unworthy, what it may bestow upon another; and in a free country it is not likely that a valuable and valued privilege will be surrendered without very great opposition. It is quite clear that the Bills of Lord Derby in 1859, and of Lord John Russell in 1860, did not satisfy the country as regards the redistribution of Parliamentary seats. Lord Derby proposed to take one member from 15 English Boroughs now returning two respectively, but having less than 5000 inhabitants according to the census of 1851. These 15 seats he thus apportioned, viz.: One member respectively to West Bromwich, Birkenhead, Burnley, Staleybridge, Croydon, Gravesend, and Hartlepool; two additional members to Middlesex, two to Lancashire, and four to Yorkshire.

The Bill of Lord John Russell (1st March, 1860), proposed to take one member from the following 25 English Boroughs now returning two respectively:—

Guildford	Andover
Hertford	Ludlow
Devizes	Lymington
Marlow	Leominster
Dorchester	Marlborough
Bodmin	Richmond
Chippenham	Wells
Huntingdon	Evesham
Cirencester	Harwich
Ripon	Totnes
Maldon	Thetford
Tewkesbury	Honiton.
Knaresborough	

All these had respectively at that period less than 500 Registered Electors, but the population of several of them, viz., of Guildford, Chippenham, Hertford, Bodmin and Devizes, exceeded 6000 at the last census. The population of Guildford was above 8000, and that of Chippenham above 7000. The number of Registered Electors in many of these Boroughs, by the returns of 1864, considerably exceeded 500; and the question naturally occurs, can this be a satisfactory criterion for disfranchisement, when the numbers are continually changing, and when it is proposed at the very same moment to extend the Franchise, and thus add considerably to the number of Electors? The 25 seats to be obtained by the Bill of Lord John Russell in 1860 were proposed to be thus distributed:—Three members respectively were to be allotted to Birkenhead, Burnley and Stalybridge; thirteen respectively to North and South Lancashire, Middlesex, Kent, W. Division; Devonshire, S. Division; Yorkshire, N. Riding; Lincolnshire, parts of Lindsey; Essex, S. Division; Somersetshire, E. Division; Norfolk, W. Division; Cornwall, W. Division; Essex, N. Division. Having thus re-distributed sixteen seats, Lord Russell proposed to give one additional member respectively to Manchester, Liverpool, Birmingham, Leeds and Glasgow; one to the Scotch Universities collectively; one to the University of London; one additional member to the County of Cork, and one to the County of Limerick.

It will be seen that neither in the Bill of Lord Derby nor of Lord John Russell was any provision made for giving additional members to some very large Boroughs which now only return one member. Nor was the single member given to a few unrepresented but important towns in any way calculated to give satisfaction. Both these statesmen, doubtless, felt the vast difficulties meeting them at every turn of this momentous question, and, not least, the natural unwillingness of the House of Commons to pass any measure which must necessarily deprive many of its own body of their seats.

It is evident that a list of Boroughs, to the amount of nearly 40, might be readily furnished, with populations small as compared with those of many great commercial towns, in favour of the partial disfranchisement of which many arguments might be adduced. I have myself proposed in former Letters on this very subject to take one member from all English Boroughs having less than 10,000 inhabitants and less than 1000 inhabited houses. It appeared to me that when the Legislature created the qualification of a £10 Householder for Boroughs, there could not be a better criterion of the condition of the Borough, or one which could more readily be ascertained, than the test of inhabited houses. But cannot we solve the difficulty in a way more acceptable to the country, than by obtaining additional representatives in proportion to our wealth, intelligence and population, through the medium of disfranchisement? Let us look for a moment at the constitution of the House of Commons. It has 658 members. It had the same number of Representatives when our political, our commercial, our domestic, our colonial interests were infinitely less numerous and important than they are now. In the time of Lord Coke the number of Representatives for England and Wales was 493,[3] at a period when the population of the whole of England was less than that of the Metropolis at the present day. The 658 members of the House of Commons are now thus made up. There are 147 members for English Counties, 15 for Welsh, 30 for Scotch, and 64 for Irish. There are 320 members for English Boroughs, 14 for Welsh, 23 for Scotch and 39 for Irish. These, with four Members for English Universities and two for the University of Dublin (one was given by the Reform Act), make up 658 Members. Taken in another way, the figures are,—For Counties, 256 Members, for Boroughs, 396, for Universities, 6—total, 658. We arrive then at length at the important question: Is there any particular charm in the figures 658, and should we not, proportionably to our increased population, our increased wealth, and the immensely diversified interests of every description to be considered by our Legislature, and especially the popular section of it, do well

252

to increase the number of our Representatives in the House of Commons? Already the labours devolving upon its members, especially as regards private legislation, are extremely onerous, and may be expected, as our commercial relations extend and become more complicated, to increase to a vast extent. Would any serious inconvenience as regards debate, or accommodation, arise by additional members being introduced? Is there not frequently no House, and is it not often counted out when made, and except on very great occasions does the House often muster more than 300 Members? I do not see any difficulty in this respect which may not be overcome.

The proposal then I have to make and respectfully to submit to the public through the medium of my Letter to you, is that the number of members of the House of Commons should be increased from 658 to 700, which will give us 42 seats to be disposed of, without interfering with the privilege of any existing Borough. These small Boroughs have their use and their value—they tend to preserve the representation of various interests in Parliament, and prevent the representatives themselves from being too much of the same form and colour.

My plan will not, however, be complete without my indicating to you in what way I would provide for the 42 additional seats. As we have already seen, England and Wales have at the present time 500 members, Ireland 105, and Scotland 53. I would apportion the 42 seats in the following manner:—I would give 30 of them to England and Wales, 7 to Scotland, making up the number of her representatives to 60, and 5 to Ireland, making her members 110. This apportionment appears to be fair when we consider the relative populations and wealth of the respective countries, as shown by the Census and the Income Tax returns. We find that the amount of Income and Property Tax charged in the year ending 5th April, 1863 (published in 1864, and there has been no return since), the total amount for England and Wales (Counties and Boroughs included, under Schedules A, B, D and E) was £8,443,906, for Scotland was £901,257, for Ireland was £754,005. For the English and Welsh Counties it was £3,537,627, for the Scotch £444,101, for the Irish £493,155. For the English and Welsh Boroughs it was £4,906,279, for the Scotch £457,156, for the Irish £260,850. The aggregate of Property and Income Tax for the United Kingdom amounted to £10,099,168. Taking the above figures relatively, and also the relative populations of the three sections of the United Kingdom, the above distribution (not a re-distribution) of the 42 seats seems to be fair and just.

Let us now proceed to point out to what constituencies additional members should be given, and what new Boroughs created, keeping in view their several qualifications as regards local importance, wealth, and population. First in the list I submit should come certain English Boroughs, to which one member was given by the Reform Act, but which show since that period an enormous advance in wealth and commercial importance. There is Salford, with an increase in population since 1831 of 51,639; Ashton-under-Lyne, with an increase of 19,882; Rochdale, with 19,143, and other Boroughs, not all of them identical in their features or commercial character. The following are ten in number, on which I propose to confer a second member, giving you the increase of population since 1831:—

Salford, Lancashire - - -	51,639
Walsall, Staffordshire - - -	23,340
Dudley, Staffordshire - - -	21,545
Ashton-under-Lyne, Lancashire	19,882
Rochdale, Lancashire - - -	19,143
Bury, Lancashire - - -	18,423
Gateshead, Durham - - -	17,970
Cheltenham, Gloucestershire -	16,751
Huddersfield, Yorkshire - -	15,842
Tynemouth, Northumberland -	10,815

Total increase since 1831–205,350

In many of these the number of registered electors has very greatly increased since 1832. Salford shows an increase of 3640, Cheltenham of 3233, Huddersfield of 1268, Walsall of 653. For the year ending 5th April, 1863, Salford contributed to the Income and Property Tax under Schedules A, B, D and E, £27,220; Cheltenham, £14,328; Dudley, £9870; Bury, £12,001.

It seems more desirable that these flourishing Boroughs should have their second representative, than that certain great trading cities should, as proposed by the Bill of Lord John Russell in 1860, be singled out for a third member. Ten of the 30 seats reserved for England having been thus allotted (for Wales proportionably to her population and the amount of her contribution towards taxation may be said to be adequately represented), let us go on to certain unrepresented towns fully entitled to the privilege of sending a single representative to Parliament. They are ten in number, respectively having populations by the last Census of upwards of 10,000, and upwards of 2000 inhabited houses each. Ten may be very fairly selected for Parliamentary honours, and they are the following, with their populations and number of inhabited houses respectively:—

	P. 1861.	H. 1861.
Barnsley, Yorkshire - - -	17,890	3565
Burnley, Lancashire - - -	28,700	5085
Croydon, Surrey - - - -	20,325	5338
Doncaster, Yorkshire - - -	16,406	3594
Gravesend, Kent - - - -	18,782	3062
Hartlepool, Durham - - -	12,603	2190
Leamington, Warwickshire -	17,958	3257
Staleybridge, Lancashire - -	24,921	4864
Torquay, Devon - - - -	16,419	2183
West Bromwich, Staffordshire -	17,024.	3363

In many of these towns the population and number of inhabited houses have greatly increased in the last ten years. Barnsley shows an increase in population since 1851, of 4353, and in inhabited houses, of 945; Doncaster in population, of 4354, and in inhabited houses, of 1011; Staleybridge in population, of 4161, and in inhabited houses, of 1194; Leamington in population, of 424, and in inhabited houses, of 2266; the others in much the same proportion. We must not, however, while recognising the claims of the above towns to send a member to the House of Commons, forget those of a large district of the Metropolis, at present comprised in the representation of the County of Middlesex—I allude to Chelsea and Kensington, with populations respectively of 63,439 and 70,198 according to the Census of 1861. I have always advocated the claims of these large and influential Parishes, and I would allot to them collectively two members. If Hammersmith were united to them, there would be an additional population of 24,519. Having thus disposed of 22 Borough seats, I would pass on to the Counties, and I propose to give an additional member to the following County and Divisions of Counties:—

```
Middlesex   -    -    -    -    -    -   - 1
Derbyshire (S. D.)    -    -    -    -   - 1
Essex (S. D.)    -    -    -    -    -   - 1
Gloucestershire (W. D.)   -    -    -   - 1
Lincolnshire (parts of Lindsey)-    -   - 1
Norfolk (W. D.) -    -    -    -    -   - 1
Somerset (W. D.)-    -    -    -    -   - 1–7
```

The following figures will show their population, exclusively of represented Cities and Towns, the number of members at present returned by each County and Division, and the amount of Income and Property Tax charged on each, exclusively of their Boroughs:—

	Population in 1861, exclusive of Boroughs.	Total Number of Members.	Amount of P. and Income Tax per year ending April '66.
Middlesex*	368,424	14	£127,670.
Derbyshire (S. D.)	220,229	4	£31,897.
Essex (S. D.)	207,270	4	£73,042.
Gloucestershire(W.D.)	143,410	4	£36,509.
Lincolnshire (N. D.)	193,757	5	£80,059.
Norfolk (W. D.)	161,218	6	£60,270.
Somerset (W. D.)	159,551	6	£53,130.

* Middlesex shews an increase of Population since 1832, independently of its cities and boroughs, of 175,878; Derbyshire, S. D., of 25,885; Essex, S. D., of 61,869; Gloucestershire, W. D., of 23,428; Lincolnshire, N. D., of 38,175; Norfolk, W. D., of 14,542; Somerset, W. D., of 13,566.

Most of these Divisions show a large increase in the number of Registered Electors since 1832. Middlesex exhibits an increase of 7373; North Lincolnshire, of 3162; West Gloucestershire of 2808; West Somerset, of 828; West Kent, of 2394; West Norfolk, of 2240.

Perhaps if we were to look carefully at the results of the Census of 1861, we might be called upon to recognise the claims of the English Counties to a greater extent than we have done; at all events, the statistics we find there form a conclusive answer to those, who maintain that the Counties have at present more than their share of the National Representation. In the first place, there are 200 English and Welsh Boroughs returning at the present time 338 members, 324 for England, and 14 for Wales; while there are 162 members returned for English and Welsh Counties, that is, 147 for England and 15 for Wales. On the other hand, if we take the population collectively of England and Wales, we find that the population of the Boroughs is 8,638,569, and of the Counties, exclusively of the Boroughs, 11,427,655, making in the aggregate, 20,066,224; of this the Welsh population is 1,111,780, made up of 345,250 for the Boroughs, and 766,530 for the Counties.

Then taking some of the English Counties separately; except a very few, for example, the Southern Division of Lancashire and the West Riding of Yorkshire, the population exclusively of the Boroughs is considerably larger that that of the Boroughs collectively. Take, for example, the Southern Division of Staffordshire, the population exclusively of represented towns, is 162,986. Including its Boroughs, it has a population of 289,663. The Boroughs show a population of 126,679 as compared with that of the Division of the County at 162,986. The East Division of Somerset has a population, exclusive of its Boroughs, of 172,717; with its Boroughs it has 259,335. The Boroughs are thus 86,618, as compared with the population of the Division for County election purposes, at 142,717. Berkshire has a population of 128,590, exclusively of its Boroughs; with its Boroughs it has 176,256. Its Boroughs are as 47,666 compared with the County population at 128,590.

With these figures before us, it may be asked, why allot so scanty a proportion of the thirty additional members to the Counties? The reply is, that there are other elements to be taken into calculation besides population. The amount charged upon the English and Welsh Counties for Income and Property Tax, for the year ending April 1853, was £3,537,627; whereas the amount contributed under the same head by the English and Welsh Boroughs was £4,906,279, and the strongest Conservative cannot disguise from himself that, valuable as our land is, and with all the improvements in cultivation, it is our trade and commerce, gathered up and issuing from the great hives of industry in our cities and towns, which constitute the chief ingredients of our national prosperity and wealth. With these convictions, we shall not go far wrong if we strengthen the cords of their representation, and to a certain extent add to the popular character of the State. One member yet remains for distribution, and I would complete the list of thirty members for England by conferring it, as was proposed by Lord Russell, upon the University of London.

Proceeding to Scotland, the representation of which I propose to increase to 60, I cannot do better than commence with the Universities of Edinburgh and

Glasgow, upon which I would confer respectively two members. Desirable as it would be to introduce the Educational principle into the Registration, there are great difficulties attending it on the score of definition and limit. What is to be an Educational vote? Where is it to begin, and where is it to leave off? Therefore, although I believe I was the first who in 1853 suggested an Educational Franchise, yet upon the whole I prefer recognising the principle of Education as conferring a right of representation, by extending it in the path already sanctioned by law, and by the usage of the Constitution, namely, by increasing the number of members for the Universities. Under my present plan England and Wales would have five University members, Scotland four, and Ireland two. Our Northern brethren are fully entitled to stand so near ourselves by their proficiency in National Education, and by their distinguished attainments in scholarship and science. Leaving the Scotch Universities, we find a very large city and a very large town, to which the Reform Act gave a single member, viz., Aberdeen and Dundee. Their population respectively, by the Census of 1861, was 73,805, and 90,417. The number of registered electors for 1864, was for Aberdeen 3586, and for Dundee 2716. The population of Aberdeen has increased by 15,786 since 1831; that of Dundee by 45,062, while the registered electors of Dundee are more than in 1831 by 1094. Aberdeen was charged for the year ending April, 1863, under the head of Income and Property Tax, £29,260, and Dundee £22,218. The remaining member I propose to allot to Lanarkshire, now only returning a single member, but having a population of 631,506, and 5183 registered electors; also paying an annual Income Tax (1863) of £59,823, exclusively of its Boroughs. I may mention in this place that the amount of Income and Property Tax charged for the year ending 5th April, 1863, was, for the Scotch Counties, £444,101, and for the Scotch Cities and Boroughs £457,156. The amount charged upon the English Metropolitan Boroughs alone for the same period was £2,291,979. You will recollect that I proposed to raise the representation of Ireland from 100 to 105, and I remarked that in proportion to her population and the amount contributed by her in taxation, the addition of five members to her Parliamentary phalanx (at present a very strong and compact one) could not well be found fault with. Ireland, for the year ending April, 1863, contributed £754,005 towards the Income Tax, viz., £493,155 her Counties, and £260,850 for her Boroughs.[4]

The five members for Ireland I propose to distribute thus:—Two additional members to Dublin, and one respectively to the Counties of Cork, Tipperary, and Down. These stand first in the list of Irish Counties as regards the payment of Property and Income Tax; and the following were the amounts charged upon them respectively for the year ending April, 1863:—

Cork - - - - -	£40,836.
Tipperary - - - -	£28,710.
Down - - - -	£27,850.

257

This is exclusively of represented towns; for the returns for the City of Cork alone show £22,068 for that year, and for the City of Dublin £143,533.

Having disposed of the five seats destined for Ireland, I will furnish you with a recapitulation of the whole plan as referring to the increase of the Representation of the People.

658 seats to be increased to 700. The forty-two additional seats to be thus allotted:—

ENGLAND.

10   English Boroughs, now returning one member, to return two respectively.
10   Unrepresented English Towns to return respectively one member.
2.   Chelsea and Kensington (and query Hammersmith) to return collectively two members.
1.   The University of London to return one member. (The qualification to be the same as at the English Universities).
7.   One English County and six Divisions of English Counties to return one additional member each.

      Total—30 additional seats.

SCOTLAND.

2.   One City and one Borough, now returning respectively one member, to return two members each.
1.   One County now returning one member to return two members.
4.   The two Universities of Edinburgh and Glasgow to return two members each. (The qualification to be as nearly as possible the same as at the English Universities returning members).

      Total—7 additional seats.

IRELAND.

2.   The City of Dublin to return two additional members.
3.   The Counties of Cork, Tipperary, and Down, to return respectively one additional member.

      Total—5 additional seats.
      658   Present Members for the United Kingdom.
       42   Additional.

Total,   700.

I have thus furnished you both as regards the extension of the suffrage, and the provision for enlarging the national representation, with a plan, which may not be without its use at the present time, when everybody is exclaiming that something must be done; but when, in consequence of the difficulty of the question, and the labour necessary to be undergone in an endeavour to grapple with and master it, few are prepared with any definite plan for its solution. I respectfully submit that an extensive scheme of wholesale disfranchisement, such as was proposed by Mr. Bright in 1858, and on a much smaller scale by an eminent scholar, the Rev. Dr. Temple,[5] in May last, is wholly adverse to the wishes and feelings of the reflecting part of our community. We are desirous to correct existing anomalies in our representative system, and to enlarge its area, at the same time strengthening the legislative body in the State; but we are anxious to retain, as far as possible, existing privileges, and to conciliate and secure the support so long given to our national institutions, by giving to every man his right, but to no man more.

With this view, my plan is one of uniform Enfranchisement throughout, and as such I propound it for consideration by both parties in the country, the interest and object of all being, in the words of Locke, "the fair and equal representation of the people."

I am, Dear Sir,

Your faithful Servant,

J. E. EARDLEY-WILMOT.

London, November, 1865.

Notes

1 In 1864 the number of County Electors for England and Wales was 534,085.
2 *Note.*—The number of Registered Electors in England and Wales for Counties and Boroughs for the year 1863 was 1,012,532,—of these 534,085 were for Counties, and 478,447 for Cities and Boroughs. In 1833 (the year after the Reform Act) there were 370,379 Registered Electors for Counties, and 285,077 for Cities and Boroughs, total 655,456, showing a net increase in thirty years for both Counties and Boroughs of 357,056. Under the present plan, it is calculated that there would be an aggregate increase of at least 250,000, although it is not possible to calculate the precise number with any degree of certainty.—(See *Returns from Register Office, Somerset House, May* 3, 1864.
3 4 Inst. i. In the time of Fortescue they were in number 300. See Hume's History of England, Appendix 3. Coke said in the House of Commons, that he was employed with Chief Justice Popham to take a survey of all the people of England, and found them to be 900,000 of all sorts. Guicciardini, however, makes the inhabitants in the reign of Queen Elizabeth, to amount to two millions.
4 The population of Scotland by the census of 1861, was 3,062,294. That of Glasgow in 1831 was 193,030, and in 1861, was 394,864. The population of Ireland in 1861, was 5,798,967, shewing a decrease since 1831 of 1,968,434. The property in Ireland assessed in 1860 under the income and property tax, was £12,893,829.
5 Dr. Temple's proposal was to disfranchise all Boroughs with populations under 5000, and take one member from all with populations under 10,000; 161 seats would thus be left for re-distribution. The county constituencies were to be doubled, and the new members to be elected by the rate payers only.

259

C. B. Adderley, *Europe Incapable of American Democracy* (London, 1867)

Bodleian Library, (OC) 200h.87(1)

Charles Adderley (1814–1905) became Conservative MP for North Staffordshire in 1841. A strong Anglican with a reputation as a progressive landowner, he also acquired an interest in colonial affairs and helped to found the Colonial Reform Society in 1849, promoting self-government in colonies settled by British emigrants. In 1858, Derby appointed Adderley Vice-President of the Education Committee of the Privy Council. In 1866, Adderley became Under-Secretary for the Colonies in Derby's third government. In his *Letter to the Rt Hon Benjamin Disraeli MP on the Present Relations of England with the Colonies* (1867), Adderley discussed the progress of colonial freedom.

In 1867, Adderley also published *Europe Incapable of American Democracy* outlining his view of constitutional development. Providential progress was fundamental to Adderley's belief. Linear advancement was evidence of God's plan in the constant onward movement of human affairs.

On this foundation, Adderley placed three working principles. First, that constitutional advancement moved through distinct stages, as defined by Aristotle and Polybius. These were monarchy, rule by one person; oligarchy or aristocracy, government by a select few; and democracy, government by the people. This mirrored the stadial development of civilisation proposed by Scottish Enlightenment philosophers such as John Millar, tracing the advance of society from agricultural communities, to feudal societies and finally commercial societies; the progress from rudeness to refinement. For Adderley, the advance from monarchy to aristocracy and then democracy related to the scale and density of the human population. The larger and denser human settlements became the greater the requirement to evolve systems of government.

Second, Adderley saw this constitutional development possessing a clear geographical impetus. As exemplified in Confucianism and legalism, Asia was the historical root of autocracy and despotism, while Europe was the constitutional birthplace of aristocracy, and America the home of democracy. The progressive advance of political economy had a clear Westward direction. However, Africa, for Adderley, was not a consideration because it appeared to be cut off from the mainstream of history. It was the French philosopher Baron de Montesquieu (1689–1755) who, in his *Persian Letters* (1721) and the *Spirit of the Laws* (1748), proposed that Asia, because of its climate and geography, naturally acquired an Oriental genius for servitude, while Europe, with its greater geographic diversity and more temperate climate, acquired a greater Occidental spirit of freedom. Oriental inertia was distinguished from European dynamism. Upon this scheme

Adderley grafted the land mass of America as the natural home of democratic habits and attitudes.

Third, another type of government could not wholly replace the constitutional foundations of a continent. All forms of Asian government retained features of despotism, resistant to aristocracy and democracy. All aristocratic European governments ultimately defied absolute monarchy and pure democracy. Systems of government changed. Revolutions occurred. However, the fundamental nature of indigenous political practice and habit always eventually reasserted itself, reinforced by religious belief. This amplified the theocratic principle prevalent in Asia, the chiefly hierarchical forms of religion in Europe, and the religious universalism of North America.

The purpose of Adderley's analysis was to repudiate those contemporary British radicals who cited the example of American democracy as a model for constitutional change in Britain, and to counter writers, such as Matthew Arnold and Alexis de Tocqueville, who lamented the irresistible triumph of democracy over other forms of government. Britain, Adderley asserted, was incapable of embracing pure democracy. Only by the study of their own distinctive history and particular institutions, not by seeking their substitution by other forms of government, could the British safeguard the onward progress of their constitution.

10

C. B. ADDERLEY,
EUROPE INCAPABLE OF AMERICAN DEMOCRACY

(London, 1867)

Constitutional stages of history

THE track of human affairs, though traversed by a thousand cloudy theories of each passing day, comes out wonderfully simple in review. There is little of intricacy in the mighty plans of Providence. Broad-featured, slow in process, and to be recognized by all, are the ways of God in the affairs of men.

The world has plainly exhibited a regular development of social economy, progressing from its first inhabitation by man, taking one westward direction as the sun, never ceasing, and never reverting.

Political constitutions have been based on one of three principles successively, and in three several stages of experiment.

Human government naturally began as monarchy, and Asia was the first scene of its action.

In its westward course, Europe saw its next development on the wider basis of aristocracy.

It is now spreading itself in broad democracy, over the gigantic area apparently prepared for its utmost expansion, in America.

I mean by Monarchy, in principle, the sovereignty of one; by Aristocracy, that of leaders; and by pure American Democracy, that of the whole people making and unmaking their own administration, from time to time, at their will.

To each of three great divisions of the globe in turn, a special type of government seems to have mainly attached itself as a native and ineradicable growth—capable indeed of admixture and variety, but incapable of entire extirpation, or even of extensive transplantation whether by way of reversion or repetition of the sequence.

Russia appears to form a connecting link between the two first stages of this series; and England between the second and the third. I hope there may be special vitality about nations imbibing life from both past and present sources, and showing a capacity to draw new inspiration into ancient forms.

Irrespectively of these connecting links, monarchy will probably be for ever the peculiar characteristic of Asiatic government, aristocracy of European, and pure democracy will remain the perennial and prevalent, as it was the indigenous, growth of the Western world.

I do not mean to say that the science of government has ever been confined to any one of these principles—or that the forms of government have ever been wholly restricted to the type of any age or period—or that different circumstances allow of universal identity of characteristics. Monarchy, Aristocracy, and Democracy have always been recognized in the philosophy of Government as its three elementary principles; and the spirit of one may pervade and vary the forms special to another; but it has required the particular circumstances of successive eras to set up each principle in turn as a primary element, to elaborate each form in its chief distinctive features, and to establish each as a prevalent and perpetual type of government in three great divisions of the world.

The progress has been incessant from the adoption of the first principle, towards the development of the last, and from the most concentrated to the most distributed form of government; and always connectedly, in one westward course, unfolding itself. Constitutional expansion has in fact kept pace and direction with the increase of the world's population, (interrupted only by violent reactions and revolutions), and during the dominance of each successive principle the onward process has never wholly stagnated. No one of the three distinctive principles of government has ever long retained a pure realization of its unmitigated essence in any quarter. Some mixture is always resulting from the very process of development, and from the perpetual changes in human conditions. Some mixture, indeed, is not only inevitable, but indispensable for tolerable government on any principle. No human power can long remain unchecked without abuse.

The popular disintegration of original monarchy was a necessary concomitant with the increase of numbers, levelling distinctions, expanding forms, introducing new adaptations. The ideas of men on all subjects have widened with their increasing multitude. The religions of Asia partook of its political concentration. The theocratic principle confounded its earthly and heavenly sovereignties, and identified its priests and nobles. The more developed religious forms of Europe have been chiefly hierarchical, while American universalism points to the Church of the Future in which the inheritors of the dominant Puritan inspiration claim for every man his own priesthood, as their civil constitutions provide self-government for every citizen.

Upon each successive stage of this general development of ideas the incessant tide of human progress has been ever bearing in its one direction, but never so as to obliterate any of the essentially distinct types of thought and action from its own stage.

Diverse constitutional forms and principles may mingle, but foundations will be found true to their own ground. The basements of the world's three constitutional structures, even in ruins, still remain where they were first laid. Millar considers circumstances of origin to be among the chief elements of national history.

The social conditions which attended the original settlement of each quarter of the globe necessitated peculiar modes of government.

The sovereign control of all by one man, the partnership in sovereignty of many leaders, or the power of the whole people without distinction to make and unmake their own administration at will—each in its own theatre of history—have been, are, and we may suppose ever will be, the predominant principle, with mainly corresponding forms, of government.

The practical inference from this general view is that such great writers as Arnold, De Tocqueville, and others erred in supposing that Democracy, in the sense defined, is destined to universal conquest over every former kind of government, as Christianity has been a dissolvent of heathendom; and that they wrongly warned Europeans to look ahead to America for their future, instead of reforming and adapting their own institutions to admit the full progress of contemporary requirements within themselves. De Tocqueville wrote to Europeans that to attempt to check Democracy would be to resist the will of God. He warned his countrymen, "launched in a rapid stream, not obstinately to fix their eyes on the ruins they had left, whilst the current swept them backwards to the gulf."— (Reeve's Translation, Preface xxii.) The consequence of so doing, he added, to France had been that democratic revolutions had been effected only in the material parts of society, with no concomitant change in laws, ideas, customs, and manners. He did not see that this very fact upset his theory so far as it connected a change in social condition with a necessary change of government. The apparent democratic revolutions in France have not affected the fundamental principle of its constitution in the least. The people do not govern themselves the more; but the old government governs more in their name. Hereditary Monarchy, endorsed by universal suffrage, but still checked by a semi-suppressed yet influential Aristocracy, remains.

M. Chevalier, in his recent work on Mexico, says, "We are now witnessing the dissolvent power of democracy on old forms of government, from east to west." Lord Brougham, in his "Political Philosophy," argues that as democracy is the only power constantly increasing, it must therefore supersede all others. The Emperor of the French is one of the few writers of the day who recognize the successive developments, by stages, of human government. He depreciates indeed, what he calls the middle era of European institutions, as composite and not thorough: possessed neither of the unity of the Oriental type, nor the universality of the Occidental; but he considers all three as distinct, local, and permanent types. Bancroft, and American writers generally, look upon their own new era, not as a sequence and development, but as a protest against darker preceding ages; reflecting its purer light upon them—a light which is dawning upon all. Such also is the ordinary language of modern demagogues, vilifying the past as incapable of the future without a radical substitution of the new forms for the old: though, after all, the old were the parents of the new of which they so much boast. History discredits these claims of an all-conquering democracy, and cautions England not to break up her old institutions for the sake of new, which have sprung out of hers, but which depend upon circumstances and materials which have never belonged to her, can never occur to her, and which, if they could, would in her case produce different results.

Let us trace in outline this lesson of history: and first we must remove wholly out of our consideration the fourth quarter of the globe—Africa—excepting Egypt, which is of Asiatic destiny; and Carthage, and Cyrene, which are of European. Africa appears to have been kept apart from the stream of history, under a doom of inferiority, by itself. Left aside from the course of social development, it may be wholly omitted from our present study. It may, like many portions of the Southern Hemisphere, afford outlets such as Algeria for the enterprise of the Northern nations, or constitute supplements such as the Cape to their career; but it can never rank among the great self-stages of human progress, as an integral part of the sequence of history. The series, indeed, must cease with the completion of the present chapter. Constitutional development can go no further than to the point of popular self-control. The globe itself is encircled by the course that has been run, and the races that inhabit it are incapable of further development or extension beyond their present territorial limits. It is Arnold's "last age." In his view the amalgamation of the Greek and Roman character with the Teutonic, which qualified the European materials of emigration to the West, is the last modification which the world can accomplish. The world can afford no new race after this.

We begin our tracing of history from

ASIA.

I assume, from the double testimony of revelation and history, concurrent with the indications of probability, that Asia was the first scene of man's existence on this earth, and that we have all descended from a first family placed somewhere in that quarter of the globe. The first form of human government was therefore necessarily paternal. Its origin was the headship of a family. As men increased, each offset-family circled round its centre in instinctive imitation, and nations naturally formed themselves under monarchies. Every new community assumed the accustomed form of government. The Patriarch of the original family became the head of many tribes, and ultimately hereditary Chieftainship became the normal Asiatic constitution, and the type of every kind of government in the East, such as it has remained to this day. Aristotle, in his general theory of Government, assumes that the earliest sources of obedience among mankind must have been personal. The idea was paternal supremacy, and nature designated the kingly government, not in form only, which might be accidental, but in essence, to be the first established everywhere.

Every government in Asia, whether fixed or roving, settled or migratory, great or small, has retained this original character indelibly as its basis. The nomadic tribes, whose separation from the main stream of nationality is also matter both of revelation and history, were always grouped under chieftainship graduating to a central head. In this organization lay the germ of subsequent European aristocracies, when the chief became no more than *primus inter pares*. (See Gibbon, c. xxvi. Manners of Pastoral Nations—and Lord Brougham's Polit. Phil. i. 261.) There were also emigrant tribes who soon scattered broadcast the seeds of future nations, far beyond the first narrow limits of organized society. In the words of Gibbon (c. viii.) "In the early ages of the world, whilst the forests that covered Europe afforded a retreat to a few savages, the inhabitants of Asia were already collected into populous cities, and reduced under extensive empires, the seat of the arts, of luxury, and of despotism." "Pure monarchy," remarks Lord Brougham (i. 101) "is the special type of Asiatic government, not to be confounded with the modified monarchy which has entered more or less at times, and by admixture, into European constitutions."

We shall see by and bye how different Roman Emperors were from Asiatic despots; and the electors to the kingly office among Germans and Gauls bore no resemblance to the Eastern aristocracies, such, for instance, as the priest-nobles of the Dalai Lama in Thibet.

There may have been absolute monarchies elsewhere, but Asia gives the type, and is the native field of them, and has adopted them as the prevailing and permanent form of all its governments. A Turkish Sultan may delegate his power to Viziers, but they do not divide the government with him; they are simply his creatures, depositaries of his single power. In the East the Prince alone rules, and so absolutely that he designates his successor at will, of course from among his own extensive progeny.

I do not suppose there was any natural predisposition in Oriental races to be governed despotically; their institutions have given them a good deal of their submissive fatalistic character; but despotism was the natural form of primitive constitution, the result of circumstances of origin, and the habit became inveterate and infectious throughout its neighbourhood, so far as its limits stretched by mere expansion without the rupture of national emigration.

The household of Abraham in all his wanderings from Chaldea to Egypt, and back to Canaan, grew into the Jewish monarchy.

In Egypt, whose history is Asiatic, and race Caucasian, though of African locality, the invading Shepherd-kings of Memphis, themselves perhaps of Arab tribes or Philistines, did not in five centuries of abnormal domination shake the habit of ancient monarchy, of which the emblem remains in the tapering Pyramid, whose whole structure but enshrines a king. They only drew out, says Lepsius, the martial spirit of the race without changing their form of government.

The Pharaohs, derived originally from the immortal Isis and Osiris, ended with Sesostris, overshadowed by the first Assyrian empire, which in its turn sank with Sardanapalus, the ruins of whose luxurious palace entombed in his person the wide empire from the Hellespont to the Indus. Out of the flames which consumed this imperial palace sprang three fresh monarchies, the second Assyrian, the Mede, and the Babylonian, till Cyrus engrossed them all in universal Persian empire. The detail of this part of Oriental history may be matter

of dispute and uncertainty, but the general truth that despotic monarchy succeeded despotic monarchy, with perhaps some sort of aristocracy underneath,
remains unassailable.

The Merchant Princes of Tyre and Sidon did not lose even by the spirit of
commerce the habit of Oriental unity of government. ("Thou art the anointed that
covereth." Ezek. 28.) Their sea-girt monarchy, whose very existence depended on
the contributions of universal trade, presented its united front as a king against the
kings of Assyria, and against Alexander—still retained its government under the
Ptolemies, and only sank under imperial Roman conquest.

China, on the other side of this Continent of despotisms, has kept the largest
population ever united under one Government for the longest historical national
period, under the most perfect exclusion from other people. It has preserved
strictly to the present day the paternal chiefship of government with which it
began its history, taking its very name from one of its earliest dynasties. The central potentate, the Son of Heaven, offers protection and care in return for implicit
obedience and universal service. The only result which time and pressing numbers have wrought in China is the stereotyping of its original government by the
reduction to agriculture of the old Tartar population of hunters and shepherds. The
Emperor is High Priest also—sole mediator with Heaven—and, as father of his
people, literally rules them with the rod. Modern commerce has opened to view
some of the sealed interior of China; and we find all power centred at Pekin, and
not even any aristocracy existing beyond the mere servile delegates of its administration. The recent rebellion, and efforts of the patriotic party, contemplate only
the subversion of a dynasty, and that on the ground of its too recent origin, for the
purpose of restoring the older.

The same Tartar race of Turcomans established the Turkish empire, which
has maintained an absolute monarchy through many centuries, whose power,
bounded only by the law of the Koran, is practically arbitrary, now seated in the
Eastern metropolis of the Cæsars, Asiatic at heart, though with limbs stretching
into Europe. There is no hereditary nobility, and all the people's devotion centres
on the family of Osman.

Thibet, the central territory of Asia, illustrates at once the religious and political
unity of Oriental government. The Dalai Lama is the Pope of the Buddhist hierarchy, and contains within himself the supreme executive and legislative power. The
provinces are governed by Lamas, who receive all their authority from the Dalai.

Persia remains a more pure and perfect despotism than ever; in her long and
varied history, never varying in this characteristic, that the life and liberty of every
subject are at the mercy of the sovereign.

India, even now, governed as it has been for a century by the freest of European
powers, must be governed autocratically, and the chief danger to the permanence
of its existing rule lies in the nearer access of the expansive spirit of its foreign
Rulers—nearer than its oriental nature may be able to endure, being utterly unable
to conform with it, though what is aristocratical in India we may find it worth
while, as far as possible, to develope.

268

All that the tide of human progress has effected in Asia has been to break down some of its exclusiveness. Europe has thrown back some of its more popular spirit on the paternal East, and mixed itself up with Asiatic commerce, and even dominion. But European habits are none the less exotic there; and the indigenous institution of despotism remains unchangeably the prevalent and characteristic feature of Asiatic Government.

Europe

Was the scene of the second phase of human government. As despotic government had naturally sprung from the first roots of society; so aristocracy resulted naturally from the first severance of the clustering layers about those roots. Asiatic tribes emigrated to the new field of Europe; or heroes and adventurers led out new plantations thither. Increase of population pressed on the western boundary of settlement, burst the original limits, spread forth to a new career, in new relations, in novel circumstances, and on fresh territory. Absolute power resents the pressure of a crowded people. The two are incompatible, unless the people be hermetically sealed up as the Chinese. Despotism requires either a small, or scantily enlightened, people for its subjects: nor could an absolute Monarchy retain its hold upon an exuberant people allowed freely to occupy a large extent of new territory. The characteristic government of Europe became necessarily, from its origin, a disintegrated Monarchy; fraternal rather than paternal; enlisting not the whole of society yet, but its leaders into the administration of common affairs.

The change, being an emanation from the preceding condition of things, naturally carried much of its origin with it. Herodotus traces the names and institutions of Greece from Egyptian and Phœnician sources. Cadmus strove to revive the Thebes he came from, in his new settlement. The Egyptian god Heracles was claimed as the head of most of the chief Grecian descents. (Grote, i. 528, and ii. 354.) Greece and Rome, both deriving their settlements from the East, were founded under Monarchies not purely Asiatic, but modified in the very act of transplantation. In the legends of early Greece, which are all of Oriental derivation, the king was the individual authority, supposed to possess every accomplishment, and to command, by personal ascendancy, complete obedience. The subordinate Chiefs and armed Freemen were an European accretion. The Eastern habits quickly Europeanized; kings became Archons, first for life, and then for ten years, lastly by annual election. It was not till Greece entered fully on European history that she required a Constitution, and branded every power outside it with the stigma of tyranny. Aristotle could hardly understand the implicit obedience of early tradition. The Council of Chiefs, and the General Assembly of Freemen were the essential and characteristic innovation. By these features Greece lost her Oriental physiognomy. The Asiatic Greek of the earliest time became the free Greek citizen of Herodotus and Aristotle. The struggle between the Grecian States and the Persian king was a characteristic antagonism. The mutual rivalries of Athens, Sparta, and Thebes never yielded more than partial and temporary supremacy to any one of them. Their nearest approach to empire was confederation. The soil resented tyranny. The Macedonian conqueror confessed that his victories rather took Greece into Asia, than made an Asiatic power in Greece, and no sooner was his individual destiny accomplished than his empire dissolved in obedience to the local destiny.

The Roman Monarchy, like the Grecian, soon gave way to a mixed constitution of Consuls, Senate, and People. Even Carthage, though only incidentally connected with European history—more in rivalry than brotherhood with Rome—found her Kings soon checked by an elected Magistracy, called Suffetes. She also caught the aristocratic infection. Absolute monarchy could not live in Europe, whose middle destiny alike rejected the repetition of despotism, and the anticipation of democracy. When the popular power outran the destiny of European history, Sylla led it back to empire. Finally, the constitutional freedom of Rome declined also in empire. Its face turned eastward, and in Constantinople found a semi-oriental repose.

Then came upon Europe a fresh westward tide of nationality, depositing perennial roots of aristocracy over it in its course. Thence sprung the nobility which ultimately spread over the whole continent, and became the characteristic growth of the middle ages. "From the patricians and nobles of the Roman Republic, says Hallam (Mid. Ages, i. 157), to the feudal nobility introduced by the German tribes, and which fused finally into an European aristocracy, the whole constitutional growth of Europe has been distinguished from the monarchical habits of Asia."

European history, speaking broadly, consists of two parts only. First, the conquest of that quarter of the globe by the Romans; and secondly, the conquest of them by the Barbarians, from whom we modern Europeans are descended, and whose institutions are the real basis of ours. (Lord Brougham, i. 257.) The west-northern language and customs, distinguishable from though cognate with the Latin, indicate that both were members of the same Indo-European family. The Romans founded European Government, the Gothic invaders originated our characteristic institutions. "The most civilized nations of modern Europe, says Gibbon (c. xxvi.), issued from the woods of Germany, and in the rude institutions of those Barbarians we may distinguish the original principles of our present laws and manners." The institutions of the German Tribes who overthrew the Roman Empire, though modified by long intercourse with the Romans between the ages of Tacitus and Clovis, remained fundamentally the same. The feudal system was a modification of the patriarchal institutions of the East, by the territorial grants incident to military service in the actual invasion of the west. (Stephen's Lectures, ii. 464.) Chiefships, first elective, became hereditary. The mediæval sovereignty of Europe was patriarchal, the modern became territorial. Henry IV. of France is considered by Sir J. Stephen the last of the mediæval sovereigns, and the first of modern European kings. He takes his reign as the final passage out of patriarchal ideas, and the commencement of our modern notions of Courts, Officials, and territorial Nobility.

The rear-guard of western invasion were Scythians, and Sarmatians, from whom we shall by and bye trace the semi-oriental Europeanism which still makes Russia a link between the two first stages of the world's progress, as in like manner we find an Anglo-American fusion uniting now the two last stages of history.

The essential distinction of European from Asiatic constitutions has been in the introduction of an independent Aristocracy, in the place of a mere Satrapy, reducing the "sic volo" of the Legislature and Executive all in one, under the consent of the leaders of the people. The dissolvents of individual tyranny were the Councils of Legislature which were universal among the northern nations, and carried by them into all the countries of Europe. (Hallam, Mid. Ages, ii. 348.) Limited Monarchy, and Feudal Aristocracy, are the intervening growth of Europe between Asiatic despotism and American democracy.

If we would realize to ourselves the unity and consecutiveness of God's Providence in the world's career, let us for a moment reflect how impossible would have been an abrupt transition from Despotism to Democracy—how natural the intervening act in the sequence of the drama—how wise that each stage should have had an area to itself, clear for the experiment, and, as historians have remarked, suited in natural features and conformation, as well as in relative locality, for each successive innovation. How would the new wine have burst the old bottles if the process had ever reverted! How would the thread of history have been broken if the progress had not been gradual, each stage working itself out from its precursor! How, also, could the elements of a continuous growth have reproduced the earlier forms on the later stages of development?

Tribal allegiance to a chief, connected with sub-allegiance of individuals within the tribe or barony, was a development of governmental form from the concentrated subjection of all alike to one; but so great a development as to constitute something wholly new and distinct. The change was fundamental and essential, and the new constitution could neither replace the old ones on their ground, nor relapse into the forms they sprang from on their own. The feudal system which synchronized with the division of lands amongst new settlers, was an original product of the circumstances. The feudatories, first at will, afterwards hereditary, and occupying land transmitted to the first born, had no essential relationship with the allottees of land under any of the Oriental autocracies, such as the Birmese or Indian. The lots of conquest given to Roman soldiers on the Danube was probably rather in imitation of the Barbarian customs, than by any tradition from the East. The Roman Colony was a body of soldiers planted in a conquered spot, and holding its lands on the tenure of defending the Roman territory at that point. But what could least of all have ever grown up in Asia, or travelled thither, or, once established, ever returned to their narrower origin, were the General Assemblies for the affairs of a community, which first breathed life in Europe, and were first embodied in the entire framework of government by the feudal system, in which the Chief was only *primus inter pares*—the first of an essentially military and territorial aristocracy. Autocracy was then a thing of the past; ranks and classes were largely distributed; individual equality was yet to come; conventional distinctions were rigidly defined; nobility was set up, not as the automata of a central will, but as depositaries of national rights, of recognized functions, and of established jurisdictions.

The Oriental "ipse dixit," with its Vizier executive and judicial bowstring, was succeeded by the German Assembly of freemen, warriors, and landholders, who gave public grievances at least an external organ to make themselves effectually heard from outside, and who imposed on the Government some responsibility in check of mere volition. The extension of power, and the command of the resources of a nation, became controlled by an independent judgment, and consent.

Why could not this European development react on Asia? The theory of M. Chevalier (Mexico, i. 57) is that the sons of Japhet are to possess the whole world. "It belongs to them to intervene in the affairs of people of Oriental civilization, and overthrow the barriers they obstinately maintain." The commerce of Europe has forced the gates of China. Let us see if it has forced its Government out of its Oriental habit. Surely as American democracy is expected to supersede European Constitutions by the force of universal popular expansion; the same cause ought to throw back some of its influence on the Constitution of Asia also, and at least burst open their despotisms, and disperse them into the wider range of aristocracies. The commerce of Europe has searched out Asia. Its enterprise and intercourse have affected and controlled its fortunes; but they have never changed its forms or ideas of government. The institutions of six thousand years are not to be eradicated. The inveterate Oriental habit and the fixed necessity of primæval order can never be put in circumstance to change. Europe may infuse its wider spirit into Asia, and its own spirit may expand with the expansion of the West, but it will never efface the native growth of Eastern forms, nor revolutionize the original foundations of history.

We have spoken of Russia as a connecting link between Asia and Europe, retaining the despotism of the one in connection with the aristocracy of the other. Mr. Grant Duff (Studies of Europ. Polit. 77) calls the "commune" of Russia an arrested social development—a form of the Indo-Germanic village institution, modified by connexion with the great Seignory of Russia, under the autocracy of the Czar. The Emperor of the French (Life and Works, i. 254) has argued that it is only from Russia that the East can receive the amelioration that it is awaiting. But how does he propose that Russia should use her Eastern influence? By centralizing as closely as possible in the hands of her autocrat the force of the State, in order to destroy all the abuses which lie under the shelter of feudal franchises. In any fusion of the composite character of Russia—that of constitutional despotism—the newer elements would be less likely to predominate than the old.

But where is there a symptom of Asiatic despotism yielding to the influence of European freedom? India can only be autocratically governed even by England; and Egypt talks of a Parliamentary constitution in the hands of its Pacha! Ismail says he is bringing things in harmony with modern society. The old Sheiks are to be elected for consultation. The Council is about as much like the House of Commons, as the German Federation is like the United States.

Suppose European civilization infused into the corruption of Turkey to the utmost, and a wider sense of public spirit made to penetrate, if possible, its civil and religious thraldom; the Sultan might distribute his power, but it would be the Sultan's power still.

But if Europe could not indoctrinate Asia, could not Asia pursue and overtake emancipated Europe? Are the destinies of the two continents so distinct that the forms of both could not live together in either? *Has Europe shown itself intolerant of Asiatic despotism?* We are not without historical tests wherewith to try this point of our inquiry. There have been several attempts to set up absolute and universal empire in Europe. We shall find, I think, that every one of them has, both in process and result, illustrated the total incompatibility of European foundations with Oriental superstructure.

So far was Charlemagne from setting up tyranny in Europe, that his Empire was, as Stephen shows, the triumph of real Constitutionalism over the ideal royalism of the Merovingians. He sustained his power by reviving among the people the free assemblies of their German ancestors (i. 82). Pope Leo's hailing him as *Imperator semper Augustus* is said to have been the epoch of his decline. The scheme of marriage between the Western Emperor and the Empress of the East, planned between the Roman, German, and Byzantine Courts came to nothing. He was essentially Kyning, not Autocrat. When he tried to regulate the state of his people, their obligations to himself and to each other, the spirit of centralization was opposed by an antagonistic power with which not even he could successfully contend.

The great Papal attempt at universal empire was an exceptional kind of dynasty; and what it achieved can hardly be considered amongst the constitutional processes of Europe. But it may be contrasted with the similarly anomalous achievement of Mahomet in the East—a dynasty alike exceptional, and in every sense its rival, and opposing the Oriental to the Mediæval destiny.

We may compare, in the fortunes of each, the Eastern and Western influences and characteristics. The Mahometan empire was one of military conquest, and subjection of Eastern powers under autocratic government—the Papal power was the opposition of Constitutional governments, the one against the other, contrived so as to acquire a moral control and supremacy over all. Territorial dominion was rather claimed than possessed; the dispute was of rights, not of possessions; Kings, as our John, surrendered their kingdoms in feudal submission to the Ecclesiastical Seignory in chief, and held them under it as fiefs. But the Papal Empire, though it had all the force of religion, then the strongest of known forces, on its side, never held the European Aristocracy down for a day.

Charles V. next attempted empire in Europe. He combined in his own person, by aristocratic alliances, the greatest inheritance of dominion in the old world with the first acquisitions in the new. But what approach did even he make to tyranny? His whole career was a struggle with a similarly constituted European aristocratic kingdom, and with the more popular Leagues of the Reformation, and his royal rival significantly assumed in the final contest with him the title of Defender of the rights of Germany, and of Princes.

273

In the plenitude of the power of Louis XIV., and indeed from one epoch to another, says Guizot, the States General were a living protestation against political servitude—an impassioned assertion of great military principles. Louis XIV. may have degraded, but he did not suppress, his Noblesse, and by the force of his own character he so stamped the government of France with centralization that it retains it to this day: still it is a pretty good evidence of the aristocratic groundwork of the French constitution that the social equality he produced about him, and the political unity he collected in himself, so balanced each other, as it were, upon it as a stationary fulcrum, that neither tendency prevailed. After all the subsequent revolutions in France no one can say whether the Government has become more absolute or more democratic. I heard Mr. Cobden declare that his impression from travelling through the country was, that self-administration had not practically been approached one iota; while others, perhaps deceived by the show of universal suffrage in the original election of the Emperor, would call the Government a Republic. The old French monarchy was a collection of aristocracies, and the Monarch himself was Count, Duke, or King in various parts of his dominions. Titles descended to all the children of the family, but the property to the eldest. No country was so saturated with nobility under the security of primogeniture. Over the process of the French Revolution the "rights of man" passed but as a meteor; the orders of society were only temporarily eclipsed, and remained in their orbits. Napoleon achieved, on the basis of the restored Monarchy, an Empire of rapid growth. In the climax of the success of his ambition, however, he never changed, nor even affected the Constitutional basis of European Governments. He set his brothers on established thrones, and even those Constitutions which had been temporarily revolutionized, were restored the same as before. When he attempted to unite Europe against England by his Berlin Decrees of commercial excommunication, it was by no Oriental edict he could make the attempt, but by cajoling Russia, compelling Denmark, and persuading his brother Louis, King of Holland, in spite of his remonstrance, to consent to his plan. He dealt not with subject powers, but confederacies; and even when he assumed the Imperial diadem the squibs of the day went no further than to Cæsar or Cromwell for parallels to compare him with. The question was not of constitutional difference, but only between upstart occupancy and hereditary succession. He actually said, "France might have a better constitution, but bad as the system is we must execute it." Call the present government of France a Democracy organized in Imperial form. But this would be to designate its present phasis an European *mezzo-termine* between Occidental and Oriental governments.

So far we have found the course of constitutional history refuse to revert, or to repeat itself.

What is called Constitutional Monarchy began in Europe from the very circumstances of European settlement. It has been its peculiar form of government ever since. In spite of its greater vigour and intelligence it has never recoiled upon the governments of Asia so as to supplant its ancestral constitutions, nor has it ever sunk back itself into Oriental despotism within the precincts of its own domain.

AMERICA.

In approaching the consideration of the third, and last stage of constitutional history, and the widest possible form of human government, we may again remark that while the three stages of development required three successive periods, as well as areas, for their complete establishment, a progressive growth of one into the other has been constantly going on from the first; and never, but by temporary revolutions, ceasing to advance. The incipient Monarchies of Greece and Rome became speedily aristocratic Republics. Lamartine likens England to what he calls those "patrician republics" of antiquity. Sir C. Lewis describes them as a mixed form of democracy at home, and oligarchy towards their surrounding subjects. No sooner had the feudal system established itself in Europe, than the westward tendency to dispersion of power, and ultimate democracy, infected it. But the utmost extension of popular government in Europe has effected nothing more popular than the aristocratic Republics of Italy and Holland, which never even approached the American ideal, and were almost a mockery of democratic Constitutions. Venetian government never advanced beyond an oligarchy. Even in Florence, scarcely for a moment of her republican history, had the people any sway except as the partisans of aristocratic factions. Switzerland at this day, and only for a few years past, may seem an exceptional democracy in Europe—and, if a solitary exception, no disproof of the prevalent rule—but there is a strong centralizing party already threatening, from many Cantons, the democracy of the Centre. It required the clear, new, wide western field beyond the Atlantic, and the first ripe seed of popular equality to be sown upon it, to produce a genuine democracy, by which I mean a government resting immediately and constantly on the people, without any aristocracy, and making and unmaking their legislature and executive, from time to time, by indiscriminate voting.

The vast increase of mankind in the world, as it was a perpetual cause of overflowing to fresh space, so also was it an element in itself of democracy, especially when the overflow became an united rushing of an intelligent people on a common enterprise of freedom. Democracy is peculiarly the government of large numbers, and of distributed intelligence. It consorts with towns, or thickly populated districts, in preference to the country. Multitudes of people, habituated to combined action, holding intercourse in common assemblies, and living under a necessity of commerce, constitute a democratic interest wherever they exist.

The chief and characterizing European exodus to North America, in the seventeenth century, was therefore only the precipitation of a process which had been long preparing by natural causes in the world, but which required a new field and special circumstances to unfold itself. There are very few instances of pure forms of government realizing any distinct theory completely; and this precipitation of democracy was not effected at once. Various combinations may take place on fundamental principles, which are established rather by the gradual dominance of one of the mixed elements of government, and subsidence of the others, than by a sequence of nakedly distinct forms. In America the democratic element became by circumstances the basis of its characteristic institutions, but it very slowly asserted its supremacy. The first adventures were under adverse auspices, and in the cause, not of freedom but, of discovery and enterprise combined with slavery. The first introduction of Europe to America almost capriciously fell into the hands, or under the patronage, of the most autocratic of her monarchs. Spain has the honour of having first connected the middle stage of the world's history with its last dénouement. But she opened this last era in a spirit the least congenial with its ultimate destiny. A century before England breathed expansive freedom into North America, Spain had communicated a very different inspiration of European life in the softer climate of the Antilles. Spain brought not in her train the genius of the western future. The ultimate destiny of the new world was pioneered but not inaugurated by Castilian enterprise. The later and much stronger influence of English freedom supervened and took the lead. The Council of the Indies set up in Mexico the aristocratic elements of the Spanish constitution, but America as a whole found her true affinity with the popular elements which afterwards escaped to her northern shores from England. England's freedom-seeking and self-sown colonies, were left to govern themselves. In them, therefore, lay the germ of America's destiny— the democracy of self-sovereignty, and of collective popular will. Not till long afterwards, did England cross the freedom she had propagated; and the severed layers of colonisation became independent nations. Blind to her warning, she only recognized still less the freedom of her remaining colonies. Her colonial administration became only more like the Council of the Indies—a governing power, so far as English institutions would admit of distant government. Indeed, there was only this whimsical difference between the Offices of Downing Street and Madrid, that England spent home treasure in colonial government while Spain amassed colonial treasure to the government at home. But the ultimate destiny of America was developing itself among the various European experiments made upon her territory. In the French, Spanish, and Portuguese colonies a Royal government was attempted more monarchical than that of the parent states—monarchy with mimic orders, unnaturally applied to a novel and remote agency. The Dutch never settled, but made commercial factories, their genius being trade. In the British colonies, whether North or South, transplanted offsets of constitutional liberty grew with a vigour proportionate to their distance from the aristocracy with which they were only theoretically connected. Grahame remarks (Hist. U. S. iii. 348), that in the struggle between France and England for the colonization of North America, that power which attempted to plant monarchy and hereditary nobility there was inevitably fated to be the victim. It was English freedom that found affinity in American soil, and germinated so as to characterize the whole continent. Spanish Colonies were not of a kind to become seedlings of new nationalities. Even their emancipation has only led to anarchy and confusion. Their first idea was that of Agencies, rather than of Settlements. A large portion of their population was Indian, so rendering republican institutions in the first instance impossible. Their Captains-General and Audiencias continue such as they were first set up. If Columbus came to life again he would find Cuba, for instance, under much the same sort of administration as he and Velasquez gave her. A Spanish colony is a plant that will not grow. That cramped old stock does not suit the new soil. It scarcely keeps alive, and becomes by time only more corrupt. The pious care of Queen Isabella, and self-devotion of Las Casas, could not sweeten the breath of European domination in the destined atmosphere of popular freedom. At this moment an attempt at Monarchy in South America floats on the elements of Democracy. In vain Brazil would borrow from Europe an hereditary throne to cover her republican blunders. The last development of human government was not in the gift of Spanish functionaries. What, meanwhile, have not the offsets of English freedom grown into in America; and what do they not promise still further to become?

When English freedom escaped from too narrow limits at home to the west, and sowed itself in a soil which intensified its nature even so as to produce new forms of life, it grew so rapidly that on the first attempt of the mother country to treat her emigrant freemen not as partners but as subordinates in legislation they shook off the protection which only stifled their breath, shaded their light, and damped their national vigour.

The enfranchisement of New England stirred such movement in the West as to rouse even the Spanish dependencies, and to make the drowsiest inhabitants of the new world feel the pulsations of a common destiny, and breathe an aspiration for a conscious future. Napoleon, master of Spain—the hero of revolution in the home of old dominion—unlocked the genius of the West, the self-sovereignty of the dependant nations. Even Spanish America was left to its own government. We are not yet assured that she is capable of the gift. It remains, indeed, for all America to prove whether to any the gift is a blessing, either to themselves or to the world around them. It is, however, her special gift, and apparently her inalienable possession. The instinct of the Monroe doctrine is that republicanism is to be left to America, as her peculiar portion; and that Europe is not to interfere, as of alien principles. The experiment of the French Emperor in Mexico was one of his temptings of destiny (to whose frown he has now instantly bowed) to introduce the Latin race and institutions in juxta-rivalry of the democracies which have sprung from Anglo-Saxon planting in that democratic soil. It has failed, and we shall see if the genius loci of self-government can strike some stable root among the *débris* of paternal anarchy there, or mould into its own federation the wrecks of European experiments.

The course of history refuses to repeat the forms of Europe among her western progeny.

The Provinces of British North America derived from their French origin institutions the least congenial with democracy. Only gradually, and at this moment, has the recognition by England of their local and now national destiny, led them to assume their own true position. But this present scheme of Confederate Vice-monarchy is a novelty in the world; and in the new world must practically assume a democratic basis. Who, for instance, would dream of an hereditary or territorial aristocracy there, however possible or desirable it may be to add to the official titles common already in America, life-titles from the British fountain of honour?

This link between America and the freest of European nations must partake of the character of both. The spirit of English institutions may adapt to itself the exigencies of American government, as the spirit of American democracy may expand without violating English institutions, which first embodied it. The growing numbers and intelligence of the world's last age will spread as vigorously over the British territory of western democracy as over the rest, and find special strength perhaps in English administration.

The Sovereign will remain hereditary—as the Canadian Attorney-General said in debate on the subject—the Sovereign of the nation, not the elected and electioneering Head of a Party. The Government will be, as the English, under the check of responsible advisers. The whole Legislature, central and local, will not vacillate perpetually with every breath of popular agitation: an incessant appeal to a mere ordeal of indiscriminate numbers will not keep in hourly hazard, and discredit, every public and private relation. The Legislature will not be the organ of universal suffrage. It is remarkable how the British North Americans have avoided, and even shrunk back from, that basis for their Representative Body, and sought for the distinct local representation of interests—such as the Western Agriculture; the Lower Canadian speciality; the Maritime Provinces' interests—and preferred nomination to election for their Upper Chamber. This monarchical democracy, and our democratic monarchy, may long work together.

We know not how many phases of democracy America may yet exhibit, though the democratic foundation of all is sure. The late triumph of union seems to be the inauguration only of fresh disunion among the confederate democracy. That bond of heterogeneous elements, which even the genius of Washington could scarcely unite, and which if ever parted was then pronounced incapable of re-union, at this moment, by civil conquest, has become a mere paradox of federation of conquering and conquered States. But should the whole body disintegrate, each part would only re-create a new democracy. The special growth of the giant hemisphere is the giant power of the people, for which the last chapter of the world's history is reserved.

We may probably include Australia in the same destiny as the Western world, from similarity of origin.

But, *Europe is incapable of American Democracy.* If circumstances, such as are of invincible result, such as can occur nowhere else, nor ever again, least of all in retrocession on the course of history, rooted and spread democracy throughout America, it is almost a corollary that America cannot throw back the product she has so received upon a previous stage. Original social conditions lie at the root of political institutions, and when was there ever such a social condition as that in which New England originated? Is the democratic government which largely sprung from it likely to find a parallel? It is a remark of De Tocqueville's, that "if we examine the social and political state of North (*i.e.* typical) America, we shall find not an opinion, not a law, not a custom, not an event on record which the origin of that people will not explain." (Reeve's Transl. i. 19.) The inference is that the same result is not likely to be derived from other origin. American Democracy is not to be reasonably expected in Asia or Europe. The potential Founders of American institutions were not like the Parents of the first human institutions—a single pair—concentrating in themselves the sole possible idea of government; nor Tribes settling under the ready-made aristocracy of Chieftainship, such as originated the second series of human Constitutions; but they were societies of equally civilized freemen, under a common impulse, of the same language, race, and political as well as social independence, and of greater intelligence than the mass of any former people. They were the scatterings abroad of the seeds of freedom from a storm in the freest spot of Europe, over a free and unencumbered soil. There was not even any admixture of the aristocratic element in the composition of such a settlement as this. It was a pure democracy in form and spirit, without alloy, without precedent, without likelihood of repetition elsewhere.

There are, indeed, traces of European aristocracy even in New England institutions. No men can quite shake off the past; but the direction of public affairs by the people themselves immediately, numerically without distinction, and independently except of such external influences as can be brought to bear on such a mass, has been the essential characteristic, and novelty arising from this last social condition; and the circumstances and scene were necessary for its establishment.

There is in old England much tendency towards democracy, even more than the normal tide of history in that direction can account for. Increase of population and intelligence, rapid intercourse and invention, large towns and growing manufactures have here even more than elsewhere, owing to our special freedom, disturbed old arrangements, rendered unmeaning conventional distinctions, and tried the tenacity of the most elastic traditions. England, moreover, contains within herself much of actual American democracy. She gave to America her municipal and local distribution of self-government, and if you scratch the Norman crust from England you will find the germ of America in the Saxon core within. But it is clear from the case that the foundations which underlie the Constitution of old England must be something very different from what was established in America. Even if the thousand elements which combine to make up American democracy could be introduced into this most congenial of European countries, the inveterate habits of ten centuries, the ligaments and fibres of long associations, recollections, and attachments would have to be wholly cleared away to give space for the new creation. As for the new Constitution so produced, it would first be an European anachronism, and secondly an American caricature. The cooperation of the Legislative and Executive Bodies, which superseded the tyrannical identification of the two in Asia, would have itself to be superseded by their total separation, such as the sages who founded the free Constitution of the American States saw to be inevitable in pure democracy. In America the Executive Ministry, and the double Legislature are all elected, only differently with the special view to their having no contact or inter-dependence with each other. At this moment we see them in mutual antagonism. As Mr. Lowe said in Parliament, "so long as we retain our present Constitution such a state of things as this could not possibly exist for a moment in this country." The American democracy grafted upon our Constitution

279

would simply render the Executive the ready and helpless tool of every passing whim of the popular Assembly, and result in the necessity of the same separation between them as in America, by an independent appointment of the Executive for a number of years certain, whether in harmony or not with the Legislature; that is, in something essentially different from our present Constitution.

It is, further, a remark of Mr. Tremenheere's (Const. of United States, p. 19) that if such a change, as democratizing the English constitution, could be effected while our form of Parliamentary Government by Queen, Lords, and Commons remained, the result would be far more democratic even than anything existing under the constitution of the United States. Theirs would be a limited and balanced democracy compared with ours.

The independent powers of the President, the coordinate authority of the Judiciary with the Legislature, are checks and safeguards in their case, which would have no equivalent in the reckless race of imitation. Unless our whole machinery of government were radically altered, it is remarkable that the House of Commons, in whose apparent interests reform is sought, would be the first to suffer, and probably to succumb. Ministerial responsibility ceasing, either the Sovereign must be a temporary power, or else the Commons must lose all control.

Is it then likely that England, and if not England I need not ask the question of other European powers, will ever take to elective and periodical Sovereigns? Does any demagogue, however intent upon his single view, think it his interest to suggest in words such a change? Is not popular feeling itself all the other way? Is England ever likely to wish for an elective Senate? Is she even at heart inclined so to democratize the House of Commons as to change her inveterate habit of local representation for a mere representation of a quotient of her numbers as counters in a Parliamentary division?

But, to pass from England, can any one seriously think that France has at all more of a democratic Constitution in the essential meaning of the term—the government of the people by themselves—for all her revolutions, or for the semblance of universal suffrage now allowed to flatter her? The casual consent of a people to adopt, once for all, a dynasty does not make the dynasty democratic. It is only popular in a very restricted sense, as being the temporary and solitary choice of a particular servitude by the people at one particular period. The Emperor of the French may style himself Prince by the grace of God and will of the people, but I suspect he would make the first tenure good against any defect in the second.

To make France really democratic, the people should be able to exercise the right not of one consent to an hereditary Emperor, but of making and unmaking from time to time the depositary of its own sovereignty at its will. At this moment perhaps we may say France never was more absolutely Monarchical—never more nearly despotically governed. Even the aristocracy are in suspense, and the people have as little to do with the government of their country as in the days of Louis XIV.

What has Spain done in half a century of almost annual revolutions? If she had realized her Constitution, it would have been no democracy. She has, like other European nations, acquired sometimes more, sometimes less, of freedom on the basis of Monarchy. The lamp of freedom has, in her case, burnt very low—from the days of her grandeur the night of the Inquisition has sat heavily over her; but the extremes of her political vicissitudes have never even tried the limits of constitutional freedom.

Consider the most staunchly aristocratic of European monarchies, Austria, and the soi-disant liberal Prussia; and see how little difference all the popular convulsions they have both suffered since 1848, have effected in the essentially aristocratic basis of the constitutions of each. Austria has lately been moved to her foundations; Prussia has received the shakings of other nations into her lap, but in vain do democrats seek the traces of democracy in any of the constitutional changes which have resulted. In vain a confused orator the other day compared the manhood suffrage set up "under the rule of Bismark" to that which he was advocating for this country. That "Europe has been casting off the cerements of the feudal system" (Speech, Goldwin Smith), may be the pleasant dream of a philosopher, but it is not the true record of history.

Let us rather expect a grand development of democratic government where alone it has had its birth, and the means to grow and expand. Its power must be great, and influence over the elder nations constant as that of the moon's upon the earth; but those elder powers will balance, and not be neutralized by, its action; and even if disturbing influences, eccentric and disordered, intervene, the destined relations will in the end maintain themselves.

What we Englishmen have to do, as we feel the influence of increased population and intelligence telling upon all human institutions, and the parallel growth of science and invention levelling distinctions, and producing new social relations, perhaps with wider gaps though fewer eminences, is to shape our special course accordingly. It were to evince an utter ignorance of history, of which some are not ashamed, to assume an inevitable prevalence of democratic institutions over all that have gone before, and to expect a dissolution of established orders to make way for the last influx of a course of progress which has accompanied them all from the first. All the world's established constitutional forms have adapted themselves to the ever rarifying atmosphere about them, and have refused to die or to remove from their own places.

We may adapt our ancient forms to the extremest future. There is nothing in the hereditary sovereignty and peerage, or in the local representation of property and interest in the legislature established in England which is incompatible with the utmost popular freedom and improvement. These things, after all, are not matters of choice, but of a destined order. We cannot submit it to a numerical majority whether we will assume this fashion or that. Being such as we are, and have been time out of mind, and by circumstances of indelible consequence, we have to confront ourselves with new events, and to admit the acquisitions of constant progress. To suppose that the old nationalities can boil themselves up into the new forms of youth which have sprung from the inheritance of their vigour is a dream which may lead men to sacrifice their own capacities of freedom in vain hopes of acquiring new.

281

The roots of European Constitutions cannot be swept away to introduce a new plant of pure democracy. The delusive expectation might be held out to the ignorant so as to awaken passions enough for the destructive part of the problem; but the substitutive part all history pronounces to be impossible; far more likely would be the further relapse into a primitive despotism. Aristocracy must remain, or will recur, and a healthy development of it is our true aim. Expel it, and it will return inevitably in some shape, probably through an ordeal of violence. To adapt European Constitutions to take in, as no doubt they may, the utmost increase of popular power, that is the work of European statesmen, not empirics—of men conversant with the history of the past, and the materials of the future, conscious that their business is to meet, not to make events, and that the last thing for a sane man to attempt is to set up a future irrespectively of the past.

The English demagogues of the day see no difference between these two courses of adaptation and substitution. They say, what matters the form if we get the democratic spirit? But the substitution of American forms for our own is obviously their object—probably unconsciously to themselves, for their single eye is incapable of discrimination. Their ready-reckoner is the standard of the West, by simple comparison with which they measure and value all other institutions. They idealize the new, and condemn the old. For instance, they only tolerate an hereditary Throne for the popularity of its present occupant. The Person, not the Institution, is what they are ready to maintain. The Lords "are not yet elective," say they, but may be kept out of harm's way till they are. The House of Commons is worthless, and always has been mischievous to their minds, however glorious its history; and must be so until it becomes something wholly different, a simple index, as in America, of conclusions resulting from processes outside its walls, in an ever-seething vortex of popular agitation, and subversion of all real representation.

But there are Englishmen who have not yet become weary or unworthy of their history, and still prize it; who, in our hereditary Monarchy, and Aristocracy, and elected representatives of local interests, see nothing inconsistent with the constant development of popular progress, according to the day.

The former politicians could easily break up our old framework, and our best luck would then be if the wreck got into the pilotage of another Cromwell. In vain snatching at Democracy they may break up our Aristocracy; but through anarchy and temporary dictatorship, it would return to some mutilated form of its former self.

The latter study organic permanence, historic destiny, and sustained vitality of progressive freedom.

If a certain common character is traceable in the forms of government which have prevailed in Asia, Europe, and America respectively, and apparently arising, in each case, from peculiar social conditions of first settlement, the statesmen who study the expansion of their own institutions are more to be trusted than those who prefer or predict the substitution of others.

Part 5

CONSERVATISM IN THE COUNTRY, 1866–1874

William Busfeild Ferrand,
The Speech of Mr Ferrand, President of the Bradford Working Man's Conservative Association, at the Inaugural Banquet, on the 20th November, 1866, in St. George Hall (London, 1866), 2–12

Duke Humphrey Reserve Counter (OC) 200h.63(1)

Born in 1809, William Busfeild took the name Ferrand in 1839 on his mother inheriting the St Ives estate, near Bradford, from her uncle. After standing unsuccessfully for Bradford in 1837, Ferrand was elected Conservative MP for Knaresborough in 1841. He opposed the Anti-Corn Law League, supported the Ten Hours Factory Act, vigorously exposed the harshness of the Poor Law, and was a fierce denouncer of corruption among public men. He did not contest the 1847 election, but was elected MP for Devonport in 1863, a notable success given that Devonport had returned either Whigs or Liberals since 1832 and that the influence of the government in the constituency, through employment in the dockyard, was very strong. Unseated in 1865, Ferrand stood unsuccessfully in by-elections for Coventry in 1867 and again for Devonport in 1868.

Known for his commitment to working men, Ferrand was President of the Bradford Working Men's Conservative Association at its Inaugural Banquet, St George's Hall, in November 1866. Ferrand's speech, on that occasion, was a forceful appeal to the educated working men of Bradford to recognise that their true interests were aligned with the Conservative party and to resist the inflammatory rhetoric of John Bright, W. E. Forster (MP for Bradford), and Gladstone. The interests of employers and employees, Ferrand declared, were entwined in mutual support. Ferrand praised the vigorous Commons statements of Robert Lowe attacking the Liberal Reform bill of 1866. The intellectual leader of the 'Adullamites', those Whigs and moderate Liberals opposed to extensive Reform, Lowe rejected moral arguments for extending the vote to those uneducated lower classes who would be subject to bribery, influence, and the blandishments of demagogues. A utilitarian meritocrat, Lowe declared property and intelligence as the essential practical requirements for possession of the vote, supporting intelligent and disinterested government free from class monopoly. In contrast, Gladstone, echoed by Bright, portrayed working class enfranchisement as a moral entitlement irresistibly carried forward by great social forces. For Ferrand, such language was an incitement to social revolution, class warfare, and the overthrow of the nation's institutions.

11

WILLIAM BUSFEILD FERRAND, *THE SPEECH OF MR FERRAND, PRESIDENT OF THE BRADFORD WORKING MAN'S CONSERVATIVE ASSOCIATION, AT THE INAUGURAL BANQUET, ON THE 20TH NOVEMBER, 1866, IN ST. GEORGE HALL*

(London, 1866), 2–12

The CHAIRMAN was received with quite an ovation on rising, and some time elapsed before silence was sufficiently restored to enable him to proceed. He said:—Ladies and Gentlemen, some 70 years ago the Inhabitants of Bradford elected my grandfather to command her volunteers—(hear, hear,)—who, with a million of their fellow countrymen, rose up to defend their native land against the invasion of the French revolutionists. (Hear, hear.) You have been pleased on this occasion to elect his grandson to preside over this assembly—(hear, hear,)—of the deliberating and educated working men—(hear, hear, and applause,)—who have united together to defend the institutions of their country from revolutionary demagogues. (Hear, hear, and loud cheers.) And did you not believe your country was in danger, not one man now present would have been here to-night. (Hear, hear.) Gentlemen, when bad men combine to destroy, it is the duty of good men to unite for protection. (Hear, hear, and applause.) And perhaps there is not within these realms a community which has more at stake at the present moment than this great emporium of the worsted trade—(hear, hear,)—for if the revolutionary demagogues who are now so busily at work could for forty-eight hours carry out their intention of revolutionising our Institutions, the trade of this district would be shaken to its foundations. (Hear, hear.) Soon would your palatial warehouses be empty, your factories—those busy hives of industry—be closed—(hear, hear.)—and your merchants and manufacturers would carry their capital and trade to a foreign land; your work people would be starved and ruined by those who are now professing to be their best friends. (Hear, hear.) Believe me, my friends, there is nothing so timid as trade, and believe me also, working

287

men, there is nothing you ought to have so much at heart, or in which you are so deeply interested as successful trade in this county. (Hear, hear.) Gentlemen, I thank you for placing me in the proud position I occupy to-night—(hear, hear,)—that of presiding over an assembly of thinking, educated, working men—(hear, hear,)—and I ask your kind indulgence this evening until I bring under your notice, and the notice of your fellow-countrymen, the working men of England, the present state of affairs connected with the agitation now going on. (Hear, hear.) The prime movers in this agitation are Mr. Gladstone and Mr. Bright—(hear, hear,)—both of them men of marvellous talent, of wonderful oratorical powers. I have sat listening to them both for hours, and amazed and confounded have I been to find two such men perverting one of the greatest gifts which they could receive from the Almighty to the worst of purposes. (Hear, hear, and loud applause.) Now, in 1859, Lord Derby's Government introduced a Reform Bill into the House of Commons which would have enfranchised some 200,000 or 300,000 educated, frugal,—[hear, hear,]—industrious working men; but these are the very men that Mr. Bright did not wish to be enfranchised. (Hear, hear, and "Shame.") His power rests entirely amongst the ignorant and dangerous classes of the community—(hear, hear,)—and therefore he assisted Lord Palmerston by the base coalition in Willis's Rooms to defeat Lord Derby, and to rob you of the franchise. (Hear, hear.) In 1860 Mr. Bright went to Birmingham, and he made there a bitter speech against the Conservative party, and did all in his power to excite the working classes into rebellion. (Hear, hear.) He there set the Trades' Union ball a-rolling, which has now increased to a dangerous size, by making use of the following language. He said:—

> "Working men have associations: they can get up formidable strikes against capital; sometimes it may be upon real, sometimes upon fancied grievances; sometimes for things that are just, sometimes for things that are impossible. They have associations, trade societies, organizations; and I want to ask them why it is that all these various organizations throughout the country could not be made use of for the purpose of obtaining their political freedom."

Now, gentlemen, the working men of England have a right to their trade societies, their organizations, and their trades' unions, for the purpose of protecting their labour, so long as they do not deprive or deny to any man the right to sell his labour where he likes, and how he likes—(hear, hear,)—but when working men combine to compel working men to be their slaves and do their bidding, then they become a curse to their country. (Hear, hear.) Mr. Bright called upon the working men to use their trades' unions and their organizations to compel Parliament to be subservient to numbers, and had he succeeded then, or if he succeed now, the star of England's glory will set for ever, and we shall soon be a conquered nation. (Hear, hear, and cheers.) Between 1860 and 1864, Mr. Bright was comparatively speaking, quiescent; he and his colleagues, in their democratic movement, were waiting for Lord

Palmerston's death; but he did not die. In 1864 it was well known that Mr. Bright and Mr. Gladstone had become intimate political friends—in fact, it was said in the House of Commons that Mr. Gladstone had literally become the scholar of Mr. Bright, and I have seen him myself in the House of Commons sitting at Mr. Bright's feet and looking up into his face to hear his mutterings. (Laughter, and hear, hear.) Mr. Gladstone, on the advice of Mr. Bright, or some other person, consented to receive Mr. Potter, and several men of Trades' Unions of London, at his house as a deputation, and it was said immediately afterwards that he had become a convert to their political views, and that in a few days he was coming down to the House to make a revolutionary speech in support of Mr. Baines's Reform Bill. I attended, with many other members of Parliament, deeply interested in seeing to what lengths Mr. Gladstone would go, as the pupil of Mr. Bright and Mr. Potter. He said, on May 11th, 1864, that—"a deputation representing the most extensive among all existing combinations of the working classes had waited upon him," and added,

> "We are told for instance that the working classes are given to strikes. I believe it is the experience of the employers of labour that these strikes are more and more losing the character of violence and compulsory inter-ference with the free will of their own comrades and fellow-workmen, and are assuming that legal and under certain circumstances legitimate character which they possess as the only means by which as a last resort, labour can fairly assert itself against capital in the peaceful strife of the labour market. Let us take too that which in former times I believe to have been the besetting sin of labour—the disposition of the majority not to recognise the right of the minority, and, indeed of every single individual to sell his labour for what he thinks fit."

I believe no man ever did more mischief in a single speech in the House of Commons than Mr. Gladstone in the remarks which he made that evening upon strikes. (Hear, hear, applause, and a voice, "that is true.") I see my name honourably associated on that flag (pointing to a banner on the wall) with Oastler, Ashley, Bull, and Fielden. (Cheers.) I have frequently heard these men declare, that no more bitter curse can befal a neighbourhood than a strike, and that it was the duty of all working men, before they strike against their masters, to do all they possibly could to bring about an amicable arrangement. (Hear, hear.) Depend upon it, working men, that unless the employers and employed look upon each other as entwined like the ivy on a tree, supporting and consolidating each other, there is no chance of permanent commercial prosperity. (Applause.) Now, mark, that ever since Mr. Gladstone made this mischievous speech, the whole of England has been torn to its centre with strikes; every neighbourhood almost has suffered lamentably; millions have been lost to trade by the folly of this man. (Hear, hear.) Well, Mr. Gladstone that night made a revolutionary speech; his friends stood aghast; the Conservative party were astounded that the member for the University of Oxford should thus have dared to violate his principles and his pledges. Mr. Forster, the member for Bradford, was in the wildest state of excitement. He rushed out of the house exclaiming, "Thank God, we (the Radicals) have got a leader at last;" but let me tell you, that in my opinion they will find it is the blind leading the blind. (Laughter and applause.) Well, in the following autumn of 1865, Mr. Forster, I think at Leeds, made a violent revolutionary speech. He talked about five millions of down-trodden people in this country deprived of the franchise, and said that he was prepared to give the franchise to one million of them. Mark, Mr. Forster, was only prepared to give the franchise to one million of the down-trodden people; he was therefore himself prepared to tread down the other remaining four millions. (Applause.) Now, what I have always said to Mr. Forster—and let me tell you that he is an able and a deep-thinking man, holding a high position in this borough and in this country—when he speaks of the million who ought to be enfranchised, is this, "Point out to the Parliament and to the country the million that are worthy of the franchise, and mark the severance between them and the four millions, and then we have some chance of legislation." (Applause.) What I complain of is this, that men in Mr. Forster's influential position should so forget themselves and their duty to their country as to go before vast assemblages of their countrymen and call them "a down-trodden people," and tell them that they are "robbed of the franchise," for, begging Mr. Forster's pardon, there is no truth in the statement. (Laughter, hear, hear, and applause.) Now, in the whole world there is no country where the working men and the working women, too, are so protected as in England. (Hear, hear.) There is no privilege which the working men cannot enjoy; there is no right which any man possesses in this country that a working man does not possess. There is no enforced service in the army or the navy; there is no public office in England which is not open to him. The franchise is not refused. The House of Commons welcomes the working men within its walls, and the House of Peers is recruited from their ranks. What said Mr. Brotherton, the member for Salford? "I myself worked in a factory when a boy, and I stand here to plead the factory boy's cause." What said John Fielden? "I am proud of having been a factory operative, and I know the tortures they have endured." Mr. Fox, the Norwich weaver boy, has frequently elicited the hearty cheers of the House of Commons by his oratory. Mr. Hume himself said there was not an instance of a working man having risen from the ranks in the army to be a general. Sir John Elley rose from his seat and said:—Mr. Speaker, I rise to give the flattest contradiction to the statement of the hon. member for Montrose. I entered the army as a private soldier. I advanced through every rank until I became colonel in the regiment in which I enlisted, and I now hold that distinguished post. I am a general in the army, and have the honour of representing the borough in which my sovereign resides. (Hear, hear, and applause.) Sir John Elley was born on Clayton Heights, he was the son of a delver, and a delver himself. He came down with his comrades to Bradford on the spree, enlisted in the Oxford Blues, and on the field of Waterloo was proclaimed, "Elley, the terrible swordsman." Don't tell me that the working men are down-trodden! If the Constitution and the Government trod down the working men, the people of England would soon tread them under their feet. The glory and the power of England is this—that no man is trodden-down within these realms unless he does it with his own feet. (Applause.) The demagogues who are now inciting the people of this country to rebellion, use no arguments but threats, abuse, and intimidation, and if any man dares to oppose them he is held up to his countrymen in language unequalled since the French Revolution, and marked out for the assassin's trigger. (Applause.) The other day I saw this Riding placarded in every direction, with the announcement of a great Reform demonstration which was to take place at Leeds, and I say the language used in that placard was revolutionary. (Hear, hear.) The working men were told "not to be found wanting in the future," and they were given to understand that they would have "to fight for their rights." (Hear, hear.) Now, mark my words, if the working men of England should be deluded into such madness as to resist the responsible Government of this country and come into collision with her forces, there is not a man amongst those who are giving this advice that will "not be found wanting." Mr. Bright may tell the working men "to fight for their rights," but will he head them and stand by them in the hour of peril? (Hear, hear, and cries of "No, no.") I have watched Mr. Bright for years; and, although, as I have told you, he is possessed of marvellous powers of eloquence, a greater political coward never entered the House of Commons. (Hear, hear, and loud cheers.) He has talked of finding a better House of Commons in a few minutes from the people that pass through Temple Bar, but I tell you they will never find a worse than himself. He never comes down to the House of Commons to make a speech, unless it is to stir up strife and bad blood throughout the country. (Hear, hear.) I never heard him make a speech which inculcated peace and good will amongst men; but, on the contrary, he has always tried to set the different classes of the country against each other, and thereby to encourage bloodshed. (Hear, hear.) For twenty-five years I have worked with you working men of Bradford, in obtaining many great and conciliating measures from Parliament—(hear, hear)—while he has opposed them all. (Hear, hear.) During that time I never heard him speak a word in favour of working men in the House of Commons. (Hear, hear.) You have been reminded of what his conduct was in Lancashire during the cotton famine. He took no part either in purse or person, to relieve the distress in his native county—hear, hear—but when I met at Manchester a great assembly of delegates from the cotton districts of Cheshire, Lancashire, Staffordshire, and Yorkshire, they unanimously declared that England had no more bitter enemy than Mr. Bright, and that he was detested by all the working men of Lancashire. (Hear, hear.) Now, the question is, will the educated working men of Bradford and of this country be the tools of designing demagogues? (Hear, hear, and "No, no."] Will they, the educated working men of England, unite with the gentry, the merchants, the manufacturers, the higher ranks, the middle classes, and all those who are educated—and will they aid them in supporting measures which will strengthen our institutions? For that is the question I ask you to decide to-night. (Hear, hear.) You have done so here to-day, and you have been requested by your Vicar to talk these matters over in private with your fellow workmen. I have never asked a favour from you in all my life, but

I have received much kindness from you. I have often given you advice, and on my conscience I tell you that I believe, as your worthy Vicar has told you, that seed will be sown in this hall which will spring up and bring forth a great harvest throughout the length and breadth of the land. (Hear, hear, and cheers.) The leaven which you have kneaded here to-night will leaven the whole of England, and a spirit will be exhibited which will show that England is yet herself, and that she will not be led astray by designing demagogues. (Hear, hear, and loud applause.) Mr. Bright tells you that he wants no monarchy but a republic. That has been the doctrine and the gospel he has preached throughout his life. (Hear, hear.) Well, I admire Mr. Bright for being an honest man in telling us what he means, and if England does not checkmate him, he will carry out what he means. (Hear, hear.) He has even impugned the Sovereign of this country, and we all know that a more virtuous woman never lived than our beloved Queen—[loud applause]—but when we remember that that Queen is a widow, borne down with a heavy burden of affliction, we feel indignant that Mr. Bright should be throwing out vile insinuations at her neglect of duty "in the neighbourhood of Windsor Castle." [Hear, hear.] Now, Mr. Bright not only abuses the Monarch, but the House of Lords, and House of Commons as well—the two great bulwarks of the freedom of the nation. [Hear, hear.] At Glasgow, the other day, he told the people there that Lord Elcho was not fit to represent Haddingtonshire. Who made Mr. Bright the judge? [Hear, hear.] The electors are the men to decide that question. But from these facts you see the spirit of the man. [Hear, hear.] His abuse of Mr. Lowe has been most scandalous and disgraceful. I heard his marvellous speech, and a more brilliant oration was never delivered in the House of Commons. [Hear, hear.] And let me tell you, working men, that I myself am prepared to endorse every word of that speech. [Hear, hear, and applause.] And there is not one educated working man in this room if he reads it fairly and honestly but will say on his conscience that Mr. Lowe spoke the truth. [Hear, hear.] Mr. Lowe's argument was this:—The present franchise is a property qualification:—manhood suffrage would be in the man alone, therefore no class should receive the suffrage, which as a class is largely disqualified to exercise it. I agree with Mr. Lowe, and also in the remark that fell from your Vicar—I think you will do so too—that if you do enfranchise these classes you endanger the institutions of the country. Now, Mr. Lowe has been abused not only by Mr. Bright, but by many other men throughout the country; for having made that speech he has been unfairly criticised, and words placed in his mouth which he never uttered. I will call into this assembly to-night a witness to support Mr. Lowe's opinions; and who do you think he is?—Mr. Forster, the member for Bradford. He, during the same debate, made use of these words, "there has been a great deal of talk about setting class against class, but there were certain classes against which it was desirable to set all classes: he meant the dangerous classes." Well, that was exactly what Mr. Lowe said; that there were dangerous classes in this country who were unfitted for the franchise, and against whom it was his duty to set the House of Commons and the country. [Hear, hear.] Mr. Forster says exactly the same thing, and instead of Mr. Lowe being abused, he ought to be thanked by every loyal Englishman for his eminent services, for Mr. Bright and Mr. Gladstone would arm those dangerous classes with the franchise. [Hear, hear.] We are anxious to keep them from it, because we know full well that they are unfitted to exercise it, and that if they did exercise it they would soon destroy the institutions of the country. [Hear, hear.] I believe there is another large class in this country—and not a dangerous class—which is equally unfitted to possess the franchise. Now if you and I next Saturday night could go and visit all the public houses and beer shops in the manufacturing districts of the north, how many thousand men should we find in them, some of them drinking the wages earned by their wives and children, who, I do not hesitate to say, would sell their votes if they had them for a quart of ale, or a leg of mutton for their Sunday dinner. [Hear, hear.] Now I say that that class is unfit to possess the franchise. [Hear, hear.] When Mr. Disraeli introduced into the House of Commons his Reform Bill, he guarded against the admission of those classes to the franchise, but he intended to enfranchise and would have enfranchised most of those I see before me to-night. [Hear, hear.] The men who have robbed you of the right to possess the franchise are not Lord Derby and his Government, but Lord Palmerston, Mr. Bright, Mr. Gladstone, and a host of other liberals who voted against that measure. [Hear, hear, and loud applause.] It is high time my friends, that you should be aroused to a sense of the danger that is threatening you. Many gentlemen who have addressed this large assembly this evening have appeared to me to view this matter in a trivial light. [Hear, hear.] They are trusting too much to what they call the good feeling and the sound sense of England; but recollect this, that water by constant dropping upon a stone will wear it away—[hear, hear]—and if those insidious demagogues who are now stirring up sedition and bad blood in the country are to have their way unchecked, uncontradicted and unopposed, they will triumph in the end. [Hear, hear.] What is the state of things at present with regard to trades' unions? They are attempting to dictate to Parliament and the country what is henceforth to be the constitution, and a more dangerous course was never pursued in this land of freedom. [Hear, hear.] I may tell you they are arranging in London, that when Parliament meets, Mr. Potter and his Trades' Union men are to march down and surround the House of Commons, and prevent the members entering into the house who are opposed to their political views. [Hear, hear.] Now, if this state of things is to be allowed, there will be no freedom of discussion, and the Parliament of England will no longer be a deliberative assembly. [Hear, hear.] Numbers will govern England, instead of common sense. [Hear, hear.] The meetings which are taking place in this country at present are like those which were carried out after the Reform Bill of 1832 was passed. Then Mr. O'Connell went through the country exciting to sedition and rebellion. Now Mr. Bright is doing the same. In 1837 Glasgow rallied round the the institutions of this country; in 1866 she has had a large meeting of her citizens, who have cried out, "Away with them." [Hear, hear.] In 1837 she elected the greatest statesman England possessed to represent her loyalty: in 1866 she has elected one of the greatest demagogues to represent her disloyalty. [Hear, hear.] On the 13th January 1837, the Statesman I allude to, Sir Robert Peel, was elected Lord Rector of Glasgow University. The Conservative working men of that city presented him with its freedom. The merchants' House of Glasgow presented him with an address, unanimously agreed to, and which I will read to you, as it is of the greatest importance at the present day:—

"To you, sir, the nation looks up as one of her best protectors, confident that whether directing the councils of your Sovereign, or leading a powerful and independent party in Parliament, while you proceed in the cause of cautious and practical reform which has distinguished your career as a statesman, you will employ the splendid talents bestowed upon you by Divine providence in resisting all reckless changes of innovation, and in upholding those free and liberal institutions which form the valuable constitution in Church and State handed down by our forefathers, and which we trust to hand down unimpaired to posterity."

At the dinner in the evening to which Sir Robert Peel was invited, there were present 2298 persons; with those admitted afterwards, the number was increased to 3432. (Applause.) Now, gentlemen, I am afraid I am taking up too much of your time—(No, no, and applause)—but with your permission I will read to you the warning words of Sir Robert Peel, delivered in that room, in which he warned the country against the hope of permanence in a Radical constitution. In a time like this, when a more violent agitation is taking place than even that carried on in 1837, it is well you should hear Sir Robert Peel's views. Recollect there is not in the north of England a large manufacturing town where the merchants, manufacturers, and the workmen, have not erected a statue in honour of Sir Robert Peel. You in Bradford have especially looked up to him for counsel and advice, considering him one of the greatest statesmen that England ever possessed. Now listen to what Sir Robert Peel says:—

"When you have formed your new Constitution: when you have relieved your electoral body from all disagreeable publicity; when you have them voting in secret, acting on the shameful advice which is already offered to them,—to hurrah for one candidate on the hustings, but to put the name of the other into the balloting box; when you have got your single popular assembly returned by such means, owing no allegiance, no responsibility, except to the select corps of secret voters, controlled by no check but theirs;—what is the ground upon which you rest your hope of steady, permanent, efficient government? What should exempt you from the state of France? Why should you expect to avert the bloody and debasing servitude which she endured? Will your constitutional assembly open under fairer auspices than hers? or will the offspring of the ballot be men of higher attainments, or purer or more generous views, than the assembly of France presented? Do you hope there will be fewer elements of resistance and struggle here? or that resistance and struggle here, as in France, will not produce the same results—proscription, confusion, annual constitutions, anarchy, military despotism? Do not believe that the bloody miscreants who chased each other in rapid succession from the slippery heights of power to the scaffold, were monsters peculiar to France; that the Dantons, the Marats, and the Robespierres, were *lusus naturæ,* which other times and other countries can never engender. No, these men were the foul, but legitimate spawn of circumstances. Their murders and their crimes were not the mere wanton gratification of an original, inherent, supernatural thirst for blood. They were the necessary instruments for getting and maintaining power—the arts of self defence in the time of anarchy—and if you consent to unloose the bonds of authority in a society constituted like ours, you will have the same consequences, the same men, and the same crimes here as in France.

The scum will gather when the nation boils

Then will crawl forth the men whose names and persons are now utterly obscure and unknown, shocking to you, if they could be revealed, succeeding to each other in a short-lived dominion, according to their gradations in effrontery and audacity, and reckless vice. Then will be the wide-spread grinding tyranny, not confined to capital cities, but having its sanguinary agent in every village, calling himself "the People," and proscribing and murdering in the cause of liberty, humanity and virtue." (Loud cheers.)

Now these were the words of warning delivered by Sir R. Peel. Some men might say, "Oh, but the French Revolution was over long ago, and such horrors would not again occur." Why, since these words were uttered in 1837, the streets of Paris have been repeatedly deluged with revolutionary blood. In 1851 the atrocities perpetrated by the Manhood Suffrage Revolutionists in the south of France were too horrible to be mentioned in the presence of women. I myself saw in one of the small towns an aged veteran, with white locks flowing around his head, his breast covered with medals in honour of the battles he had fought in his country's service, who commanded a small detachment of *gendarmerie*. Before that day week he was burnt to death for the crime of defending his post. Believe me, Sir Robert Peel knew full well the dangerous classes of England, which Mr. Forster advised all classes to set themselves against, and also what would be the result of a Radical revolution. (Applause.) But Sir Robert Peel's was not the only voice of warning raised on that occasion in Glasgow. He was accompanied by a rising statesman, his beloved pupil, whom he looked upon as his right-hand man, to whom the future government of England, when he was gone should revert, and who would govern the country under the guidance of his conservative principles. Listen to what this talented statesman then said:—that

"The present great struggle in which the country was engaged was not a party but a national contest; the institutions of the country were threatened with destruction, and the assault now openly made on the Constitution which had been so long the boast of Britain—offered to men of all parties—whether called by the forgotten name of Whig or Tory—a neutral ground upon which they might meet to withstand the insidious attacks of their common enemy. (Great cheering.) He felt convinced that from the walls of this building a voice would reverberate which had already been sounded to them from England—the voice of fearless and resolute attachment to the institutions of this country."

Who was the man who thus warned his countrymen? Mr. Gladstone. (Applause.) Well, Mr. Lowe selected this neutral ground in the House of Commons to warn his fellow-countrymen against the insidious attacks of the enemies of the constitution, led by Mr. Gladstone himself; but who was the man that first denounced him for his loyalty and his patriotism? Mr. Gladstone, who rushed down to Liverpool, grossly misrepresented Mr. Lowe, and told the people there that he had burnt the boats and broken down the bridges behind him, and would never rest until he had destroyed "the institutions of the country." [Applause.] Mr. Lowe's speech was the "voice of fearless and resolute attachment to the institutions of this country," and the cheers which resounded through this room to-night, like the cheers at Glasgow on that occasion, proclaim throughout the length and breadth of the land the determination of the thoughtful and educated working men of Bradford never to be the tools of Mr. Gladstone. The present struggle is no more a party one than the struggle in 1837. It is a national contest, with the principles of our glorious Constitution at stake, which the merchants of Glasgow unanimously called upon Sir Robert Peel to protect. Already thousands of our countrymen are flinging aside the worn out names of Whig and Tory and are becoming constitutionalists; they are taking up their position upon this neutral ground, which you have so nobly done. [Loud cheers.] I see many gentlemen here to-night who would not have joined this party as a conservative party, or if it had assembled for merely party objects. Working men of Bradford, the Working Men's Conservative Associations from 1837 to 1841 were Sir Robert Peel's right arm, by which he fought the battle of the Constitution on every hustings, and in every polling booth, and throughout the country, and who won for him on that occasion a great and glorious victory. They greatly aided in sending him to Parliament with a majority of 90, by which for several years he governed this country supported by the patriotism, the good will, and the good feeling of every class, and whose wise policy had endeared him not only to the people living in his time, but also will endear his memory for ages to come. I believe that you working men of Bradford have to-night set an example which will be largely followed throughout Great Britain and Ireland. I believe that Lord Derby, should he be driven by factious opposition to dissolve Parliament, will find, like Sir Robert Peel, the educated working men his right arm of defence, and that by your Conservative Associations springing up in every quarter you will give him as triumphant a victory as was given to Sir Robert Peel. [Loud applause.]

R. S. S., *The Tory Reform Act. What Must We Do with It? Register! Register!! Register!!!, By a Member of the Council of the 'National Union'*
National Union of Conservative and Constitutional Associations, Publication No 4, (London, 1868), 3–19

British Library, General Reference Collection 8138.aaa.56

Following its inaugural meeting in November 1867, the National Union of Conservative and Constitutional Associations (NUCCA) began publishing pamphlets intended to educate and inform the approximately 969,000 new voters in England and Wales enfranchised by the 1867 Reform Act. *The Tory Reform Act. What Must We Do with It? Register! Register!! Register!!!* outlined an historic Tory commitment to Reform going back to William Pitt, a tradition most recently stated by Lord Derby at Manchester on 17 October 1867. It portrayed Disraeli as Leonidas, heading a Spartan force of 300, in the battle of Thermopylae over Reform against the mass Persian forces led by Gladstone and Bright. Citing Peel's cry of 1837, that Conservative voters needed to 'register, register, register', it declared that it was in the Registration Courts that the great institutions of the country must be defended.

12

R. S. S., *THE TORY REFORM ACT.* *WHAT MUST WE DO WITH IT?* *REGISTER! REGISTER!! REGISTER!!!,* *BY A MEMBER OF THE COUNCIL OF* *THE 'NATIONAL UNION'*

National Union of Conservative and Constitutional Associations, Publication No 4, (London, 1868), 3–19

WHEN, in 1832, "The Bill, the whole Bill, and nothing but the Bill" had become the law of the land, as far as the "Great Revolution houses" would permit, (and it was not the "parvula cælestes pacavit mica" that typified the stipulations of the illustrious and celestial "blue blooded," as represented by Lord John Russell), it was supposed that an extinguisher had been put upon the Tory party. Certainly it was not intended that that measure should "dish the Whigs," but, notwithstanding the "Chandos Clause," it was fondly hoped that it would "dish" the Tories. And it did—for a longer time than was sweet and wholesome for the sound interests of the country. Due regard being observed towards the fact that so small a number of Tories was returned to the first reformed Parliament, it cannot be rationally supposed that they fretted and fumed because they were doomed to sit, and did sit, in the "cold shade" of opposition. They felt that their principles were just and most thoroughly *English*. And they were content, for the time, to comfort themselves by the always fresh and green traditions of true political and Constitutional liberty that had, but recently (in the life of nations) been handed to them by their great leader, William Pitt—the most illustrious and soundest "Reformer" in theory, and in earnest and fixed intention, that ever lived in this country, and, we will take the bold liberty to say, that ever *will* live.

To digress just a little, what were these traditions? A brief but expressive summary of them was presented to the reader two years and a half ago, in a speech just then delivered at Ashton-under-Lyne, and we hope that we may be excused if we present an epitome of them, in order that the public may be seized of the simple and most undoubted truth. The Tory statesman, Pitt, was a more earnest, practical reformer than any of his Whig contemporaries, who, having "tasted the sweets of office" (and wished to lie down to many banquets of them), were. He was solicitous, not only for Parliamentary reform, but for commercial freedom, while those who were opposed to him sat in sullen silence, with folded hands, when either of those great topics were broached. In 1783, Pitt proposed to disfranchise thirty-six small boroughs, and transfer the seats to populous places like Manchester, Leeds, Birmingham, and other great towns that had achieved commercial and manufacturing importance in England by their splendid thrift and enterprise. The genius of Pitt's measure undoubtedly was (and no one, as we suppose, will dare to deny it), that the basis of representation might widen and be made to correspond with the progress of population, and consequently of wealth. What was the fate of this wise and most statesman-like and truly "liberal" measure? The Bill was thrown out by 293 to 149 votes—scarcely a solitary one of the "great Revolution houses," of which Lord John Russell speaks with such conscientious complacency, having supported it.

We are willing to give the utmost credit for sincerity to Charles Fox, whose genius and astuteness compelled even the first Napoleon, when Fox visited Paris, to approach him at an audience with something very like subserviency, for he was the only man who gave in his adhesion to that measure. In the following year Pitt brought forward a similar measure. Again, the great bulk of the Whig party, joined by a small, but nevertheless influential, section of those who ought to have been his own supporters (as, indeed, happened last year to Lord Derby—for history "repeats itself," and there are always conscientious "obstructives" to be found in the curious history of *all* political parties), opposed Pitt, and his Bill was thrown out by a majority of 248 to 174. We might carry the record, as regards Parliamentary Reform in Pitt's time, much further, but it is quite unnecessary to go beyond this point. We have proved enough; and it can never be wise to push inquiry beyond the point of truth and conviction. It is a fault of our political adversaries; and, to those who allow others to think and reason for them in a way that may be agreeable to barbaric passion, which possesseth not the power to think before it acts, we can make no hopeful appeal. Oddly and incongruously enough, to "move our special wonder," Mr. Gladstone began, some time ago, to found himself upon Pitt. When the Right Honourable gentleman was Chancellor of the Exchequer he continually claimed the great minister as his model and prototype of economic and fiscal statesmanship. He plucked him out, as it were, from those sweet and wholesome pastures of Tory management and culture which so entirely won the love and devotion of an admiring country, even in the midst of a ruinous but glorious war—a war waged to vindicate the integrity of all Europe and the inviolable freedom of the British soil—war which Pitt, on his solitary death-bed on "the Heath," drew from him with his last breath the agonised ejaculation, "Oh, my country!" though the splendid triumph of that country, owing to his own wisdom and foresight, and unknown to him, was so near at hand.

Amidst all these painful distractions, the "Tory" statesman had ever an eye to the commercial advancement of his country, and he had reserved a large space in his mind for it, though the whole and undivided powers of an inferior genius would have been devoted to the one grand purpose—the safety of the country. We positively cannot commit ourselves to fritter away our space upon so small a theme as Mr. Gladstone's abortive attempt to adjust gracefully and becomingly upon his own shoulders the shining mantle of Pitt. He sank to his knees under it when he tried it on. The appropriated panoply was too heavy for him to carry. Well, this is a digression, and we will not push it any further than to say this—that if Mr. Gladstone had lived in Pitt's time he would have run the hazard of being put in a kind of political pillory by a populace that had an abiding objection to a political adventurer, who strutted and swaggered in borrowed plumes that could never belong to him after he had performed the Hibernian feat of "turning his back upon himself," and become a renegade to the principles which he professed when he was a promising lieutenant under Peel. We are accustomed in this country to look for something like consistency in political principle among those who aspire to be our leading statesmen; and public opinion seldom hesitates in the end to invoke the First Lictor to perform his dread functions upon an offender. Against this wholesome principle even the youthful orator cannot always escape,—

"At juveni oranti subitus tremor occupat artus."

When Mr. Gladstone was "young and curly" he escaped this horrid sensation; but at a later period of his life he was expelled from the representation of the dwellers in the classic groves of his *Alma Mater,* and within four and twenty hours of his expulsion he was discovered on a Manchester platform; and something like a voice as of "[Illegible Text] [Illegible Text] [Illegible Text]," as old Homer hath it,[1] was distinctly heard, and it is even averred that some "bitter tears were shed." But we may dismiss all this about the ex-Chancellor of the Exchequer, with the simple observation that no man of truly liberal tendencies need have deserted the Conservative party any time within the last quarter of a century. For we have certainly followed in the footsteps of Pitt. We have followed him, for instance, in promoting the freedom of trade and all fiscal relaxations. It cannot be disputed that a considerable number of the Conservative party were opposed to a repeal of the Corn Laws, but a large portion of the party, including Sir Robert Peel, who brought the measure forward and carried it, were in favour of repeal. In fact, it ought never to have been made a party question at all, and never would have been, had it not been taken up by that reactionary and even revolutionary party, which numbered in its ranks Mr. Bright and other admirers of that American democracy (which was recently displayed in the Fenian murders at Manchester and Clerkenwell), who keep up their *rôle* to this day, and still mean to push their un-English craze to an extremity. Even the late Mr. Cobden declared, in his place in the House of Commons, in February, 1845, that the larger portion—"4–5ths" he said—of the Conservative party in the North of England had always been in favour of free trade. We will not now undertake to say whether these Conservatives were right or wrong; but when the party is charged wholesale with "obstructing" every measure of Reform (a charge, by the way, which was brought by Mr. Bright against the late Lord Palmerston, with respect to Parliamentary reform—and perhaps rather more justifiably, seeing that when the late Premier was badgered by his constant tormentor, the Tiverton tradesman, on the hustings, and asked why he and his colleagues had "not brought forward a Reform Bill," the noble Viscount, with his characteristic shrewdness, and readiness of repartee, replied, "because we are not such geese"), have we not the clear right to quote the evidence of men who are connected with the party of our opponents? Among other things, an attempt has been made to identify the Tory party as opponents of the abolition of slavery. But who was it that brought forward that humane and beneficent measure? Who was it that invited and persuaded the country, through its representatives in Parliament, to devote twenty millions of money to compensate the planters for the heavy loss which they must inevitably sustain by this noble christian act? Need we remind the world that it was the Lord Stanley of that day, now the First Minister of Great Britain? What party repealed the Test and Corporation Act? The Test Act was passed in March, 1673, in the reign of Charles II., and it provided that all officers, civil and military, under Government, should receive the Holy Eucharist, according to the forms of the Church of England, and take the oaths against Transubstantiation, and so forth. This Act was repealed by statute 9th George IV., chapter 17, on the 9th of May, 1828, and was intituled, "An Act for repealing so much of several Acts as impose the necessity of receiving the Sacrament of the Lord's Supper as a qualification for certain office and emoluments." And who were in office in 1828? Why, the Duke of Wellington and Sir Robert Peel, and all the "Tories" of mark in that day. And they also brought forward and passed, amidst enormous opposition, even from royal personages and the Court, the Roman Catholic Emancipation Act. To come down some years later, it may be well to remember that the Act providing for the abolition of the property qualification of Members of Parliament was introduced by Mr. Secretary Walpole, and passed into law under the auspices of Lord Derby's administration. The Jews are likewise the debtors of this much-abused Tory party of ours, that "never did and never will do anything in the way of Reform."

We protest that it is a good, and wholesome, and eminently just thing to lay these fair and comely traditions of the "Tory party" before a forgetful people— forgetful, because mainly by reason of the all-absorbing thriftiness and marvellous prosperity of a commercial and manufacturing community like ours, which is very apt to look only to the present, and perhaps not much to the *future,* and be too much given to overlook all the blessings and honours and glories of the past. It is wise, to borrow the tender phrase of one of our favourite novelists, Mr. Dickens (who, by the way, is a professing Liberal, though he is evidently quite insensible of the absolute fact that he is preeminently a "Conservative"), to keep the "memory green" of our "pensive public," on these most remarkable, but (in a party sense) much perverted points.

And now let us crown all these brave achievements of this much-abused party of public usefulness with that resplendent chaplet which we suppose must be divided between Lord Derby and Mr. Disraeli. Here we come at last to "The Representation of the People Act, 1867," such is the technical title of the great "Tory Reform Act" of the last session. For our immediate and very practical purpose, we shall go into its main provisions presently. In the meantime let us just see what our own friends here, out of doors, say about it. On Thursday the 27th of June there was held in the large room of the Town Hall at Manchester (the very hot-bed of Radicalism) a great "Conference" of "Conservative and Constitutional Associations," and the beautiful hall was crowded by an audience that thought deeply and strongly. An old and a devoted adherent of the great Constitutional Party moved the first resolution, which was in these terms:

"That this Conference desires to record its satisfaction at the formation and development of the Constitutional Association and its numerous branches throughout the country, and this Conference hereby resolves to aid to the utmost of its ability the extension and *consolidation of the same*." The Speaker said in effect, for we do not profess to *borrow his precise words*,[2] "At first the Conservatives were called "obstructives," but they were called "obstructive" no longer; in fact, it was made a reproach against them that they were *more liberal than the Liberals*." He happened to get hold of a newspaper that morning and he found that Mr. Bright had been addressing the Fishmongers at London, and that among other things he said, "It cannot be concealed, I shall not attempt to conceal it from myself or anybody else, that a very rapid and extraordinary stride is being made to what men call democratic and, if you like, even republican institutions." He, the Speaker, was afraid that the democracy that Mr. Bright spoke of was not exactly the democracy he, the Speaker, liked. If the Conservative Party had brought forward democratic measures, they had taken care to frame them on the "old lines of the Constitution," and not upon those "lines" which had been the subject of Mr. Bright's modern discovery. He had no hesitation in confessing that he had heard many Conservatives complain of the measure of Parliamentary reform that had been brought forward by the present government. *His answer was that the measure was founded on sound constitutional principles, (hear, hear,) and if the Conservative Party had not brought forward this measure of reform the opposite party would have done so, and it would have been that kind of Parliamentary Reform leading on to republicanism. (Applause.)* Therefore he held that, as a *patriotic party,* the Conservative Party of this country had only *done its duty* by bringing forward this measure. *If it had been less liberal there would have been no resting place;* as it was, he hoped and believed that the reform question was now *settled for a generation at least.* He could not help thinking it was gall and wormwood to their opponents to know that they had taken it out of their *mouths,* and had by *the same act* taken from their *hands* a weapon which they wished to use not for the common good of their country, but for the purpose of placing their party in the ascendant." Is it not true that the Tory party, under Lord Derby and Mr. Disraeli, have placed the representation of the people on a sound basis? We have discovered a firm foundation, and we cannot with safety to the Constitution of an old country like this spread ourselves into a "sweezy" bog of democratic adventure, the only lights of which are at the best an "ignus fatuus" that can lead us to nothing but utter destruction. If we were a young state we could try all sorts of experiments, as the Americans have, very much to their sorrow, or we grievously misread those "signs of the times" which point to the mournful result that *must* come of the present utter exclusion of all the wealth and cultivated intelligence of the western shores of the Atlantic. We think that the Reform measure of the Government requires no further justification whatever beyond that which we have quoted. But just listen to bluff and shrewd old Mr. Henley, one of the members for Oxfordshire. He said, only a a few months ago, at an Agricultural Dinner at Bicester, that the question of Reform was now "settled," "all they could hope now was that it had been settled in a way which was satisfactory to the country. This question had been agitated for the last fourteen years, and he, Mr. Henley, was one of those who thought that when successive Prime Ministers had put words into the mouth, and told the people that an extension of the franchise was necessary, they ought no longer to play the humbug, and that it was necessary to settle the question if they could. *We believed that the question had now been settled, not bit by bit, but in the only mode in which it could be settled with any prospect of permanence;* and all they could do now was to look forward with confidence to the good sense and feeling of the country to use fairly the great trust which had been placed in their hands. It was impossible to shut their eyes to the vast spread of independence and energy which had taken place in the country, especially in the lifetime of some of the oldest among them; and they had not only to take into consideration that independence and energy, but to turn the tide for the benefit and advantage of the people. *They had done so, not by adopting a temporary cure, but by passing a great and strong measure; and they could not be too thankful if that which had taken place should be vastly for the better.* There had been an enormous increase to the wealth of the country, and that had been accompanied by enormous temptations, for while some had been put up, others were longing for it; but amidst all the discouraging circumstances by which they were surrounded, which had grown up during the last fifty years, he looked with confidence to the good sense of the people of this country, and he trusted he might live to see his hopes fulfilled. The question of education was now prominently before Parliament and the country, and he trusted that in the settlement of the question the Legislature would endeavour to accomplish thorough education of the labourer without taking him away from useful occupations, and at the same time that he should not go to labour until he arrived at a proper age, so that those who have the proper opportunities may make the best of them during the time they are under their care. He believed that education would make a man a better labourer and more useful to his employer, and the only way to get that was to train them in good schools."

We have now, as we most conscientiously believe, fairly stated the pretensions of the Tory Party, and vindicated the soundness and security of their great Reform Bill. Anybody who has been a moderately fair and attentive student of the history of this country, during the last fifty years, must perceive that we have *understated* the case which would have been in our own favour. But we would much rather understate than overstate, because the truth always surprises and fascinates the most when it appears to us in a modest garb.

And now what have our "Revolution Houses" to say? We cannot suppose that they will allow what we must be permitted to name, and with conspicuous justice too, "The Tory Reform Act" to swamp them. They have already given strong evidences that they mean nothing of the sort,—nothing so like political suicide. The ultra members of the party intend this great Act to be useful as a party, and not merely as a party, but as a democratic "lever" to bring all things *down* in a grand crash to their own ignoble level, by that easy descent of the Avernus that may land the Monarchy, the Church, and all the constituent and essential members of the constitution in a hopeless limbo in which no light can shine. We cannot misunderstand Mr. Gladstone when he tells those who invited him to the Reform Fete at the Crystal Palace, (which, by the way, was a memorable and most deplorable failure!) that although he cannot come he does not consider he has fulfilled the whole of his mission. Writing from Hawarden he says, "I beg, however, to say that *in all that remains unaccomplished* I shall labour to *complete the settlement* of this great question in the same spirit which has hitherto guided me." There is nothing that his opponents can more ardently desire than that he *will* still be guided and governed by that same spirit which impelled him to hector and domineer over his supporters in the House of Commons, and insult his opponents. Nor could his bitterest enemy wish to take more effectual means of completing his unpopularity with the substantial and responsible members of society, than he certainly will if he persist in re-opening a question that for so long a time has been a grevious obstruction to much valuable and greatly-needed legislation of another sort. As far as he is personally concerned, it would be far better, if he would reduce to sober reality that transpontine figure illuminated by a confiagration of "boats," in which he indulged at Liverpool. And yet it would seem as if he and Mr. Bright were both of a mind as to "completing the settlement" of the "great question" at the earliest available opportunity,—though that may not be in the present Parliament; for we find Mr. Bright in another letter of excuse for *not* being present (what conscientious instincts these men of mark have!) at the Crystal Palace failure of the League, stating that "It is quite natural and most just that the working man should rejoice at what has been gained, but I hope that they will not forget that without a re-adjustment of members to population, and without the security of the Ballot, the House *of Commons will still be for the most part but a delegation from the rich,* and *not a real and free representation of the people.*" The Honorable Gentleman says something more which we shall not fail to quote presently in the right place, because it strongly supports the main purport of our present paper. Let us just observe, however, how forgetfully inconsistent with himself is the Member for Birmingham. In the very first line of his letter he speaks of "those that rejoice with us in the wide extension of the suffrage." *Other* Members of "The Great *United* Liberal Party" think that enough has already been done to ensure the most sweeping and destructive reforms in Church and State. We will show presently what Mr. Grant Duff expects to be done in the way of destruction and spoliation; but in the meantime, if we may be permitted a slight digression, we shall be glad to present his brief but vivid history of what occurred to the Liberal party at Carlton House Terrace on the 5th of last April. He gives Mr. Gladstone credit for having "yielded to the remonstrances of a large body of his own followers, and throwing over the preposterous and suicidal "instruction" that had been placed in the innocent hands (Heaven bless all these "innocents!") of Mr. Coleridge;" but then he goes on to say "there is something surpassingly foolish in asking a number of gentlemen to come and talk over the next move in a campaign, and then all but pitching down stairs the first that ventures to disagree with you by a hair's breadth," &c., &c., &c. This was on the 5th of April, but then came the memorable 17th, and we should very much like to know whether, in the opinion of the Liberals Mr. Gladstone's "blunder" was retrieved on the latter occasion. It will be remembered that the Liberals defeated themselves on Friday night the 12th of April on Mr. Gladstone's amendment on the Government Reform Bill by a majority of 21. This "shocking event" brought forth the following correspondence—

20, EATON SQUARE, S.W.,
April 17*th.*

DEAR MR. GLADSTONE,

I find that many Members of the House, who supported you on Friday evening, are anxious like myself to know what course you propose to take with regard to the remaining amendments to the Reform Bill standing in your name. It would be very useful, I am sure, if you could let me have a line from you on the subject before you leave town for the recess.

Believe me, yours faithfully,
R. W. CRAWFORD.

THE RIGHT HON. W. E. GLADSTONE, M.P.

Hawarden, Chester,
April 18*th.*

MY DEAR MR. CRAWFORD,

I thank you for giving me an opportunity, which enables me to make known to you and to others the course I propose to take with regard to the amendments

306

on the Reform Bill, as yet standing in my name on the notice paper of the House of Commons. I need not state what must be in the minds of all the nature of the amendment which the House rejected on Friday the 12th by 21 voices, or the composition of the body of noes by which it was rejected.

"The country can hardly fail now to be aware that those gentlemen of liberal opinions, whose convictions allow them to act unitedly upon this question, are not a majority but a minority of the existing House of Commons, and that they have not the power they were supposed to possess of limiting or directing the action of the administration, or of shaping the provisions of the Reform Bill. Still, having regard to the support which my proposal, with respect to personal rating, received from so large a number of Liberal members, I am not less willing than heretofore to remain at the service of the party to which they belong, and when any suitable occasion shall arise, if it shall be their wish, I shall be prepared again to attempt concerted action upon this, or any other subject for the public good. But until then, desirous to avoid misleading the country and our friends, I feel that prudence requires me to withdraw from my attempts to assume the initiative in amending a measure which cannot, perhaps be effectually amended except by a reversal, either formal or virtual, of the vote of Friday the 12th, for such attempts, if made by me, would, I believe, at the present critical moment, not be the most likely means of advancing their own purpose. Accordingly, I shall not proceed with the amendments now on the paper in my name, nor give notice of other amendments, such as I had contemplated, but I shall gladly accompany others in voting against any attempt, from whatever quarter, to limit yet further the scanty modicum of enfranchisement proposed by the Government, or in improving, where it may be practicable, the provisions of the Bill."

I remain, my dear MR. CRAWFORD,

Most faithfully yours,

W. E. GLADSTONE.

R. W. CRAWFORD, ESQ., M.P.

Time wears away, and sometimes erases entirely the most unpleasant reminiscences;[3] and we must hold Mr. Grant Duff responsible for "keeping our memory green," as Mr. Dickens hath it. When we come, very shortly, to the really practical part of this paper, we shall have a word or two to say to Mr. Grant Duff. In our humble judgment, no one contributed more to the success of Ministers in carrying through the new Reform Act, than Mr. Gladstone himself. He "lost his head" when he lost his temper, and perpetrated an endless series of blunders. It would be but a poor compliment to the leader of the House of Commons to say that he mainly owed his success to the miserable *tactique* of the leader of the Opposition; but that Mr. Disraeli was largely indebted to the mismanagement of his opponent, no one seriously doubts. It can be as little doubted that the Government Reform Act is the greatest party and political victory of modern times; in fact it is Mr. Disraeli's Thermopylæ. The Leonidas of the situation, he, by his fine temper, his coolness, prudence, and courage, inspirited his 300 followers (the Spartans of the occasion) in such a manner, that they beat back Mr. Bright's and Mr. Gladstone's boasted five millions or more of the large towns—nor can we see how any Ephialtes can arise to undo, by treachery, that which has been so well accomplished by loyalty and valour. The only way in which such a catastrophe could happen, would be by the great Conservative party being untrue to itself; and it is the main purpose of this pamphlet to avert, by timely advice, so great a calamity to the country.

The extreme Liberal party can hardly hope to induce the present parliament to undo any portion of the great work of last session, or even to add to it. In fact, Mr. Bright in the letter from which we have already quoted, confesses as much. He says to Mr. George Potter, "The destruction of the popular power of the great Boroughs by the vote at the end of the session, will show you how little Parliament is now to be trusted on any question of Reform, on which it may think it safe to go wrong. The Legislature has been driven in one direction by forces too strong for it, but its temper is not changed." We have seen, however, that the Honourable Gentleman talks about a prospective "readjustment of members to population, and the security of the Ballot." His coadjutor, the Junior Member for South Lancashire, has evidently something of the same kind in his mind also, for have we not already detected him muttering from Hawarden Castle: "in all that *remains unaccomplished* I shall labour to *complete* the settlement of this great question in the same spirit which has hitherto guided me?" Nor does this brace of political agitators, of the extreme school, stand alone in the expression of ulterior objects and purposes. A month ago, Mr. Grant Duff in the address to his constituents at Elgin, already referred to, is reported to have said, referring to Ireland, "*I am for general disendowment;* the maintenance of the national system of education, the retention of the Queen's University in its present unsectarian shape, and *the throwing open of Trinity College, as we desire to throw open Oxford and Cambridge.* Further, I advocate *a cheaper system of land transfer; encouragement to leases, and an equitable compensation for tenants' improvements;* nor if those mild measures failed to settle the land question and pacify the country, should I shrink from more sweeping changes. Don't fancy Fenianism is killed, it is hardly even scotched. * * * Lord Russell has mistaken the clock; pray heaven his mistake may not break up the Liberal party. I, for one, am wholly *opposed* to his scheme for *endowing the Roman Catholic Clergy,* and to the cry for giving Ireland denominational education, because we have it in England; as well might they clamour against us for not importing that ornament of our English hearths—the viper. [Anticipating that questions relating to land will occupy a more important place in discussion in the new Parliament than they have done hitherto, and that Mr. Locke King's bill will be carried, he proceeded]." It seems more than probable that the good sense of all parties will lead to some attempt being made to bring the House of Lords into closer harmony with the new House of Commons, by the disuse of proxies, by insisting upon a larger quorum, and, above all, by the creation of life Peers. Further organic changes may well be postponed till we have cured some of the functional disorders of the body politic, I should be *glad to see* *the ballot kept in reserve* as a thing to be agitated for with the whole strength of the Liberal party, *if we find that we don't get our own way under the new state of things,* so, too, with the question of the further re-distribution of seats. If it can be effected, by a general understanding next year, so much the better, and that is not impossible, for nothing but the shortness of time prevented the Lord's carrying the re-distribution further, and the House of Commons was more than prepared to follow suit; but if it cannot be done without fighting and loss of time, let us leave it alone till we see whether we cannot get some substantial fruits from our recent three-parts accomplished success. I think the immediate results of Reform have all along been over estimated by both parties, but I entertain no shadow of a doubt that, as an ultimate result, partly of this great electoral change, but still more of the change going on in men's minds, *every institution which has only antiquity or custom to plead for it, too will go by the board.* Sooner or later the interest of the majority will sweep away every vestige of mere historical as distinguished from philosophical right. Democracy lies before us on a not very distant horizon. Our duty during the next thirty years will be to prepare for it."

So far, the outspoken Mr. Grant Duff. We do not employ the expletive adjective in an invidious or a reproachful sense. On the contrary, we regard this candour on the part of our opponents as a virtue of the highest utility, for it enables us to know what they would be at, and consequently sets us upon devising the requisite methods of resistance. About the same time Mr. Baxter, Member for the Montrose District of Burghs, addressed his constituents at Arbroath; and it is astonishing to find how both he and Mr. Duff agree with their English confrères. Quoth Mr. Baxter, according to a palpably accurate summary before us, "I rejoice much at the passing of the Reform measure. I do not question for a moment the sincerity of the Chancellor of the Exchequer in promoting a great enfranchisement of the people. I am persuaded that that Right Hon. Gentleman believes that he has done a great and good thing for the country. (The Honourable Gentleman advocated the *dis-establishment of the Irish Church* and the *appropriation of its revenues to secular purposes*; he condemned the proposal to endow the Roman Catholic priesthood out of its revenues). It might, however, be *possible,* though *not wise, to delay doing justice to Ireland,* but we could not, without absolute danger, refuse to provide, and that immediately, for the education of England. *It was high time that Oxford and Cambridge should be opened up to all classes of Her Majesty's subjects, without distinction of either creed or social rank. The laws of entail or primogeniture are relics of the middle* ages, which we must *get rid of very soon, and he looked upon the continued aggregation of vast properties in the hands of one man as a most serious evil.* Such, in his humble opinion, was the programme likely to be adopted by the Liberal party. Who was to be the leader? In point both of intellect and oratorical power, Mr. Gladstone was head and shoulders above every one on their side, except Mr. Bright; but there should be no misunderstanding that no temporising measures would do; *and that if he, Mr. Gladstone, intended to lead on the party to Liberal victories, he must throw himself heart and soul into the cause, cut himself loose from all ecclesiastical trammels, and regard the Oxford of his youth as a mere house of bondage.*" Mr. Baxter also expressed his belief that "we shall be driven to adopt the *ballot,* not so much as a means of preventing bribery and intimidation, as in order to facilitate the process of voting. He disapproved of the proposal to increase the number of members in the House in order to provide for the necessary additional representation of Scotland. To gain the needed seats, the second member should be taken from every borough in the United Kingdom having less than 12,000 inhabitants. He was *gradually* inclining to the adoption of the American system of equal electoral votes."

We have so frequently gone over the topics so lightly and yet so earnestly touched upon by these two Scottish representatives, that we can only detain the reader by a very slight commentary upon the mode in which these representatives have dealt with them when brought face to face with their constituents. It was indispensable to their political existence, and more requisite still to the continued favour of those whom they represent, that they should say something. As respects Reform, why, the present administration has almost taken the breadth of political life out of them. Of course they have something of an "ulterior" kind to say on that topic, but, unless for fell purposes of destruction, that must be delayed for another year at least; it is a stale and an unprofitable topic. They rake up old grievances, which are at the best imaginary, and liable to a very violent explosion, to their utter horror and destruction, at any moment. But they must "live," said the pamphleteer who had libelled Richelieu,— "I must live." "I cannot see the necessity," replied the Cardinal. Well, we are more merciful. We are content, in the fewest possible words, to show, once more, how hollow and impracticable is the whole of this "*residuum*" of political grievance. We have not the smallest doubt that Mr. Grant Duff is perfectly right when he says that Lord Russell has "mistaken the clock" if the noble Earl supposes that he can spoliate the Irish Church by endowing the Roman Catholic clergy out of its revenues. His former colleague, Sir George Grey, most distinctly stated in the House of Commons that any attempt to divert the revenues of the Established Church in Ireland to either Romish or secular use would produce a "Revolution." Why? Because, after that, no description of real property would be safe either in Ireland or any other part of the United Kingdom. The old Catholic Church existed in Ireland in 432—eleven hundred years before the doctrines of Romanism were enforced upon the adherents of the Roman See by the promulgation of the decrees of the Council of Trent in 1561, after which the supremacy of the Pope was *renounced,* and that of Henry VIII. had been affirmed in 1537. In the meantime, says Archdeacon Mant,"[4] except only during the reign of Queen Mary (providentially very short), the authority of the Pope had virtually been superseded in many places, idolatry had been abolished, and a purified form of public worship, together with the preaching of the Gospel, had prevailed. So that, on the accession of Elizabeth, not only did all the Bishops of the Church of Ireland, except two, take the oath of supremacy, but they and the clergy generally accepted the Book of Common Prayer, and thereby, in form at least, renounced the superstitions of Rome. But very little of this most ancient property of the Irish Church ever emanated from, or was ever conferred by, the Government and people. It was for the most part given and demised by pious members of the good old "Catholic"

310

Church long before the Popes ever even dreamed of laying their paws upon it. It was just as much the property of the *real* old Church of Christ before the disfigurements of a selfish hierarchy and chancery on the "seven hills," (for the ingenious purpose of claiming and appropriating everything on the face of the earth), were made essential to the religion of our Saviour, as the property of the Duke of Bedford in Covent Garden and Woburn Abbey. Mr. Guinness, within the last few years, has restored, out of his own pocket, and the resources of his enormous wealth, the Cathedral of Saint Patrick, in Dublin. Is *he* to be robbed of his pious intentions and of his wealth so piously and so worthily bestowed? What say Messrs. Duff and Baxter to this? Whether their contemplated new law be the law of right or the law of wrong, it will prove to be a precedent that will be inexorable in its effect upon all sorts of property; for, if the thing be *really right* as respects the property of ecclesiastic or any other bodies—corporations sole or corporations aggregate—how can they possibly resist the rule that will have been established? If they *have* estates—and who can doubt the position of men who have leisure so far to establish themselves in this world as great politicians, aspiring to be statesmen?—why should not *their* title be disputed and confiscated to the State? If they succeed in their most unholy mission against the Irish Church, the least they can do is to assent at once to their substance being devoted by Parliament to the "secular" use of "educating" and maintaining, in comfort, the benighted and pinched thousands around them. According to *their* theory, they only hold their possessions, whatever they may be, for the common good. Therefore, why should they not issue a proclamation, "Come ye *all,* and enjoy the blessings which have been vouchsafed to us! Let us realise the visions of the late Robert Owen, and enjoy a common property in everything." Is *this* what they mean? Because, if they give themselves the trouble to think and mean *anything,* this is the logical and most inevitable result of all that they, as politicians (*"pour vivre,"* as Richelieu's libeller pleaded), now urge as an argument for unsettling the established institutions that have made this country the freest and happiest in the known universe. Talk of the Irish branch of the United Church being looked upon by the Romanists as a "badge of servitude!" that badge was never fixed upon Ireland until Henry II. made the good "old" Church a vassal of the Pope. The history of the Church in Ireland begins with the fifth century.[5] It was only four hundred years under the Roman Pontiff, and for the remaining centuries has been free, and restored to that original purity which existed before the novelties and corruptions of Rome were forced upon it. It was, indeed, inconsiderately and ignorantly said by Mr. Dillwyn that the foundation of the Irish Church took place in 1172; but Mr. Gladstone (now that he has been rejected by Oxford), a lukewarm friend, if not a cold and calculating enemy of the Church, has corroborated the statement which ascribes the more "remote" antiquity of the property and pretensions of the Irish Church. Ah! but this attack upon the Irish outworks is but the prelude to an assault upon the English "Establishment," which the Puritan element detests, as it always has detested, with a most cordial hatred. When we find "The Liberation Society" declaring that it is filled with the conscientious impiety of destroying the English Church, and "scattering its dust to the four winds of heaven," as Mr. Miall once said, at a "Conference," we know pretty well what is meant by attacking the Irish branch. At all events, we should be deplorable idiots if we didn't. It comes to this; none of these things can be done without tumbling into hopeless confusion, and a second chaos, all those Institutions that are the envy of Europe, and that have made the British Nation the greatest, and the freest upon earth. As for the Irish land question, we think that it is right worthy to be discussed well, and wisely dealt with, (if only the ultra-Liberal Irish Members will permit it), for it most richly deserves a very dispassionate consideration. Ireland has been badly dealt with—but not by the Tories; it's disorders and wrongs are *internal,* and are the effect of the *customs* of the country, not in any respect *external* as far as the Imperial Government of the United Kingdom is concerned. We lay especial emphasis upon the customs of the country, because we believe them to be the "Fountain and origin of the evil." To a certain extent, many of these evils have been repaired. But just see what destructive folly existed only a few years (comparatively) ago. There existed in the country Tipperary, what was known and painfully understood as the *con-acre* system. And what was that? It was a system, prevalent among the landlords and occupiers of the larger sort of farms, of letting to the peasantry, or cotters, small slips of land, varying from a perch to half an acre, for a single season, to be planted with potatoes, or cropped. Old grass land was frequently let out on this system, and then it was usual to allow the surface to be "pared" and "burned." Would anybody in this country believe that the rent of this land ran from £7. to £12. or £13. an acre? And yet it really was so, and, if the iniquity had not, in a great measure, been removed in consequence of modern protests, it must really have constituted (and, to some extent still does) a pregnant part of the wrongs of Ireland. It is those "middlemen," the "Squireens" who are the curse of the country, and whom we must get rid of as soon, but still as gently and equitably, as we can. For the rest, we really ought to borrow the language of Queen Elizabeth's statute, with respect to the poor-law, to "take order" that the Irish tenant-farmers, great and small, shall be amply compensated for all improvements. It is utter madness, however, to suppose that any re-distribution of lands in Ireland can eventually help the Irish tenantry. If you robbed all the landlords in Ireland to-morrow, and distributed their possessions among the multitude, things would come back to their present, or a worse state, in ten years hence; for those who hold the money-bags are sure to win in the end, and, therefore, it is the greatest nonsense that ever was heard of, for Mr. Bright, and Mr. Grant Duff, and Mr. Baxter, to talk of a "re-distribution of property." Pray what would it lead to? Just take the example of Cromwell's soldiers, who were rewarded, when the Republican Army was reduced to 25,000 men, by allotments of land in Ireland;[6] Non-Commissioned Officers got so many acres spiece—say ten to a Serjeant, six to a Corporal, and smaller quantities to the rank and file. What was the consequence? Just this:—that in a wonderfully short space of time the land changed hands—the title deeds of one Nobleman consisting, to this day, of the grants made by Cromwell, which this Nobleman purchased from the holders. Who can doubt, that, unless we could select a "model population," free from improvidence, and haters of whisky, as the new possessors of the broad acres of Ireland, precisely the same thing would happen again? We have not the requisite space at our command, even if we had the inclination, to go through all the points of attack, comprised in the ulterior aims of Messrs. Grant Duff, and Baxter. Facts and figures in abundance are ready to our hand, and some day we may take an opportunity to make use of them. At present it is sufficient for us know that the Church and Universities of both countries are to be assailed and plundered, and handed over to the everythingarians. And we must just be permitted to say, in passing, that the pestilent race of *doctrinaires* that has sprung up of late years in the "Common Rooms" of Oxford and Cambridge has encouraged these destructive designs in no small degree. Let the evil spirit prevail and meet with a few early successes, and who shall say that Mr. Grant Duff's "democratic" prophecy will not have embraced the Monarchy itself before the expiration of his prescribed "thirty years!" He, in common with Mr. Bright, confidingly looks forward to the establishment of the ballot (which is now only "kept in reserve"), and probably universal suffrage at the same time. Then, down go the laws of primogeniture and entail, to be followed, doubtless, by a proposal to seize and divide the whole property of the country. Once let loose the demon of confiscation, and what man can tell when and where the devastation will end? Only put a period to the accumulation of property in the hands of men and families of birth and high honour and intelligence, and nothing will remain of that social power which has made England's greatness, and caused her to be the envy and admiration of those countries from which, in her self-contained forces, she has been so long and so happily distinguished. The late Lord Macaulay's figure of the "New Zealander" perched on the broken arch of the bridge, inspecting the ruins of St. Paul's, will no longer be a myth, but a mournful reality. We trust, however, that these calamities will be averted; but they can only be so by the zeal and devotion of the great party of the Constitution. It is in order that they may be kept in mind of the perils that beset them that we have put once more upon record the foregoing facts and arguments in as lucid a manner as we are capable of. They are simply intended to *lead up* to the question which we have placed at the head of this paper. Having secured the Tory Reform Act, "*what must we do with it?*" A timely warning has more than once appeared in the pages of *Blackwood's Magazine* and the *Standard* with respect to the duty which now presses on Conservatives. "More than ever," they have been told, "duty requires that Sir Robert Peel's dictum should be treated by the gentlemen of England as their battle-cry. In the Registration Courts the great institutions of the country are to be defended." Sound advice at a critical moment, though *we* say so. We are old enough to remember that for some years the Reform Act of 1832 put the Conservative party under a cloud. It was almost useless for them to protest that, while they were determined to maintain unimpaired the great institutions of the country, they were ready to remove "all proved abuses." They might have talked until they were dumb, and have got no nearer to the righteous end which they had in view. At last, they began to *act,* and the movement, which afterwards so rapidly spread throughout the country, was commenced in South Lancashire. Squire Hulton, of Hulton Park; Squire Entwisle, of Foxholes, Rochdale; John Roby (the gifted author of "The Tradition of Lancashire"); John Clare, of Warrington; Joseph Wagstaff, of the same place; and other Lancashire worthies—now, alas! (for the most part) "gone to their rest," met together at Newton-in-the-Willows, midway between Manchester and Liverpool, and established the afterwards famous "South Lancashire Conservative Association." The main purpose of this institution was to bring together the known members of the Conservative party in the south of the county, and to devise a systematic method of attending to the registration of qualified voters. The success of this well-organised scheme was astonishing. A Conservative Association, subsidiary to the parent institution, was speedily established in every town and district of the division, and "Operative Conservative Associations" sprung up everywhere. The consequence, when the efforts of these societies were fairly put to the test, was that Lord Francis Egerton (afterwards the Earl of Ellesmere), and the Hon. R. Bootle Wilbraham, supplanted Lord Molyneux and Mr. George William Wood in the representation of the Southern Division of Lancashire. The Conservative members kept their places for years. But then came that unhappy disruption of the party which attended and followed the repeal of the Corn Laws. However, the party rallied again afterwards, and, in the persons of the Hon. Algernon Egerton and Mr. Legh, of Lyme Park, and subsequently of Mr. Charles Turner, formerly member for Liverpool, secured the representation. These, however, are bygones; and since Mr. Gladstone, the rejected of Oxford University, got in by a "fluke" at the last election, it is hardly necessary to carry any further what is, at best, but a digression. We can only hope that the "fluke" will not be repeated; and we have some sound reasons for believing that it will not—mainly because, as we are informed, the Oxford parsons of the district, who were moved by Mr. Gladstone's great tribulation, have since come to their senses [for we are solely guided by documents that have been put in our possession]. To proceed, we learn from a *brochure*[7] now before us, which, at the time, was held to be eminently practical and useful, and of which many thousands were circulated, that "a course of procedure similar to that adopted with perfect success by the South Lancashire Conservative Association," was generally resorted to by the Conservative party throughout the country. It is suggested that out of the members of each society a County and Borough Registration Committee should be instituted; "and" says the writer, "let it be the province of the County Registration Committee to extract from the published list of county voters the names of all persons who appear to have voted in opposition to the Conservative cause, (or, whose principles, if they have not voted, have been ascertained to be hostile), to inspect the books of the Overseers of the various townships within the division of the county, and prepare therefrom a list of persons apparently qualified to vote, to support Conservative claims in the Revising Barristers Courts, to which objections can or shall be made; to procure the registration of those Conservatives who have not claimed to be inserted in the lists of voters; to serve a legal notice of objection upon every political opponent whose right to vote is questionable; to prepare a distinct series of questions applicable to every description of qualification, to which answers can be obtained respecting any vote in order that the acquisition of information for its support or opposition may be facilitated, and, to the end that such proceedings may be placed on record, it will be advisable to prepare a BOOK, in which the names of all the voters polling in each district, the nature of qualification, and other important information may be entered from 'time to time.)' " It will be seen that these practical observations refer exclusively to *county* voters, and an appropriate tabular heading for a book is appended. The same remarks, according to their appropriate significance, are made with respect to *borough* voters. And we now proceed to lay before our readers similar headings for registration books for counties and boroughs respectively in accordance with the provisions of the "*Representation of the People Act,* 1867," (passed the 16th of August, 1867), we shall make this difference however,—we shall distinguish by consecutive numbers, in a note to each head of the tables the requirements of the recent Act. We will take the county qualification first in order, because, according to the new qualifications which, though differing in amount, although very nearly identical in character, are of prime importance. The "heading" of the book should be in this wise or something like it:—

Candidates voted for at last election.	Voter.	Residence.	Freeholds (1).	Copyholds (2).	Freeholds for lives (1)	Copyholds (2).	Leaseholds (3).	Tenancy or any other tenure whatever (4).	Leasees or Assignees (3).	Conservative.		Anti-Conservatives.		Observations. (Provisos in Section 6, especially †)
										Objection	Objector.	Objection	Objector.	

30th and 31st Victoria, cap. 102, sec. 5, "Every man of full age," &c., shall, &c., be entitled to be registered as a voter * * * for a county, "who is of full age," &c., and is "seized at law or in equity of any lands or tenements *Freehold* (1) *Copyhold* (2), or any other tenure whatever, for his *own life,* or [Illegible Text] the *life of another,* or for *any lives whatsoever* (1), or for any larger estate of the clear *yearly value of not less than five pounds, over and above all rates and charges,* payable out of or in respect of the same, or who is entitled, either as *lessee* (3), or *assignee* (3), to any lands or tenements of Freehold or of any other tenure whatever (4), for the unexpired residue, whatever it may be, of any [Illegible Text] originally created for a period of *not less than sixty years* (whether determinable on a life or lives or not,) of the clear yearly value of not less than *five pounds over and above all rents and charges,* payable out of or in respect of the same."

† Observe the Provisos in Section 6.—(1) full age; (2) been "occupier as owner or tenant" for 12 months next preceding July 31st, of rateable value of "twelve pounds or upwards"; (3) has been rated during that time to relief of poor; and (4) has, before the 20th July, paid all poor rates up to the preceding 5th of January.

This may be a useful *guide* for the construction of a book essential to a due watchfulness of county representation. Of course we do not pretend, for the capacities of a single page will not permit of it, to set forth all the *minutiæ*. Practical men will, however, supply all deficiencies,—if there be any. Now for a similar heading of a book devoted to *Borough* representation.

If any vote at that time, Candidates voted for at last election.	Name of Voter.	Place were house is situate.	Nature of qualification, Householder or Lodger.	Disqualifications.				Remarks.
				Not rated to relief of poor during 12 months previously (2).	Not occupied house previously to the 21st of July for 12 months (2).	Not paid on or before 20th of July in the same year an "equal amount" of poor's rates paid by other ordinary occupiers (3)	Lodger not occupied for 12 months at rate of £10, a year before 31st July, and not having claimed before 31st of July as a 12 months Lodger. (4).	

30th and 31st Victoria, cap. 102, sec. 3: Every man of (full age) who, on the 31st of July, has, during the whole of the preceding 12 months (1), been "an inhabitant occupier, as owner or tenant" of any "dwelling house" within the borough, and has during the time of such occupation been rated to the relief of the poor (2), and has on or before the 20th July "*bona fide*" paid an equal amount in the pound to that payable by other ordinary occupiers in respect of all Poor Rates that have become payable by him in respect of the said premises up to the preceding *fifth day* of *January*." (3) *Joint occupiers of a dwelling house* NOT *to be entitled to vote*. Section 4. (The Lodger Franchise). "Every man (of full age, &c.) who for 12 months previously to the 31st of July has occupied "separately and as sole tenant" the same lodgings, such lodgings being part of one and the same dwelling-house, and of a clear yearly value, if let *unfurnished,* of ten pounds or upwards," and that he "has resided in such lodgings during the 12 months immediately preceding the 31st of July (4), and has claimed to be registered as a voter at the next ensuing Registration of Voters." *N.B.* OCCUPIERS in Boroughs are to be rated, and NOT OWNERS!

In abstracting from the Act of Parliament these forms for the guidance of our friends, we do not pretend to have done more than follow (with certain requisite variations) the old examples set us by our friends thirty years ago; and we cannot, and will not, pledge ourselves to exact accuracy of detail. What we have presented, however, is abundantly sufficient to lead the great "Tory" party (for we love the old name the longer we live, *so much for the country* has been done under it,) into the right track. We warn them, and we insist upon it, with becoming deference, that they must, AT ONCE, and WITHOUT ANY LOSS OF TIME WHATEVER, adopt some such systematic action as we have indicated. They owe it to themselves; they owe it to the integrity of their country; they owe it to their illustrious leaders, to do so. Only think what sacrifices of personal case and comfort, Lord Derby, with the besetting assaults of his inexorable "enemy," the Gout, has made to his Sovereign and his country! It is perhaps, his great misfortune that he is ("facile princeps") the great orator of the British Isles; and that as at the great ovation in the Free Trade Hall, at Manchester, on the memorable 17th of October, he was called from his well earned comfortable privacy and case to address an audience, hundreds upon hundreds of whom had, until then, only heard of his entering the murky city week after week, for years, in order to devise and keep in activity—means to relieve the working people of Lancashire from that terrible cotton "famine" that befell them when, North and South were tearing each other to pieces, on the western shores of the Atlantic, so by his constancy and his advice, and counsel, he was, (certainly without meaning to be so), the giant among the sympathisers with the poor of that memorable epoch,—as indeed he towers above contemporary orators in the legislative chamber which he adorns:

> "—Mox sese attolit in auras,
> Ingrediturque solo, et caput inter nubila condit."

Under a leader so richly endowed with public and private virtues, the great Tory party can be at no loss to know "what they must do with it." At all events, we have pointed out to them a method which has, in times past, done it's work well, and which is the most feasible that has yet been suggested; and we trust that our friends will lose no time in putting it once more into operation.

TEMPLE,   R. S. S.

December, 1867.

Notes

1 Iliad B', 209.
2 Reported in the Manchester Courier of Friday, June 28th, 1868,—the speech of Mr. Sowier, Q.C.
3 For instance, we are reminded by Mr. Gladstone's reply to the very short note of Mr. Crawford (possibly preconcerted and written "to order") of a pungent satire on Mr. Gladstone's letter written off hand, by an esteemed friend of ours, a ripe scholar. We cannot resist the temptation to print it here for the first time. It runs—"*Verbosa et Grandis Epistolavenit A Capreis.*"

> "What means th' epistle sent from Wales?
>
> Echo—Ails.
>
> What liquid marks when Statesmen sink?
>
> Echo—Ink.
>
> What Instrument a line misshapen?
>
> Echo—A pen.
>
> What does the Statesman who composes?
>
> Echo—poses.
>
> What choice of syllables which vex?
>
> Echo—*Ex.*
>
> What would he change men to what wins?
>
> Echo—*Ins.*

What would he rather be without?

Echo—*Out.*

What makes a following conspire?

Echo—Ire.

What brings about such disorders?

Echo—Orders.

What liquid best smoothes down turmoil?

Echo—Oil.

And what brings in such vile distemper?

Echo—*Temper!*

How leads a man who's stern and Godly.

Echo—Oddly.

What† "Room" undoes majority?

Echo—Tea.

What needs must be a Derby bill?‡

Echo—Ill.

How can a Parliament best mend it?

Echo—End it.

What makes "Reformers" so irate?

Echo—Hate.

What is the "fine" at which they scold

Echo—Old.

What are the "checks" men nonsense call?

Echo—All.

* Juvenal, Sat. X, 71.
† That "Tea-room" in the House of Commons.
‡ For the "dished" Whigs.

4 See his admirable Paper in the "*Churchman's Shilling Magazine*" for October, 1867. See, also, the forcible and impartial paper in the January number of the same periodical, entitled, "A Plea for the Irish Church." By a Nonconformist.
5 See the powerful pamphlet of the Rev. Alfred T. Lee, entitled, "Tracts respecting the [Illegible Text] State of the Church in Ireland," (London: Rivingtons); and the Charge of the Most Rev. Dr. Trench, Archbishop of Dublin.
6 See the late Sir Archibald Alison's History.
7 Thoughts on the state of, and prospects of, Conservatism, with especial reference to the [Illegible Text] of the Gentry, Tradesmen, and Operatives. Bp R.S.S., Author of a "Word to the Operative Conservatives," "Another Word," &c., &c., London: James Fraser, 213, Regent St., 1837.

Practical Suggestions to the Loyal Working Men of Great Britain, on Points of Policy and Duty at the Present Crisis. By a Member of the Committee of the London and Westminster Working Men's Constitutional Association (London, 1868), 3–8

British Library, 000000427

Published in March 1868 by the NUCCA, on the retirement through illness of Derby from the premiership and his succession by Disraeli, *Practical Suggestions to the Loyal Working Men of Great Britain* called for newly enfranchised working men, through constituency Conservative Associations, to support the Conservative government. Unlike the Whig oligarchic faction, the Conservatives were a national patriotic party carrying forward the historic Tory commitment to the people and the harmony of all social classes.

13

PRACTICAL SUGGESTIONS TO THE LOYAL WORKING MEN OF GREAT BRITAIN, ON POINTS OF POLICY AND DUTY AT THE PRESENT CRISIS. BY A MEMBER OF THE COMMITTEE OF THE LONDON AND WESTMINSTER WORKING MEN'S CONSTITUTIONAL ASSOCIATION

(London, 1868), 3–8

THE Political situation in which we are now placed is one of singular importance. Nothing approaching it for the magnitude of the results which must arise has existed within the memory of any of us. The last Reform agitation— recommenced nearly twenty years ago, with what motives and under what pressure of circumstances it is not now necessary to discuss—had brought about such a block and complication in public business as to render a settlement of the question absolutely necessary in the interest of the community. The death of Lord Palmerston, who had so long trifled with all great subjects of State policy, closed a prolonged season of administrative inactivity. Lord Russell's Government brought in a Reform Bill which failed through its inadequacy, its inconsistency, its unfitness, and through the discords prevailing between the various sections of Whigs and Whig-Radicals. Lord Russell and his friends left office, to resume it, as they hoped, after a short and futile struggle on the part of the Constitutional party to carry on the business of the country. This expectation was disappointed by the patriotic and self-sacrificing firmness of Lord Derby, and the surpassing ability, courage, and sagacity of Mr. Disraeli. These statesmen recognised and accepted the necessities of the situation. They perceived that the time had arrived when serious injury would be caused by any further delay in passing an extensive measure of Parliamentary Reform. To this object they addressed themselves with all the energy imparted by the consciousness of a great duty, and by unflinching resolution to perform it. And it has been performed—performed amid and against enormous difficulties—with a completeness which has won expressions of surprise and admiration from some of the most prominent opponents of Government. If factious tactics and schemes of personal ambition were laid aside, the Irish and Scotch Bills would now be the only points to be settled in connection with Parliamentary Reform, and these could be arranged so easily as to engross but little of the time so urgently required for the transaction of other important affairs.

The main business of Parliamentary Reform may now, however, be regarded as brought to a satisfactory and permanent adjustment, though it is just possible that vexatious and harassing controversies may be raised, in accordance with the policy—all but avowed in certain quarters—of doing everything possible to impede and embarrass Government. The principle of the Irish and Scotch Bills is substantially the same as that of the English. This principle is so broad and comprehensive that some leading men of advanced Liberal opinions have declared it to be tantamount to the establishment of a democracy—to the preponderance of the popular element over the influence of the aristocratic, the middle, and all other classes and subdivisions of society. This description is not accurate. The principle of the Reform Bill carried by Constitutional statesmen is more just and impartial. It does not give the multitude—the strictly working and industrial class—supremacy over the rest of their countrymen, but it gives them their just share of influence and ungrudgingly; it restores to them the ancient power of which they were deprived 36 years ago; and, in addition to this, it invests them with very great additional power, to which they have become entitled by improved intelligence, and—let it be said plainly—by improved morality; for, without disparagement of the qualities of those who have gone before us, it is a manifest fact that the English artizan and workman of the year 1868 is, in most of those attributes which make up the qualification of a good citizen, the superior of his progenitor in the earlier portion of the century.

In short, the Act of 1868 is one of faith and trust in the good feeling and good sense of the great mass of Englishmen. It entrusts them with privileges which, beyond doubt, will enable them to exercise a leading influence in the government of the empire. This influence will be so great as to give them the means of frequently turning the scale in favour of either of the alternative courses which must be taken by any possible Administration. One of these courses is that of vigorous and substantial improvement in our laws, institutions, and social arrangements, combined with scrupulous regard for the fundamental principles upon which they are based, and which have endowed us, on the whole, with greater liberty, greater security, greater opportunities for rising in the world, for "bettering our condition" and enjoying the fruits of our industry, than are possessed by any other nation. Another course—the one contemplated by the majority of those who are opposed to Mr. Disraeli's Government—is that of what is called "Radical"—that is to say, uprooting and destructive—changes; the ignoring of all our old national maxims, political, social, and religious; the repudiation of the possibility of reconciling the interests of different orders; the internicine warfare of class against class.

If I call the promoters of the last designs an anti-national party, I do them no injustice. They are incessantly engaged in ridiculing principles on which the greatness of England has been erected, and their ridicule is always pointed by pretended and fallacious contrasts of our own inferiority with the assumed superiority of the system or systems existing in foreign countries. We hear fierce, unqualified condemnations of the higher ranks, who are described not merely as an aristocratic grade, but as vampires, plunderers, and oppressors, preying on the life's-blood of all who have to work. "Kings, priests, and lords," the Throne, the Church, the Peerage, the Gentry, are represented as the people's natural enemies. It would be absurd to measure the objects of the extreme movement party, or the results to which these objects tend, by the language of such men as Lord Russell, Mr. Gladstone, or even Mr. Bright, engaged as they are in the dangerous work of playing with edged tools. The events of the first French Revolution teach a lesson upon the folly of this. In the earlier stages of that convulsion, men like Mirabeau spoke and worked energetically to bring the upper classes into contempt and ridicule. They succeeded in doing so, but they little dreamed of the eventualities to which their agitation was destined to lead. They little dreamed that their own career was, in almost every instance, to end on the scaffold; that anarchy, rapine, universal terror; the most horrible scenes of wholesale murder, misery and starvation; the most [Illegible Text] and ruthless despotism, upon record; the decimation of the populace, the destruction of the lives of millions of Frenchmen; the literal depopulation of the country by civil war, foreign war, and famine; the degradation of the very standard of health, stature, and vigour, leaving France far behind neighbouring countries both in the growth of numbers and the physical capacity of the people;—the agitators of 1789, I say little imagined that this would be the result of their proceedings. Mirabeau died early, but he lived long enough to discern, to dread, to deprecate the coming ruin he had wrought. Most of his colleagues perished miserably, and France, after 80 years of blood, distraction, and disappointment, is now governed more arbitarily—I do not say more unjustly—but practically more oppressed and enslaved—than she was even in the days when the Bastile still existed, to subserve the absolute will of the sovereign.

We have no such grievances to complain of as those which existed in France prior to 1789. For every abuse, for every grievance, there is a known remedy; and there are men in high places, men in the very highest places, able and willing to apply the remedy effectually, but carefully and constitutionally, without disturbance and violence. The Ministry of Lord Derby took office to carry forward this wise policy—the Ministry of Mr. Disraeli retains office in order to continue and realise it. Shall we support these statesmen with heart and head and hand, or shall we permit them to be overthrown by the intrigues of those who, if not actually by act, still by connivance, identify themselves with agitators whose language is more violent than that of the Mirabeaus, and Baillys of the first French revolution. We must calculate the fruits of a Government of which Lord Russell or Mr.

Gladstone should be the nominal head, not merely by the strongest expressions to which these public men have given utterance, but by the most advanced—that is to say, the most revolutionary and practically treasonable declamations frequently reported from the neighbourhood of the Adelphi, and by which even the "League" President, Mr. Beales, is sometimes so alarmed as to enter his protest.

It is a happy occurrence that at a time so full of anxiety and perplexity,— when vicissitudes and trials at home are accompanied by ominous shadows in the aspect of foreign affairs, and the Ministerial programme embraces measures of the utmost moment, and of no small difficulty, for amelioration and reform in various directions—it is fortunate that at this juncture the working men of the kingdom have had a call made upon them—a call originating in their own body—to prepare themselves for the exercise of the power with which they are now endowed. It is fortunate that they are responding to that call in their tens of thousands, with a spirit and activity which inspire better anticipations of the future. It is clear that they begin to understand the character and disposition of what I will call the Tory party, as contra-distinguished from the Whigs and self-styled Liberals. The personal constitution of Ministries formed by the two parties respectively suggest some instructive reflections upon this very point. Looking back through the history of two hundred years, we may in vain seek for a Whig Prime Minister connected immediately with the ranks of the people. Tory or Conservative Ministries, on the contrary, show a liberal proportion of Premiers sprung from the ranks. Sir Robert Peel, though a rich man, was essentially and thoroughly a plebeian in blood; Mr. Canning was a poor man and the son of a poor man, who died when he was quite young; Mr. Perceval was a practising barrister; Mr. Disraeli is a literary man,—a man to whom money honourably earned by his pen is understood to have one time formed the main source of his income. He is entirely a man of the people, but one who thinks and acts in perfect appreciation of the fact that the aristocracy is a great and essential portion of the people. This is the doctrine which Mr. Disraeli has inculcated from his youth upwards, and which he has illustrated in practice in the great measures of 1868. His maxim is, I will not say the fusion, but the [Illegible Text] and harmony of classes, instead of the isolation, jealousy, and exclusiveness upon which the Whigs have always acted. It would be difficult to name a single statesman of the first rank who has risen from the ranks to an eminent position through the Whig connection; but the history of the other party abounds in such instances—in fact, they make up a considerable proportion of that history. Mr. Disraeli himself might not have attained his high and deserved reputation were it not that his rare gifts and high endowments were generously recognised by the heads of the national party with which he identified himself soon after his entry into active political life. Lord Derby, himself an aristocrat of the aristocrats—a representation of the most illustrious of England's old nobility—was amongst the first and most cordial of those who did justice to the present Premier's great qualities; but then Lord Derby has from his own youth been the friend, not the supercilious, condescending patron, but the frank, hearty, sympathising friend of the people; and it is only a few weeks—just before the last prostrating attack of the illness which led to his retirement—that he declared his implicit confidence and respect for them. In fine, the policy of the Whigs in dealing with the people, has ever been to amuse them with plausible generalisations and professions of unmeaning "Liberalism," but always to keep them outside the charmed circle of "the family interests," and exclude them from the paths to high and supreme advancement. The policy of the Tories is to fraternise with the people to diminish and mitigate social differences, not by lowering themselves, but by elevating their humbler fellow-countrymen, and on all occasions to afford free scope and facility for the advance of merit to the highest position. The distinction perhaps is, that the Tory is a member of a party, the Whig a member of a faction; that the former is an aristocracy, the characteristic of which is the recognition and admission of worth and ability, that the other is an oligarchy, the characteristic of which is to exclude all who were not born within its particular pale.

Still we find the Whigs, through their leaders, tampering, for paltry temporary purposes, with the theories of sedition and treason, whilst the Tories honestly declare that with sedition and treason there shall be no compromise, and that above all things social order and the majesty of the law shall be maintained. Now, even waiving for a moment those considerations of tremendous danger involved in the conduct of the former—supposing that nothing worse should follow from their return to office than the re-enactment of those scenes of shuffling, bungling, trifling, meddling, and promise without performance which stopped all progress, humiliated us in the eyes of the world, and sunk us in the esteem of all foreign powers, during the lazy and ignoble administrations which preceded that of Lord Derby—would not this contrast furnish urgent reason for regarding a change of Government as a severe misfortune, to avert which no effort should be omitted? With Mr. Gladstone in office, be it observed, there would be no security for gaining anything, and no security for preserving anything. In every department of official duty the Whigs have betrayed an utter incapacity for vigorous initiation. Their abortive attempt at bankruptcy reform, their peddling with poor-law anomalies, their trickery and truckling with the Irish difficulty, always saying the very contrary of what they mean, their imbecile maunderings upon a subject so important and definite as that of national education, exemplify their general helplessness upon questions of home policy, whilst the Polish, the Danish, the Brazilian, the Italian, the North American episodes have proved their capability for getting us into positions, always of embarrassment, not unfrequently, it is to be regretted, of mortification and something like ignominy. To all this it may be added that, but for the fantastic tricks of the Foreign Office under the sway of that redoubtable "complete letter-writer," Earl Russell, the ever present "Eastern question" would now be involved in less difficulty, and but for the incomprehensible negligence, infatuation, and stupidity which prevailed in that office at the same period, we should be spared the cost and vexation of the Abyssinian expedition. Going still further off, it is certain that, with Sir Stafford Northcote at the India Office, such a calamity would have been impossible as the loss of 1,000,000 lives by famine in the district of Orissa, in consequence of the neglect of the most obvious precautions.

At home and abroad with the arduous task of contending against the accumulated effects of previous mismanagement with the work of carrying Reform and checkmating Fenianism upon its hands, with the unfavourable circumstances of stagnant trade and unprosperous industry, and many other exceptional difficulties which it is unnecessary to recapitulate, the present Government has already accomplished an unusual amount of useful legislation; and it is evident from the language and acts of the members of the Cabinet, that all that has been done is only a fractional instalment of what is to come. There has hitherto been no clear stage for working out the great plans contemplated by them, nor, indeed, will there now be until the meeting of the Reformed Parliament. The practical work which they have carved out for themselves will not commence until next year. But, whilst during this period of transition, so much good service has already been done at home, it is moderate to say that the wise and dignified management of our Foreign relations, since Lord Stanley has held Office, has raised England again to her natural high station in the councils of Europe—from a predicament as like degradation as any into which it is conceivable that she could fall. On few occasions in her modern career has she stood lower than when Lord Russell went out,—at no time has she possessed more influence and respect than at present.

What, then, is the policy and duty of loyal Englishmen? We have on one side a Government able and determined to preserve and improve,—we have on the other a medley of discordant factions, not one of which has any plan of definite and tangible improvement, whilst between one and another, they are in the aggregate pledged to all kinds of revolutionary destruction. There is not an existing institution—not the throne itself—to the maintenance of which the Whig-Radicals are bound as to a principle; indeed the virtual abrogation of the Royal prerogative is one of the favourite theories of Whig philosophists. And again there is not an existing institution—not the Throne itself—which some of their sections or allies would not willingly destroy.

What, then, is the duty and policy of loyal Englishmen? Clearly to unite more zealously than ever in support of an Administration, which, whilst unchanged in its views upon all great public subjects, is at this moment subjected to additional trial and labour in consequence of the inevitable retirement of its late distinguished chief. Lord Derby is heart and soul with the Government. Health permitting, his support of their policy, his defence of their measures, his vindication of their pure [Illegible Text] patriotic motives would probably be still more emphatic, pointed, and uncompromising than it was when his language was necessarily modified by official responsibilities. Nevertheless his withdrawal from these responsibilities has increased the difficulty of circumstances already critical, and should make us, as Constitutional loyalists, anxious to show that our confidence in our great statesmen is firm and unswerving. We should neglect no occasion to evince our resolution to sustain and uphold them; we should make themselves know this, and we should make their enemies know it. This is one of the modes in which we can best prove the reality and strength of our organization. The opponents of Government will not [Illegible Text] "making a handle" of Lord Derby's retirement for their own purposes. They will not fail to descant upon it as a premonitory sign of weakness—as "the beginning of the end" of Conservative Government. Directly and indirectly this card will be played assiduously during the present session. It will be used to encourage our antagonists, to discourage our friends. We must meet it by the process of counteraction, or, in medical phraseology, by counter-irritation. We must show our strength, our increasing strength, our increasing knowledge how to use that strength, and our intention to devote it to the support of a Ministry of Constitutional statesmen.

For such manifestations of opinion and intention the meetings of the Associations throughout the country will afford frequent opportunities. These should be turned to account and resolutions passed, not only declaring confidence in Government, but intimating the avowal of such confidence to be an indispensable test of the claims of candidates at the hustings. By this test mistakes and mystifications will be avoided, would-be trimmers revealed in their true colours, the wheat separated from the chaff, and men of sterling principles returned to form a loyal majority in the new House of Commons. Irrespectively of minor differences, the genuine sentiment of the nation is so truly represented by the present Cabinet, that, at a juncture of peculiar emergency like the present, when the all-important necessity is to keep our party compact, harmonius, and unanimous, it is not expedient to dwell too much on isolated questions. Let us keep our eyes fixed on the beacon—the maintenance and permanent strengthening of the Government—and we cannot go wrong. Any other course than this, any hair-splitting or internal divisions, may land us in disappointment and defeat. This course alone will ensure the object we have at heart. This is the course of duty, policy, and patriotism.

Let this, then, be the goal of our individual and united efforts. We can work for it at the registrations, we can work for it at the periodical and extraordinary meetings, we can work for it amongst our friends and neighbours, we can work for it through the press. I am endeavouring to do so in this statement of plain facts, which, unvarnished and unadorned as it is, will, I trust, strike a chord in the best feelings of the loyal, truthful, and prudent majority of the people.—I am, fellow working-men, your faithful and sincere Servant,

E. A.

London, March 1868.

The Political Future of the Working Classes, or, Who Are the Real Friends of the People, by a Member of the Committee of the London and Westminster Working Men's Constitutional Association
(London, 1868), 3–7

British Library, 000157260

The Political Future of the Working Classes was published by the NUCCA in anticipation of a general election in 1868 based on the greatly extended electorate created by the Reform Acts of 1867–1868. The pamphlet declared the Conservative party 'the real friend of the people'. The Conservative government had settled Reform and improved workhouse and factory working conditions. Matters Whig-radical politicians, over the previous 20 years, had proved unable or unwilling to redress. The institutions of the country required protection from destructive radicalism, a patriotic duty best fulfilled by working men supporting progressive Conservatism.

14

THE POLITICAL FUTURE OF THE WORKING CLASSES, OR, WHO ARE THE REAL FRIENDS OF THE PEOPLE, BY A MEMBER OF THE COMMITTEE OF THE LONDON AND WESTMINSTER WORKING MEN'S CONSTITUTIONAL ASSOCIATION

(London, 1868), 3–7

In the present state of political transition, it is the duty of every man to state clearly and fearlessly his views upon the political future of the working classes. More especially should the working men themselves calmly and impartially consider their present and future political position. They have large and increasing interests at stake. They have to protect those interests, which, it is suggested, can best be done—not by listening to the clap-trap of Radical agitators—but by having respect for the interests of others. What good can come out of Radical teachings, which excite the jealousy of one class against another? We must not forget that by these continued agitations we destroy the confidence of the classes above us, nor must we forget that the income of the working classes (which is said to be £400,000,000 per annum in time of prosperity), would be considerably reduced if the capitalist, having no confidence, chooses to withdraw his capital. We contend that the interests of all classes are so intimately connected that they cannot be separated without disastrous consequences to the country, and great misery to the working man. Capitalists can seek other spheres wherein to work their capital; but the working man, whose labour is his capital, has no field of action but his own country, in the prosperity and harmony of which he is therefore vitally concerned. The radical cries of the last two years are mere clap-trap, set forth by men seeking their own interests, regardless of the interests of the country. Never has any class of politicians dealt so freely in misrepresentations as they have, and misrepresentations so glaring in themselves, that we are no less astonished at their impudence in advancing them, than at the ready manner in which they have been received as fact. We can account for this only by ascribing it to the general apathy of the working men upon political affairs. Such apathy may be lamentable; yet in one sense we may be thankful that it exists, for were it otherwise—if Messrs. Bright, Beales, & Co. were the true expounders of the opinions of the people, if the pot-house politicians, "spouters of stale sedition," were the real representatives of the working men,—then the political future would indeed be gloomy; but as a working man I emphatically deny such to be the fact. I have been connected with the Constitutional movement in the metropolis from the first, and I distinctly declare it as my belief that we are liable to the charge of apathy, but not to the charge of folly. I believe that if my fellow men would look into the history of the last twenty years, Radicalism and its degrading influences, together with its advocates, would sink into oblivion. If we would only look into history—but this is apparently too wearisome and unnecessary a task, and yet I contend that the first duty of a citizen is to thoroughly understand the politics of his country, which will teach him that the vote he holds is sacred, for upon it depends the future prosperity of the nation, that he holds it in trust, and that posterity will hold him responsible for the good or the evil that may spring out of his use of it.

In a few months we shall be called upon to exercise the franchise, many of us for the first time. How shall we use it? Shall we accept the misrepresentations of the Liberal party and vote for them? or shall we support that party, who, by their actions, have proved themselves the real friends of the people, viz.,—the Conservatives? These are momentous questions to us.

Let the past be some guide for the future. Have we not witnessed during the last few years, the Liberal party climbing to power upon the question of Reform, and then cruelly deceiving us and shelving the question for seven years? Have we not witnessed, during the same period, their masterly inactivity upon all questions, political and social? Did they attempt any reform in the poor laws, to relieve the aged and infirm of the Metropolis, whose state had been a crying evil during the whole of their administration? Did they attempt any legislation between master and workman, which had then become, and is now, a great public question? Did they manage our Foreign Affairs creditably to the country? No; both at home and abroad they showed themselves incapable of directing the business of the nation; and the people acknowledge the fact by the manner in which they received the government of Lord Derby. No sooner was the noble lord in power, than a marked change for the better took place in the government of the country. The Reform Bill was settled in a far more liberal spirit than ever the Liberals dreamt of, and, unlike their measures, in accordance with the constitution of the country. The Conservative Bill of 1867 restored to the working man the franchise of which he had been robbed by the bill of 1832. No sooner were the Conservatives in power, than a bill was prepared to relieve the aged and infirm in the workhouses of London. Upon the assembling of parliament, it was the first bill before the house, gave general satisfaction, and in a few weeks became the law of the land. At the earliest opportunity the attention of Parliament was called to the question of master and workman with the view of bringing about a better understanding between them. The Factory Acts—which had first been carried by the Conservatives some 20 years ago, and opposed by Mr. Bright and the Radicals—were extended. These Acts had proved a great benefit to the operatives of the north, and the present government felt it their duty to extend the operation of them to all trades. The Foreign Affairs of the country—which, under the guidance of Lord Russell, had been conducted in a manner far from creditable to the nation—have, under the statesman-like administration of Lord Stanley, been so conducted as to call forth the admiration of even his political opponents. On the other hand, the true political character of the liberal party has been specially shown by their conduct since they have been in opposition. As we said before, they were content to sit upon the Treasury benches for seven years, and do nothing towards the settlement of the great political and social questions of the day; but, no sooner are they in opposition, than out comes their liberality. If the Irish question must be settled now—as they say—why did they not find it out before? Almost for twenty years has the government of the country been in the hands of the liberal party, with a majority in the House of Commons. Such being the case, is it not strange—if they are so politically honest as they would have us believe—that they never found out all these so-called causes of Irish discontent? Again, to suit their purpose upon the Reform question, the Liberals were continually dinging into our ears the great intelligence of the working classes; now, that the question has been taken out of their hands, their cry is "Educate, educate, educate," and Lord Russell expresses his fears of the great reduction of the franchise, if we do not educate the working man.

This is our experience of a "Liberal" policy at home; if we look abroad, there, also, the history of the last twenty years proves that the Conservatives, and not the Liberals, are the real friends of the working man. Foreign affairs, we may be told, are not our business; nevertheless let us look well to these questions ourselves; they concern us as much or more than any other class. No country on earth has greater liberties than we have under our (so-called) oligarchic Constitution. Look on the democracies of the Continent and compare the condition of the people of France and other countries with ourselves. In France, where is the liberty of the subject—where no meeting of any sort can be held unless the authorities will sanction it with their presence? Where is the liberty of the press—that great defender of the liberties of the people—when they are not allowed to criticise the policy of the Government, or give a report of the proceedings of the Legislature, except that put forth by the official *Moniteur?* The Radicals have been very fond of holding up France as a specimen of Liberty and Equality. Is there an Englishman who would barter the liberties of his country for those of France? In England the intelligence of the country rules; in France one man. In England the Government is responsible to the people, through their representatives, for the policy by which they may govern the country; in France the representatives must petition the Emperor to allow his Ministers to attend the Legislature to answer certain questions, the nature of which must be mentioned in their petition. In England the Army is recruited on the voluntary system; in France, by the new Bill, all the manhood of the country is to be driven into the service. The same in Prussia. I apprehend if such is the produce of universal suffrage, we had better be without it.

Space will not allow me to go more into these matters; but, from the facts here set forth, What should be the future policy of the working man? Shall it be to support the Whig-Radical party, which has always played with their interest, and in every department showed its incapacity to govern? or shall it be for the progressive Conservatism which is being carried out by the present Government? Surely we will not let ourselves be deluded by a senseless cry or deluded by an effete nickname. No doubt the Conservatives have been called obstructives, opposed to all progress, and the natural enemies of the people; but, I ask, Are such statements true? Let us remember there are two sides to every question, but that on this question we have as yet heard only one. By a monopoly of the platform and the press, the Liberals have been able to go on making these assertions without contradiction, until they are now accepted as facts, notwithstanding that they are gross misrepresentations, so palpable, indeed, that we are astonished so many have been deluded by them.

The time has now arrived for us to throw off our apathy. We have tremendous responsibility thrown upon us; the Constitution of England has, in no small degree, been placed in our hands. Let us defeat the expectation of a noisy few, and support at the poll those Candidates who will support Constitutional principles. A great deal has been said about the inconsistency of a working man being Conservative. Why he should not be so I cannot understand. My definition of Conservatism is, to conserve all that is good in the existing institutions, to reform that which is proved to be bad, and "to resist any attempt to subvert the Constitution of the country"— a Constitution which has existed 1,000 years, grown with the intelligence of the people, and placed England at the head of the civilized world. I contend that it is as consistent for a working man to defend Constitutional principles as for any other class, and I am convinced they will not readily throw them over for any newfangled schemes of dreamy philosophers. We are not asked blindly to follow any man's lead; we are asked to approach our political position fairly and without prejudice before deciding upon the course we shall take at the coming general election. Do this, and we have the greatest confidence in the success of the Constitutional cause. We have great faith in the principles on which that cause is founded, sincerely believing they are best for the interests of the country generally. Radicalism, on the other hand, can produce nothing but a war of classes and ultimate ruin to the country. It is but the expression of a senseless and causeless discontent. Let us show that independent men, who making themselves respected, can respect others in their turn. Above all we must remember that under the new franchise, we shall more than ever combine two characters; we shall be the rulers in a sense, but we shall also be the ruled; and we must learn to combine the peculiar virtues of each. We must ever bear in mind the maxim which history testifies, that they are least fitted to rule who cannot be ruled—self-government and justice in the governors being no less essential than subordination and respect for superiors in the governed. This is not the doctrine of Radicalism; and therefore to avoid

Radicalism is the obvious interest as well as the first duty of a working man. His prosperity lies in the prosperity of the country, and that can be best attained by an intimate and hearty connection among all classes of the community, each one of us actuated by the same desire—the future welfare of our common country. These are the principles of Conservatism which demand not only the serious attention, but the active co-operation of every working man.

E. B.

Shall We Give It Up? A Political Correspondence Dedicated to the Conservative Associations of the United Kingdom (London: Robert Hardwicke, 1871), 3–32

Bodleian Library, (OC) 200h.80(1). Post-1701 Weston

The general election of November/December 1868 returned a large Liberal Commons majority of 110 MPs. In the years that immediately followed, Disraeli's leadership of the Conservatives was fragile and vulnerable. The responsibility for electoral failure, in the wake of the 1867–1868 Reform Acts, and ineffective opposition to major Liberal reforms was placed at his door, 1871 marking a low point in Conservative morale.

The 1871 pamphlet *Shall We Give It Up?* was a response to the despondency pervading Conservative circles. Presented as an exchange of letters between a disenchanted Conservative supporter and his long-standing political friend, the Secretary of the 'Pedlington Constitutional Association', it discussed the state of Conservative activism. Both correspondents agreed that Disraeli's leadership was a calamitous failure. Lord Salisbury, Gathorne Hardy, Lord Cairns, and the 15th Earl of Derby were possible replacements. But principles and measures were more important than men. The country could not be consigned to Democracy and the Church robbed of all rights and privileges. Zeal and energy were urgently required.

15

SHALL WE GIVE IT UP? A POLITICAL CORRESPONDENCE DEDICATED TO THE CONSERVATIVE ASSOCIATIONS OF THE UNITED KINGDOM

(London: Robert Hardwicke, 1871), 3–32

Part I. Reasons for giving it up

IN replying to your invitation to attend the annual meeting of the Pedlington Constitutional Association, I am aware, my dear Leonard, that I shall excite your astonishment, and I am not at all sure that I shall escape your serious displeasure. The fact is, I have resolved, or nearly resolved, to give up politics. What pursuit I shall adopt to supply the vacuum created by so great a change in my habits of thought and action I have not yet definitely determined; but I have scarcely read a leading article for months, and meditate a material saving in my expenditure for newspapers and reviews. As for the Pedlington Constitutional Association, it has, I believe, received my last subscription. I, who used to be one of its most enthusiastic members, have come to regard it with a strange indifference, fast ripening, I am afraid, into positive disgust. Now, my good friend, pray refrain from flying into a passion, or tearing my letter, at this point, into a thousand pieces, but hear my reasons, and by all means answer them if you can.

I freely confess I am unable to express my feelings on this subject to one by whose side I have stood on so many public occasions, and in whose views I have generally participated, without that sort of reluctance which comes from a crowd of old recollections and associations. You know what intense interest I have hitherto taken in political movements. You know how, from my boyhood upwards, I have read parliamentary debates with greater avidity than young ladies read sensational novels. You know how, at general elections, you and I have, time after time, thrown our private business to the winds, and worked hard for the Constitutional cause, both in borough and county. And although the fun and frolic of electioneering have, to a great extent, disappeared with youth, I would do the same, and more than the same, if I felt that the slightest good would come of it. But that is the point. The question of *cui bono?* has of late presented itself to my mind with disagreeable persistence, and at last has quite mastered me. It appears

339

to me, after mature consideration, that I could scarcely spend my time in a more foolish and ridiculous manner than by attending the annual meeting of the Pedlington Constitutional Association.

I am aware, indeed, that I make these remarks at a time when we, the Tories, the Conservatives, the Constitutionalists—call us what you please—are supposed to be in excellent spirits. The parliamentary session of 1871 is known to have materially damaged the reputation of the "Ins," and has, therefore, as a matter of course, communicated all manner of fluttering sensations to the "Outs." That Mr. Gladstone has several times lost his temper, that Mr. Lowe has exasperated the matchmakers, that Mr. Bruce has stirred up the enmity of the licensed victuallers, that Mr. Cardwell cannot march a few thousand men from one county to another, that the horses of the Life Guards have broken loose, that the *Captain* has gone down, that the *Agincourt* has struck upon a rock, that the *Megæra* has been driven ashore—these and a number of other facts are supposed to constitute important items of congratulation to all who dislike a so-called Liberal policy. And then the East Surrey, Truro, and Plymouth elections. Think of a Conservative obtaining a majority of 1,200 votes in a suburban constituency hitherto Radical! Think of Colonel Hogg storming a Whig seat after three days' canvass! Think of Mr. Bates' extraordinary triumph! Surely the wheel of fortune is about to bring us once more to the top, and we shall be able to rival the achievements of 1852, 1859, and even 1867.

The jubilant strain prevalent among the wire-pullers of our party, and echoed with great faithfulness and unwearied pertinacity by that portion of the press which is under their influence, is utterly repugnant to my reason, and to the reason of very many of our best friends. If I were a Liberal I think I should be well satisfied with the session of 1871. The administrative failures of my leaders would weigh but little against the steady triumph of my principles. The passing of the University Tests Bill would in itself reconcile me, I am quite certain, to a great many minor blunders. Here is a most important controversy, in which the two great parties of the day have long been in direct antagonism, authoritatively settled in favour of the Liberals, with scarcely more than a faint protest from their opponents. The colleges at Oxford and Cambridge, although founded by Churchmen, and intended to be homes of religious education as well as of sound learning, are for the future to exhibit no foolish attachment to the Church of England, or, indeed, for any religion at all, but just to go the way which chance or indifferentism may happen to lead them. Those chapels which stand in their midst, and around which halls, lecture-rooms, and libraries so significantly cluster, have clearly become so many anomalies, not, perhaps, to be pulled down just at present, or to be alienated for the next few years from existing uses, but to be dealt with by-and-by as time, circumstances, and Liberalism may combine to dictate. Nor is the University Tests Bill the only slap in the face which the Church of England has received during the last session. The Commons have again passed a Bill to enable ministers of all denominations to officiate in churchyards; and for the Commons to have passed it is, as we all know, a tolerably sure token of ultimate success. The so-called Conservatives, who would have rallied bravely upon any personal matter between Mr. Gladstone and Mr. Disraeli, did not think it worth while to make a party fight of it. In that impossible hypothesis of my being a Liberal, possessed with the usual Liberal hatred to the Church of England, I can scarcely conceive a fact more calculated to give me pleasure than the approaching triumph of this measure. The churchyard is on the way to the Church. When the funeral service is performed by a clergyman, a considerable portion of it is generally said within the building itself. Now, are the doors of the venerable fabric to be irrevocably closed against the Dissenting minister? The weather may, perchance, be unpropitious: the rain may beat, the wind may howl, the hail may discharge its myriads of icy pellets, the snow may lie thick upon the ground. You have already welcomed him into the consecrated enclosure; what miserable hair-splitting to keep him out of the consecrated building! Then, when you have once conceded to him the use of the Church, is there any good reason why the indulgence should not be extended? There is no service at such and such a time; if you will kindly allow him to hold one, he will pay for his own gas, and guarantee that the fittings shall not be injured. You have admitted the principle, you know; the rest is a mere matter of detail, which a little charitable feeling and enlightened catholicity can readily arrange. I cannot think, my dear Leonard, what a Conservative party is for, if it does not put forth all its strength in opposing such a bill as this, and if it looks with complacency upon a session in which the House of Commons has sanctioned it. Nor was it only in legislation affecting the Church of England that the Liberals were marvellously successful. For the first time Vote by Ballot was passed by the Lower House, and though it was rejected by the Upper, it was apparently on the mere grounds of its being sent up somewhat late for considering details. Vote by Ballot! Still, supposing myself to be a Liberal, thoroughly impregnated by the conviction that Tory triumphs are invariably gained by the tyranny of landlords, how I should exult in the knowledge that a proposal lately laughed at by the leading statesmen of all schools is now on the very eve of accomplishment! And even more. The session of 1871 was made further remarkable by the Prime Minister hinting to us, in no obscure terms, that we must shortly prepare for Universal Suffrage. The House of Commons stared, and perhaps thought the Premier a little injudicious, but continued its confidence in him, and is probably ready, after a modest interval, to adopt that, or any other proposition in a similar direction. How long is it since Universal Suffrage was looked upon as the most extreme nostrum of the most extreme Radicals, not in the least likely to be seriously entertained in our own time, and scarcely in the time of our great grandchildren? Yes, I think I should be well content with the session of 1871, if only I were a Liberal. A faster gallop towards Secularism and Democracy I can scarcely imagine. Being a Conservative, I am unable to find comfort in those blunders and misfortunes of the Liberal Cabinet which our newspapers keep dinning into our ears.

As for the East Surrey, Truro, and Plymouth elections, I certainly regard them as remarkable proofs of a sound and healthy feeling among our constituencies which, under other circumstances, and under brighter auspices, might be made to do wonders. But you and I are old enough to have seen many single elections won by our party, and to have been assured on numerous occasions that a great reaction was undoubtedly setting in. Somehow it never came. The next dissolution of Parliament effectually settled *that* matter. I have no faith whatever that it will come now. A local triumph may here and there be within our grasp, but a victory all along the line is quite beyond our powers. Taking the country generally, I believe that, while Conservatism is gaining very few fresh adherents, many, like myself, who have hitherto been its strongest supporters, are meditating an early retreat from all further political efforts, and are unwillingly, but decidedly, giving it up.

But you will tell me that all this is mere grumbling, and that I have failed, so far, to put my motives for deserting the Pedlington Constitutional Association into a distinct shape. Before I conclude, however, you shall have no reason to blame me on that score, insomuch as I am very anxious you should perceive I am not acting through laziness or caprice, but simply because I cannot get over the difficulties which appear to me to stand in the way of any further political action on my part. I have deserted the Pedlington Constitutional Association from a conviction, battled against for a long while, but ultimately irresistible, that the objects I have all along had in view, and which gave me my only interest in politics, will never be accomplished by the Conservative party as at present constituted. You are aware that, as a man of comparatively little influence, I have no power of altering its existing organization. I must take it as it is, and either work in the same groove with it, or stand aloof. I infinitely prefer to stand aloof. Let me tabulate my reasons, as I have often tabulated them in my own thoughts.

We cannot, I think, look back in any spirit of candour upon the history of the last half century without perceiving that the party with which we are connected has frequently made terrible blunders. Again and again it has denounced measures as fraught with the utmost danger to the country, which, on being carried, have proved not only harmless, but positively beneficial. Nor have its mistakes been only in the way of resistance. In that sort of blindness there would have been a species of consistency which would have ensured respect, even where it excited pity. But along with the most persistent opposition to changes which ought not to have provoked the hostility of a wise Conservatism there has gone a strange facility to yield in matters of principle. Did you ever happen to be shut up in a country house during wet weather, and to be driven to study long shelves of "Annual Registers," or old files of *The Times?* I have, and the result to me, as a Conservative, was not pleasant. Turn to what year I would, I found the Liberals with a clear and definite policy, always knowing towards what point to advance next, and making for it with firm and resolute footsteps. The Conservatives, on the contrary, have been at one time provokingly obstinate, and at another sensationally yielding. They have entirely failed, as it seems to me, to recognize the difference between useful reform and dangerous innovation. They have been perpetually eating their own words, perpetually discarding fair argument for personal abuse of opponents, perpetually striving to account for notorious inconsistencies by a species of quibbling. The plain fact is, the history of the Tory party for the last half century will scarcely bear writing. In appealing to the support of the country, it is laden with such a pitiable past as places it at a serious and apparently inevitable disadvantage. "Remember what you did at such a time, and again at such time, and yet again at such a time," is often enough to neutralize the soundest position we take up. When Mr. Mill calls us "the stupid party," is he so far wrong? Does not our inclination from time to time to change our name—to call ourselves at one period Tories, at another Conservatives, at a third Constitutionalists, at a fourth (if I remember right) the Country party—betray an uncomfortable consciousness that we have been "stupid?" You and I cannot be held responsible for events which took place when we were in the nursery or the school-room, and only to an infinitely small extent for those which have occurred since we entered the arena of politics. But I confess I ardently long to throw off all names which seem to mix me up with a history I cannot deny, and certainly will not defend.

This feeling, however, though bitter, I would try to get over, if I had any trust in the Conservative party of the present day. Did I see the slightest prospect that it would redeem its character, that it would shake itself free from an unfortunate past, that it would make itself respected, that it would enunciate distinctive principles and stick to them, then I would make a great gulp and swallow those unwelcome facts of which I have been speaking. But all expectation of the sort has died out of my mind. I see constant battling between the Ins and the Outs, but whether the Ins or the Outs would go furthest in the direction I deprecate, is with me a doubtful question. Whether I read the debates in the House of Commons, or the extra parliamentary utterances of Opposition notabilities, or the leading articles in *The Standard,* I find myself continually saying to myself, "If this is Conservatism, I am not a Conservative." In short, I am connected, or supposed to be connected, with a knot of politicians up in London who appear to me to be playing fast and loose with what loyal and constitutional feeling is still left in the country: whose opinions, at all events, are not my opinions, whose objects are not my objects, whose manner of fighting is not my manner of fighting, and whose triumph would probably advance what I consider genuine Conservatism not a single jot.

What are the objects which you and I—for I feel confident that so far there is no difference between us—have always proposed to ourselves in our political life? First and foremost, I have no hesitation in saying, the protection and development of the Church of England, and the re-adjustment of her relations with the State in such a way as to secure her fair and reasonable independence. After that, the defence of the Throne, the maintainance of the House of Lords, the integrity of endowments, the extension of religious and secular education, the arrangement of the franchise so as to guard against the tyranny of mere numbers, the preservation of our colonies, the efficiency of our army and navy, the promotion of proper but not cheese-paring economy in the public expenditure, the diminution of pauperism, the improvement of the dwellings of the labouring classes, the gradual amendment and codification of our laws, and generally, the adoption of a policy at once tolerant of reasonable change, and impervious to restless innovation. Now, my dear Leonard, can you look me gravely in the face, and tell me that these ends are likely to be advanced, especially those of them which are more distinctly Conservative, by our again putting the author of "Lothair" in the position of Prime Minister? Have you read that celebrated novel? Have you further read that "brilliant manifesto of his matured opinions" (see *Standard*) which he prefixed to a recent edition? As far as you can follow the mind of the writer of these productions, I want you to say candidly whether it is a mind which you would like to see impressed upon the future policy of the country? And if you reply that "Lothair," preface and all, was simply an attempt to amuse and mystify the public, and must not be looked upon in any serious light, then, quite content that such an extraordinary explanation should go by without comment, I should like further to ask you if you seriously defend and admire Mr. Disraeli's ordinary leadership of the Conservatives? That he is one of the most clever men of the age I freely admit. If you ask me to praise his genius, his pluck, his good temper, his powers of debate, his knowledge of the House of Commons, you will not find me behindhand. But I am sure that I carry your judgment with me, even if I fail to elicit the concurrence of your words, when I say that Mr. Disraeli's leadership of the Conservatives is a great practical joke. That the chief originator of the most democratic measure which ever received the sanction of the English Parliament should lead the gentlemen of England against Democracy is in itself more remarkable than the wildest combination in his own works of fiction. But take him session by session, and I am unable to perceive in him more than the most hollow and conventional sympathy with those deep-rooted convictions on the part of the nation which have placed some two hundred and seventy gentlemen at his back. How few of his orations strike the faintest chord in the hearts of his reputed adherents! How little we care for those stilted sentences, those elaborate sneers, those carefully prepared aphorisms, those sharp cuts and thrusts of parliamentary warfare, all of which go to prove the cleverness of the man, but very few of which have the remotest connection with Conservative principles! How often have we laid down the newspaper, after one of his finest efforts, with a feeling which can only be described in Scriptural language, "The whole head is sick, and the whole heart faint!" Leonard, I will help to send no more supporters of Mr. Disraeli to the House of Commons. The exertions of parliamentary agents, the manipulations of the London clubs, and the influence of a well-drilled press, have hitherto done much to suppress the thorough distrust with which he is regarded by the mass of Conservatives throughout the country, and I dare say will continue to do so. But I should like to know how many members of the Pedlington Constitutional Association, for example, have really the slightest confidence in him. I never happen to have met with a single one. Did you?

You will tell me, however, that the lead of Mr. Disraeli cannot last for ever. I suppose not; but it seems likely to last long enough to make Conservatism more and more ridiculous and unintelligible in the eyes of the nation, and so to secure the easy triumph of the Liberals. His acknowledged ability, coupled with the authority of the late Lord Derby, has given him a *locus standi* of which it is exceedingly difficult to deprive him; and he is not at all the sort of person to retire of his own accord into private life, nor yet to take up any such independent position as Lords Grey and Russell. Like Sinbad's old man, his arms are round the neck of the Conservative party, and, however terrible the weight, he is not to be shaken off. But suppose him away, and who is to succeed him? The present Lord Derby?—the Marquis of Salisbury?—Lord Cairns?—Mr. Gathorne Hardy? It must be allowed that all these statesmen have been placed during the last few years in extraordinary and unwonted positions. Some of the great contests in which they have been engaged, notably the Reform Bill and the Irish Church Bill, have involved complications and surprises most difficult to be wisely dealt with. We certainly ought not to pass stern sentence upon mere mistakes, where we have seen honesty and integrity of purpose. As a simple matter of fact, however, no one of these statesmen has, up to the present time, so commended himself to the judgment of his party as to give rise to any general desire for his leadership. Lord Salisbury and Mr. Gathorne Hardy would probably command most suffrages: but Lord Salisbury is cross and crotchety, and Mr. Gathorne Hardy has seldom had the courage to take a different line to Mr. Disraeli. Nor does there seem to be any "coming man" among the younger members of either House. It is astonishing how few of the nobility and gentry train themselves to statesmanship. They go on the turf, they devote themselves to field sports, they travel in distant lands, they collect moths, they mount fire-engines, they shoot pigeons, they practise mesmerism, but they utterly refuse, for the most part, to assume their natural position as leading politicians. And as you can hardly expect me to rest my hopes upon that knot of independent but eccentric skirmishers which embraces Mr. Newdegate, Mr. Beresford Hope, and the two Mr. Bentincks, it follows that even the retirement of Mr. Disraeli would not be likely, in my judgment, to effect a satisfactory re-arrangement of the Conservative party. How earnestly I have longed and how patiently I have waited for some rising star to guide us out of the quagmire, I can hardly express to you; but I have longed and waited in vain.

But now, my dear Leonard, I will imagine what is not in the least likely to come to pass, namely, that the Conservative party is placed ere long upon a fresh basis; that it takes to itself a distinct creed; that it has leaders in whom it can trust; and that such enthusiasm is communicated to its ranks as only comes from a steady and well-defined purpose. I will imagine all that, and even then I have grave doubts whether the labour and anxiety of a stand-up fight with the Liberals would not be utterly useless. The fact is, our chance has got by. Partly by its own inherent strength (for in this wicked world that spirit of restlessness and anarchy which is called Liberalism will always be strong), and still more by the blindness and inefficiency of its opponents, Liberalism has acquired too great an impulse to be successfully resisted. Whether the plunder of the Church of England, the abolition of the House of Lords, the overthrow of the Throne, the establishment of a republic, the re-distribution of private property, and other processes of a similar description will happen in our time I will not undertake to say, because human life is uncertain; but that they will happen, and happen ere long, I have not the shadow of a doubt. Why, what is to stop them? The Pedlington Constitutional

Association? A mere pebble thrown in the way of a torrent. Five hundred Constitutional Associations? Five hundred pebbles piled into a little heap, and intended to block up Niagara. The common sense of the moderate Liberals? The moderate Liberals have no common sense which will not be swept aside by the necessities of their party. We are clearly in for a Democracy, and our wisest course is probably to "grin and bear it." You laugh at me; but so you laughed when I told you a few years ago that household suffrage would shortly be adopted, and that the first result would be the Disestablishment and Disendowment of the Irish Church. Instead of laughing, be kind enough to give me your close attention for a few moments longer.

The Liberal party is not the Liberal party unless it is in constant motion. Incessant change, and always in one direction, is the first principle of its existence. No doubt a large proportion of its members entertain views comparatively moderate. They are Liberals rather from habit and from disgust at Toryism, than because they want to see any violent alterations in the constitution of the country. But they are not their own masters. However ready they may be from time to time to "rest and be thankful," their political position will allow them neither rest nor thankfulness. Let a single session of Parliament pass by without a fresh onslaught upon the established order of things, and there would be the utmost danger of the "great Liberal party" going to pieces. Accordingly, the Moderates find themselves in a perpetual process of conversion to advanced opinions. In order to avoid the awful alternative of becoming Conservatives, it is absolutely essential that they should respond to the new cry, whatever it be, of their political friends. As fast as one cry is rendered nugatory by legislation in obedience to its demand, another is necessarily adopted. The Liberalism of yesterday is the Toryism of to-day, and the Liberalism of to-day will be the Toryism of to-morrow. The point, or points, therefore, to which the Liberal party will ultimately drift is not to be inferred from the present opinions of its Granvilles, its Argylls, its Lowes, or even its Gladstones, but rather from that of its Bradlaughs, its Odgers, its Lucrafts, and its Applegarths.

You will scarcely meet with a better specimen of a moderate Liberal than our borough member, Mr. Pumpkin. The other day I happened to observe to him that one of the next cries of his party will doubtless be the Disestablishment and Disendowment of the English Church. You should have seen the indignation with which he repudiated the idea, and, no doubt, as far as his present feelings are concerned, repudiated it honestly. The angry expostulation of one of old, "Is thy servant a dog, that he should do this thing?" could hardly have been more emphatic. Yet I know perfectly well what will happen. At the next general election the support of the Nonconformists will depend upon his giving them a distinct pledge that he will carry out their wishes in this matter, and without the support of the Nonconformists he could never again be M.P. for Pedlington. Then will Mr. Pumpkin become convinced that "in the interests of the Church herself, you know," it is highly desirable that she should be freed from the shackles of the State, and relieved of the property committed to her by our ancestors. The moderate Liberals are mostly such men as Mr. Pumpkin. They will not lead the way down the hill, but they will follow with tolerable smartness. As time goes on, a few of them may possibly become Conservatives; but the greater number will glide almost insensibly into Republicanism, and even Communism, with the same facility with which we have seen them glide into vote by ballot and the confiscation of Church property.

If anything could save England from the fate to which a reckless Liberalism is leading her, it would be the formation and development of a real Conservative party. In the improbable event of such a movement, I do not say but that, win or lose, I would fling myself into the fight. But sitting quietly in my arm-chair, and thinking of things as they are, I repeat that the time has gone by. England must have a taste of the horrors of Democracy, and of the still greater horrors of irreligion, before she regains her senses. There are two reasons which, without by any means standing alone, are sufficient in themselves to justify me in this conviction. The first is, the state of the public press; the second, the inevitable working of household suffrage.

The public press of this country is thoroughly steeped in Liberalism. I appeal to your candour whether nearly all ths best writing is not on the Liberal side. I further appeal to your knowledge of facts whether twenty copies of Liberal publications are not sold, week by week, to one of Conservative. How it has come to pass that Conservatism, the creed of education, is so badly represented by public writers, and that Liberalism, the creed of ignorance, is proportionately well off, is a separate question. My own persuasion is, that the Conservatism of the period, shifty, unintelligible, inconsistent, destitute of any quality commanding confidence, has effectually alienated from it the intellect and enthusiasm which, under happier circumstances, would have been put forth in defence of the Church and Constitution. But whether that opinion be correct or not, the bitter truth is the same, and is surely most fatal to the prosperity of a healthy reaction. To contend against the press is, as you are aware, to contend against the chief means of influencing all classes of society. And if you are disposed to suggest that instead of contending against it, we should try to convert it, I will merely remark that such a process of conversion, even if possible, would be exceedingly slow, and that long before it is accomplished we shall be so utterly be-Liberalized as to have little to fight for. The next time you travel by railway, go to one of Smith's stalls, and purchase, as a matter of curiosity, a copy of all the periodicals you find there, whether daily, weekly, or monthly. When you have taken the trouble to look them over, and have noted not only on which side is the large preponderance of political opinion, but what is still more remarkable, on which side are unquestionably the minds of the greatest calibre and the pens most gifted with the trick of literary composition, you will be driven, I think, to admit the terrible disadvantage at which any revival of sound Constitutional principles would have to be attempted.

The inevitable working of household suffrage is a subject which Conservatives treat very differently in public and in private. In public they generally claim for their party great credit for the Act of 1867, enlarge upon the political wisdom of the labouring classes, and cling, or seem to cling, to that delightful fiction of a loyal and constitutional substratum. In private this sort of talk is usually laid aside, and

347

it is confessed that household suffrage has permanently lost us the large majority of the boroughs. Mr. Disraeli, indeed, told us a short time back that a moiety of the new voters polled at the general election for Conservative candidates. It is just possible that the undoubted Conservatism of the twelve-pound householders in the counties so far balanced the increased Liberalism of the towns as to render such an assertion literally correct; but inasmuch as the towns send the greater number of members to Parliament, and must always determine the destinies of the country, the fact, if fact it be, leaves the real danger of our position untouched. The representation of our boroughs is unquestionably at the mercy of that section of the electors who are least qualified to form an opinion on public affairs, and least likely to respect existing institutions. The voice of our merchants, our bankers, our manufacturers, our professional men, and even our shopkeepers, is completely drowned by the roar of our back lanes. You and I, during the autumn of 1868, canvassed a considerable portion of the town of Pedlington in the interest of our late Conservative member. Need I remind you how beautifully our promises told up, so long as we kept to our High Street, our Crescent, our Parades, and our Terraces, but what long faces we pulled when we had traversed Scavenger's Buildings, Swine Street, and Mud Lane? That Mr. Pumpkin should throw out our man by so large a majority was the more provoking because really the latter had talked almost as much "bunkum" as his opponent, and had buttered the labouring classes, after the new fashion of his party, with the most unscrupulous liberality. But why, when we came to think of it, should the ordinary working man be a Conservative? As he rarely considers it necessary to attend public worship of any sort, it can hardly be supposed that he has much sympathy with the Church of England. Gathering his chief impressions of the aristocracy from his Sunday newspaper, or from the leading orator at his trades' union, he looks upon the upper classes as a body of men who, in some way or other, are trampling upon his rights. Change—wide, sweeping, immediate change—has to him a pleasant and attractive sound. The Act of Parliament which practically transferred to him the government of the country, rendered it in the highest degree improbable that Conservative principles should for the future direct our interests.

But I must have mercy upon your time. Though I have not written down all that is in my mind, I have probably said enough to make you understand my determination. Tell any of our friends who enquire after me that I have by no means lost faith in my political creed, but that I have very decidedly lost faith in the power of the Pedlington Constitutional Association to advance it. Sorrowfully, but not the less decidedly, I have arrived at the conclusion that circumstances are too strong for us; that to fight for a good cause "like one that beateth the air," is even worse than not to fight for it at all; and that, consequently, it is safest and wisest to give it up.

Part II. Reasons for not giving it up

TWENTY years ago, my dear and valued friend, you stood by my side at a great public meeting, and, in one of the very best speeches I ever heard, proposed the formation of a Pedlington Constitutional Association. Of that political confederacy you have till quite lately been the most active and energetic member. From our personal intimacy, and my consequent acquaintance with the recent workings of your mind, I was prepared in part for the communication you now make; but it has not the less filled me with emotions to which a variety of public and private considerations join to contribute.

Some hopes I venture to build upon a single word in your letter. You tell me you have resolved, or "nearly" resolved, to give up politics. I cling to the "nearly" with a pertinacity which may be desperate, but is at least pardonable. Many misfortunes have "nearly" come to pass, which at the last have been happily averted. In any case, I feel certain that you will allow me to have my "say," and that you will give to such arguments as I place before you a frank and patient attention.

You have expressed with great clearness the reasons which urge you to retire from political life. I am the more pleased that you have done so, because I am quite aware that in this matter you are a representative man, and that your impressions are shared to a considerable extent by vast numbers of the Conservative party. My position as Secretary to the Pedlington Constitutional Association, as well as my connection with a similar society for the southern division of our county, brings me into frequent contact with hundreds of our political friends; and I will make you a present of the fact that much of what you say would be generally and even eagerly endorsed. Nay, more, official though I am, I am not going to defend either the past or present of the Conservative party. Such a task as that I must emphatically decline. The one is eminently inconsistent, and the other eminently incomprehensible.

Let me postpone for another moment the point at which I am compelled to differ from you. Your enumeration of the objects we have always had in view is admirable. In the London clubs, and the little world which surrounds them, I suppose that a variety of personal considerations and a whole crowd of private interests mix themselves up with the turmoil of political life, and often render it a question of men rather than of measures. In the country it is otherwise. We care very little about the men. We can get up no sort of enthusiasm for one set of administrators above another, unless we believe that they stand committed to distinctive principles. For the programme you sketch out we would work hard; for a mere change in the occupants of Downing Street the vast majority of us would not care to work at all.

But agreeing with you thus far, I must protest with all the energy I possess against your avowed disposition to allow the events of the next few years to determine themselves without interference. Scarcely can I bring myself to believe that with the clear knowledge of their importance which your letter indicates, and with the full conviction that they involve the fate of the Church of England, the Throne, the House of Lords, and all our most valuable institutions, you are really content to stand by with your arms folded. "Better," say you, "not to fight at all than to fight to no purpose." Indeed! If it be true, as you think, that our beloved country is shortly to be consigned to the tender mercies of a Democracy, and our

349

Church to be robbed of her rights and privileges, I, for my part, should much prefer to be able to say, "I did my best to hinder all this, but I failed," to—"I saw it coming on, but I sulked, like Achilles, in my tent." The quietness with which you consign England to the purgatory of a second Commonwealth would be amusing if it were not also sorrowful. Believe me, my good friend, we cannot thus shake off our political responsibility. So long as we have even that infinitesimal share in the government of the kingdom which consists in the possession of borough and county votes, it is positively incumbent upon us to exercise it to the best of our judgment and ability. Blundering is vexatious; want of confidence in our leaders is distressing; defeat is hard to bear; but inactivity—stolid, peevish, faint-hearted inactivity—is surely the worst of all.

It will be my main object, however, to convince you that our cause is by no means so desperate as you seem to suppose, and that though the political horizon is undoubtedly dark and portentous at the present moment, it does not quite follow that an early storm will sweep us to destruction. And here I will plunge at once *in medias res* by dealing with that fact which undoubtedly constitutes our chief danger, namely, the absence of leaders in whom we can place full confidence. If this difficulty can only be got over, and the Conservative party placed on a sound and intelligible basis, I am prepared to prove, before the close of this letter, that the good feeling of the nation and its attachment to existent institutions are far too strong to necessitate, or even to justify, despondency. In the meantime, I am quite aware that a question of great awkwardness and delicacy blocks the way, and that its removal, or at the very least, its careful and unflinching treatment, is essential to our success.

A series of extraordinary circumstances, which I will not attempt at the present moment to analyse, has placed the nominal lead of the Conservative party in the hands of one who never has possessed, and who never will possess, the confidence of his reputed followers. Friends and foes alike give Mr. Disraeli credit for the possession of many brilliant qualities; but friends and foes alike believe him to be tricky, unreliable, destitute of fixed convictions, utterly incapable of giving effect to the principles with which he has accidentally become connected. The continued predominance of Mr. Disraeli is disastrous to the Conservative party in more ways than can readily be described. It prevents distinct issues being placed before the country. It degrades what ought to be a great cause into a perpetual snarl against the personal and administrative abilities of opponents. It forces other Conservative statesmen, time after time, into false and embarrassing positions. It utterly damps that enthusiasm which a leader of another sort would readily evoke. It hinders Moderate Liberals, although alarmed at the ever-lengthening programme of their own associates, from joining our ranks. It alienates old supporters like yourself, who begin to talk moodily of giving up politics. It holds out no sort of attraction to the young or the wavering. It is the origin of three-fourths of the foolish talk we hear about all parties and all public men being alike. It withholds the Conservative leadership in the House of Lords from the eloquent and accomplished peer who of all others is most fitted for it. In a word (for I do not pretend to follow the difficulty into all its details), the very worst enemy to the Conservative party could scarcely wish to see an arrangement at our head-quarters other than the one which unfortunately exists.

Such is our position, and I have no wish whatever to underrate its disadvantages. But it should be asked, in all fairness, is Mr. Disraeli the only person to blame for it? If that gentleman is of opinion that the creed of Conservatism begins and ends with the conviction that he is the greatest statesman of the age, has not such an impression been fostered by the general attitude of his supporters, and the remarkable docility with which they have acquiesced with every course he has adopted? True, there has been abundance of private grumbling. As far as my experience goes, Conservatives scarcely ever meet together in social life without bewailing their unlucky fate in being tied to such a leader as Mr. Disraeli. But surely never has so much private dissatisfaction met with so little public utterance. Who would judge from our newspapers, our reviews, and our Conservative meetings, that we are otherwise than a united and happy party, deeming ourselves extremely fortunate in the men who preside over our interests in the Palace at Westminster?

It must, indeed, be conceded that the forbearance of Conservatives towards Mr. Disraeli has been caused by a very proper aversion to appear disunited. It is confessedly difficult to effect a change of front in presence of an enemy; and our enemy has kept us so hard at work that the moment has always appeared inopportune for forcing an alteration. But surely this sort of feeling may be carried too far. The present unreality of our position is a much greater evil than a fair and open confession of uneasiness. We are come to a point where an over-sensitive dread of disunion may spread disunion in every direction. What will happen if, at the next dissolution of Parliament, we have nothing but Disraelism to oppose to the war-cries of the Liberals?

Let me point out to you what a strong contrast to the position of affairs in the Conservative camp is afforded us by the relations which exist between Mr. Gladstone and his supporters. If Mr. Gladstone failed to represent the feelings and opinions of the mass of the Liberals, there can be no question that he would not hold his present office for many weeks. He is head of his party, and just now Premier of England, on the tacit understanding that he will execute the behests of the Radicals and political dissenters as expeditiously as possible. In one sense he is their leader, but in another sense they are his. He has taught them comparatively little: they have taught him almost every point in his political creed. Under their tuition he constantly proposes measures at which, a few years ago, he would have stood aghast; and as time goes on he will doubtless propose other measures at which he would stand aghast now. Is there no similar power in Conservatism? Are we utterly incapable of making our influence felt at head-quarters? Is it fated that a party which includes so large a proportion of the intelligence of the country should still submit to be "educated" by the adroit but shifty schoolmaster of Hughenden Manor, instead of thinking and acting for itself?

Suppose that, instead of deserting the Pedlington Constitutional Association, you were to give notice of a series of resolutions, expressive of our dissatisfaction at the present position of the Conservative party, and our conviction that an early reconstruction is absolutely necessary. Suppose you were to submit these resolutions to a special meeting of our club, in one of those speeches which you well know how to make, and the true ring of which invariably raises the enthusiasm of your auditors. What would be the result of such a proceeding? In the first place, as far as I know the feelings of our members, your resolutions would be carried by a very large majority, even if anyone cared to oppose them. Then the fact of their being so carried would find its way into the public papers, and would certainly provoke a good deal of comment and criticism. I am much mistaken if other Conservative Associations would not soon follow our example, and if our little spark would not fall upon a great quantity of material quite ready to burst into flame. Would not this course be far better than giving it up? It might, possibly—I am inclined to think probably—bring about important consequences: but, in any case, it would satisfy your conscience, and prevent your taking a step which, I feel certain, would not stand the test of subsequent reflection.

But, say you, a satisfactory reconstruction of the Conservative party appears to be all but impracticable. Even if Mr. Disraeli were out of the way, whom have we to put in his place? Now, I am obliged to agree with you, that no Conservative statesman "has, up to the present time, so commended himself to the judgment of his party as to give rise to any general desire for his leadership." I am rejoiced, however, to find you admit that "public men have been placed, during the last few years, in extraordinary and unwonted positions;" that "there have been complications and surprises most difficult to be wisely dealt with;" and that "we ought not to pass sentence upon mere mistakes, where we have seen honesty and integrity of purpose." My own opinion is, that the two eminent persons you mention as "probably commanding most suffrages," Lord Salisbury and Mr. Gathorne Hardy, would soon gain that confidence which they can scarcely be said as yet to enjoy, and which, indeed, they have had no fair opportunity of winning. It is true that at a certain critical juncture these gentlemen took opposite courses, the one breaking loose from the then Lord Derby and Mr. Disraeli, the other deeming it best, all things considered, to remain at their side. Perhaps neither on the part of him who broke loose, nor of him who stayed, can we discern a line of policy in all respects consistent. But it appears to me that both the Peer and the Commoner have qualifications which, once freed from the disturbing influences of Disraelism, would speak to the hearts of Conservatives, and give powerful effect to their distinctive opinions. Lord Salisbury would probably cease to be "cross and crotchety," and Mr. Gathorne Hardy would probably cease to muffle up his right impulses, if they were supported by a great and influential party. Be these things as they may, however, I feel confident that the question of leadership is not one about which we need be painfully anxious. I have intense faith in that old proverb, "God helps the men who help themselves." If we of the rank and file do our duty bravely, the leaders will come. Either the best of our present statesmen will throw themselves into the movement, or else clever and eloquent politicians will rise up from unexpected quarters, and place themselves at our head.

I contend, then, that there is nothing whatever in the present state of the Conservative party but what a little zeal and energy would set right. The Constitutional Associations throughout the country, as well as that large mass of good men and true who ought to form themselves into similar societies, have the matter in their own hands. Instead of being the mere tools of a "knot of politicians up in London," let them adopt a course more consistent both with their convictions and their self-respect. Let them insist that the battle between the two great parties of the day should not be a miserable and unscrupulous scramble for office, but shall be fought out on broad and intelligible issues. Let them make it clearly understood that Conservatism means the defence and freedom of the Church of England, while Liberalism means her robbery and degradation; that Conservatism involves the preservation of the House of Lords, while Liberalism, whatever disclaimers may be made by individuals, is fast being committed to its overthrow; that Conservatism advocates the fair influence of all classes in the government of the country, while Liberalism demands the predominance of the lowest; that Conservatism respects religious and charitable endowments, while Liberalism looks upon them as fair plunder; that Conservatism labours for the social and practical benefit of the poor, while Liberalism is content to dangle before them political concessions. Let them openly declare their opinion that Conservatism, being thus connected with great principles, and relying for support upon their truth and expediency, is not helped, but is rather injured and disgraced, by an unlimited amount of mere personal antagonism and the incessant depreciation of political opponents. Until our Constitutional Associations have taken some such steps as I have suggested, their members have no right to indulge in private abuse of Mr. Disraeli, and— excuse me, my good friend, but I cannot help saying it—most certainly no right to give up a contest in which the happiness and prosperity of the country are clearly at stake.

I now come to that part of your letter in which you express your pursuasion that even if the Conservative party could be put on a satisfactory basis, the complete triumph of the Liberals can no longer be averted. Well, were I unhappily forced to take that gloomy view, I should still strongly urge that the more trouble we give them in doing their disgraceful work, and the longer we can defer the evil day, the better. If, for example, the Church of England is to be disestablished and plundered (for, of course, disestablishment means plunder), it will make a wonderful difference whether the process is to be effected at once, or a quarter of a century hence. The Church is growing stronger and stronger every year. She is feeling her way towards a system of representation and self-government. Her members are gradually learning the duty and privilege of liberality. That cruel blow which our adversaries contemplate would be most unjustifiable and sacrilegious at any time; but the hour may come when it will be far less injurious than if struck within the next lustrum. So again with regard to the growing power of the populace. Education may not be advancing in the precise way we could wish, but it is unquestionably advancing. The Act of 1870, with all its imperfections and inconsistencies, did certainly strike a blow at ignorance, the effects of which have yet to be developed. I think it may be safely assumed that the next generation will be better qualified to exercise their judgment on political matters than the present. A democracy A.D. 1900, however much to be deprecated, will be less alarming than a democracy A.D. 1875. Although, therefore, we may be unable in the long run to defeat the Liberals, it is well worth our while to thwart them, baffle them, impede them. The more manfully we can fight, and the longer we can keep them at bay, the less gloomy need be our anticipations of what the future will produce.

But I utterly refuse to allow that your surmise as to the certain triumph of Liberalism is irrefragable. After giving due weight to the two powerful reasons by which you support it—namely, the condition of the public press, and the probable working of household suffrage—and entirely agreeing with you that nothing whatever is to be expected from the moderation of our opponents, I must, nevertheless, express my firm belief that a Conservatism cleared from an unhappy past, and presented to the nation in an intelligible form, would have a fair chance of ultimate success. You may look upon this opinion as the mere product of a sanguine temperament; but I hope to show you that it has not been adopted without careful thought, and an honest endeavour to see things as they are, rather than as I wish them to be.

The more I examine polls and investigate statistics, the more astonished I am, not at the weakness of the Conservative party, but at its strength. When we take into consideration the heavy and unparalleled discouragements under which we have so long laboured, the amount of sound feeling still existing in the country is simply marvellous. You tell me, and I have no reason to doubt the accuracy of your information, that twenty copies of Liberal publications are constantly circulated to one Conservative. How remarkable, then, that when a general election occurs, even under that enlarged system of franchise which Mr. Disraeli has given us, the proportion of Liberal voters to Conservative is not twenty to one, or ten to one, or five to one, or even two to one, but scarcely six to five! The fact seems to be that people are not influenced by newspapers and other periodicals to the extent, or anything like the extent, you imagine. They take in Liberal journals for much the same reason that I myself (perhaps I ought to be ashamed to confess it) take in *The Times,* the *Saturday Review,* and the *Guardian,* namely, that there are no similar publications on the Conservative side which exhibit an equal amount of carefully collected news or editorial ability. Surely, however, it is a strange thing, a thing which speaks volumes for the good sense of the English people, that despite this perpetual flood of Liberalism, nearly half of them walk quietly to the polls, and vote for the Church and Constitution. What might not be expected of them if we had our fair share in the public press, and if Conservatism were known to be a more genuine article than that which has hitherto excited such bewilderment and suspicion!

Disastrous as was the last dissolution of Parliament to the Conservative cause, there were certain features about it which startled our opponents, and even gave rise in the minds of some of them to serious forebodings. Such a feature was the verdict of the English counties. The Liberals had supposed that the extension of the suffrage to twelve-pound householders would result in the transfer to their side of at least twenty or thirty seats. It resulted in nothing of the sort. The new county electors were discovered to be at least as Conservative as the old, and the balance of gains and losses, so far as these contests were concerned, was decidedly in our favour. Such a feature, again, was the decision of some of our largest cities and boroughs. No doubt household suffrage, on the whole, told fearfully against us; and yet, if such places as Liverpool, Manchester, Westminster, Portsmouth, Blackburn, Southampton, Bolton, Coventry, Salford, York, Worcester, and Preston made choice of Conservatives, what guarantee have the Liberals that the example of these important constituencies may not at some future time be extensively followed? Such a feature, once more, was the strong constitutional feeling displayed even by many large towns which returned supporters of Mr. Gladstone. The contests which were undertaken in the greater number of these localities were from the first hopeless, and that very fact alienated from the Conservative side whole droves of waverers and well-wishers. Yet the raising of the Constitutional standard was followed by an amount of support which was as significant as it was unexpected. That the Tower Hamlets should have had their 7,500 Conservative voters, Lambeth its 7,000, Finsbury its 6,100, Chelsea its 4,200, Bristol its 6,700, Birmingham its 8,700, Oldham its 6,100, Hull its 5,400, Greenwich its 4,700, Brighton its 3,000, and so forth, displays a state of things wholly inconsistent with the supposition that such constituencies must of necessity remain Radical till the end of time. Let me add that many contests which have occurred since the general election have shown how soon Liberal majorities, even when apparently formidable, may be beaten down by a little pluck and determination on the part of Conservatives.

It is proved by the irresistible logic of the polls that the large majority of the upper and middle classes of England are opposed to those alterations in the Constitution which you look upon as inevitable. The universities and counties have delivered their opinion with tolerable plainness; and after taking the trouble to analyse the poll-books of some six or seven Liberal boroughs, our own among the number, I have found in every case that the present members owe their seats to the votes of the back streets. When you remark that Conservatism is the creed of education, and Liberalism of ignorance, you are at least backed by some curious and instructive facts. The English Liberals would have been literally nowhere at the last general election if it had not been for the support of those classes whom it has been recently found so necessary to teach to read.

"All that may be very interesting," I think I hear you respond, "but it is scarcely to the purpose. The convictions of the upper and middle classes in these days are nothing; the convictions of the lower everything." Well, I must, of course, admit that the working men now form by far the largest element in our borough constituencies, and that, as a body, they vote heavily against us. And the question resolves itself into this: is it utterly unreasonable to expect that Conservative principles will make sufficient progress among working men to prevent property and education being swamped? The upper and middle classes are certain to become more and more Conservative in proportion as Conservatism makes itself respected, and in proportion as Liberalism enlarges and amplifies its programme; but will they be joined, and joined before irretrievable mischief is done, by such a number of artisans and labourers as shall enable them to form an effective barrier against wild and sweeping innovations?

Conscious that to deal fully with this most important point would carry me beyond the limits of a letter, I will merely glance at a few considerations which seem to me to justify a more hopeful view than the one which has presented itself to your mind. To begin with, in some boroughs—not many, it may be, but still some, including one or two of the largest—a clear majority of the operatives already vote for the Conservatives. This shows, at all events, that there is nothing in Conservatism violently alien to the feelings of the working classes, and that when it is presented to them in a genial form, and with the earnestness of intense conviction, they will sometimes prefer it to Liberalism. Next, we may fairly hope that the advance of education will expose many of those fallacies which are the stock-in-trade of political agitators, but which are often found to give way before even a moderate amount of intelligence and information. If you believe Conservatism to be the creed of education, you must, of necessity, believe that to educate is to make Conservative. Further, it is earnestly to be desired that any reconstruction of the Conservative party will bring prominently into the front a real sympathy with the working classes, and an honest effort to improve their condition. We may not believe that the happiness of our operatives would be promoted by a subverted constitution, or a ruined church; but we may believe (and the generality of us do believe) that there are social problems which should be bravely, though carefully, dealt with, and upon the successful elucidation of which, the welfare of the whole community is in a great measure dependent. Granted that the poor will never cease out of the land: it does not at all follow that the poor shall always live in narrow and unhealthy houses, that they shall be forced to labour from early morning to late evening, that no means of innocent recreation should be within their reach, that their lives should be monotonous, or their prospects hopeless. The Conservatives all over the country—the Conservative nobility, the Conservative parsons, the Conservative squires, the Conservative manufacturers—have, I believe, been invariably foremost in every good work affecting the moral and social condition of the poor. But I confess I should like to see more attention paid to the possibility of sound legislation coming to the assistance of private effort. And I have yet to mention my strongest reason for anticipating an increasing Conservative contingent among the working classes, and that is, the steady progress and influence of the Church of England. It is so much the fashion of politicians to snub the Church of England—to assume that she has lost her hold over the laity of all ranks—to pretend to regard her as an effete institution—that they appear purposely to blind their eyes to what is going on all over the country, with a quietness, but, at the same time, a reality, which forms one of the greatest facts of the age. The Church

356

of England, so far from losing ground, is rapidly gaining it; gaining it with strides which a few years back would have been deemed impossible; gaining it in spite of the bullying of statesmen, the sneers of shallow philosophers, and the miserable divisions among her own children; gaining it, as with all classes, so emphatically with the one where she has hitherto failed. It is no doubt an uncomfortable suspicion of this fact which makes Dissenters so averse to a religious census, and incites Liberals, with their accustomed intolerance, to use the power of the State to empty Church schools. Whether we collect statistics or trust to our own observation, the work which the Church has been doing during the last few years, and is still doing, is prodigious, and consists not merely in bricks and mortar, but in those ever-extending influences of which bricks and mortar are but the external expression. "Why, it we let you alone," a candid Dissenter and Liberal lately observed to me, "the next generation will be clean under your thumb. You are covering the land in every direction with ecclesiastical network; and unless we can take away your school-grants and your endowments, it will be impossible for us to maintain for any length of time the ground we at present occupy." And when I say that the onward march of the Church of England is the onward march of Conservatism, I do not mean that the Church is herself political, or that her clergy are in the habit of preaching political sermons. There can be no doubt, as a matter of fact, that vast numbers of the clergy have been alienated from the Conservative cause by the apparent inability of its leaders to appreciate Church questions, and have drifted off into all manner of unnatural opinions and combinations. But the sort of disposition engendered by the teaching of the Church of England will always, in the long run, be Conservative. We need not fear the votes of operatives who attend church, lead sober lives, refrain from bad language, send their children to national schools, and cherish habits of frugality and independence. Such operatives grow more numerous every year, and in their increase I see great hopes for the prosperity of the country and the stability of its institutions.

On the whole, therefore, without approving of the Act which gave to the working classes so large and, as I think, so unfair a preponderance of political power, I perceive no sufficient cause to adopt your tone of despondency. I am aware, indeed, that I have said nothing of those strongholds of the Liberals—Wales, Scotland, and Ireland. It would take many sheets to discuss with the slightest accuracy the currents of feeling prevalent in those several countries, and I have already trespassed too long upon your patience. I will only observe that any summons to support a real and intelligible Conservatism would be sure to find a responsive echo, not merely in England, but throughout the whole electoral area of the British Isles. There is everywhere a wonderful amount of patriotism which will never be roused to battle so long as the trumpet gives an uncertain sound, but which will wake into energy the moment a trusted general sends forth a clear signal.

Despite the restless tendencies of the age, despite the apparent insincerity of public men, despite the tweedledom and tweedledee of parliamentary recrimination, depend upon it there is a Conservatism so suited to the necessities of the times—so just, so noble, so rational, so completely in accordance with the convictions of intelligent Englishmen—as to contain within it all the elements and conditions of success. There is yet time, and only just time, to proclaim such a Conservatism, and to rally round it the flower and respectability of the nation. A few more years of Disraelism, and we are undone. That grand political party which has its eager representatives in every town and every hamlet in the kingdom cannot understand it, feel no enthusiasm for it, fight for it (if they fight for it all all) with half-hearted allegiance, and will never be led to victory under its banner. Let you and I do our little best to place the "good old cause" on a more reasonable footing. Instead of giving it up, let us induce our Constitutional Association, and by its example other Constitutional Associations, to demand a rectification of our line of battle, and the appointment of commanders in whom we can confide. If we fail, we fail in a great work; if we succeed, England's Church and England's Constitution may yet be preserved, to pour their blessings upon our children, and our children's children.

The Principles and Objects of the National Union of Conservative and Constitutional Associations (London, 1872), 5–15

British Library, General Reference Collection 8138.aaa.56

In 1870, the Conservative Central Office was established in Parliament Street, Westminster, under the temperamental and prickly John Eldon Gorst (1835–1916), who had chaired the inaugural meeting of the NUCCA in November 1867. The NUCCA was also housed in Parliament Street, bringing it under Gorst's control. As stated in its *Principles and Objects* of 1872, the purpose of the NUCCA was to organise Conservative feeling in the country, advise on voter registration, and monitor the selection of parliamentary candidates and the use of campaign funds. It provided speakers for public meetings, posters for hoardings, leaflets for letterboxes, and a rapidly growing list of publications. The brief of the NUCCA was confined to England and Wales, and it was obliged to liaise with the County Conservative Registration Association and its Secretary, Charles Keith-Falconer. By 1872, 151 local Conservative Associations had affiliated with the NUCCA and, by 1874, 59% of all English and Welsh constituencies had Conservative or Conservative Working Men's Associations. In 1877 a total of 791 local Conservative Associations were affiliated with the NUCCA.

16

THE PRINCIPLES AND OBJECTS
OF THE NATIONAL UNION
OF CONSERVATIVE AND
CONSTITUTIONAL ASSOCIATIONS

(London, 1872), 5–15

THE NATIONAL UNION was established for the purpose of effecting a systematic organisation of Conservative feeling and influence throughout the country, by helping in the formation and work of the Constitutional Associations which have so rapidly increased in numbers. It is notorious that the Constitutional cause has suffered much from the want of organisation amongst its supporters. Through this want the great Conservative strength, which has existed in all parts of the country and in every class of the people, has been deprived of its just influence upon public affairs. It is now obvious that the measure of Reform achieved for the nation by the late Lord Derby and Mr. Disraeli, widening the basis and deepening the foundations of the Constitution, has greatly strengthened the hold of Constitutional principles upon the important constituencies. In all directions—and especially among working men—old Associations have been enlarged and new ones sprung into vigorous life. All that is needed to make them a source of great and abiding strength to the Constitutional cause is that there shall be some National organisation ready at all times to give information and advice; to strengthen each Association by combining the influence of all; and to supply a means of bringing to bear upon any public question the united weight of the Constitutional party.

That organisation is found in the NATIONAL UNION.

It was founded in the Autumn of 1867, and its rules were framed at a Conference, in November of that year, at which many Conservative and Constitutional Associations, in every part of the country, were represented.

The Council, with its various special Committees, has since been meeting constantly, and its work is of a threefold nature.

In the first place, it keeps a register of all existing Conservative and Constitutional Associations, with the number of their members, their rules of action, the names and addresses of their officers, and all other particulars which may enable the National Union to act promptly and effectively as their London agency. In the second place, it is always ready to assist with advice, or the personal co-operation of its members, in the service of the existing Associations or the formation of new ones. It will from time to time offer suggestions, where they are required, as to the direction of local effort—suggestions which the Associations will, of course, be perfectly free to accept or reject. And when any Association wishes to have a speaker to take part in its meetings and address it upon political matters, the Council will endeavour to send an efficient representative. Its third class of work is the publication from time to time of short pamphlets on important political questions, and the re-printing of speeches and lectures which may be of enduring and universal interest. It is confidently hoped that these publications, supplied to the affiliated Associations at a merely nominal price, and circulating far and wide amongst working men, will aid in the spread of sound political education, and therefore in the extension of Constitutional principles. It also hopes to be able to afford gratuitous Lectures to such Associations as may desire such aid. In carrying out its work, the Council carefully avoids any unsought interference with local action, and strives simply by every means at its disposal to gather up the whole strength of the Constitutional party throughout the kingdom into one compact organisation.

The aid of the National Union has been cordially welcomed by the local associations, and it has secured both from them and from individual members of the party, support so large and influential, that its permanence and usefulness may be now considered as certain.

The Vice-Presidents now number 367, amongst whom are 66 noblemen and 143 past and present members of the House of Commons, in whose names an ample guarantee is afforded of the value attached to the Union by leading members of the Party. The Honorary Members number 219.

The Council has printed 120,000 pamphlets, over 90,000 of which have been distributed gratuitously. Besides these, nearly 160,000 circulars, handbills, and broadsides have been printed and distributed with good effect, principally during the general election of 1868, in every place contested throughout the kingdom.

During the debate on Mr. Gladstone's Irish Church Resolutions in 1868, upwards of 37,000 letters and circulars were issued from the office, and 864 petitions, bearing 61,792 signatures, were presented through the Union, a considerably larger number being forwarded direct to Members of Parliament; and during the recent debates on the Ballot Bill, in the House of Lords, 150 petitions praying the Peers to abide by their amendments, with upwards of 21,500 signatures, were prepared and forwarded to the Hon. Secretaries for presentation in little more than six days, thus affording a gratifying proof of the energy and organisation existing among the Associations.

Many lectures and addresses have been delivered in different towns by Members of the Council and others, and there is abundant proof of the good effect thereby produced.

The Annual Conference for 1872 was held in London, under the presidency of Lord George Hamilton, M.P., and was largely and influentially attended, and it was followed by a Banquet at the Crystal Palace, given under the auspices of the Union, at which Mr. Disraeli, the Duke of Abercorn, the Earl of Shrewsbury, the Earl of

Abergavenny, and many of the leading members of the Party, in all upwards of 1,500, were present, the whole proceedings resulting in a brilliant success.

Early in 1869 the late Earl of Derby, who had for a considerable time interested himself in the prospects of the Union, consented to connect himself officially with it by becoming its Patron, and on his decease the Duke of Rich-consented to accept the office.

The following noblemen and gentlemen have been elected and have consented to act as Vice-Patrons:—

Vice-Patrons

THE EARL OF ABERGAVENNY.
THE RIGHT HON. LORD JOHN MANNERS, M.P.
THE RIGHT HON. SIR J. PAKINGTON, BART., G.C.B., M.P.
THE RIGHT HON. SIR STAFFORD NORTHCOTE. BART. C.B., M.P.
THE RIGHT HON. GATHORNE HARDY, M.P.
THE RIGHT HON. G. WARD HUNT, M.P.
COLONEL THE RIGHT HON. T. E. TAYLOR, M.P.

After the Conference held at Liverpool, under the presidency of Lord Skelmersdale, in June, 1869, it was resolved to invite several of the principal Vice-Presidents to take an active part in directing the operations of the Union, and a General Consultative Committee was formed, on which the following Noblemen and Gentlemen have agreed to act, under whose guidance it is hoped the movement so well commenced may be developed in the most effective manner:—

General Consultative Committee

THE PRESIDENT, TRUSTEES, AND HON. TREASURER (ex officio).

MARQUIS OF BATH.
MARQUIS OF EXETER.
MARQUIS OF HAMILTON, M.P.
EARL OF ABERGAVENNY.
EARL OF COURTOWN.
EARL OF DARTMOUTH.
LORD CLAUD J. HAMILTON, M.P.
RT. HON. LORD JOHN MANNERS, M.P.
LORD HENRY SCOTT, M.P.
VISCOUNT HAWARDEN.
VISCOUNT CRICHTON, M.P.
VISCOUNT SANDON, M.P.
LORD GARLIES, M.P.

LORD COLCHESTER.
LORD COLVILLE OF CULROSS.
LORD REDESDALE.
LORD SKELMERSDALE.
HON. E. W. DOUGLAS.
HON. A. EGERTON, M.P.
MAJOR HON. C. KEITH-FALCONER.
HON. GERARD NOEL, M.P.
HON. MARK ROLLE.
RT. HON. SIR STAFFORD NORTHCOTE, BART. C.B., M.P.
RT. HON. GATHORNE HARDY, M.P.
RT. HON. G. WARD HUNT. M.P.
COLONEL RT. HON. T. E. TAYLOR, M.P.
SIR H. DRUMMOND WOLFF, K.C.M.G.
E. B. EASTWICK, Esq., C.B., M.P.
HUGH BIRLEY, Esq., M.P.
HENRY CHAPLIN, Esq., M.P.
MONTAGU CORRY, Esq.
R. ASSHETON CROSS, Esq., M.P.
R. DIMSDALE, Esq., M.P.
W. HART DYKE, Esq., M.P.
JOSHUA FIELDEN, Esq., M.P.
J. C. S. FREMANTLE, Esq.
HARDINGE GIFFARD, Esq., Q.C.
J. E. GORST, Esq.
COLONEL HONYWOOD.
E. K. HORNBY, Esq., M.P.
H. CECIL RAIKES, Esq., M.P.
LEONARD SEDGWICK, Esq.
W. H. SMITH, Esq., M.P.
ROWLAND WINN, Esq., M.P.

Henry Cecil Raikes, Esq., M.P., is Chairman, and Lord Colchester Vice-Chairman of the Council.

The Council appeals to all Conservatives for steady and earnest support.

In the House of Lords the Constitutional party enjoys a commanding influence. In the House of Commons it is strong in its unity of purpose and in confidence in its leaders.

But besides trusted leaders and an united Parliamentary party, it is necessary to have that steady popular support upon which the success of any political combination must depend. With a number of Associations founded on the same principles, working in the same manner, and striving after the same results, in communication with each other and with the National Union, the Conservative party will be strengthened, and the maintenance of the Constitution secured.

Rules

I.—The name of the Society shall be the National Union of Conservative and Constitutional Associations, and its object to constitute a centre for such bodies.

II.—Every such Association, subscribing One Guinea or more per annum to the funds, may, by vote of the Council, be admitted a Member of the Union, but the Council shall have the power to place on the Register of the Union gratuitously the names of any Conservative or Constitutional Associations which may desire it. Such Association, unless subscribing, being not thereby entitled to take any part in the government of the National Union.

III.—Any Branch or Affiliated Association, consisting of not less than 100 Members, may, either in common with its Chief or Parent Association, or alone be admitted, on a separate subscription as an individual Member of the Union.

IV.—Each Association shall be entitled to send two Representatives to attend and vote at any conference of the Union.

V.—Every person subscribing not less than One Guinea per annum to the funds shall be an Honorary Member of the Union.

VI.—The regulation and control of the affairs of the Union shall be vested in a Conference, to consist of:—(1) The President, Vice Presidents, Treasurer, and Trustees of the Union: (2) The Representatives of Subscribing Associations (3) and such Honorary Members as shall also be Members of the Council.

VII.—The Council may, and if required by not less than Twenty Subscribing Associations, shall, at any time, call a Conference, to be held at such time and place as the Council shall think fit.

VIII.—An Annual Meeting of the Conference shall be held at such time and place as the next preceding Annual Meeting shall have appointed; but the Conference may vary, and in the absence of any appointment fix the time and place of any Annual Meeting.

IX.—Notice of the time and place of any Meeting of the Conference shall be given by the Council by a circular letter, to be despatched by the post not less than seven days previously, and to be addressed to the Subscribing Associations, or their Secretaries, or other responsible officers respectively, and by advertisement to be published at least seven days previously in two London daily newspapers.

X.—The President and Vice-Presidents shall be elected at the Annual Meeting of the Conference, and retain office until the close of the next Annual Meeting after election. Any person who has served the office of President of the Union shall, if willing, remain without further election a Vice-President of the Union.

XI.—There shall be a General Consultative Committee formed out of the Vice-Presidents and Honorary Members of the Union, to whom questions of importance and difficulty shall be from time to time referred by the Executive.

XII.—The executive powers of the Union shall be vested in a Council, to consist of:—(1) The President, Treasurer, and Trustees of the Union; (2) [Illegible Text]

Members of the Consultative Committee as are willing to act; (3) Twenty four Members to be elected annually by the Conference from the officers and delegates of Subscribing Associations, and the Vice Presidents and Honorary Members of the Union; and, in addition, a certain number of Members, not exceeding twenty, to be nominated annually, on the request of the Council, by the principal Provincial Associations, or Unions of Associations connected with the National Union.

XIII.—The Council shall have power to fill up vacancies in their numbers as they occur.

XIV.—There shall be a Patron and not more than ten Vice-Patrons of the Union. The Patron and six Vice-Patrons to be elected by the Conference, and four Vice-Patrons by the Council at their discretion.

XV.—The Council shall appoint a Finance Sub-Committee of not less than two, and not more than four Members of Council; and no expenditure shall be incurred or sanctioned on behalf of the Union without a written authority to that effect, signed by at least two Members of the Finance Sub-Committee.

XVI.—The Council shall submit at the Annual Conference a Report of the Proceedings, and a Statement, certified by two Auditors to be elected by the Conference, of the Receipts and Expenditure of the Union, for the previous year.

XVII.—The Statement of Account, as audited, shall be printed, and he open for the inspection of all representatives and Honorary Members, at the Offices of the Union, for ten days at least before the Annual Conference, and a copy of the same shall be sent to each Subscribing Association.

XVIII.—After 1st January, 1869, Subscribers of Twenty Guineas may be Vice-Presidents for Life, and of Ten Guineas, Honorary Members for Life; and the ordinary Subscription of any Vice-President who shall be elected after 1st January, 1869, shall be fixed at not less than Five Guineas.

XIX.—These Rules may be altered at any Conference by a majority of two-thirds of the persons present and entitled to vote, provided that notice of the proposed alteration be given with the notice of the Meeting by circular despatched, as mentioned in Rule 9.

Associations

WHICH HAVE JOINED THE UNION.

Abingdon Working Men's Conservative Association.
Alston Constitutional Association.
Armley Working Men's Conservative Association.

Barnsley Working Men's Conservative Association.
Bath General and Working Men's Conservative Association.
Batley Working Men's Conservative Association.
Bedworth Conservative Association.
Birmingham Liberal-Conservative Association.
Birstal Working Men's Conservative Association.

Bolton Conservative Registration Association.
Bradford Conservative Association.
Brecon and Llywel Working Men's Conservative Association.
Bridgnorth Working Men's Literary and Constitutional Association.
Brighton Constitutional and Conservative Association.
Bristol Working Men's Conservative Association.
Brompton and South Kensington Conservative Association.
Burnley Constitutional Association.

Cambridge Conservative Club.
Cambridge Junior Conservative Club.
Cardiff Constitutional Association.
Castleton Conservative Burgess Association.
Chatham Conservative Association.
Chelsea Working Men's Constitutional Association.
Chelsea and Brompton Conservative Association.
Cleckheaton Working Men's Conservative Association.
Coventry Working Men's Conservative Association.
Crewe Constitutional Association.

Deal, Sandwich, and Walmer Working Men's Constitutional Association.
Dewsbury Working Men's Conservative Association.
Doncaster Working Men's Conservative and Constitutional Association.
Dover Working Men's Constitutional Association.
Durham Constitutional Association.

Exeter Working Men's Conservative Union.

Fulham Conservative Association.

Gateshead Conservative Association.
Gloucester Working Men's Conservative and Constitutional Association.
Gosport Working Men's Conservative Association.
Grantham Conservative Association.
Gravesend Conservative Association.
Guildford Conservative Association.

Halifax Conservative Association.
Hanley Branch of Staffordshire Potteries' Constitutional Association.
Haslingden Conservative and Constitutional Association.
Heckmondwike Constitutional Association.
Hereford Conservative Working Men's Association.
Heywood Constitutional Association.
Holbeck Pitt Club.
Horbury Working Men's Conservative Association.
Horsham Conservative Association.
Huddersfield Working Men's Conservative Association.

Hull Conservative Association.
Hyde Conservative Association.

Ipswich Working Men's Conservative Association.

Kensington (North) Conservative Association.
Kidderminster Working Men's Conservative Association.
King's Lynn Loyal and Constitutional Association.
Kirkstall Working Men's Conservative Association.
Knaresborough Working Men's Conservative Association.

Leamington—Conservative Alliance.
Leicester Working Men's Conservative Association.
Lewes Conservative Association.
Little Lever Conservative Association.
Liverpool Working Men's Conservative Association.
Loyal Orange Institution of Conservative Working Men, Liverpool.
London (City of) Conservative Association.
London and Westminster Working Men's Constitutional Association.

Manchester Conservative Union.
Metropolitan Conservative Alliance.
Middlesbrough Constitutional Association.
Middlesex Conservative Registration Association
    (Bethnal Green Branch).
Do. (Mile End Branch).

Newark Constitutional Association.
Newbury and West Berks Constitutional Association.
Newport (Monmouth) Conservative Association.
Newton-in-Mackerfield District Constitutional Association.
Norwich Conservative Association.
Norwood and South Penge Conservative Association.
North Ormesby Constitutional Association.
Northampton Operative Conservative Association.
Nottingham Working Men's Constitutional Association.

Oldbury Conservative Association.
Openshaw and Gorton Constitutional Association.
Ossett Working Men's Conservative Association.
Oxford Conservative Club.
Oxford Constitutional Association.

Paddington Conservative Association.
Peterborough Conservative and Constitutional Association.
Portsmouth Conservative Club.
Portsmouth Working Men's Liberal-Conservative Association.

Plymouth Working Men's Conservative Association.
Pudsey Working Men's Conservative Association.

Radford Branch of Nottingham Working Men's Constitutional Association.
Rawtenstall Conservative and Constitutional Association.
Reading Working Men's Conservative Association.
Rochdale Conservative Association.
Rochester Conservative Association.
Rotherhithe Conservative Association.
Royton Working Men's Conservative Association.

Saddleworth Operative Conservative Association.
Salisbury Conservative Union and Working Men's Association.
Scarborough Working Men's Conservative Association.
St. Helen's Working Men's Conservative and Constitutional Association.
St. Maryleboue Conservative Association.
St. Pancras Conservative Association.
Shipley Working Men's Conservative Association.
Southampton Conservative and Constitutional Association (All Saints' Ward).
Do. do. (St. Mary's Ward).
Southport and District Working Men Conservative Association.
Staffordshire Potteries Constitutional Association.
Stalybridge Constitutional Association.
Stroud Constitutional Association.
Sunderland Conservative Association.
Surrey (Mid) Conservative Association.
Swansea Constitutional Association.

Taunton Working Men's Conservative and Constitutional Association.
Torquay Conservative Association.
Tiverton Working Men's Conservative Association.
Torrington Conservative Association.
Tower Hamlets Constitutional Association.
Tynemouth Working Men's Cosmopolitan Conservative Association.

Wakefield Working Men's Conservative Association.
Wardleworth Conservative Burgess Association.
Warwick Conservative Association.
West Bromwich Conservative Association.
Whitby Conservative Association.
Wigan Working Men's Conservative Club.
Winsford Conservative Association.
Wolverhampton Constitutional Association.
Wortley Working Men's Conservative Association.

York Working Men's Conservative Association.

PUBLICATIONS ISSUED BY THE NATIONAL UNION,

COPIES OF WHICH CAN BE OBTAINED ON APPLICATION AT THE OFFICE, AND ARE SUPPLIED AT COST PRICE TO AFFILIATED ASSOCIATIONS.

IRISH CHURCH QUESTION.

	PRICE.
SPEECH of Mr. GATHORNE HARDY, March 31, 1868	9s. 6d. per 100.
SPEECH of Right Hon. The EARL of DERBY, K.G., June 25, 1868 ...	9s. 6d. per 100.
SPEECH of The Most Honourable The MARQUIS of SALISBURY, June 26, 1868	5s. 0d. per 100.
SPEECH of The Right Hon. LORD CAIRNS, June 29, 1868	12s. 0d. per 100.

GENERAL PUBLICATIONS.

No.		... ...
1.	"Principles and Objects of the National Union."	
2.	"Conservative and Liberal Foreign Policy; or, Who is Responsible for Recent Wars?"...	5s. 0d. per 100.
3.	"The Ballot—its Uses and Effects."	(Out of print.)
4.	"The Tory Reform Act. What must we do with it? Register! Register! Register!"...	9s. 6d. per 100.
5.	"Practical Suggestions to the Loyal Working Men of Great Britain; or, Points of Policy and Duty at the Present Crisis."	(Out of print.)
6.	"Conservative Legislation for the Working Classes.—No. 1. Mines and Factories." By W. T. CHARLEY, Esq., M.P.	9s. 6d. per 100.
7.	"The Political Future of the Working Classes; or, Who are the Real Friends of the People?"	(Out of print.)
8.	"Judgment of Judge Keogh in the Drogheda Election Petition."	(Out of print.)
9.	"The Irish Land Question."	10s. 6d. per 100.
10.	"Conservative Legislation for the Working Classes. No. 2. The Truck Acts." By W. T. CHARLEY, Esq., M.P.	9s. 6d. per 100.
11.	SPEECH of The EARL of DERBY, at Liverpool, January 9, 1872	7s. 0d. per 100.
12.	"Debate in a Republican Parliament."	2s. 0d. per 100.
13.	"The Alabama Claims."	7s. 0d. per 100.
14.	SPEECH of The Right. Hon. B. DISRAELI, M.P., at Manchester, April 3, 1872	15s. 0d. per 100.
15.	Report of Sixth Annual Conference of the National Union and Banquet at Crystal Palace, June 24, 1872, with Speeches of The DUKE of ABERCORN, The Right Hon. B. DISRAELI, M.P., &c., &c.	10s. 6d. per 100.
16.	SPEECH of Right Hon. B. DISRAELI, M.P., at Crystal Palace, June 24, 1872.	6s. 6d. per 100.
17.	A Review of the principal Measures passed by the present Government since their accession to office in 1868.	

(Will appear shortly.)

*The Policy of the Conservative Party. The Speech of the Earl
of Derby, at the Annual Meeting of the Liverpool Working
Men's Conservative Association, January 9th, 1872*
NUCCA Publication No 11, (London, 1872), 3–14

British Library, General Reference Collection 8138.aaa.56

The 15th Earl of Derby succeeded his father (the Conservative prime minister and party leader) to the title in October 1869. During the 1850s and 1860s, as Lord Stanley, he was a rising star of the party, though recognised as an untypical Conservative in his views. High-minded, earnest, and conscientious, he had little patience for what he saw as the rural fatuousness of the Tory squirearchy. An admirer of Disraeli in his youth, he had welcomed the abandonment of Protection in 1852. The liberality of his views disturbed some Conservative backbenchers. They came to see him as a closet Liberal who was only a Conservative out of filial loyalty, suspicions aggravated by his reclusive shy manner, partly enforced by ill health. His mother described him as 'a sort of political monk' (Angus Hawkins, *The Forgotten Prime Minister: Achievement, 1851–1869*, (Oxford, 2008), p. 261) . Nevertheless, as early as 1853, some prominent Conservatives were pointing to the young Stanley as a possible replacement for Disraeli as party leader in the Commons. In October 1855, he declined an invitation from Palmerston to join his cabinet. The same year he hosted a large meeting of Mechanics Institutions at Knowsley, the Derby family seat, declaring his enthusiastic support for educational reform and all measures conducive to the moral and intellectual welfare of the people.

First as Colonial Secretary and then President of the Board of Control in his father's 1858–1859 government, Stanley strengthened his reputation for business-like capability. In June 1859, Disraeli suggested to Derby that, if they wished Whigs and moderate Liberals to merge with the Conservatives, then Stanley was the only politician who could achieve it. The Liberal chief whip, in private conversation with Stanley, floated the possibility of such a fusion in February 1861. Russell, in November 1865, invited Stanley to join his cabinet. Rejection of the offer caused Stanley no regret.

In July 1866, Derby appointed Stanley Foreign Secretary. Stanley strictly adhered to the foreign policy declared by his father as prime minister. Entanglements in European conflicts were to be avoided and there would be no engagement in diplomatic threats or menace, the internal affairs of other nations being matters in which Britain should not meddle. During the war between Prussia and Austria in July 1866 and following the Prussian victory at Sadowa, Stanley abstained from diplomatic interference.

In the Amphitheatre near Lime Street, in Liverpool, Derby (as Stanley had become) spoke to an audience of about 3,000, made up of members of the

371

Liverpool Working Men's Conservative Association on 9 January 1872. His carefully considered speech lasted about 75 minutes and ranged over a variety of topics. He advised against the Conservatives taking office without an assured majority, but pointed out the influence Conservatives might exercise in the Commons, given the divided state of the Liberal party. In his diary, Derby noted that after his speech he was weary, but well satisfied.

17

THE POLICY OF THE CONSERVATIVE PARTY. THE SPEECH OF THE EARL OF DERBY, AT THE ANNUAL MEETING OF THE LIVERPOOL WORKING MEN'S CONSERVATIVE ASSOCIATION, JANUARY 9TH, 1872

NUCCA Publication No 11, (London, 1872), 3–14

The Earl of DERBY said: Gentlemen, I have more than once, on former occasions, been asked to attend the annual meeting of this Association, and though not very fond of discussing purely political questions in the recess, still I could not but feel that you had claims on me, both as a neighbour and as a member of a political party. Now, I hope I shall not disappoint some of my friends if I say I am not here to make observations on the departmental failings or mistakes of our present Government. There are ample materials for criticism of that kind if one cared to go into it. When unseaworthy ships are sent to the end of the world; when prerogative is strained as it has not been strained for generations before; when a Minister in the recess violates, by a transparent evasion, the provisions of an Act of Parliament passed six months before, in order to find a place for one of his law officers; when financial arrangements are brought forward which—to speak mildly—are eccentric and unfortunate; when things of this sort happen, and a good many more like them, we may thank heaven that the power of public men—both for good and evil—is far more limited than they are willing to believe, and that an energetic and prosperous people will survive a good many administrative blunders. Nor have I come here, gentlemen, like some sanguine parties who have been of late before the public, with a patent plan in my pocket for making everybody happy—for fixing the rate of wages and the hours of work by Act of Parliament, and turning all the artisans of great towns into the country districts. I may have a word to say about schemes of that kind by-and-bye; but what, if we are to meet at all, seems to me the use of our meeting is, that we may be able to take stock of our position, to see how we stand, what is the work we have got before us to do, and what are our means and prospects of being able to do it. First of all, one word as to the position of the Conservative party. There are friends of ours who are inclined to grow slack and indifferent about public affairs, because, they say, "What can we do when we are in a minority of [Illegible Text] I don't take that view. Certainly, if political life were what some people consider it—a "soaped pole," with £5,000 a year and lots of patronage at the top; if the end and object of all party efforts were the holding of office for a longer or shorter time, I might agree with them, though even in that point of view the Conservative position is very different from what it was three years ago. But, gentlemen, the holding of office is only a means; power is the end—power over the legislative and administrative conduct of affairs; and a party which, at the very lowest estimate of its strength, includes two-fifths of the House of Commons, may exercise very great power when those who sit opposite to it are notoriously divided into sections which have hardly an idea in common. Take, as an illustration, the Education Bill of 1870. Do you suppose that measure—a fair and honest attempt, as I hold it to be, to keep the balance even between conflicting interests—would ever have passed if there had not been a Conservative opposition to back up the Minister against his own followers? And, depend upon it, what was done then will have to be done again. How much sympathy do you suppose there is between a Whig duke or a Liberal millionaire, on the one hand, and a politician like Mr. Odger, or Mr. Auberon Herbert, or Sir Charles Dilke, on the other? When we are told that the great Liberal party is all-powerful, let us first know what the great Liberal party is. Is it in favour of putting Irish education into Ultramontane hands, which is what Irish Liberals want, or of purely secular education, which is what English Radicals want? Is it in favour of Mr. Miall's scheme for ecclesiastical disestablishment and disendowment for England? Is it prepared to vote for breaking down all large accumulations of property by graduated taxation, and of confiscating the land under one pretext or another, which is what the Republican clubs want? Is it in favour of colonial separation, which is the theory of Mr. Goldwin Smith's school; or of colonial federation, which is the cry of another party? I don't put these questions by way of taunt or reproach to those who sit opposite to us. What I contend for is this, that with the Ballot Bill, about which I shall have a word to say, presently, the old Liberal programme will have disappeared; that new subjects of controversy in their turn are cropping up; and that upon those new questions we have fair ground to hope that the view taken by the present, and still more by the next, House of Commons will be a Conservative rather than a Radical view. Only don't let us spoil our own game; don't let us lose power by running after place. If we become the majority, as we may, it is our duty to accept the responsibilities of that position. But for myself, I tell you frankly, though I should rejoice to see a strong Conservative Government in power, I had infinitely rather, in the public interest and that of our party, see the Conservatives forming a strong and compact opposition than have them, for the fourth time in the last twenty years, holding office without the support of an assured majority. That is my conviction, and I believe it is that of most Conservatives who have had any experience in affairs. Now, how do we stand as regards the great institutions of the country? The Crown is safe enough. We have had evidence on that point within the last few weeks that is worth any amount of argument. As to the

House of Lords, I am very far from saying that it is perfect, or that we could not do something to improve and strengthen it. Undoubtedly, if we were framing the Constitution for the first time, we should not select by a rather arbitrary process some 400 or 500 heads of families, and constitute them a separate branch of the Legislature. This much only I will say in defence of the hereditary principle, that you cannot condemn it in the peerage without condemning it in the monarchy also; because among 400 well-educated men, it is by the law of chances a matter of absolute certainty that you will find a certain number competent to take a leading and active part in public affairs, whereas in the case of royalty it is a pure question whether the Sovereign for the time being be personally competent or not. But there are other considerations to be borne in mind. Many people think—I do for one—that it would not be exactly safe to attempt to carry on affairs by a single Chamber without any check, even the check of a temporary delay, on the impulses and passions of the moment. Despotic power is not good for any man or any set of men; and you have to take into account also this historical fact, that every attempt made in modern times to create an effective second Chamber has been a failure. If that Chamber is composed of Crown nominees appointed for life, they are looked upon—perhaps in most cases not unjustly—as mere Government hacks or worn-out officials. If it is elective, you have then two similarly constituted bodies, liable to exactly the same impulses, and therefore unfit to control one another. The American Senate, which is sometimes referred to, is an institution by itself, because it represents separate and sovereign States, each of which has its own Legislature for internal affairs. That is a condition which we have not, and cannot have, here. In one word, what I would suggest to the gentlemen who agitate against the House of Lords, and who lately sat in judgment upon it at Birmingham—though somehow that agitation went off in an unexpectedly quiet manner—what I would say to them is: Don't content yourselves with finding fault with the Lords as they are, but tell us first whether you want a second Chamber at all; and next, if you do, give us your opinion how it should be framed. If they take the first of these alternatives, they will be in a small minority, and if they adopt the second, they will find they have a tougher job on their hands than they are aware of. For my own part, while I should utterly object to an unlimited creation of peerages for life, and especially to any renewal of the attempt of fourteen years ago to create them by reviving an antiquated prerogative, I see no harm and some advantage in a limited number of peerages of that class. And I say so mainly for this reason: Under an hereditary system, paper peerages are a misfortune. They create a temptation to jobbing and place-hunting; and, as matters stand, it will often happen that an able man, with a family and without a fortune, either refuses to go into the House of Lords, and so his services are lost to that body, or accepts a peerage, which is merely an encumbrance and a disadvantage to his successors, because it cuts them off from many legitimate means of pushing their own fortune, while it places them politically and socially in a false position. The next great institution against which attacks are directed is the Church, and it is perfectly natural that the success of the party of disestablishment in Ireland should have encouraged the supporters of a similar policy here. Logically, I don't see much difference between the two cases. The ground on which the Irish Church was abolished was, that it is an insult and an injury to any man that a religious persuasion which is not his should be endowed and connected with the State. Well, if that is so, I don't know that it makes much difference whether the persons so insulted and injured are a majority or a minority of the nation. I am not surprised that Protestant Dissenters should argue that as much consideration is due to their scruples as to those of the Catholic hierarchy. As against Mr. Gladstone and his friends, I think they have the best of the argument; but legislation is not guided by logic, and practically, I believe the position of the Church Establishment to be unassailable, at any rate, for as long a period as we need look to, provided only that those who belong to it can manage to keep the peace among themselves. I look on that question as one which is entirely in their own hands. Nonconformists and Secularists combined will not bring about disestablishment; but the real question is whether the contending parties within the Church itself can keep their hands off one another. If they cannot, if there is any considerable secession on one side or the other, I should begin to fear that the end was not far off. But, so far, English common sense has been too strong for the spirit of faction, and I hope it will be so still. The battlefield for the moment is the education question; and, as to that, I think our Nonconformist friends are a little unreasonable. If they can shew that in any one particular, that in any—the slightest—degree they were put by the Act of 1870 in a worse position than their rivals, I should at once admit that they had a fair ground of complaint. But that is not alleged. It is not even contended that the schools belonging to the Establishment get any help which is refused to theirs. The point on which the present agitation has arisen is one which was hardly noticed in debate when the Act was passed. It is impossible not to see that the real grievance lies deeper; that they have been startled, and perhaps disappointed, to find how large an amount of wealth and social influence belonging to the Establishment could be brought to bear on the setting up and maintenance of schools. Well, I am not here to speak as a partisan of any system. I wish all to have fair play; but I must observe that I think they have fair play under the present arrangement. Wherever Nonconformists are strong enough to set up a school of their own, that school gets a share of public help; where they are not strong enough for that, they have all the security that a stringent conscience clause can give them against any doctrine being taught to their children of which they disapprove; and if in any district Churchmen are in a small minority, the same security—no less, but no more—is conceded to them. Parliament has undoubtedly maintained what is called the "denominational system;" but it has done so only in deference to the clearly-expressed opinion of the great majority of the people, and for my part I think the popular instinct has been right. You cannot ignore the existence of strong sectarian and ecclesiastical feeling, whether you like it or not. The practical alternative is either to use the services of men who are guided to some extent by that feeling, and who, under its influence, will make large sacrifices of time and money to help in the work of popular teaching, or to try and set up a contrary system in the face of a most determined and violent opposition, and with comparatively little private help. I am quite sure that any attempt to adopt the latter plan would have thrown back the cause of popular teaching half a century, and on that ground—leaving other reasons aside—I rejoice that it has not been attempted. Just one word more on this subject. I am afraid that some of our School Boards are rather too ambitious, and are aiming at much more than can usefully be taught in the great majority of cases. They are not likely to take any hint of mine; but I think they hardly make allowance for the short-ness of time, for the stupidity of the average human intellect, and for the wonderful facility with which boys and men forget quickly and completely what they have only half learnt. That will settle itself; and or the general question of education all I have to say comes to this: You have got a system which promises to work fairly well. That, under all the difficulties of the case, is much to have accomplished. Don't be in a hurry to alter it; at any rate, let it work for some years, and then if there is a real grievance anywhere—which I don't admit there is—we shall see more clearly where the shoe pinches. There is another matter of great social interest, with which Parliament will probably have to deal next session: I mean the Licensing Question. It is not a very easy or simple one, and, as usually happens, those who see its difficulties least are most confident that they have found the way to settle it. There is a general feeling, and I am afraid one cannot deny that it is well founded, that as a nation we are a little too fond of good liquor. I think there is great exag-geration in what is commonly said about drunken habits, because we must remem-ber that a perfectly sober, temperate man of the middle or upper classes, who consumes his three or four glasses of wine daily, and never is the worse for them, gets through a great deal more drink in the course of the year than most of the poor fellows who go in for too much beer on Saturday night, and get into trouble in con-sequence. Still, making allowances of that kind, there is no doubt that a good deal of crime and disease is due to intemperance. We all want to check that, if we only knew how; and every year various plans are put forward for that purpose. One of those plans is that preposterous scheme framed by a body of men calling themselves the United Kingdom Alliance. Their theory is, that if by any means you could persuade two-thirds of the ratepayers of a district that beer is objectionable, they shall have the right to impose that rule of diet on the remaining third. Now that is sheer tyranny and intolerance of the worst sort. It would be just as reasonable to lay it down that where two-thirds of the population of any district were Protestants, no Catholic should be allowed to open a place of worship; or that where two-thirds were Liber-als, no Conservative should be allowed to set up a newspaper. But I won't waste your time in discussing that theory. We have our national faults, but a sour and morose fanaticism is not one of them. If those Puritans of the nineteenth century were to carry their point, they would find, like the Puritans of the seventeenth cen-tury, that they had only produced, during a few years, an apparent conformity, which would be followed by a reaction of excess which everybody would deplore. Well, the other proposals are, in various ways, to cut down the number of licensed houses by refusing fresh licences, and gradually cancelling the old ones. That is the direc-tion which the last attempt at legislation took. But there is one very awkward feature attending it, that the more you follow the policy of limiting numbers, the more you are putting into a few hands a close and profitable monopoly, with the inevitable result, that a worse article is supplied at a higher price. Another course, again, is to leave the trade open to all competitors, but to enforce stricter regulations as to hours of management. That is a policy which, just now, is out of fashion, though it is easier to abuse it than to shew that it is wrong. On the whole, I do not think that we shall this year pass any large measure, or do what is called "settle the question"; but something will be tried, and I think it will be the duty of Conservatives to help as far they can. For myself I have no great faith in this kind of legislation, except as a temporary expedient. Time, and teaching, and the force of opinion will do more than any Act of Parliament. The passion for drink is a disease rather than a vice—a disease generated sometimes by bad air, sometimes by excessive labour, often by poor and ill-chosen diet, and often, again, by inherited morbid tendencies. To believe that you could cure it throughout the country in a year, or even in a few years, is to go against all the teachings of experience. That there will be improvement I do not doubt, but I believe it will be a work of time, and that in the poorer classes, as in the richer classes, a reform of social habits will come about gradually and almost imperceptibly. Well, gentlemen, I am addressing you under great physical difficulties, and I will not take you through the probable legislation of next session; but there are one or two measures to which you will expect me to advert. We are promised a Mines Regulation Bill, and I think it will be only fair to ask that it shall be brought forward at a time when it can have full and deliberate consideration. We are promised a Scotch Education Bill, and I have no doubt, from the practical good sense which characterises Scotchmen of all parties, that question will be brought to a satisfactory issue. We are threatened with a renewal of last year's Rating Bill, and I can only say that if it in any degree resembles the plan brought forward by Mr. Goschen, I hope it will be as speedily and summarily disposed of as that was. We are led to expect that something will be done for sanitary improvement; and of all agitations that can be set on foot or imagined, I can conceive none more entirely justifiable than an agitation for pure air, pure water, and freedom from poisoning from bad drainage. Sanitary reformers have a very wide field before them; but I must pass over that class of questions with only one observation. What we want in sanitary matters is not so much better laws as more effective machinery for enforcing the laws we have. There is power in the law as it now stands to put down most kinds of nuisances, but there is nobody to take the initiative. Very few men like to put themselves in the invidious position of public prosecutors, and I never noticed that they got thanks from anybody if they did. But while I say that, I am no advocate for rushing into vast and costly plans at the shortest notice. It is quite on the cards that the next generation may find out that the gigantic drainage works, on which so many millions have been spent, are comparatively useless, and what we want now is, not so much a few schemes of national dimensions, as a more minute and careful supervision of little local details, which do not make any particular show, but which being looked after, or neglected, constitute the whole difference between a healthy and an unhealthy district. Well, we are to have the Ballot over again, probably, as soon as Parliament meets; and on that subject I would merely repeat the opinion which I have expressed more than once in former years—that there is no question in the whole range of politics the practical importance of which appears to me to have been so much exaggerated. The cry for the Ballot was raised forty or fifty years ago, when there were many exceedingly small constituencies in which half a dozen votes might turn the scale, and where the owners of those votes were mostly in an entirely dependent condition. I don't believe that, even then, it would have made the change which was supposed, because you must remember this, that no system of secret voting can ever be more than a half protection. Those who can bribe, or those who can intimidate, if there are any, cannot indeed, where votes are secret, ensure a vote being given in their favour, but they can always ensure the absence from the poll of a voter who they know is determined to go against them; nor have I any great faith in bribery being checked by that method. Payment by results may be applied to elections as well as to schools, and, odd as it may seem, I believe there are very many men so constituted that their consciences, or their sense of duty, will not prevent their taking a bribe, but who yet will have honour enough left (if honour you can call it) to give their vote so paid for, either in secret or openly, for the candidate to whom they promised it. However, I don't think this is the time or place to go into the argument. I believe that even if secret voting is carried, you will still know how 99 men out of 100 have voted. They will think it a mean and cowardly thing to use any disguise in the matter, and as to the hundredth—the prudent, cautious, timid individual—who won't let his wife or his friend know what his politics are, why, he is not likely to be a dangerous revolutionist. And let me just observe, in passing, I do not think our Liberal friends pay themselves a high compliment, when they assume, as a matter of course, that all persons of that description, that is all the cowards and all the sneaks, are likely to be on their side. They are quite welcome to have them; but I expect, as a fact, the number will not be great anyhow. What seems to me to be the practical part of the question, is how to prevent personation, and it is to that point, I think, that our consideration ought now to be mainly directed. We want an effectual check against men voting, as the phrase goes, "early and often," and we have fair ground for objecting to any measure that does not give us security on that point. There is an infinitely larger subject to which I should like to see the attention of Parliament directed, but whether it will be so or not, during the present year, I have no means of judging—the reform of judicial administration. Our bench and bar are, for learning, for ability, and for high professional honour, unsurpassed in the world. In that respect there is no improvement to ask for. But I don't think we can deny that, notwithstanding all that has been done of late years, justice is still sometimes very slow and often very costly. I speak under reserve as a layman, but I don't think it ought to be difficult to establish a single and supreme court of appeal, which the stopgap measure of last year does not give us. I don't see why the highest equity judge of the land should be placed in the wholly anomalous and inconsistent position of being also a member of the Cabinet, and therefore a political partisan. Nor can I understand why, when there is no want of competent men to relieve one another, so large a part of our judicial machinery should stand still for four months out of the twelve. There is much useful work to be done in this line, and I don't see why Conservatives should not help to do it. In finance—a question which touches

379

our feelings very nearly—all we need ask of our rulers is not to play tricks. We are doing well now, and if we continue at peace, we shall do still better. But it is possible to be *too* ingenious; and a great many people will be relieved from anxiety if the Chancellor of the Exchequer next April condescends to give us a commonplace Budget. If I were to throw out a suggestion on that subject, it would be that we ought to turn our thoughts more than we do to the reduction of the debt. Our present prosperity may not last for ever. I speak advisedly when I tell you that we are not, any of us, rich or poor, paying, in proportion to our income, one-half the burdens which were borne by our grandfathers in the time of the great war. Probably one-third would be nearer the mark; and I don't think it is altogether satisfactory to anticipate that our descendants 150 or 200 years hence may still be paying the bill for Waterloo and Trafalgar. If we could be sure of perpetual peace, we might be content to allow the cost of former wars to remain a perpetual charge. But this is not the case; and we may reasonably utilise a time—it may be only an interval—of safety and prosperity to clear ourselves from at least some part of this old inherited burden. If we don't do that; if every war is to add to the debt, and every interval of peace is to leave it undiminished, or very nearly so, there is only one ending; and I, for one, am not reconciled to the thought of bankruptcy or repudiation merely by the consideration that it will not come in my time. In regard to material resources and prospects, we have nothing just now to complain of. Trade is flourishing, the people are employed, and pauperism has perceptibly diminished. Very much more remains to be done in that respect; but I am expressing to you one of the deepest and strongest convictions of my mind when I say that for those social improvements which we all desire, and which are in everybody's mouth, we must look to the community acting for itself in the first instance, and to Governments and legislators only in rare and exceptional cases. I know that is with many people an unpalatable doctrine; but bear with me for a moment while I state it. What are the characteristic national achievements of which Englishmen in the present day are most apt to boast? I think anyone would name—next to our free government—our unparalleled commerce, our unlimited command of capital, the manufactures in which we excel and with which we supply the whole world, our railway system—the first-established and the most complete which any country possesses—and our newspaper press, to which I will not pay a compliment, because compliments of that kind from public men are always suspicious, but of which you may judge for yourselves. Well, is not every one of these things the work, the unassisted work, of individual enterprise, as distinguished from State agency. Take, again, your trade unions, by which working men have obtained in so many branches of business their demand for higher wages and shorter hours of work. They did not ask help from Parliament to found those unions or to carry them on. They acted more sensibly—they did the work themselves. Well, cannot you do the same with the great majority at least of those wants which are reasonably and properly being put forward? Artisans, we are told, require better houses—I agree in that—and foolish and fantastic schemes are afloat for some State machinery which is to empty the towns into the country. Well, are there no such things as land companies and building companies? And is there any reason why in every town, and why in every part of the country, artisans should not be able to build and buy their own houses, paying for them gradually, as in many thousand cases they have done already? But, it is asked, why should not the State undertake this work? What is the objection? I answer that State agency is not wanted to give you a house or anything else at the fair market price; and if the proposal is to give it for less than a fair price, for less than it costs, then you are opening a door which will let in more than you think for. If houses are to be supplied on those terms, why not clothes? why not meat? why not bread? And so you come by a sharp and easy process to what is simply universal and undisguised pauperism. Again, there are great outcries about the adulteration of articles of food. By all means punish adulterators if you can catch them; and I should agree that, as the law stands, they get off too easily; but surely for that abuse—and it is a very great one—the best and simplest remedy is the co-operative store, which you can set up for yourselves without asking help or fearing hindrance from any man. I don't tell you in so many words that the State should take on itself no functions except those which it actually performs; but I do tell you that the tendency to enlarge indefinitely the scope of its operations is one to be watched with great jealousy. There is risk of extravagance and jobbery; there is discourage-ment of individual enterprise; there is loss of individual self-reliance; there is the inevitable discontent caused by the disappointment of unreasonable expectations; and, if time allowed, a good deal might be said as to the way in which these evils have been and are felt in other countries in which governmental interference is car-ried further than here. Well, gentlemen, you will be glad to hear that I am getting to the end of a long story. I need not detain you by discussing the state of our foreign relations, because at this moment there is no foreign question that is particularly urgent. The warmest friends of the Ministry will not claim for them that either the Black Sea negotiations or the settlement with the United States has been a diplo-matic victory. And on the other hand, it is fair to tell you that I do not see any reason-able ground for apprehending that we are likely to be involved in foreign complications. No man can predict the future, and no doubt it seems probable enough that a struggle for military supremacy on the Continent will not be ended by the war of last year; but we were neutrals in the European wars of 1860, of [Illegible Text] and of 1870, and with ordinary prudence and common sense—I do not [Illeg-ible Text] [Illegible Text] on the part of our officials, but also on the part of the nation, with which the ultimate decision of peace or war must rest—I see no reason why we should not continue to hold a neutral position when the next great [Illegible Text] comes off. This only I will add, that we must be consistent, and not expect things which are incompatible with one another. Moral influence is very well in its way, but between combatants it does not go far. If we hold it our duty, as I do for one, to keep this country out of the risks and miseries of an unnecessary war, we must not complain that we do not dictate the conditions of peace. The least satisfac-tory part of our national position is, to my mind, the state of Ireland. We have exhausted the list of what, rightly or wrongly, have been considered remedial mea-sures. The Church is disestablished and disendowed; the land has been practically handed over to the peasantry. No further sacrifice of that kind remains to be made.

And what are our thanks? Why, the disaffected party tell you every day that but for the Fenian movement, the Irish Church would still have been on its legs, and but for the shooting of landlords and agents, the demands of the peasantry would never have been listened to. And, don't let us deceive ourselves, gentlemen; when they say that, they are not very far from the truth. If Ireland had remained quiet, you would have heard nothing, at least for many years to come, of a Church Act or a Land Act. Well, that state of things is not exactly discouragement to future agitation. You are now face to face with two claims which you must resist—one the claim of the Ultramontane party to control all education; the other the demand for what is called "Home Rule," which, as every child can see, practically means Irish independence. Nobody supposes that an Irish Parliament would confine itself for a single session to purely local affairs, or that anything short of the Constitution of 1782 would satisfy those who have raised the cry. I do not argue that point because, happily, it is one on which there are not two opinions in England. But I do think that the other question to which I refer—that of education—will require to be closely watched. There are a good many politicians—not on our side the House—who believe in the theory of governing Ireland through the Catholic clergy, and I think some leanings in that direction may be observed in very high quarters. Now, that is a system to which there are two objections: One, that the English nation—which, after all, has a voice in the matter—will not endure it; the other, that, even if it could be acted upon, the Catholic clergy do not by any means possess the power which is commonly ascribed to them. Their strength has always lain in following the popular movement which they seem to lead, and if that feeling points in the direction of repeal, they can't help themselves, and will be repealers to a man. I have no great scheme to propose, nor do I believe in any remedy of that sort. I agree with Lord Hartington that there is nothing to be done except to shew patience and firmness—we shall know, I suppose, in a few [Illegible Text] what is meant by that utterance—and I hope that when we come to learn what is intended, we may find that the policy of Ministers is such as we are able honestly to support. Well, gentlemen, I think I need detain you no longer. I thank you for the patience with which you have listened to rather a dry discourse. Let us keep together as a political connection; let us work and wait; let there be no quarrels among ourselves—let there [Illegible Text] no apathy on the one hand, and no undue precipitation on the other; and, depend upon it, whatever benches we sit upon, we shall not have been without influence on the future destinies of this country, nor shall we fall to enjoy those opportunities of doing public service which constitute the chief inducement to any honest and rational man to engage in the labours and anxieties of political life.

Benjamin Disraeli, *Speech of the Right Hon. B. Disraeli, MP, at the Banquet of the National Union of Conservative and Constitutional Associations at the Crystal Palace, on Monday June 24, 1872* (London: R. J. Mitchell and Sons, 1872)

British Library, General Reference Collection 8138.aaa.56

In April 1872, Disraeli gave a major speech in the Free Trade Hall, Manchester, marked by a great NUCCA parade. In June, he delivered a second major speech to a NUCCA audience at the Crystal Palace, Sydenham. Disraeli rarely made public speeches to mass audiences. His Manchester and Crystal Palace speeches, however, strengthened his hold on the party leadership. In January 1872 a group of leading Conservatives had gathered at Lord Exeter's Burghley estate to discuss Disraeli's deficiencies as party leader. The Commons chief whip stated that Disraeli's replacement by Derby (who was not present) would gain the Conservatives 40 or 50 MPs. Orchestrated by Gorst and drawing on the resources of the NUCCA, Disraeli's speeches at Manchester and the Crystal Palace were the spirited response to such private sedition. They were powerful demonstrations of Disraeli's call upon Conservative feeling in the constituencies. They resurrected Disraeli's authoritative claim to the leadership of the party.

At Manchester, Disraeli spoke for over three hours. The Conservatives, he declared, were a great national party, in contrast to the cosmopolitanism of the Liberals. The Conservatives were committed to maintaining the constitution of the country and to the need for health legislation. This culminated in Disraeli's description of the Liberal cabinet, formed on the principle of violence and under the influence of some deleterious drug, as a range of exhausted volcanoes. Delivered without notes and with Disraeli fortifying himself with white brandy, the over three-hour speech was a remarkable oratorical feat. On leaving Manchester, the horses drawing Disraeli's carriage were unhitched and a crowd pulled it to the railway station, where a celebratory crowd mobbed Disraeli and his wife.

A large meeting of the NUCCA was held at the Westminster Palace Hotel on 24 June. In the evening, the delegates dined at the Crystal Palace. Disraeli's shorter Crystal Palace speech presented the same themes he had elaborated at Manchester. The Tory party, unless it was a national party, was nothing and the Tory party had three great objects. The first was to maintain the institutions of the country. The House of Lords had all the virtues required of a Senate. It possessed independence, great local influence, and a public sense of duty no theory could supply. Able to defy both despots and the mob, the peerage were a class whose patriotism sprang from its intimate connection with the soil of the nation. The established Church was a national profession of faith combined with the enjoyment of private judgement in all matters spiritual. The second great object of the party was to

383

uphold the Empire. Disraelian swagger invested the British Empire with the durability of classical Rome and the adventurism of Carthage. The third great object of the party was to elevate the condition of the people. Disraeli's rhetorical alchemy transformed the base metal of social reform into the gold of party triumph. The immediate future, he predicted, presented a fundamental contest between national and cosmopolitan principles – a choice between the patriotism of Conservatism and the alien abstract ideals of Liberalism. The advanced guard of Liberalism had openly announced itself Republican. The cause of Conservativism was the commitment to England as a great Imperial country commanding the respect of the world.

18

BENJAMIN DISRAELI, *SPEECH OF THE RIGHT HON. B. DISRAELI, MP, AT THE BANQUET OF THE NATIONAL UNION OF CONSERVATIVE AND CONSTITUTIONAL ASSOCIATIONS AT THE CRYSTAL PALACE, ON MONDAY JUNE 24, 1872*

(London: R. J. Mitchell and Sons, 1872)

At the Banquet of the NATIONAL UNION OF CONSERVATIVE AND CONSTITUTIONAL ASSOCIATIONS, at the Crystal Palace, on Monday, June 24, 1872, the LORD MAYOR proposed the toast of "The Constitutional Cause," to which Mr. DISRAELI, whose name was coupled with the toast, replied as follows:—

My Lord Duke and Gentlemen,—I am very sensible of the honour which you have done me in requesting that I should be your guest to-day, and still more for your having associated my name with the important toast which has been proposed by the Lord Mayor. In the few observations that I shall presume to make on this occasion I will confine myself to some suggestions as to the present state of the Constitutional cause and the prospects which you, as a great Constitutional party, have before you. Gentlemen, some years ago—now, indeed, not an inconsiderable period, but within the memory of many who are present, the Tory party experienced a great overthrow. I am here to admit that in my opinion it was deserved. A long course of power and prosperity had induced it to sink into a state of apathy and indifference, and it had deviated from the great principles of that political association which had so long regulated the affairs and been identified with the glory of England. Instead of the principles professed by Mr. Pitt and Lord Grenville, and which those great men inherited from Tory statesmen who had preceded them not less illustrious, the Tory system had degenerated into a policy which found an adequate basis on the principles of exclusiveness and restriction. Gentlemen, the Tory party, unless it is a national party, is nothing. It is not a confederacy of nobles, it is not a democratic multitude; it is a party formed from all the numerous classes in the realm—classes alike and equal before the law, but whose different conditions and different aims give vigour and variety to our national life.

Gentlemen, a body of public men distinguished by their capacity took advantage of these circumstances. They seized the helm of affairs in a manner the honour of which I do not for a moment question, but they introduced a new system into our political life. Influenced in a great degree by the philosophy and the politics of the Continent, they endeavoured to substitute cosmopolitan for national principles; and they baptized the new scheme of politics with the plausible name of "Liberalism." Far be it from me for a moment to intimate that a country like England should not profit by the political experience of Continental nations of not inferior civilisation; far be it from me for a moment to maintain that the party which then obtained power and which has since generally possessed it did not make many suggestions for our public life that were of great value, and bring forward many measures which, though changes, were nevertheless improvements. But the tone and tendency of Liberalism cannot be long concealed. It is to attack the institutions of the country under the name of Reform, and to make war on the manners and customs of the people of this country under the pretext of Progress. During the forty years that have elapsed since the commencement of this new system—although the superficial have seen upon its surface only the contentions of political parties—the real state of affairs has been this: the attempt of one party to establish in this country cosmopolitan ideas, and the efforts of another—unconscious efforts, sometimes, but always continued—to recur to and resume those national principles to which they attribute the greatness and glory of the country. The Liberal party cannot complain that they have not had fair play. Never had a political party such advantages, never such opportunities. They are still in power; they have been for a long period in power. And yet what is the result? I speak not I am sure the language of exaggeration when I say that they are viewed by the community with distrust and, I might even say, with repugnance. And, now, what is the present prospect of the national party? I have ventured to say that in my opinion Liberalism, from its essential elements, notwithstanding all the energy and ability with which its tenets have been advocated by its friends—notwithstanding the advantage which has accrued to them, as I will confess, from all the mistakes of their opponents, is viewed by the country with distrust. Now in what light is the party of which we are members viewed by the country, and what relation does public opinion bear to our opinions and our policy? That appears to me to be an instructive query; and on an occasion like the present it is as well that we should enter into its investigation as pay mutual compliments to each other, which may in the end, perhaps, prove fallacious. Now, I have always been of opinion that the Tory party has three great objects. The first is to maintain the institutions of the country—not from any sentiment of political superstition, but because we believe that it embodies the principles upon which a community like England can alone safely rest. The principles of liberty, of order, of law, and of religion ought not to be entrusted to individual opinion or to the caprice and passion of multitudes, but should be embodied in a form of permanence and power.

We associate with the Monarchy the ideas which it represents—the majesty of law, the administration of justice, the fountain of mercy and of honour. We know that in the Estates of the Realm and the privileges they enjoy, is the best security for public liberty and good government. We believe that a national profession of faith can only be maintained by an Established Church, and that no society is safe unless there is a public recognition of the Providential government of the world, and of the future responsibility of man. Well, it is a curious circumstances that during all these same forty years of triumphant Liberalism, every one of these institutions has been attacked and assailed—I say, continuously attacked and assailed. And what, gentlemen, has been the result? For the last forty years the most depreciating comparisons have been instituted between the Sovereignty of England and the Sovereignty of a great Republic. We have been called upon in every way, in Parliament, in the Press, by articles in newspapers, by pamphlets, by every means which can influence opinion, to contrast the simplicity and economy of the Sovereignty of the United States with the cumbrous cost of the Sovereignty of England. Gentlemen, I need not in this company enter into any vindication of the Sovereignty of England on that head. I have recently enjoyed the opportunity, before a great assemblage of my countrymen, of speaking upon that subject. I have made statements with respect to it which have not been answered either on this side of the Atlantic or the other. Only six months ago the advanced guard of Liberalism, acting in entire unison with that spirit of assault upon the Monarchy which the literature and the political confederacies of Liberalism have for 40 years encouraged, flatly announced itself as Republican, and appealed to the people of England on that distinct issue. Gentlemen, what was the answer? I need not dwell upon it. It is fresh in your memories and hearts. The people of England have expressed, in a manner which cannot be mistaken, that they will uphold the ancient Monarchy of England, the Constitutional Monarchy of England, limited by the co-ordinate authority of the Estates of the Realm, but limited by nothing else. Now, if you consider the state of public opinion with regard to those Estates of the Realm, what do you find? Take the case of the House of Lords. The House of Lords has been assailed during this reign of Liberalism in every manner and unceasingly. Its constitution has been denounced as anomalous, its influence declared pernicious; but what has been the result of this assault and criticism of forty years? Why, the people of England, in my opinion, have discovered that the existence of a second Chamber is necessary to Constitutional Government; and, while necessary to Constitutional Government, is, at the same time, of all political inventions, the most difficult, not to say the most impossible. Therefore, the people of this country have congratulated themselves that, by the aid of an ancient and famous history, there has been developed in this country an Assembly which possesses all the virtues which a Senate should possess—independence, great local influence, eloquence, all the accomplishments of political life, and a public training which no theory could supply. The assault of Liberalism upon the House of Lords has been mainly occasioned by the prejudice of Liberalism against the land laws of this country. But in my opinion, and in the opinion of wiser men than myself, and of men in other countries beside this, the liberty of England depends much upon the landed tenure of England—upon the fact that there is a class which can alike defy despots and mobs, around which the people may always rally, and which must be patriotic from its intimate connection with the soil. Well, gentlemen, so far as these institutions of the country—the Monarchy and the Lords Spiritual and Temporal—are concerned, I think we may fairly say, without exaggeration, that public opinion is in favour of those institutions, the maintenance of which is one of the principal tenets of the Tory party, and the existence of which has been unceasingly criticised for forty years by the Liberal party. Now, let me say a word about the other Estate of the Realm, which was first attacked by Liberalism. One of the most distinguishing features of the great change effected in 1832 was that those who brought it about at once abolished all the franchises of the working classes. They were franchises as ancient as those of the Baronage of England; and, while they abolished them, they proposed no substitute. The discontent upon the subject of the representation which has from that time more or less pervaded our society dates from that period, and that discontent, all will admit, has now ceased. It was terminated by the Act of Parliamentary Reform of 1867–8. That Act was founded on a confidence that the great body of the people of this country were "Conservative." When I say "Conservative," I use the word in its purest and loftiest sense. I mean that the people of England, and especially the working classes of England, are proud of belonging to a great country, and wish to maintain its greatness—that they are proud of belonging to an Imperial country, and are resolved to maintain, if they can, their empire—that they believe, on the whole, that the greatness and the empire of England are to be attributed to the ancient institutions of the land. Gentlemen, I venture to express my opinion, long entertained, and which has never for a moment faltered, that this is the disposition of the great mass of the people; and I am not misled for a moment by wild expressions and eccentric conduct which may occur in the metropolis of this country. There are people who may be, or who at least affect to be, working men, and who, no doubt, have a certain influence with a certain portion of the metropolitan working classes, who talk Jacobinism. But, gentlemen, that is no novelty. That is not the consequence of recent legislation or of any political legislation that has occurred in this century. There always has been a Jacobinical section in the city of London. I don't particularly refer to that most distinguished and affluent portion of the metropolis which is ruled by my right hon. friend the Lord Mayor. Mr. Pitt complained of and suffered by it. There has always been a certain portion of the working class in London who have sympathised—perverse as we may deem the taste—with the Jacobin feelings of Paris. Well, gentlemen, we all know, now, after eighty years' experience, in what the Jacobinism of Paris has ended, and I hope I am not too sanguine when I express my conviction that the Jacobinism of London will find a very different result. I say with confidence that the great body of the working class of England utterly repudiate such sentiments. They have no sympathy with them. They are English to the core. They repudiate cosmopolitan principles. They adhere to national principles. They are for maintaining the greatness of the kingdom and the empire, and they are proud of being subjects of our Sovereign and members of such an Empire. Well, then, as regards the political institutions of this country, the maintenance of which is one of the chief tenets of the Tory party, so far as I can read public opinion, the feeling of the nation is in accordance with the Tory party. It was not always so. There was a time when the institutions of this country were decried. They have passed through a scathing criticism of forty years; they have passed through that criticism when their political upholders have, generally speaking, been always in opposition. They have been upheld by us when we were unable to exercise any of the lures of power to attract force to us, and the people of this country have arrived at these conclusions from their own thought and their own experience.

Let me say one word upon another institution, the position of which is most interesting at this time. No institution of England, since the advent of Liberalism, has been so systematically, so continuously assailed, as the Established Church. Gentlemen, we were first told that the Church was asleep, and it is very possible, as everybody, civil and spiritual, was asleep forty years ago, that that might have been the case. Now we are told that the Church is too active, and that it will be destroyed by its internal restlessness and energy. I see in all these efforts of the Church to represent every mood of the spiritual mind of man, no evidence that it will fall, no proof that any fatal disruption is at hand. I see in the Church, as I believe I see in England, an immense effort to rise to national feelings and recur to national principles. The Church of England, like all our institutions, feels it must be national, and it knows that, to be national, it must be comprehensive. Gentlemen, I have referred to what I look upon as the first object of the Tory party—namely, to maintain the institutions of the country, and reviewing what has occurred, and referring to the present temper of the times upon these subjects, I think that the Tory party, or, as I will venture to call it, the National party, has everything to encourage it. I think that the nation, tested by many and severe trials, has arrived at the conclusion which we have always maintained, that it is the first duty of England to maintain its institutions, because to them we principally ascribe the power and prosperity of the country.

Gentlemen, there is another and second great object of the Tory party. If the first is to maintain the institutions of the country, the second is, in my opinion, to uphold the Empire of England. If you look to the history of this country since the advent of Liberalism—40 years ago—you will find that there has been no effort so continuous, so subtle, supported by so much energy, and carried on with so much ability and acumen, as the attempts of Liberalism to effect the disintegration of the Empire of England. And, gentlemen, of all its efforts, this is the one which has been the nearest to success. Statesmen of the highest character, writers of the most distinguished ability, the most organised and efficient means have been employed in this endeavour. It has been proved to all of us that we have lost money by our Colonies. It has been shewn with precise, with mathematical demonstration, that there never was a jewel in the Crown of England that was so truly costly as the possession of India. How often has it been suggested that we should at once emancipate ourselves from this incubus. Well, that result was nearly accomplished. When those subtle views were adopted by the country under the plausible plea of granting self-government to the Colonies, I confess that I myself thought that the tie was broken. Not that I for one object to self-government. I cannot conceive how our distant Colonies can have their affairs administered except by self-government. But self-government, in my opinion, when it was conceded, ought to have been conceded as part of a great policy of Imperial consolidation. It ought to have been accompanied by an Imperial tariff, by securities for the people of England for the enjoyment of the unappropriated lands which belonged to the Sovereign as their trustee, and by a military code which should have precisely defined the means and the responsibilities by which the Colonies should be defended, and by which, if necessary, this country should call for aid from the Colonies themselves. It ought, further, to have been accompanied by the institution of some representative council in the metropolis, which would have brought the Colonies into constant and continuous relations with the Home Government. All this, however, was omitted because those who advised that policy—and I believe their convictions were sincere—looked upon the Colonies of England, looked even upon our connection with India, as a burden upon this country, viewing everything in a financial aspect, and totally passing by those moral and political considerations which make nations great, and by the influence of which alone men are distinguished from animals. Well, what has been the result of this attempt during the reign of Liberalism for the disintegration of the Empire? It has entirely failed. But how has it failed? Through the sympathy of the Colonies with the Mother Country. They have decided that the Empire shall not be destroyed, and in my opinion no Minister in this country will do his duty who neglects any opportunity of reconstructing as much as possible our Colonial Empire, and of responding to those distant sympathies which may become the source of incalculable strength and happiness to this land. Therefore, gentlemen, with respect to the second great object of the Tory party also—the maintenance of the Empire—public opinion appears to be in favour of our principles—that public opinion which, I am bound to say, thirty years ago, was not favourable to our principles, and which, during a long interval of controversy, in the interval had been doubtful.

Gentlemen, another great object of the Tory party, and one not inferior to the maintenance of the Empire, or the upholding of our institutions, is the elevation of the condition of the people. Let us see in this great struggle between Toryism and Liberalism that has prevailed in this country during the last forty years what are the salient features. It must be obvious to all who consider the condition of the multitude with a desire to improve and elevate it, that no important step can be gained unless you can effect some reduction of their hours of labour and humanise their toil. The great problem is to be able to achieve such results without violating those principles of economic truth upon which the prosperity of all States depends. You recollect well that many years ago the Tory party believed that these two results might be obtained—that you might elevate the condition of the people by the reduction of their toil and the mitigation of their labour, and at the same time inflict no injury on the wealth of the nation. You know how that effort was encountered—how these views and principles were met by the triumphant states-men of Liberalism. They told you that the inevitable consequence of your policy was to diminish capital, that that, again, would lead to the lowering of wages, to a great diminution of the employment of the people, and ultimately to the impov-erishment of the kingdom. These were not merely the opinions of Ministers of State, but those of the most blatant and loud-mouthed leaders of the Liberal party. And what has been the result? Those measures were carried, but carried, as I can bear witness, with great difficulty and after much labour and a long struggle. Yet they were carried; and what do we now find? That capital was never accumulated so quickly, that wages were never higher, that the employment of the people was never greater, and the country never wealthier. I ventured to say a short time ago, speaking in one of the great cities of this country, that the health of the people was the most important question for a statesman. It is, gentlemen, a large subject. It has many branches. It involves the state of the dwellings of the people, the moral consequences of which are not less considerable than the physical. It involves their enjoyment of some of the chief elements of nature—air, light, and water. It involves the regulation of their industry, the inspection of their toil. It involves the purity of their provisions, and it touches upon all the means by which you may [Illegible Text] them from habits of excess and of brutality. Now, what is the feel-ing upon these subjects of the Liberal party—that Liberal party who opposed the Tory party when, even in their weakness, they advocated a diminution of the toil of the people, and introduced and supported those Factory Laws, the principles of which they extended, in the brief period when they possessed power, to every other trade in the country? What is the opinion of the great Liberal party—the party that seeks to substitute cosmopolitan for national principles in the govern-ment of this country—on this subject? Why, the views which I expressed in the great capital of the county of Lancaster have been held up to derision by the Liberal Press. A leading member—a very rising member, at least, among the new Liberal members—denounced them the other day as the "policy of sewage." Well, it may be the "policy of sewage" to a Liberal member of Parliament. But to one of the labouring multitude of England, who has found fever always to be one of the inmates of his household—who has, year after year, seen stricken down the children of his loins, on whose sympathy and material support he has looked with hope and confidence, it is not a "policy of sewage," but a question of life and death. And I can tell you this, gentlemen, from personal conversation with some of the most intelligent of the labouring class—and I think there are many of them in this room who can bear witness to what I say—that the policy of the Tory party—the hereditary, the traditionary policy of the Tory party, that would improve the condition of the people—is more appreciated by the people than the ineffable mysteries and all the pains and penalties of the Ballot Bill. Gentlemen, is that wonderful? Consider the condition of the great body of the working classes of this country. They are in possession of personal privileges—of personal rights and liberties—which are not enjoyed by the aristocracies of other countries. Recently they have obtained—and wisely obtained—a great extension of political rights; and when the people of England see that under the constitution of this country, by means of the constitutional cause which my right hon. friend the Lord Mayor has proposed, they possess every personal right of freedom, and, according to the conviction of the whole country, also an adequate concession of political rights, is it at all wonderful that they should wish to elevate and improve their condition, and is it unreasonable that they should ask the Legislature to assist them in that behest as far as it is consistent with the general welfare of the realm? Why, the people of England would be greater idiots than the Jacobinical leaders of London even suppose, if, with their experience and acuteness, they should not long have seen that the time had arrived when social, and not political improvement is the object which they ought to pursue. I have touched, gentlemen, on the three great objects of the Tory party. I told you I would try to ascertain what was the position of the Tory party with reference to the country now. I have told you also with frankness what I believe the position of the Liberal party to be. Notwithstanding their proud position, I believe they are viewed by the country with mistrust and repugnance. But on all the three great objects which are sought by Toryism—the maintenance of our institutions, the preservation of our Empire, and the improvement of the condition of the people—I find a rising opinion in the country sympathising with our tenets, and prepared, I believe, if the opportunity offers, to uphold them until they prevail.

Before sitting down, I would make one remark particularly applicable to those whom I am now addressing. This is a numerous assembly; this is an assembly individually influential; but it is not on account of its numbers, it is not on account of its individual influence, that I find it to me deeply interesting. It is because I know that I am addressing a representative assembly. It is because I know that there are men here who come from all districts and all quarters of England, who represent classes and powerful societies, and who meet here not merely for the pleasure of a festival, but because they believe that our assembling together may lead to national advantage. Yes, I tell all who are here present that there is a responsibility which you have incurred to-day, and which you must meet like men. When you return to your homes, when you return to your counties and to your cities, you must tell to all those whom you can influence that the time is at hand, that, at least, it cannot be far distant when England will have to decide between national and cosmopolitan principles. The issue is not a mean one. It is whether you will be content to be a comfortable England, modelled and moulded upon Continental principles and meeting in due course an inevitable fate, or whether you will be a great country,—an Imperial country—a country where your sons, when they rise, rise to paramount positions, and obtain not merely the esteem of their countrymen, but command the respect of the world. Upon you depends the issue. Whatever may be the general feeling, you must remember that in fighting against Liberalism or the Continental system you are fighting against those who have the advantage of power—against those who have been in high places for nearly half a century. You have nothing to trust to but your own energy and the sublime instinct of an ancient people. You must act as if everything depended on your individual efforts. The secret of success is constancy of purpose. Go to your homes, and teach there these truths, which will soon be imprinted on the conscience of the land. Make each man feel how much rests on his own exertions. The highest, like my noble friend the chairman, may lend us his great aid. But rest assured that the assistance of the humblest is not less efficient. Act in this spirit, and you will succeed. You will maintain your country in its present position. But you will do more than that—you will deliver to your posterity a land of liberty, of prosperity, of power, and of glory.

Benjamin Disraeli, *The Inaugural Address and Speeches of the Rt Hon B. Disraeli, MP, at Glasgow, November 1873* (London: Longmans, Green and Co, 1873). 2ⁿᵈ edition, 1–69

Bodleian Library

Elected Lord Rector of Glasgow University two years earlier, in November 1873 Disraeli visited Glasgow. On 19 November, he attended his installation as Lord Rector, held at the Kibble Crystal Palace in the Botanical Gardens, a large circular glass building capable of holding an audience of 4,000. Before the ceremony, the large number of students attending sang snatches of patriotic songs, indulging in repeated rounds of applause for their favourites. Disraeli's entrance was hailed with loud and enthusiastic applause. Throughout his Address and at its close Disraeli was keenly cheered. At a Banquet given to him by the City that evening in City-hall, the Lord Provost introduced Disraeli as a man of genius and brilliant talents. The next day Disraeli, again at the City-hall, received the Freedom of the City. On 22 November, he spoke to a meeting of the Conservative Association of Glasgow and at 5 o'clock the next afternoon he received at Maclean's Hotel a deputation of operatives, the Short Time Committee, campaigning for the Nine Hours' Factory bill. Prior to leaving Glasgow on 24 November, Disraeli launched a new steamship, the *Beta*, for service with the Cunard Company carrying the Royal Mail from Britain to Halifax, Bermuda and St Thomas. It was reported that an immense crowd of workers in the shipyard enthusiastically cheered him.

The most politically partisan speech Disraeli gave at Glasgow was to the Conservative Association. He asked why, in their own estimation, the Liberal government, distinguished by its self-proclaimed talent and success in passing measures of immense magnitude, was, by their own admission, unpopular? The reason, Disraeli answered, was that the Liberal ministry had harassed trades and worried professions, attacked every class and institution, introduced legislation for Ireland that had caused veiled rebellion, pursued an urge for yet further parliamentary Reform, and allowed relations between capital and labour to sour. This relentless and restless Liberal exertion, moreover, have been pursued against the background across Europe of a fundamental contest between spiritual truths, moral certainties, and temporal power. The anxiety, uncertainty, and agitation created by Liberal restlessness denying that deeper yearning for stability and calm desired by the British people.

19

BENJAMIN DISRAELI, *THE INAUGURAL ADDRESS AND SPEECHES OF THE RT HON B. DISRAELI, MP, AT GLASGOW, NOVEMBER 1873*

(London: Longmans, Green and Co, 1873),
2nd edition, 1–69

Inaugural address delivered at the College of Glasgow, November 19, 1873

MR. PRINCIPAL, PROFESSORS, AND STUDENTS—

MY first duty, and my deepest gratification, is to thank you for the honour which you conferred on me two years ago. It is a high one. No one can be insensible to sympathy from the unknown, but the pleasure is necessarily heightened when it is offered by the educated and refined; when that body is representative, and, above all, when it represents the youth of a famous country.

My next duty, and one of which the fulfilment is scarcely less gratifying, is to avail myself of the privilege attendant on the office to which you have raised me, and to offer you some observations either on the course of your studies or the conduct of your lives, which, if made by me, will be made without pretence or presumption, quite satisfied if, when we are separated, any chance remark of mine may recur to your memory, and lead you to not altogether unprofitable meditation.

Were I to follow my own bent, I would dwell on those delightful studies which occupy a considerable portion of your time within your academic halls, studies which, while they form your taste and strengthen your intelligence, will prove to you in future years both a guide and a consolation; but when I recollect the illustrious roll of those who have preceded me in this office, and remember how fully and how recently many of them have devoted their genius and their learning to such an enterprise, I am inclined to think that the field, though in my opinion inexhaustible, has been for the present sufficiently cultivated, and that as you are about to enter life at a period which promises, or rather which threatens, to be momentous, it would not be inappropriate were I to make some observations which may tend to assist you in your awaiting trials.

He who would succeed in life, and obtain that position to which his character and capacity entitle him, has need of two kinds of knowledge. It would seem at the first blush that self-knowledge were not very difficult of attainment. If there be any subject on which a person can arrive at accurate conclusions, it should be his own disposition and his own talents. But it is not so. The period of youth in this respect is one of great doubt and difficulty. It is a period alike of false confidence and unreasonable distrust, of perplexity, of despondency, and sometimes of despair. It has been said by an eminent physician that there are very few persons of either sex who have attained their eighteenth year who have not contemplated withdrawing from the world—withdrawing from that world which, in fact, they have never entered. Doubtless, this morbid feeling is occasioned in a great degree by a dread of the unknown, but it is also much to be attributed to, and it certainly is heightened by, an ignorance of themselves.

How, then, is this self-knowledge to be acquired, and where are we to obtain assistance in this quest? From the family circle? Its incompetency in this respect is a proverb. Perception of character is always a rare gift, but around the domestic hearth it is almost unknown. Every one is acquainted with the erroneous estimates of their offspring which have been made even by illustrious parents. The silent, but perhaps pensive, boy is looked upon as a dullard, while the flippancy of youth in a commonplace character is interpreted into a dangerous vivacity which may in time astonish, perhaps even alarm, the world. A better criterion should be found in the judgment of contemporaries who are our equals. But the generous ardour of youth is not favourable to critical discrimination. Its sympathy is quick, it admires and applauds; but it lavishes its applause and admiration on qualities which are often not intrinsically important, and it always exaggerates. And thus it is that the hero of school and of college often disappoints expectation in after life. The truth is, he has shown no deficiency in the qualities which obtained him his early repute, but he has been wanting in the capacity adapted to subsequent opportunities.

Some are of opinion that the surest judge of youthful character must be the tutor. And there is a passage in Isocrates on this head not without interest. He was an accomplished instructor, and he tells us he always studied to discover the bent of those who attended his lectures. So, after due observation, he would say to one, 'You are intended for action, and the camp is the life which will become you;' to another 'You should cultivate poetry;' a third was adapted to the passionate exercitations of the Pnyx; while a fourth was clearly destined for the groves and porticoes of philosophy. The early Jesuits, who were masters of education, were accustomed to keep secret registers of their observations on their pupils, and generations afterwards, when these records were examined, it is said the happy prescience of their remarks was strikingly proved by the subsequent success of many who had attained fame in arts and arms. But the Jesuits, gentlemen, whatever they may be now, were then very clever men; and I must confess that I am doubtful whether the judgment of tutors in general would be as infallible as that of Isocrates.

398

In the first place, a just perception of character is always a rare gift. When possessed in a high degree it is the quality which specially indicates the leader of men. It is that which enables a General or a Minister to select the fit instrument for the public purpose; without which all the preparations for a campaign, however costly and complete, may be fruitless, and all the deliberations of councils and all the discussions of Parliament prove mere dust and wind. Scholars and philosophers are in general too much absorbed by their own peculiar studies or pursuits to be skilled in the discrimination of character, and if the aptitude of a pupil is recognised by them, it is generally when he has evinced a disposition to excel in some branch of acquirement which has established their own celebrity.

No, gentlemen, I believe, after all, it will be found that it is best and inevitable, in the pursuit of self-knowledge, that we should depend on self-communion. Unquestionably, where there is a strong predisposition, it will assert itself in spite of all obstacles, but even here only after an initiation of many errors and much self-deception. One of the fruitful sources of that self-deception is to be found in the susceptibility of the youthful mind. The sympathy is so quick that we are apt to transfer to our own persons the qualities which we admire in others. If it be the age of a great poet, his numbers are for ever resounding in our ears, and we sigh for his laurels; if a military age, nothing will content us but to be at the head of armies; if an age of oratory and politics, our spirit requires that we should be leaders of parties and Ministers of State. In some instances the predisposition may be true, but it is in the nature of things that the instances must be rare. In ninety-nine cases out of one hundred the feeling is not idiosyncratic but mimetic, and we have mistaken a quick sensibility for creative power. Then comes to a young man the period of disappointment and despondency. To publish poems which no one will read; to make speeches to which no one will listen; after reveries of leading armies and directing councils, to find yourself, on your entrance into the business of life, incapable of influencing the conduct of an ordinary individual,—all this is bitter; but all depends upon how the lesson is received. A weak spirit will not survive this catastrophe of his self-love. He will sink into chronic despondency, and, without attempting to rally, he will pass through life as a phantom, and be remembered, as an old man, only by the golden promise of his deceptive youth. But a man of sense will accept these consequences, however apparently mortifying, with courage and candour. He will dive into his own intelligence, he will analyse the circumstances of his failure, he will discriminate how much was occasioned by indigenous deficiencies, and how much may be attributed to external and fortuitous circumstances. And in this severe introspection he may obtain that self-knowledge he requires; his failures may be the foundation of his ultimate success, and in this moral and intellectual struggle he may discover the true range of his powers, and the right bent of his character and capacity.

So much, gentlemen, for self-knowledge, a subject that for ages has furnished philosophers with treatises. I do not pretend to be a philosopher, and I have not offered you a treatise, but I have made some remarks which are, at least, the result of my own observation.

But assuming that you have at length attained this indispensable self-knowledge, and that you have an opportunity, in the pursuits of life, of following the bent of your disposition, we come now to the second and not less important condition of success in life: have you that other kind of knowledge which is required?—do you comprehend the spirit of the age in which your faculties are to be exercised? Hitherto you have been as explorers in a mountain district. You have surveyed and examined valleys, you have penetrated gorges, you have crossed many a ridge and range, till at length, having overcome all obstacles, you have reached the crest of the commanding height, and, like the soldiers of Xenophon, you behold the sea. But the sea that you behold is the Ocean of Life! In what vessels are you going to embark? With what instruments are you furnished? What is the port of your destination?

It is singular that though there is no lack of those who will explain the past, and certainly no want of those who will predict the future, when the present is concerned—the present that we see and feel—our opinions about it are in general bewildered and mistaken. And yet, without this acquaintance with the spirit of the age in which we live, whatever our culture and whatever our opportunities, it is probable that our lives may prove a blunder. When the young King of Macedon decided that the time had arrived when Europe should invade Asia, he recognised the spirit of his age. The revelations of the weakness of the Great King, which had been made during the immortal expedition of the Ten Thousand, and still more during the campaigns of Agesilaus, had gradually formed a public opinion which Alexander dared to represent. When Caius Julius perceived that the colossal empire formed by the Senate and populace of Rome could not be sustained on the municipal institutions of a single city, however illustrious, he understood the spirit of the age. Constantine understood the spirit of his age when he recognised the Sign under which he was resolved to conquer. I think that Luther recognised the spirit of the age when he nailed his Theses against Indulgences to the gates of a Thuringian church. The great Princes of the House of Tudor, and the statesmen they employed, were all persons who understood the spirit of their age.

But it may be said, 'These are heroic instances. A perception of the spirit of their age may be necessary to the success of princes and statesmen, but is not needful, or equally needful, for those of lesser degree.' I think there would be fallacy in this criticism, and that the necessity of this knowledge pervades the whole business of life. Take, for example, the choice of a profession; a knowledge of the spirit of the age may save a young man from embracing a profession which the spirit of the age dooms to become obsolete. It is the same with the pursuits of commerce. This knowledge may guard a man from embarking his capital in a decaying trade, or from forming connexions and even establishments in countries from which the spirit of the age is gradually diverting all commercial transactions. I would say a knowledge of the spirit of the age is necessary for every public man, and in a country like ours, where the subject is called upon hourly to exercise rights and to fulfil duties which, in however small a degree, go to the aggregate of that general sentiment which ultimately governs States, every one is a public man, although he may not be a public character.

But it does not follow, because the spirit of the age is perceived and recognised, it should be embraced and followed, or even that success in life depends upon adopting it. What I wished to impress upon you was that success in life depended on comprehending it. The spirit of the age may be an unsound and injurious spirit; it may be the moral duty of a man, not only not to defer to, but to resist it, and if it be unsound and injurious, in so doing he will not only fulfil his duty, but he may accomplish his success in life. The spirit of the age, for instance, was in favour of the Crusades. They occasioned a horrible havoc of human life; they devastated Asia and exhausted Europe; and, in all probability, in acting in this instance according to the spirit of the age, a man would have forfeited his life, and certainly wasted his estate, with no further satisfaction than having massacred some Jews and slain some Saracens.

What then, gentlemen, is the spirit of the age in which we ourselves live; of that world which in a few years, more or less, you will have all entered; where you are to establish yourselves in life; where you have to encounter in that object every conceivable difficulty; perplexities of judgment, material obstacles, tests of all your qualities, and searching trials of your character; and all these circumstances more or less affected by the spirit of the age, an acquaintance with which will assist you in forming your decisions and in guiding your course?

It appears to me that I should not greatly err were I to describe the spirit of this age as the spirit of equality; but 'equality' is a word of wide import, under which various schools of thought may assemble and yet arrive at different and even contradictory conclusions. I hold that Civil equality—that is, equality of all subjects before the law, and that a law which recognises the personal rights of all subjects—is the only foundation of a perfect commonwealth—one which secures to all liberty, order, and justice. The principle of Civil equality has long prevailed in this kingdom. It has been applied during the last half-century more finely and completely to the constantly and largely varying circumstances of the country; but it had prevailed more or less in Britain for centuries, and I attribute the patriotism of our population mainly to this circumstance, and I believe that it has had more to do with the security of the soil than those geographical attributes usually enlarged upon.

Another land, long our foe, but now our rival only in the arts of peace, thought fit, at the end of the last century, to reconstruct its social system, and to rebuild it on the principle of Social equality. To effect this object it was prepared to make, and it made, great sacrifices. It subverted all the institutions of the country: a Monarchy of 800 years whose traditionary and systematic policy had created the kingdom; a National Church—for, though Romanist, it had secured its liberties; a tenure of land which maintained a valiant nobility, that never can be restored; it confiscated all endowments, and abolished all corporations; erased from the map of the soil all the ancient divisions, and changed the landmarks and very name of the country. Indeed, it entirely effected its purpose, which was to destroy all the existing social elements and level the past to the dust. This experiment has had fair play, and you can judge of its results by the experience of eighty years.

It is not in Scotland that the name of France will ever be mentioned without affection, and I will not yield to any Scotchman in my appreciation of the brilliant qualities and the resplendent achievements of its gifted people. We are not blind to their errors, but their calamities are greater than their errors, and their merits are greater than their calamities. When I heard that their bright city was beleaguered, and that the breach was in the wall, I confess I felt that pang which I remember, as a child, I always experienced when I read of Lysander entering the City of the Violet Crown. But, gentlemen, I may on this occasion be permitted to say that of all the many services which France has rendered to Europe—Europe, that land of ancient creeds and ancient Governments, and manners and customs older than both—not the least precious is the proof she has afforded to us that the principle of Social equality is not one on which a nation can safely rely in the hour of trial and in the day of danger. Then it is found that there is no one to lead and nothing to rally round. There is not a man in the country who can assemble fifty people. And rightly: since for an individual to direct is an usurpation of the sovereignty of the many. Those who ought to lead feel isolated, and those who wish to obey know not to whom to proffer their devotion. All personal influences are dead. All depends on the Central Government, a sufficient power in fair weather, but in stormy times generally that part of the machine which first breaks.

Civil equality prevails in Britain, and Social equality prevails in France. The essence of civil equality is to abolish privilege; the essence of social equality is to destroy classes. If the principle of equality at the present day assumed only these two forms, I do not think there would be much to perplex you in your choice, or in your judgment as to their respective results. But that is not so. The equality which is now sought by vast multitudes of men in many countries, which is enforced by writers not deficient in logic, in eloquence, and even learning, scarcely deigns to recognise civil equality, and treats social equality only as an obsolete truth. No moral or metaphysical elements will satisfy them. They demand physical and material equality. This is the disturbing spirit which is now rising like a moaning wind in Europe, and which, when you enter the world, may possibly be a raging storm. It may, therefore, be as well that your attention should be called to its nature, and that you may be led to consider its consequences.

The leading principle of this new school is that there is no happiness which is not material, and that every living being has a right to a share in that physical welfare. The first obstacle to their purpose is found in the rights of private property. Therefore, they must be abolished. But the social system must be established on some principle; and, therefore, for the rights of property they would substitute the rights of labour. Now, the rights of labour cannot be fully enjoyed if there be any limit to employment. The great limit to employment, to the rights of labour, and to the physical and material equality of man, is found in the division of the world into states and nations. Thus, as civil equality would abolish privilege, social equality would destroy classes; so material and physical equality strikes at the principle of patriotism, and is prepared to abrogate countries.

Now I am addressing a race of men who are proud, and justly proud, of their country. I know not that the sentiment of patriotism beats in any breast more strongly than in that of a Scotchman. Neither time nor distance, I believe, enfeebles that passion. It is as vehement on the banks of the Ganges as on the banks of the Clyde, and in the speculative turmoil of Melbourne as in the bustling energy of Glasgow. Why is a Scotchman proud of his country? Because the remembrance of it awakes a tradition of heroic exploits and inspiring emotions; of sacrifices for its sake in the field and on the scaffold; of high examples of military skill and civil prudence; of literary and scientific fame; of commanding eloquence and profound philosophy, and of fascinating poesy and romance; all of which a Scotchman feels ennoble his existence, and all of which he is conscious have inevitably sprung from the circumstances of his native land. So that the very configuration of the soil and the temper of the clime have influenced his private virtues and his public life, as they unquestionably have given a form and colour to those works of creative genius which have gained the sympathy and admiration of the world.

No, gentlemen, it is not true that the only real happiness is physical happiness; it is not true that physical happiness is the highest happiness; it is not true that physical happiness is a principle on which you can build up a flourishing and enduring commonwealth. A civilised community must rest on a large realised capital of thought and sentiment; there must be a reserved fund of public morality to draw upon in the exigencies of national life. Society has a soul as well as a body. The traditions of a nation are part of its existence. Its valour and its discipline, its religious faith, its venerable laws, its science and erudition, its poetry, its art, its eloquence and its scholarship, are as much portions of its life as its agriculture, its commerce, and its engineering skill. Nay, I would go further, I would say that without these qualities material excellence cannot be attained.

But, gentlemen, the new philosophy strikes further than at the existence of patriotism. It strikes at the home; it strikes at the individuality of man. It would reduce civilised society to human flocks and herds. That it may produce in your time much disturbance, possibly much destruction, I pretend not to deny; but I must express my conviction that it will not ultimately triumph. I hold that the main obstacles to its establishment are to be found in human nature itself. They are both physical and moral. If it be true, as I believe, that an aristocracy distinguished merely by wealth must perish from satiety, so I hold it is equally true that a people who recognise no higher aim than physical enjoyment must become selfish and enervated. Under such circumstances the supremacy of race, which is the key of history, will assert itself. Some human progeny, distinguished by their bodily vigour or their masculine intelligence, or by both qualities, will assert their superiority, and conquer a world which deserves to be enslaved. It will then be found that our boasted progress has only been an advancement in a circle, and that our new philosophy has brought us back to that old serfdom which it has taken ages to extirpate.

But the still more powerful—indeed, I hold the insurmountable—obstacle to the establishment of the new opinions will be furnished by the essential elements of the human mind. Our idiosyncracy is not bounded by the planet which we inhabit. We can investigate space and we can comprehend eternity. No considerations limited to this sphere have hitherto furnished the excitement which man requires, or the sanctions for his conduct which his nature imperatively demands. The spiritual nature of man is stronger than Codes or Constitutions. No Government can endure which does not recognise that for its foundation, and no legislation last which does not flow from this fountain. The principle may develope itself in manifold forms—shape of many Creeds and many Churches; but the principle is divine. As time is divided into day and night, so religion rests upon the providence of God and the responsibility of man. One is manifest, the other mysterious; but both are facts. Nor is there, as some would teach you, anything in these convictions which tends to contract our intelligence or our sympathies. On the contrary, religion invigorates the intellect and expands the heart. He who has a due sense of his relations to God is best qualified to fulfil his duties to man. A fine writer of antiquity—perhaps the finest—has recorded in a beautiful passage his belief in Divine Providence, and in the necessity of universal toleration:—

'Ἐγὼ μὲν οὖν, καὶ ταῦτα, καὶ τὰ πάντ' ἀεὶ,
Φάσκοιμ' ἂν ἀνθρώποισι μηχανᾶν θεούς·
Ὅτῳ δὲ μὴ τάδ' ἐστὶν ἐν γνώμῃ φίλα,
Κεῖνός τ' ἐκεῖνα στοργέτω, κἀγὼ τάδε.'

These lines were written, more than two thousand years ago, by the most Attic of Athenian poets. In the perplexities of life I have sometimes found in them a solace and a satisfaction; and I now deliver them to you, to guide your consciences and to guard your lives.

Speech at the banquet given by the City of Glasgow to the Lord Rector on the Same Day

MR. DISRAELI, who on rising to return thanks was loudly cheered, said—

MY LORD PROVOST AND GENTLEMEN,—I must thank you most cordially for the kind manner in which you have received the toast which his Lordship has just proposed, and for the courteous and munificent hospitality you have extended to me, without any reference to political opinion, as the Lord Provost has very properly intimated.

I have always thought it to be one of the happiest circumstances of public life in England that we have not permitted our political opinions to interfere with our social enjoyments. I believe it is a characteristic of the country; at least, I am not aware that it is shared by any other. For instance, if you are on the Continent and wish to pay your respects to a Minister and go to his Reception, you are invited by the Minister. The consequence is you find no one there except those who follow him. It is not so in England. I remember some years ago meeting under the charming roof of one of the most accomplished women of the time the most celebrated diplomatist of certainly this half century, and he said to me, 'What a wonderful

404

system of society you have in England! I have not been on speaking terms with Lord Palmerston for three weeks, and yet here I am; but you see I am paying a visit to Lady Palmerston.'

It is unnecessary to dwell now on what may be the causes that produce this happy state of society in this country, which is essentially a political country, and therefore the circumstance is more to be valued. At the same time there is no doubt that by mixing together with this freedom both parties become acquainted with some political traits with which they might not otherwise be conversant. I did not know until to-night, for example, when we have heard it from a great authority, that it was a leading principle of the Liberal party not to give their opponents credit either for talents or patriotism. I may have heard it before, but I thought it must be the assertion of some malignant Tory. What I wish to say for the Conservative party is that it is not the principle which we adopt. We all give our opponents credit for the greatest abilities and the best intentions, although we may intimate our occasional regret that those abilities are misapplied, and that, whatever may be their good intentions, they meet that destiny which is proverbially provided for that kind of article.

Gentlemen, I thank you for the kindness with which you have received the intimation of the Lord Provost with regard to my own political career. I would not trouble you with touching on it further, but after the allusion which has been made perhaps you will permit me to say that it has been my fortune to be the leader in the House of Commons of one of the great parties of the State for twenty-five years, and that there is no record, I believe, in the Parliamentary history of the country of the duration of a leadership equal to it. There have been in my time two illustrious instances of the great parties being led by most eminent men; one was the instance of Sir Robert Peel, who led the Tory party for eighteen years, though unfortunately it twice broke asunder; there was also the instance of one who is still spared to us, and who, I hope, will be long spared to us, for he is the pride of this country as he was the honour of the House of Commoms—Lord John Russell. He led one of the great parties seventeen years, though at last it slipped out of his hands.

Do not suppose I make these observations in any vain spirit. The reason why I have been able to lead any party for such a period, and under circumstances of some difficulty and discouragement, is that the party with which I am connected is really the most generous and the most indulgent party that ever existed. I cannot help smiling sometimes when I hear of those convenient intimations given by those, who know all the secrets of the political world, of the extreme anxiety of the Conservative party to get rid of my services. The fact is, the Conservative party can get rid of my services whenever they give me any intimation that such is their desire. All I can say is, whenever I have desired to relieve them of it, they have only too kindly insisted on my retaining the lead, and the only difference to me has been that they were more indulgent and more kind. I will not trespass on the rule of the evening by making any further political allusion, but I hope you will allow me to think that I was justified in making these remarks.

Unfortunately the Lord Provost has touched on a subject, with great kindness and even minuteness, which is one I cannot even allude to. I think that an author who speaks about his own books is almost as bad as a mother who talks about her own children. You know what happens under those circumstances. Everybody present soon gets wrapt in abstraction—one looks at the ceiling, another at the fire, one sighs, and another, perhaps, yawns. That is the general result of the introduction of such a topic, and I have always thought that a literary man who talks of his own writings must be put in the same category of boredom as the mother who dilates on the qualities of her darlings. Allow me now to express my surprise and delight that a rhapsody in 'Vivian Grey,' written nearly fifty years ago, has received the high honour, in one of the greatest cities of the kingdom, of being introduced to your indulgence. Gentlemen, on this subject I will merely say that, whatever the merits or demerits of my works, they were at least the result of my own feelings and my own observation.

Gentlemen, it is my fate, unfortunately, to pay a visit to one of the greatest commercial communities, I may say of the world, at a time when the commercial world is a little agitated. I have always found in my own experience that when the Bank rate of interest was at a minimum of 9 per cent., or something of that kind, my correspondence with Glasgow immensely increased. Therefore, I will make one or two remarks on that subject, because I must say that I cannot myself give my adhesion to the alarm which some feel at what some think a collapse in our commercial prosperity. I cannot myself see any signs of such declension; and I would rather attribute the somewhat startling results which have been recently witnessed to other causes.

I do not observe myself that there are any symptoms in Britain of reckless speculation, or any circumstances which can justify the alarm which has lately prevailed and the inconveniences which no doubt have been very generally felt. I see that there is no reduction in the returns of the railways or the wages of those connected with them, and I have always found that a very good sign as to the national prosperity and the general state of trade. I do not find that there are any dangerous commitments to foreign loans, which are generally so abundant, but less at this moment than usual, nor do I see any evidence of reckless speculation of any kind.

No doubt our young relations on the other side of the Atlantic—with that ardour which is characteristic of youth—have been doing some things somewhat improvident; no doubt they have commenced many undertakings without any capital whatever. We may perhaps attribute this outburst of speculation to the unexpected receipt of the 'Alabama' money. I have known young people, when they came into a fortune unexpectedly, playing rigs of that kind, and quite astonished at what it ends in. But the commercial system of this country is now so vast and various that, with the greatest respect for our Transatlantic cousins—and no one has a greater respect and regard for them than myself—I do not believe that the disorders which have arisen there could have occasioned, or were adequate to occasion, the disorders that have occurred in our own country with reference to the value of money. I attribute them to quite another cause, and if I touch on that cause, which I shall very briefly, I do it because I think the cause is not exhausted, and is deserving the grave attention of men who are so deeply interested in the prosperity of the country and the action of commerce as those I have the pleasure of meeting to-day.

I attribute the great monetary disturbance that has occurred, and is now to a certain degree acting very injuriously to trade—I attribute it to the great changes which the Governments in Europe are making with reference to their standard of value. You, of course, are perfectly acquainted with all these circumstances to which I allude. I attribute the present state of affairs very much to a Commission that was sitting in Paris at the time of the great Exhibition. That was a Commission the object of which was to establish a uniform coinage throughout the world—a beautiful idea of cosmopolitan philanthropy, which probably if it could be fulfilled would do no great harm; though I think it would be difficult to attain. The Commission of Paris never came to a definite recommendation on this subject, but they did on another subject, and that was that no time should be lost by any of the States of Europe in taking steps to establish a uniform gold standard of value. This, I know myself, arose from an opinion extremely prevalent among the statesmen of Europe and among distinguished economists and merchants abroad, that the commercial prosperity and preponderance of England were to be attributed to her gold standard. Now, our gold standard is, I think, an invaluable arrangement. I think that any country which has a gold standard of value should, to use a celebrated expression, think once, twice, and thrice before it gives it up. But it is the greatest delusion in the world to attribute the commercial preponderance and prosperity of England to our having a gold standard. Our gold standard is not the cause of our commercial prosperity, but the consequence of our commercial prosperity; and it is very well for us to have it: but you cannot establish a gold standard by violent means. It must arise gradually from the large transactions of the country, and the consequent command it may have over the precious metals. When the various States of Europe suddenly determined to have a gold standard, and took steps to carry it into effect, it was quite evident we must prepare ourselves for convulsions in the money-market, not occasioned by speculation or any old cause, which has been alleged, but by a new cause with which we are not yet sufficiently acquainted, and the consequences of which are very embarrassing; and that is the reason I have taken the opportunity of calling your attention to it.

Take the case of Germany. At this moment it is most remarkable, when there has been such a want of a gold standard in various parts of Europe, and even in England, where the strain has been so great, Germany has at this moment fifty millions sterling of gold coin virtually locked up; and it is locked up because it is the object of Germany to substitute a gold coinage for a silver coinage. While it has fifty millions value in gold coinage locked up, it has eighty or ninety millions of silver circulating, and they know very well, if they were to attempt to substitute violently the gold for the silver coinage—fifty millions of gold against ninety millions of silver—the consequence would be that the silver, already reduced in value, would become reduced still more, and the fifty millions of gold would all leave Germany. The consequence is that Germany is taking violent steps to get rid of this silver. The other day Germany sent a large amount of silver to Calcutta, and Germany could only by artificial means transmit it. The result was for a considerable time you could not buy a single bill on England. These are all circumstances calculated to disturb the course of commerce and manufacturing arrangements.

Then, again, take the case of France and America, which are floating on inconvertible paper; but France has also at this moment ninety millions sterling in silver coin. What must be the position of France with all her silver already depreciated, if Germany, to establish a gold standard, forces her own silver into France? France would be in a position of much embarrassment, and would make violent efforts to establish as soon as she can a gold coinage at any cost. Vast disturbance and fluctuations must arise from such circumstances. I regret to treat matters of this kind at a moment like this, because they require to be treated with more precision of language and with greater patience than either I or you can afford at this moment, but it did appear to me a subject to which I ought to call your attention.

You are commercial men, interested in the monetary system of the world; you ought to have your eye carefully upon the efforts which are making to establish a gold standard of value in Germany, in France, and, soon you will find, also in America. Legally, of course, there is a gold standard in America, but virtually there is not. Holland and all the Scandinavian States have also established a gold standard, probably to protect themselves from a depreciated currency; and when countries inundated with silver are trying to get rid of it, convulsions must come, and no one would be able to form an adequate idea of the monetary arrangements of the times in which he lives if he omits from his consideration the circumstances to which I have called your attention. I have drawn your attention to it today because you must know it is very difficult for me to address you under the conditions in which we meet. Munificent as is your hospitality, and cordial as may be your reception, it would scarcely do that our meeting to-day should be a mere interchange of compliments. To a certain degree that is very agreeable; one glass of liqueur is appropriate, but none of you would like to dine off a bottle of maraschino. A famous monarch, King Louis-Philippe, once said to me that he attributed the great success of the British nation in political life to their talking politics after dinner. Gentlemen, unfortunately to-day that is the only subject on which I may not enter, and therefore I hope that will be some excuse if I have touched on a question which is not a party question.

Let me, however, before I sit down, thank you, with my utmost heart, for the most cordial manner in which you have received me in your great city. I assure you the events of this day, both in the morning and evening, will not be easily erased from my memory. It is my first visit to your city. I think it is nearly half a century since I first visited Scotland. I remember it well, not only because I saw for the first time a memorable country, but because I made the personal acquaintance and became the guest of one of the best and greatest of men, the Lord of Abbotsford. He was a friend of my father, and he received me with that kindness which the illustrious do not, unfortunately, always bestow on the young. I remember walking with him in those new plantations of which he was so proud, by the banks of that River Tweed which he loved so well. He poured out all the treasures of his fancy and his memory, all the fire and music of his mind; he took as much pains to interest and entertain me as if, instead of being an unknown youth, I had been the Lord Rector of a famous University. That was the good nature of the man, which was as great as his genius.

How much has happened in those fifty years—a period more remarkable than any, I will venture to say, in the annals of mankind? I am not thinking of the rise and fall of empires, the change of dynasties, the establishment of governments. I am thinking of those revolutions of science, which have had much more effect than any political causes; which have changed the position and prospects of mankind more than all the conquests and all the codes, of all the Conquerors and all the Legislators that ever existed. In that time, gentlemen, you and your society have not been idle. You have raised your town to a position among the great cities of the world. Long may you retain that position; long may you retain that energy which has rendered your Clyde as famous as the Thames and the Seine; long may your factories be full of creative life; long may you appropriate the metallic treasures of your teeming soil; long may your docks and harbours receive and furnish navies. Under Divine Providence that prosperity will remain if you retain your public spirit. That depends upon your patriotism and your self-respect, and those sentiments can never in the British isles assume a more legitimate and fairer form than when they take the shape of loyalty and freedom. Gentlemen, I drink to your healths—all.

Speech on receiving the freedom of the City of Glasgow, in a Gold Box, Nov. 20, 1873, in the City Hall

MR. DISRAELI, who was received with loud and prolonged cheering, said—

MY LORD PROVOST AND GENTLEMEN,—Notwithstanding the kind and considerate terms in which the Lord Provost has alluded to the public accidents of my life, whether political or literary, and notwithstanding the cordial manner in which you have received those observations, I cannot for a moment permit any feeling of personal vanity to misinterpret the cause why I have received to-day this distinguished honour, bestowed in a manner which I cannot forget. I feel that it is owing to my connection with the University of Glasgow. I feel that you, the citizens of Glasgow, have, wisely and well, taken the opportunity of expressing the entire sympathy which subsists between the city and the University, and that you could do it in no manner more agreeable to them at this moment, and more convenient, than in honouring the individual whom they have so much honoured.

Gentlemen, I look upon that connection between the city and the University of Glasgow as a most valuable one, and which should be ever cherished. There is not any city connected with a University which has not become illustrious. The mutual influence of both institutions is most beneficial. On the one hand, it softens the habits of those who are devoted to the busy purposes of life; while the contiguity of the University to a great city like Glasgow infuses a knowledge of the world which those who are secluded in cloisters cannot command. I am happy to remember that this connection of affection between these two great institutions has always prevailed. I have read, at least certainly in works of the last century, that there existed in this city an example of a commercial and literary association, which may, perhaps, even now survive, which was illustrious from its members, and in which the merchants of Glasgow met names not second to any in the roll of British worthies. Adam Smith, known to the whole world as the highest authority on one of the highest of subjects, celebrated men of science, philosophers like the ingenious Reid and the illustrious Hutchinson, were members of that association, and exercised their influence upon the public mind and spirit of this community. Nor need I remind you that the connection with the University has not been wanting in material advantage to this great city. The discoveries of philosophers in the University have influenced most advantageously the material fortunes of Glasgow. I need not allude to the inventions of Black and others which you have carried into practice, and which have given such an impetus to your industrial life, but I may perhaps be permitted to say, as Lord Rector of the University, that it would be most delightful to me if I could hear of some public acknowledgment on the part of some distinguished citizen of Glasgow on that subject, so that I might see the hall of our University raised with becoming splendour from the ground which is, unfortunately, now unoccupied.

I have observed that it is characteristic, a happy characteristic, of the age in which we live that men become their own executors, and I should be delighted to hear of some munificent endowment which would place our University in the position which it deserves. I feel confidence in appealing to the wealthy citizens of this opulent city, because it is, after all, in cities that enlightenment looks for its natural home; it is here, it is in great cities, especially those that have been intellectually influenced by the existence of Universities, that we find letters and arts and science flourish. The city, indeed, is the natural home of civilization. It is in cities that have been discovered those inventions which have given an impulse to the education of the human mind. Priests and princes may have devised hieroglyphics and cuneiform writing, but nobody will deny that the alphabet was invented by merchants and manufacturers. Therefore, gentlemen, I trust that my election to the great office to which I have been raised may not be any impediment to the natural flow of the dispositions of the citizens of Glasgow, and that during the period that I may exercise any influence over the conduct of the University it will not be recorded as one in which it made no advance in its material fortunes.

Now, my Lord Provost and gentlemen, let me offer you my thanks for the distinction which you have conferred on me to-day. There is nothing which animates public men more than the prospect that they may obtain the sympathy and respect of their fellow citizens. It is acts like these and scenes like these that sustain men in the turmoil and struggle of public life. Here we meet that approbation which is the great meed of public efforts; to live in the affections and afterwards in the memory of our fellow subjects is what every man looks to as the chief object of

410

his career. I shall not forget the new position which I have occupied this day. I shall show at all times, not only that I am proud of the distinction which you have conferred upon me, but that I am faithful to the duties which it entails, and if ever the rights and interests of the city of Glasgow are invaded or imperilled there will be at least, I assure you, one Burgess on whose efforts to maintain them you need not fail to rely.

Reply to the address of the Short Time Committee of Scotch Operatives, Nov. 23, 1873

Mr. Disraeli said—

Gentlemen,—I remember my support of the Ten Hours Bill as one of the most satisfactory incidents of my life, and therefore I need not say that I sympathize generally with your views. That measure was opposed by persons of great influence and by many parties in the State, and at one time it seemed impossible that it could have succeeded, because then neither of the two great parties avowedly upheld it. But as time advanced it was successful in its progress, and I am glad to say that those with whom I act generally in public life uniformly and unanimously upheld it; and they have been repaid for the great effort which they made—because it was not made without sacrifice—by the results. It has tended to the elevation of the working classes of this country. That elevation depends upon two causes. If their wages rise and their hours of labour diminish they are placed in a most favourable position; and if they do not avail themselves of the position they only prove that they are unworthy of it.

With regard to the first point, involving financial considerations—I refer to wages—no legislation can interfere. The rate of wages must be left to those inexorable rules of political economy to which we must all bow. They depend on demand and supply; but when you come to the hours of labour you then enter into social considerations, and in these the Legislature can interfere, and, if we use discretion and wisdom, no doubt to the advantage of the country and the working classes.

With regard to the particular point brought before me, it is not for the first time. Two years ago, in the centre of British industry, the great county of Lancaster, the glory of England, I received many communications and many deputations on the subject. I said at that time that it was unnecessary for me to state that I was favourable to the general policy, but as regarded the details of their particular proposal I requested that I should have confidence placed in me by the working classes; that they would allow me to consider its details when brought before Parliament in the shape of a practical measure, and that I could not pledge myself beyond a general sympathy with their cause. Since that time I have omitted no opportunity of making myself acquainted with the details of the subject brought before me to-day. I have communicated with great employers of labour. I have received from them much information, and I have made myself acquainted with their views, and all I can say now is that the result of my deliberations and of my researches

411

is favourable to the views which you uphold; but I reserve to myself the right, for your interests as much as my own, to take care that whenever this subject is discussed I should be considered perfectly free.

I should be opposed to any change in which the general sympathies of the employers were not with the employed. I believe, myself, that with dispassionate discussion, and with those inquiries proceeding in an impartial spirit to which I have referred, the result would be that there would be very little difference of opinion between the working classes generally and their employers; but I should desire that in making any alterations of this kind there should be a general concurrence of sentiment. I only wish to make one reference to an observation made by one member of this deputation, that I should subserve the interests of the Conservative party by carrying out the views which you have expressed. That member of the deputation may rest assured that in upholding these views I am not guided by the interests of any party. My views on this subject were formed long before I was in the responsible position I have the honour to hold as the leader of a party. My opinions have never changed. And it is to me a subject of gratification that the large majority of those with whom I act in public life have the same opinion on this subject as myself. But I could not for a moment consider this question with reference to the interest of a political party.

I believe it is for the welfare of the country that the working classes should rise, as I think they are rising, in social and political consideration. I have confidence in the working classes. I do not know any other order of men which is so interested in maintaining the glory and greatness of this country. I have long been of opinion that if that state of things is brought about which seems fast approaching, when, with the increased remuneration for their toil which they now possess, they have reasonable diminution of their labour, nobody will be placed in a more happy position than the intelligent and educated working classes of this country.

It is only by labour and constant employment that life really is endurable. It is delightful with constant occupation—without it, it is intolerable. Your life is a life of happiness so long as your labour is not so excessive that you cannot cultivate your intelligence, while you enjoy those recreations of existence which the working classes to a great degree at present enjoy, and which fifty years ago they did not possess. In answer to your address to-day, I do not wish to pledge myself in any detail to what you request, but I am sure your own reflection will convince you from my past conduct that when the subject is brought before the Legislature, I shall take that course which I think best for the interests of the country and for your advantage.

Speech, in the City Hall, on receiving an address of confidence from the Conservative Association of Glasgow, November 22, 1873

Mr. Disraeli, on rising to address the meeting, was received with the most enthusiastic cheers. He said—

Mr. Chairman and Gentlemen,—I am not using merely conventional language when I express to you the high honour that I feel in receiving this address from the Conservative Association of Glasgow. The gratification is increased by the chair being filled this day by one who was formerly a colleague of mine in Parliament, and whom, with others around me, I learnt to respect, and more than respect, for he gained the heart of the House of Commons while he sat there.

Gentlemen, I will not conceal from you, and, indeed, many and most of you know it, that when it was first suggested to me to receive this distinction, and to meet you here, after great reflection, I felt it my duty—though with pain—to refuse the honour which was intended for me. I did so, because I thought that, upon the whole, as my visit to Glasgow was an academic and neutral visit, it would be better that nothing should occur that might in any way make an exception to that general sentiment of respect which it is my pride and pleasure to say I have received from all classes and all parties in this city. And I must take this opportunity, as it may be the last I shall have, without reference to any political opinions, of expressing to the citizens of Glasgow my lively sense of the kind and considerate manner in which they have received me, and I must say the too great indulgence even of those who do not generally agree with me in political opinion.

But, Gentlemen, when I had been here some little time it was represented to me by those who spoke for a large body of my fellow countrymen that it seemed very hard upon them who, from their pursuits and other reasons, could take no part in august academical functions, or in the splendour of civic banquets, that, feeling deeply as they did on political subjects, one whom, however unworthy he may be of their confidence, they still regard as their chief, should be resident for nearly a week in this great city, in communication, apparently, with all but his humbler friends, who perhaps looked on him with not less confidence and affection. And I confess to you that although it had been my original hope that not a word should have fallen from these lips during my visit to Glasgow which should have been discordant to any individual in the city, I could not resist this appeal. It did appear to me to be so unfair, I would say so unkind and ungenerous, that I assented, after due consideration, to receive this address and meet you as we meet today, on terms which will permit me to make some observations to you on the present state of public affairs.

And I will here say, that there may be no misunderstanding with reference to some paragraphs I have seen in the public papers, that I never was asked and never assented to meet any separate body particularly styled 'Conservative Working Men.' I have never been myself at all favourable to a system which would induce Conservatives who are working men to form societies confined merely to their class. In the church and at the polling-booth all are equal. All that concerns Conservative working men and interests them concerns and interests the great body of Conservatives of whom they form a portion. Therefore, it is to the Conservative Association I see before me, of whom a very considerable majority consists of working men—it is to that Association that I address myself.

Mr. Chairman and Gentlemen,—I believe I may describe the position of this country as one of great prosperity. There is no doubt that during the last three years that prosperity has been generally acknowledged. There are some who suppose that it may have now received a check. If it has received a check it will increase, I hope, our circumspection, but I must express my own opinion that no substantial diminution in the sources of the prosperity so apparent during the last three years has occurred. I think we may fairly say the state of this country is one of great prosperity, and although I believe and know that it is a prosperity for which we are not indebted either to Whigs or Tories, although I know that it has been occasioned in a considerable degree, under Providence, by fortuitous though felicitous circumstances, I am perfectly ready, speaking to-day, as I hope to speak, in the fairest terms on public affairs, which I believe to be quite consistent with the position of the leader of a party—I am ready to give to Her Majesty's Government credit for the prosperity we feel and acknowledge.

With regard to Her Majesty's Ministers themselves, I will be equally candid, equally fair—I will take them at their own estimate. They have lost few opportunities of informing the country that they are men distinguished for commanding talent, admirable eloquence and transcendent administrative abilities. I dispute none of these propositions any more than I do the prosperity of the country. They also tell us that the country being so prosperous, and they having all these personal advantages, they have taken the opportunity during the last few years of passing measures of immense magnitude, only equalled by the benefit they have conferred upon the people.

Now, gentlemen, I will not question their own estimate of their ability, or even for a moment their own description of their achievements; but I ask this question,—What is the reason, when the country is so prosperous, when its affairs are administered by so gifted a Government, and when they have succeeded during five years in passing measures so vast and beneficent—what is the reason that Her Majesty's Ministers are going about regretting that they are so unpopular? Now, gentlemen, I beg you to observe that I did not say Her Majesty's Ministers are unpopular. It is they who say so. I stated their own case and their own position; I say that, under the circumstances I have put fairly before you, it is a remarkable circumstance, and the question must be inquired into—why persons in the position of Her Majesty's Government should on every occasion deplore the unpopularity they have incurred.

Now my opinion, gentlemen, is that that is not a question of mere curiosity—it is one that, as I think I shall show you, concerns the honour and the interests of the country. If the country is so prosperous—if Her Majesty's Ministers are so gifted—if they have had such an ample opportunity of showing the talents which they possess—if they have done all this good—if they have availed themselves of this signal opportunity to effect such great results, then the only inference we can draw from the unpopularity which they themselves deplore is that the people of this country is a fickle and ungrateful people. Therefore it is not a question of mere curiosity. It is a question that ought to be answered.

If there be those who suppose that the people of this country, as I hold, is not a fickle or ungrateful people—that they are a people who may be mistaken—that may be misled, but that they are a people who, on the whole, are steadfast in their convictions, and especially in their political convictions, then this question, if left unanswered, as Her Majesty's Ministers have placed the circumstances before the country, is a slur on the character of the people of this kingdom. I say it ought to be answered; and a short time since—some two months ago—I answered it.

It appeared to me, at that moment especially, when Her Majesty's Government, by their ablest and most powerful representatives, were deploring their unpopularity, and asking the reason why, or rather intimating by inference that it was the fault of the people, not of the Government, that some one should give an answer to that question. I gave it, and in a very brief form—in the most condensed and the most severely accurate form. There is not an expression in that description of the conduct of the Government which was not well weighed; there is not a word for which I had not warranty, and for which I could not adduce testimony ample and abounding. There was only one characteristic of that description which was not noticed at the time, and which I will now confess—it was not original, for six months before, in the House of Commons, I had used the same expressions and made the same statement—not in a hole or corner, but on the most memorable night of the Session, when there were six hundred members of the House of Commons present, when on the debate then taking place avowedly the fate of the Ministry depended.

It was at midnight that I rose to speak, and made the statement almost similar in expression, though perhaps stronger and more lengthened than the one which has become the cause of recent controversy. The Prime Minister followed me in that debate. The House of Commons knew what was depending upon the verdict about to be taken, and with all that knowledge they came to a division, and by a majority terminated the existence of the Government. Gentlemen, it surprises me, then, that having repeated that statement six months after, with the advantage of six months' more experience and observation, it should have so much offended Her Majesty's Government. The Ministers sighed and their newspapers screamed. The question I have to ask, and in this your interests are vitally concerned—the question is, was the statement I made a true and accurate one?

You cannot answer statements of this kind by saying 'Oh, fie! how very rude.' You must at least adduce arguments in order to prove that the statement which you do not sanction is one that ought not to have been made. And therefore I ask you to-day, in the first place, is it or is it not true that the Irish Church has been despoiled? Is it or is it not true that the gentlemen of Ireland have been severely amerced? Is it or is it not true that a Royal Commission has been issued which has dealt with the ancient endowments of this country in so ruthless a manner that Parliament has frequently been called upon to interfere, and has addressed the Crown to arrest their propositions? Are these facts or are they not?

Well, I did then venture to say that the Ministers had 'harassed trades and worried professions,' as reasons why men naturally become unpopular. Was that true

415

or was it not? Because, after all, everything depends on the facts of the statement. I will not enter into a long catalogue of trades, commencing with the important trade of which we have heard so much, and which has made itself felt at so many elections, down to the humblest trade—the lucifer match makers who fell upon their knees in Palace-yard. I suppose there are some Scotch farmers present, or, at least, those who are intimately connected with them. I want to know whether their trade was harassed when a proposition was brought before the House of Commons to tax their carts and horses, and all the machinery of their cultivation? I know how the proposition was received in England, and I doubt not the Scotch farmers, like the English, felt extremely harassed by it. I want to know what is the reason why there is this crusade throughout the country against Schedule D of the Income Tax. The Income Tax has been borne for 30 years with great self-sacrifice, and endured with great loyalty by the people of this country. It is at this moment at the lowest pitch it ever reached; how is it, then, that it is at this moment more unpopular than it was at any time during the long period we endured it, and at a much higher figure? It is on account of the assessment of the trades of England under that schedule. It is the vexatious and severe assessment that has harassed all trades under that Act, who are not particularly pleased when, after paying five quarters of Income Tax in one year, they learn also that they are in arrears.

Then, have the professions been worried? Is it not true that at this moment a Royal Commission is examining in London into the grievances of six thousand officers? Ask the Naval profession whether they have not been worried. During the course of the present Government the whole administrative system of the Admiralty, the Council that had always a wise and vast influence in the management of the Navy, and the peculiar and important office of the Secretary, were all swept away; and in spite, I may say, of the nightly warnings of a right hon. friend of mine now lost to us all and his country, the ablest Minister of the Admiralty during the present reign—notwithstanding his nightly warnings that they were so conducting the administration of the Navy that they would probably fall into some disaster. His remonstrances were in vain, and it was not till the most costly vessel of the State foundered, and the perilous voyage of the 'Megæra' had been made, that the country resolved to stand it no longer, they rescinded the whole of this worrying arrangement, and appointed a new First Lord to re-establish the old system. Is that worrying a profession, or is it not?

Well, gentlemen, I can speak of another profession—a profession not the least considerable in the State—the Civil Service profession. Has it been worried or is it now in a process of worrying, or is it not? There are many even in this room well acquainted with the Civil Service in all its departments. Let them decide. I might say the same of the legal profession, for I have heard the lawyers on both sides of the House in the debates of last Session agree in imploring the Government not to continue propositions which would infallibly weaken the administration of justice in this country. But with professions and trades it is not merely those directly attacked, but it is every one that is harassed and worried, because no one knows whose turn will come next.

Well, I did say to the House of Commons, and I afterwards expressed it in another form—I said the Ministers had attacked every class and institution, from the highest to the lowest in the country. Is that true or is it not? Is it not a fact that Her Majesty's Government on every occasion of which they could avail themselves during the last three years attacked the House of Lords—scoffed at the existence of its high functions, and even defied its decisions, until the result proved that the House of Lords was extremely popular in the country, and Her Majesty's Government were obliged themselves to confess that they were exceedingly unpopular. But you must also remember this,—that the same body of men who thus attacked the House of Lords also brought in a bill which attacked the poor inheritance of the widow and the orphan.

Now, I think I have shown that from the highest to the lowest the same system prevailed. What occurred in the interval? The Churches of England and Scotland have been threatened. It has been publicly stated by the highest authority in the House of Commons that he did not believe that the present House of Commons would sanction the views of those who wished to pull down these venerable establishments, but he recommended them to agitate out of doors and endeavour to excite public opinion against them.

Then, again, I said jobs were perpetrated that outraged public opinion. Is that true, or is it not? Is it not the fact that two years ago public opinion was outraged by persons being appointed to important offices in Church and State in direct violation of the language of Acts of Parliament?—that a dispensing power in that respect was exercised by the Minister, that dispensing power which forfeited the crown of James II. Was not public indignation roused to the highest pitch upon the Collier appointment? Were these acts perpetrated or not, and did they outrage public opinion? Every one knows that public opinion was outraged.

I have said, also, that they stumbled into errors which were always discreditable and sometimes ruinous. That was called violent language. Gentlemen, I never use violent language. Violent language is generally weak language; but I hope my language is sometimes strong. Now, let us look at this statement. I said that they stumbled into errors which were always discreditable and sometimes ruinous? Was the Zanzibar contract an 'error,' and was it not 'discreditable?' Was the conduct of the Treasury in allowing a subordinate officer to misappropriate nearly a million of the public money an 'error,' and was it not 'discreditable?' When the Government had referred the Alabama Claims to the arbitrament of a third State, was not the change of the Law of Nations by the Three Rules an 'error,' and was that not 'discreditable?' And besides being 'discreditable,' was it not ruinous?

Now, I have given an answer to the question why the Government, with transcendent abilities, as they tell us, with magnificent exploits which they are always extolling, and with a country whose prosperity is so palpable, are unpopular. I tell them why. They have harassed and worried the country, and there was no necessity for any of the acts they have committed. I have put it in condensed and, I am sure, accurate language. There was a celebrated writer, one of the greatest masters of our language, who wrote the history of the last four years of the reign of Queen

Anne, which was the duration of an illustrious Ministry. I have written the history of a Ministry that has lasted five years, and I have immortalized the spirit of their policy in five lines.

And now, gentlemen, I will tell you what is the unfortunate cause of this political embarrassment. Why, with such favourable circumstances as the present Government have experienced; why with the great ability which no man is more aware that they possess than myself; why, with the most anxious and earnest desire for which I give them entire credit to do their duty to their Sovereign and their fellow countrymen, the result has been so mortifying. I told it two years ago to the assembled county of Lancaster, when I met not only the greatest proprietors of its soil, but deputations and delegations of its choicest citizens from every town and city of that great county. I told them, speaking with the sense of the deepest responsibility, which I trust also animates me now—I told them that the cause was, that this Government, unfortunately, in its beginning had been founded on a principle of violence, and that fatal principle had necessarily vitiated their whole course.

And what have we gained by that principle of violence? Let us consider it, here even, with impartiality and perfect candour. I am now referring to the Irish policy of the Ministry. I say it is quite possible for public men, with the view of obtaining some great object advantageous to the country, to devise and pass measures which may utterly fail in accomplishing their purpose; and yet, however mortifying to themselves, however disappointing to the country, there would be no stain upon their reputation. We cannot command, but we must endeavour in public life to deserve, success. If, therefore, it is said that the Government proposed the large measures which they did with respect to Ireland in order to terminate the grievances of years and the embarrassment to England—which the state of Ireland certainly was—although they may have failed, their position was one which still might be a position of respect. That they have failed in this instance no one can doubt. A great portion of Ireland at this moment is in a state of veiled rebellion.

But what I charge upon the Government is this, not that their measures have failed—for all measures may fail—not that their measures failed to prevent or to suppress this veiled rebellion in Ireland, but that the measures, which they brought forward to appease and settle, to tranquillize and consolidate Ireland, are the very cause that this veiled rebellion has occurred.

For, gentlemen, what was the principle upon which the whole of their policy with respect to Ireland was founded? What was the principle upon which they induced Parliament to confiscate and to despoil the Church and private property in Ireland? It was that Ireland must be governed on Irish principles—the administration of Ireland must be carried on with reference to Irish feeling. If that is a sound principle and a sound sentiment in politics, it is a perfect vindication of what is occurring in the city of Dublin at this moment—viz. an assembly of men whose avowed object is to dissever the connection between the two countries. If we are not to legislate for Ireland with reference to Imperial feelings and general and national interests—if we are only to legislate with reference to Irish feelings, it is perfectly evident that if a majority of the Irish people take any idea in the world into their heads, however ruinous to themselves, and however fatal to the Empire, that policy must be recognized by this country. It is, therefore, to the principle avowedly, ostentatiously, brought forward by the Ministry as the basis of their Irish policy that I trace the dangerous condition in which Ireland is placed. Well, then, I say this policy of violence, for which such sacrifices were made, for which institutions and interests which were at least faithful to Britain were sacrificed—this policy of violence has led only to a state of affairs, unfortunately, more unsatisfactory than that which prevailed before.

Now, gentlemen, I observe in the papers that the day is fixed for the re-assembling of Parliament. The time is not yet very near, but when you find Her Majesty has appointed the day for our re-assembling, it is an intimation that we must begin to consider the public business a little, and, therefore, it is not altogether inconvenient that we should be talking upon these matters to-day. Now, when we meet Parliament I apprehend the first business that will be brought before us will be the Ashantee war. Upon that subject my mouth is closed. I will not even make an observation upon the railway, which I believe has been returned to England. Whenever this country is externally involved in a difficulty, whatever I may think of its cause or origin, those with whom I act, and myself, have no other duty to fulfil but to support the existing Government in extricating the country from its difficulties, and vindicating the honour and interests of Great Britain. The time will come, gentlemen, no doubt, when we shall know something of the secret history of that mysterious mess of the Ashantee war; but we have now but one duty to fulfil, which is to give every assistance to the Government in order that they may take those steps which the interests of the country require.

I should, indeed, myself, from my own individual experience, be most careful not to follow the example which one of the most distinguished members of the present Administration pursued with respect to us when we had to encounter the Abyssinian difficulty. Mr. Lowe thought proper to rise in Parliament when I introduced the necessity of interference in order to escape from difficulties which we had inherited and not made—Mr. Lowe rose in Parliament and violently attacked the Government of the day for the absurdity, the folly, the extreme imprudence of attempting any interference in the affairs of Abyssinia. He laughed at the honour of the country, he laughed at the interests of a few enslaved subjects of the Queen of England being compared, as he said, with the certain destruction and disaster which must attend any interference on our part. He described the horrors of the country and the terrors of the clime. He said there was no possibility by which any success could be obtained, and the people of England must prepare themselves for a horrible catastrophe. He described not only the fatal influences of the climate, but I remember he described one pink fly alone, which he said would eat up the whole British army. He was as vituperative of the insects of Abyssinia as if they had been British workmen.

Now, gentlemen, there is a most interesting and important subject which concerns us all, and which it is not impossible may be submitted to the consideration of Parliament by Her Majesty's Ministers, because I observe a letter published in a newspaper, by the authority of the Prime Minister, which is certainly calculated to arrest public attention. That is a letter respecting the subject of Parliamentary Reform. Now, gentlemen, I think it is not undesirable that at a moment when letters of this kind are circulated, and when there is a good deal of loose talking prevalent in the country on the subject, that I should take this opportunity of calling your attention to some considerations on this subject which may occupy you after my visit to Glasgow has terminated, and may not be, I think, unprofitable. Her Majesty's Government are not pledged, but after the letter of the Prime Minister announcing his own opinion, and the intention of the Government, probably, to consider the question, Her Majesty's Government may at this moment be considering the question of further Parliamentary Reform.

Now, there are two points which the Government ought to consider when they come to that question. The first is the expediency of having any further Parliamentary Reform. They will have to remember that very wise statesmen have been of opinion that there is no more dangerous and feebler characteristic of a State than perpetually to be dwelling on what is called organic change. The habit, it has been said in politics, of perpetually considering your political constitution can only be compared to that of the individual who is always considering the state of his health and his physical constitution. You know what occurs in such circumstances—he becomes infirm and valetudinarian. In fact, there is a school of politics which looks at the English Constitution as valetudinarian. They are always looking at its tongue and feeling its pulse, and devising means by which they may give it a tonic. The Government will have to consider that very important point, first of all, whether it is expedient. I am not giving any opinion upon it—being only a private member of Parliament that is quite unnecessary—but I am indicating that the consideration would occur to a responsible statesman. They will also have to consider this important point, that whatever Minister embarks in a campaign of Parliamentary Reform must make up his mind that he will necessarily arrest the progress of all other public business in the country.

I will show you to what extent that consideration should prevail. Parliamentary Reform, as a new question, was introduced in the House of Commons in 1852 by Lord John Russell, and from 1852 to 1866 or the end of 1865 it was introduced annually; four Prime Ministers had pledged themselves to the expediency of Parliamentary Reform; the subject made no progress in Parliament, but took up a great deal of time; a great portion of the Parliamentary Sessions for these twelve or thirteen years was taken up by discussions on Parliamentary Reform; and the country got very ill-tempered, finding that no reform was ever advanced, and other and more important subjects were neglected. At last it was taken up by men determined to carry it: first by Lord Russell, who did not carry it, and afterwards by others; but observe, the whole of 1866, 1867, and 1868 were entirely absorbed by the subject of Parliamentary Reform. Therefore, you will observe that when important subjects in legislation are pressing, you must be prepared to discourage any further demand for Parliamentary Reform

420

unless you feel an insuperable necessity for it, because if you want Parliamentary Reform you cannot have any of those large measures with regard to local taxation or other subjects in which you are all so much interested. That is the first consideration for the Government of the present day to determine, whether they shall embark in the question of Parliamentary Reform. Is it necessary? Is the necessity of such a character that it outweighs the immense inconvenience of sacrificing all other public and progressive measures for the advancement of this particular measure?

Then there comes another subject of consideration. I dwell upon these matters because I apprehend that one of the reasons of our meeting this evening is that upon questions which are likely to engage the public attention so far as those whom you honour with your confidence can give you any guidance, it is as well that I should indicate to you briefly my general views of the situation. Now, the next point, therefore, that Government will have to consider if they make up their minds to bring forward a measure of Parliamentary Reform is the character of the measure, and that will be a most anxious question for them to decide.

I think I may say without conceit that the subject of Parliamentary reform is one that I am entitled to speak upon at least with some degree of authority. I have given to it the consideration of some forty years, and am responsible for the most important measure on the subject that has been carried. I would say this, that it is impossible to go further in the direction of Parliamentary Reform than the Bill of 1867–68 without entirely subverting the whole of the borough representation of this country. I do not mean to say that if there was a place disfranchised to-morrow for corruption it would not be possible to enfranchise a very good place in its stead; but, speaking generally, you cannot go beyond the Act of 1867 without making up your mind entirely to break up the borough representation of this country. The people of Great Britain ought to be aware that that is the necessary consequence.

So far as I am concerned I never could view the matter in a party light. If I were to accustom myself to view it in a party light I might look with unconcern on this difficulty, for the smaller boroughs of the country are not, on the whole, favourable to our views. I am proud to think our party is supported by the great counties, and now to a great extent by great towns and cities; but I do not consider the small boroughs favourable to Conservative views. It is the national sympathies and wide sentiments of those who live in our great cities that are much more calculated to rally round the cause in which we are deeply concerned—the greatness and glory of our country. This ought to be known, that if you really intend to have a further measure of Parliamentary Reform, and have digested that large meal which you had a few years ago, there is no borough in England with under forty thousand inhabitants that would have any claim to be represented even by one member. Now that is a very important consideration, if, as we are told, the small boroughs of between ten and thirty thousand inhabitants are the backbone of the Liberal party. They may be, and I think they are. But I should be very sorry to see them disfranchised. They are centres of public spirit and intelligence in the country, influencing much the districts in which they are situated, and affording a various representation of the mind and life of the country. But it is inevitable that should occur, and I think, therefore, it ought to be well understood by the country when you have persons, without the slightest consideration, saying they are prepared to vote for this, or who are all in favour of that, whereas they have not really mastered the question.

So far as I am concerned, any proposition to change the representation of the people brought forward by Her Majesty's Government will have my respectful and candid consideration. But I say at once that I will vote for no measure of that kind, or of that class that is brought forward by some irresponsible individual who wants, on the eve of a general election, to make a clap-trap career. I think it perfectly disgusting for individuals to jump up in the House of Commons, and without the slightest responsibility, official or moral, make propositions which demand the gravest consideration of prolonged and protracted Cabinets, with all the responsibility attaching to experienced statesmen.

Now, gentlemen, although I have rather exceeded the time I had intended, there are one or two more remarks I should like to make on subjects which interest us all. And first, as the only feature in our domestic life that gives me uneasiness, are the relations at present between capital and labour, and between the employers and the employed—I must say one word upon that subject. If there are any relations in the world which should be those of sympathy and perfect confidence, they always appear to be the relations which should subsist between employers and employed, and especially in manufacturing life. They are, in fact, much more intimate and more necessary relations than those which subsist between landlords and tenants. It is an extremely painful thing that of late years we so frequently hear of misunderstandings between the employers and the employed—that they look upon each other with suspicion—with mutual suspicion—as if each were rapaciously inclined either to obtain or retain the greater share of the profits of their trade; those incidents with which you are all acquainted, of a very painful nature, being the consequence.

Now I am not talking of demands for an increase of wages when men are carrying on what is called a roaring trade—I believe that is the classical epithet. When a roaring trade is going on, I am not at all surprised that working men should ask for an increase of wages. But the trade sometimes ceases to roar, when wages naturally, on the same principle, assume a form more adapted to the circumstances. But, no doubt, during the last twenty years there appears to have been, not a passing and temporary cause of disturbance, like the incidents of trade being very active or reduced, but some permanent cause disturbing prices, which alike confuses the employer in his calculations as to profits and embarrasses the employed from the greater expenditure which they find it necessary to make.

Now, I cannot but feel myself—having given to the subject some consideration—I cannot help feeling that the large and continuous increase of the precious metals, especially during the last twenty years, has certainly produced no inconsiderable effect on prices.

I will not on an occasion like this enter into anything like an abstruse discussion. I confine myself to giving my opinion and the results; and this moral, which

422

I think is worthy of consideration. If it can be shown accurately and scientifically that there is a cause affecting a prominent class, reducing the average remuneration of the employed, and confusing and confounding the employer in his calculations as to profits—if that can be shown, and if it is proved to be the result of inexorable laws, far beyond the reach of legislatures, and of circumstances over which human beings have no control—I think if that could be shown, and employers and employed had sufficient acuteness and knowledge—and I am sure that in Scotland there is no lack of both—it would very much change those mutual feelings of suspicion and sentiments of a not pleasant character which occasionally prevail when they find that they are both of them the victims, as it were, of some inexorable law of public economy which cannot be resisted. I think, instead of supposing that each wanted to take advantage of the other they would feel inclined to put their shoulders to the wheel, accurately ascertain whether this be true, and come to some understanding which would very much mitigate the relations which subsist between them. I have little doubt the effect would be to increase the average rate of wages, with my views as to the effect of the continuous increase of the precious metals. But, at the same time, I have not the slightest doubt the employer would, in the nature of things, find adequate compensation for the new position in which he would find himself.

There is one point, before I sit down, to which I wish to call your attention. Because, if I am correct in saying that the question of the relations between the employer and employed is the only one that gives me anxiety at home, there is a subject abroad to which I think I ought, on an occasion like this, to draw your notice; and that is the contest that is commencing in Europe between the spiritual and temporal power.

Gentlemen, I look upon it as very grave, as pregnant with circumstances which may greatly embarrass Europe. A religious sentiment is often and generally taken advantage of by political causes which use it as a pretext; and there is much going on in Europe at the present moment which, it appears to me, may occasion soon much anxiety in this community. I should myself look upon it as the greatest danger to civilization if in the struggle that is going on between faith and free thought, the respective sides should only be represented by the Papacy and the Red Republic. And here I must say that if we have before us the prospect of struggles— perhaps ultimately of wars and anarchy—caused by the struggle now rising in Europe, it will not easily be in the power of England entirely to stand apart. Our connection with Ireland will then be brought painfully to our consciousness, and I should not be at all surprised if the visor of Home Rule should fall off some day and you beheld a very different countenance.

Now, gentlemen, I think we ought to be prepared for these events. The position of England is one, which is indicated, if dangers arise, of holding a middle course upon these matters. It may be open to England again to take her stand upon the Reformation, which three hundred years ago was the source of her greatness and her glory, and it may be her proud destiny to guard civilization alike from the withering blast of atheism and from the simoom of sacerdotal usurpation. These things may be far off, but we live in a rapid age, and my apprehension is that they are nearer than some suppose. If that struggle comes, we must look to Scotland to aid us. It was once, and I hope is still, a land of liberty, of patriotism, and of religion. I think the time has come when it really should leave off mumbling the dry bones of political economy and munching the remainder biscuit of an effete Liberalism. We all know that a General Election is at hand. I do not ask you to consider on such an occasion the fate of parties or of Ministers. But I ask you to consider this, that it is very probable that the future of Europe may depend greatly on the character of the next Parliament of England. I ask you, when the occasion comes, to act as becomes an ancient and famous nation, and give all your energies for the cause of faith and freedom.